HONG KONG

22nd Edition

Fodor's Travel Publications · New York, Toronto, London, Sydney, Auckland

www.fodors.com

Be a Fodor's Correspondent

Your opinion matters. It matters to us. It matters to your fellow Fodor's travelers, too. And we'd like to hear it. In fact, we *need* to hear it.

When you share your experiences and opinions, you become an active member of the Fodor's community. That means we'll not only use your feedback to make our books better, but we'll publish your names and comments whenever possible. Throughout our guides, look for "Word of Mouth," excerpts of your unvarnished feedback.

Here's how you can help improve Fodor's for all of us.

Tell us when we're right. We rely on local writers to give you an insider's perspective. But our writers and staff editors—who are the best in the business—depend on you. Your positive feedback is a vote to renew our recommendations for the next edition.

Tell us when we're wrong. We're proud that we update most of our guides every year. But we're not perfect. Things change. Hotels cut services. Museums change hours. Charming cafés lose charm. If our writer didn't quite capture the essence of a place, tell us how you'd do it differently. If any of our descriptions are inaccurate or inadequate, we'll incorporate your changes in the next edition and correct factual errors at fodors.com *immediately*.

Tell us what to include. You probably have had fantastic travel experiences that aren't yet in Fodor's. Why not share them with a community of like-minded travelers? Maybe you chanced upon a beach or bistro or B&B that you don't want to keep to yourself. Tell us why we should include it. And share your discoveries and experiences with everyone directly at fodors.com. Your input may lead us to add a new listing or highlight a place we cover with a "Highly Recommended" star or with our highest rating, "Fodor's Choice."

Give us your opinion instantly at our feedback center at www.fodors.com/feedback. You may also e-mail editors@fodors.com with the subject line "Hong Kong Editor." Or send your nominations, comments, and complaints by mail to Hong Kong Editor, Fodor's, 1745 Broadway, New York, NY 10019.

You and travelers like you are the heart of the Fodor's community. Make our community richer by sharing your experiences. Be a Fodor's correspondent.

Happy traveling!

Tim Jarrell, Publisher

FODOR'S HONG KONG

Editors: Stephanie Butler, Carolyn Galgano

Editorial Contributors: Jo Baker, Cherise Fong, Doretta Lau, Samantha Leese, Dorothy So

Production Editor: Carrie Parker

Maps & Illustrations: David Lindroth, *cartographer;* Bob Blake, Rebecca Baer, *map editors;* William Wu, *information graphics*

Design: Fabrizio La Rocca, *creative director;* Guido Caroti, Siobhan O'Hare, *art directors;* Tina Malaney, Nora Rosansky, Chie Ushio, Jessica Walsh, Ann McBride, *designers;* Melanie Marin, *senior picture editor*

Cover Photo: (Chinese Junk and skyline of Central District and Victoria Harbor): SCPhotos/Alamy

Production Manager: Steve Slawsky

22nd Edition

ISBN 978-1-4000-0521-5

ISSN 1070-6887

SPECIAL SALES

This book is available at special discounts for bulk purchases for sales promotions or premiums. Special editions, including personalized covers, excerpts of existing books, and corporate imprints, can be created in large quantities for special needs. For more information, write to Special Markets/Premium Sales, 1745 Broadway, MD 6-2, New York, New York 10019, or e-mail specialmarkets@randomhouse.com.

AN IMPORTANT TIP & AN INVITATION

Although all prices, opening times, and other details in this book are based on information supplied to us at press time, changes occur all the time in the travel world, and Fodor's cannot accept responsibility for facts that become outdated or for inadvertent errors or omissions. So **always confirm information when it matters,** especially if you're making a detour to visit a specific place. Your experiences—positive and negative—matter to us. If we have missed or misstated something, **please write to us.** We follow up on all suggestions. Contact the Hong Kong editor at editors@fodors.com or c/o Fodor's at 1745 Broadway, New York, NY 10019.

PRINTED IN SINGAPORE

10 9 8 7 6 5 4 3 2 1

CONTENTS

1 EXPERIENCE HONG KONG.....9

What's Where. 10

Hong Kong Planner 12

Hong Kong
Top Attractions 14

Free Things to Do 16

Feasts and Fêtes 17

On the Move 18

Feng Shui Structures. 20

The Peak Experience 22

To Your Health 23

Beaches 26

Island Hopping 30

Sail Away:
Sampans and Junks 32

Hiking. 33

Very Amusing 35

Cinema Hong Kong 38

Off to the Races 40

**2 HONG KONG
NEIGHBORHOODS 41**

Western 43

Central 48

Wan Chai, Causeway Bay, and
Beyond. 58

Southside 66

Lantau Island 71

**3 KOWLOON
NEIGHBORHOODS 77**

Kowloon 79

The New Territories 91

4 SHOPPING 101

Shopping Planner 102

Nathan Road 104

SoHo and NoHo 106

Causeway Bay 108

Hong Kong Island 111

Kowloon Peninsula 145

5 WHERE TO EAT 159

Where to Eat Planner 162

Best Bets for
Hong Kong Dining 164

Central 166

Causeway Bay 168

Yau Ma Tei, Mong Kok, and
Jordan 170

Hong Kong Island 172

Kowloon Peninsula 192

**HONG KONG DINING AND
LODGING ATLAS 205**

6 WHERE TO STAY 213

Hong Kong Lodging
Planner. 216

Best Bets for
Hong Kong Lodging 218

Hong Kong Island 219

Kowloon 236

7 AFTER DARK 249

After Dark
Planner. 250

Hong Kong Island 252

Kowloon 266

CONTENTS

8 SIDE TRIP TO MACAU 269

Welcome to Macau 270

Macau Planner 272

Exploring Macau 275

Casinos. 289

Where to Eat 295

Where to Stay. 302

After Dark 311

Shopping. 313

TRAVEL SMART
HONG KONG 315

Getting Here and Around. 316

Essentials 323

INDEX. 336

ABOUT OUR WRITERS. 352

MAPS

Hong Kong Beaches 28

Western. 44–45

Central District. 50–51

Wan Chai, Causeway Bay, and
Beyond 60–61

Southside. 68–69

Lantau Island. 72–73

Kowloon. 82

Kowloon Districts 85

The New Territories. 94–95

Nathan Road Shopping 105

SoHo and NoHo Shopping 107

Causeway Bay Shopping. 109

Hong Kong Dining. 161

Macau 279

Taipa and Coloane Islands 288

ABOUT
THIS BOOK

Our Ratings

Sometimes you find terrific travel experiences and sometimes they just find you. But usually the burden is on you to select the right combination of experiences. That's where our ratings come in.

As travelers we've all discovered a place so wonderful that its worthiness is obvious. And sometimes that place is so unique that superlatives don't do it justice: you just have to be there to know. These sights, properties, and experiences get our highest rating, **Fodor's Choice**, indicated by orange stars throughout this book.

Black stars highlight sights and properties we deem **Highly Recommended,** places that our writers, editors, and readers praise again and again for consistency and excellence.

By default, there's another category: any place we include in this book is by definition worth your time, unless we say otherwise. And we will.

Disagree with any of our choices? Care to nominate a place or suggest that we rate one more highly? Visit our feedback center at www.fodors.com/feedback.

Budget Well

Hotel and restaurant price categories from ¢ to $$$$ are defined in the opening pages of each chapter. For attractions, we always give standard adult admission fees; reductions are usually available for children, students, and senior citizens. Want to pay with plastic? **AE, D, DC, MC, V** following restaurant and hotel listings indicate whether American Express, Discover, Diners Club, MasterCard, and Visa are accepted.

Restaurants

Unless we state otherwise, restaurants are open for lunch and dinner daily. We mention dress only when there's a specific requirement and reservations only when they're essential or not accepted—it's always best to book ahead.

Hotels

Hotels have private bath, phone, TV, and air-conditioning and operate on the European Plan (aka EP, meaning without meals), unless we specify that they use the Continental Plan (CP, with a continental breakfast), Breakfast Plan (BP, with a full breakfast), or Modified American Plan (MAP, with breakfast and dinner) or are all-inclusive (including all meals

and most activities). We always list facilities but not whether you'll be charged an extra fee to use them, so when pricing accommodations, find out what's included.

Listings

★	Fodor's Choice
★	Highly recommended
✉	Physical address
✢	Directions or Map coordinates
⌂	Mailing address
☎	Telephone
🖷	Fax
⊕	On the Web
✍	E-mail
☞	Admission fee
☉	Open/closed times
Ⓜ	Metro stations
▭	Credit cards

Hotels & Restaurants

⛊	Hotel
⇲	Number of rooms
⌣	Facilities
¶◎¶	Meal plans
✕	Restaurant
⌣	Reservations
🏛	Dress code
⌇	Smoking
⌘	BYOB

Outdoors

🏌	Golf
⛺	Camping

Other

☾	Family-friendly
⇨	See also
✉	Branch address
☞	Take note

Experience
Hong Kong

1

WHAT'S WHERE

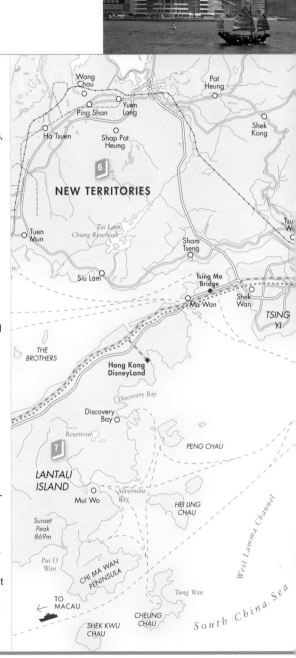

1 Western. Just west of the skyscrapers, this older and quieter neighborhood of Hong Kong Island is known for its steep and narrow roads, Chinese medicine markets, antiques shops, temples, and the tram. On Connaught Road, Central, the century-old Western Market is an iconic example of colonial architecture in Sheung Wan.

2 Central. Hong Kong's world-famous finance hub extends through Admiralty and boasts skyline high-rises, luxury-brand flagship stores, and grand hotels with gourmet restaurants, all connected by footbridges. Head up the midlevels escalators and take the funicular to Victoria Peak for postcard views of the city and harbor.

3 Wan Chai and Causeway Bay. Wan Chai still has its strip of harmless red-light venues. Not so far away are design shops and wine bars. Hip and trendy young locals flock to Causeway Bay's shopping hubs, Sogo and Times Square.

4 Southside. Stanley, with its colonial remnants, outdoor market, waterfront restaurants, and annual Dragon Boat races, may be Southside's obvious destination. But don't let it stop you from visiting

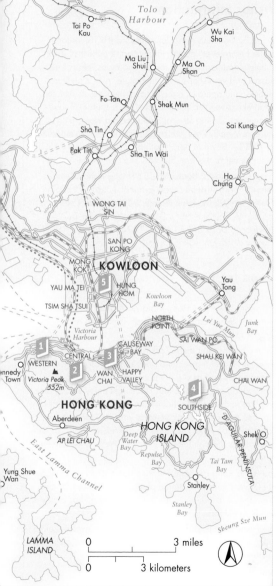

beaches, from Repulse Bay to Shek O, at the start (or finish) of the Dragon's Back scenic hiking trail. Or play with the pandas at Ocean Park.

5 Kowloon. It begins at the 50-year-old Star Ferry Terminal in Tsim Sha Tsui, followed by the eastward promenade along the Avenue of Stars, which offers front-row views of the famous Hong Kong Island skyline. Kowloon continues up the Golden Mile of Nathan Road Mong Kok is the epicenter of day and night markets.

6 New Territories. Hong Kong's least developed areas are the sites of still-inhabited historic villages and relatively unspoiled natural beauty, in addition to the Ten Thousand Buddhas Monastery and Hong Kong Heritage Museum in the new town of Sha Tin.

7 Outlying Islands. Of the Hong Kong archipelago of 260 islands, Lantau is by far the largest. No wonder that it is home to the Big Buddha and spectacular mountain views from hiking trails beyond the Ngong Ping 360 cable car ride. It's also where you'll find Disneyland as well as endangered pink dolphins swimming in the bay.

HONG KONG PLANNER

Looks Deceive

On the surface Hong Kong is a big chaotic Chinatown punctuated by imposing skyscrapers and shopping malls. A closer look reveals the marks of a century of colonialism and several thousand years of Chinese ancestry. Then, notice that rural mountains, forests, and outlying islands comprise more than 70% of Hong Kong's land mass.

Wording It Right

Learn to recognize a few basic Cantonese expressions such as "*lei-ho?*" ("hello, how are you?") and "*mm-goi*" ("excuse me" or "thank you"). Hong Kong's official languages are Chinese and English, but the native dialect is Cantonese. Mandarin Chinese has gained popularity here and in Macau.

In hotels, large stores, international restaurants, and clubs, most people speak English. Many taxi and bus drivers and staffers in small shops, cafés, and market stalls do not.

Ask MTR employees or English-speaking policemen, identifiable by their red striped epaulets, for directions. Get your concierge to write down your destination in Chinese if you're headed off the main trail.

Visitor Information

Swing by the Hong Kong Tourist Board (HKTB) visitor center before even leaving the airport. It publishes stacks of helpful free exploring booklets and maps, offers free classes and workshops on local culture, runs a plethora of tours, and operates a multilingual helpline. Its detailed, comprehensive Web site is a fabulous resource. If you're planning on visiting several museums in a week, pick up a Museum Weekly Pass, which gets you into seven museums for HK$30. Buy it at participating museums or at the HKTB visitor center at the Tsim Sha Tsui Star Ferry Concourse.

Hong Kong Tourist Board (*HKTB ⊠ Hong Kong International Airport, Arrivals Level, Terminal 1, Lantau ⊙ Daily 7 AM–11 PM ⊠ The Peak Piazza, Victoria Peak Central ⊙ Daily 9–9 ⊠ Star Ferry Concourse, Tsim Sha Tsui, Kowloon ⊙ Daily 8–8 ☎ 2508–1234 [hotline daily 9–6] ⊕ www.discoverhongkong.com*).

Good for Kids

Top your list with the Hong Kong Zoological & Botanical Gardens, Symphony of Lights, Peak Tram, and a skyscraper climb.

On the Southside, Ocean Park offers a balance of toned-down thrills and high-octane rides suitable for toddlers to teenagers as well as a giant aquarium and the popular giant-panda enclosure. Older kids might enjoy seeing pink dolphins in their natural habitat on a Dolphinwatch half-day trip. See tropical birds close-up as you walk through the Edward Youde Aviary in Hong Kong Park, or watch bigger, wilder birds through telescopes at the Wetland Park in the New Territories.

The Hong Kong Heritage Museum has a Children's Discovery Gallery with educational playzones designed for children ages 4 to 10, while the Science Museum has plenty of hands-on exhibits.

The Festival Walk and Elements malls both have ice-skating rinks, while Kowloon Park has a massive outdoor multipool swimming complex.

And of course, there's always Disneyland.

Navigating

Hong Kong's streets may seem utterly chaotic, but its public transport system is not. On the northern side of Hong Kong Island, look for the tracks or listen for the "ding-ding" of the tram, which runs straight across the island west to east. This is the same route that the MTR (underground railway) follows, so you should be able to walk to an MTR station from any tram stop between Sheung Wan and Shau Kei Wan. In Kowloon, orient yourself in relation to Nathan Road: Most buses running southbound down Nathan Road terminate at the Star Ferry Concourse in Tsim Sha Tsui, unless they're crossing over to Hong Kong Island.

The MTR, which links most of the areas you'll want to visit, is quick, safe, clean, and user-friendly. Signs and announcements are in both Chinese and English, and exits often lead directly into shopping malls.

Pay with a rechargeable Octopus card. You can use it on the MTR, buses, trams, the Star Ferry, the Peak Tram, and even at vending machines, convenience stores, fast-food restaurants, public swimming pools, and the racetrack.

It's often not worth taking the MTR for one stop, as stations are close, so walk or take the tram. The MTR paid areas also include underground pedestrian passageways between nearby stops such as Tsim Sha Tsui and East Tsim Sha Tsui or Central and Hong Kong Station.

Most MTR stations have multiple exits, so consult the detailed station maps to determine which exit lets you out closest to your destination.

If you're crossing Central, use the covered walkways that link its main buildings, thus avoiding stoplights, exhaust fumes, and weather conditions (but not crowds). The same can apply to the pedestrian overpasses in Mong Kok. Note that signs marked "subway" refer to a subterranean passageway, not to the MTR.

On Hong Kong Island, Queen's Road changes its suffix every so often, resulting in Queen's Road East, Queen's Road Central, and Queen's Road West. However, these suffixes don't exactly correspond with the districts, so part of Queen's Road Central is actually in Western. As street numbers start again with each new section, be sure you know which part you're headed for, or better still, the intersecting street. The same goes for Des Voeux Road.

When to Go

Hong Kong's high season, from September through late December, sees sunny, dry days and cool, comfortable nights. January and February are mostly cool and dank, with long periods of overcast skies. March and April are fairly pleasant, and by May the temperature is consistently warm and comfortable.

June through August are the cheapest months for one reason: they coincide with the hot, sticky, and very rainy typhoon (hurricane) season. Hong Kong is prepared for blustery assaults; if a big storm approaches, the airwaves crackle with information, and your hotel will post the appropriate signals (a No. 10 signal indicates the worst winds, and a black warning means a rainstorm is brewing). This is serious business—bamboo scaffolding and metal signs can come hurtling through the streets like spears, trees can break or fall, and large areas of the territory can flood. Museums, shops, restaurants, and transport shut down at signal No. 8, but 7-Elevens and cinemas typically stay open.

HONG KONG TEMPERATURES

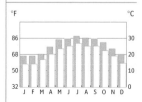

HONG KONG TOP ATTRACTIONS

Star Ferry

(A) The iconic Star Ferry has been shuttling passengers across Victoria Harbour for more than a century. Today's green and white boats are relics of the 1950s and '60s. Take one from either Wan Chai or Central to Tsim Sha Tsui, then turn around and admire that famous Hong Kong skyline. At night, catch the 8 PM Symphony of Lights show.

Tram

(B) The *ding-ding*, whose rattling cars have become giant rolling advertisements, carries everyone from schoolboys to grannies through all the main street action straight across Hong Kong Island. Climb aboard at off-peak hours on an early weekday afternoon for a leisurely ride from the busy Western Market terminus to the green fields of Happy Valley or Victoria Park.

Midlevels Escalators

(C) The longest outdoor covered escalator system in the world covers half a mile of moving stairs, walkways, and passageways from the business hub of Central to the residential heights of Midlevels. Step off a few flights up from Central in SoHo or on Hollywood Road for gallery hopping, fine dining, or club crawling.

Victoria Peak

(D) At 1,810 feet above sea level, the Peak is Hong Kong Island's highest hill above the harbor. Buy a ticket for the 123-year-old Peak Tram, take in the postcard views, then take a scenic nature walk or bus ride back down to Central.

Mong Kok Markets

(E) Flowers, birds, goldfish, turtles, and jade by day; clothes, sneakers, toys, and knickknacks by night. And there's always food around Temple Street. Visit the stronghold of the Triads (secret-society gangs) on Nathan Road, or wander down

Sai Yeung Street, which is full of snacks, buskers, and touts.

Kowloon Walled City Park

(F) Exempted from British rule and abandoned by the Chinese following their treaty in 1842, the Walled City grew into a lawless, labyrinthine slum occupied by Triads, gambling houses, brothels, and disease. Only in 1995 was it resurrected as this peaceful and expansive Qing Dynasty–style garden. The documentary photos and restored South Gate remnants exhibit how far the park has come.

Tian Tan Buddha

(G) The Ngong Ping 360 cable car ride can only take you so far. The true path to divine ascension is by way of 268 steps leading up to the 275-ton Tian Tan Buddha statue (the Big Buddha), which sits on a hill next to the Po Lin Buddhist Monastery. Nearby is the Wisdom Path, a beautiful walk that offers splendid views.

Stanley

Come here to see classic colonial buildings, wander through the eclectic market, dine on the waterfront, and swim at the beach where hundreds of Dragon Boats race every spring.

Dragon's Back Trail

(H) This is one hiking trail that will give you a whole new perspective of Hong Kong. You don't need to be an athlete to walk along the undulating Dragon's Back ridge, which runs across the southeast end of Hong Kong Island.

Duk Ling

(I) Sail Victoria Harbour on Hong Kong's last authentic red-sailed junk. The Duk Ling was built in Macau over half a century ago and was restored to her original glory in the late 1980s. It's now the symbol of the Hong Kong Tourist Board, which offers HK$50 one-hour rides exclusively for tourists.

FREE THINGS TO DO

It's easy to spend money in the big city: shopping, entrance fees, food, shows, late-night cocktails. But if you'd like to put your wallet away for a while, here are some of our favorite options.

Art

Visitors are free to browse antiques and art works by Asian prodigies at private galleries in Central, SoHo, and Sheung Wan. Kowloon Park's winding Sculpture Walk features 20 works—including an Eduardo Paolozzi—against a leafy backdrop. And be sure to keep your eyes open at the malls, most notably Harbour City and Times Square, where you'll see Hong Kong's version of public art.

Bright Lights

Victoria Harbour's Symphony of Lights is performed every evening at 8 to a crowd of mesmerized visitors and proud residents. Music and narration blast through low-fi outdoor speakers as 44 skyscrapers are synchronized to light up on cue. Watch from the waterfront promenade in Tsim Sha Tsui, Golden Bauhinia Square in Wan Chai, or the InternContinental hotel's lobby lounge.

Culture Classes

The tourist board runs free classes on feng shui, traditional Chinese medicine, Cantonese Opera, and Chinese tea appreciation. If you prefer a more immersive experience, a tai chi master will guide you through the moves at the Sculpture Court, just outside the Hong Kong Museum of Art, every Monday, Wednesday, and Friday morning at 8. Contact the HKTB (☎2508–1234) for details.

Enlightenment

Inner peace is priceless, and though it's customary to make a small donation, all of Hong Kong's temples are free. So is the peaceful Chi Lin Nunnery in Kowloon, as well as the Big Buddha and Wisdom Path on Lantau Island, although you have to pay to get there first.

Bird-Watching

See our feathered friends up close and personal without leaving town—either at the Yuen Po Street Bird Garden in Kowloon, or at the Edward Youde Aviary in the heart of Hong Kong Park.

Heritage

Visit the Hong Kong Heritage Museum in Sha Tin on a Wednesday, when admission is free of charge for the whole family. This expertly curated museum chronicles Hong Kong's changing face, from scattered fishing and farming communities to booming towns. Hong Kong's Museum of Art, Museum of History, Museum of Coastal Defence, Science Museum, Space Museum, and Dr. Sun Yat-sen Museum also offer free admission on Wednesday.

Walkabouts

In town, you can take in colonial architecture during an hour-long stroll through Western between the University of Hong Kong and Western Market. Or, try walking across Central through buildings linked by covered pedestrian passages. You can also head for the hills and hike along the Dragon's Back or up to Lion Rock.

Views

It doesn't cost a cent to ride up to the Bank of China's 43rd-floor observation deck or to visit the Hong Kong Monetary Authority on the 55th floor of the International Finance Centre, for fabulous harbor views over to Kowloon. Get the reverse vista from the Tsim Sha Tsui waterfront promenade. For a glorious panoramic bay view of Victoria Park, visit the 5th and 6th floors of the main library in Causeway Bay.

FEASTS AND FÊTES

The loudest and proudest traditional festival, **Chinese New Year,** brings Hong Kong to a standstill each year. Shops shut down, and everywhere you look there are red and gold signs, kumquat trees, and pots of yellow chrysanthemums, all considered auspicious. On the lunar new year's eve the crowds climax at the flower market and fair in Victoria Park; on the first night there's a colorfully noisy parade; on the second night the crowds ooh and ahh at the no-costs-spared fireworks display over the harbor. (1st day of 1st moon, usually late Jan.–early Feb.)

The Chinese New Year festivities end with the overwhelmingly red **Lantern Festival.** Hong Kong's green spaces—especially Victoria Park—become a sea of light as people, mostly children, gather with beautifully shaped paper or cellophane lanterns. It's also a traditional day for playful matchmaking, so it's particularly auspicious for single people. (15th day of 1st moon, usually Feb.)

Ancestor worship is important, and on **Ching Ming** families meet to sweep the graves of departed relatives and burn paper offerings in respect for them. (3rd moon, Apr. 4 or 5)

Thousands make the yearly trip to Cheung Chau Island for the exuberant **Cheung Chau Bun Festival,** a four-day-long Taoist thanksgiving feast. A procession of children dressed as gods winds its way toward Pak Tai Temple, where 60-foot towers covered in buns quiver outside. (8th day of 4th moon, usually May)

The **Dragon Boat Festival** pits long, multi-oared dragon-head boats against one another in races to the shore; the biggest event is held at Stanley Beach. It commemorates the hero Qu Yuan, a poet and scholar who drowned himself in the 3rd

century BC to protest government corruption. These days it's one big beach party. (5th day of 5th moon, usually June)

Smoldering piles of paper are everywhere during the **Hungry Ghosts Festival.** Replicas of houses, cars, and Monopoly-style "hell money" are burned as offerings to the ancestral spirits allowed to roam the earth for these two weeks, when the gates of hell are opened. (15th day of 7th moon, usually Aug.–Sept.)

During the **Mid-Autumn Festival,** families and friends gather to admire the full moon while munching on moon cakes, which are traditionally stuffed with red-bean or lotus-seed paste. Colorful paper lanterns fill Hong Kong's parks, and a 220-foot-long "fire dragon" dances through the streets of Tai Hang near Victoria Park. (15th day of 8th moon, usually Sept.–Oct.)

ON THE MOVE

The city's transport options are as varied—old and new, fast and slow, land and sea—as they are clean, safe, and easy to use. There's no timetable for the MTR because trains run so frequently. Buses are air-conditioned, with cushioned seats, and often an upper level. On the water, enjoy a quick scenic trip across the harbor on the iconic Star Ferries, or take a fast ferry to an outer island or even Macau. For a leisurely ride harking back to the days of old, nothing beats a double-decker tram ride across Hong Kong Island. So when hitting the hot spots, skip taxis and take public transport.

Double-Decker Trams. Tall, thin, and rumbling, the trams have efficiently, albeit slowly, moved passengers across Hong Kong Island since 1904. This is the world's largest fleet of double-deckers in operation, also offering prime advertising real estate, so look out for some colorful cars. As of March 2010, the tramways were completely acquired by a French company, which promises to preserve their unique historical status, affordability, and sustainability. The beloved trams, which locals affectionately call "ding-ding" after the onomatopoeic sound of their bell, are a fun and inexpensive way to cruise the island. Enter from the rear, head straight up the narrow staircase, and grab a seat at the very front for the best views. At this height, you can almost reach out and touch the neon signs. One 15-minute journey takes you through Central's forest of skyscrapers east to Wan Chai's wet markets and clothing shops, ending at Southorn Playground, where kids play basketball and soccer and the older folk play chess. ■ TIP→ For history and lists of attractions and places to eat along the tram line, see HKTB's 'Ding Ding' Hong Kong Tram Guide: www.discov-

FLY THE FRIENDLY SKIES

With 2.9 km (1.8 mi) of moving walkways, 14 acres of glass, and around 30 acres of carpeting, the international terminal at Chek Lap Kok Airport is the world's largest. At $20 billion to build, it's also the world's most expensive. A super-efficient express train runs between the city and this modern marvel in 24 minutes.

erhongkong.com/tramguide. ☎ 2548–7102 ⊕ *www.hktramways.com* ⊗ 6 AM–midnight ☒ *HK$2.*

Midlevels Escalator. A practical human mover, this 800-meter-long (½-mi-long) combination of escalators and walkways provides free, covered transport up or down the steep incline between Central and Midlevels. Along the way, the trip offers a view of small Chinese shops, the Jamia Mosque at Shelley Street, and gleaming residential high-rises. You're often so close to the apartments that it's impossible to avoid peering in. Starting at Staunton Street, the escalator cuts through the fashionable SoHo area, filled with cafés, bars, and boutiques.

Plan to ride the escalators up between 10:30 AM and midnight. From 6 to 10 AM they move downhill only, so commuters from Midlevels can get to work. After midnight the escalators shut down, and that equates to a long walk on steep steps. You can get off at any point and explore the side streets. ✉ *Enter across from Central Market, at Queen's Rd. Central and Jubilee St., Central* ⊗ *Daily 6 AM–11:30 PM.*

Ngong Ping 360 Cable Car. The meditative 5.7-km (3.5-mi) suspended cable-car journey takes you above Lantau Island's greenery, from Tung Chung to the Ngong

Ping plateau, home of the Pol Lin Monastery. The 25-minute ride includes panoramic vistas of the South China Sea, North Lantau Country Park, Hong Kong International Airport, and a glimpse of the Big Buddha, sitting and smiling on the mountaintop. ☎ 2109–9898 ⊕ *www. np360.com.hk* ⊗ *Weekdays 10–6; weekends and holidays 9–6:30* 🚋 *HK$74 oneway; HK$107 round-trip.*

★ **Fodor's Choice** **Peak Tram.** Hong Kong is proud that its funicular railway is the world's steepest. On the way up, grab a seat on the right-hand side for the best views of the harbor and mountains. The trams, which look like old-fashioned trolley cars, are hauled the whole way in seven minutes by cables attached to electric motors. En route to the Upper Terminus, 1,300 feet above sea level, the cars pass four intermediate stations, with track gradients varying from 4 to 27 degrees.

At the top you enter the Peak Tower, a mall full of restaurants and shops; there's a viewing platform on the roof. Outside the Tower, another mall faces you. Well-signed nature walks around the Peak are wonderful respites from the commercialism.

Bus 15C, usually but not always a red double-decker with an open top, shuttles you between the Peak Tram Lower Terminal and Central Bus Terminal near the Star Ferry pier, every 15 to 20 minutes, for HK$4.20. ⊠ *Between Garden Rd. and Cotton Tree Dr., Central* ☎ 2522–0922 ⊕ *www.thepeak.com.hk* 🚋 *HK$25 oneway, HK$36 round-trip* ⊗ *Daily every 10–15 mins, 7 AM–midnight.*

★ **Fodor's Choice** **Star Ferry.** Since 1898 the Star Ferry pier has been the public gateway to Hong Kong Island from Kowloon. If it's your first time in the

city, taking the Star Ferry across Victoria Harbour and back is a must. It's a beautiful and relaxing 10-minute trip on vintage vessels, whose average age is 50 years old. An evening ride is the most spectacular, when the city's neon and skyscrapers light up the skyline across the water, especially if you can time your ride to coincide with the 8 PM Symphony of Lights show.

The new Central Star Ferry Terminal is at Piers 7 and 8 of the Outlying Islands Ferry Piers. On ferries between Central and Tsim Sha Tsui there are two classes: first-class seats (HK$2.50–HK$3) on the roomier upper deck have more of a breeze, and an air-conditioned compartment in front; second-class seats (HK$2–HK$2.40) on the lower deck tend to be stuffier and noisy because they're near the engine room. ■ TIP→ For trips from Central to Tsim Sha Tsui, seats on the eastern side have the better views. ⊠ *Central* ☎ 2367–7065 ⊕ *www.starferry.com.hk* ⊗ *Central to/from Tsim Sha Tsui, daily 6:30 AM–11:30 PM.*

FENG SHUI STRUCTURES

There's a battle going on in Central, a battle between good and evil forces. Feng shui (pronounced *foong soy* in Cantonese, *fung shway* in Mandarin, and literally translated as "wind" and "water") is the art of placing objects to bring about yin–yang balance. In the West, feng shui seems like just another interior-design fad; here it's taken very seriously.

One school looks at buildings in relation to mountains or bodies of water. It's ideal, for example, for a building to face out to sea with a mountain behind it. (Is it coincidence that this allows for the best views and breezes?) Another school focuses on shapes in the immediate environment; triangles, for instance, give off bad feng shui. Both schools are concerned with the flow of energy. Entrances are placed to allow positive energy to flow in, and objects such as mirrors are used to deflect negative energy. Cities are often short of such natural feng shui improvers as babbling brooks, but not to worry: a fish tank is a fine alternative.

Case Study 1: Bank of China

Bank of China Tower. In the politics of Hong Kong architecture, the stylish art deco building that served as the old Bank of China headquarters was the first trump: built after World War II, it was 20 feet higher than the adjacent Hongkong & Shanghai Bank (HSBC). In 1985 HSBC finished a steel-and-glass structure that dwarfed the old Bank of China, whose officials in turn commissioned the Chinese-American architect I.M. Pei to build a bigger, better headquarters, which opened in 1990.

Architectural Assessment: Although it's not as innovative as the HSBC skyscraper, the Bank of China Tower is a masterful, twisting spire of replicating triangles

(uh-oh). As the first building to break the ridgeline of Victoria Peak, it dominates Hong Kong's landscape and embodies the post-handover balance of power. Its 43rd-floor observation deck also offers panoramic, uncrowded Central views.

Feng Shui Assessment: The tower has some of the worst feng shui in town. Some say that because the building thins at the top, it resembles a screwdriver—one that's drilling the wealth out of Hong Kong; others prefer the metaphor of a knife into the heart of the SAR (Special Administrative Region). The two antennas sticking out of the top are said to resemble the two incense sticks burned for the dead. Circles, which look like coins, bring prosperity. The opposite effect is supposedly caused by the building's triangular angles and sharp edges—indeed, many believe that it has had a negative effect on nearby structures. The Lippo Centre, which faces one of the triangles, was formerly the Bond Centre, owned by disgraced Australian businessman Allen Bond, who was forced to sell the building because of financial troubles. Local gossip

has it that Government House—still the residence of colonial governors when the bank was built—was the target of these bad vibes. After the 1997 handover, Hong Kong's first chief executive, Tung Chee-Hwa, refused to live there, citing its bad feng shui. ⊠ *1 Garden Rd., Central* ☎ *No phone* 🎫 *Free* 🕐 *Observation deck: weekdays 8–6, Sat. 9–1* Ⓜ *Central, Exit J2.*

Case Study 2: HSBC

Hongkong & Shanghai Bank (HSBC) Main Building. Designed by Sir Norman Foster, the headquarters of Hong Kong's premier bank (it's depicted on most of the territory's paper money) was completed in 1985 at a whopping cost of more than US$1 billion. At a time of insecurity vis-à-vis China, it was a powerful statement that the bank had no intention of taking its money out of the territory.

The two bronze lions outside the building also guarded HSBC's previous headquarters, built in 1935. The one with the gaping mouth is named Stephen, after the Hong Kong branch manager at the time; the other's called Stitt, after the manager in Shanghai. If you look closely, you can see bullet marks in them from the 1941 Battle of Hong Kong.

Architectural Assessment: With its distinctive ladder facade, many consider this building a triumph—a landmark of modern architecture, even. It sits on four props that allow you to walk under it and look up through its glass belly into the soaring atrium within. Even more interesting is Foster's sensitive treatment of high-tech details: the mechanics of everything, from the elevators' gears and pulleys to the electric signs' circuit boards, are visible through smoked glass. Because of all these mechanics, irreverent locals call this the Robot

Building. ■TIP→ Computer-controlled glass mirrors—480 of them—change position throughout the day to reflect natural light into the bank. You can get an insider perspective by taking the escalators through the public banking hall up to the third-floor atrium.

Feng Shui Assessment: Rumor has it that during construction the escalators were reset from their original straight position so that they would be at an angle to the entrance. Because evil spirits can only travel in a straight line, this realignment was thought to prevent waterborne spirits from flowing in off Victoria Harbor. The escalators are also believed to resemble two whiskers of a powerful dragon, sucking money into the bank. Atop the building and pointing toward the Bank of China Tower are two metal rods that look like a window-washing apparatus. The rods are a classic feng shui technique designed to deflect the negative energy—in this case, of the Bank of China's dreaded triangles—away and back to its source. ⊠ *1 Queen's Rd., across from Statue Sq., Central* 🎫 *Free* 🕐 *Weekdays 9–5:30, Sat. 9–12:30* Ⓜ *Central, Exit K.*

THE PEAK EXPERIENCE

★ Fodor's Choice ☼ **Victoria Peak's** Chinese name, Tai Ping Shan, means Mountain of Great Peace, and it certainly seems to inspire momentary hushed awe in visitors at the viewing point, a few yards left along the road from the tram terminal. Spread below you is a glittering forest of skyscrapers; beyond them the harbor and—on a clear day—Kowloon's eight mountains. On a rainy day wisps of cloud catch on the buildings' pointy tops; at night both sides of the harbor burst into color. Consider having dinner at one of the restaurants near the Upper Terminus.
■TIP➜ Forsake all else up here and start your visit with the lookout point: there are a hundred other shopping ops in the world, but few views like this.

Before buying a return ticket down on the tram, consider taking one of the beautiful low-impact trails back to Central. Buses also go down. You'll be treated to spectacular views in all directions on the **Hong Kong Trail**, an easygoing 40- to 60-minute paved path that begins and ends at the Peak Tram Upper Terminus. Start by heading north along fern-encroached Lugard Road. There's another stunning view of Central from the lookout, 20 minutes along, after which the road snakes west to an intersection with Hatton and Harlech roads. From here Lantau, Lamma, and—on incredibly clear days—Macau come into view. The longer option from here is to wind your way down Hatton to the University of Hong Kong campus in Western District.

The tacky but immediately recognizable **Peak Tower** (✉ *128 Peak Rd., The Peak* ☎ *2849–0668* ⊕ *www.thepeak.com.hk* ☼ *Weekdays 10 AM–11 PM, weekends and holidays 8 AM–11 PM*) is where you'll find the panoramic-view Australian restaurant

PEAK OF EXCLUSIVITY

A trip to Victoria Peak puts you within spitting distance of some *very* expensive real estate, including the infamous Severn Road, though prices have halved since the property boom of the late 1990s, when houses fetched up to $130 million. But money couldn't always get you into this club—in the 19th century you needed the governor's permission to have a home on the Peak, because his summer residence was here. Local Chinese people weren't allowed to live here until 1947.

Pearl on the Peak. Local heroes Bruce Lee, Jackie Chan, and Michelle Yeoh are some of the famous faces resisting meltdown at Asia's first branch of London's famous wax works, **Madame Tussaud's** (☎ *2849–6966* ⊕ *www.madametussauds.com/hongkong* ✉ *HK$160* ☼ *10–10*), which specializes in Asian stars of all categories, in addition to the usual international celebrities. The neighboring upscale restaurant **Peak Lookout** (✉ *121 Peak Rd., the Peak Central* ☎ *2849–1000* ⊕ *www.thepeaklookout.com.hk* ☼ *Sun.–Thurs. 10:30 AM–11:30 PM, Fri., Sat., and eve of holidays 10:30 AM–1 AM*) emerged in 2001 from the site of the beloved Peak Café, which first opened in 1947. It offers fine dining in a heritage-theme setting with an open garden terrace overlooking Aberdeen.

■TIP➜ Bypass the overpriced tourist traps inside Sky Terrace and Gallery and head straight up the escalators to the rooftop, which looks down over the Pok Fu Lam country park and reservoir, and, on a clear day, Aberdeen.

TO YOUR HEALTH

In recent years Traditional Chinese Medicine (TCM) has caused a lot of holistic hype in the West. Around here, though, it's been going strong for a while—more than 2,000 years, to be precise. Although modern Hong Kongers may see western doctors for serious illnesses, for minor complaints and everyday pick-me-ups they still turn to traditional remedies.

To get to the root of your body's disequilibrium, a TCM practitioner takes your pulse in different places, examines your tongue, eyes, and ears, and talks to you. Your prescription could include herbal tonics, teas, massage, dietary recommendations, and acupuncture.

Learning to Balance

Taoists believe that the world is made up of two opposing but interdependent forces: negative *yin*, representing darkness and the female, and positive *yang*, standing for light and masculinity. Both are essential for good health: when one becomes stronger than the other in the body, we get sick.

Another concept is *qi*, the energy or life force behind most bodily functions. It flows through channels or meridians: if these are blocked, ill health can ensue. Acupuncture along these meridians is a way of putting your qi in order.

It's not all inner peace—to be healthy you need to be in harmony with your environment, too. The Five Elements theory divides up both the universe and the body into different "elemental" categories: water, wood, fire, earth, and metal. Practitioners seek to keep all five elements in balance.

If you don't know your qi from your chin, and you're not sure if you need a dried seahorse or a live snake, head to the **Eu Yan**

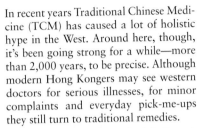

Sang Medical Hall. Glass cases at this reputable store display reindeer antlers, dried fungi, ginseng, and other medicinal mainstays. Grave but helpful clerks behind hefty wooden counters will happily sell you purported cures for anything from the common cold to impotence (the cure for the latter is usually slices of reindeer antler boiled into tea). ■TIP→ The Hong Kong Tourism Board organizes free introductory classes on Chinese medicine here every Wednesday at 2:30 PM. From Sheung Wan MTR, walk left along Wing Lok Street, right into Wing Wo Street, then left onto Queen's Road Central. There are other smaller branches all over Hong Kong; try the one on 18 Russell Street in Causeway Bay for over-the-counter consultations in English. ✉ *152 Queen's Rd. Central, Central* ☎ *3521–1233, 3521–1236 hotline* ⊕ *www.euyansang.com* ⊗ *Mon.–Sat. 10–2, 3–7* Ⓜ *Sheung Wan, Exit E2.*

⚠ Chinese medicines aren't regulated by the Hong Kong government. Anything that sounds dubious or dangerous might be just that.

Brush up on traditional treatments at the **Hong Kong Museum of Medical Sciences.** The least morbid and most enlightening exhibits compare Chinese and western medical practices, and show Chinese medicines of both animal and plant origin. Elsewhere, dusty displays of old medical equipment send macabre thrills up your spine. Reaching this museum is a healthy experience in itself: you pant up several blocks' worth of stairs to the Edwardian building in which it's located. ■TIP→ The cheat's way of getting here is on the Mid-levels Escalator: alight at Caine Road and walk west a few blocks to Ladder Street. The museum is just down the first flight of stairs, on the left. ✉ *2 Caine La., Midlevels,*

Central ☎ *2549–5123* ⊕ *www.hkmms.org. hk* ✉ *HK$10* ⊙ *Tues.–Sat. 10–5, Sun. 1–5* Ⓜ *Sheung Wan.*

Taking the Cure

Therapeutic massages are the specialty at **Charlie's Acupressure and Massage Centre of the Blind.** An hour-long massage costs around HK$250. ✉ *Room 205, 2nd fl., Tung Ming Building, 40–42, Des Voeux Rd. Central, Central* ☎ *2810–6666* Ⓜ *Central.*

The **Hong Kong University Chinese Medicine Clinic and Pharmacy** is a training clinic run by the most respected med school in town. It also has master practitioners of acupuncture and orthopedics on hand. Consultations start at HK$100, visits to the masters at HK$300 (not including medication). ✉ *Admiralty Centre, 2nd fl., Unit 50–53, Harcourt Rd., Admiralty* ☎ *3761–1188* ⊙ *Tues.–Sat. 10–2, 3–8, Sun. 9:30–1:30* Ⓜ *Admiralty, Exit A.*

Acupuncture, acupressure, and herbal medicine are just some of the offerings at the **Quality Chinese Medical Centre.** Consultations start at HK$70; expect to pay around HK$250 for acupuncture. ✉ *Jade Centre, 5th fl., Unit A, 98 Wellington St., Central* ☎ *2881–8267 English hotline* ⊕ *www.qualitytcm.com* Ⓜ *Central.*

Established in 1669, **Tong Ren Tang** has long been one of mainland China's most respected traditional medicine companies. ✉ *Watsons, Haiphong Mansion, 2nd fl., 101 Nathan Rd., Central* ☎ *3153–5059* ⊕ *www.tongrentang.com.*

At the root of Chinese acupressure and acupuncture is reflexology, which is based on the theory that there are reflex points on the feet, hands, and head linked to every part of the body. Thus, a good foot, hand, or head massage is believed to effectively relieve tension or even treat illness. Foot massage need not be torture in the gentle hands of **Reflexology at Happy Foot,** where the goal is to make your whole body feel relaxed, from the feet up. Massages cost HK$198 for 50 minutes. ✉ *Jade Centre, 11th fl., 98–102 Wellington St., Central* ☎ *2544–1010* ⊙ *Daily 10–midnight* Ⓜ *Central.*

Healthy Ways

In colonial times **Bonham Strand,** a curving thoroughfare in Sheung Wan, was a major commercial hub. Sadly, its wooden shop fronts are fast falling victim to real-estate development. The few that remain are medicinal mother lodes: wood-clad walls are lined with shelves of jars filled with pungent ingredients such as fungi, barks,

SMOOTH MOVES

Tai Chi (A Centuries-Old Art)

Just before dawn you'll see young businesspeople and retirees alike practicing tai chi: slow, steady, flowing movements with moderate postures designed to improve physical and mental well-being. There's no better advertising for tai chi than seeing an octogenarian balance on one leg, with the other outstretched. Although the health and philosophical aspects of tai chi may be common knowledge, few people know that it's also a subtle, sophisticated, and scientific method of self-defense.

and insects. These are consumed dried and ground up—infused in hot water or tea or taken as powder or pills. West of the intersection with Wing Lok Street, the original facades give way to those with big plate-glass windows displaying bundles of hairy-looking forked yellow roots—this is the heart of the ginseng wholesale trade. Ginseng is a broad-spectrum remedy that's a mainstay of Chinese medicine.

A sharp, musty smell fills the air when you turn down **Wing Lok Street** or **Des Voeux Road West**, Sheung Wan streets renowned for their dried-seafood stores. Out of shop fronts spill sacks filled to bursting with dried and salted fish, seahorses, shrimp, and abalone—a shellfish that is to China what oysters are to the West. Foot-wide fungi, gleaming beans, wrinkly red prunes, nuts, and even rosebuds make up the rest of the stock. A grimmer offering lurks behind a few shop windows: highly prized shark's fins, purported to be an aphrodisiac.

At Possession Street, where Queen's Road Central becomes **Queen's Road West**, shop windows display what looks like clumps of fine vermicelli noodles, ranging in color from pale gold to rich chestnut. These are birds' nests, which are used to make

NO GIN, JUST TONIC

Downing a glass of herbal health tonic is a normal part of many a Hong Konger's day. There are blends for flu, headaches, colds, and coughs. Many stores have English labels; if not, tell the server your troubles, and he or she will run you off a glass of whatever works best. Most cost HK$6–HK$20 a dose.

a much cherished (and correspondingly expensive) soup that tastes rather disappointingly like egg white.

In herb shops on Queen's Road West beyond the intersection with Hollywood Road, herbs, dried mushrooms, and other more mysterious ingredients offer the promise of longevity.

Don't poke your fingers into the grubby cages outside shops on **Hillier Street,** the center of the snake trade. A snake's meat is used in winter soups to ward off colds, and its gallbladder reputedly improves vigor and virility.

Tai Chi Masters (AD 1247-New Millennium and Beyond)

Tai chi's founder was Chang San Feng, a Taoist born in AD 1247. One of the greatest masters, however, was Yang Lu Chan (1799–1872), known as Invincible Yang, who served as the chief combat instructor to the Imperial Guard during the Qing Dynasty. To follow in their footsteps you must study under an accomplished master. To try tai chi while you're in town, contact the HKTB (☎ 2508–1234), which offers free classes at Sculpture Court outside the Hong Kong Museum of Art.

BEACHES

Hong Kong has many fantastic beaches with gorgeous views of the sea dotted with small green islands. On the southern coast of the main island, the most accessible and most popular are Stanley and Repulse Bay. Just to the west is the smaller, less-crowded Deep Water Bay, and farther west is the more intimate South Bay. On the southeast coast of the island, Turtle Cove is isolated and beautiful, and Shek O's beach has a community feel. Day trips to the outlying islands (⇨ *Island Hopping*) can also include sunbathing on a clean beach. You can reach most beaches by bus or taxi (HK$150 and up).

The waters off beaches in the New Territories, particularly the Sai Kung Peninsula, are crystal clear. Pollution can be a problem on the Southside, though that doesn't deter the thousands who flock seaside for respite from the summer heat. ■TIP→ Hong Kong's Environmental Protection Department has set some tough guidelines and goals for cleaning up area waters. For more info, including beach-by-beach pollution ratings, check out the EPD's Web site: www.epd.gov.hk/epd.

Southside

Deep Water Bay. On Island Road, just to the east of Ocean Park and all its amusements, this bay was the setting for the William Holden film *Love Is a Many Splendored Thing* (1955). Nearby are the manicured greens of the Deep Water Bay Golf Course, which is owned by the Hong Kong Golf Club. The area has become a multimillionaires' enclave, and is home to Hong Kong's richest man, Li Ka-shing, a real-estate tycoon. *From Exchange Square Bus Terminus in Central, take Bus 6, 64, 260, or 6A.*

■TIP→ For a scenic route to Deep Water Bay, take Bus 70 from Central's Exchange Square to Aberdeen and change to Bus 73, which passes the beach en route to Stanley.

Repulse Bay. It's named after the British warship HMS *Repulse* and not, as some say, after its slightly murky waters. It was home of the now demolished Repulse Bay Hotel, which gained notoriety in December 1941, when Japanese clambered over the hills behind it, entered its gardens, and overtook the British, who were using the hotel as headquarters. **Repulse Bay Verandah Restaurant & Bamboo Bar** (⊠ *109 Repulse Bay Rd., Southside* ☎ *2292–2822* ⊕ *www.therepulsebay.com*)—a great place for traditional English afternoon tea—is a replica of the eating and drinking establishment that once graced the hotel. High tea is served Tuesday to Saturday from 3 to 5:30 and Sunday from 3:30 to 5:30. There are several Chinese restaurants and snack kiosks on the beach. The Lifesaving Club at the beach's east end has large statues of Tin Hau, goddess of the sea, and Kwun Yum, goddess of mercy. ⚠ If you opt for a meal in a seafood restaurant here or at any beach, note that physicians caution against eating raw shellfish because of hepatitis outbreaks. *From Exchange Square Bus Terminus in Central, take Bus 6, 6A, 6X, 66, 64, or 260.*

Shek O. This wide beach is almost Mediterranean in appearance, with its low-rise houses and shops set prettily on a headland. In Shek O village you can find old mansions, small shops selling inflatable toys and other beach gear, and a few popular Chinese and Thai restaurants. Follow the curving path from the town square across a footbridge to the "island" of Tai Tau Chau, really a large rock with

a lookout over the South China Sea. Also near town are the Shek O Golf and Country Club and the superb Shek O Country Park, with great trails and bird-watching: look for Kentish plovers, reef egrets, and black-headed gulls, as well as the colorful rufus-backed shrike and the ubiquitous chatty bulbul. *From Central, take MTR to Shau Kei Wan, then take Bus 9 to last stop (about 30 min).*

Stanley. Notorious during World War II as the home of Japan's largest POW camps in Hong Kong, Stanley is now known primarily for its market, a great place for deals on knickknacks, ceramics, paintings, casual clothing, and sporting goods. Past the market, on Stanley Main Street, a strip of restaurants and pubs faces the bay. On the other side of the bay is a temple honoring Tin Hau.

Stanley's wide main beach is the site of Hong Kong's official Dragon Boat races, usually held in June, in which teams paddle out into the sea, turn around, and, at the sound of the gun, race ferociously back to shore. The beach is popular with the windsurfing, waterskiing, and wakeboarding crowd. **Patrick's Water-skiing** (⊠ *Tai Tam, Stanley* ☎ *2813–2372*) is run by the friendly, laid-back man himself. Patrick will take you to the best area waters and give you pointers on your technique. The fee—HK$700 per hour on weekdays, HK$800 on weekends—includes a range of equipment. *From Exchange Square Bus Terminus in Central, take Bus 6, 6A, 6X, 66, 64, or 260.*

The New Territories

Hap Mun Wan. Half Moon Bay is a brilliant, golden-sand beach on a grassy island near Sai Kung Town. It's one of the many small beaches among dozens

WINDSURFING

Windsurfing has grown dramatically in popularity since Hong Kong's Lee Lai-shan sailed off with a women's Olympic gold medal at the 1996 Summer Olympic Games in Atlanta, inspiring a generation of youngsters to take up the sport, which is further popularized on ESPN and MTV. Now windsurfing centers at Tai Tam on Hong Kong Island, Sha Ha beach in Sai Kung, and Tung Wan Beach (Lee's home on Cheung Chau Island) will gladly start you on the path to glory with some lessons.

of small islands near Sai Kung that are popular and easy to reach. **Bunn's Divers Institute** (⊠ *188 Johnston Rd., Chuen Fung House, Wan Chai* ☎ *3422–3322 or 2574-7951* ⊕ *www.bunnsdivers.com*) runs outings for qualified divers to areas like Sai Kung. Sampans to Half Moon depart from the Sai Kung waterfront, beside the bus station. If you're sharing a sampan with other passengers, remember the color of the flag on the roof: that's the color you need for your return ferry. Shared sampans cost HK$40. ■TIP→ To cruise around the harbor, rent a *kaido* (pronounced "guy-doe," one of the small boats run by private operators for about HK$130 round-trip), and stop at tiny Yim Tin Tsai Island, which has a rustic Catholic mission church built in 1890. *From Central, take MTR to Hang Hau, then Exit B1 and Minibus 101M to Sai Kung Town.*

Sha Ha. The sand isn't fine and golden, but the main reason people visit this beach is for the windsurfing. Sha Ha's waters are shallow, even far from shore, and ideal for beginning windsurfers. Grab something to eat at the restaurants and bars that dot

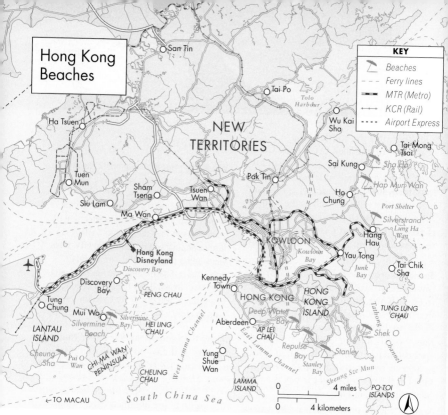

KEY

Beaches	
Ferry lines	
MTR (Metro)	
KCR (Rail)	
Airport Express	

San Tin

Tai Po

Tolo Harbour

Ha Tsuen

Wu Kai Sha

NEW TERRITORIES

Tai Mong Tsai

Sai Kung

Sha Ha

Tuen Mun

Sham Tseng

Tsuen Wan

Pak Tin

Ho Chung

Hap Mun Wan

Port Shelter

Siu Lam

Ma Wan

Silverstrand

Lung Ha Wan

KOWLOON

Hang Hau

Hong Kong Disneyland

Discovery Bay

Kowloon Bay

Yau Tong

Tai Chik Sha

Discovery Bay

Kennedy Town

Junk Bay

Tung Chung

PENG CHAU

HONG KONG ISLAND

HONG KONG ISLAND

TUNG LUNG CHAU

Mui Wo

Silvermine Bay

HEI LING CHAU

Deep Water Bay

Aberdeen

AP LEI CHAU

Shek O

LANTAU ISLAND

Silvermine Beach

Yung Shue Wan

Repulse Bay

Stanley

Cheung Sha

Pui O Wan

CHI MA WAN PENINSULA

CHEUNG CHAU

LAMMA ISLAND

Stanley Bay

Sheung Sze Mun

PO TOI ISLANDS

←TO MACAU

South China Sea

0   4 miles

0   4 kilometers

the beach. You can take lessons or rent a board or even a kayak at the **Windsurfing Centre Hong Kong** (✉ Shop 13, 1/F, Ko Shing Bldg., 9 King Man St., Sai Kung ☎ 9733–1228 ⊕ www.windsurfing.com.hk). Ask for Eddy. From Central, take MTR to Hang Hau, then Exit B1 and Minibus 101M to Sai Kung Town. It's a 10-min walk along the shore to Sha Ha.

Silverstrand. Though a little rocky in spots, this beach at the east end of Sai Kung near Clear Water Bay has soft sand and is crowded on summer weekends. Walk down a steep set of steps to reach the small stretch of beach where families enjoy all manner of floating beds and tubes in the sea. Despite the heat, barbecuing is a popular beach activity, where the local style is to hold long forks laden with sausages, chicken wings, fish balls, or other finger food over the coals. From Central, take MTR to Hang Hau, then Exit B1 and Minibus 11M toward the University of Science and Technology.

Lantau Island

An often-overlooked fact is that when visitors arrive, they land on Lantau Island—on a large stretch of reclaimed land purposely built for the airport called Chep Lap Kok. Twice the size of Hong Kong Island, Lantau is also home to the giant Tian Tan Buddha statue, which sits majestically on a hilltop next to the Po Lin Monastery. The Ngong Ping 360 cable car whisks you here in 25 minutes. Also on Lantau is Hong Kong Disneyland, a small version of its American counterparts, as well as the charming Tai O fishing village.

Cheung Sha. Popular Cheung Sha is only a short taxi or bus ride from the Silvermine Bay ferry pier. Its mile-long expanse is excellent for swimming. The Stoep

REGION/BEACH	Travel Time from Central	Peaceful	Swimmable	Lifeguards	Showers/ Restrooms
Southside					
Deep Water Bay	20 mins.	crowded	often	yes	yes
Repulse Bay	30 mins.	crowded	often	yes	yes
South Bay	30 mins.	crowded	yes	yes	yes
Shek O	60 mins.	crowded	yes	yes	yes
Stanley	40–45 mins.	crowded	yes	yes	yes
New Territories					
Hap Mun Wan	60–75 mins.	often	yes	yes	yes
Sha Ha	60–75 mins.	often	yes	no	no
Silverstrand	60 mins.	crowded	yes	yes	yes
Clear Water Bay	70–80 mins.	crowded	yes	yes	yes
Outer Islands					
Cheung Chau: Tung Wan	60–75 mins.	crowded	yes	yes	yes
Lamma: Hung Shing Ye	60–75 mins.	often	yes	yes	yes
Lamma: Lo So Shing	60–75 mins.	often	yes	yes	yes
Lantau: Cheung Sha Wan	60–75 mins.	often	yes	yes	yes
Tap Mun	90–120 mins.	yes	yes	no	no

restaurant on the beach serves great Mediterranean and South African fare. Watching the sunset here is a perfect end to a sun-drenched day. ■TIP→ There are only 30 taxis on the entire island, so on weekends, when things get busy, make sure you ask the restaurant to get you one back to the pier. *Take ferry from Central's Pier 6 to Mui Wo. Buses meet ferry every half hour on weekdays and Sat.; on Sun., buses leave when full.*

Silvermine Beach. The stretch of beach can be seen from the ferry as you approach the island, though because of its proximity to the pier and other fishing boats, the waters aren't as clean as those at Cheung Sha. You can rent bikes at the Silvermine

Beach Hotel and explore the village of Mui Wo. *Take ferry from Central's Pier 6 to Mui Wo. Buses meet ferry every half hour on weekdays and Sat.; on Sun., buses leave when full.*

ISLAND HOPPING

Hong Kong comprises 260 outlying islands, and several of them are great escapes from the city for the waterfront views, some seafood, and a little peace. Island villages are up to speed (to the regret of many, cell phones work), but they run at a more relaxed pace. Hong Kong ferries travel from Central to many of the islands, where beaches are often a short walk from the pier.

Cheung Chau. This small, carless island southwest of Hong Kong is best known as the home of windsurfing Olympic gold medalist Lee Lai-shan. At the tip of the beach is a lovely outdoor restaurant owned by relatives of San-San (as she's affectionately called), who have proudly hung a large framed picture of the athlete in her golden moment. The island community lives mostly on the sandbar that connects the two hilly tips of this 1.2-mile-long, dumbbell-shape landmass. It's a one-hour ferry ride from Central's Pier 5 outside Two IFC, and the town harbor is lined with seafood restaurants and shops.

On weekends Tung Wan, Cheung Chau's main beach, is so crowded that its sweep of golden sand is barely visible. At one end of the beach is the Warwick Hotel. Plenty of nearby restaurants offer refreshments, seafood, and shade. There are no private cars allowed on this island, so the air is noticeably cleaner.

Lamma Island. Lamma is as close to a 1960s bohemian scene as Hong Kong gets—full of laid-back expats driven out of Central by high rents. They've spawned a subculture of vegetarian restaurants, health-food shops, and craft stores. The ferry from Central's Pier 4, in front of Two IFC, to the village of Sok Kwu Wan or to Yung Shue Wan takes about 25 minutes.

It doesn't matter which village you go to first—time spent on beaches near them and on the hour-long walk through rolling green hills between them is what a leisurely afternoon on Lamma is all about.

"Beach" overstates the scale of the sandy strip known as Hung Shing Ye. It's also called Power Station Beach because of the massive power plant visible from it. The view doesn't deter the young locals, who materialize whenever the rays shine down. They even swim here—sometimes. Stay on shore if you see plastic bags or other refuse on the water. Or just head to Yung Shue Wan, the former farming and fishing village that's been an expat enclave since the early 1980s. Main Street is lined with handicraft shops, though the smell of the fish markets is a reminder of Lamma's humbler, less cosmopolitan origins.

Popular with families, Lo So Shing beach is an easy 20- to 30-minute hike on a paved path from Sok Kwu Wan, the smaller and grittier of Lamma's two villages and one that's notable mainly for the string of cavernous seafood restaurants that line the path leading from the pier. ■TIP→ Arrive on foot from Yung Shue Wan; your first glimpse of the bay from the hills will be stunning.

Tung Ping Chau. Inaugurated in November 2009, Hong Kong's very own Geopark confirms its efforts to promote eco-tourism through geo-science—more specifically, by encouraging people to check out fascinating rock formations on the outlying islands. On the archipelago, eight geosites are identified and introduced, including Tung Ping Chau, a tiny crescent-shaped island, which boasts the youngest rocks in Hong Kong, estimated at a mere 55 million years old. One of its famous landforms is named Dragon Diving into

the Sea. The island is also known for its distinctive shale beds, which make the ground look like a layered sponge cake with faint ripple marks, often reflecting vivid colors. Ferries to Tung Ping Chau depart every weekend from Ma Liu Shui Pier, about a 15-minute walk from the Chinese University (University MTR station) along Tai Po Road in Sha Tin. Call 2527–2513 to confirm ferry times and price (⊕ *www.geopark.gov.hk*).

Po Toi Islands. Three barren little fishing islands, virtually unchanged since medieval times, sit in the extreme southeast of Hong Kong. The largest, Po Toi, offers spectacular walks and a fine seafood restaurant. Walk uphill past primitive dwellings, many deserted, to the 150-year-old Tin Hau Temple, or walk east through the hamlet of Wan Tsai, past banana and papaya groves, to some geometric rock carvings, believed to have been carved during the local Bronze Age, about 2,500 years ago.

A trip to the Po Toi Islands is an all-day affair. Ferries leave Aberdeen on Tuesday, Thursday, and weekends at 8:15 AM and from Blake Pier in Stanley at 10 or 11:30 AM. Ferries return at 3 and 4:30 PM directly to Blake Pier, or at 6 PM to Aberdeen via Blake Pier. A round-trip costs HK$40.

Tap Mun Island. Ma Liu Shui Ferry Pier is the starting point for a ferry tour of the harbor and Tap Mun Island, whose east side is home to Tap Mun Cave and some of the territories' best-kept beaches. The ferry makes many stops; if you take the 8:30 AM trip you'll have time to hike around Tap Mun Island and be back in the city by late afternoon. The last ferry returning from the island is at 5:30 PM. A round-trip costs HK$32 on weekdays and HK$50 on weekends.

The New Fisherman's Village, on the island's southern side, is populated mainly by Hakka women. About 1 km (½ mi) north, near the western shore, is the ancient village of Tap Mun, where you'll see old women playing mah-jongg. The Tin Hau Temple, dedicated to the goddess of the sea, is less than ½ km (¼ mi) north of the village. It's atop steps that lead down to the harbor; inside are old model junks and, of course, a veiled figure of the goddess.

SAIL AWAY: SAMPANS AND JUNKS

Named after an English lord, not the Scottish city, the Southside town of Aberdeen (30 minutes from Central via Bus 70 or 91) was once a pirate refuge. After World War II it became commercial, as the *tanka* (boat people) attracted visitors to their floating restaurants. Today the harbor is home to some 3,000 junks and sampans, still interspersed with floating restaurants, among them the famous Jumbo Kingdom, with its faux-Chinese decorations covered in lights. The tanka still live on houseboats, and though the vessels look picturesque, conditions are depressing.

Elderly women with sea- and sun-weathered skin and croaking voices may invite you aboard a sampan for a harbor ride. It's better to go with one of the licensed operators that depart from the seawall opposite Aberdeen Centre. A tour lets you see how the fishing community lives and works and how sampans are also homes, sometimes with three generations on one small vessel. Ironically, about 110 yards away are the yachts of the Marina Club and the slightly less exclusive Aberdeen Boat Club.

You can also hire a junk to take you to outer islands: Cheung Chau, Lamma, Lantau, Po Toi, or the islands in Port Shelter, Sai Kung. Sailing on a large (up to 80-feet-long), well-varnished, plushly appointed, air-conditioned junk—which can serve as a platform for swimmers and water-skiers—is a unique Hong Kong experience. Many local "weekend admirals" command these floating rumpus rooms, which are also known as "gin junks" because so much alcohol is often consumed aboard them.

Ap Lei Chau (Duck's Tongue Island), accessible via sampan or Buses 90B or 91 along the bridge that connects it with Aberdeen, has a yard where junks, yachts, and sampans are built, almost all without formal plans. With 86,800 people living on 1.3 square km (½ square mi), Ap Lei Chau is the world's most densely populated island.

■TIP→ Look to your right when crossing the bridge to Ap Lei Chau for a superb view of the harbor and its countless junks.

The ritzy bar **aqua luna** (☎2116–8821 ⊕ *www.aqualuna.com.hk*) is on the *Cheung Po Tsai,* an impressive junk named for a pirate and created by an 80-year-old local craftsman. It's slow but impressive, with magnificent red sails. A 45-minute cruise around Victoria Harbour costs HK\$150 by day and HK\$180 at night. Departures are every afternoon at 1:30 and 2:30, then every hour on the half hour from 5:30 PM to 10:30 PM from Tsim Sha Tsui Pier 1, near the Cultural Centre, and 15 minutes later from Pier 9 in Central.

The **Duk Ling** (☎2573–5282 ⊕*www. dukling.com.hk*) is a fully restored authentic fishing junk, originally built in Macau in the 1950s, whose large red sails are a sight to behold. For HK\$50, the HKTB offers visitors aged 3 to 75 one-hour sails from Kowloon Pier (Thursday at 2 PM and 4 PM, Saturday at 10 AM and noon) and from Central's Pier 9 (Thursday at 3 PM and 5 PM, Saturday at 11 AM and 1 PM). Register first at the HKTB Visitor Centre in Tsim Sha Tsui, and bring your passport to prove you're from out of town.

HIKING

Most visitors don't come for the lush lowlands, bamboo and pine forests, rugged mountains with panoramas of the sea, and secluded beaches, but nature is never very far from all the skyscrapers. About 40% of Hong Kong's territory is protected in 23 parks, including three marine parks and one marine reserve.

Don't expect unspoiled wilderness, however. Few upland areas escape Hong Kong's plague of hill fires for more than a few years at a time. Some are caused by dried-out vegetation; others erupt from small graveside fires set by locals to clear the land around ancestors' eternal resting spots. Partly because of these fires, most of Hong Kong's forests, except for a few spots in the New Territories, have no obvious wildlife other than birds—and mosquitoes. Bring repellent.

Gear

Necessities include sunglasses, hat, bottled water, day pack, and sturdy hiking boots. Weather tends to be warm during the day and cool toward nightfall. The cliff sides get quite windy. If you need some basics, there are several options.

Although it doesn't sell the same range of equipment you'd find back home, **Great Outdoor Clothing Company** (⊠ *Shop LG48, Silvercord Bldg., 30 Canton Rd., Tsim Sha Tsui, Kowloon* ☎ *2730–9009* ⊕ *www.theoutdoorshop.com.hk*) will do in a pinch.

Timberland (⊠ *Shop 116, Pacific Place, 88 Queensway, Admiralty* ☎ *2868–0845* ⊕ *www.timberland.com*) sells hiking boots, backpacks, and appropriate togs.

World Sports Co., Ltd. (⊠ *1st fl., 83 Fa Yuen St., Mong Kok, Kowloon* ☎ *2396–9357*) caters to your every outdoor need.

Pick up guides such as *Hong Kong Hikes* from any bookstore.

You can buy trail maps at the **Government Publications Centre** (⊠ *Pacific Place, Government Office, ground fl., 66 Queensway, Admiralty* ☎ *2537–1910* ⊕ *www.bookstore.gov.hk*). Ask for blueprints of the trails and the Countryside Series maps. Note that the HM20C series has handsome four-color maps, but they're not very reliable. The HKTB also provides maps with good walking trails and hikes.

Trails

★ Fodor's Choice **Dragon's Back.** One of the most popular trails crosses the "rooftop" of Hong Kong Island. Take the Peak Tram from Central up to Victoria Peak, and tackle as much or as little of the range as you feel like—there are numerous exits "downhill" to public-transport networks. Surprisingly wild countryside feels a world away from the urban bustle below, and the panoramas—of Victoria Harbour on one side, and Southside and outlying islands on the other—are spectacular. You can follow the trail all the way to the delightful seaside village of Shek O, where you can relax over a casual evening dinner before returning to the city by bus or taxi. The most popular route, and shorter, is from Shek O Country Park. Take the MTR from Central to Shau Kei Wan, then Bus 9, alight after the first roundabout, near the crematorium.

Lion Rock. The easiest way to access the trail to Lion Rock, a spectacular summit, is from Kowloon. The hike passes through dense bamboo groves along the Eagle's Nest Nature Trail and up open slopes to Beacon Hill for 360-degree views over hills and the city. The contrasting vistas of green hills and the cityscape are extraordinary. There's a climb up the steep rough track to the top of Lion Rock, a superb vantage point for appreciating Kowloon's setting between hills and sea. The trail ends at Wong Tai Sin Taoist Temple, where you can have your fortune told. To start, catch the MTR to Choi Hung (25 minutes from Tsim Sha Tsui) and a 10-minute taxi ride up Lion Rock. From Wong Tai Sin, return by MTR.

★ **Fodor's Choice** **MacLehose Trail.** Named after a former Hong Kong governor, the 97-km (60-mi) MacLehose is the grueling course for the annual charity event, the MacLehose Trailwalker. Top teams finish the hike in an astonishing 15 hours. Mere mortals should allow three to four days or simply tackle one section or another on a day hike or two.

This isolated trail through the New Territories starts at Tsak Yue Wu, beyond Sai Kung, and circles High Island Reservoir before breaking north. A portion takes you through the Sai Kung Country Park and up a mountain called Ma On Shan. Turn south for a high-ridge view, and walk through Ma On Shan Country Park. From here, walk west along the ridges of the mountains known as the Eight Dragons, which gave Kowloon its name.

After crossing Tai Po Road, the path follows a ridge to the summit of Tai Mo Shan (Big Hat Mountain), which, at 3,140 feet, is Hong Kong's tallest mountain. On a clear day you can even see the spire of the Bank of China building in Central from here. Continuing west, the trail drops to Tai Lam Reservoir and Tuen Mun, where you can catch public transport back to the city. To reach Tsak Yue Wu, take the MTR to Hang Hau, then Exit B1 and Minibus 101M to Sai Kung Town. From Sai Kung Town, take Bus 94 to the country park.

■ **TIP→** An easier way to access Tai Mo Shan is via an old military road. En route you'll see the old British barracks, now occupied by the People's Liberation Army. Take the MTR to Tsuen Wan and exit the station at Shiu Wo Street, then catch Minibus 82.

Wilson Trail. The 78-km- (48-mi-) long trail runs from Stanley Gap on the south end of Hong Kong Island, through rugged peaks that have a panoramic view of Repulse Bay and the nearby Round and Middle islands, and to Nam Chung in the northeastern New Territories. You have to cross the harbor by MTR at Quarry Bay to complete the entire walk. The trail is smoothed by steps paved with stone, and footbridges aid with steep sections and streams. Clearly marked with signs and information boards, this popular walk is divided into 10 sections, and you can easily take just one or two (figure on three to four hours per section); traversing the whole trail takes about 31 hours.

Section 1, which starts at Stanley Gap Road, is only for the very fit. Much of it requires walking up steep mountain grades. For an easier walk, try Section 7, which begins at Sing Mun Reservoir and takes you along a greenery-filled, fairly level path that winds past the eastern shore of the Sing Mun Reservoir in the New Territories and then descends to Tai Po, where there's a sweeping view of Tolo Harbour. Other sections will take you through the monkey forest at the Kowloon Hill Fitness Trail, over mountains, and past charming Chinese villages.

VERY AMUSING

As one child's buzz is another child's bore, it's best to vary the amusements to keep them entertained. Hong Kong has two major amusement parks, but many more opportunities to laugh and learn from observing live animals close-up, whether in captivity or in the wild.

Thrills and Spills

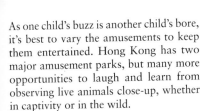

Hong Kong Disneyland. If you're expecting an Asian take on the Magic Kingdom, think again—this park on Lantau Island is aimed at mainland Chinese hungry for apple-pie Americana. It's as polished as all the other Disneys, but much smaller in scale. You can easily go on every ride at least once and see all the attractions in a day. If your kids are theme park–savvy, the tame rides here won't win their respect, but there are loads for little kids. Space Mountain is the only attraction with a height restriction, and it's by far the most thrilling, as you speed through pitch darkness. Otherwise, watch the *Lion Festival of the King* show, or just wait for the fireworks. ■TIP→ Hong Kong Disneyland operates a Fastpass system, which lets you jump the lines at the most popular attractions.

The MTR is the quickest way here: take the Tung Chung line to Sunny Bay, then change to the Disneyland Resort Line, whose special trains have royal-blue plush seating and Mickey-shape windows. Check opening hours online first, as they change monthly. ■TIP→ Shade is limited, so take the lead from locals and make an umbrella your No. 1 accessory— use it as a parasol if the sun blazes down or the traditional way if it rains. ☒ *Lantau Island* ⊕ *www.hongkongdisneyland.com* ☜*HK$350 peak days (weekends and school holidays); HK$295 other days* ☺ *Daily 10–9* Ⓜ *Disneyland Resort.*

Ocean Park. When it comes to amusement parks, there's no question where Hong Kongers' loyalties lie. Opened in 1977, this homegrown marine-theme park embraces both high- and low-octane buzzes along with fascinating animal attractions. The park often does renovations, acquires new creatures, and hosts special events to keep it competitive. Every Halloween night, for example, the park transforms into one giant spooky costume party. Furthermore, Ocean Park's conservation program was the first in the world to successfully breed dolphins by artificial insemination, and is primarily focused on the conservation of Asian wildlife, such as critically endangered reptiles. The park stretches out over 170 hilly acres, which you can gaze down at from the serenely silent cabins of the mile-long cable car that connects the tamer Low-lands area to the action-packed Headland. ■TIP→ If all you fancy is roller-coasting, enter the park at the Tai Shue Wan entrance. Beginning your visit on this side also tends to avoid the heftier crowd flow in the opposite direction. But if you really came to see the pandas, start at the main entrance.

Hong Kong's biggest roller coaster, the Dragon, is at the **Headland**, where the cable car stops, along with a ferris wheel, swinging pirate ship, and the Abyss Turbo Drop, consisting, simply, of a 185-foot vertical plunge. In **Adventure Land,** the geographically far-out Wild West–theme Mine Train was purposely designed to feel rickety and screw-loose; it also offers a truly exceptional view of the Aberdeen coastline as you scream. Expect a light spraying or a heavy drenching at the Raging River: it all depends on your seat (and your luck).

More than 2,000 fish inhabit the four-story Atoll Reef in **Marine Land,** where newer exhibits include the Chinese Sturgeon Aquarium and Pacific Pier, featuring more than 20 resident seals and sea lions. For sheer visual delight, the Sea Jelly Spectacular offers a colorful display in a dark environment.

The rock stars of the **Lowland Gardens** are the giant pandas. An An and Jia Jia, gifted to Hong Kong from Beijing in 1997, were once the main act, but now Le Le and Ying Ying, siblings who arrived in 2007, are now in the spotlight. Paths wind to other enclosures, including a cantilevered butterfly house where rare species are bred, an aviary, a goldfish pavilion, and a gator marsh. Cross a rickety bridge to the lush undergrowth of the Amazing Amazon, where you'll find toucans and flamingos.

Ocean Park is 30 minutes from Admiralty MTR or Central Star Ferry Pier by Citybus 629. Buses 70, 75, 90, 97, 260, 6A, and 6X also run from Central. ⊠ *Tai Shue Wan Rd., Aberdeen* ☎ *3923–2323* ⊕ *www.oceanpark.com.hk* ⊠ *HK$250* ⊙ *Daily 10–7.*

Animal Pursuits

Yuen Po Street Bird Garden. The air fills with warbling and tweeting about a block from this narrow public garden. Around 70 stalls stretch down one side of it, selling various species of birds, mostly smaller ones, in addition to cages, seed, and accessories. Ironically, the birds' cramped living conditions mirror those of many Hong Kong residents in the poorest parts of Kowloon. Plenty of wild birds swoop in to gorge on spilled food and commiserate with imprisoned brethren. Look for talking mynahs, budgies, and parrots toward the far end of the garden, where they also have more space to perch on independent stands to which they're chained. The garden was built to replace the old Bird Market, which was closed down during the worst avian-flu outbreaks. (Government sanitation programs mean the flu is no longer a threat, though all the vendors here ignore signs warning against contact with birds.) From the MTR station, walk east along Prince Edward Road for three short blocks, then turn left onto Sai Yee Street, then right onto Flower Market Road, for an aromatic approach. The Bird Garden is at the end of this flower-market street. ⊠ *Yuen Po St., Prince Edward, Kowloon* ☎ *2302–1762* ⊕ *www.lcsd.gov. hk/parks/ypsbg* ⊠ *Free* ⊙ *Daily 7 AM–8 PM* Ⓜ *Prince Edward, Exit B1.*

☯ **Edward Youde Aviary.** Built over a natural valley on the northern slope of Victoria Peak in 1992, this sprawling aviary is home to about 600 birds of 90 species indigenous to the endangered Malesian rainforests around Southeast Asia. As caws, chirps, and warbles fill your ears, and vibrant flashes of color swoop down or settle in nearby branches, you may spot broadbills, bulbuls, and leafbills, if not pheasants, partridges, and thrushes on the ground. Visitors walk through the tropical environment on timber walkways elevated to canopy level that rise up to almost 100 feet at their highest viewing point. On the valley floor below, pelicans rest at a swamp, which is contiguous with a small lake that lies outside the mesh. The aviary was named for a bird-loving colonial governor and is located in the southwest of Hong Kong Park, which you reach by walking up through Pacific Place shopping mall. ⊠ *Hong Kong Park, 19 Cotton Tree Dr., Admiralty Central* ☎ *2521–5041* ⊕ *www.lcsd.gov.hk/parks/*

hkp/en/edward_youde_intro.php ✉ *Free* 🕙 *Daily 9–5* Ⓜ *Admiralty, Exit C1.*

🍃 **Hong Kong Zoological & Botanical Gardens.** The city has grown around these noble gardens, which opened in 1864, and although they're now watched over by skyscrapers, a visit to them is still a delightful escape. Paths lined with semi-tropical trees, shrubs, and flowers wind past cramped zoo enclosures. Burmese pythons, Chinese alligators, Bali mynahs, Bornean orangutans, ring-tailed lemurs, and lion-tailed macaques are among its 400 birds, 70 mammals, and 50 reptiles. The Garden houses more than 1,000 species of plants indigenous to tropical and subtropical regions. Albany Road slices the park in half: birds and the greenhouse are on the eastern side, the other animals are to the west. A pedestrian underpass connects the two sides. ✉ *Albany Rd., Central* ☎ *2530–0154* ⊕ *www.lcsd.gov. hk/parks/hkzbg* ✉ *Free* 🕙 *Zoo: daily 6 AM–7 PM. Gardens: daily 6 AM–10 PM. Greenhouse: daily 9–4:30.*

A CHANGE OF PACE

Hong Kong Wetland Park. It may be a trek on the MTR and Light Rail, or at least one very long bus ride to get out to Tin Shui Wai in the New Territories, but it's worth it. While Tin Shui Wai is known for being one of Hong Kong's poorest communities, the Wetland Park's opening in 2006 helped raise its image with a 61-hectare Wetland Reserve home to numerous species of native wildlife—featuring birds, butterflies, dragonflies, fireflies, and flowers, as well as Hong Kong's own star crocodile Pui Pui, found a few years ago puttering around a swamp in Yuen Long. The reserve itself is a natural open marsh area over which are laid wooden footpaths, and so offers little shade, but its main highlights are the many wooden viewing houses in which you can observe birds unseen at a respectful distance through telescopes. Most of the houses have two stories, with plenty of bench area to sit and rest, but can get crowded quickly, as they're quite small. The park also has a visitor center, which includes an auditorium and several indoor galleries offering edutaining exhibits, as well as a café, play area, resource center, and souvenir shop. Take the MTR to Tin Shui Wai, then transfer to the Light Rail 705 or 706 and get off at Wetland Park Station. You can also take Bus 967 from Admiralty, and get off at Tin Yan Estate on Wetland Park Road. ✉ *Wetland Park Road, Tin Shui Wai, New Territories* ☎ *2708–8885 or 3152–2666* ⊕ *www.wetlandpark.com* ✉ *HK$30* 🕙 *Wed.–Mon. 10–5.* Ⓜ *Tin Shui Wai.*

CINEMA HONG KONG

Hong Kong cinema still projects an image of classic martial arts and prolific triad flicks, with a few auteurs capturing the nuanced poetry of life in the former British colony. Inside the territory, however, silly romantic comedies with Cantopop stars, gory/sexy ghost films, cheesy slapstick throwaways, and a handful of thoughtful independent films also populate the screens. It goes without saying that you can learn a lot about Hong Kong by watching its local flicks in-situ.

Post-1997

The Hong Kong film industry churned out more than 200 local features a year in the early 1990s; but by 1997 that number had plummeted to 85, and in 2007 Hong Kong released a mere 50 films. This decline in an empire can be credited, not only to changing audience tastes, but to increasing pressure from the "motherland" to target the mainland Chinese market. The result is often big-budget, epic-proportion, crowd-pleasing, censor-friendly co-productions, such as 2009's blockbuster *Bodyguards and Assassins*. But many local filmmakers have complained about the homegrown industry losing its distinct Hong Kong character.

Among the most popular Hong Kong films expressing post-1997 angst are Fruit Chan's *Made in Hong Kong, Durian Durian*, and *Little Cheung*, as well as Johnnie To's *Election* and *Election 2*. For a typical Hong Kong movie about Hong Kong, see Samson Chiu's *Golden Chicken*; for a less typical one, see Toe Yuen's animated *My Life as McDull*.

Meanwhile, don't forget to pay tribute to the legend Bruce Lee, whose bronze statue is frozen in stance on the eastern end of Kowloon's Avenue of Stars.

A Night at the Movies

An engaging cinema is an integral part of the Hong Kong movie-going experience. Except for children's and other niche-market films dubbed in Cantonese, all non-English-language films have both Chinese and English subtitles. For show times and theaters, check the Web sites of the movie chains or theaters directly, where you can usually see the seating chart updated in real time, before either booking online by credit card or buying your tickets at the counter later. Prime-time tickets range from HK$60 to HK$80, while most cinemas offer a discount of around 20% on Tuesday and morning matinees. Concession stands usually sell two kinds of popcorn—salty and sweet. ■TIP→ Some theaters can be notoriously frigid. Bring a sweater or borrow a shawl from the cinema if available.

Broadway Cinematheque. The train-station design of this art house has won awards; inside the foyer a departure board displays primarily foreign and independent films, with a few Hollywood productions to round out the sales. You can read the latest reel-world magazines from around the globe at Kubrick, the café-bookshop next door, which also sells film books, comics, and other alternative literature. An oasis of culture in a Kowloon housing estate, this one shouldn't be overlooked, especially if you're in the neighborhood. To get here, take the MTR to Yau Ma Tei, Exit C and browse through the Temple Street trinkets on your way over. ✉ *Prosperous Garden, 3 Public Square St., Yau Ma Tei, Kowloon* ☎ *2388–3188 ticketing hotline* ⊕ *www.cinema.com.hk* Ⓜ *Yau Ma Tei.*

Palace IFC. Large, sink-into brown leather seats and ushers in black suits make this intimate boutique cinema seem more like a private screening room than a multiplex. Five screens show new releases, foreign and independent films, and occasionally even restored celluloid classics. The adjoining bookshop and upscale café fit right into IFC's business-posh atmosphere, making it especially popular with the Central after-work crowd. It's pricier than most picture houses, but also much classier. ⊠ *IFC Mall, 8 Finance St., level 1, Central* ☎ *2388–6268* ⊕ *www.cinema. com.hk* Ⓜ *Hong Kong or Central.*

JP Cinema. When it's good old popcorn action fare you're after, JP treats its patrons right, without the shopping-mall multiplex madness. Past the snack bar you'll enter one of two theaters equipped with panoramic screens, surround sound, and a combined total of 658 red-cushioned seats for your all-round movie experience. It even projects 3-D movies digitally at 4K super-high resolution. Hollywood and Asian action thrillers, epic adventures, and blockbuster comedies rule the lineup. As you come up out of Causeway Bay MTR exit E, walk left and watch for the giant posters. ⊠ *22–36 Paterson St., Causeway Bay* ☎ *2881–5005, 3413–6688 booking* ⊕ *www.mclcinema. com* Ⓜ *Causeway Bay.*

President Theatre. This is one place on the Island where you can still see all the cheesy, vulgar, slapstick, sexy, scary, and silly local romantic comedies, triad films, and Category III (under 18 not allowed) horror flicks. Within walking distance of JP Cinema and UA (*www.cityline.com. hk*) Times Square multiplex in Causeway Bay, it's also another entertaining place to cool down on a hot day. Just point to the poster of the movie you want to watch when you get to the street-level ticket office. ⊠ *517 Jaffe Rd., Causeway Bay* ☎ *2836–5581* ⊕ *www.theatre. hk* Ⓜ *Causeway Bay.*

★ **Fodor's Choice** | **Hong Kong Film Archive.** Still wondering who all those handprints belong to on the Avenue of Stars? This is the place to see the faces behind the names, among an audience of elderly locals come to reminisce. Don't underestimate the popularity of old black-and-white picture shows in a modern auditorium; it's best to buy your movie ticket in advance to avoid sold-out disappointment. Not only does the theater screen rare classics from the history of Hong Kong cinema and beyond, but the building houses a genuine, living archive of film reels and documents dating back several decades. Conscientiously curated film programs are accompanied by an exhibition in a separate gallery downstairs. The Archive is a 10-minute walk from Sai Wan Ho MTR exit A. Several open cafés and restaurants overlooking the northeastern waterfront promenade are nearby. ⊠ *50 Lei King Rd., Sai Wan Ho, Eastern* ☎ *2739–2139* ⊕ *www. filmarchive.gov.hk* Ⓜ *Sai Wan Ho.*

OFF TO THE RACES

Even if you're not a gambler, it's worth going to one of Hong Kong's two tracks just to experience the phenomenon. The "sport of kings" is run under a monopoly by the Hong Kong Jockey Club, one of the territory's most powerful entities. It's a multimillion-dollar-a-year business, employing thousands of people and drawing crowds that approach insanity in their eagerness to rid themselves of their hard-earned money. Profits go to charity and community organizations.

The season runs from September through June. Some 65 races are held at one or the other of the two courses—on Saturday or Sunday afternoon 1 to 6 at Sha Tin and Wednesday night 7:30 to 11 at Happy Valley—which must rank among the world's great horse-racing experiences.

In the public stands the vibe is electric and loud, thanks to feverish gamblers shouting and waving their newspapers madly. Both courses have huge video screens at the finish line, so you can see what's happening every foot of the way. ■TIP➔ Contact the HKTB about Come Horseracing Tours, which begin at HK$690 and include transfers, guide, buffet with unlimited drinks, and tips on picking a winner.

★Fodor's Choice **Happy Valley Racecourse.** Hong Kong punters are the world's most avid horse-racing fans, and the beloved track in Happy Valley—opened on reclaimed marshland soon after the British first arrived in the territory—is one of their headquarters. The exhilarating blur of galloping hooves under jockeys dressed in bright silk jerseys is a must-see. The joy of the Happy Valley track, even for those who aren't into horses, is that it's smack in the middle of the city and surrounded by towering apartment blocks—indeed, people whose balconies hang over the backstretch often have parties on racing days. Dine with a view at Moon Koon restaurant, or stand in the open space right next to the track, with the roar of the crowd at your back and a front-row view of the finish line. The public entrance to the track is a 20-minute walk from Causeway Bay MTR Exit A (Times Square), or simply hop on the Happy Valley tram, which terminates right in front. ⊠ *Hong Kong Jockey Club, 1 Sports Rd., Happy Valley, Causeway Bay* 🕿 *2966–8111* ⊕ *racecourses.hkjc. com* ✉ *HK$10* Ⓜ *Causeway Bay.*

Sha Tin Racecourse. Whether you enter Sha Tin by road or rail, you'll be amazed to find this metropolis in the middle of the New Territories. One of the so-called "new towns," Sha Tin underwent a population explosion starting in the mid-1980s that transformed it from a town of 30,000 to a city of more than a half million. The biggest attraction is the racecourse, which is newer and larger than the one in Happy Valley, opened in 1978 with a capacity of 83,000. In fact, it's one of the world's most modern courses and, as such, is the venue for all championship events, including the official equestrian events during the 2008 Olympics. On race days you can take the MTR to the Racecourse station, where a walkway takes you directly to the track. ⊠ *Tai Po Rd., Sha Tin, New Territories* 🕿 *2966–6520* ⊕ *racecourses.hkjc. com* ✉ *HK$10* Ⓜ *Racecourse.*

Hong Kong
Neighborhoods

WORD OF MOUTH

"You can spend hours in Hong Kong Park—watching or joining the morning crowd doing their Tai Chi, having a great run, and being struck by the contrasting harmonies of the non-stop frenzy of HK side-by-side with the serenity of the park."

—rizzuto

Updated by
Doretta Lau

The Hong Kong Island skyline, with its ever growing number of skyscrapers, speaks to the triumph of ambition over fate. Whereas it took Paris and London 10 to 20 generations and New York 6 to build the spectacular cities seen today, in Hong Kong almost everything you see has been built in the time since today's young investment bankers were born.

On Hong Kong Island the central city goes only a few kilometers south into the island before mountains rise up. In the main districts and neighborhoods luxury boutiques are a stone's throw from old hawker stalls.

When you're on Hong Kong Island and feeling disoriented, remember that the water is always north. Central, Admiralty, and Wan Chai, the island's main business districts, are opposite Tsim Sha Tsui on the Kowloon Peninsula. West of Central are Sheung Wan and the other (mainly residential) neighborhoods that make up Western. Central backs onto the slopes of Victoria Peak, so the districts south of it—the Midlevels and the Peak—look down on it. Causeway Bay, North Point, Quarry Bay, Shau Kei Wan, and Chai Wan East run east along the shore after Wan Chai. Developments on the south side of Hong Kong Island are scattered: the beach towns of Shek O and Stanley sit on two peninsulas on the southeast; high-tech Cyberport, industrial Aberdeen, and Ap Lei Chau are to the west.

West of Hong Kong Island lie Lamma, Cheung Chau, and Lantau islands. Lantau is connected by a suspension bridge to west Kowloon. More than 200 other islands also belong to Hong Kong.

Hong Kong's older areas—the southern side of Central, for example—show erratic street planning, but the newer developments and reclamations follow something closer to a grid system. Streets are usually numbered odd on one side, even on the other. There's no baseline for street numbers and no block-based numbering system.

WESTERN

Sightseeing
☆★★★
Dining
☆☆★★
Lodging
☆☆★★
Shopping
☆☆☆★

Western has been called Hong Kong's Chinatown, and though it's a strange-sounding epithet, there's a reason for it. The area is light-years from the dazzle of Central, despite being just down the road. And although developers are making short work of the traditional architecture, Western's colonial buildings, rattling trams, Old World medicine shops, and lively markets still recall bygone times.

TOP ATTRACTIONS

Fodor's Choice
★

University Museum and Art Gallery, The University of Hong Kong. Chinese harp music and a faint smell of incense float through its peaceful rooms. The small but excellent collection of Chinese antiquities includes ceramics and bronzes, some dating from 3,000 BC; fine paintings; lacquerware; and carvings in jade, stone, and wood. There are some superb ancient pieces: ritual vessels, decorative mirrors, and painted pottery. The museum has the world's largest collection of Nestorian crosses, dating from the Mongol Period (1280–1368). These belonged to a heretical Christian sect who came to China from the Middle East during the Tang Dynasty (618–907).

There are usually two or three well-curated temporary exhibitions on: contemporary artists who work in traditional mediums are often featured. ■TIP➔ Don't miss part of the museum: the collection is spread between the T. T. Tsui Building and the Fung Ping Shan Building, which you access via a first-floor footbridge. The museum is out of the way—20 minutes from Central via Buses 3A, 23, 40, 40 M, or 103, or a 15-minute uphill walk from Sheung Wan MTR—but it's a must for the true Chinese art lover. ✉ *94 Bonham Rd., Pokfulam, Western* ☎ *2241–5500* ⊕ *www.hku.hk/hkumag* 🗺 *Free* ☉ *Mon.–Sat. 9:30–6, Sun. 1–6* Ⓜ *Sheung Wan.*

WORTH NOTING

Hollywood Road. Hong Kong's best antiques shops and classical-art galleries are on Hollywood Road, named for the holly trees that once grew here. The farther west you go, the less genuine things get. Porcelain, curios, and not-very-old trinkets masquerading as artifacts make up most of the offerings on Upper Lascar Row, a flea market commonly known as Cat Street. ✉ *Hollywood Rd. between Arbuthnot Rd. and Queen's Rd. Wes, Sheung Wan, Western* Ⓜ *Sheung Wan, Exit A2.*

GETTING ORIENTED

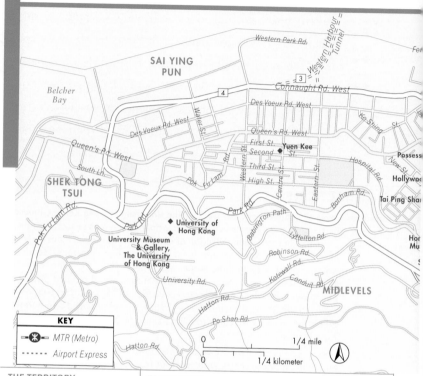

KEY

- ━❌━ *MTR (Metro)*
- ------ *Airport Express*

THE TERRITORY

The Midlevels Escalator forms a handy boundary between Western and Central. Several main thoroughfares run parallel to the shore, each farther up the slope: Des Voeux Road (where the trams run), Queen's Road, Hollywood Road (where SoHo starts), and Caine Road (where the Midlevels begin).

As to how far west Western goes, it technically reaches all the way to Kennedy Town, where the tram lines end, but there isn't much worth noting beyond Sheung Wan.

TAKING IT IN

Colonial Architecture. You can see Western's colonial buildings on an hour-long stroll from the University of Hong Kong (take a cab or bus out). East along Bonham Road, which becomes Caine Road, are Victorian apartments. The Museum of Medical Sciences is at Caine Lane. Head downstairs, then left onto Hollywood Road to Possession Street. Follow this downhill, doglegging right and left through Bonham Strand, onto Morrison, and to the Western Market.

Traditional Goods. An hour is enough time to wander Sheung Wan's traditional shops. In the morning, when trade's brisk, take the tram to Wilmer Street. Walk a block south and turn left onto Queen's Road West (herbal remedies, temple goods). Walk left for a block at Possession, then loop left through Bonham Strand West (ginseng), right for a block at Des Voeux, then back along Wing Lok (dried seafood). Continue on Bonham Strand (bird's nest), dipping left onto Hillier (snakes) and beyond to Man Wa Lane (chops).

2

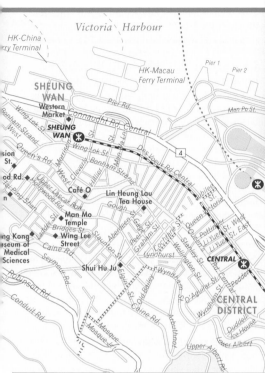

GETTING AROUND

The most scenic way to Sheung Wan is on a tram along Des Voeux Road. From Central or Admiralty it's probably the quickest, too: no traffic, no subway lines, or endless underground walks. There are stops every two or three blocks. The Sheung Wan MTR station brings you within spitting distance of Western Market.

The Macau Ferry Terminal is behind the MTR (use Exit D). **Turbojet** (☎ 2859–3333 ⊕ www.turbojet.com.hk) vessels run every 15 minutes with a reduced schedule from midnight to 7 AM. You can usually buy tickets on the spot (from HK$134), but reservations are recommended on weekends. ■TIP→ **You need your passport to go to Macau.**

The Midlevels Escalator is fun up as far as SoHo. Buses 3B, 40, and 40M run between the university and Jardine House in Central, as does green Minibus 8. Both pass the top of Ladder Street. Expect a taxi from Central to the Midlevels to cost HK$20.

QUICK BITES

Sit on weathered wooden benches at **Classified** (✉ 108 Hollywood Rd., Sheung Wan, Western ☎ 2525–3445), and sample cheeses from their vast selection. Or have a coffee, a glass of wine, or a hearty pasta.

Cracked Formica tabletops, cranky waiters, old men reading the newspapers: There's nothing fancy about **Lin Heung Lau Tea House** (✉ 160 Wellington St., Sheung Wan, Western ☎ 2544–4556). But it's been doing great dim sum for years, as locals will testify.

Café O (✉ 284 Queen's Rd. Central, Sheung Wan, Western ☎ 2851–0890) has pizza by the meter, and an assortment of salads and rice dishes, but the mega-breakfasts (served all day) are fierce competition. Fresher-than-fresh juices and smoothies help you keep your energy up.

Hong Kong Museum of Medical Sciences. You can find out all about medical episodes at this private museum, which is housed in a redbrick building at the top of Ladder Street that references Edwardian style architecture. The 11 exhibition galleries cover 10,000 square feet, and present information on both Western and Chinese medical practices. ✉ *2 Caine La., Midlevels, Western*☎ *2549–5123* ⊕ *www.hkmms.org.hk* 🍴 *$5–$10* ⊙ *Tues.–Sat. 10–5, Sun. and holidays 1–5* Ⓜ *Sheung Wan, Exit A2.*

Man Mo Temple. It's believed to be Hong Kong Island's oldest temple, though no one knows exactly when it was built—the consensus is sometime around the arrival of the British in 1841. It's dedicated to the Taoist gods of literature and of war: Man, who wears green, and Mo, dressed in red. The temple bell, cast in Canton in 1847, and the drum next to it are sounded to attract the gods' attention when a prayer is being offered—give it a ring to make sure yours are heard. ■TIP→ To check your fortune, stand in front of the altar, ask a question, select a small bamboo cylinder, and shake it until a stick falls out. The number on the stick corresponds to a written fortune. Then go next door, where an English-speaking fortune-teller can tell you what it means for HK$20. ✉ *Hollywood Rd. at Ladder St., Sheung Wan, Western* ⊙ *Daily 8–6* Ⓜ *Sheung Wan, Exit A2.*

Possession Street. A sign here marks where Captain Charles Elliott stepped ashore in 1841 to claim Hong Kong for the British empire. This was once the waterfront, but aggressive reclamation has left it several blocks inland. At the top of the street stands Hollywood Centre, home to a number of shops and galleries and the non-profit contemporary art space Asia Art Archive. ✉ *Possession St., between Queen's Rd. Central and Hollywood Rd., Sheung Wan, Western* Ⓜ *Sheung Wan, Exit A2.*

Tai Ping Shan. The maze of streets west of Man Mo Temple is known as Tai Ping Shan (the Chinese name for Victoria Peak, which towers above it). It's a sleepy area filled with small shops. One of the city's oldest residential districts, Tai Ping Shan was badly hit by plague outbreaks in the 1890s. ✉ *Tai Ping Shan St. between Upper Station St. and Square St., Sheung Wan, Western* ⊕ *www.lcsd.gov.hk/ce/Museum/Monument/en/trails_sheungwan1.php?tid=26* Ⓜ *Sheung Wan, Exit A2.*

The University of Hong Kong. It's worth a trip out to the western end of the Midlevels to see the imposing Edwardian buildings, most along Bonham Road, of the University of Hong Kong, where competition for a place is fierce. The institution opened in 1912 with the Faculty of Medicine. Today the exteriors of University Hall, Hung Hing Ying Building, and Tang Chi Ngong Building are on the government's "Declared Momument List." ✉ *Bonham Rd. at Pok Fu Lan Rd., Pok Fu Lam, Western* ☎ *2859–2111* ⊕ *www.hku.hk.*

Western Market. The Sheung Wan district's iconic market, a hulking brown-and-white colonial structure, is a good place to get your bearings. Built in 1906, it functioned as a produce market for 83 years. Today it's a shopping center selling trinkets and fabrics—the architecture is what's worth the visit. Nearby are the Chinese herbal medicine on Ko Shing Street and Queen's Road West; dried seafood on Wing Lok Street and Des Voeux Road West; and ginseng and bird's nest on Bonham Strand West. ⊠ *323 Des Voeux St. Central, Sheung Wan, Western* ☉ *Daily 10* AM*–midnight* Ⓜ *Sheung Wan, Exit B or C.*

Wing Lee Street. Just minutes away from Man Mo Temple is one of the last streets in Hong Kong where every building features 1950s architecture. In 2010 the buildings on this tucked-away street were saved from being demolished, following a series of protests and a plea from the filmmakers of the award-winning local film Echoes of the Rainbow. ⊠ *Wing Lee St., above Hollywood Rd. between Ladderand Shing Wong Sts., Sheung Wan, Western* Ⓜ *Sheung Wan, Exit A2.*

2

A PERFECT DAY

A CULINARY ADVENTURE

From Sheung Wan's markets to the hip international eateries (and drinkeries) of SoHo, Western is a foodie's heaven. Here's how to make a culinary adventure of it.

The breakfast of champs in Hong Kong is dim sum. Head for the old **Lin Heung Lau Tea House** (⇨ *Quick Bites)* any time after 6 AM and fill up on things like *ha gau* (steamed shrimp dumplings) and *cha siu bau* (barbecue pork buns), washed down with lots of tea.

Get to Sheung Wan Wet Market early to watch expert shoppers in action. Earn their respect by examining fish gills for freshness and picking up a bag of lychees or cherries to munch on the go. Take time to browse the dried delicacies—abalone, bird's nest, sea cucumbers, mushrooms—in shops around Wing Lok Street and Des Voeux Road. You might want to invest in an herbal indigestion cure, just in case.

Got a sweet tooth? Try a traditional dessert at **Yuen Kee** (⊠ *32 Centre St., Western* ☎ *2548–8687*)—the almond soup is divine.

Take a tram and head over to Gage Street for a steaming bowl of wonton noodles at any *dai pai dong* (street-stall restaurant). Wander more stalls on chaotic Graham Street—the meat stalls aren't for the fainthearted—then go for some liquid sustenance. Many SoHo bars along the Midlevels Escalator start happy hour in midafternoon and go until 8 or 9 PM.

Wind up the day with top-notch Shanghainese, Sichuan, or Beijing dishes amid lots of lacquered wood at **Shui Hu Ju** (⊠ *68 Peel St., SoHo, Western* ☎ *2869–6927*).

CENTRAL

Sightseeing
★★★★
Dining
☆★★★
Lodging
☆★★★
Shopping
★★★★

Shopping, eating, drinking—Central lives up to its name when it comes to all of these. But it's also Hong Kong's historical heart, packed with architectural reminders of the early colonial days. They're in stark contrast to the soaring masterpieces of modern architecture that the city is famous for. Somehow the mishmash works. With the harbor on one side and Victoria Peak on the other, Central's views—once you get high enough to see them—are unrivaled. It's a hot spot for both locals and expatriates, packed with people, sights, and life.

TOP ATTRACTIONS

Central Star Ferry Pier. Take in the view of the Kowloon skyline from the pier. For arguably the best panorama of Central's architecture, start on the Kowloon side at the Tsim Sha Tsui pier and take one of the sturdy green-and-white Star Ferries to this pier; enjoy the skyline along the way. ⊠ *Man Kwong St. between Rumsey and Man Yiu Sts., Central* ☎ *2367–7065 for ferries, 2118–6201 for tours* ⊕ *www.starferry.com. hk* ⌖ *round-trip HK$55 (day) or HK$110 (night); Symphony of Lights Harbour Cruise HK$150* Ⓜ *Hong Kong Station, Exit.*

Fodor's Choice ★ **Flagstaff House Museum of Tea Ware.** All that's good about British colonial architecture is exemplified in the simple white facade, wooden monsoon shutters, and colonnaded verandas of Flagstaff House. More than 600 pieces of delicate antique teaware from the Tang (618–907) through the Qing (1644–1911) dynasties fill rooms that once housed the commander of the British forces. ■TIP→ Skip the lengthy, confusing tea-ceremony descriptions; concentrate on the porcelain itself. Look out for the unadorned brownish-purple clay of the Yixing pots: unglazed,

2

their beauty hinges on perfect form. There's a carved wooden booth on the first floor where you can listen to Chinese tea songs. Head to the **Lock Cha Tea Shop** (☎ 2801–7177 ⊕ *www.lockcha.com*), in the K.S. Lo Gallery annex, where you can sample teas before you buy. The Hong Kong Tourist Board runs tea appreciation classes at the shop—phone the shop to book a place. Try the Tie Guan Yin, a highly aromatic green tea. ⊠ *Hong Kong Park, 10 Cotton Tree Dr., Admirality, Central* ☎ 2869–0690 ⊕ *www.lcsd.gov.hk/ce/Museum/Arts/english/tea/intro/eintro.html* 🎟 *Free* ☉ *Wed.–Mon. 10–5* Ⓜ *Admiralty, Exit C1.*

🔄
Fodor's Choice
★

Hong Kong Park. The 8-hectare park, which opened in 1991, is a respite from the skyscrapers that spill over into Admiralty from Central. Previously it was the site of Victoria Barracks, a garrison, and the buildings from 1842 and 1910 still stand. The park is home to the Flagstaff House Museum of Tea Ware and the Edward Youde Aviary. ⊠ *19 Cotton Tree Dr., Admirality, Central* ☎ 2521–5041 ⊕ *www.lcsd.gov.hk/parks/hkp/en/index.php* 🎟 *Free* ☉ *Daily 6 AM–11 PM* Ⓜ *Admiralty, Exit C1.*

Midlevels Escalator. The unimaginatively named Midlevels is midway up the hill between Victoria Peak and the Western and Central districts. Running through it is the escalator, which connects the now-defunct Central Market (at the border of Central and Western) with several main residential roads. Free of charge and protected from the elements, this series of moving walkways makes the uphill journey a cinch. Before 10 AM they move only downward, carrying yuppies bearing coffee to work. ⊠ *Next to 100 Queen's Rd. Central, Central* ☉ *6–midnight* Ⓜ *Central, Exit D1.*

SoHo. The area south of (i.e., above) Hollywood Road is the epicenter of Hong Kong's latest gastro revolution. The bars here are a chiller alternative to the crowded drinking spots in Lan Kwai Fong and generally close by 2 AM. There are also trendy boutiques tucked between the eateries, some featuring local designers and one-of-a kind goods. ⊠ *South of Hollywood Rd. and north of Caine Rd., just off Midlevels Escalator, SoHo, Central* ⊕ *www.ilovesoho.hk* Ⓜ *Central, Exit D1.*

Fodor's Choice
★

Victoria Peak. Soaring 1,805 feet above sea level, the peak looks over Central and beyond. Residents here take special pride in the positions to which they have, quite literally, risen; theirs is the island's most exclusive address. The steep tracks up to it start at the **Peak Tram Terminus,** near St. John's Cathedral on Garden Road. ⊠ *Tram between Garden Rd. and Cotton Tree Dr., Central* ☎ 2522–0922 ⊕ *www.thepeak.com.hk* 🎟 *HK$25 one-way, HK$36 round-trip* ☉ *7 AM–midnight.*

WORTH NOTING

Bank of China. Along Statue Square's southern end are the three buildings of Hong Kong's note-issuing banks. The art deco building is the former headquarters of the Bank of China, which was built in the 1950s and renovated in 1998. The building now houses offices, as well as the exclusive China Club, a member's only restaurant. ⊠ *1 Bank St., Central* Ⓜ *Central, Exit K.*

GETTING ORIENTED

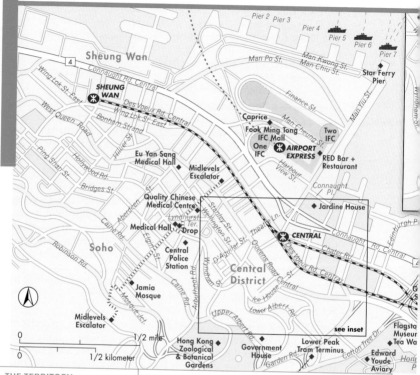

THE TERRITORY

The Midlevels Escalator forms the boundary of Central with Western. Streets between Queen's Road Central and the harbor are laid out more or less geometrically. On the south side of Queen's Road, however, is a confusion of steep lanes. Overhead walkways connect Central's major buildings, an all-weather alternative to the chaotic streets below.

QUICK BITES

At lunchtime people flood the cul-de-sac that is known as Rat Alley (Wing Wah Lane off D'Aguilar Street). Choose from Thai, Malay, Indian, Chinese, or American places.

No visit to Central is complete without a bowl of noodles at **Tsui Wah** (⊠ Ground fl., 15–19 Wellington St., Central ☎ 2525–6338 ⊕ www.tsuiwahrestaurant.com) down the hill from Lan Kwai Fong. It's open 24 hours.

Need an instant sushi fix? Pull up a stool at the conveyor belt at **Genki Sushi** (⊠ Ground fl., Far East Finance Centre, 16 Harcourt Rd., Admiralty ☎ 2865–2933 ⊕ www.genkisushi. com.hk).

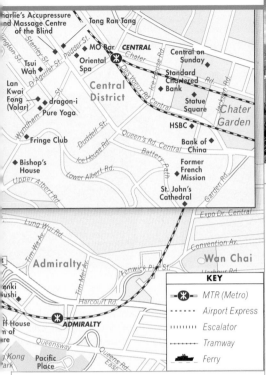

2

TAKING IT IN

Colonial Central. *South China Morning Post* columnist Jason Wordie (⊕ *www.jasonswalks. com*) leads three-hour tours loaded with anecdotes.

The Urban Runway. Cross Central without touching street level. Start in the IFC Mall; leave by Pret a Manger on the southeast side, turn right into the walkway, pass the General Post Office and Jardine House and into the Armani floor of the Chater Building. The door between Emporio and Fiori leads to Alexandra House; take the stairs left of Dolce & Gabbana and into the Landmark. Turn right past Jimmy Choo, go downstairs and cross over to the Central Building, turn left, go up the stairs past Clarins, and into the Central Building. Cross to the back right of the elevator lobby, through the bridge into the Entertainment Building, which drops you in Lan Kwai Fong. Time your 15-minute walk to finish at 6 PM—happy hour.

KEY

✪	MTR (Metro)
- - - - -	Airport Express
⁞⁞⁞⁞⁞	Escalator
········	Tramway
🚢	Ferry

GETTING AROUND

Central MTR station is a mammoth underground warren with a host of far-flung exits. A series of travelators join it with Hong Kong Station, under the IFC Mall, where Tung Chung Line and Airport Express trains arrive and depart. Rattling old trams along Des Voeux Road have you at Sheung Wan, Admiralty, and Wan Chai in minutes.

Star Ferry (☎ *2367–7065* ⊕ *www.starferry.com.hk*) vessels to Kowloon leave Pier 7 every 6–12 minutes 6:30 AM–11:30 PM; the nine-minute trip costs HK$2.50 (upper deck) on weekdays, HK$3 on weekends.

New World First Ferry (☎ *2131–8181* ⊕ *www.nwff.com. hk*) goes to Lantau (from Pier 6) and Cheung Chau (Pier 5). Crossings take 35–55 minutes and cost HK$11.50–HK$32.20.

Discovery Bay Transportation Service (☎ *2987–7351* ⊕ *www.hkri.com/icms2/template?series=88*) has high-speed boats for the northeastern coast of Lantau Island every 20–30 minutes from Pier 3 around the clock. Trips take 25–30 minutes and cost HK$27.

From Victoria Peak, Hong Kong Island's multiple levels of skyscrapers stretch out below.

Bishop's House. The big gray Victorian building across the road from the Fringe Club is Bishop's House, official residence of the Anglican bishop since 1851. Lower Albert Road forks in two; the lower branch is Ice House Street, which curves down the hill to Queen's Road. Before the bend are the magnificent balustrades of the stone staircase that becomes Duddell Street; it's adorned with four old-fashioned gas lamps that have been lighting the way since the late 1870s. ⊠ *1 Lower Albert Rd., Central* Ⓜ *Central, Exit D1.*

Central Ferry Pier. The pier juts out into the harbor in front of the International Finance Centre. Ferries regularly leave from here to Lantau, Lamma, and Cheung Chau islands. The Star Ferry Pier is just steps away (⇨ *See above*). ⊠ *Man Kwong St. between Rumsey and Man Yiu Sts., Central* Ⓜ *Hong Kong Station.*

Central Police Station. The colonial building just after Wyndham Street becomes Hollywood Road is a must-have location in any self-respecting Hong Kong cop movie. It was the neighborhood headquarters from 1864—when part of it was built—through 2004. Currently it is closed except during special events. ⊠ *10 Hollywood Rd., Central* ⊙ *Not open to public except during events* Ⓜ *Central, Exit D1.*

Edward Youde Aviary. In Hong Kong Park, the aviary boasts numerous varieties of birds in an environment filled with plants, trees, and even a forest streambed. ⊠ *10 Cotton Tree Dr., Admirality, Central* ☎ *2521–5041* ⊕ *www.lcsd.gov.hk/parks/hkp* 🖃 *Free* ⊙ *Daily 9–5* Ⓜ *Admiralty, Exit C1.*

Former French Mission Building. A narrow tree-lined lane called Battery Path runs uphill parallel to Queen's Road Central behind the HSBC

2

building. The British built it when they arrived in 1841 to move their cannons uphill—hence the name. At the top of Battery Path sits the Former French Mission Building, an elegant redbrick building with white stone windows and green shutters. Finished in 1917, the government declared monument is now home to the Court of Final Appeal. ⊠ *1 Battery Path, Central* Ⓜ *Central, Exit D1*

Government House. The handsome white Victorian occupying the land between Upper and Lower Albert roads was constructed in 1855. It was the official residence of British governors, but is shunned by the new chief executives—some say because it has bad feng shui. During the Japanese occupation it was significantly rebuilt, so it exhibits a Japanese influence, particularly in the roof eaves. The gardens are opened to the public once a year in March, when the azaleas bloom. ⊠ *Upper Albert Rd., Midlevels, Central* ⊕ *www.ceo.gov.hk/gh/eng* ☉ *Not open to public except during special occasions* Ⓜ *Central, Exit D1.*

Hong Kong Zoological & Botanical Gardens. Farther uphill on Central's eastern edge is this welcoming green breathing space. It includes a children's playground and numerous gardens, but the real attractions are the dozens of mammals, birds, and reptiles housed in zoological exhibits. Buses 3B, 12, and 13 run from Central; the walk from the Central MTR stop is quite a distance and uphill. ⊠ *Albany Rd. between Robinson and Upper Albert Rds., Central* ☎ *2530–0154* ⊕ *www.lcsd.gov.hk/parks/hkzbg/en/* 🎟 *Free* ☉ *Daily 6 AM–10 PM* Ⓜ *Central.*

HSBC. The spectacular strut-and-ladder facade of this Norman Foster building is one of the most important structures in 20th-century architecture. Walk under it and look up into the atrium through the curved glass floor, or go inside for a view of the building's mechanics. ⊠ *1 Queen's Rd. Central, across from Statue Square, Central* 🎟 *Free* ☉ *Weekdays 9–5:30, Sat. 9–12:30; closed Sun. and holidays* Ⓜ *Central, Exit K.*

International Finance Centre. One building towers above the rest of Central's skyline: Two IFC, or the second tower of the International Finance Centre. The tall, tapering structure has been compared to at least one—unprintable—thing and is topped with a clawlike structure straight out of Thundercats. Designed by Argentine architect Cesar Pelli (of London's Canary Wharf fame), its 88 floors measure a whopping 1,362 feet. Opposite stands its dinky little brother, the 38-floor One IFC. The massive IFC Mall stretches between the two, and Hong Kong Station is underneath. If you wish to see the breathtaking views from Two IFC, you can visit the Hong Kong Monetary Authority (⊠ *55/F, Two IFC* ☎ *2878–1111* ⊕ *www.info.gov.hk/hkma*). Upon arrival, you may need to register your passport with the concierge. ⊠ *8 Finance St., Central* ⊕ *www.ifc.com.hk* 🎟 *Free* ☉ *Hong Kong Monetary Authority weekdays 10–6, Sat. 10–1* Ⓜ *Hong Kong Station, Exit A2.*

Jamia Mosque. The Midlevels Escalator goes right by the gray-and-white religious institution on Shelley Street. The original 1840s structure was rebuilt in 1915 and shows its Indian heritage in the perforated arches and decorative facade work. The mosque isn't open to non-Muslims, but it occupies a small verdant enclosure that's a welcome retreat.

✉ *30 Shelley St., above Caine Rd. next to escalator, Central* Ⓜ *Central, Exit D1.*

Jardine House. Just behind the IFC is a notable '60s skyscraper recognizable by its many round windows. The 52-level building is home to Jardine, Matheson & Co., the greatest of the old British *hongs* (trading companies) that dominated trade with imperial China. Once an establishment linked to opium trafficking, it's now a respected investment bank. The shops on the lower ground and ground floors include the Oxfam Shop, Starbucks, and the art gallery iPreciation. ✉ *1 Connaught Place, Central* Ⓜ *Hong Kong Station, Exit 2A.*

Lan Kwai Fong. In Hong Kong the word "nightlife" is synonymous with LKF, a few narrow lanes filled with bars and clubs just up the hill from the intersection of Queen's Road Central and Pedder Street. Veering right at the top gets you to Wyndham Street and the start of a series of high-caliber antiques and Oriental-rug shops. ✉ *Lan Kwai Fong and D'Aguilar St. between Wyndham and Wellington Sts., Central* ⊕ *www.lankwaifong.com* Ⓜ *Central, Exit D1.*

Queen's Road. Hong Kong's answer to New York's 5th Avenue and London's King's Road are the first few blocks of Chater Road, Des Voeux Road Central, and Queen's Road Central (the thoroughfares that stretch west from Statue Square). Most high-end designers have boutiques in the priceless über-posh minimalls like the Landmark, Alexandra House, or the Pedder Building. A stone's throw away, but at the other end of the income scale, are Li Yuen Street East and Li Yuen Street. Known as the Lanes, they're packed with stalls selling cheap *cheongsams* (sexy, slit-skirt, silk dresses with Mandarin collars) and Hello Kitty merchandise. On the south side of Queen's Road is steep Pottinger Street, a haberdasher's dream street. ✉ *Queen's Rd. Central, Chater Rd., and Des Voeux Rd. Central, between Peel and Bank Sts., Central* Ⓜ *Central, Exit D1.*

St. John's Cathedral. A peaceful gap in the skyscrapers—on Garden Road and up from Queen's Road Central—accommodates the graceful Gothic form of this Anglican church. Completed in 1849, it's made of Canton bricks in the shape of a cross. Among the World War II relics it houses are the cathedral doors themselves, made from timber salvaged from the British warship HMS *Tamar.* ✉ *4–8 Garden Rd., Central* ☎ *2523–4157* ⊕ *www.stjohnscathedral.org.hk* ☐ *Free* ◷ *Daily 7–6* Ⓜ *Central, Exit K.*

Standard Chartered Bank. The rose-color wedgelike building was completed in 1990 and designed by P&T Architects and Engineers. A pair of stained-glass windows by Remo Riva represents visions of "Hong Kong Today" and "Hong Kong Tomorrow." ✉ *4 Des Voeux Rd., Central* Ⓜ *Central, Exit K.*

Statue Square. The land it's on was gifted to the public by the Hongkong & Shanghai Bank (HSBC, whose headquarters dominate the southern end), with the proviso that nothing built on it could block the bank's view of the water. The Victorian–Chinese hybrid building on Statue Square's east side is the Legislative Council Building. Built for the Supreme Court in 1912, it's now home to the 60-member Legislative Council (LegCo). It's often the focus of the demonstrations that have

Spend a few minutes, an hour, or a day people-watching in Hong Kong Park.

become a fixture of Hong Kong life since 1997. In front of the council building is the Cenotaph, a monument to all who lost their lives in the two World Wars. ⊠ *Between Chater Rd. and Des Voeux Rd. Central, next to Prince's Building at 10 Chater Rd., Central* Ⓜ *Central, Exit K.*

DID YOU KNOW?

Statue Square took its name from bronze figures of British royalty that stood here before the Japanese occupation, when they were removed and melted down. The only figure exempt was stern Sir Thomas Jackson (1841–1915), who looks over the square toward HSBC—he was the chief manager for more than 30 years.

A PERFECT DAY (AND NIGHT)

NINE HOURS OF LUXURY

With boutiques, spas, and coffee shops galore, Central has everything you need to be a *tai-tai*—localspeak for ladies who lunch—even if you're a man. There's *so* much more to do than lunch, so take a page out of their book and spend some time (and lots of money) on—who else?—yourself.

Start off by harmonizing the inner you with an early-morning yoga class (a trial class is free, or it's HK$2,000 for a monthlong visitor pass) at **Pure Yoga** (⊠ *The Centrium, 16th fl., 60 Wyndham St., Central* ☎ *2971–0055* ⊕ *www.pure-yoga.com*).

Head to the **Oriental Spa** (⊠ *Landmark Mandarin Oriental, 15 Queen's Rd. Central, Central* ☎ *2132–0011* ⊕ *www.mandarinoriental.com/landmark*) for the 170-minute Urban Retreat package (HK$2,100–

HK$2,350), which includes a facial, massage, and foot treatment, as well as a juice, smoothie, or tea. It's best to make reservations several days ahead.

Relaxing is hungry work. But not just anyone should be allowed to prepare your lunch, so book a table at **Caprice** (⊠ *8 Finance St., Central* ☎ *3196–8860*) in the Four Seasons hotel. It's hard to know whether to gaze at the view of the harbor, the French chandeliers, or the chefs in the open kitchen cooking up some of the best French food in town.

What better way to work off lunch than shopping? The Landmark and Chater House are packed with international designers, but don't neglect the Pedder Building, where local luxury brands such as Shanghai Tang sell made-to-measure Chinese-style suits and cheongsams.

Reflect on your busy day over Bellinis at **MO Bar** (⊠ *15 Queen's Rd. Central, Central* ☎ *2132–0077*) in the Landmark Oriental.

TEN HOURS ON THE TOWN

When the neon lights up, office-Central transforms into party-Central.

Boozing is an expensive pastime, so keep costs down with a happy-hour bar crawl through Lan Kwai Fong. While the sun sets, sip a quirky cocktail at an open-air table in the **RED Bar + Restaurant** (⊠ *Level 4, Two IFC, 8 Finance St., Central* ☎ *8129–8882*).

Don't worry about losing your party momentum by stopping for dinner. Just head to celebrity haunt **dragon-i** (⊠ *Upper ground fl., The Centrium, 60 Wyndham St., Central* ☎ *3110–1222* ⊕ *www.dragon-i.com.hk*), where there's sushi, dim sum, *and* cocktails to nourish you.

Pace yourself at **Drop** (⊠ *On Lok Mansion, 39–43 Hollywood Rd., basement [entrance off Cochrane St.], Central* ☎ *2543–8856* ⊕ *www.drophk.com*), where the fab cocktails are tempting and the funky sounds are mesmerizing. You could easily overindulge. Be sure to hit ultratrendy club **Volar** (⊠ *Basement fl., 38–44 D'Aguilar St., Central* ☎ *2810–1510* ⊕ *www.volar.com.hk*) for dancing.

Stumble out and head to **Tsui Wah** (⇨ *Quick Bites*) for a restorative 3 AM bowl of noodles.

WAN CHAI, CAUSEWAY BAY, AND BEYOND

Sightseeing
☆★★★
Dining
★★★★
Lodging
☆★★★
Shopping
☆★★★

The Happy Valley horse races are a vital part of Hong Kong life, so it's only fitting that they're in one of the city's most vital areas. A few blocks back from Wan Chai's new office blocks are crowded alleys where you might stumble across a wet market, a tiny furniture-maker's shop, or an age-old temple. Farther east, Causeway Bay pulses with Hong Kong's best shopping streets and hundreds of restaurants. At night the whole area comes alive with bars, restaurants, and discos, as well as establishments offering some of Wan Chai's more traditional services (think red lights and photos of seminaked women outside).

WAN CHAI

TOP ATTRACTIONS

Hong Kong Arts Centre. The Arts Centre is a vibrant building housing several galleries, including the Goethe Institute, a cinema, and two performing arts venues. ⊠ *2 Harbour Rd., Wan Chai* ☎ 2582–0200 ⊕ *www.hkac.org.hk/en/index.php* 🎫 *Free* ⊙ *Daily 8* AM–11 PM Ⓜ Wan Chai, Exit C.

WORTH NOTING

Central Plaza. Clad in reflective gold, silver, and copper-color glass, the triangular building at Harbour and Fleming roads is glitzy to the point of tastelessness. On completion in 1992 it was briefly the city's tallest building, but then Two IFC beat it by a mere 130 feet. Note the colorful fluorescent tube lights atop the building; they actually make up a clock so complicated that no one knows how to tell time using it. ⊠ *18 Harbour Rd., Wan Chai* ☎ *2586–8111* ⊕ *www.centralplaza.com.hk.*

Hong Kong Convention & Exhibition Centre. Land is so scarce that developers usually only build skyward, but the HKCEC is an exception. It sits on a spit of reclaimed land jutting into the harbor. Its curved-glass walls and swooping roof make it look like a tortoise lumbering into the sea or a gull taking flight, depending on whom you ask. Of all the international trade fairs, regional conferences, and other events held here, by far the most famous was the 1997 Handover ceremony. An obelisk commemorates it on the waterfront promenade, which also affords great views of Kowloon.

Outside the center stands the *Golden Bauhinia*. This gleaming sculpture of the Bauhinia flower, Hong Kong's symbol, was a gift from China celebrating the establishment of the Hong Kong SAR in 1997. The police hoist the SAR flag daily at 7:50 AM. ⊠ *1 Expo Dr., Wan Chai* ☎ *2582–8888* ⊕ *www.hkcec.com.hk* Ⓜ *Wan Chai, Exit A.*

Johnston Road. Trams clatter along this busy road, which is choked with traffic day and night. It's also packed with shops selling food, cell phones, herbal tonic, and bargain-basement clothes. Rattan furniture, curtains, picture frames, paper lanterns, and Chinese calligraphic materials make up the more traditional assortment at Queen's Road East, which runs parallel to Johnston Road. The lanes that stretch between the two roads are also lined with stalls, forming a mini-market of clothing and accessories. ⊠ *Johnston Rd. between Heard and Gresson Sts., Wan Chai* Ⓜ Wan Chai, Exit A.

The Pawn. In its previous incarnation, this heritage building was home to a pawnshop. It is now a refurnished dining establishment serving modern British cuisine. The rooftop is official public space; you may visit it even if you are not a patron of the restaurant. ⊠ *62 Johnston Rd., Wan Chai* ☎ *2866–3444* ⊕ *www.thepawn.com.hk* ⊘ 11 AM–2 AM Ⓜ Wan Chai, Exit A.

Yan Yuen Shek. High above Wan Chai halfway to Victoria Peak is the suggestively shaped monolith known as **Yan Yuen Shek**, or Lovers' Rock. It's a favorite with local Bridget Joneses, who visit it to burn joss sticks and make offerings in hope of finding a husband. The easiest way up is on Minibus 24A from Admiralty. ⊠ *South of Bowen Rd. between Wan Chai Gap and Stubbs Rds.*

DID YOU KNOW?

Wan Chai was once one of the five *wan*—areas the British set aside for Chinese residences—but it developed a reputation for vice and attracted sailors on shore leave during the Vietnam War. How times have changed: Wan Chai is still as risqué an area as Hong Kong has to offer, but that says more about the city's overall respectability than it does about the available indulgences. For all its bars and massage parlors, Wan Chai is now so safe that it seems a pale version of the "Wanch" of Richard Mason's novel *The World of Suzie Wong.* Today many venture to the area for arts and culture at Hong Kong Academy for Performing Arts and the Hong Kong Arts Centre.

GETTING ORIENTED

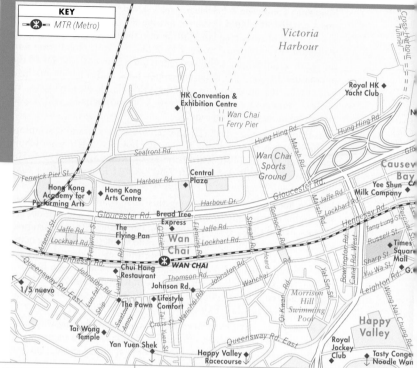

KEY
✳ MTR (Metro)

THE TERRITORY

Wan Chai's trams run mostly along Hennessy Road, with a detour along Johnston Road at the neighborhood's western end. Queen's Road East runs parallel to these two streets to the south, and a maze of lanes connect it with Hennessy.

The thoroughfares north of Hennessy—Lockhart, Jaffe, and Gloucester, which is a freeway—are laid out in a grid. Causeway Bay's diagonal roads make it hard to navigate, but it's small; wander around, and before long you'll hit something familiar.

TAKING IT IN

Once Upon a Time in the East. There were settlements here long before the British arrived, and the area was strategically important after colonization. Find out about it all from local historian Jason Wordie (☎ 2476–3504 ⊕ www.jasonswalks.com), who runs tours through Wan Chai, Causeway Bay, and Shau Kei Wan.

A Wan Chai Wander. Rattle to Wan Chai by tram along roads dense with jutting signs, just like in the movies. Get off at Southorn Playground, and wander the lanes south of Johnston Road before heading up Luard Road and over walkways to the Hong Kong Academy for Performing Arts and Hong Kong Arts Centre, in adjacent buildings. The Hong Kong Convention & Exhibition Centre is a few minutes away—wander its harborside promenade. If you time this part for dusk, Wan Chai's drinking holes will be lighting up as you walk back to the MTR along Fleming Road. Look up at Central Plaza on your right.

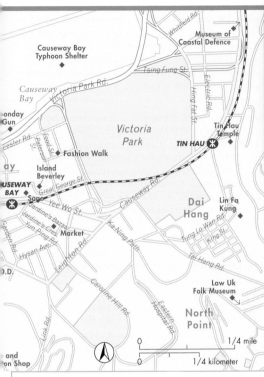

GETTING AROUND

Both Wan Chai and Causeway Bay have their own MTR stops, but a pleasant way to arrive from Central is on the tram along Hennessy Road. All the lines go through Wan Chai, but check the sign at the front if you're going beyond. Some continue to North Point and Shau Kei Wan, via Causeway Bay, while others go south to Happy Valley.

The underground stations are small labyrinths, so read the signs carefully to find the best exit. Traffic begins to take its toll on journey times farther east—the MTR is a better option for Shau Kei Wan and Chai Wan.

The Star Ferry runs between Tsim Sha Tsui and Wan Chai every 8–20 minutes. They leave from the ferry pier just east of the convention center.

Like all of Hong Kong, Wan Chai isn't really dangerous at night, but single women strolling the streets in the wee hours might get unwanted attention from groups of drunk expats. Taxis are a good idea late at night.

QUICK BITES

In a nightspot-packed district, a café serving breakfast round-the-clock is bound to be a hit. The **Flying Pan Wan Chai** (⊠ *3rd fl., 81–85 Lockhart Rd., Wan Chai* ☎ *2528–9997*) has waffles, blintzes, 16 different omelets, bagels, muffins, grilled sandwiches—the list goes on. Throw in squishy sofas and a jukebox, and it's perfect—be it 3 AM or 3 PM.

Hong Kong–style baked pastas, sandwiches, and inexpensive tea sets are oh-so satisfying at **Bread Tree Express** (⊠ *G/F 134 Jaffe Rd., Wan Chai* ☎ *2529–8848*). Seating is limited at lunch, but this is the perfect spot for a late afternoon nibble.

Yee Shun Milk Company (⊠ *506 Lockhart Rd., Causeway Bay* ☎ *2591–1837*) sounds kooky, but you can't leave Causeway Bay without dessert at this crowded little diner. The signature dish is steamed milk with ginger juice. Alternatively, there's steamed egg, a local custard.

CAUSEWAY BAY

Shoppers crowd the streets of Causeway Bay, the area east of Wan Chai, seven days a week. There are also lots of restaurants and the odd sight. The action happens in a five-block radius of the intersection of Hennessy Road and Percival Street. Another of the area's specialties are upstairs cafés (non-ground-floor spots inside combo commercial/residential buildings), often populated by teens and twentysomethings, and mazelike micromalls of independent fashion, jewelry, and gadgets.

TOP ATTRACTIONS

Happy Valley Racecourse. The biggest attraction east of Causeway Bay for locals and visitors alike is this local legend, where millions of Hong Kong dollars make their way each year. The races make great Wednesday nights out on the town. Aside from the excitement of the races, there are restaurants, bars, and even a racing museum to keep you amused. The easiest way to reach the racecourse is to take the tram to Happy Valley. ⊠ *Sports Rd. at Wong Nai Chung Rd., Happy Valley, Causeway Bay* ⊕ *www.racecourses.hkjc.com/english/come_racing/racecourses/happy_valley* ⊠ *$10* ⊙ *Wed. 5:15 or 5:30 during racing season* Ⓜ *Causeway Bay, Exit A.*

Victoria Park. Hong Kong Island's largest park is a welcome breathing space on the edge of Causeway Bay and bounded by Hing Fat, Gloucester, and Causeway roads. It's beautifully landscaped and has recreational facilities for swimming, lawn bowling, tennis, and rollerskating. At dawn every morning hundreds practice tai chi chuan here. It's also the site of midautumn's Lantern Carnival, with the trees a mass of colorful lights. Just before Chinese New Year (late January to early February), the park hosts a huge flower market. On the eve of Chinese New Year, after a traditional family dinner at home, much of Hong Kong happily gathers here to shop and wander until the early hours of the new year. ⊠ *Causeway Rd. between Hing Fat St. and Gloucester Rd., Causeway Bay* 🕾 *2890–5824* ⊕ *www.lcsd.gov.hk/parks/vp/en/index.php* ⊠ *Free* ⊙ *24 hours* Ⓜ *Tin Hau, Exit A2.*

WORTH NOTING

Causeway Bay Typhoon Shelter. Hong Kong's maritime past and present are much in evidence on Causeway Bay's waterfront. Sampan dwellers and old-fashioned junks once gathered during bad weather in the Causeway Bay Typhoon Shelter. Most boat-dwellers have moved to dry land, so these days it's mainly yachts and speedboats that moor here. A few traditional sampans, crewed primarily by elderly toothless women, still ferry owners to their sailboats. ⊠ *Near entrance of Cross Harbour Tunnel, Causeway Bay* Ⓜ *Causeway Bay, Exit D1.*

Fashion Walk. The more upscale mall Fashion Walk is on the Sogo side of Hennessy Road. Marc by Marc Jacobs, Michael Kors, and Burberry all have shops here. ⊠ *9 Kingston St., Causeway Bay* 🕾 *2890–5200* ⊕ *www.lcx.com.hk* ⊙ *Daily noon–10* Ⓜ *Causeway Bay.*

Noonday Gun. A block east of the Royal Hong Kong Yacht Club stands the Noonday Gun, which Noël Coward made famous in his song *Mad Dogs and Englishmen*; it's still fired at noon every day. It is said that

Hope that luck will be a lady and stick with you at Happy Valley Racecourse.

the tradition began when a Jardine employee fired a gun in salute of the company's head arriving at the port, angering a member of the Royal Navy. ⊠ *Kellet Island, Causeway Bay* Ⓜ *Causeway Bay, Exit D1.*

Royal Hong Kong Yacht Club. Most of the facilities are for members only, but the posh yacht club is a great place to get a drink or dine. Note that there is a dress code for dining in the Compass Room. ⊠ *Kellett Island, Causeway Bay* ☏ *2832–2817* ⊕ *www.rhkyc.org.hk* Ⓜ *Causeway Bay, Exit D1.*

Times Square. The 13-story megamall features the high-end favorite Lane Crawford, as well as a host of other boutiques such as Anna Sui and Marks & Spencer. Its Food Forum is comprised of four levels of restaurants, ranging from Thai to American-style Italian fare. A couple of blocks south is trendy hot spot Yiu Wa Street, with small, thoughtfully designed bars that are conducive to good conversation. ⊠ *1 Matheson St., Causeway Bay* ☏ *2118–8900* ⊕ *www.timessquare.com.hk* ⊗ *Daily 11–10* Ⓜ *Causeway Bay, Exit A.*

DID YOU KNOW?

Opium-smuggler-turned-investment-bank Jardine Matheson once had its warehouses in Causeway Bay. The company moved to Central decades ago, but left a legacy of street names: there's Jardine's Bazaar and Jardine's Crescent, two of Causeway Bay's best shopping streets, and Yee Wo Street with the firm's Chinese name.

EASTERN

Law Uk Folk Museum. This restored Hakka house was once the home of the Law family, who arrived here from Guangdong in the mid-18th century. It's the perfect example of a triple-*jian*, double-*lang* residence. Jian are enclosed rooms— here, the bedroom, living room, and workroom at the back. The front storeroom and kitchen are

HEADING EAST

The island's far eastern districts— North Point, Quarry Bay, Shau Kei Wan, and Chai Wan—are all undeniably parts of the "real" Hong Kong, which means they're full of offices, apartment blocks, and factories.

the *lang*, where the walls don't reach up to the roof, and thus allow air in. Although the museum is small, informative texts outside and displays of rural furniture and farm implements inside give a powerful idea of what rural Hong Kong was like. It's definitely worth a trip to bustling industrial Chai Wan, at the eastern end of the MTR, to see it. Photos show what the area looked like in the 1930s—these days a leafy square is the only reminder of the woodlands and fields that once surrounded this buttermilk-color dwelling. ⊠ *14 Kut Shing St., Chai Wan, Eastern* ☎ *2896–7006* ⊕ *www.lcsd.gov.hk/CE/Museum/History/ en/luf.php* 🎫 *Free* ☉ *Mon.–Wed., Fri. and Sat. 10–6, Sun., holidays 1–6* Ⓜ *Chai Wan, Exit B.*

Museum of Coastal Defence. Shau Kei Wan is home to the Museum of Coastal Defence in the converted Lei Yue Mun Fort. The museum is in the redoubt, a high area of land overlooking the narrowest point of the harbor; you take an elevator and cross an aerial walkway to reach it. As well as the fascinating historical displays indoors, there's a historical trail complete with tunnels, cannons, and observation posts. ⊠ *175 Tung Hei Rd., Shau Kei Wan, Eastern* ☎ *2569–1500* ⊕ *hk. coastaldefence.museum* 🎫 *HK$10; free Wed.* ☉ *Fri.–Wed. 10–5* Ⓜ Shau Kei Wan.

A PERFECT DAY (AND NIGHT)

A DAY FOR THOSE WHO CAN'T AGREE

If your group includes both shopaholics and history buffs, there's no need to squabble: Causeway Bay's the perfect place to divide and conquer. Start the day in perfect harmony with midday dim sum at Chung's Cuisine (☎ *2506–9218*) on the 10th floor of Times Square shopping mall. The pickings are top-notch, and the sleek booths and silk cushions seem made for lingering—other diners think likewise, so book a table on weekends.

Time to part company. Retail therapists have a whole afternoon to mall- and stall-trawl. Pickings at Times Square Mall are not particularly unusual, so don't dawdle too long before rifling through the micromall stalls for quirky street wear, followed by Fashion Walk and its surrounding streets, and then bargain-hunt along Jardine's Crescent and Jardine's Bazaar.

Meanwhile, the more studious can take the MTR or a tram to Chai Wan for a brief visit to Law Uk Folk Museum. If boats are your bag, take the MTR or a cab to Shau Kei Wan, where the Museum of Coastal Defence will keep you busy for a good couple of hours. Then a waterfront cab ride brings you to the Royal Hong Kong Yacht Club to check out the rich boys' toys and the Noonday Gun and Typhoon Shelter.

Rendezvous near Times Square, and sweeten things up with a dessert at Hui Lau Shan—nothing beats the sago in mango juice with extra mango. Hours on your feet will have taken their toll, so counter the effects together with a foot massage and back rub at one of the massage places *without* a red light outside—there are lots in the Bartlock Centre at 3 Yiu Wa Street in Causeway Bay.

A NIGHT IN THE EAST

When the sun goes down, all kinds of other lights fill the sky: in Wan Chai, the neon signs of bars (both reputable and otherwise); on the waterfront, the beams illuminating skyscrapers in the Symphony of Lights; and in Happy Valley, the floodlighting at the racetrack.

If it's race night, grab an early, stabilizing meal around the corner at the **Tasty Congee and Noodle Wonton Shop** (⊠ *21 King Kwong St., Happy Valley, Wan Chai* ☎ *2838–3922*), a Cantonese restaurant with a retro decor. Then, dressed comfortably but chicly, be at the track by 8 for turf 'n' tippling. Take some throat lozenges if you plan to bet—you'll want to scream as loudly as the thousands around you. Wait for the crowds to ease, and then get a cab over to Wan Chai for drinking and dancing. There are plenty of feel-good beery boozers where you know the words to every song—Carnegie's, Delaney's, Joe Bananas, and From Dusk Till Dawn, to name a few.

If you fancy something sophisticated, look the part and make your way to **1/5 nuevo** (⊠ *9 Star St., Wan Chai* ☎ *2529–2300*), pronounced "one-fifth," where martinis are shaken to house music. When you're done? Why, breakfast at the **Flying Pan** (⇨ *Quick Bites*), no matter the hour.

SOUTHSIDE

Sightseeing
☆★★★

Dining
☆☆★★

Lodging
☆☆☆★

Shopping
☆☆☆★

For all the unrelenting urbanity of Hong Kong Island's north coast, its south side consists largely of green hills and a few residential areas around picturesque bays. With beautiful sea views, real estate is at a premium; some of Hong Kong's wealthiest residents live in beautiful houses and luxurious apartments here. Southside is a breath of fresh air—literally and figuratively. The people are more relaxed, the pace is slower, and there are lots of sea breezes.

TOP ATTRACTIONS

☙ **Ocean Park.** Most Hong Kongers have fond childhood memories of this aquatic theme park. It was built by the omnipresent Hong Kong Jockey Club on 170 hilly acres overlooking the sea just east of Aberdeen. Highlights include the four resident giant pandas; Marine Land's enormous aquarium; Ocean Theatre, where dolphins and seals perform; and such thrill rides as the gravity-defying Abyss Turbo. The park is accessible by a number of buses including the 72, 72A, 260, and M590; get off at the stop after the Aberdeen tunnel. ⊠ *Ocean Park Rd., Aberdeen, Southside* ☎ *3923–2323* ⊕ *www.oceanpark.com.hk* 🖃 *HK$250 adults; HK$125 kids* ☉ *Daily 10–7.*

Stanley. This peninsula town lies south of Deep Water and Repulse bays. There's great shopping in the renowned Stanley Market, whether you want casual clothes, sneakers, cheap souvenirs, cheerful bric-a-brac—even snow gear. Stanley's popular beach is the site of the Dragon Boat Races held every June. ⊠ *Stanley, Southside.*

WORTH NOTING

2

Aberdeen. On side streets you'll find outdoor barbers at work and any number of dim sum restaurants. You'll also see traditional sights like the Aberdeen Cemetery with its enormous gravestones, and yet another shrine to the goddess of the sea: the Tin Hau Temple. During the Tin Hau Festival in April and May, hundreds of boats converge along the shore here.

Aberdeen's harbor contains about 3,000 junks and sampans. Several generations of one family can live on each junk (you may recall when Angelina Jolie's character, Lara Croft, stepped aboard such a boat in *Tomb Raider 2*). ⊠ *Southside.*

Ap Lei Chau Island. A bridge connects Aberdeen with this island (Duck's Tongue Island in English), where boat-builders work in the old way. Unspoiled just a decade ago, Ap Lei Chau is now covered with public housing, private estates, and shopping malls. ⊠ *Southside.*

Repulse Bay. The tranquil area is home to a landmark apartment building with a hole in it. Following the principles of feng shui, the opening was incorporated into the design so the dragon that lives in the mountains behind can readily drink from the bay. The popular Repulse Bay Verandah Restaurant and Bamboo Bar (⇨ *Quick Bites)* is a great place for a meal with majestic bay views. The beach is large and wide, but be warned: it's the first stop for most visitors. At the beach's east end, huge statues of Tin Hau—Goddess of the Sea and Goddess of Mercy—border on gaudy. In the 1970s, when worshippers were planning to erect just one statue, they worried she'd be lonely, so an additional statue was created to keep her company. ⊠ *Beach Rd. at Seaview Promenade, Repulse Bay, Southside* ☎ 2812–2483.

DID YOU KNOW?

The Chinese name for Stanley translates as "Red Pole." Depending on who you talk to, it refers to the red flowers on two silk-cotton trees here or to a nearby hill that turns red at sunset, acting as a beacon for sailors. The English name comes from Lord Stanley, a 19th-century British official.

Shek O. The seaside locale is Southside's easternmost village. Weekend beachgoers and hikers crowd the Thai restaurant on the left as you enter town. Every shop here sells the same inflatable beach toys—the bigger the better, it seems. Cut through town to a windy road that takes you to the "island" of Tai Tau Chau, really a large rock with a lookout over the South China Sea. Little more than a century ago, this open water was ruled by pirates. You can hike through nearby Shek O Country Park, where the bird-watching is great, in less than two hours. ⊠ *Southside.*

GETTING ORIENTED

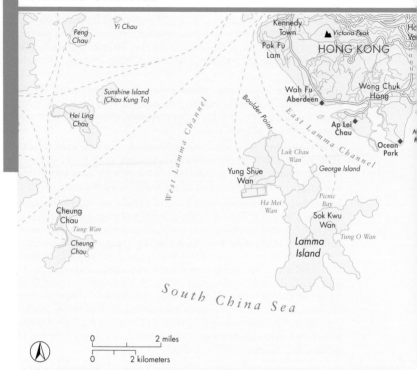

TAKING IT IN	TRANSPORTATION FROM CENTRAL TO . . .
If you travel independently, pick one hub and explore in and around it: Aberdeen with its junks and sampans on the southwest coast; Stanley and its market on the south central coast; or, perhaps, Shek O with its beaches and parkland far to the southeast. **Gray Line Tours** (☎ 2368–7111 ⊕ www.grayline.com.hk) has seven-hour day trips of Hong Kong Island including Man Mo Temple, the Peak, Aberdeen, Repulse Bay, Stanley Market, and dim sum lunch at Jumbo Kingdom for HK$490 per adult.	**Aberdeen:** 30 minutes via Bus 70 or 91. (Ap Lei Chau is 15 minutes from Aberdeen on Bus 90B or 91; 10 minutes by sampan). **Deep Water Bay:** 20 minutes via Bus 6, 64, 260, or 6A. **Ocean Park:** 30 minutes via Central Pier #7 and Bus 629. **Repulse Bay:** 30 minutes via Bus 6, 6A, 6X, 66, 64, or 260. **Shek O:** 50 minutes via MTR to Shau Kei Wan and then Bus 9 to the last stop. **Stanley:** 40 minutes via Bus 6, 6A, 6X, 66, 64, or 260. Note that express buses skip Aberdeen and Deep Water Bay, heading directly to Repulse Bay and Stanley. Buses run less frequently in the evening, so it's more convenient to grab a taxi (they're everywhere).

2

QUICK BITES

In **Stanley Market** there are dozens of cheap local and international eateries. For more upscale yet still casual joints, head to Stanley Main Road.

Treat yourself to British high tea at the **Repulse Bay Verandah Restaurant & Bamboo Bar** (✉ *109 Repulse Bay Rd., Southside* ☎ *2292–2822* ⊕ *www. therepulsebay.com*). Tea is served Tuesday to Saturday from 3 to 5:30 and Sunday from 3:30 to 5:30.

A favorite place for lunch, drinks, or just alfresco lounging is Shek O's **Black Sheep Restaurant** (✉ *Ground fl., 330, Southside, Shek O* ☎ *2809–2021*), a small place with an eclectic menu and a relaxed vibe.

The **Top Deck at the Jumbo** (✉ *Jumbo Aberdeen Pier, Shum Wan Pier Dr., Wong Chuk Hang, Southside* ☎ *2552–3331* ⊕ *www.cafedecogroup.com*) was built on the previously unused upper deck of the Jumbo Kingdom floating restaurant. It's a fantastic alfresco spot on the water, serving international cuisine.

GOLFERS TAKE NOTE

Deep Water Bay is flanked to the north by the **Deep Water Bay Golf Club** (✉ *19 Island Rd., Deep Water Bay* ☎ *2812– 7070* ⊕ *www.hkgolfclub.org*), which is owned by the Hong Kong Golf Club. The most convenient course to play if you're staying on Hong Kong Island has nine challenging holes. It's a members' club (some of Hong Kong's richest businessmen play here), but it's casual, and visitors with handicap certificates are admitted on weekdays from 9 to 2 (walk-in only).

Greens fees are HK$500 for 18 holes. Club rental will cost you another HK$300; a caddy, still another HK$150. The club also has two restaurants (one serving Chinese fare, the other western dishes), plus a members-only fitness center and swimming pool.

Repulse Bay is one of Hong Kong's lovely but frequently overlooked beaches.

A PERFECT DAY (OR SO)

Grab breakfast at your hotel, and get off from Central to Aberdeen for a sampan ride. Be prepared for the strong smell of drying fish and the noise of boat women shouting over engine noise. Afterward hop a cab or bus for a 10-minute ride to Repulse Bay beach for a swim and some sunbathing.

Refuel on the terrace of the Repulse Bay Verandah Restaurant (⇨ *Quick Bites*), before taking a cab or bus to Stanley Market, 10 to 15 minutes away. Enjoy sundowners at a restaurant or bar on Stanley's Main Street overlooking the bay. Take a taxi or bus back to Aberdeen for dinner at the Top Deck at the Jumbo Kingdom floating restaurant (⇨ *Quick Bites*).

If you have kids, spend the whole day at Ocean Park. Afterward high tea at the Repulse Bay Verandah Restaurant is a must.

If you only have a half day, take a sampan ride around Aberdeen, followed by a dim sum lunch at the Jumbo Kingdom floating restaurant. Take a taxi to Stanley Market.

LANTAU ISLAND

Sightseeing
★★★★
Dining
☆☆☆★
Lodging
☆☆☆★
Shopping
☆☆☆★

A decade of manic development has seen Lantau become more than just "the place where the Buddha is." There's a mini-theme park at Ngong Ping to keep the Buddha company. Not to be outdone, Disney has opened a park and resort on the northeast coast. And, of course, there's the airport, built on a massive north coast reclamation. At 55 square mi, Lantau is almost twice the size of Hong Kong Island, so there's room for all this development and the laid-back attractions—beaches, fishing villages, and hiking trails—that make the island a great getaway.

TOP ATTRACTIONS

🟢 **Hong Kong Disneyland.** Though Hong Kong's home to Mickey Mouse is tame compared to other Magic Kingdoms, it's fast bringing Mai Kei Lo Su—as the world's most famous mouse is known locally—to a mainland audience. ⊠ *Fantasy Rd., Lantau Island* ⊕ *park.hongkongdisneyland. com* 🎫 *HK$350 adults, HK$250 kids* ☉ *Daily 10–8 or 9* Ⓜ *Disneyland Resort.*

Fodor'sChoice **Tian Tan Buddha.**
★ ⇨ *See highlighted listing in this chapter.*

WORTH NOTING

Cheung Sha Beach. Two miles of golden sand 5 mi southwest of Mui Wo make this Hong Kong's longest. It gets breezy here, but that's why windsurfers love it; it rarely gets too crowded. Upper Cheung Sha Beach is equipped for barbecues, and there is also a refreshment stand. ⊠ *South Lantau Rd., Lantau Island* ☎ *2852–3220.*

GETTING ORIENTED

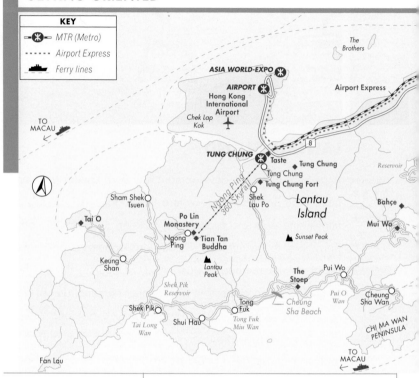

KEY
- MTR (Metro)
- Airport Express
- Ferry lines

The Brothers

ASIA WORLD-EXPO
AIRPORT
Hong Kong International Airport
Chek Lap Kok
Airport Express
8

TO MACAU

TUNG CHUNG · Taste · Tung Chung
Tung Chung
Tung Chung Fort
Reservoir

Sham Shek Tsuen
Tai O
Po Lin Monastery
Ngong Ping · Tian Tan Buddha
Keung Shan

Shek Lau Po
Lantau Island
Bahçe
Mui Wo

Ngong Ping 360 Skyrail

Sunset Peak

Lantau Peak

The Stoep
Pui Wo
Pui O
Cheung Sha Wan
Shek Pik Reservoir
Shek Pik
Shui Hau
Tong Fuk
Tong Fuk Miu Wan
Cheung Sha Beach
Pui O Wan
CHI MA WAN PENINSULA

Tai Long Wan

Fan Lau

TO MACAU

THE TERRITORY	TAKING IT IN
Most Lantau roads lead to Tung Chung, the north shore new town, close to Hong Kong International Airport. It's connected to Kowloon by the lengthy Tsing Ma Bridge, which starts near Hong Kong Disneyland, on Lantau's northeast tip. The Tung Chung Road winds through mountains and connects north Lantau with the southern coast. Here, the South Lantau Road stretches from the town of Mui Wo in the east to Tai O in the west, passing Cheung Sha Beach, and Ngong Ping.	Candy-pink dolphins might sound like something Disney cooked up, but Lantau's cutest residents are the endangered species *Sousa chinensis*, native to the Pearl River estuary. Only a few hundred are left, but ecotourism company **Hong Kong Dolphinwatch** (☎ 2984–1414 ⊕ *www.hkdolphinwatch.com*) guarantees you a sighting on their 2½-hour cruises (HK$320)—or a free second trip. To see Lantau's big sights whistle-stop style, try **Splendid Tours** (☎ 2316–2151 ⊕ *www.splendid.hk*). A daylong trip (HK$650, including lunch) takes in the Tsing Ma Bridge, Cheung Sha Beach, Tai O village and Ngong Ping.

GETTING AROUND

The speediest way to Lantau from Central is the MTR's Tung Chung line (HK$18), which takes about half an hour. A trip by ferry is a 35-minute crossing from Central with great views.

New World First Ferry (☎ 2131–8181 ⊕ www.nwff.com.hk) vessels to Mui Wo leave every 30–40 minutes from Central's Pier 6 (HK$13–HK$25.50).

Bus routes are winding, and rides can be heart-stopping. There's service every half hour from Tung Chung and Mui Wo to Ngong Ping, more frequently to Tai O.

The most direct (and daring) way to Ngong Ping is the 25-minute trip on the **Ngong Ping 360 Skyrail** (☎ 2109–9898 ⊕ www.np360.com.hk ☎ HK$74 one-way; HK$107 round-trip ☉ Weekdays 10–6, Sat. 10–6:30, Sun. 9–6:30).

You can reach Tung Chung by a red taxi from Kowloon or Central, but the long, toll-ridden trip will cost around HK$340 from Central. Blue taxis travel Lantau (but can't leave it)—and hairpin bends make costs add up.

QUICK BITES

If you're hiking, stop off in Tung Chung for provisions. Deli counters in the huge branch of the local supermarket **Taste** (✉ Citygate Mall, Basement fl., 20 Tat Tung Rd., Lantau) have sushi, sandwiches, salads, baked goods, and precut fruit.

For lunch on Cheung Sha Beach—or on Lantau in general—everyone agrees: **The Stoep** (✉ 32 Lower Cheung Sha Village Rd., Lantau ☎ 2980–2699) is the place. Its name means "patio," appropriately: tables are outside, facing the beach. It's run by South Africans, and the food's a mix of Mediterranean standards and South African–style barbecued meat—try the mixed grill.

You're spoiled for choice on the Mui Wo waterfront, but cozy Turkish café **Bahçe** (✉ Shop 19, ground fl., Mui Wo Centre, Lantau ☎ 2984–0222) is a good bet. You can make a meal out of several *meze* (small snacks)—the flaky filo triangles are delicious—or beef up with a kebab. At night, the place is more like a bar.

TIAN TAN BUDDHA

✉ *Ngong Ping, Lantau Island* ☎ *2109–9898 Ngong Ping hotline* ⊕ *www.plm.org.hk/ eng/home.php* 🖾 *Monastery and path free. Walking with Buddha: HK$35* ☾ *Buddha daily 10–5:30. Monastery and path daily 8–6* Ⓜ *Tung Chung.*

TIPS

■ You can get here on the Ngong Ping 360 Skyrail or via Buses 2 and 23 from Mui Wo and Tung Chung, respectively. To reach Lantau Island from Central take the MTR to Tung Chung or the New World First Ferry from Pier 6 to Mui Wo.

■ The only way to the upper level, right under the Buddha, is through an underwhelming museum inside the podium. You only get a couple of feet higher up.

■ The booth at the base of the stairs is only for tickets for lunch—wandering around the Buddha is free.

■ The monastery's vegetarian restaurant is a clattering canteen with uninspiring fare. Pick up sandwiches at the Citygate Mall, Tung Chung, or eat at a restaurant in Ngong Ping Village.

Hong Kongers love superlatives, even if making them true requires strings of qualifiers. So the Tian Tan Buddha is the world's largest Buddha—that's seated, located outdoors, and made of bronze. Just know its vast silhouette is impressive. Steep stairs lead to the lower podium, essentially forcing you to stare up at all 202 tons of Buddha as you ascend. At the top, cool breezes and fantastic views over Lantau Island await.

HIGHLIGHTS

Po Lin Monastery. It's hard to believe today, but from its foundation in 1927 through the early '90s, this monastery was virtually inaccessible by road. These days, it's at the heart of Lantau's biggest attraction. The monastery proper has a gaudy, commercial, orange temple complex. Still, it's the Buddha people come for.

Wisdom Path. This peaceful path runs beside 38 halved tree trunks arranged in an infinity shape on a hillside. Each is carved with Chinese characters that make up the Heart Sutra, a 5th-century Buddhist prayer that expresses the doctrine of emptiness. The idea is to walk around the path—which takes five minutes—and reflect. Follow the signposted trail to the left of the Buddha.

Ngong Ping Village. People were fussing about this attraction before its first stone was laid. Ngong Ping Village is a moneymaking add-on to the Tian Tan Buddha. Walking With Buddha is intended to be an educational stroll through the life of Siddhartha Gautama, the first Buddha, but it's more of a multimedia extravaganza that shuns good taste with such kitsch as a self-illuminating Bodhi tree and piped-in incense. No cost has been spared in the dioramas that fill the seven galleries—ironic, given that each represents a stage of the Buddha's path to enlightenment and the eschewing of material wealth.

Lantau Peak. The most glorious views of Lantau—and beyond—are from atop Fung Wong Shan, or Lantau Peak, but at 3,064 feet it's not for the faint-hearted. It's a strenuous 7½ mi west from Mui Wo, or you can begin at the Po Lin Monastery—still a demanding two hours. You can also elect to take a bus to a trail that is closer to the summit, and climb from stage three of the Lantau Trail. ⊠ *Lantau Island.*

Mui Wo. Mui Wo is a sleepy little town, but it has some good waterfront restaurants. Silvermine Bay Beach, a pleasant sandy stretch, is a half-mile northeast of the ferry pier. A gentle uphill trail leads to the Silvermine Caves and Waterfall, the small 19th-century mine that gave the bay its English name. ⊠ *Lantau Island.*

Tai O. Tucked away on the west of Lantau is this fishing village inhabited largely by the tanka (boat people), whose stilt houses have mostly been replaced by government-funded high-rises. Similarly, an old rope-pulled ferry connecting the village proper with a small island has been replaced with a metal bridge. Aging Hakka women, however, haul the ferry back into action on weekends. You can also see salt pans and a 16th-century temple dedicated to Kwan Tai, god of war. ⊠ *Lantau Island.*

DID YOU KNOW?

Lantau is connected to the Kowloon Peninsula by the world's longest suspension bridge, the 4,518-foot Tsing Ma Bridge. Airport Express and MTR trains run through its sheltered lower level; a highway runs atop it, with stunning views of the Pearl River Delta to the west.

Tung Chung New Town. Looking at the tower blocks and perfectly planned avenues of Tung Chung New Town, home to around 80,000 people, it's hard to imagine that only 15 years ago this was a small village. Over the MTR station is a mall filled with outlet stores for big local brands. All that remains of the old Tung Chung is the hulking granite **Tung Chung Fort** (⊠ *Tung Chung Rd., Lantau* ⊕ *www.lcsd.hk/CE/Museum/Monument/en/monuments_07.php* ☉ *Wed.–Mon. 10–5*). The first fortification on this spot was built during the Song Dynasty; the current structure dates from 1832. ⊠ *Lantau Island.*

A PERFECT (SUNNY) DAY

Leave Central on the Mui Wo ferry at around 11 AM—bag a window seat for the views. From Mui Wo Ferry Pier catch Bus 1 or a cab to Cheung Sha Beach for an early lunch at The Stoep (⊲ *Quick Bites*) and a stroll on the sands. Bus 2 from here takes you up to Ngong Ping, where you need a good hour or two to visit the Buddha and monastery, more if you plan to tour Ngong Ping Village. Stock up on water here.

There are stunning views from the Wisdom Path. From here, it's an hour's easy hiking to Tung Chung Fort. There'll be views of the airport to your left. After a quick visit to the fort, you can walk (or catch a cab) into Tung Chung town center. Refuel with a juice or a coffee at a Citygate Mall café before taking the MTR back to Hong Kong Island.

DID YOU KNOW?

Despite its image as a hyper-modern cityscape, seventy percent of Hong Kong's land is rural, rugged, undeveloped terrain. Lantau is the territory's largest island and about double the size of Hong Kong Island. Though home to Disneyland, it's still known as the "lungs of Hong Kong" because of the abundant indigenous forests and relative lack of skyscrapers.

Kowloon Neighborhoods

WORD OF MOUTH

"Hop on the Star Ferry to Tsim Sha Tsui (TST). The Star Ferry and the tram, by the way, might be the two best transportation bargains on earth. When you reach TST, walk over to the Promenade, and take in the view of the harbor—the most spectacular cityscape you may ever see."

—rizzuto

Updated by
Doretta Lau

Though some call Kowloon "The Dark Side," there are many spots on the peninsula that glow with neon, sparkle with new developments, and boast breathtaking cultural sights. In this part of town, where the water lies to the south, there are ample museums, temples, mosques, art spaces, shopping centers, and nature to keep anyone busy for days, and nights as well.

Kowloon's southern tip is the Tsim Sha Tsui district, famous for its boutiques and malls, which gives way to Jordan, Yau Ma Tei, Mong Kok, and Prince Edward. Northeast are the New Kowloon districts of Kowloon Tong, Kowloon City, and Wong Tai Sin, beyond which lie the eastern New Territories—mostly made up of mountainous country parks and fishing villages, but also home to a modern, high-tech horseracing track that isn't far from a temple housing more than 10,000 buddhas. The Sai Kung Peninsula juts out on the east, and massive Sha Tin New Town is north of New Kowloon, over Lion Rock Mountain. The Kowloon–Canton Railway and a highway run north of this to the Chinese border at Lo Wu. Industrial Sham Shui Po lies west of Prince Edward, and the urban sprawl continues northwest to the New Territories' New Town Tsuen Wan. The western New Territories is a mixture of country parks and urban areas.

KOWLOON

Sightseeing
☆★★★
Dining
★★★★
Lodging
★★★★
Shopping
☆★★★

3

There's much more to the Kowloon than rock-bottom prices and goods of dubious provenance. Just across the harbor from Central, this piece of Chinese mainland takes its name from the string of mountains that bound it in the north: *gau lung,* "nine dragons" (there are actually eight mountains, the ninth represented the emperor who named them). Although less sophisticated and wilder than its island-side counterpart, Kowloon's dense, gritty urban fabric is the backdrop for Hong Kong's best museums and most interesting spiritual sights. And there's street upon street of hard-core consumerism in every imaginable guise.

TSIM SHA TSUI

One of the best things to see in Tsim Sha Tsui (TST) is, well, Central. There are fabulous cross-harbor views from the **Star Ferry Pier** as well as from the ferries themselves. The sweeping pink-tile **Hong Kong Cultural Centre** and the Former KCR (Kowloon–Canton Railway) Clock Tower are a stone's throw away, the first stop along the breezy pedestrian **TST East Promenade,** which starts at the Avenue of Stars and stretches a couple of miles east. ■TIP➔ **Try to visit the promenade once in the daytime and once at 8 PM for the Symphony of Lights, a nightly show in which 44 skyscrapers light up on cue as a commentator introduces them in time to a musical accompaniment.**

TOP ATTRACTIONS

Fodor's Choice **Hong Kong Museum of Art.**

★ *See highlighted feature in this section.*

Hong Kong Museum of History. A whopping HK$156 million went into making this museum engaging and educational. The permanent Hong Kong Story re-creates life as it was rather than simply displaying relics of it: indeed, actual artifacts are few. The museum's forte is clear explanations of spectacular life-size dioramas, which include village houses and a Central shopping street in colonial times. The ground-floor Folk Culture section is a Technicolor introduction to the history and customs of Hong Kong's main ethnic groups: the Punti, Hakka, and Hoklo. Upstairs, gracious stone-walled galleries whirl you through the Opium Wars and the beginnings of colonial Hong Kong. ■TIP➔ **Unless you're with kids who dig models of cavemen and bears, skip the prehistory and dynastic galleries. Reserve energy for the last two galleries: a chill-**

HONG KONG MUSEUM OF ART

✉ *10 Salisbury Rd., Tsim Sha Tsui, Kowloon* ☎ *2721–0116* ⊕ *hk.art.museum* 💰 *HK$10* ⏱ *Fri. and Sun.–Wed. 10–6, Sat. 10–8* Ⓜ *Tsim Sha Tsui MTR, Exit E.*

TIPS

■ Traditional Chinese landscape paintings are visual records of real or imagined journeys—a kind of travelogue. Pick a starting point and try to travel through the picture, imagining the journey the artist is trying to convey.

■ There are educational rooms tucked away on the eastern side of every floor. Kids can emboss traditional motifs on paper or do brass rubbings; there are also free gallery worksheets in English. A good selection of reference books makes them useful learning centers for adults, too.

■ Guided tours can help you to understand art forms you're not familiar with. There are general museum tours in English Tuesday through Sunday at 11

■ . Check the Web site for the schedule of more detailed visits to specific galleries—they change every month.

■ If you prefer to tour alone, consider an English-language audio guide: it's informative, if a little dry, and it costs only HK$10.

An extensive collection of Chinese art is packed inside this boxy tiled building on the Tsim Sha Tsui waterfront in Kowloon. The collections here contain a heady mix of things that make Hong Kong what it is: Qing ceramics, 2,000-year-old calligraphic scrolls, kooky contemporary canvases. Thankfully it's organized into thematic galleries with clear, if uninspired, explanations. Hong Kong's biggest visiting exhibitions are usually held here too. The museum is a few minutes' walk from either the Star Ferry or Tsim Sha Tsui MTR stop.

HIGHLIGHTS

The Chinese Antiquities Gallery is the place to head if Ming's your thing. A series of low-lit rooms on the third floor houses ceramics from Neolithic times through the Qing dynasty. Unusually, they're displayed by motif rather than by period: dragons, phoenixes, lotus flowers, and bats are some of the auspicious designs. Bronzes, jade, lacquerware, textiles, enamel, and glassware complete this collection of decorative art.

In the Chinese Fine Art Gallery you get a great introduction to Chinese brush painting, often difficult for the Western eye to appreciate. Landscape paintings from the 20th-century Guangdong and Lingnan schools form the bulk of the collection, and modern calligraphy also gets a nod.

The Contemporary Hong Kong Art Gallery showcases a mix of traditional Chinese and western techniques—often in the same work. Paintings account for most of the pieces from the first half of the 20th century, when local artists used the traditional mediums of brush and ink in innovative ways. Western techniques dominate later work, the result of Hong Kong artists' having spent more time abroad.

ing account of life under Japanese occupation and a colorful look at Hong Kong life in the '60s.

Budget at least two hours to stroll through—more if you linger in each and every gallery. Pick your way through the gift shop's clutter to find local designer Alan Chan's T-shirts, shot glasses, and notebooks. His retro-kitsch aesthetic is based on 1940s cigarette-girl images. To get here from the Tsim Sha Tsui MTR walk along Cameron Road, then left for a block along Chatham Road South. A signposted overpass takes you to the museum. ⊠ *100 Chatham Rd. S, Tsim Sha Tsui, Kowloon* ☎ *2724–9042* ⊕ *hk.history.museum* ⊠ *HK$10; free Wed.* ☼ *Mon. and Wed.–Sat. 10–6, Sun. and holidays 10–7* Ⓜ *Tsim Sha Tsui, Exit B2.*

☾ **Kowloon Park.** Just behind Nathan Road, at TST's north end, are the 33 acres of park, which opened in 1970 and received a $300 million face-lift in 1989. It's crisscrossed by paths and landscaped to within an inch of its life but is still refreshing after a day of shopping. In addition to a fitness trail, soccer pitch, playgrounds, an aviary, and a maze garden, there are stalls with arts and crafts on Sundays and public holidays. ⊠ *22 Austin Rd., Tsim Sha Tsui, Kowloon* ☎ *2724–3344* ⊕ *www.lcsd. gov.hk/parks/kp/en* ⊠ *Free* ☼ *5* AM*–midnight* Ⓜ *Tsim Sha Tsui MTR, Exit A1, Jordan, Exit C1.*

WORTH NOTING

Avenue of Stars. You have to look down to appreciate the city's walk of fame. Over the past several decades countless local film stars have pawed the wet concrete—you won't recognize many names unless you're a fan, but it goes to show how old Hong Kong's film industry is. ⊠ *TST East Promenade outside New World Renaissance Hotel, Tsim Sha Tsui, Kowloon* Ⓜ *Tsim Sha Tsui, Exit E.*

☾ **Hong Kong Science Museum.** The exhibits are kid-friendly and hands-on and include an energy machine, a miniature submarine, and cognitive and memory tests. That said, it's more of a rainy-day time-killer than a must-see. ⊠ *2 Science Museum Rd., corner of Cheong Wan Rd. and Chatham Rd., Tsim Sha Tsui East, Kowloon* ☎ *2732–3232* ⊕ *hk. science.museum* ⊠ *HK$25–35; free Wed.* ☼ *Mon.–Wed., Fri. 1–9, Sat., Sun., and holidays 10–9, closed Thurs.* Ⓜ *Tsim Sha Tsui, Exit B2.*

☾ **Hong Kong Space Museum.** Looking like an oversize golf ball sliced in half, the space museum stands behind the art museum. Despite many attractions—a planetarium, a solar telescope, an Omnimax theater—it's fairly unremarkable, and children under 3 aren't allowed to view the Omnimax shows. ⊠ *10 Salisbury Rd., Tsim Sha Tsui, Kowloon* ☎ *2721–0226* ⊕ *hk.space.museum* ⊠ *HK$10* ☼ *Mon. and Wed.–Fri 1–9, Sat.–Sun. 10–9, closed Tues.* Ⓜ *Tsim Sha Tsui MTR, Exit E.*

Kowloon Mosque and Islamic Centre. Built in 1984, Hong Kong's largest Islamic worship center stands in front of Kowloon Park. Visitors can call ahead to arrange for a tour of the premises or simply drop by to see the building, which is also known as the Kowloon Masjid and Islamic Centre, and was designed by architect I. M. Kadri. In addition to prayer halls, it includes a medical clinic and a library. ⊠ *105 Nathan Rd., Tsim Sha Tsui, Kowloon* ☎ *2724–0095* ⊠ *Free* ☼ *5* AM*–10* PM Ⓜ *Tsim Sha Tsui, Exit A1.*

GETTING ORIENTED

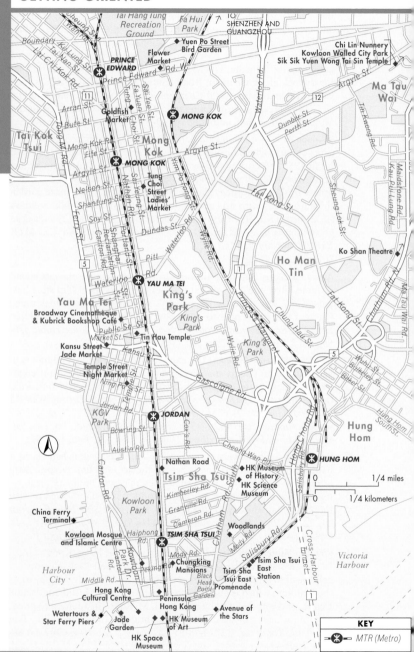

Cheung Sha Wan

Tai Hang Tung Recreation Ground

Fa Hui Park

TO SHENZHEN AND GUANGZHOU

Boundary St.

Kowloon

Tai Nan St.

Lai Chi Kok Rd.

Yuen Po Street Bird Garden

Chi Lin Nunnery
Kowloon Walled City Park
Sik Sik Yuen Wong Tai Sin Temple

PRINCE EDWARD

Flower Market

Prince Edward Rd. W.

Ma Tau Wai

11

Arran St.

Bute St.

Goldfish Market

MONG KOK

Fa Yuen St.

Tung Choi St.

Sai Yee St.

Dunbar St.

Perth St.

Argyle St.

12

Tai Kok Tsui

Mong Kok Rd.

Fife St.

Mong Kok

MONG KOK

Argyle St.

Tai Kong St.

Ko Shan Theatre

Argyle St.

Sai Yeung Choi St.

Nathan Rd.

Shanghai St.

Nelson St.

Shantung St.

Soy St.

Tung Choi Street Ladies' Market

Dundas St.

Waterloo Rd.

Wylie Rd.

Sheung Lok St.

Ho Man Tin

Portland St.

Reclamation St.

Canton Rd.

5

Pitt Rd.

Waterloo Rd.

YAU MA TEI

Shanghai St.

Yau Ma Tei

King's Park

Princess Margaret Rd.

Fat Kong St.

Ma Tau Wai Rd.

Broadway Cinematheque & Kubrick Bookshop Café

King's Park

Chung Hau St.

Wuhu St.

Bulkeley St.

Baker St.

5

Public Sq.

Market St.

Tin Hau Temple

Wylie Rd.

King's Park

Kansu Street Jade Market

Kansu St.

Temple Street Night Market

Ning Po St.

Gascoigne Rd.

Hung Hom South St.

KGV Park

Jordan Rd.

Bowring St.

JORDAN

Cox's Rd.

Hung Hom

Austin Rd.

Cheong Wan Rd.

HUNG HOM

Nathan Road

HK Museum of History

HK Science Museum

0   1/4 miles

Canton Rd.

Tsim Sha Tsui

Kimberley Rd.

Nathan Rd. South

Hong Chong Rd.

0   1/4 kilometers

China Ferry Terminal

Kowloon Park

Granville Rd.

Cameron Rd.

Cross-Harbour Tunnel

Kowloon Mosque and Islamic Centre

Haiphong Rd.

TSIM SHA TSUI

Woodlands

Mody Rd.

Salisbury Rd.

Victoria Harbour

Harbour City

Kowloon Park Dr.

Canton Rd.

Peking Rd.

Chungking Mansions

Mody Rd.

Tsim Sha Tsui East

Tsim Sha Tsui East Station

Middle Rd.

Black Head Point Garden

Tsim Sha Tsui East Promenade

Hong Kong Cultural Centre

Peninsula Hong Kong

Watertours & Star Ferry Piers

Jade Garden

HK Museum of Art

Avenue of the Stars

HK Space Museum

KEY
☀ MTR (Metro)

GETTING AROUND

The most romantic way from Hong Kong Island to southern Tsim Sha Tsui (TST) is by Star Ferry. There are crossings from Central every 6–12 minutes and a little less often from Wan Chai.

TST is also accessible by MTR. Underground walkways connect the station with the Tsim Sha Tsui East station on the East Rail Line, where trains depart every 10–15 minutes for the eastern New Territories. The Kowloon Airport Express station is amid a construction wasteland west of TST, connecting with Austin station on the West Rail; for now hotel shuttles link it to the rest of Kowloon.

The MTR is your best bet for Jordan, Yau Ma Tei, Mong Kok, Kowloon Tong, Lok Fu, and Wong Tai Sin. But you'll need a bus or cab to reach Kowloon City from Wong Tai Sin or TST East.

QUICK BITES

Woodlands (✉ *1st fl., Wing On Plaza, 62 Mody Rd., Tsim Sha Tsui East, Kowloon* ☎ *2369–3718*) is a find. Expect fabulous South Indian food—all vegetarian—and fantastic mango lassi. The HK$65/75/85 *thalis* (10 tiny curry dishes served with rice and chapatis) are perfect for the indecisive, uninitiated, or just plain greedy.

Arty tomes surround the tables at the **Kubrick Bookshop Café** (✉ *Broadway Cinemathèque, 3 Public Square St., Yau Ma Tei, Kowloon* ☎ *2384–8929*). It's attached to the city's best art-house cinema. Tuck into sandwiches, pasta dishes, and cakes. The coffee's great, too.

Jade Garden (✉ *4th fl., Star House, opposite Star Ferry Concourse, Tsim Sha Tsui, Kowloon* ☎ *2730–6888*) is a popular dim sum chain. Come early on weekends.

THE TERRITORY

Kowloon's southernmost district is Tsim Sha Tsui (TST), home to the Star Ferry Pier. The waterfront extends a few miles to TST East. Shops and hotels line Nathan Road, which runs north from the waterfront through the market districts of Jordan, Yau Ma Tei, and Mong Kok.

New Kowloon is the unofficial name for the sprawl beyond Boundary Street. The district just north is Kowloon Tong. Two spiritual sights—Wong Tai Sin and Lok Fu—are a little farther east. The tongue sticking out into the sea to the south was the runway of the old Kai Tak Airport. Kowloon City is a stone's throw west.

TAKING IT IN

Walk the Talk (⊕ *www.walkthetalk.hk*) tours use your mobile phone or its iPhone App as an audio guide. The TST tour is packed with serious history and kooky anecdotes.

Kowloon looks great from the harbor, and the **Hong Kong Tourist Board** (*HKTB* ✉ *TST Star Ferry Concourse* ☎ *2508–1234* ⊕ *www.discoverhongkong.com*) runs cruise combos that include visits to fishing communities or markets. Plain old cruises depart morning, afternoon, and evening.

3

Nathan Road. The famous Kowloon road runs several miles north from Salisbury Road in TST. It's filled with hotels, restaurants, and shops—indeed, retail space is so costly that the southern end is dubbed the Golden Mile. The mile's most famous tower block is ramshackle Chungking Mansions, packed with cheap hotels and Indian restaurants. It was the setting for arty local director Wong Kar-Wai's film *Chungking Express*. To the left and right are mazes of narrow streets with even more shops selling jewelry, electronics, clothes, souvenirs, and cosmetics. Skulking individuals chanting "copy watch" and "copy suit" are on every street corner—at least they're honest about the "Rolexes" they sell. ⊠ *Nathan Rd. between Salisbury Rd. and Boundary St., Tsim Sha Tsui and Mong Kok, Kowloon* Ⓜ *Tsim Sha Tsui, Jordan, Yau Ma Tei, Mong Kok, Prince Edward.*

The Peninsula Hong Kong. The grand building on the other side of Salisbury Road from the Hong Kong Space Museum is the famed.hotel. The fleet of Rolls-Royce taxis outside indicates the heights of luxury here. You can have tea in the colonnaded lobby and stroll through the shopping arcade. As you take afternoon tea in the soaring grand lobby, a string quartet plays as liveried waiters pour from silver pots. Three tiers' worth of salmon sandwiches, petit fours, and Valrhona truffles will keep you munching for a while. There's clotted Devonshire cream for the airy scones—so popular the Pen makes 1,000 a day. All this comes to a snip of what a suite here costs: HK$398 for two. ■TIP→ You can't make reservations for tea at the Peninsula; to avoid lines, come at 2 on the dot or after 5:30. ⊠ *Salisbury Rd., Tsim Sha Tsui, Kowloon* ☏ 2920–2888 ⊕ *www.peninsula.com* ▭ *AE, DC, MC, V* ☉ *Tea served daily 2–7* Ⓜ *Tsim Sha Tsui, Exit E.*

YAU MA TEI, MONG KOK, AND NORTHERN KOWLOON

TOP ATTRACTIONS

Fodor'sChoice   **Chi Lin Nunnery.**

★   *See highlighted listing in this section.*

Kowloon Walled City Park. Arguably Hong Kong's most beautiful park, designed in Qing-dynasty style, is near the old Kai Tak Airport, between Tung Tau Tsuen and Tung Tsing roads. The park opened in 1995, and in previous centuries it was a walled strategic military site, home to numerous offices and soldiers' quarters. Today the major attraction is the Yamen, an example of southern Chinese architecture of the 19th century, and is the only remaining structure from the original Walled City. There are also a number of traditional gardens on the grounds, and eight walks showcasing different flora, as well as free 45-minute guided tours. Hong Kong's Thai community is based in the streets south of the park, and there are countless hole-in-the-wall Thai restaurants. Bus 113 stops nearby, or take the MTR to Kowloon Tong and take a cab. ⊠ *Tung Tau Tsuen Rd. between Junction Rd. and Tung Tsing Rd., Kowloon City, Kowloon,Hong Kong* ☏ 2716–9962 ⊕ *www.lcsd.gov.hk/ parks/kwcp/en/* ▭ *Free* ☉ 6:30 AM–11 PM.

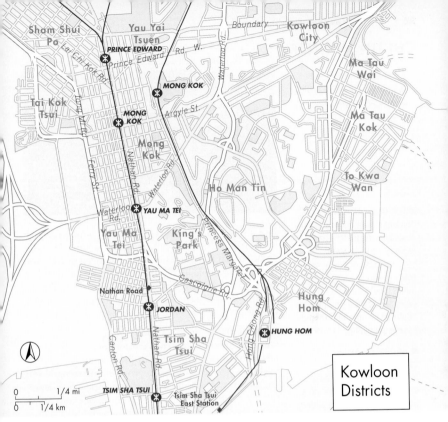

Kowloon
Districts

0   1/4 mi
0   1/4 km

Only the occasional patch of daylight was visible from the labyrinthine alleys of the Kowloon Walled City, Hong Kong's most notorious slum. Originally a 19th-century Chinese fortress, the city wasn't included in the British lease of the New Territories, thus it remained part of China and out-of-bounds to the Hong Kong police. The Triads ruled its unlicensed doctors and dentists, opium dens, brothels, gambling houses, and worse.

Fodor's Choice ★ **Sik Sik Yuen Wong Tai Sin Temple.** There's a practical approach to prayer at one of Hong Kong's most exuberant places of worship. Here the territory's three major religions—Taoism, Confucianism, and Buddhism—are all celebrated under the same roof. You'd think that highly ornamental religious buildings would look strange, with highly visible vending machines and LCD displays in front of them, but Wong Tai Sin pulls it off in cacophonous style. The temple was established in the early 20th century, on a different site, when two Taoist masters arrived from Guangzhou with the portrait of Wong Tai Sin—a famous monk who was born around AD 328—that still graces the main altar. In the '30s the temple was moved here; continuous renovations make it impossible to distinguish old from new.

Start at the incense-wreathed main courtyard, where the noise of many people shaking out *chim* (sticks with fortunes written on them) forms

CHI LIN NUNNERY

✉ 5 Chi Lin Dr., Diamond Hill, Kowloon ☎ 2354–1789 🎟 Free ⏱ Nunnery daily 9–4:30, lotus-pond garden daily 7–7 Ⓜ Diamond Hill, Exit C2.

TIPS

■ Left of the Main Hall is a don't-miss hall dedicated to Avalokitesvra, better known in Hong Kong as Kwun Yum, goddess of mercy and childbearing, among other things. She's one of the few exceptions to the rule that bodhisattvas are represented as asexual beings.

■ Be sure to keep looking up—the latticework ceilings and complicated beam systems are among the most beautiful parts of the building.

■ Combine Chi Lin Nunnery with a visit to Sik Sik Yuen Wong Tai Sin Temple, only one MTR stop or a short taxi ride away.

Not a single nail was used to build this nunnery, which dates from 1934. Instead, traditional Tang Dynasty architectural techniques involving wooden dowels and bracket work hold its 228,000 pieces of timber together. Most of the 15 cedar halls house altars to bodhisattvas (those who have reached enlightenment)—bronze plaques explain each one.

HIGHLIGHTS

Feng shui principles governed construction. The buildings face south toward the sea, to bring abundance; their backs are to the mountain, provider of strength and good energy. The temple's clean lines are a vast departure from most of Hong Kong's colorful religious buildings—here polished wood and gleaming Buddha statues are the only adornments.

The Main Hall is the most imposing—and inspiring—part of the monastery. Overlooking the smaller second courtyard, it honors the first Buddha, known as Sakyamuni. The soaring ceilings are held up by 28 cedar columns, measuring 18 feet each. They also support the roof—no mean feat, given that its traditionally made clay tiles make it weigh 176 tons.

Courtyards and gardens, where frangipani flowers scent the air, run beside the nunnery. The gardens are filled with bonsai trees and artful rockeries. Nature is also present inside: the various halls and galleries all look onto two courtyards filled with geometric lotus ponds and manicured bushes.

a constant rhythmic background. After wandering the halls, take time out in the Good Wish Garden—a peaceful riot of rockery—at the back of the complex. At the base of the complex is a small arcade where soothsayers and palm readers are happy to interpret Wong Tai Sin's predictions for a small fee. At the base of the ramp to the Confucian Hall, look up behind the temple for a view of Lion Rock, a mountain in the shape of a sleeping lion. ■TIP→ If you feel like acquiring a household altar of your own, head for Shanghai Street in Yau Ma Tei, the Kowloon district north of Tsim Sha Tsui, where religious shops abound. ⊠ *Wong Tai Sin Rd., Wong Tai Sin, Kowloon* ☎ *2327–8141* ⌨ *Donations expected. Good Wish Garden: HK$2* ☻ *Daily 7–5:30* Ⓜ *Wong Tai Sin, Exit B2 or B3.*

WORTH NOTING

Cattle Depot Artist Village. A former location for the slaughter of cattle, the venue was transformed into a home for a number of artists' studios, a theater, and some of Hong Kong's best galleries, including 1a Space and Videotage, in 2001. Take the MTR to Jordan and catch a cab, or take a bus that goes through To Kwa Wan, such as the 101. ⊠ *63 Ma Tau Kok Rd.</str>, To Kwa Wan, Kowloon* ⌨ *Free* ☻ *10 AM–8 PM.*

Fa Yuen Street. Parallel to Tung Choi Street Ladies' Market, between Argyle Street and Shan Tung Street, is sneaker central; its sports shops sell some brands you know and lots you don't. If you're not sporty, the stretch between Mongkok Road and Nullah Road offers cheap versions of the latest clothing fashion trends. ⊠ *Fa Yuen St. between Mongkok Rd. and Shan Tung St., Mong Kok, Kowloon* ⌨ *Free* Ⓜ *Mong Kok.*

Flower Market. Stalls containing local and imported fresh flowers, potted plants, and even artificial blossoms cover Flower Market Road, as well as parts of Yuen Po Street, Yuen Ngai Street, Prince Edward Road West, and Playground Field Road. ⊠ *Flower Market Rd. between Yuen Ngai St. and Yuen Po St., Mong Kok, Kowloon* ⌨ *Free* ☻ *7–7* Ⓜ *Mong Kok East, Exit C; Prince Edward, Exit B1.*

ⓒ **Goldfish Market.** A few dozen shops on Tung Choi Street and Nullah Road sell the ubiquitous fish, which locals believe to be lucky. In addition to feed and aquariums, the market is home to other varieties of animals. ⊠ *Tung Choi St. and Nullah Rd., Mong Kok, Kowloon* ⌨ *Free* ☻ *10:30–10* Ⓜ *Mong Kok East, Exit C; Prince Edward, Exit B2.*

Kansu Street Jade Market. From priceless ornaments to fake pendants, if it's green and shiny, it's here. Quality and prices at the stalls vary hugely, so if you're not with a jade connoisseur, stick with the cheap and cheerful. Chaotic street markets continue in Mong Kok, technically the last Kowloon district (Boundary Street marks the beginning of the New Territories, though these days the urbanized areas are known as New Kowloon). ⊠ *Kansu St. between Battery St. and Reclaimation St., Yau Ma Tei, Kowloon* ⌨ *Free* ☻ *Daily 10–5* Ⓜ *Yau Ma Tei, Exit C.*

Shanghai Street. Traditional trades are plied along this street. There are blocks dominated by tailors or shops selling Chinese cookware or everything you need to set up a household shrine. Nearby Ning Po Street is known for its paper kites and for the colorful paper and bamboo models of worldly possessions (boats, cars, houses) that are burned at Chinese funerals. ⊠ *Shanghai St. between Jordan Rd. and Argyle St., Yau Ma Tei, Kowloon* Ⓜ *Yau Ma Tei.*

Temple Street. The heart of Yau Ma Tei, north of TST, is home to Hong Kong's biggest night market. Stalls selling kitsch of all kinds set up in the late afternoon in the blocks north of Public Square Street. Fortune-tellers, prostitutes, and street doctors also offer their services here. ⊠ *Temple St. between Jordan Rd. and Kansu St., Yau Ma Tei, Kowloon* Ⓜ *Yau Ma Tei, Exit C; Jordan, Exit A.*

Tin Hau Temple. This incense-filled site is dedicated to Taoist sea goddess Tin Hau, queen of heaven and protector of seafarers. The crowds here testify to her being one of Hong Kong's favorite deities—indeed, this is one of around 40 temples dedicated to her. Like all Tin Hau temples, this one once stood on the shore. Kowloon reclamation started in the late 19th century, and now the site is more than 3 km (2 mi) from the harbor. The main altar is hung with gold-embroidered red cloth and usually piled high with offerings. There are also two smaller shrines inside the temple honoring earth god Tou Tei and city god Shing Wong. Both the temple and stalls in the eponymous market outside are fortune-telling hot spots: you may well be encouraged to have a try with the chim. Each stick is numbered, and you shake them in a cardboard tube until one falls out. A fortune-teller asks you your date of birth and makes predictions from the stick based on numerology. Alternatively, you could have a mystically minded bird pick out some fortune cards for you. ■TIP➔ It's a good idea to agree on prices first; bargaining with fortune-tellers is common. ⊠ *Market St. between Temple St. and Nathan Rd., Yau Ma Tei, Kowloon* ⊙ *Daily 7–5:30* Ⓜ *Yau Ma Tei, Exit C.*

Tung Choi Street Ladies' Market. As you head north it's mostly tourists browsing this length of the street. The shopping is best between Dundas and Argyle. Despite its name, stalls are filled with no-brand clothes and accessories for both sexes. ⊠ *Tung Choi St. between Dundas St. and Argyle St., Mong Kok, Kowloon* ⊒ *Free* Ⓜ *Mong Kok.*

♺ **Yuen Po Street Bird Garden.** Next to the Flower Market, over 70 stalls sell different types of twittering, fluttering birds of numerous colors, shapes and sizes. Birdcages and food, from seeds to live grasshoppers, are also for sale. ⊠ *Yuen Po St. between Boundary St. and Prince Edward Rd. West, Mong Kok, Kowloon* ⊙ *7 AM–8 PM* Ⓜ *Mong Kok East, Exit C; Prince Edward, Exit B1.*

PERFECT HOURS IN KOWLOON

Only have a couple of hours between meetings? Your kids—or you—haven't the stamina to keep going all day? Kowloon's fragmented layout means it's perfect for breaking up into short-tour-size chunks. Hard-core sightseeing masochists can lump them all into one tourist feast.

A FEW HOURS OF . . .

. . . the Movies. Start at Chungking Mansions, which starred in the art-house classic *Chungking Express*. It's a short walk to the Avenue of Stars and the handprints of Jackie Chan and company. From here you'll have a great view of the harbor, which Pierce Brosnan appeared out

Wong Tai Sin Temple is one of Hong Kong's most famous Taoist temples.

of in *Die Another Day* (not to be tried on your own; the water is very polluted). On the other side is the IFC building that Angelina Jolie jumped from in *Tomb Raider 2*, as well as the Centre and the Hong Kong Exhibition & Convention Centre that had Batman cameos in *The Dark Knight*. Catch the MTR to the Broadway Cinemathèque in Yau Ma Tei for an art flick and a bite at Kubrick Café.

. . .Indulgence. When it comes to luxury, the **Peninsula Hong Kong** (✉ *Salisbury Rd., Tsim Sha Tsui, Kowloon* ☎ *2920–2888* ⊕ *www.peninsula.com*) is your one-stop shop. Start with afternoon tea in the lobby (HK$398 for two); have a 50-minute body massage (HK$990) at the spa; buy a dinner outfit at Chanel or Fendi; take the elevator to 28th-floor Felix for harbor-view cocktails; then book a table downstairs at Gaddi's for a fabulous French dinner. A suite here (from HK$6,800) would be a fitting finish.

. . .Spiritual Stuff. Only one MTR stop apart, Wong Tai Sin Temple and Chi Lin Nunnery are two of Hong Kong's must-do spiritual sights. One's a clattering, chaotic temple-turned-spiritual-mall, the other a peaceful haven. If your soul's still hungry, there's the Tin Hau Temple in Yau Ma Tei; the Shanghai Street altar shops are just up the road.

. . .the Old Days. Start at the top by taking a cab or bus to Kowloon Walled City Park, where the old walled city stood: there's a model inside the renovated almshouse. Then take a couple of hours to wise up at the History Museum in TST East, before strolling to the old KCR Clock Tower (built in 1915) near the Star Ferry, which has run since 1888.

3

THE NEW TERRITORIES

Sightseeing
☆★★★

Dining
☆☆☆★

Lodging
☆☆☆★

Shopping
☆☆☆★

Rustic villages, incense-filled temples, green hiking trails, pristine beaches—the New Territories have a lot to offer. Until a generation ago the region was mostly farmland with the occasional walled village. Today, thanks to a government housing program that created "new towns" like Sha Tin and Tuen Mun with up to 500,000 residents, parts of the region are more like the rest of Hong Kong. Within its expansive 518 square km (200 square mi), however, you'll still feel far removed from urban congestion. Here you can visit the area's lushest parks and glimpses traditional rural life in the restored walled villages and ancestral clan halls.

TOP ATTRACTIONS

Fodor's Choice
★

Hong Kong Heritage Museum.
See highlighted feature in this section.

Temple of Ten Thousand Buddhas. You climb some 400 steps to reach this temple: but look on the bright side, for each step you get about 32 Buddhas. The uphill path through dense vegetation is lined with life-size golden Buddhas in all kinds of positions. If you're dragging bored kids along, get them to play "Spot the Celebrity Lookalike" on the way. ■TIP➔ In summer bring water and insect repellent. Prepare to be dazzled inside the main temple: its walls are stacked with gilded ceramic statuettes. There are actually nearly 13,000 Buddhas here, a few more than the name suggests. They were made by Shanghai craftsmen, and have been donated by worshippers since the temple was built in the 1950s. Kwun Yum, goddess of mercy, is one of several deities honored in the crimson-walled courtyard.

HONG KONG HERITAGE MUSEUM

✉ *1 Man Lam Rd., Sha Tin, New Territories* ☎ *2180–8188*
⊕ *hk.heritage.museum*
🎟 *HK$10; free on Wed.*
🕙 *Mon. and Wed.–Sat. 10–6, Sun. and holidays 10–7* Ⓜ *Che Kung or Sha Tin.*

TIPS

■ Look for the audio tours in English, which are available for special exhibitions.

■ There's lots of ground to cover: Prioritize the New Territories Heritage, the T. T. Tsui Gallery, and the Cantonese Opera Halls, all permanent displays, and do the temporary history and art exhibitions if energy levels permit.

■ Don't miss the opera hall's virtual makeup display, where you get your on-screen face painted like an opera character's.

■ The museum is a five-minute signposted walk from Che Kung Temple station. If the weather's good, walk back along the leafy riverside path that links the museum with Sha Tin station, in New Town Plaza mall, 15 minutes away.

This fabulous museum is Hong Kong's largest, yet it still seems a well-kept secret: chances are you'll have most of its 10 massive galleries to yourself. They ring an inner courtyard, which pours light into the lofty entrance hall.

HIGHLIGHTS

The New Territories Heritage Hall is packed with local history—6,000 years of it. See life as it was in beautiful dioramas of traditional villages—one on land, the other on water (with houses on stilts). The last gallery documents the rise of massive urban New Towns. There's even a computer game where you can design your own.

In the T. T. Tsui Gallery of Chinese Art, exquisite antique Chinese glass, ceramics, and bronzes fill nine hushed second-floor rooms. The curators have gone for quality over quantity. Look for the 4-foot-tall terra-cotta *Horse and Rider*, a beautiful example of the figures enclosed in tombs in the Han Dynasty (206 BC–AD 220). The Tibetan religious statues and *thankga* paintings are unique in Hong Kong.

The Cantonese Opera Hall is all singing, all dancing, and utterly hands-on. The symbolic costumes, tradition-bound stories, and stylized acting of Cantonese opera can be impenetrable: the museum provides simple explanations and stacks of artifacts, including century-old sequined costumes that put Vegas to shame.

Kids love the Children's Discovery Gallery, where hands-on activities for 4- to 10-year-olds include putting a broken "archaeological find" together. The Hong Kong Toy Story charts more than a century of local toys.

Look southwest on a clear day and you can see nearby **Amah Rock,** which resembles a woman with a child on her back. Legend has it that this formation was once a faithful fisherman's wife who climbed the mountain every day to wait for her husband's return, not knowing he'd been drowned. Tin Hau, goddess of the sea, took pity on her and turned her to stone.

The temple is in the foothills of Sha Tin, in the central New Territories. Take Exit B out of Sha Tin station, walk down the pedestrian ramp, and take the first left onto Pai Tau Street. Keep to the right-hand side of the road and follow it around to the gate where the signposted path starts. ■TIP→ Don't be confused by the big white buildings on the left of Pai Tau Road. They are ancestral halls, not the temple. ⊠ *Off Pai Tau St., Sha Tin, New Territories* ☎ *Free* ☉ *Daily 9–5:30* Ⓜ *Sha Tin, Exit B.*

3

WORTH NOTING

The Chinese University of Hong Kong Art Museum. Located in the Institute of Chinese Studies building, the museum has paintings and calligraphy from the Qing period to modern times. There are also collections of bronze seals, carved jade flowers, and ceramics from South China. Take the East Rail line to University station, then a campus bus or taxi. ⊠ *Tai Po Rd., Sha Tin, New Territories* ☎ *2609–7416* ⊕ *www.cuhk.edu.hk/ ics/amm* ☎ *Free* ☉ *Daily 10–5. Closed holidays* Ⓜ *University.*

Ching Chung Koon Taoist Temple. Adjacent to the Ching Chung LRT station near the town of Tuen Mun, this temple has room after room of altars filled with the heady scent of incense. On one side of the main entrance is a cast-iron bell with a circumference of about 5 feet—all large monasteries in ancient China rang such bells at daybreak to wake the monks and nuns for a day of work in the rice fields. On the other side of the entrance is a huge drum that was used to call the workers back in the evening. Inside, some rooms are papered with small pictures; people pay the temple to have these photos displayed so they can see their dearly departed as they pray. Colorful plants and flowers, hundreds of dwarf shrubs, ornamental fishponds, and pagodas bedeck the grounds. The temple's entrance isn't obvious, so ask for directions. ⊠ *Tuen Mun, New Territories* ⊕ *www.discoverhongkong.com/eng/ attractions/nt-chingchungkoon.html* Ⓜ *Siu Hong, Exit B.*

Lam Tsuen Wishing Trees. Featured in Hong Kong's chapter of *The Amazing Race* TV show, these trees are an important Chinese New Year pilgrimage site. People from throughout Hong Kong come to the two banyan trees to make wishes and offerings. Some people burn joss sticks and incense; others throw an orange—tied to a wish written on a piece of paper—up into a tree (if it catches on a branch the wish will come true). Unfortunately, the weight of the oranges has caused several branches to fall off. People also visit the trees during exam time or when their health or that of a loved one is in jeopardy. Take the East Rail line to Tai Po Market train station, then take Bus 64K or 65K, or Minibus 25K. ⊠ *Lam Tsuen Village, New Territories* ⊕ *www.discoverhongkong. com/eng/attractions/nt-lamtsuen-wishing-trees.html.*

GETTING ORIENTED

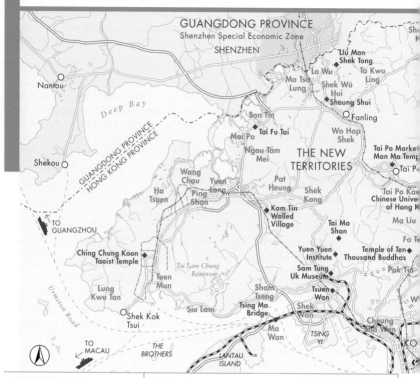

THE TERRITORY	QUICK BITES
The New Territories borders mainland China to the north and Sai Kung Peninsula to the east. Places worth visiting are a fair distance from each other, so day trips here take some planning—and some patience. Note that fewer people speak English away from the city center. It's best to choose two or three sights to visit in a day, allowing 15–30 minutes of travel time between each, depending on whether you're going by bus or taxi.	Sai Kung Town's waterfront has a plethora of outdoor seafood restaurants. If you have a sweet tooth, drop by the famous **Honeymoon Dessert Shop** (✉ Ground fl., 10C Po Tung Rd., Sai Kung ⊕ www.honeymoon-dessert.com/en_us) for such saccharine delights as mango pudding, chilled sago coconut soup, and banana crepes. Go on, you deserve it. On Castle Peak Road near Tuen Mun, the **Miu Fat Buddhist Monastery** is a popular place for a vegetarian lunch. Dishes have lots of greens, mushrooms, and "meat," which is actually made from rice flour. Lunch is served between noon and 3:30. Take the MTR to Tsuen Wan, then a taxi to the monastery. Alternatively, take the Tung Chung line to Tsing Yi station and then Bus 53, 63M, 63X, or 68A.

3

KEY

- ━●✱● MTR (Metro)
- ━•↗• KCR stops
- ----- Light rail
- 🚢 Ferry lines

Mirs Bay

CROOKED ISLAND

CRESCENT ISLAND

Crook Harbour

Starling Inlet

Luk Keng Village

Double Haven

North Channel

PORT ISLAND

Middle Channel

Plover Cove Reservoir

Plover Cove

Tolo Channel

Tolo Harbour

Tap Mun Island

Wu Kai Sha

Mo On Shan

Art Museum

Hong Kong Heritage Museum

Tin

Amah Rock

g Tai

n

n Po

ong

LOON

Kowloon Bay

Yau Tong

Tai Mong Tsai

Sai Kung

Inner Port Shelter

Sai Kung Peninsula

KAU SAI CHAU

Ho Chung

Port Shelter

Hang Hau

Lung Ha Wan

Chek Keng

High Island Res

Tai Long Wan

HIGH ISLAND

Rocky Harbour

JIN ISLAND

BLUFF ISLAND

BASALT ISLAND

0 ———— 3 miles
0 ———— 3 kilometers

GETTING AROUND

Between the bus and MTR, you can get close to many sights. Set off on the MTR from Central to Tsuen Wan; from there, taxis, buses, and minibuses will take you to places such as the Yuen Yuen Institute and Tai Mo Shan. For Sha Tin and other spots in the east, take the MTR to Kowloon Tong; transfer to the East Rail line to Sha Tin station. To reach the Sai Kung Peninsula, take the MTR from Central to Choi Hung, then the green Minibus 1A to Sai Kung Town.

To tour at your own pace, consider hiring a car and driver.

Ace Hire Car (☎ 2893–0541) charges HK$220 per hour (three-hour minimum), exclusive of tunnel tolls.

For a HK$5 call charge, you can hire a cab from the **Hong Kong Kowloon Taxi Knowledge Association** (☎ 2574–7311) to pick you up and take you anywhere in Hong Kong.

TAKING IT IN

Even if you don't think of yourself as a tour type, the best way to see some of the smaller villages is on one of the Hong Kong Tourist Board's organized tours that loop through the region. The guides are extremely knowledgeable and helpful.

Gray Line Tours (☎ 2207–7235 ⊕ www.grayline.com.hk) has full- and half-day tours that stop at the Yuen Yuen Institute and Tai Mo Shan lookout, among other places. Full-day tours (HK$490, including lunch) depart at about 9 AM; exact time and location are confirmed upon booking. Half-day tours (HK$350) depart at about the same time and return two hours earlier, without lunch.

Gray Line's five-hour Heritage Tour (HK$350) takes you to the Man Mo Temple, Lam Tsuen Wishing Trees, and other cultural sights. Tours depart from the Kowloon Hotel in Tsim Sha Tsui at 8:45 AM Monday, Wednesday, Friday, and Saturday.

Liu Man Shek Tong. In the far northern New Territories—just south of Shenzhen—a small unmarked path in the village of Sheung Shui leads to this ancestral hall. It was built in 1751 and was one of few such halls that survived the Cultural Revolution. A restoration preserved the spectacular original roofs and ornamentation, but substituted concrete walls to take the weight off rickety pillars—at some cost to the site's aesthetic unity, unfortunately. The Liu clan, for whom this hall was built, was obsessed with education: the wood panels hung in the rear hall indicate the education levels achieved by various clan members under the old imperial civil-service-exam system of the Qing Dynasty. Take the East Rail line to Sheung Shui, then Bus 73K and alight at Sheung Shui Wai on Jockey Club Road. ⊠ *Mun Hau Tsuen, Sheung Shui, New Territories* ☎ *2208–4400* ⊕ *lcsd.hk/CE/Museum/Monument/en/monuments_30. php* ☜ *Free* ⊙ *Wed., Thurs., and weekends 9–1 and 2–5* Ⓜ *Sheung Shui.*

Man Mo Temple. Adjacent to the Tai Po Market is the 100-year-old temple that was built to commemorate the establishment of the town of Tai Po. As you draw near, you'll smell the incense offered by worshippers. This historic site was fully restored in 1985. ⊠ *Fu Shin St.</str>, Tai Po, New Territories* ⊕ *www.lcsd.gov.hk/ce/Museum/Monument/en/ monuments_23.php* ☜ *Free* ⊙ *Daily 9–6* Ⓜ *Tai Wo station.*

Sam Tung Uk Museum. A walled Hakka village from 1786 was saved from demolition to create this museum. It's in the middle of industrial Tsuen Wan, in the western New Territories, so its quiet whitewashed courtyards and small interlocking chambers contrast greatly with the nearby residential towers. Hakka villages were built with security in mind, and this one looks more like a single large house than a village. Indeed, most Hakka village names end in *uk*, which literally means "house"—Sam Tung Uk translates as "Three Beam House." Rigid symmetry dictated the village's construction: the ancestral hall and two common chambers form the central axis, which is flanked by the more private areas. The front door is angled to face west–southwest, in keeping with feng shui principles of alignment between mountain and water. Traditional furniture and farm tools are displayed in each room. ■ TIP➔ **Head through the courtyards and start your visit in the exhibition hall at the back, where a display gives helpful background on Hakka culture and pre-industrial Tsuen Wan—explanations are sparse elsewhere. You can also try on a Hakka hat.** ⊠ *2 Kwu Uk La., Tsuen Wan, New Territories* ☎ *2411–2001* ⊕ *www. heritagemuseum.gov.hk/english/branch_sel_stu.htm* ☜ *Free* ⊙ *Wed.– Mon. 9–5* Ⓜ *Tsuen Wan, Exit B3.*

Pak Tai Temple. In the 19th century, Cheung Chau Island was a haven for pirates like the notorious Cheung Po Tsai, whose name translates as Cheung Po the Kid, and whose treasure cave is reportedly on the island's southwest tip. The temple here is dedicated to Pak Tai, the god of the sea, who is supposed to have rid the island of pirates. He's thanked during the weeklong springtime Bun Festival. Expect parades of the island's deities, huge towers of buns, and lots of color. The renovated temple originally dates to 1783, when an image of Pak Tai was brought to appease the spirits of people killed by pirates, thought to be the source of bubonic plague outbreaks. Apparently he did the trick: he remains the island's favorite deity. Beside the main altar are four whalebones

The road is paved with golden Buddhas on the path to the Temple of Ten Thousand Buddhas.

from the nearby sea. ■**TIP→** Make a full day of your trip to Cheung Chau. It's a gorgeous island with several temples. Kwan Yu Pavilion, the biggest, is dedicated to war god Kwan Tai. There's also a Kwun Yum temple and four shrines honoring sea goddess Tin Hau. A walk takes in most places of worship as well as the pirate cave. New World First Ferry sails to Cheung Chau twice hourly from Central Ferry Pier 5. Normal ferries take 50 minutes, fast ones 30. Turn left from the Cheung Chau ferry pier and walk ½ km (¼ mi) along waterfront Praya Street, until you see the temple to your right, over a playground. ⊠ *Pak She St., Cheung Chau Island, New Territories* ⊕ *www.ctc.org.hk/en/directcontrol/temple23. asp* ⌷ *Free* ⊙ *Daily 7–5.*

Sai Kung Peninsula. To the east of Sha Tin, this landmass has a few small towns and Hong Kong's most beloved nature preserve. The hikes through the hills surrounding **High Island Reservoir** are spectacular, and the beaches are among the territory's cleanest. Seafood restaurants dot the waterfront at Sai Kung Town as well as the tiny fishing village of Po Toi O in Clear Water Bay. Take the MTR to Choi Hung and then Bus 92 or 96R, or Minibus 1 to Sai Kung Town. Instead of taking the bus, you can also catch a taxi along Clearwater Bay Road, which will take you into forested areas and land that's only partially developed with Spanish-style villas overlooking the sea. At Sai Kung Town you can rent a sampan that will take you to one of the many islands in the area for a day at the beach. Sai Kung Country Park has several hiking trails that wind through majestic hills overlooking the water. This excursion will take a full day, and you should only go if it's sunny. ⊠ *Sai Kung Peninsula, Kowloon.*

Sha Tin. Whether you enter by road or East Rail, you'll be amazed by this new town metropolis that's smack dab in the middle of the New Territories. It's home to Sha Tin Park and the fantastic Hong Kong Heritage Museum, which is devoted to Chinese history, art, and culture. Exhibitions are housed in a five-story building surrounded by a traditional Chinese courtyard. ⊠ *Sha Tin, New Territories.*

Sha Tin Racecourse. The popular track is Hong Kong's largest, and a spectacular place to watch a race. Racing season is from September through June. The racecourse has its own stop on the East Rail line (Racecourse) that only operates on race days. ⊠ *Near Tai Po Rd., Sha Tin, New Territories* ⊕ *racecourses.hkjc.com/english/come_racing/racecourses/shatin/* 🎫 *HK$10* Ⓜ *Racecourse.*

Tai Fu Tai. It's worth the trek almost to the Chinese border to visit this preserved 1865 home of New Territories merchant and philanthropist Man Ching-luen. The surefire path to becoming a big shot in Imperial China was passing civil service examinations, but few people from Hong Kong—which was hicksville at the time—made the grade. Man Ching-luen proved the exception in 1875. Congratulatory tablets from the emperor hang in the house's entrance hall. The room layout, beautifully decorated doors, and roof ridges are all characteristic of Qing-dynasty architecture. Stained glass and rococo moldings reflect European influences, a result of the British victory over China in the Opium War of 1841. Women could watch guests unobserved from an upper gallery here, which also has an enclosed courtyard for stargazing, charmingly called a "moon playing chamber." To reach the house, cross over the road outside Sheung Shui station and take Bus 76K toward Yuen Long—alight at San Tin, 5½ km (3½ mi) away. The five-minute walk to the mansion is signposted from there. Alternatively, get a taxi from the station—one-way costs HK$35; for under HK$100 the taxi will wait for you and take you back, too. ⊠ *Wing Ping Tsuen, San Tin, New Territories* ⊕ *www.lcsd.gov.hk/CE/Museum/Monument/en/ monuments_32.php* 🎫 *Free* ⊙ *Wed.–Mon. 9–1 and 2–5.*

Tai Mo Shan. The name means Big Hat Mountain, and it is Hong Kong's highest point at 3,140 feet. Made of volcanic rock, it's located north of Tsuen Wan in Tai Mo Shan Country Park, which was established in 1979. The "Foggy Mountain" is covered in clouds almost daily. When the mist—and pollution—clears, the view stretches all the way to Hong Kong Island. Take bus 51 from Tsuen Wan and get off at the intersection of Route Twisk and Tai Mo Shan Road ⊠ *Rte. Twisk and Tai Mo Shan Rd., New Territories* ⊕ *www.afcd.gov.hk.*

Tai Po. The name means "shopping place," which it more than lives up to. In the heart of the region's breadbasket, the town is fast becoming a utilitarian "new town," but its main open-air market is a feast for the eyes, with baskets of lush green vegetables, freshly cut meat hanging from great racks overhead, fish swimming in tanks awaiting selection, and all types of baked and steamed treats. To reach the village, take the MTR East Rail line to the Tai Po Market stop. ⊠ *Tai Po, New Territories* Ⓜ *Tai Po Market.*

Tap Mun Island. Also known as Grass Island, this locale makes a great day trip. Most people have a seafood lunch at the New Hon Kee Seafood Restaurant (☎ 2328–2428), run by Loi Lam, a stocky, vivacious fellow who speaks fluent English with a fantastic accent from Manchester, England. There are a couple of temples and shrines dotting the island, as well as beautiful beaches. A sampan from Wong Shek Pier in Sai Kung Country Park will speed you here (☎ 9134–6248). ⊠ *New Territories.*

Yuen Yuen Institute. Made up of pavilions and prayer halls built in the 1950s to bring together the three streams of Chinese thought: Buddhism (which emphasizes nirvana and physical purity), Taoism (nature and inner peace), and Confucianism (following the practical and philosophical beliefs of Confucius). The main three-tier red pagoda is a copy of the Temple of Heaven in Beijing, and houses 60 statues representing the full cycle of the Chinese calendar—you can look for the one that corresponds to your birth year and make an incense offering. To reach the institute, take the MTR to Tsuen Wan, exit the station, and walk five minutes to Shiu Wo Street, then catch green Minibus 81 to To Lo Wai. ⊠ *Lo Wai Village, Tsuen WanNew Territories* ☎ 2492–2220 ⌁ *Free* ⊙ *Daily 9–5* Ⓜ *Tsuen Wan, Exit B1.*

TWO-AND-A-HALF PERFECT DAYS

Catch the MTR from Central to Tsuen Wan, then take Minibus 81 to Lo Wai Village to reach the Yuen Yuen Institute, one of the only temples in Hong Kong devoted to all three Chinese religions: Buddhism, Confucianism, and Taoism. For lunch, take a taxi to the Miu Fat Buddhist Monastery, a popular restaurant serving vegetarian dishes. Take a break from history and culture and walk off the lunch by heading to Tai Mo Shan by taxi, and hiking through the country park, experiencing the greener side of Hong Kong.

Alternatively, head to Tap Mun Island for a day of sunbathing on a pristine beach, punctuated only by a delicious seafood lunch. You can take the MTR from Central to the Chinese University station and then walk 15 minutes along Tai Po Road in Sha Tin to the Ma Liu Shui Ferry pier, where a vessel will take you to the island. Or you can take the MTR from Central to Choi Hung, then Bus 92 or 96R or Minibus 1 to Sai Kung Town. From there, jump in a taxi to Wong Shek pier in Sai Kung Country Park and then board a sampan for the island.

If you have only half a day to spend in the New Territories, then Sha Tin is the place to be. Take the MTR to Kowloon Tong, then the East Rail line to Tai Wai to visit the Hong Kong Heritage Museum, dedicated to Chinese history, art, and culture. From here, take a taxi to Sha Tin station and follow the signs to the Temple of 10,000 Buddhas. Hike up the steps to reach the temple where thousands of gold statues sit in various poses. End the day at Sha Tin Racecourse (via taxi or the East Rail line to the Racecourse station).

Shopping

WORD OF MOUTH

"Luxury items can be much cheaper in Hong Kong: Prada bags, Cartier watches, etc., etc. But you should identify the exact item you want (as with the electronics, by the way) and price it at home before you leave. Buy bags and other accessories in proper stores or the brand's own shop—there are plenty of fakes around."

—Peter N-H

SHOPPING PLANNER

Pace Yourself

Shopping streets and malls are packed with people. In summer, pounding the streets weighed down by bags quickly starts to feel like an exercise from *Survivor*. Then, the minute you step into a mall, arctic a/c blasts have you shivering. Dress comfortably, carry a water bottle and light sweater, and stop frequently to rest and refuel.

Way Up

With space at a premium, shops and small businesses are tucked into all sorts of places—up the back staircase of a scruffy building, down an alleyway, or on an office tower's 13th floor.

Shopping Tours

Asian Cajun (☎ 9278–4174 ⊕ *www.asiancajun.com*) runs tours to choice shops, including little-known stores and private dealers.

Malls, markets, and outlets are a part of tailor-made tours led by **Shopping 4 U**. Book through **Concorde Travel** (☎ 2524–5121 ⊕ *www. concorde-travel.com*). Daylong tours cost HK$480 per person (10-person minimum).

Best Buys

Brushing Up. Granted, becoming a master brush painter takes years. But calligraphy equipment makes a wonderful display, even if your brushwork doesn't. Boxed sets of bamboo-handled brushes, porcelain inkwells, and smooth inkstones start at HK$200 at Yue Hwa.

Kung-Fu Fighting. You've seen *Enter the Dragon* a hundred times, and you practice your karate chops daily. Time to get the drum cymbal, leather boots, sword, whip, double dagger, studded bracelet, and *kempo* gloves. **Kung Fu Supplies Co.** (⊠ *192 Johnston Rd., Wan Chai* ☎ *2891– 1912* ⊕ *www.kungfu.com.hk*) can kit you out.

On the Table. Remind yourself of all those dim sum meals by dressing up your dining room. Black-lacquer chopsticks and brocade place mats are in street stalls all over. Stanley Market has beautiful appliqué table linen. Department stores like Wing On sell cheap bamboo dim sum baskets— good for cooking or storage.

Opium Den Chic. Silk dressing gowns and basic *cheongsams* (silk dresses with Mandarin collars) are a bargain in markets and at Yue Hwa or Chinese Arts & Crafts. For more luxurious versions, try Shanghai Tang or Blanc de Chine, who also do men's Mao jackets. Get some brocade cushion covers for a matching bedroom.

Seal of Approval. Have your name engraved in Chinese, English, or both on traditional chops (seals). Made of wood, stone, or even jade, they're usually ornately carved, often with animals of the Chinese zodiac. Sets come with a tub of sticky red ink. Man Wa Lane in Sheung Wan is a great place to find them.

Tea for Two. Yixing teapots like those from homegrown brand Fook Ming Tong (⊕ *www.fookmingtong.com*) will melt even coffee-guzzlers' hearts. For the best brews head to the Lock Cha Tea House in the K.S. Lo Gallery, in Hong Kong Park, where you can sample vegetarian dim sum as well as tea. Lock Cha has a retail outlet in Sheung Wan (⊠ *U/G 290B Queens Road Central., Sheung Wan* ☎ *2805–1360* ⊕ *www.lockcha.com*), which also holds weekly tea classes. Standard leaves come in pretty tins at local supermarkets like Park 'n' Shop. Yue Hwa does cheap porcelain tea sets.

Shop Around

Prices vary hugely. For big items, do research before the trip and then comparison shop in different districts. Ask clerks to record prices on store business cards: it helps you to keep track and ensures that you get the quoted rate if you return to buy. Keep expectations realistic. A US$5 (about HK$40) pure silk shirt probably isn't pure silk. That said, it may still be a good shirt at a great price.

Sales

Hong Kongers look forward to sales like other people look forward to summer vacation. From late December through February and July through September, prices plummet. It may be retail heaven, but it isn't therapy—shoppers all but wrestle bargains from each other at hot sales like Lane Crawford's or Joyce's. Many shops frown on trying things on during sales. Stand your ground, and you'll probably swing a fitting room.

The Perfect Fit

There are no two ways about it: most Americans stand a few inches taller (and wider) than the average Hong Konger. Finding bigger sizes, particularly at cheap shops, can be frustrating. Tailoring—thank goodness it's afford-able here—may be the only way to go.

Tricks of the Trade

Be wary of absurd discounts, designed purely to get you in the door. Product switches are also common—after you've paid, they pack a cheaper model. Avoid electronics shops in Tsim Sha Tsui, whose fearsome reputation is well earned. Check purchases carefully, ensuring that clothes are the size you wanted, jewelry is what you picked, and electronics come with the accessories you paid for. *Always* get an itemized receipt. Without one, forget about getting refunds. Shops displaying the **Hong Kong Tourism Board's (HKTB)** QUALITY TOURISM SERVICE sticker (an easily recogniz-able junk boat) are good bets. You can complain about prices or treatment at them to the HKTB (☎ 2508–1234). For complaints about all shops not approved by the Hong Kong Tourism Board, call the **Hong Kong Consumer Council** (☎ 2929–2222).

Bargaining Power

Prices are always negotiable at markets, and you can expect discounts in small shops, too, especially for electronics or if you buy several things at once. The norm ranges from 10% to 50% off. Be firm and decisive—walking away from a stall can often produce a radical price drop.

Don't let anyone guilt-trip you; no Hong Kong salesperson will sell you anything that doesn't cut them a profit.

Faking It

The Hong Kong government has seriously cracked down on designer fakes. Depending on how strict the police are being when you visit, you may not find the choice of knockoffs you were hoping for.

Bear in mind that designer fakes are illegal, and as such you could get into trouble if you get caught with them going through customs.

Cash or Plastic

In spite of the credit-card decals on shop doors (every card you could possibly imag-ine and more), many smaller stores will insist on cash or add 3% to 5% to the total if you pay by credit card.

If you plan to use plastic, ask if there's a charge before gloating over your "bargain."

NATHAN ROAD

With its frenetic forest of clashing neon signs, Nathan Road is a postcard image of a busy Hong Kong street. It's also the main artery through a throbbing cluster of markets and shopping streets.

If it's a rarified shopping experience you're after, forget it: this 'hood is all about bargains, and it's a different world from the organized chaos of Central's covered walkways. Once you step off poker-straight Nathan Road, you can become lost in the perpetual stream of humanity weaving through the streets. But focus on all the amazing finds, and it's easier to fend off claustrophobia. Whether you're after classic Chinese souvenirs, jewelry, gadgets, clothes, shoes, or brand-name rip-offs (naughty you), it's all here. Keep your valuables tucked away safely, and keep that map in your hand. Nathan Road itself is the best landmark. Chinese street names are totally different from the anglicized versions, and many local people don't speak English.

BEST TIME TO GO

Arrive early to see communes of old men hanging their birdcages and chatting in the morning sunlight as the Bird, Goldfish, and Jade markets gather momentum at around 9 AM. Mong Kok's clothing markets open at midday and specialize in cheap bags, jeans, and toys. Temple Street's Night Market comes alive after dark.

BEST GIFT FOR MOTHER-IN-LAW

Just because it looks like antique jade doesn't mean it is. Keep her having happy thoughts for years to come with a carved soapstone coaster or trivet, around HK$90, from **Kansu Street Jade Market**.

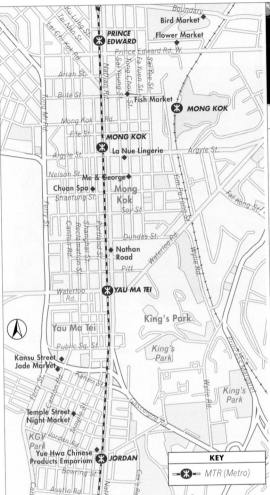

4

WHAT YOU WANT

BARGAINS

Fa Yuen Street. Feast your eyes on all the kicks you've ever wanted.

La Nue Lingerie. Despite the shabby exterior, La Nue is a chic boutique with inexpensive lingerie in probably Hong Kong's greatest size range.

Me & George. Rummage for vintage treasures including tea dresses and men's leather jackets.

Yuen Po Street Bird Garden. These delicate birdcages make perfect planters to hang outside your window back home.

SOUVENIRS

Yue Hwa Chinese Products Emporium. If haggling isn't your thing, this long-standing institution offers all manner of "Made in China" items at set prices.

Temple Street Night Market. Although Temple Street stalls peddle a lot of kitschy souvenirs and knockoffs this market is worth a visit for the atmosphere alone.

REJUVENATING

If it's a quiet moment you're after, your best bet is **Chuan Spa** (✉ *Langham Place Hotel, 555 Shanghai St., Mong Kok Kowloon* ☎ *3552–3501* ⊕ *www.chuanspa.com.hk*), which overlooks the city from the top floor of arctic oasis Langham Place Mall and Hotel. In five-star spa surroundings, consult with a Traditional Chinese Medicine (TCM) practitioner: you'll likely be prescribed cupping (an ancient Chinese acupressure technique), acupuncture, or myofascial therapy (a gentle massage and stretching technique), all of which aim to distribute chi (energy) throughout the body and promote health and balance. (Or you could just have a massage.)

SOHO AND NOHO

When it comes to big malls, big labels, and big spenders, Central is true to its name. However, ride three minutes uphill on the Midlevels Escalator, step off into Hollywood Road, and you'll find a different world. This century-old antiques hub bisects the districts known as SoHo (South of Hollywood Road) and NoHo (North of Hollywood Road).

On SoHo's winding, low-rise streets independent designers, hole-in-the-wall boutiques, and international restaurants coexist with antiques shops, incense-heady shrines, and Chinese doctors.

NoHo runs from Gage Street's outdoor food market at the Central end, with its photogenic charm and olfactory assault, through Gough Street's boutiques and interior design stores, down to Cat Street Market, a more affordable alternative to the five-figure antiques on Hollywood Road, in Sheung Wan.

BEST TIME TO GO

Shops here open and close late, operating from around 11 AM to 11 PM, seven days a week.

BEST GIFT FOR YOUR SIBLING

Earth-friend relations will love a stylish reusable shopping bag from G.O.D. Made of canvas and synthetic leather, the totes are printed with classic Hong Kong images.

Get "Clocky" at design shop **Homeless** (✉ Ground fl., 28 Gough St., NoHo, Central ☎ 2851–1160 ⊕ www.homeless.hk), for oversleepers. An extra tap on the snooze button sends the clock's monster-truck wheels bumping around the room.

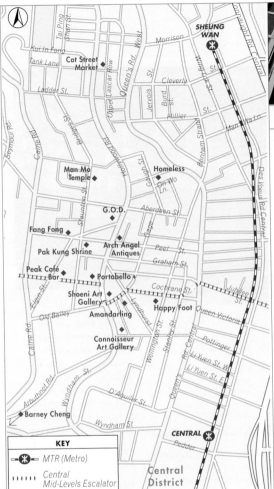

WHAT YOU WANT

ART AND ANTIQUES
Connoisseur Art Gallery. Past the ubiquitous bazooka-wielding nymphs is a superlative collection of Chinese artwork. Seek out future stars at sister gallery Connoisseur Contemporary, next door.

Schoeni Art Gallery. Here you'll find the big names in Chinese avant-garde, including Yu Chen, Chen Yu, and Zhang Lin Hai. The Hollywood Road site is a showcase; the main gallery is a minute's walk away on Old Bailey Street.

Arch Angel Antiques. This shop specializes in Chinese rarities, from pocket-size marvels to multistory statues of horses, warriors, and porcelain vases.

BEST BOUTIQUES
Amandarling. Locally designed beachwear collections include printed cotton beach dresses and sexy Bond-girl bikinis.

Fang Fong. Small but perfectly formed collection of affordable, sophisticated vintage and Asian-influenced designs include silk day dresses and sequined cocktail attire.

REFUELING AND REJUVENATING

Step off the Midlevel Escalator and enjoy delicious tea and cake at **Portobello+** (✉ *9 Staunton St., SoHo, Central* ☎ *2523–8999* ⊕ *www.stauntonsgroup.com/portobello* ⏱ *9 AM–late*). Or, mainline G&Ts as you recline at decadent **Peak Café Bar** (✉ *9–13 Shelley St., SoHo, Central* ☎ *2140–6877* ⊕ *www.cafedecogroup.com* ⏱ *11 AM–2 AM*).

A foot massage is the ultimate post-shopping treat. Don't be put off by the NO SCREAMING signs at **Happy Foot** (*6th fl., 11th fl., and 13th fl., Jade Centre* ✉ *98–102 Wellington St., Central* ☎ *2544–1010*), next to the escalator. A lighter touch can be applied on request.

CAUSEWAY BAY

From local celebrities to mall rats, shoppers flowing through the streets of Causeway Bay are from all walks of life, but they're united by a common mission: to drop some cash on the three Rs (retail, restaurants, and recreation).

If Hong Kong is the gateway to China, then Causeway Bay is the shortcut to her cash-filled wallet. Retail sky-scrapers tower over micromalls and scruffy low-rises bursting with independent boutiques and restaurants. High-end flagships occupy the malls of Hysan Avenue, often called Hong Kong's Rodeo Drive. Times Square is a 16-floor midrange mall and includes the sleek, western-style Lane Crawford department store. Japanese department store Sogo carries many big brands, and Fashion Island is the place to go for lines like Armani Exchange and DKNY.

The adjacent streets are lined with painfully hip concept malls such as LCX and midrange boutiques such as Ztampz and Pink Martini. And if all this label talk is hurting your wallet, head to the stalls at Jardine's Crescent for budget fashion.

BEST TIME TO GO

Opening times vary, but noon is the most common. Shoppers are still going strong at 10 PM on weekdays and till 11 PM on weekends. Sale seasons run from December to February and July to September.

BEST SOUVENIR

Milan Station is the city's largest, most discerning chain for pre-owned designer handbags.

Hipster magnet D-mop showcases items from the hottest international alternative fashion lines.

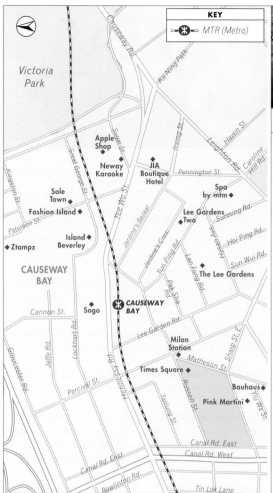

WHAT YOU WANT

HIGH-END HEAVEN
Lee Gardens & Lee Gardens Two. Lee Gardens houses classic blueblood labels including Hermès, Chanel, and Christian Dior, while Lee Gardens Two features funkier brands such as Miu Miu, Joseph, and Agnès b.

ROCK-STAR STYLE
Bauhaus. For the best rock-star duds in town, this multistory fashion gallery is a favorite of former Jane's Addiction front man Perry Farrell.

Pink Martini. This tiny boudoir gets more ink in fashion magazines than its size would dictate, thanks to its affordable tea dresses, shoes, and vintage jewelry.

Sole Town. Imagine a gigantic space-age sweet shop, but replace the candy with colorful shoes and bags for every occasion.

BARGAINS
Aroma Natural Skin Care. Housed in mazelike minimall Island Beverly, this tiny store sells cult skin-care products at low direct-import prices.

REJUVENATING

Spa by mtm (⊠ *Shop A, 3 Yun Ping Rd., Causeway Bay* ☎ *2923–7888* ⊕ *www.spamtm.com* ⊘ *11:30–11:30*), a Japanese spa, is a sanctuary, where products are custom-blended on-site. The aesthetic is as important as the physical treatments, and each room has a specific identity.

As a home-away-from-home for Japanese nationals, Causeway Bay is also the spiritual center of karaoke in Hong Kong. **Neway Karaoke** (⊠ *2-8 Sugar St., Causeway Bay* ☎ *2196–2196* ⊕ *www.newaykb.com* ⊘ *10:30–5:30*) is among the most popular places to belt out a tune, and boasts a pretty good English song menu.

Updated by Jo Baker

They say the only way to get to know a place is to do what the locals do. When in Rome, scoot around on a Vespa and drink espresso. When in Hong Kong, shop. For most people in this city, shopping is a leisure activity, whether that means picking out a four-figure party dress, rifling through bins at an outlet, upgrading a cell phone, or choosing the freshest fish for dinner.

Shopping is so sacred that sales periods are calendar events, and most stores close on just three days a year—Christmas Day and the first two days of Chinese New Year. Imagine that: 362 days of unbridled purchasing. Opening hours are equally conducive to whiling your life away browsing the racks: all shops are open until 7 or 8 PM; many don't close their doors until midnight.

It's true that the days when everything in Hong Kong was mind-bogglingly cheap are over. It *is* still a tax-free port, so you can get some good deals. But it isn't just about the savings. Sharp contrasts and the sheer variety of experiences available make shopping here very different from back home.

You might find a bargain or two elbowing your way through a chaotic open-air market filled with haggling vendors selling designer knockoffs, the air reeking of the *chou tofu* ("stinky" tofu) bubbling at a nearby food stand. But then you could find a designer number going for half the usual price in a hushed marble-floor mall, the air scented by designer fragrances worn by fellow shoppers. What's more, in Hong Kong the two extremes are often within spitting distance of each other.

Needless to say, thanks to travelers like you running out of space in their suitcases, Hong Kong does a roaring trade in luggage. No need to feel guilty, though—shopping here is practically cultural research. All you're doing is seeing what local life is really like.

HONG KONG ISLAND

WESTERN

The past is very much alive in Western, Hong Kong Island's most traditional neighborhood, and nowhere more than in its shops. Different streets are known as centers for particular trades. Along Hollywood Road, between Sheung Wan and Central, antique Chinese furniture and collectibles fetch high prices in upscale showrooms. You can get similar-looking items half their price (and less than half their age) in Upper Lascar Row, which also does a brisk trade in communist retro paraphernalia, mah-jongg tiles, and fans.

Man Wa Lane is the place for chops (seals carved in stone with engraved initials). Traditional Chinese medicine is the commercial lifeblood of Sheung Wan proper: ginseng, snake musk, birds' nests, and shark's fins are some of the delicacies available. *(For more information, see To Your Health in Chapter 1.)* Locals stock up on less exotic household goods at Sincere and Wing On, two of Hong Kong's largest department stores.

DEPARTMENT STORES

Wing On. Great values on household appliances, kitchenware, and crockery have made Wing On a favorite with locals on a budget since it opened in 1907. It also stocks clothes, cosmetics, and sportswear, but don't expect to find big brands (or even brands you know). You *can* count on rock-bottom prices and an off-the-tourist-trail experience, though. ✉ *211 Des Voeux Rd., Central, Sheung Wan, Western* ☎ *2852–1888* ⊕ *www.wingonet.com* Ⓜ *Sheung Wan, Exit E3* ✉ *Cityplaza, 18 Tai Koo Shing Rd., Tai Koo, Eastern* Ⓜ *Tai Koo, Exit D2* ✉ *Wing On Kowloon Centre, 345 Nathan Rd., Jordan, Kowloon* Ⓜ *Jordan, Exit A.*

MARKETS

Western Market. This redbrick Victorian in the Sheung Wan district is a declared monument and the oldest existing market building in Hong Kong; when built in 1906 it was used as a produce market. These days the first floor has a few unmemorable shops selling crafts, toys, jewelry, and collectibles; second-floor shops sell a remarkable selection of fabric. A more surreal experience is lunch, dinner, or high tea in the Grand Stage Chinese restaurant and ballroom on the top floor. After a great Chinese meal you can while away the afternoon with the old-timers trotting around the room to a live band belting out the cha-cha and tango. ✉ *Des Voeux Rd., Western* ⊕ *www.westernmarket.com.hk* Ⓜ *Sheung Wan.*

SPECIALTY SHOPS

ANTIQUES
DEALERS **Lok Man Rare Books.** This shop's wooden shelves and cases are packed with an impressive collection of rare books that are still in

---

TOP SHOPS

Best Upscale Mall: IFC

Biggest Selection Under One Roof: Harbour City

Chinese Chic: Shanghai Tang

Gifts Galore: Yue Hwa

Best Custom Suit: Sam's Tailor

Best Designer Outlet: Joyce Warehouse

The dried seafood shops on Des Voeux Road West promise traditional Chinese cures for all your ailments.

very good condition. Browse around for first- and second-edition copy of books, including children's favorites, or ask the owner to show you around. The collection includes some rare pre-1900 finds, like a first edition of *Oliver Twist*. Also check out vintage board games and antique chess sets. ⊠ *129A Hollywood Rd., Sheung Wan, Western* ☎ *2868–1056* ⊕ *www.lokmanbooks.com.*

BEAUTY AND COSMETICS

HONG KONG
GOODIES

Eu Yan Sang. The Sheung Wan area is a quaint and pungent place to shop for traditional Chinese herbs and medicines. But this reliable Asia-wide chain—in operation since 1879—is a more straightforward and seemingly sanitized option. There are branches all over Hong Kong, including one past immigration in the airport's Terminal One. ⊠ *152–156 Queens Rd., Sheung Wan, Western* ☎ *2544–3870, 2544–3308 customer service and branch information* ⊕ *www.euyansang.com* ⊠ *Ground fl., 2–4 Russell St., Causeway Bay* ☎ *2573–2038* Ⓜ *Causeway Bay* ⊠ *Ground fl., 11–15 Chatham Rd. S, Tsim Sha Tsui, Kowloon* Ⓜ *Tsim Sha Tsui.*

CLOTHING

HONG KONG
COUTURE

Sin Sin Atelier. Sin Sin's conceptual, minimalist clothes, jewelry, and accessories retain a Hong Kong character, while drawing from other influences—especially Japanese. She also has an art space directly across the road and a fine art gallery up the hill in SoHo. ⊠ *Ground fl., 52 Sai St., off Hollywood Rd. at Cat St. end, Western* ☎ *2521–0308* ⊕ *www. sinsin.com.hk.*

CRAFTS AND CURIOS

Sang Woo Loong. At more than 90 years old, Mr. Leung Yau Kam is Hong Kong's oldest lantern maker, and he has refused to move his workshop across the border like all the others. These intricate, hand-made works in paper take fantastical forms such as bright-orange goldfish. Their role has changed over his long career from functional to purely decorative, but lanterns are still important in Chinese society. This is especially true during the Mid-Autumn Festival, when children carry their special lanterns outdoors to view the full moon. Ask for one that can pack flat. ⊠ *Ground fl., 28 Western St., Sai Ying Pun, Western* ☎ *2540–1369.*

> **ART SCOOP**
>
> The **Asia Art Archive** saw it before the rest of us: contemporary Asian art is big. In 2000 the AAA set out to address the lack of information on the emerging field and to record its growth. It provides comprehensive research resources through its Web site, library, and reading facilities, which are open to the public. ⊠ *11th fl., Hollywood Centre, 233 Hollywood Rd., Sheung Wan, Western* ☎ *2815–1112* ⊕ *www.aaa.org.hk* Ⓜ *Central.*

CENTRAL

New York, London, Paris, Milan . . . Central. When it comes to designer labels, the district's name says it all. Where else can you find a mall with a whole floor dedicated to Armani or calculate the Pradas per square mile? Spacious, golden-hue centers like the IFC Mall, the Landmark, Prince's Building, and the Galleria are the fashion hunting grounds of Hong Kong's well-to-do, and all places to head to if your shopping list reads like *Vogue's* directory pages.

Platinum taste but no platinum card? Cut-price designer outlets fill the Pedder Building, also home to iconic local store Shanghai Tang. There's offbeat urban attire—jeans, in particular—at the hip boutiques scattered through Lan Kwai Fong and SoHo. Hong Kong's coolest art galleries are also here, if it's your walls you're looking to dress.

Central may be fashion heaven, but there's an earthier side to it, too. Head out of the air-conditioned malls and down to the stalls on Li Yuen streets East and West for cheap souvenirs like silk dressing gowns. Ribbons, buttons, and sequins come in colors you didn't know existed on steep Pottinger Street, a haberdasher's dream.

DEPARTMENT STORES

Fodor's Choice
★

City'super. Wherever you're from and whatever you're missing, whether it's fresh oysters from France or Japanese cosmetics, this gourmet supermarket and international variety store is the place to begin your search. Locals and tourists looking for gadgets, inexpensive jewelry and accessories, and quirky products like bottled water for pets often find what they're looking for here, and this store will never bore you. The Times Square location often has international-theme food festivals. Be sure to check out the Japanese imported sweets like Royce Chocolate's unusual chocolate chips. ⊠ *IFC Mall, 8 Finance St., Central* ☎ *2234–7128* ⊕ *www.citysuper.com.hk* Ⓜ *Hong Kong, Exit A1* ⊠ *Times Square, 1*

CLOSE UP

That's a Wrap

Wander into the pretty Edwardian-style Western Market (⊕ www.westernmarket.com.hk) in Sheung Wan, and you'll find the entire second floor bursting with pure silk shantung, cotton-piqué shirting, French lace, silk brocade, velvet, damask, and printed crepe de chine—just some of the exquisite, reasonably priced fabrics available in Hong Kong. Although professional sourcing agents spend most of their time in Sham Shui Po on Kowloon side, Western Market's vast selection is more than adequate. Thai silk costs a bit more here than in Bangkok, but is still much cheaper than in the United States or Europe.

Chinese Arts & Crafts and Yue Hwa Chinese Products Emporium have great selections of Chinese brocades and other fabrics. Look also for Chinese hand-embroidered and -appliquéd linen and cotton in Stanley Market. ■TIP→ When buying a hand-embroidered item, check that the edges are properly overcast; if

not, it's probably machine made. You'll be looking for reasons to buy lots of the blue-and-white, patterned Chinese country fabrics at Mountain Folkcraft. Just check to see that you can bring your bolts on the plane; shipping costs may cancel out any discount.

The **Textile Society of Hong Kong** (⊕ www.textilesocietyofhk.org) hosts talks, expeditions, and events to explore all aspects of traditional and contemporary textiles. It counts as its members design professionals, museum curators, collectors, historians, textile conservators, dealers, and craftspeople. Textile Society of Hong Kong member Edith Cheung's atelier, **Cloth Haven** (⊠ Ground fl., 43–45 Square St., Sheung Wan ☎ 2546–0378 ⊕ www.clothhaven.com), not far from the Man Mo temple, hosts weaving classes on looms right on the shop floor—amid a mix of textiles, vintage clothing, and design inspirations.

Matheson St., Causeway Bay Ⓜ Causeway Bay, Exit A ⊠ Harbour City, 3 Canton Rd., Tsim Sha Tsui, Kowloon Ⓜ Tsim Sha Tsui, Exit A1.

Harvey Nichols. When this legendary British retailer announced its Hong Kong opening, locals were skeptical, saying nothing would ever live up to the original London store. But Harvey Nicks quickly had them eating their (Phillip Treacy) hats with the sheer volume of hyper-cool labels the store stocks. The menswear section has been a particularly big hit with local celebs, while local *tai-tais* (ladies who lunch) have declared the fourth-floor restaurant *the* place for mid-shopping-spree coffee breaks. ⊠ The Landmark, 15 Queen's Rd., Central ☎ 3695–3388 ⊕ www.harveynichols.com Ⓜ Central, Exit G.

Marks & Spencer. Classic, good-quality clothing is what this British retailer has built an empire on—its underwear, in particular, is viewed as a national treasure. Although basics are on the staid side, the newer Per Una, Autograph, and Limited collections are decidedly trendier. This is one of the few stores in town to stock a full range of sizes, which includes shoes up to a US size ten. There are branches in many of Hong Kong's malls; most of the shops have a British specialty food section, too, with a good range of wines. ⌧ *28 Queen's Rd., Central* ☎ *2921–8323* Ⓜ *Central, Exit D1* ⌧ *Times Square, 1 Matheson St., Causeway Bay* Ⓜ *Causeway Bay, Exit A* ⌧ *Harbour City, 5 Canton Rd., Tsim Sha Tsui, Kowloon* Ⓜ *Tsim Sha Tsui, Exit E.*

Sincere. Hong Kong's most eclectic department store stocks everything from frying pans to jelly beans. Run by the same family for more than a

WHY PAY RETAIL?

As Central becomes Sheung Wan, a little lane called Wing Kut Street (between Queen's Road Central and Des Voeux Road) is home to costume jewelry showrooms and wholesalers, many of whom accept retail customers and offer bargain-basement prices.

century, Sincere has several local claims to fame: it was the first store in Hong Kong to give paid days off to employees, the first to hire women in sales positions—beginning with the founder's wife and sister-in-law—and the first to establish a fixed-price policy backed up by the regionally novel idea of issuing receipts. Although you probably won't have heard of its clothes or cosmetic brands, you might come across a bargain. ⌧ *173 Des Voeux Rd., Central* ☎ *2544–2688* ⊕ *www.sincere. com.hk* Ⓜ *Sheung Wan, Exit E3.*

MALLS AND CENTERS

Fodor'sChoice
★

IFC Mall. The people at the International Finance Centre love superlatives: having made Hong Kong's tallest skyscraper (Two IFC), they built the city's poshest mall under it. A quick glance at the directory—Tiffany, Kate Spade, Prada, Gieves & Hawkes—lets you know that the IFC isn't for the faint of pocket. Designer department store Lane Crawford has its flagship store here, and agnès b.'s whimsical multi-boutique fashion and lifestyle flagship sits under a large skylight styled after the shop owner's summer house in the south of France. Even the mall's cinema multiplex is special: the deluxe theaters have super-comfy seats with extra legroom and blankets for those chilled by the air conditioning. If you finish your spending spree at sunset, go for a cocktail at RED or Isola, two rooftop bars with fabulous harbor views. The Hong Kong Airport Express station (with in-town check-in service) is under the mall, and the Four Seasons Hotel connects to it. Avoid the mall between 12:30 and 2, when it's flooded with lunching office workers from the two IFC towers. ⌧ *8 Finance St., Central* ⊕ *www.ifc.com.hk* Ⓜ *Hong Kong, Exit A1.*

The Landmark. If you haven't got a boutique in the Landmark, you clearly haven't made it in the fashion world, darling. Central's most prestigious shopping site houses Celine, Loewe, Gucci, Joyce Boutique, Hermès, and Harvey Nichols, among others. Even if your credit-card limit isn't up to a spree here, the hushed atrium café is the best place in town to watch well-coiffed tai-tais on the prowl. The large gourmet grocery store and food court, Three Sixty, serves up Hong Kong's widest selection of organic produce and eco-friendly household products like detergent and utensils. A pedestrian bridge links the Landmark with shopping arcades in Jardine House, the Prince's Building, the Mandarin Oriental Hotel, and 9 Queen's Road. ⌧ *Pedder St. and Des Voeux Rd., Central* Ⓜ *Central, Exit G.*

Pedder Building. Although dwarfed by flashy skyscrapers, the Pedder Building is one of Hong Kong's few remaining true colonial-style buildings; the elegant stone construction houses a mix of outlets and shops with local luxury brands that line hushed wood-paneled corridors. Shanghai Tang's flagship store takes up the ground floor and basement.

> ### LAW ON YOUR SIDE
>
> Although mainland law forbids that any item more than 120 years old leave China, the SAR isn't held to this rule. It's perfectly legal to ship your antique treasures home.

Upstairs, Blanc de Chine does clothes in similar styles to Shanghai Tang but in subtler colors. Floors 4, 5, and 6 are packed with small designer outlets, with 30% or more off retail prices. Labels Plus has some men's fashions as well as women's daytime separates. La Place has Prada bags and a large selection of Chanel jackets at about 20% off retail. Look at discounted items carefully; some have defects. ⊠ *12 Pedder St., Central* Ⓜ *Central, Exit D1.*

SPECIALTY SHOPS
ANTIQUES DEALERS

Altfield Gallery. If only your entire home could be outfitted by Altfield. Established in 1980, the elegant gallery carries exquisite antique Chinese furniture, Asia-related maps and topographical prints, Southeast Asian sculpture, and decorative arts from around Asia, including silver artifacts and rugs. Altfied Home, on the same floor, features a selection of larger furniture pieces and china. ⊠ *2nd fl., Prince's Bldg., 10 Chater Rd., Central* ☎ *2537–6370* ⊕ *www.altfield.com.hk* Ⓜ *Central.*

Arch Angel Antiques. Ask for Bonnie Groot, who will enthusiastically and knowledgeably guide you through the three floors of fine ceramics, furniture, ancestor portraits, and more. Across the road, the Groots have opened Arch Angel Art Gallery, which specializes in contemporary Vietnamese and Southeast Asian art. ⊠ *Ground fl., 53–55 Hollywood Rd., Central* ☎ *2851–6848* Ⓜ *Central* ⊠ *58 Hollywood Rd., Central* Ⓜ *Central.*

Chine Gallery. Dealing in antique furniture and rugs from China and furniture from Japan, this dark, stylish gallery accommodates international clients by coordinating its major exhibitions with the spring and fall auction schedules of Christie's and Sotheby's. ⊠ *42A Hollywood Rd., Central* ☎ *2543–0023* ⊕ *www.chinegallery.com* Ⓜ *Central.*

The Green Lantern. Irish expat Olive Forrest has cleverly retained original elements of the former print shop in which her store is housed. With her unique sense of style, Forrest brings together Chinese and Tibetan antiques, contemporary lighting designed in-house, silk soft furnishings, high-quality OM Living bed linens, and home accessories, such as contemporary lamp stands in brass. It also carries the statement-making bags by Hong Kong–based designer Tomoko Okamuru. The collection is handmade with Chinese metalwork, vintage Japanese fabrics, Thai silks, and bamboo. Of all the artisanal Asian fabric bags, these are the best. ⊠ *72 Peel St., SoHo, Central* ☎ *2526–0277* Ⓜ *Central.*

Cat Street antiques shops in Sheung Wan offer cheaper wares than those on Hollywood Road.

Hanlin Gallery. For Japanese works of art and woodblocks, visit this refined, calm gallery run by specialist Carlos Prata since 1986. His collection and expertise extend to furniture, textiles, silver, and European glass. ⊠ *Ground fl., Wilson House, 19–27 Wyndham St., Central* ☎ *2522–4479* ⊕ *www.hanlingallery.com* Ⓜ *Central.*

Honeychurch Antiques. Highly respected dealers Lucille and Glenn Vessa (one of the few accredited appraisers here) were the first to set up shop on Hollywood Road. The landscape has changed, but this shop still provides fine Chinese, Japanese, and Southeast Asian antique silver, porcelain, and unaltered furniture. ⊠ *Ground fl., 29 Hollywood Rd., Central* ☎ *2543–2433* Ⓜ *Central.*

Oi Ling Fine Chinese Antique. This beautiful showroom displays Chinese antique furniture, scholar's items, and archaeological stone works. Owner Oi Ling Chiang gives frequent talks. Succinct books on collecting by type are also sold here. A second branch, just down the road, sells terra-cotta, pottery, and bronze antiques. ⊠ *Ground fl., 52 Hollywood Rd., Central* ☎ *2815–9422* ⊕ *www.oilingantiques.com* Ⓜ *Central* ⊠ *Ground fl., 85 Hollywood Rd., Central* ☎ *2964–0554* Ⓜ *Central.*

Picture This Gallery. It's a one-of-a-kind source for vintage posters—mainly with travel and movie themes—early photography of Hong Kong and elsewhere in China, antique maps, prints and engravings, antiquarian books, and limited-edition reproductions or works by artists such as Dong Kingman. You might imagine a dusty library, but Christopher Bailey's welcoming shop and gallery is spacious, bright, and organized. ⊠ *13th fl., 9 Queen's Rd., Central* ☎ *2525–2820* ⊕ *www.*

picturethiscollection.com Ⓜ *Central* ✉ *2nd fl., Prince Bldg., 10 Chater Rd., Central* Ⓜ *Central.*

Teresa Coleman Fine Arts Ltd. You can't miss the spectacular textiles hanging in the window of this busy corner shop. Specialist Teresa Coleman sells embroidered costumes from the Imperial Court, antique textiles, painted and carved fans, jewelry, lacquered boxes, and engravings and prints. ✉ *79 Wyndham St., Central* ☎ *2526–2450* ⊕ *www. teresacoleman.com* Ⓜ *Central.*

The Tibetan Gallery. At this extension of Teresa Coleman Fine Arts you'll find antique Tibetan *thangkas* (Buddhist paintings), bronzes, textiles, and exquisite rugs. Manager Josephine Chan is also a restoration expert. ✉ *55 Wyndham St., Central* ☎ *2530–4863* ⊕ *www.teresacoleman.com* Ⓜ *Central.*

Wattis Fine Art. Run by affable expert Jonathan Wattis and his wife Vicky for over 20 years, Wattis Fine Art specializes in antique maps and prints and photographs of Hong Kong, China, and Southeast Asia. ✉ *2nd fl., 20 Hollywood Rd., Central* ☎ *2524–5302* ⊕ *www.wattis.com.hk.*

Yue Po Chai Antique Co. One of Hollywood Road's oldest shops is at the Cat Street end, next to Man Mo Temple. Its vast and varied stock includes porcelain, stone carvings, and ceramics. ✉ *Ground fl., 132–136 Hollywood Rd., Central* ☎ *2540–4374* Ⓜ *Central.*

ART GALLERIES

Alisan Fine Arts. In a quiet corner of the sleek Prince's Building shopping arcade is this established authority on contemporary Chinese artists. Styles range from traditional to modern abstract, and mediums include oil, acrylic, and Chinese ink. Founded in 1981 by Alice King, this was one of the first galleries in Hong Kong to promote the genre. ✉ *3rd fl., Prince's Bldg., 10 Chater Rd., Central* ☎ *2526–1091* ⊕ *www.alisan.com.hk.*

Connoisseur Art Gallery. This well known gallery represents a small batch of modern, mostly figurative Chinese artists, though it also showcases the dreamlike work of Romanian painter Dorina Mocan. The gallery started to push out of its—and Hong Kong's—comfort zone with the opening of Connoisseur Contemporary a few doors down in 2008; it features the often controversial creative output of the socio-political group reffered to as the "eighties generation"—mainland Chinese emerging artists born in the 1980s and known for subversive works. ✉ *G3 Chinachem Hollywood Ctr., 1 Hollywood Rd., Central* ☎ *2868–5358* ⊕ *www.connoisseur-art.com.*

Galerie La Vong. The works of today's leading Vietnamese artists, many of whose creations reveal an intriguing combination of French Impressionist and traditional Chinese influences, are the focus here. ✉ *13th fl., 1 Lan Kwai Fong, Central* ☎ *2869–6863* Ⓜ *Central.*

Gallery on Old Bailey. Gallery director Ma Choi attracts prominent and innovative contemporary artists to display their work at this well-established gallery, which draws an appreciative crowd of local and international patrons. ✉ *Basement fl. and ground fl., 17 Old Bailey St., Central* ☎ *2869–7122* Ⓜ *Central.*

Grotto Fine Art. Director and chief curator Henry Au-yeung writes, curates, and gives lectures on 20th-century Chinese art. His hidden gallery (hence the "grotto" in the name) focuses exclusively on local Chinese artists, with an interest in the newest and most avant-garde works. Look for paintings, sculptures, prints, photography, mixed-media pieces, and conceptual installations. ⊠ *2nd fl., 31C–D Wyndham St., Central* ☎ *2121–2270* ⊕ *www.grottofineart.com* Ⓜ *Central.*

Hanart TZ Gallery. This is a rare opportunity to compare and contrast cutting-edge and experimental art from mainland China, Taiwan, and Hong Kong selected by one of the field's most respected authorities. Unassuming curatorial director Johnson Chang Tsong-zung also cofounded the Asia Art Archive, and has curated exhibitions at the São Paolo and Venice biennials. ⊠ *2nd fl., Henley Bldg., 5 Queen's Rd., Central* ☎ *2526–9019* ⊕ *www.hanart.com* Ⓜ *Central.*

Plum Blossoms Gallery. You can't miss this gallery's unique, asymmetrical window. The airy, New York–style space displays groundbreaking contemporary Chinese art alongside ancient Asian textiles and rugs. Ask the refreshingly knowledgeable staff to escort you upstairs to see more. ⊠ *1 Hollywood Rd., Central* ☎ *2521–2189* ⊕ *www.plumblossoms.com* Ⓜ *Central.*

Sandra Walters Consultancy Ltd. Sandra Walters, a longtime figure on the art scene, represents a stable of Asian and international artists encompassing a variety of periods and styles. Make an appointment with her or one of her team to advise you on small to significant investments. ⊠ *501 Hoseinee House, 69 Wyndham St., Central* ☎ *2522–1137* Ⓜ *Central.*

Schoeni Art Gallery. Known for vigorously promoting Chinese art on a global scale, this gallery, founded by Manfred Schoeni in 1992, has represented and supported various artists from mainland China with styles ranging from neorealism to postmodernism. Manfred's daughter Nicole now pinpoints exciting new artists for her prominent clientele. Informative past exhibition catalogs are placed atop Chinese antiques, which are also presented in this huge space. You're likely to pass the Hollywood Road branch first, but the Old Baily Street gallery, up the hill, is the bigger and better of the two. ⊠ *Upper ground fl., 21–31 Old Bailey St., Central* ☎ *2869–8802* ⊕ *www.schoeniartgallery.com* Ⓜ *Central.*

Sin Sin Fine Art. Take the escalator up to Prince's Terrace, where you can't miss this corner gallery's large windows. Inside, works by diverse emerging and established artists from Indonesia, Thailand, mainland China, Hong Kong, and France reveal the aesthetic tastes of the lively Hong Kong designer and entrepreneur, Sin Sin. There are also regular exhibitions and artist talks. The Sin Sin Annex extension, near Cat Street in Sheung Wan, is a space for more progressive installations, objets, and performance art. ⊠ *Ground fl., 1 Prince's Terr., Midlevels, Central* ☎ *2858–5072* ⊕ *www.sinsin.com.hk.* ⊠ *Ground fl., 52 Sai St., Sheung Wan, Western.*

10 Chancery Lane Gallery. A visit here takes you behind the historic Central Police Station, where walls facing the gallery's distinctive loft-like space are still topped by broken glass, a common security measure. Since it opened in 2000, the white-walled gallery has focused on

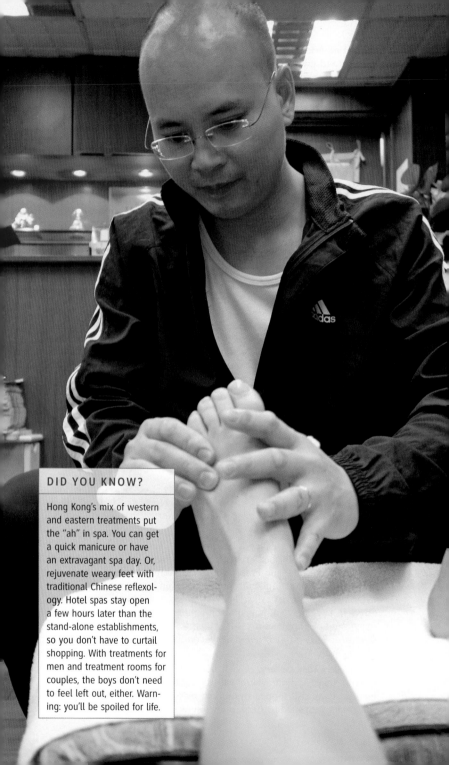

DID YOU KNOW?

Hong Kong's mix of western and eastern treatments put the "ah" in spa. You can get a quick manicure or have an extravagant spa day. Or, rejuvenate weary feet with traditional Chinese reflexology. Hotel spas stay open a few hours later than the stand-alone establishments, so you don't have to curtail shopping. With treatments for men and treatment rooms for couples, the boys don't need to feel left out, either. Warning: you'll be spoiled for life.

emerging artists from all over the world, as well as more established names, among them local expatriate painter Simon Birch and Beijing-based performance artist Li Wei. The gallery recently screened a multimedia installation by Australian film director Baz Lurhmann, and owner-curator Katie de Tilly also has a particularly keen eye for photography. ⊠ *Ground fl., 10 Chancery La., SoHo, Central* ☎ *2810–0065* ⊕ *www.10chancerylanegallery.com* Ⓜ *Central.*

Yan Gallery. This is the place for Hong Kong–based artist Hu Yongkai's charming, slightly cartoonish depictions of Chinese women in traditional settings (you've almost certainly seen fakes in a Stanley Market stall). Among emerging and established local artists the gallery, which isn't as stuffy as some and more commercial than others, also represents Bob Yan, whose extremely popular and colorful dog portraits are commissioned by private clients. ⊠ *1st fl., 1 Hollywood Rd., Central* ☎ *2139–2345* ⊕ *www.yangallery.com* Ⓜ *Central.*

Zee Stone Gallery. Massive street-level windows still hold court on what's fast becoming a sleek bar and restaurant strip. The gallery displays contemporary, often abstract, paintings from China, with a smattering of work from Burma and Vietnam. ⊠ *Ground fl., Yu Yuet Bldg., 43–55 Wyndham St., Central* ☎ *2810–5895* ⊕ *www.zeestone.com* Ⓜ *Central.*

BEAUTY AND COSMETICS

DRUGSTORES **Mannings.** Like Watsons, this chain can be found throughout the city. It sells everything from shampoo and lotions to emery boards and cough medicine (western and Chinese brands). Some stores have pharmacies. ⊠ *IFC Mall, 8 Finance St., Central* ☎ *2523–8326; 2299–3381 customer service and branch information* Ⓜ *Central.*

CLOTHING

CHILDREN'S CLOTHES

Bumps to Babes. It has everything you could possibly need for babies and children, all in one place. In addition to familiar brands of clothing, diapers, toiletries, food, and toys, look for strollers, books, maternity wear, furniture, and more. ⊠ *5th fl., Pedder Bldg., 12 Pedder St., Central* ☎ *2522–7112* ⊕ *www.bumpstobabes.com* Ⓜ *Central* ⊠ *21st fl., Horizon Plaza, 2 Lee Wing St., Ap Lei Chau, Southside.*

Lace Department Store. You might head straight for the embroidered linens, but back up and review the children's clothing by the door. You've seen these beautiful, traditional, hand-smocked cotton dresses and baby overalls in elegant European stores, sold at prices to make you faint. Here expect to pay as little as HK$198 to HK$248. As you tour the city, keep an eye out for embroidered-linens specialists who carry similar dresses. ⊠ *6th fl., Pedder Bldg., 12 Pedder St., Central* ☎ *2523–8162* Ⓜ *Central.*

Marleen Molenaar Sleepwear. When Hong Kong–based Dutch designer and mother Marleen Molenaar discovered how limited her choices were for children's pajamas and sleepwear, she founded her own label. The gorgeous 100% cotton, high-quality classic European collections are sold around the world and through her showroom, by appointment. ⊠ *502 Tak Woo House, 1–3 Wo On Lane 17–19 D'Aguilar St., Central* ☎ *2525–9872 or 9162–0350* ⊕ *www.marleenmolenaar.com* Ⓜ *Central.*

HONG KONG COUTURE

Amandarling. Think floaty and floral and you'll get the idea of this serene Central-based boutique, a winning antidote to a hot and crowded urban shopping hub on a weekend. British designer Amanda Loke specializes in resort wear, favoring loose lounge kaftan styles and light fabrics with exotic prints. ⊠ *32 Lyndhurst Ter., Central* ☎ *2545–0280* ⊕ *www. amandarling.com.*

Barney Cheng. One of Hong Kong's best-known, locally based designers, Barney Cheng creates haute couture designs and prêt-à-porter collections, infusing his glam, often sequined, pieces with wit. When the Kennedy Center in Washington, D.C., hosted an exhibition titled "The New China Chic," Cheng was invited to display his works alongside those by the likes of Vera Wang and Anna Sui. It's pretty much only open during office hours though, so call ahead for a weekend appointment. ⊠ *12th fl., World Wide Commercial Bldg., 34 Wyndham St., Central* ☎ *2530–2829* ⊕ *www.barneycheng.com* Ⓜ *Central.*

Episode. Locally owned and designed Episode collections focus on accessories and suiting and other elegant clothing for working women and ladies who lunch. Look also for the younger Jessica, the trendy Colour, and the casual Weekend Workshop collections. Though distinct, each collection pays close attention to current trends in the fashion world. ⊠ *Basement fl., Entertainment Bldg., 30 Queen's Rd., Central* ☎ *2943–2115 customer service* ⊕ *www.toppy.com.hk* Ⓜ *Central* ⊠ *Gateway Arcade, Harbour City, Canton Rd., Tsim Sha Tsui, Kowloon* Ⓜ *Tsim Sha Tsui.*

Fang Fong Projects. Fang Fong fell in love with the vintage feel of the SoHo district as a design graduate and vowed to move in. She chose a light-filled studio space to display her floaty, 1970s-inspired clothing line, with its bold prints and sexy wisps of lace and silk. She also brought her friends with her, or at least those who suited her vibe. Head here for the Japanese-inspired clutches of Mischa Designs and for pieces by U.K. brand Dialog (⊕ *www.dialogltd.net*), which works with scrap fabric from fair trade sources. ⊠ *Shop 1, 69 Peel St., SoHo, Central* ☎ *3105–5557.*

Lu Lu Cheung. A fixture on the Hong Kong fashion scene for more than a decade, Lu Lu Cheung creates designs that ooze comfort and warmth. In both daytime and evening wear, natural fabrics and forms are represented in practical yet imaginative ways. ⊠ *The Landmark, 15 Queen's Rd. Central, Central* ☎ *2537–7515* ⊕ *www.lulucheung.com.hk* Ⓜ *Central* ⊠ *Shop B, G/F, 50 Wellington St., Central* Ⓜ *Central.*

Ranee K. Designer Ranee Kok Chui-Wah's showrooms are scarlet dens cluttered with her one-off dresses and eclectic women's wear that bring new meanings to "East meets West." Known for her quirky cheongsams and dresses, she has also collaborated with brands such as Furla and Shanghai Tang. Special clients and local celebrities enjoy her custom tailoring, too. ⊠ *Ground fl., 16 Gough St., Central* ☎ *2108–4068* ⊕ *www.raneek.com* Ⓜ *Central.*

Fodor's Choice
★

Shanghai Tang. In addition to the brilliantly hued—and expensive— displays of silk and cashmere clothing, you'll find custom-made suits starting at around HK$18,000, including fabric from a large selection of Chinese silks. You can also have a cheongsam (a sexy slit-skirt silk dress with a Mandarin collar) made for around HK$8,000, including fabric. Ready-to-wear Mandarin suits are in the HK$5,000–HK$6,000 range. Among the Chinese souvenirs are novelty watches with mah-jongg tiles or dim sum instead of numbers. You can find outlets scattered across Hong Kong, including the airport's Terminal One. ⊠ *12 Pedder St., Central* ☎ *2525–7333* ⊕ *www.shanghaitang.com* Ⓜ *Central* ⊠ *1881 Heritage Bldg., 2A Canton Rd., Tsim Sha Tsui, Kowloon* Ⓜ *Tsim Sha Tsui.*

Siberian Fur Store Ltd. In general, furs sold by reputable Hong Kong dealers are the ideal combination of superior quality and low prices. This shop, owned and operated by a prominent local family, is famous for its high-quality furs and special attention to design. ⊠ *Ground fl., 29 Des Voeux Rd. Central, Central* ☎ *2522–1380* Ⓜ *Central* ⊠ *Ground fl., 21 Chatham Rd. S, Tsim Sha Tsui, Kowloon* Ⓜ *Tsim Sha Tsui.*

CRAFTS AND CURIOS

Mountain Folkcraft. A little old-fashioned bell chimes as you open the door to this fantastic old shop filled with handicrafts and antiques from around China. Amid the old treasures, carved woodwork, rugs, and curios, are stunning folk-print fabrics. To reach the store from Queen's Road Central, walk up D'Aguilar Street toward Lan Kwai Fong, then turn right onto Wo On Lane. ⊠ *Ground fl., 12 Wo On La., Central* ☎ *2525–3199* Ⓜ *Central.*

GIZMOS, GADGETS, AND ACCESSORIES

CDS, DVDS, AND VCDS

Flow. Track down this tiny, hidden gem for secondhand CDs, DVDs, magazines, and wall-to-wall used books in English. The range is extraordinary, and the organizational system baffling, but the owner is knowledgeable, friendly, and willing to poke among the shelves for you. Books here average around HK$45, compared to a few hundred new. Find it, if you can, up a flight of stairs, under the Midlevels Escalator, just across from a hot-dog stand. ⊠ *1st fl., 40 Lyndhurst Terr., SoHo Central* ☎ *2964–9483.*

HOME FURNISHINGS

ASIAN LIFESTYLE STORES

Homeless. Pleasantly quirky but with a finger firmly on the pulse of the city, this small design brand emporium has its flagship in NoHo (North of Hollywood Road), one of Central's up and coming nooks. The store showcases some of its own in-house creations, but it mostly stocks pieces from modern-day design icons. Come here to pick up a Tom Dixon bowler-hat lampshade or a Pac Man–shape oven glove by Fred. Try its basement café for brunch on Saturday. ⊠ *Ground fl., 28 Gough St., NoHo, Central* ☎ *2851–1160* ⊕ *www.homeless.hk.*

Kou. Socialite and interior designer Louise Kou's lifestyle boutique is a moody mix of dark jewel tones and silver on two floors connected by an internal staircase. Different rooms allow her to showcase chinaware, silverware, lamps, linens, fashion accessories, clothes, lingerie, and unique household items. When Kou can't find what she desires somewhere in the world, she simply has it custom-made. ⊠ *22nd fl.,*

Fung House, 19–20 Connaught Rd., Central ☎ *2530–2234* ⊕ *www. kouconcept.com* Ⓜ *Central.*

CARPETS AND RUGS

Tai Ping Carpets. Headquartered in Hong Kong, Tai Ping is highly regarded for its custom-made rugs and wall-to-wall carpets. It takes 2½ to 3 months to make specially ordered carpets; you can specify color, thickness, and even the direction of the weave. Tai Ping's occasional sales are well worth attending; check the classified section of the *South China Morning Post* for dates. ✉ *Prince's Bldg, 10 Chater Rd., Central* ☎ *2522–7138* ⊕ *www.taipingcarpets.com* Ⓜ *Central.*

CERAMICS

Lee Fung China Ware Co., Ltd. Friendly service and a decent selection of Chinese and western-style dinnerware make this a good one-stop shop, uniquely situated just off the Midlevels Escalator. It also carries vases and antique reproductions. ✉ *Ground fl., 18 Shelley St., SoHo, Central* ☎ *2524–0630.*

Wah Tung Ceramic Arts. It's a slightly slick but reliable manufacturer and retailer of predominantly handcrafted ceramics that has been in operation since the early days of trade with the West (1863). The overwhelmingly large product line includes antique replicas, vases, dinnerware, figurines, and more—all in classic Chinese motifs. ✉ *7th fl., 57–59 Hollywood Rd., Central* ☎ *2543–2823* ⊕ *www.wahtungchina. com* Ⓜ *Central* ✉ *16th fl., Chung Fat Bldg., 7–9 Hill Rd., Western.*

JEWELRY

Carat. Forget the cheesy cubic zirconium of the past. One look at its stark white showrooms, and you'll see that Carat has mastered the creation and presentation of synthetic gemstones. Hand-assembled in precious-metal settings, the large collection spans various eras of jewelry styles. The second line, Carat Emporium, is inspired by far-flung cultures and made with colorful semiprecious stones. ✉ *IFC Mall, 8 Finance St., Central* ☎ *2234–7372* ⊕ *www.carat.cc* Ⓜ *Central* ✉ *Gateway Arcade, Harbour City, 3 Canton Rd., Tsim Sha Tsui, Kowloon* Ⓜ *Tsim Sha Tsui.*

Chocolate Rain. The collections—dreamed up by a Hong Kong fine arts graduate—consist of pieces handcrafted of recycled materials, jade, crystals, precious stones, and mother-of-pearl. The showroom also displays works by the designer's friends, and it doubles as a classroom for jewelry-making courses. ✉ *Ground fl., 67a Peel St., SoHo, Central* ☎ *2975–8318* ⊕ *www.chocolaterain.com* Ⓜ *Central.*

Jan Logan. This Australian designer has celebrities wearing her youthful yet elegant designs. Pieces contrast cultured, South Seas, and Tahitian pearls with onyx, diamonds, quartz, and other stones. ✉ *IFC Mall, 8 Finance St., Central* ☎ *2918–4212* ⊕ *www.janlogan.com* Ⓜ *Central.*

Kai-Yin Lo. Kai-Yin Lo is famous for her Asian-inspired jewelry, combining contemporary style with ancient Chinese designs and materials such as jade. The *International Herald Tribune* has credited her with bridging the gap between fine and fashion jewelry. Lo acts as a consultant, lecturer, and writer on heritage, art, culture, and philanthropy; sales of her jewelry continue by appointment. ✉ *55 Garden Rd., Central* ☎ *2773–6009* ⊕ *www.kaiyinlo-design.com.*

Karen Jewel Co. Designer Karen Lee studied jewelry making in Florence before creating her own brand in 2003. She uses a variety of precious stones, including rubies, sapphires, and emeralds, in her one-of-a-kind custom-made jewelry, which tends to have an antique look. Her showroom, where you can check out some sample pieces, is worth a visit; appointments are required, so call ahead. ✉ *17A, 128 Wellington St., Central* ☎ *2151–9622* ⊕ *www.karenjewel.com* Ⓜ *Central.*

Qeelin. With ancient Chinese culture for inspiration and *In The Mood for Love* actress Maggie Cheung as the muse, something extraordinary was bound to come from Qeelin. Its name was cleverly derived from the Chinese characters for male ("qi") and female ("lin"), and symbolizes harmony, balance, and peace. The restrained beauty and meaningful creations of designer Dennis Chan are exemplified in two main collections: Wulu, a minimalist form representing the mythical gourd as well as the lucky number eight; and Tien Di, literally "Heaven and Earth," symbolizing everlasting love. Classic gold, platinum, and diamonds mix with colored jades, black diamonds, and unusual materials for a truly unique effect. A sweeter addendum to the collection was added recently in the form of Bo Bo, the panda bear. ✉ *IFC Mall, 8 Finance St., Central* ☎ *2389–8863* ⊕ *www.qeelin.com* Ⓜ *Central* ✉ *Peninsula Shopping Arcade, Salisbury Rd., Tsim Sha Tsui, Kowloon* Ⓜ *Tsim Sha Tsui* ✉ *Ocean Terminal, Harbour City, 3 Canton Rd., Tsim Sha Tsui, Kowloon* Ⓜ *Tsim Sha Tsui.*

Saturn Essentials. If you're looking for a local artisan, a reasonably priced piece of silver, semiprecious stones, and sometimes even gold jewelry—or you just want a chat with a nice lady—visit Maureen "Mo" Gerrard. Her shop is opposite the salon of her son, Paul Gerrard. The shop repairs, cleans, plates, and polishes, too. ✉ *11th fl., 51 Wellington St., Central* ☎ *2537–9335* ⊕ *www.saturnessentials.com* Ⓜ *Central.*

Tayma Fine Jewellery. Unusual colored "connoisseur" gemstones are set by hand in custom designs by Hong Kong–based jeweler Tayma Page Allies. The collection is designed to bring out the personality of the individual wearer, and includes oversize cocktail rings, distinctive bracelets, pretty earrings, and more. ✉ *Prince's Bldg., 10 Chater Rd., Central* ☎ *2525–5280* ⊕ *www.taymajewellery.com* Ⓜ *Central.*

DIAMONDS

Larry Jewellery. This is a long-established source for handcrafted jewelry made from high-grade precious stones. Catering to local tastes since 1967, the traditional company has a new push to attract younger customers. That said, there really is a wide enough range to please most tastes. ✉ *Ground fl., 72 Queens Rd. Central, Central* ☎ *2521–1268* ⊕ *www.larryjewelry.com* Ⓜ *Central* ✉ *Pacific Place, 88 Queensway, Admiralty, Central* Ⓜ *Admiralty* ✉ *Ground fl., 33 Nathan Rd., Tsim Sha Tsui, Kowloon* Ⓜ *Tsim Sha Tsui.*

Ronald Abram Jewellers. Looking at the rocks in these windows can feel like a visit to a natural history museum. Large white- and rare-color diamonds sourced from all over the world are a specialty here, but the shop also deals in emeralds, sapphires, and rubies. With years of expertise, Abrams dispenses advice on both the aesthetic merits and the investment potential of each stone or piece of jewelry. ⊠ *Mezzanine, Mandarin Oriental, 5 Connaught Rd., Central* ☎ *2810–7677* ⊕ *www. ronaldabram.com* Ⓜ *Central* ⊠ *Mezzanine, Shop 10, Peninsula Shopping Arcade Salisbury Rd., Tsim Sha Tsui, Kowloon* Ⓜ *Tsim Sha Tsui.*

JADE

Chow Sang Sang. Chow Sang Sang has more than 100 shops in China. In addition to its contemporary gold, diamond, jade, and wedding collections for the local market, the manufacturer and retailer also sources international brands. ⊠ *37 Queen's Rd. Central, Central* ☎ *3583–4150; 2192–3123 customer service and branch information* ⊕ *www. chowsangsang.com* Ⓜ *Central* ⊠ *LG2, Festival Walk, 80 Tat Chee Ave., Kowloon Tong, Kowloon* Ⓜ *Kowloon Tong* ⊠ *Ground fl., 525 Hennessy Rd., Causeway Bay* Ⓜ *Causeway Bay.*

Chow Tai Fook. Jade is not the only thing you'll see from this local chain founded in 1929. It also has fine jewelry in diamond, jadeite, ruby, sapphire, emerald, pearl, 18K gold, and more-traditional pure gold. And don't worry about tracking one down; there are 11 branches on Kowloon's Nathan Road alone. ⊠ *Ground fl., AON China Bldg., 29 Queen's Rd. Central, Central* ☎ *2523–7128 or 2526–8649* ⊕ *www.chowtaifook. com* Ⓜ *Central* ⊠ *Park Lane Shopper's Boulevard, 123 Nathan Rd., Tsim Sha Tsui, Kowloon* Ⓜ *Tsim Sha Tsui* ⊠ *Ground fl., Chow Tai Fook Centre, 580A Nathan Rd., Mong Kok, Kowloon* Ⓜ *Mong Kok.*

Edward Chiu. Everything about Edward Chiu is *fabulous,* from the flamboyant way he dresses to his high-end jade jewelry. The minimalist, geometric pieces use the entire jade spectrum, from deep greens to surprising lavenders. He's also famous for contrasting black-and-white jade, setting it in precious metals and adding diamond or pearl touches. ⊠ *IFC Mall, 8 Finance St., Central* ☎ *2525–2618* ⊕ *www.edwardchiu.com* Ⓜ *Central.*

PEARLS

Gallery One. This is the next-best option for midrange pearls if you can't make it to the Jade Market. Gallery One blends into Hollywood Road's backdrop of trinket-filled storefronts, but its selection of freshwater pearls stands out. Prices are reasonable, and they will string together whichever combination of pearls and semiprecious stones you choose. Gallery One also carries Tibetan and Buddhist beads in wood and amber as well as bronze sculptures. ⊠ *Ground fl., 31–33 Hollywood Rd., Central* ☎ *2545–6436* Ⓜ *Central.*

K.S. Sze & Sons. More salon than store, powdered elderly ladies who lunch and casually dressed tourists all come here for the same thing: quality pearls, fine jewelry, and excellent service. In addition to classic styles, K.S. Sze works closely with clients on custom orders. ⊠ *Prince's Building, 10 Chater Rd., Central* ☎ *2524–2803* ⊕ *www.kssze.com* Ⓜ *Central.*

Po Kwong Jewellery Ltd. Specializing in strung pearls from Australia and the South Seas, Po Kwong will add clasps to your specifications. They also carry pearl earrings, rings, and pendants. ⊠ *18th fl., HK Diamond Exchange Bldg., 8–10 Duddell St., Central* ☎ *2521–4686.*

Many visitors to Hong Kong come for the tax- and duty-free jewelry.

Super Star Jewellery. Discreetly tucked in a corner of Central, Super Star looks like any other small Hong Kong jewelry shop—with walls lined by display cases filled with the usual classic designs (old-fashioned to some) in predominantly gold and precious stones. What makes them stand out are the good prices and personalized service. The cultured pearls and mixed strands of colored freshwater pearls are not all shown, so ask Lily or one of her colleagues to bring them out. ⊠ *The Galleria, 9 Queen's Rd. Central, Central* ☎ *2521–0507* Ⓜ *Central.*

WATCHES
Eldorado Watch Co Ltd. At this deep emporium of watch brands, seek the advice of one of the older staffers who look like they've been there since the British landed. Brands include: Rolex, Patek Philippe, Girard-Perregaux, etc. ⊠ *Ground fl., Peter Bldg., 60 Queen's Rd., Central* ☎ *2522–7155* Ⓜ *Central.*

SHOES AND BAGS
Hop's Handbag Co. Ltd. Uh-oh. You've over-shopped, and now packing is a problem. Hop over to Hop's for cheap luggage, from generic to name brands such as Samsonite. It also sells lots of handbags: some nameless but acceptable; others, amazing throwbacks to the '80s (and now back in fashion). ⊠ *Ground fl., 18 Li Yuen St. E, Central* ☎ *2523–3888* Ⓜ *Central.*

Kow Hoo Shoe Company. If you like shoes made the old-fashioned way, then Kow Hoo, one of Hong Kong's oldest (circa 1946), is for you. It also does great cowboy boots—there's nothing like knee-high calf-skin. ⊠ *2nd fl., Prince's Bldg., 10 Chater Rd., Central* ☎ *2523–0489* Ⓜ *Central.*

Ladyplace. The prices on French Sole brand ballerinas will have you doing pirouettes. In the United States the ballet flats by British designer Jane Winkworth sell for about US$160. At Ladyplace they're HK$895—or about US$115—a pair. While you're here, browse through the second-hand shoes and apparel by famous fashion labels, all at discounted prices. ✉ *1st fl., World Trust Tower, 50 Stanley St., Central* ☎ *2854–2321* ⊕ *www.ladyplace.com* Ⓜ *Central.*

Lianca. This is one of those unique places that make you want to buy something even if there's nothing you need. Lianca, first and foremost a manufacturer, sells well-made leather bags, wallets, frames, key chains, and home accessories in timeless, simple designs. It's an unbranded way to be stylish. ✉ *Basement fl., 27 Staunton St., entrance on Graham St., SoHo, Central* ☎ *2139–2989* ⊕ *www.liancacentral.com* Ⓜ *Central.*

Mayer Shoes. Since the 1960s, Mayer has been making excellent custom-order shoes and accessories in leather, lizard, crocodile, and ostrich. Go to them for the classic pieces for which they became famous rather than this season's "it" bag. Prices start at about US$300 for shoes, US$360 for bags. ✉ *Mandarin Oriental, 5 Connaught Rd., Central* ☎ *2524–3317* Ⓜ *Central.*

Mischa Designs. Designer Michelle Lai's bags are handmade from Japanese brocade obis (sashes) and kimonos from the 1920s to the 1950s. Clutch bags such as the Dumpling or any of the reversible styles could make even the most unremarkable outfit look noteworthy. Keep an eye out for bigger totes made of obis paired with leather. You can also find her designs at Fang Fong Projects. ✉ *Shop 1, 69 Peel St., Central* ☎ *3105–5557* ⊕ *www.mischadesigns.com.*

On Pedder. This store's brand directory reads like a fashion editor's wish list of world-famous shoe, bag, accessory, and jewelry designers. The main branch can be found in Central's Joyce Boutique, but you might see the same brands at Lane Crawford—that's because they're sister companies. For the same aesthetics at lower prices, check out trendy younger sibling **Pedder Red** (✉ *The Gateway, Harbour City, Canton Rd., Tsim Sha Tsui, Kowloon* Ⓜ *Tsim Sha Tsui*). ✉ *Joyce Boutique, 1st fl., New World Tower, 18 Queen's Rd., Central* ☎ *2118–2323 for branch information* ⊕ *www.onpedder.com* Ⓜ *Central.*

Sam Wo. A veteran of this area, Sam Wo sells fashion-inspired leather bags at low prices and without the branding. You'll need a keen eye to spot the must-haves amid all the must-nots. See neighboring stalls for closer interpretations of branded bags. ✉ *Basement, 41–47 Queen's Rd. Central, Central* ☎ *2524–0970* Ⓜ *Central.*

SPAS

Acupressure and Massage Centre of the Blind. Looking for a good massage without all the glitz? Visit these skilled and affordable blind masseurs trained in acupressure, reflexology, and Chinese massage, conveniently located in the middle of the Central Business District. Expect to pay around HK$240 per hour. ✉ *2nd fl., Tung Ming Bldg., 40–42 Des Voeux Rd., Central* ☎ *2810–6666* Ⓜ *Central.*

Four Seasons. Enter via a light-wood and stark white hallway into treatment rooms that ooze modern cool. The two-hour, signature Pure

Indulgence treatment, using organic products, is head-to-toe pampering for your body and your soul. The serene steam and sauna complex, harbor views, and a Japanese garden also help to alter your mood. ⊠ 8 Finance St., Central ☎3196–8888 ⊕ www.fourseasons.com Ⓜ Central.

Fodor'sChoice ★ **Happy Foot Reflexology Center.** Who knew that pressure on your big toe could help clear your sinuses? Reflexology is Hong Kong's cheap way to relax, and Happy Foot is the legendary place to have it done. The armchairs are comfortable, and the therapists are experts, but don't expect a luxe experience. Interiors are basic, and you'll share a room with other customers. But, this is reflected in the prices too: pay about HK$250 for a 50-minute full body massage or HK$198 for just your feet. ⊠ 6th fl., 11th fl., and 13th fl., Jade Centre, 98–102 Wellington St., Central ☎2544–1010 Ⓜ Central ⊠ 19th fl., Century Square, 1–13 D'Aguilar St., Central Ⓜ Central ⊠ 1st fl., Elegance Court, 2–4 Tsoi Tak St., Happy Valley, Causeway Bay.

> ### FIX IT AND FORGET IT
>
> Shoe troubles? For basic services the shoe-repair chains in MTR stations or hotels can help. But for special cases (mauled Manolos, for instance), head to the **Top Shoes Repair & Lock Centre** (⊠ Ground fl., 35 Queen's Rd. Central, Central ☎ 2530–0978 Ⓜ Central).

Fodor'sChoice ★ **The Mandarin Spa & the Oriental Spa.** If you indulge in just one Hong Kong spa treatment, have it at one of these sister spas, at the Mandarin Oriental and the Landmark Mandarin Oriental hotels. Designed as a journey from the outer into the inner world, the experience begins on the check-in and fitness floor. You're taken up to the next level and offered a welcome tea, then guided deeper into this haven, where treatments are administered by excellent therapists in serene rooms. Try the signature Time Ritual, a holistic combination of therapies adapted to your specific needs on the day. Treatments here get you access to the vitality pool, the amethyst-crystal steam room, the authentic Turkish hammam, and more. Next door to the Mandarin, the legendary **Mandarin Beauty Salon and Barber Shop** (⊠ Mandarin Oriental, 5 Connaught Rd., Central ☎2825–4888 Ⓜ Central) offers traditional favorites. Ask for a famous Shanghainese pedicure with Samuel and his knives (yes, knives!), or see Betty for the traditional eyebrow threading. ⊠ Landmark Mandarin Oriental, 15 Queen's Rd. Central, Central ☎2132–0011 ⊕ www.mandarinoriental.com Ⓜ Central.

Quality Chinese Medical Centre. Acupuncture looks alarming but is painless. Where better to try it than in China? This reputable center is also a good place to learn more about traditional Chinese medicine and herbal remedies. ⊠ 5th fl., Jade Centre, 98 Wellington St., Central ☎2881–8267 ⊕ www.qualitytcm.com Ⓜ Central.

TAILOR-MADE CLOTHING

Blanc de Chine. Blanc de Chine has catered to high society and celebrities, such as actor Jackie Chan, for years. That's easy when you're housed on the second floor of an old colonial building (just upstairs from Shanghai Tang) and you rely on word of mouth. The small, refined tailoring shop neatly displays exquisite fabrics. Next door is the Blanc de

Chine boutique filled with lovely ready-made women's wear, menswear, and home accessories. With newer stores in New York and Beijing, it appears the word is getting out. Items here are extravagances, but they're worth every penny. You'll also find another branch just opposite on the 2nd floor of the Landmark mall. ⊠ *Pedder Bldg., 12 Pedder St., Central* ☎ *2104–7934* ⊕ *www.blancdechine.com* Ⓜ *Central.*

Linva Tailors. It's one of the best of the old-fashioned cheongsam tailors, in operation since the 1960s. Master tailor Mr. Leung takes clients through the entire process and reveals a surprising number of variations in style. Prices are affordable, but vary according to fabric, which ranges from basics to special brocades and beautifully embroidered silks. ⊠ *38 Cochrane St., Central* ☎ *2544–2456* Ⓜ *Central.*

Fodor'sChoice **Shanghai Tang—Imperial Tailors.** Upscale Chinese lifestyle brand Shanghai
★ Tang has the Imperial Tailors service in select stores, including the Central flagship. A fabulous interior evokes the charm of 1930s Shanghai, and gives an indication of what to expect in terms of craftsmanship and price. From silk to velvet, brocade to voile, fabrics are displayed on the side walls, along with examples of fine tailoring. The expert tailors here can make conservative or contemporary versions of the cheongsam. Men can also have a Chinese *tang* suit made to order. Expect to pay from between HK$6,000 to HK$20,000 ⊠ *Ground fl., 12 Pedder St., Central* ☎ *2525–7333* ⊕ *www.shanghaitang.com* Ⓜ *Central* ⊠ *1881 Heritage Bldg., 2A Canton Rd., Tsim Sha Tsui, Kowloon* Ⓜ *Tsim Sha Tsui.*

MEN'S TAILORS

A-Man Hing Cheong Co., Ltd. People often gasp at the very mention of A-Man Hing Cheong in the Mandarin Oriental Hotel. For some it symbolizes the ultimate in fine tailoring, with a reputation that extends back to its founding in 1898. For others it's the lofty prices that elicit a reaction. Regardless, this is a trustworthy source of European-cut suits, custom shirts, and excellent service. ⊠ *Mezzanine, Mandarin Oriental, 5 Connaught Rd., Central* ☎ *2522–3336* Ⓜ *Central.*

Ascot Chang. This self-titled "gentleman's shirtmaker" makes it easy to find the perfect shirt, even if you could get a better deal in a less prominent shop. Ascot Chang has upheld exacting Shanghainese tailoring traditions in Hong Kong since 1955, and now has stores in New York, Beverly Hills, Manila, and Shanghai, in addition to offering online ordering and regular American tours. The focus here is on the fit and details, from 22 stitches per inch to collar linings crafted to maintain their shape. Among the countless fabrics, Swiss 200s two-ply Egyptian cotton by Alumo is one of the most coveted and expensive. Like many shirtmakers, Ascot Chang does pajamas, robes, boxer shorts, and women's blouses, too. It also has developed ready-made lines of shirts, T-shirts, neckties, and other accessories. ⊠ *Prince's Bldg., 10 Chater Rd., Central* ☎ *2523–3663* ⊕ *www.ascotchang.com* Ⓜ *Central* ⊠ *IFC Mall, 8 Finance St., Central* Ⓜ *Central* ⊠ *Peninsula Hong Kong, Salisbury Rd., Tsim Sha Tsui, Kowloon* Ⓜ *Tsim Sha Tsui* ⊠ *New World Centre, InterContinental Hong Kong, 18–24 Salisbury Rd., Tsim Sha Tsui, Kowloon* Ⓜ *Tsim Sha Tsui.*

CLOSE UP

Tailor-Made

No trip to Hong Kong would be complete without a visit to one of its world-famous tailors, as many celebrities and dignitaries can attest. In often humble, fabric-cluttered settings, customer records contain the measurements of notables such as Jude Law, Kate Moss, David Bowie, Luciano Pavarotti, and Queen Elizabeth II.

TAILORING TIPS

If you've ever owned a custom-made garment, you understand the joy of clothes crafted to fit your every measurement. Hong Kong is best known for men's tailoring, but whether you're looking for a classic men's business suit or an evening gown, these steps will help you size things up.

■ Set Your Style. Be clear about what you want. Bring samples—a favorite piece of clothing or magazine photos. Also, Hong Kong tailors are trained in classic, structured garments. Straying from these could lead to disappointment. There are three basic suit styles. The American cut has a jacket with notched lapels, a center vent, and two or three buttons. The trousers are lean, with flat fronts. The British cut also has notched lapels and two- or three-button jackets, but it features side vents and pleated trousers. The double-breasted Italian cut has wide lapels and pleated trousers.

■ Choose Your Fabric. You're getting a deal on workmanship, so consider splurging on, say, a luxurious blend of cashmere, mink, and wool. When having something copied, though, choose a fabric similar to the original. Take your time selecting: fabric is the main cost factor. Examine fabric on a large scale; small swatches are deceiving.

■ Measure Up. Meticulous measuring is the mark of a superior craftsman, so be patient. And for accuracy, stand as you normally would (you can't suck in that gut forever).

■ Place Your Order. Most tailors require a deposit of 30%–50% of the total cost. Request a receipt detailing price, fabric, style, measurements, fittings, and production schedule. Ask for a swatch to compare with the final product.

■ Get Fit. There should be at least two fittings. The first is for major alterations. Subsequent fittings are supposed to be for minor adjustments, but don't settle for less than perfect: Keep sending it back until they get it right. Bring the right clothes, such as a dress shirt and appropriate shoes, to try on a suit. Try jackets buttoned and unbuttoned. Examine every detail. Are shoulder seams puckered or smooth? Do patterns meet? Is the collar too loose or tight? (About two fingers' space is right.)

FINDING A TAILOR

■ As soon as you arrive, visit established tailors to compare workmanship and cost.

■ Ask if the work is bespoke (made from scratch) or made-to-measure (based on existing patterns but handmade according to your measurements).

■ You get what you pay for. Assume the workmanship and fabric will match the price.

■ A fine suit requires six or more days to create. That said, be wary but not dismissive of "24-hour tailors." Hong Kong's most famous craftsmen have turned out suits in a day.

4

Jantzen Tailor. Catering to expatriate bankers since 1972, this reputable yet reasonable tailor specializes in classic shirts; it also makes suits and women's garments. The comprehensive Web site displays its commitment to quality, such as hand-sewn button shanks, Gygil interlining, and Coats brand thread. ⊠ *5th fl., 25 Des Voeux Rd., Central* ☎ *2570–5901 or 2810–8080* ⊕ *www.jantzentailor.com* Ⓜ *Central.*

Yuen's Tailor. Need a kilt? This is where the Hong Kong Highlanders Reel Club comes for custom-made kilts. The Yuen repertoire, however, extends to well-made suits and shirts. The tiny shop is on an unimpressive gray walkway and is filled from floor to ceiling with sumptuous European fabrics. It's a good place to have clothes copied; prices are competitive. ⊠ *2nd fl., Escalator Link Alley, 80 Des Voeux Rd., Central* ☎ *2815–5388* Ⓜ *Central.*

WOMEN'S TAILORS

Irene Fashions. In addition to having the same name as the W. W. Chan women's division (⇨ *See Kowloon Peninsula*), this Irene Fashions promises much of the same guidance and workmanship. But don't confuse this popular Central tailoress with her Kowloon-side counterpart; the two are *not* related. Slightly more well known, this tailor attracts many expatriate women in search of everything from suits to evening wear. Service in the cluttered atmosphere may be brusque, but it's only because they know what they're talking about. ⊠ *3rd fl., Tung Chai Bldg., 86–90 Wellington St., Central* ☎ *2850–5635* Ⓜ *Central.*

Margaret Court Tailoress. A name frequently passed on by expert Hong Kong shoppers, Margaret Wong's tailoring services span women's daywear to bridal gowns to Chinese cheongsam. Prices tend to be midrange. ⊠ *8th fl., Block A, Winner Bldg., 27–37 D'Aguilar St., Central* ☎ *2525–5596* Ⓜ *Central.*

Perfect Dress Alteration (aka Ann & Bon). Hong Kong's tai tais bring their couture here for adjustments, as evidenced by the Chanel, Escada, and Versace bags hanging overhead in this cluttered little workshop buzzing with the sound of sewing machines. Although primarily known for alterations, it also offers tailoring services for women. ⊠ *2nd fl., Melbourne Plaza, 33 Queen's Rd., Central* ☎ *2522–8838* Ⓜ *Central.*

Siriporn. Visible from the Midlevels Escalator and one of the most highly recommended Thai tailors in town, Siriporn is known for an acute sense of aesthetics, reasonable prices, and brightly colored Thai silks. It's also capable of crafting subtle garments to please minimalists. Visit by appointment only. ⊠ *1st fl., Merlin Bldg., 28 Cochrane St., Central* ☎ *2866–6668* Ⓜ *Central.*

ADMIRALTY

Shopping in Admiralty is synonymous with one thing—glitzy Pacific Place Mall. Locals come here for the designer labels, and visitors to stock up on souvenirs at Chinese Arts & Crafts. Elevated walkways connect it to three lesser shopping centers: the Admiralty Centre, Queensway Plaza, and United Centre.

CLOTHING

HONG KONG
COUTURE

Vivienne Tam. You know it when you walk into a Vivienne Tam boutique—the strong Chinese-motif prints and modern updates of traditional women's clothing are truly distinct. Don't let the bold, ready-to-wear collections distract you from the very pretty accessories, which include footwear with Asian embellishments such as jade. Tam is one of the best-known Hong Kong designers and, even though she's now based outside the SAR, the city still claims her as its own. ⊠ *Pacific Place, 88 Queensway, Admiralty, Central* ☎ *2918–0238* ⊕ *www.viviennetam.com* Ⓜ *Admiralty* ⊠ *Harbour City, Canton Rd., Tsim Sha Tsui, Kowloon* Ⓜ *Tsim Sha Tsui* ⊠ *Festival Walk, 80 Tat Chee Ave., Kowloon Tong, Kowloon* Ⓜ *Central.*

> ### ART CRAWL?
>
> The art world's version of a pub crawl, **Hong Kong Art Walk** (⊕ www.hongkongartwalk.com) is an excellent chance to experience the gallery scene. Held over the course of one evening every March, it gives ticket holders unlimited access to more than 40 galleries where food and drinks donated by neighboring restaurants help create a festive environment. Proceeds go to charity.

DEPARTMENT STORES

Fodor's Choice
★

Chinese Arts & Crafts. Head to this long-established mainland company to blitz through that tiresome list of presents in one fell swoop. It stocks a huge variety of well-priced brocades, silk clothing, carpets, and cheap porcelain. In direct contrast to the thrill of digging through dusty piles at the open-air Jade Market, it provide a clean, air-conditioned environment in which to shop for classic jade jewelry—the prices aren't too outrageous. Incongruously scattered throughout the shops are specialty items like large globes with lapis oceans and landmasses inlaid with semiprecious stones for a mere HK$70,000. Other more accessible—and more packable—gifts include appliqué tablecloths and cushion covers or silk dressing gowns. ⊠ *Pacific Place, Admiralty, Central* ☎ *2827–6667* ⊕ *www.cacgift.com* Ⓜ *Admiralty, Exit F* ⊠ *Asia Standard Tower, 59 Queen's Rd., Central* Ⓜ *Central, Exit D2* ⊠ *China Resources Bldg., 26 Harbour Rd., Wan Chai* Ⓜ *Wan Chai, Exit A5* ⊠ *Star House, 3 Salisbury Rd., Tsim Sha Tsui, Kowloon* Ⓜ *Tsim Sha Tsui, Exit F.*

Fodor's Choice
★

Lane Crawford. This prestigious western-style department store has been the favorite of local label-lovers for years—not bad for a brand that started out as a makeshift provisions shop back in 1850. The massive flagship store in the IFC Mall feels like a monument to fashion's biggest names, with exquisitely designed acres divided up into small gallery-like spaces for each designer. The phenomenal brand list includes everything from haute couture through designer denim to Agent Provocateur lingerie. Sales here are more like fashionista wrestling matches, with everyone pushing and shoving to find bargains. ⊠ *Podium 3, IFC Mall, 8 Finance St., Central* ☎ *2118–3388; 2118–7777 Lane Crawford concierge* ⊕ *www.lanecrawford.com* Ⓜ *Hong Kong, Exit A1* ⊠ *Pacific Place, 88 Queensway, Admiralty, Central* Ⓜ *Admiralty, Exit F* ⊠ *Gateway Mall, 3 Canton Rd., Tsim Sha Tsui, Kowloon* Ⓜ *Tsim Sha Tsui, Exit E* ⊠ *Times Square, 1 Matheson St., Causeway Bay* Ⓜ *Causeway Bay, Exit A.*

4

Traditional herbalists mix healing concoctions in Wan Chai shops.

Seibu. This Japanese department store is actually owned by local tycoon Dickson Poon, who counts Harvey Nichols among his other possessions. Beauty counters and Western ready-to-wear labels make up the bulk of its offerings: expect hip street wear at Langham Place and more professional looks at the Pacific Place branch. This is also home to Japanese housewares shop Loft, and the aptly named Great Food Hall, where homesick expat foodies stock up on imported delicacies. ✉ *Pacific Place, 88 Queensway, Admiralty, Central* ☎ *2971–3888* Ⓜ *Admiralty, Exit F* ✉ *Kowloon Hotel, 19–21 Nathan Rd., Tsim Sha Tsui Kowloon* Ⓜ *Tsim Sha Tsui, Exit F* ✉ *Langham Place, 8 Argyle St., Mong Kok, Kowloon* Ⓜ *Mong Kok, Exit C3.*

MALLS AND CENTERS

Pacific Place. Once Hong Kong Island's classiest mall, Pacific Place has since been upstaged by the IFC. Yet it remains popular with well-to-do Hong Kongers, perhaps because it's quieter and more exclusive than most malls. High-end international prêt-à-porter fills most of its four floors, and two department stores, Seibu and Lane Crawford, also have branches here. Live music from its resident grand piano can still sometimes be heard wafting through the floors. When your bags are weighing you down, sandwiches, sushi, and Starbucks are on hand, as is a multiplex cinema. The Marriott, the Island Shangri-La, and the Conrad hotels are connected to this plaza, all with enticing afternoon tea options. Elevated walkways join Pacific Place with three lesser arcades: the **Admiralty Centre, United Centre,** and **Queensway Plaza**. ✉ *88 Queensway, Admiralty, Central* ⊕ *www.pacificplace.com. hk* Ⓜ *Admiralty, Exit F.*

SHOES AND BAGS

Kwanpen. Famous for its crocodile bags and shoes, Kwanpen has acted as a manufacturer for famous brands since 1938, as well as being a stand-alone retailer. It also uses ostrich and leather. ⊠ *Pacific Place, 88 Queensway, Admirality, Central* ☎ *2918–9199* Ⓜ *Admiralty* ⊠ *IFC Mall, 8 Finance St., Central* Ⓜ *Central* ⊠ *1881 Heritage, 2A Canton Rd., Tsim Sha Tsui, Kowloon*⊕ *www.kwanpen.com* Ⓜ *Tsim Sha Tsui.*

SPECIALTY SHOPS

AUCTION HOUSES

Sotheby's. The respected auction house opened here in 1973. Its teams work with Chinese ceramics, jade carvings, snuff bottles, and classical and contemporary paintings. The auction house also deals in watches and jewelry, including jadeite and western pieces. ⊠ *31st fl., Pacific Place, 88 Queensway, Admiralty, Central* ☎ *2524–8121* ⊕ *www.sothebys.com* Ⓜ *Admiralty.*

4

WAN CHAI, CAUSEWAY BAY, AND BEYOND

WAN CHAI

No malls, no air-conditioning, no Prada—Wan Chai has all these things in its favor when shopping in Central starts to feel a bit samey. Tourists don't shop here much, so you can try out your Cantonese at the rock-bottom no-name clothing outlets on the lanes between Johnston Road and Queen's Road East. Everything from underwear to evening wear is on offer. On Johnston Road shops selling bamboo birdcages and kung fu gear pay homage to Wan Chai's traditional side, in contrast to the chic modern furniture stores that have mushroomed here. Find them spreading into the small meandering Star Street neighborhood behind Three Pacific Place (⊕ *www.starstreet.com.hk*). Rosewood furniture and camphor-wood chests are two of the specialties of the mid-range furniture shops on Queen's Road East and Wan Chai Road, near Admiralty. The Suzy Wong stereotype lives on in the marine-filled tattoo parlors lining Lockhart Road. Techno-happy modern Hong Kong is alive and well at the Wan Chai Computer Centre, a collection of dozens of computing outlets on Hennessy Road.

CLOTHING

HONG KONG COUTURE

Sonjia by Sonjia Norman. Walk past a local garage and snoozing dogs in this old-style Hong Kong area to find the low-key atelier of Korean-English ex-lawyer Sonjia Norman. The designer crafts quietly luxurious, one-of-a-kind pieces, and modified vintage clothing under the Sonjia label. Her clothes are the epitome of understated stealth wealth. A new adjacent store houses Norman's home and living collection, including tableware, linens, and all sorts of pillows and cushions. ⊠ *Ground fl., 1A–2 Sun St., Wan Chai* ☎ *2529–6223* ⊕ *www.sonjiaonline.com* Ⓜ *Wan Chai.*

GIZMOS, GADGETS, AND ACCESSORIES

Fodor'sChoice
★
COMPUTERS

Wanchai Computer Centre. You'll find honest-to-goodness bargains on computer goods and accessories in the labyrinth of shops here. And you can negotiate prices. Your computer can be put together by a computer technician in less than a day if you're rushed; otherwise, two days is normal. The starting price is HK$6,000 depending on the hardware, processor, and peripherals you choose. This is a great resource, whether you're a techno-buff who's interested in assembling your own computer (a popular pastime with locals), or a technophobe looking for discounted earphones. ✉ *130 Hennessy Rd., Wan Chai* ☎ *No phone* Ⓜ *Wan Chai.*

HOME FURNISHINGS

ASIAN LIFE-
STYLE STORES

OVO. Push past a giant weathered steel door to enter this atmospheric, high-ceiling showroom, which feels like a cross between a museum and a temple. The fusion and contrasts of Southeast and West permeate every surface of the minimalist furniture, home furnishings, and accessories designed by the in-house team. Items are smart and rarely fussy. Beautiful, unvarnished blocks of wood, for example, are proposed as side tables. A few min-

utes' walk away you'll also find the newer **OVO Studio** (✉ *Ground fl., 60 Johnston Rd., Wan Chai* ☎ *2529–6060* Ⓜ *Wan Chai*), or OS, with its more European mix of in-house and international contemporary designs from brands like Kartell and Andreu World. When you're done, consider dinner at OVOlogue next door to OS, which serves modern Chinese cuisine in a beautifully renovated nineteenth-century shophouse (a type of building where shops and residences shared one structure). ✉ *Ground fl., 16 Queen's Rd. E, Wan Chai* ☎ *2526–7226* ⊕ *www.ovo. com.hk* Ⓜ *Admiralty.*

JEWELRY

JADE

Wing On Jewelry Ltd. There's a nostalgic charm to the butterflies, birds, and natural forms fashioned from jade, pearls, precious stones, and gold here. Everything looks like an heirloom inherited from your grandmother. With on-site gemologists and artisans, and a commitment to post-sale service, this store has a long list of repeat customers. If, however, you lean toward Scandinavian aesthetics and clean lines, this probably isn't the place for you. ✉ *146 Johnston Rd., Wan Chai* ☎ *2572–2332* ⊕ *www.wingonjewelry.com.hk* Ⓜ *Wan Chai* ✉ *459 Hennessy Rd., Causeway Bay* Ⓜ *Causeway Bay.*

SHOES AND BAGS

LIII LIII Shoes. The Chan Brothers have an illustrious history in Hong Kong and have certainly left a trail of satisfied customers in their wake; however reviews these days speak of hit and miss experiences there. Prices have also shot up over the last few years (from around HK$1,300 for sandals and HK$2,000 for high heels). Still, when they are good, they are very, very good. ✉ *Admiralty Centre, 18 Harcourt Rd., Wan Chai* ☎ *2136–9739* Ⓜ *Admiralty.*

CAUSEWAY BAY

Hong Kong fashionistas hungry for new labels choose Causeway Bay over Central any day. Quirky-but-cool Asian brands that won't arrive stateside for years are the pull at Japanese department store Sogo and micromalls like the Island Beverley. The low-profile storefronts on Yiu Wa Street belie its being *a hot* address for homegrown clothing and housewares. Similar up-and-coming boutiques are scattered along Vogue Alley, at the intersection of Paterson and Kingston streets. Local shops that have already made their name around here include innovating lifestyle specialist G.O.D. (Goods Of Desire), which has a big branch on Leighton Street.

Megamall Times Square soars behind all this—its mix of designer and midrange gear makes it a good one-stop shop destination. Other good bets for clothing are the big branches of local chains like Giordano on Jardine's Crescent. Prices in the stalls and poky shops along here and Jardine's Bazaar are unbeatable. Cheap souvenir stalls are another boon. You can see how real Hong Kongers do their food shopping at the "wet market" (so called because the vendors are perpetually hosing down their produce) at the end of these streets. Locals also head to Hennessy Road for jewelry, watches, luggage, stereos, cameras, and electronic goods.

DEPARTMENT STORES

LCX. This spacious store combines local and international fashion, beauty products, and dining under one roof. Clothing brands like Bauhaus, Zstampz, and Killah all have their own areas here, along with Apivita and other cosmetics lines. The Harbour City store also has restaurants and cafés including the California Pizza Kitchen, Itacho Sushi, and Suzuki Cafe. ⊠ *9 Kingston, Causeway Bay* ☎ *2890–5200* ⊕ *www. lcx-group.com* Ⓜ *Causeway Bay, Exit E* ⊠ *Harbour City, 3 Canton Rd., Tsim Sha Tsui Kowloon* Ⓜ *Tsim Sha Tsui, Exit E.*

Sogo. A lynchpin of the Causeway Bay shopping scene, Japanese brand Sogo's main branch has 10 floors of clothing, cosmetics, and housewares. The vast basement-level grocery store keeps the Japanese expat community happily fed. There's a dazzling variety of Chinese, Japanese, and international brands—the store is particularly strong on street wear, makeup, and accessories. The downside is that it's all squeezed into a tiny retail space, which can make shopping here cramped work. The considerably smaller Tsim Sha Tsui branch is in the basement shopping arcade under the Space Museum. ⊠ *555 Hennessy Rd., Causeway Bay* ☎ *2833–8338* ⊕ *www.sogo.com.hk* Ⓜ *Causeway Bay, Exit D* ⊠ *12 Salisbury Rd., Tsim Sha Tsui, Kowloon* Ⓜ *East Tsim Sha Tsui, Exit J.*

MALLS AND CENTERS

Lee Gardens One and Two. These two adjacent malls are a firm favorite with local celebrities. They come as much for the mall's low-key atmosphere—a world away from the bustle of Central—as for the clothes. And with so many big names under one small roof—Gucci, Ralph Lauren, Y's Yohji Yamamoto, Jean-Paul Gaultier, and Hermès, to name but a few—who can blame them? The second floor of Lee Gardens Two is taken up with designer kiddie wear. The two buildings, one on either side of Hysan Avenue, are linked by a second-floor footbridge. ✉ *33 Hysan Ave., Causeway Bay* ⊕ *www.leegardens.com.hk* Ⓜ *Causeway Bay, Exit F.*

Fodor's Choice ★ **Times Square.** This gleaming mall packs in most of Hong Kong's best-known stores into 12 frenzied floors, organized thematically. Lane Crawford and Marks & Spencer both have big branches here, as does favored local deli City'Super. Many restaurants are located in the basement, giving way to designers like Anna Sui on the second floor, and mid-range options like Zara higher up. The electronics, sports, and outdoors selection is particularly good. An indoor atrium hosts everything from heavy-metal bands to fashion shows to local movie stars; there's also a cinema complex and a dozen or so eateries; try the innovative SML (or Small Medium Large) for its large terrace and good selection of wines. The huge Page One bookshop is on the ninth floor. ✉ *1 Matheson St., Causeway Bay* ⊕ *www.timessquare.com.hk* Ⓜ *Causeway Bay, Exit A.*

MARKETS

Jardine's Bazaar and Jardine's Crescent. These two small parallel streets are so crammed with clothing stalls it's difficult to make your way through. Most offer bargains on the usual clothes, children's gear, bags, and cheap souvenirs like chopstick sets. The surrounding boutiques are also worth a look for local and Japanese fashions, though the sizes are small. ✉ *Jardine's Bazaar, Causeway Bay* ☉ *Daily noon–10* PM Ⓜ *Causeway Bay, Exit F.*

BEAUTY AND COSMETICS

DISCOUNTS SHOPS **Sa Sa Cosmetics.** The fuchsia-pink signs that announce Hong Kong's best and largest cosmetic discounter will become familiar sights on any shopping expedition. Look for deals on everything from cheap glittery makeup to sleek designer lines. Fragrances are a particularly good buy; prices are usually even lower than those at airport duty-free shops. ✉ *Shop G01, Hang Lung Centre, 2–20 Paterson St., Causeway Bay* ☎ *2577–2286; 2505–5023 customer service and branch info* ⊕ *www. sasa.com* Ⓜ *Causeway Bay* ✉ *1st fl., Chung King Express 36–44 Nathan Rd., Tsim Sha Tsui, Kowloon* Ⓜ *Tsim Sha Tsui.*

HONG KONG GOODIES **Kwong Sang Hong.** This shop carries Hong Kong's first local cosmetics line, also known as Two Girls Brand. The colorful, old-fashioned packaging, which is reminiscent of traditional Chinese medicines, is more remarkable than the products. That said, the line's classics—including hair oil, talcum powder, and face cream—do make lovely gifts. ✉ *Causeway Place, Hong Kong Mansion, 2–10 Great George St., Causeway Bay* ☎ *2504–1811* ⊕ *www.twogirls.hk* Ⓜ *Causeway Bay.*

CLOTHING

HONG KONG CASUAL **G2000.** This inexpensive chain carries men's and women's business wear in Asian sizes. It's a great place to look for suits with matching shirts (and ties) for a good price, and it's an especially good find for anyone petit. G2000 also has a few diffusion lines, including **G2000 Pink** for a city-chic look and a casual line called **G2 Blu.** ✉ *Ground fl., Lin Fook House, Jardine Crescent, Causeway Bay* ☎ *2527–8604* ⊕ *www.g2000. com.hk* Ⓜ *Causeway Bay* ✉ *88 Nathan Rd., Tsim Sha Tsui, Kowloon* Ⓜ *Tsim Sha Tsui.*

HONG KONG **Giordano.** Hong Kong's version of the Gap is the most established and
CASUAL ubiquitous local source of basic T-shirts, jeans, and casual wear. Like its
U.S. counterpart, the brand now has a bit more fashion sense and slick
ad campaigns, but still offers reasonable prices. A few of its hundreds
of stores are listed here, but you'll have no problem finding one on
almost every major street. A new line, **Giordano Concepts,** offers more
stylish (and pricier) urban wear in neutral colors like black, gray, and
white. Customer service is generally good, even if the young, energetic
staff screeches "hello" then "bye-bye" at every customer in a particularly jarring way. ⊠ *Ground fl., Capitol Centre, 5–19 Jardine's Crescent,
Causeway Bay* ☎ *2921-2955* ⊕ *www.giordano.com.hk* Ⓜ *Causeway Bay*
⊠ *Ground fl., 43–45 Queen's Rd Central., Central* Ⓜ *Central* ⊠ *Ground
fl., 74–76 Nathan Rd., Tsim Sha Tsui, Kowloon* Ⓜ *Tsim Sha Tsui.*

HONG KONG **Giordano Ladies.** If Giordano is the Gap, Giordano Ladies is the Banana
CASUAL Republic, albeit with a more Zen approach. Find clean-line modern
classics in neutral black, gray, white, and beige; each collection is bright-
ened by a single highlight color, red one season, blue the next, and so
on. Everything is elegant enough for the office and comfortable enough
for the plane. ⊠ *1st fl., Capitol Centre, 5–19 Jardine's Crescent, Causeway Bay* ☎ *2923–7118* ⊕ *www.giordanoladies.com* Ⓜ *Causeway Bay*
⊠ *1st fl., Manson House, 74–78 Nathan Rd., Tsim Sha Tsui, Kowloon*
Ⓜ *Tsim Sha Tsui.*

HONG KONG **Olivia Couture.** The surroundings are functional, but the gowns, wed-
COUTURE ding dresses, and *cheongsams* by local designer Olivia Yip are lavish.
With a growing clientele, including socialites looking to stand out, Yip
is quietly making a name for herself and her Parisian-influenced pieces.
⊠ *Ground fl., Bartlock Centre, 3 Yiu Wah St., Causeway Bay* ☎ *2838–
6636* ⊕ *www.oliviacouture.com* Ⓜ *Causeway Bay.*

HONG KONG **Pink Martini.** Step into this blush-colored boudoir for fresh young fash-
COUTURE ions with spunk, courtesy of brands like Language and Double Standard Clothing. Find the perfect pair of animal print Wellington boots
to match your studded clutch, but be sure to add a few flouncy ruffles
to the mix. It also has a small range of costume jewelry, all nicely aimed
at bringing out your inner girl. ⊠ *Shop 2, ground fl., Bartlock Centre, 3
Yiu Wa St., Causeway Bay* ☎ *2574–1498* ⊕ *www.pinkmartini.com.hk.*

HONG KONG **Spy Henry Lau.** Local bad boy Henry Lau brings an edgy attitude to his
COUTURE fashion for men and women. Bold and often dark, with a touch of bling,
his clothing and accessories lines are not for the fainthearted. ⊠ *1st
fl., Cleveland Mansion, 5 Cleveland St., Causeway Bay* ☎ *2317–6928*
⊕ *www.spyhenrylau.com* Ⓜ *Causeway Bay* ⊠ *Shop C, ground fl., 11
Sharp St., Causeway Bay* Ⓜ *Causeway Bay* ⊠ *21 Staunton St., Soho,
Central* Ⓜ *Central.*

HONG KONG **Uniqlo.** If you are a Giordano or Bossini fan, don't miss this Japanese
CASUAL chain. Uniqlo carries a wide variety of inexpensive, fashionable casual
wear for women, men, and children. New locations have been open-
ing rapidly throughout the city since 2007. Popular items include
T-shirts, jeans, and pajamas. ⊠ *2nd fl., Lee Theatre Plaza, 99 Percival
St., Causeway Bay* ☎ *2577–5811* ⊕ *www.uniqlo.com.hk* Ⓜ *Causeway*

4

CLOSE UP

Boutique Alert: Hip

For years, fashion cognoscenti and victims alike have relied on **D-mop** (⊕ www.d-mop.com for info and locations) to bring out new generation talent, whatever the cost. **Ztampz** (⊕ www.ztampz.com) mixes cartoonish and avant-garde fashion from all over, including up-and-coming designers from Thailand and Japan. Limited-edition T-shirts printed with slick simians are what cult Japanese brand **A Bathing Ape** (⊕ www.bape.com) built

their empire on. True devotees call it "Bape."**Sistyr Moon** (⊠ Lee Garden Two, 33 Hysan Ave., Causeway Bay ☎ 2576–1930 ⊕ www.sistyrmoon.com Ⓜ Causeway Bay) shops, including Soul Sistyr and Hysteric Glamour, offer a distinct blend of cute, sexy, rock-chick fashion from Brazil to Australia. When their cool customers become mothers, they can dress the kids at Hysteric Mini.

Bay ⊠ 2nd fl., Miramar Shopping Centre, 132 Nathan Rd., Tsim Sha Tsui, Kowloon Ⓜ Tsim Sha Tsui.

GIZMOS, GADGETS, AND ACCESSORIES

Broadway. Like its more famous competitor, Fortress, Broadway is a large electronic-goods chain. It caters primarily to the local market, so some staff members speak better English than others. Look for familiar name-brand cameras, computers, sound systems, home appliances, and mobile phones. Just a few of the many shops are listed here. ⊠ 7th fl., Times Square, 1 Matheson St., Causeway Bay ☎ 2506–0228 ⊕ www. ibroadway.com.hk Ⓜ Causeway Bay ⊠ 3rd fl., Ocean Centre, Harbour City, Canton Rd., Tsim Sha Tsui, Kowloon Ⓜ Tsim Sha Tsui ⊠ Ground fl., 78 Sai Yeung Choi St. S, Mong Kok, Kowloon Ⓜ Mong Kok.

Fodor's Choice
★
Fortress. Part of billionaire Li Ka-shing's empire, this extensive chain of shops sells electronics with warranties—a safety precaution that draws the crowds. It also has good deals on printers and accessories, although selection varies by shop. You can spot a Fortress by looking for the big orange sign. For the full list of shops, visit the Web site. ⊠ Times Square, 7th fl., 1 Matheson St., Causeway Bay ☎ 2506–0031 ⊕ www. fortress.com.hk Ⓜ Causeway Bay ⊠ 3rd fl., Ocean Centre, Harbour City, Canton Rd., Tsim Sha Tsui, Kowloon Ⓜ Tsim Sha Tsui ⊠ Chung Kiu Commercial Bldg., 47–51 Shan Tung St., Mong Kok, Kowloon Ⓜ Mong Kok ⊠ Lower ground fl., Melbourne Plaza, 33 Queen's Rd. Central, Central Ⓜ Central.

COMPUTERS **DG Lifestyle Store.** An appointed Apple Center, DG carries Mac and iPod products. High-design gadgets, accessories, and software by other brands are add-ons that meld with the sleek Apple design philosophy. ⊠ Times Square, 1 Matheson St., Causeway Bay ☎ 2506–1338 ⊕ www. dg-lifestyle.com Ⓜ Causeway Bay ⊠ IFC Mall, 8 Finance St., Central Ⓜ Central ⊠ Mega Box, Kowloon Bay, Kowloon Ⓜ Kowloon Bay.

HOME FURNISHINGS

Franc Franc. This Japanese home and living store is sort of like a higher-end IKEA, with everything you'd need to equip your downtown apartment, from bookshelves to bubble bath. The funky, colorfully modern designs and intriguing gadgets will keep all types of shoppers entertained, and it's quite a feat to leave the store with empty hands. ⊠ *2nd fl., Hang Lung Centre, 2–20 Paterson St., Causeway Bay* ☎ *3427–3366* ⊕ *www.francfranc.com* Ⓜ *Causeway Bay.*

G.O.D. This pioneering lifestyle brand plays with ideas, designs, and words drawn from Hong Kong's unique heritage, with imaginative and retro, yet functional, results. Its huge product range consists mostly of home furnishings and tableware, though there are some fashion items; the men's and women's boxer shorts are particularly cute. Affordable creations, such as red rubber trays for making "double happiness" character ice cubes, Buddha statues irreverently painted in Day-Glo tones, and old-fashioned Chinese textiles reimagined in modern settings, manage to be both nostalgic and contemporary. Buy a trendy gift or unique vintage-style postcards for the folks back home. ⊠ *Ground fl. and 1st fl., Leighton Centre, 77 Leighton Rd., entrance on Sharp St. E, Causeway Bay* ☎ *2890–5555* ⊕ *www.god.com.hk* Ⓜ *Causeway Bay* ⊠ *Ground fl. and 1st fl., 48 Hollywood Rd., Central* Ⓜ *Central* ⊠ *Basement fl., Silvercord, 30 Canton Rd., Tsim Sha Tsui, Kowloon* Ⓜ *Tsim Sha Tsui.*

JEWELRY

City Chain Co. Ltd. With more than 200 shops in Asia and locations all over Hong Kong, City Chain has a wide selection of watches for various budgets, including Swatch, Cyma, and Solvil & Titus. ⊠ *Times Square, 1 Matheson St., Causeway Bay* ☎ *2506–4773* ⊕ *www.citychain.com* Ⓜ *Causeway Bay* ⊠ *Ground fl., Yat Fat Bldg., 44–46 and 60–80 Des Voeux Rd. Central, Central* Ⓜ *Central* ⊠ *L2 Shop 50, Festival Walk, 80 Tat Chee Ave., Kowloon Tong, Kowloon* Ⓜ *Kowloon Tong.*

King Fook Jewellery. When considering jewelry stores, longevity is a good thing. King Fook has been around since 1949, promising stringent quality control, quality craftsmanship, and professional service. **Masterpiece by King Fook,** the higher-end King Fook line, sells first-grade diamonds and precious jewelry. ⊠ *Ground fl., 1 Yee Wo St., Causeway Bay* ☎ *2576–1032* ⊕ *www.kingfook.com* Ⓜ *Causeway Bay* ⊠ *Ground fl., 30–32 Des Voeux Rd. Central, Central* Ⓜ *Central.*

SHOES AND BAGS

Milan Station. Even if you're willing to shell out for an Hermès Kelly bag, how can anyone expect you to survive the waitlist? Milan Station resells the "it" bags of yesterday that have been retrieved from Hong Kong's fickle fashionistas. Inexplicably, the shop entrances were designed to look like MTR stations. The concept has been so successful, unimaginatively named copycats have sprung up, such as Paris Station. Discounts vary according to brand and trends, but the merchandise is in good condition. ⊠ *Ground fl., Percival House, 77–83 Percival St., Causeway Bay* ☎ *2504–0128; 2730–8037 customer service* ⊕ *www.milanstation.net* Ⓜ *Causeway Bay* ⊠ *Ground fl., 26 Wellington St., Central* ⊠ *Ground fl., Pakpolee Commercial Centre, 1A–1K Sai Yeung*

Choi St., Mong Kok, Kowloon Ⓜ *Mong Kok* ✉ *Ground fl., 81 Chatham Rd., Tsim Sha Tsui, Kowloon* Ⓜ *Tsim Sha Tsui.*

Prestige Shoe Co. Ltd. Like the Happy Valley shoemakers, Prestige does fashion-forward, acceptable-quality, reasonably priced shoes. Unlike its valley brethren it's more convenient, with several locations around town. ✉ *Upper-ground fl., Island Beverly Ctr. 1 Great George St., Causeway Bay* ☎ *2523–3003* Ⓜ *Causeway Bay* ✉ *World Wide House, 19 Des Voeux Rd. Central, Central* Ⓜ *Central.*

Rabeanco. Hong Kong–based Rabeanco has a reasonably priced line of beautiful, quality bags in Italian leather. Expect designs that are contemporary and colorful, but never flashy or absurd. Buy yours now before the world discovers them. ✉ *Ground fl., 33 Sharp St. E, Causeway Bay* ☎ *3586–0281; 2245–5085 customer service and branch information* ⊕ *www.rabeanco.com* Ⓜ *Causeway Bay* ✉ *L1, Man Yee Arcade, 68 Des Voeux Rd., Central* Ⓜ *Central* ✉ *Ground fl., Hong Kong Pacific Centre, 28 Hankow Rd., Tsim Sha Tsui, Kowloon* Ⓜ *Tsim Sha Tsui.*

Sole Town. A godsend for the larger-footed lady, this expansive neon playground with its slightly spacey decor stocks shoe sizes up to a US 10. There's also a good range of bags and accessories. Expect appearances from Anne Klein, Arturo Chang, and Nine West. Keep an eye out for the sales too, during which you can pick up a pair of heels for as little as HK\$200. ✉ *1st fl., Hang Lung Ctr., 2–20 Paterson St., Causeway Bay* ☎ *2480–2816* ⊕ *www.soletown.com.hk.*

TAILOR-MADE CLOTHING

WOMEN'S
TAILORS
Teneel. The fume-filled thoroughfare that leads to Teneel, also known as Made to Measure, doesn't exactly put you in the mood to talk about evening wear, but you should persist. Teneel Chan is experienced in women's wear, particularly gowns. Although some of her creations are on the garish side (think T-shirts adorned with expletives in Swarovski crystals), clear direction will put her on the right track. Even better, her prices are low. Remember to ask about delivery times, as more complicated work could take two or more weeks. ✉ *Ground fl., 28C Canal Rd. E, Causeway Bay* ☎ *2892–2465* Ⓜ *Causeway Bay.*

EASTERN

SHOES AND
BAGS
Brand Off Tokyo. This Japanese chain hit town in June 2008; like Milan Station, it carries secondhand goods from luxury brands like Louis Vuitton, Hermès, Chanel, Gucci, Prada, and Dior. The shop is also a member of the Association Against Counterfeit Product Distribution, a Japanese organization that uses scientific evidence to determine whether products are genuine or knockoffs. ✉ *1st fl., Shop 120, Cityplaza, 18 Tai Koo Shing Rd., Tai Koo, Eastern* ☎ *2967–6137* Ⓜ *Tai Koo.*

MALLS AND
CENTERS
Cityplaza. An ice-skating rink, a bowling alley, and a multiplex theater are some of the reasons why Cityplaza is the city's most popular family mall. So popular, in fact, that it's best to steer clear on weekends, when you have to fight through the crowds. Toys and children's clothing labels are well represented, as are low- to midrange local and international adult brands. There are also branches of Marks & Spencer, local department store Wing On, Japanese supermarket Apita, and Japanese

Stanley Village Market draws visitors and locals with its bargain prices.

stationery and accessory shop Muji. ⊠ *18 Tai Koo Shing Rd., Tai Koo, Eastern* ⊕ *www.cityplaza.com.hk* Ⓜ *Tai Koo, Exit D2.*

SOUTHSIDE

Stanley Village Market is the reason most visitors come south. Trawling its crowded tourist-laden lanes for clothes, sportswear, and table linen can take half a day—more if you stop to eat. Classy reproductions of traditional Chinese furniture (with price tags to match) are the main draw at the Repulse Bay's shopping arcade, nearby. Farther west is Ap Lei Chau, a small residential island on reclaimed land, known for its vast furniture and antique warehouse Horizon Plaza and its designer outlets—the most famous of which is Joyce. A bridge connects it to Hong Kong Island proper.

MARKETS

Fodor'sChoice **Stanley Village Market.** This was once Hong Kong's most famed bargain
★   trove for visitors, but its ever-growing popularity means that Stanley Village Market no longer has the best prices around. Still, you can pick up some good buys in sportswear and casual clothing if you comb through the stalls. Good-value linens—especially appliqué tablecloths—also abound. Dozens and dozens of shops line a main street so narrow that awnings from each side meet in the middle, and on busy days your elbows will come in handy. Weekdays are a little more relaxed. One of the best things about Stanley Market is getting here: the winding bus ride from Central (routes 6, 6X, 6A, or 260) or Tsim Sha Tsui (route 973) takes you over the top of Hong Kong Island, with fabulous views on the way. ⊠ *Stanley Village, Southside* ☾ *Daily 11–6.*

CLOSE UP

The Choice Is Joyce

Local socialites and couture addicts still thank Joyce Ma, the fairy god-mother of luxury retail in Hong Kong, for bringing must-have labels to the city. Others may be catching up, but her Joyce boutiques are still ultrachic havens outfitted with a *Vogue*-worthy wish list of designers and beauty brands.

Joyce Beauty. Love finding unique beauty products from around the world? Then this is the place for you, with cult perfumes, luxurious skin solutions, and new discoveries to be made. Bring your credit card—"bargain" isn't in the vocabulary here. ⊠ *Ground fl., New World Tower, 16–18 Queen's Rd. Central, Central* ☎ *2367–0860* Ⓜ *Central* ⊠ *The Gateway, 3–27 Canton Rd., Tsim Sha Tsui, Kowloon* Ⓜ *Tsim Sha Tsui* ⊠ *Festival Walk, 80 Tat Chee Ave., Kowloon Tong, Kowloon* Ⓜ *Kowloon Tong.*

Joyce Boutique. Not so much a shop as a fashion institution, Joyce Boutique's hushed interior houses the worship-worthy creations of fashion's greatest gods and god-desses. McCartney, Galliano, Dolce

& Gabbana, Prada, Miyake: the stock list is practically a mantra. Joyce sells unique household items, too, so your home can live up to your wardrobe. ⊠ *New World Tower, 16 Queen's Rd., Central* ☎ *2810–1120* ⊕ *www.joyce. com* Ⓜ *Central, Exit G* ⊠ *Pacific Place, 88 Queensway, Admiralty, Central* Ⓜ *Admiralty, Exit F* ⊠ *Harbour City, Tsim Sha Tsui, Kowloon* Ⓜ *Tsim Sha Tsui, Exit F.*

Joyce Warehouse. Fashionistas who've fallen on hard times can breathe a sigh of relief. Joyce's outlet on Ap Lei Chau, the island offshore from Aberdeen in Southside, stocks last season's duds from the likes of Jil Sander, Armani, Ann Demeulemeester, Costume National, and Missoni. Prices for each garment are reduced by about 10% each month, so the lon-ger the piece stays on the rack, the less it costs. Bus 90B gets you from Exchange Square to Ap Lei Chau in 25 minutes; then hop a taxi for the four-minute taxi ride to Horizon Plaza. ⊠ *21st fl., Horizon Plaza, 2 Lee Wing St., Southside* ☎ *2814–8313* ⊗ *Mon.–Sun. 10–7.*

SPECIALTY SHOPS

ANTIQUES DEALERS

Manks Ltd. Though it had to move out of its former home, a historic house surrounded by skyscrapers and highways, Manks is now far more accessible, and has opened its doors to walk-ins seven days a week. Head to the Wong Chuk Hang industrial district for 20th-century deco-rative arts, European antiques, and Scandinavian furniture, all proffered by the delightful Susan Man. ⊠ *3/F The Factory, 1 Yip Fat St., Wong Chuk Hang, Southside* ☎ *2522–2115* ⊕ *www.manks.com.*

CLOTHING

Hoi Yuen Emporium Co. Of all the cheaper alternatives to Shanghai Tang, this is the best. It has a fantastic selection of Mao collared jackets for boys and girls. Chinese-style onesies come in muted, non-cartoonish colors, and cost less than HK$80. ⊠ *Stanley Market, 64 Stanley Main St., Stanley, Southside* ☎ *2813–0470.*

CASHMERE **Lung Sang Hong.** It's easy to miss this little shop, quite literally set up in a staircase. Although it doesn't sell the cheapest cashmere scarves in town (about HK$1,245–HK$1,400), it has some of the finest, with the quality, diamond weave, and lightness of the fabled "ring pashmina." Men's and women's cashmere knits are also sold here. Ask to go up to the first-floor showroom for more. ⊠ *Stanley Market, Ground fl., 45–47 Stanley Main St., Stanley, Southside* ☎ *2577–6802 or 9323–2360.*

CRAFTS AND CURIOS

Good Laque. These elegant lacquerwares make wonderful gifts. The reasonably priced decorative home accessories, tabletop items, and photo albums come in classic red, black, and metallic colors as well as silver or gold. ⊠ *Ground fl., Stanley Market, 40–42D Stanley Main St., Southside, Stanley* ☎ *2899–0632* ⊕ *www.goodlaque.com* ⊠ *16th fl., Horizon Plaza, 2 Lee Wing St., Ap Lei Chau Southside.*

HOME FURNISHINGS

CARPETS **CarpetBuyer.** With a modern approach to an age-old business, a son AND RUGS of the Oriental Carpet Trading House family sells high-quality carpets from China, India, and Pakistan at warehouse prices. ⊠ *17th fl., Unit 1718, Horizon Plaza, 2 Lee Wing St., Ap Lei Chau, Southside* ☎ *2850–5508* ⊕ *www.carpetbuyer.com.*

KOWLOON PENINSULA

Kowloon is home to the famous Nathan Road, where bright neon lights adorn every building. Locals usually don't shop on Nathan Road, and tourists usually get ripped off there. But when it comes to outdoor markets, Kowloon draws locals and in-the-know visitors who are willing to bargain for their bargains. In addition to good sales at outdoor vending areas such as the Temple Street Night Market and the Ladies' Market, cultural shopping experiences abound in places such as the Bird Garden or the Jade Market.

■TIP→ Visiting all the outdoor markets in Kowloon in one day may be exhausting. You're better off picking three sites you want to spend some time in rather than rushing through them all.

TSIM SHA TSUI

Lighted up in neon and jam-packed with shops, garish Nathan Road is Tsim Sha Tsui's main drag, usually crammed with tourists and sketchy salespeople alike. "What a drag" is the phrase that often comes to mind when shopping here: sky-high prices and shop assistants bent on ripping you off leave you wishing you'd gone elsewhere. Slip down the side streets, though, and things get better. Granville and Cameron roads are home to cheap clothing outlets, while Japanese imports and young designers fill the boutiques at the funky minimall called Rise. Chinese emporiums Yue Hwa and Chinese Arts & Crafts have big branches here—both are great places to stock up on cheap souvenirs.

Although Tsim Sha Tsui is known for its low-end shopping, that doesn't mean luxury goods are out of the picture. The Peninsula Arcade, Joyce,

the vast Harbour City shopping center, and the impressive, colonial-style 1881 Heritage arcade all have a big-name count fit to rival Central's. One contrast is found in the shoppers, who tend to be a bit lower key. Bespoke tailoring is another Tsim Sha Tsui specialty—quality varies enormously, so try to choose somewhere well established, like Sam's.

MALLS AND CENTERS

Elements. This upscale shopping mall is in the Kowloon West residential and commercial district, and just above Kowloon's Airport Express train and check-in station.

The mall is beautifully designed, and is divided into five different zones based on the elements: metal, wood, water, earth, and fire. This is one-stop shopping as far as international luxury brands are concerned, with Valentino, Paule Ka, Mulberry, Lanvin, Prada, and Gucci, just to name a few. A complimentary shuttle bus is available every 20 minutes from 12:30 PM to 9:30 PM outside the duty-free shop on Peking Road, Tsim Sha Tsui. ⊠ *1 Austin Rd. W, Tsim Sha Tsui, Kowloon* ⊕ *www. elementshk.com* Ⓜ *Kowloon, Exit D1.*

Fodor's Choice ★ **Harbour City.** The four interconnected complexes that make up Harbour City contain almost 700 shops between them—if you can't find it here, it probably doesn't exist. Pick up a map on your way in, as it's easy to get lost. **Ocean Terminal,** the largest section, runs along the harbor and is divided thematically, with kids' wear and toys on the ground floor and sports and cosmetics on the first. The top floor is home to white-hot street-wear store LCX *(⇨ above).* Near the Star Ferry pier, the **Marco Polo Hong Kong Hotel Arcade** has branches of the department store Lane Crawford. Louis Vuitton, Prada, and Burberry are some of the posher boutiques that fill the **Ocean Centre** and **Gateway Arcade,** parallel to Canton Road. Most of the complex's restaurants are here, too. A cinema and three hotels round up Harbour City's offerings. Free Wi-Fi is available. ⊠ *Canton Rd., Tsim Sha Tsui, Kowloon* ⊕ *www. harbourcity.com.hk* Ⓜ *Tsim Sha Tsui, Exit E.*

Rise Commercial Building. Many a quirky Hong Kong street-wear trend is born in this fabulous micromall. Don't let its grubby exterior put you off: this arcade is a haven of Asian cool. Japanese designers are particularly well represented—look out for überhip brand A Bathing Ape, which does some of the funkiest T-shirts around. Handmade shoes and oversized retro jewelry are other fixtures—and all at bargain prices. ⊠ *5–11 Granville Circuit, off Granville Rd., Tsim Sha Tsui, Kowloon* Ⓜ *Tsim Sha Tsui, Exit B2.*

MARKETS

Arts & Crafts Fair. Small stalls from local cottage industries sell handicrafts each Sunday and on public holidays outside the Cultural Centre on the Tsim Sha Tsui waterfront. Portrait artists are at hand to capture your likeness, and there's other artwork, jewelry, clothing, and knickknacks. Each stall holder is chosen by a panel of judges who look to promote Hong Kong artists and small businesses. ⊠ *Hong Kong Cultural Centre Piazza, Salisbury Rd., Tsim Sha Tsui, Kowloon* ☎ *2734–2843* ⊙ *Sun. and public holidays 2–7* Ⓜ *Tsim Sha Tsui, Exit E.*

BEAUTY AND COSMETICS

INTERNATIONAL LINES

Aroma Natural Skin Care. This well hidden store has been the secret weapon of skin regime enthusiasts for years, with stock from some of the industry's most venerated brands, many of them hard to track down. Find your Dr. Hauschka, Renee Furterer, and Skin Ceuticals here, as well as the mandatory spectrum of whitening products. ⊠ *Shop 863 Island Beverly Ctr., 20 Carnarvon Rd., Tsim Sha Tsui, Kowloon* ☎ *2506–0699.*

INTERNATIONAL LINES

FACES. FACES is a sprawling one-stop shop, just a stone's throw from the Kowloon Star Ferry terminal, carrying a long list of high-profile and niche beauty brands. It also hosts regular product launches and special presentations by international beauty experts. ⊠ *Ocean Terminal, Canton Rd., Tsim Sha Tsui, Kowloon* ☎ *2118–5622* Ⓜ *Tsim Sha Tsui.*

CLOTHING

CASHMERE

Dorfit. A longtime cashmere manufacturer and retailer, Dorfit caters to a variety of men's, women's, and children's tastes. Knitwear here comes in pure cashmere as well as blends, so be sure to ask which is which. ■TIP→ After visiting the Pedder Building branch of Dorfit, be sure to duck into other on-site discount cashmere shops, such as Aptitude Clothing International and Fabel. ⊠ *6th fl., Mary Bldg., 71–77 Peking Rd., Tsim Sha Tsui, Kowloon* ☎ *2312–1013* ⊕ *www.dorfit.com.hk* Ⓜ *Tsim Sha Tsui* ⊠ *6th fl., Pedder Bldg., 12 Pedder St., Central* Ⓜ *Central.*

Fodor'sChoice

★

Pearls & Cashmere. Warehouse prices in chic shopping arcades? It's true. This old Hong Kong favorite is elegantly housed in hotels on both sides of the harbor. In addition to quality men's and women's cashmere sweaters in classic designs and in every color under the sun, they also sell reasonably priced pashminas, gloves, and socks, which make great gifts for men and women. In recent years the brand has developed the more fashion-focused line, BYPAC. ⊠ *Mezzanine, Peninsula Hotel Shopping Arcade, Salisbury Rd., Tsim Sha Tsui, Kowloon* ☎ *2723–8698* Ⓜ *Tsim Sha Tsui* ⊠ *Mezzanine, Mandarin Oriental, 5 Connaught Rd., Central* Ⓜ *Central.*

HONG KONG COUTURE

Azalea by i'sis. A fantastic place for hip yet understated dresses and separates that will have everyone asking, "Ooh, where'd you get that?" At first glance, this looks like all the other trendy little boutiques in the area, but everything here is just that much better made—and better looking—with a fit that accounts for curves. You can find the same items at select U.S. boutiques, but prices may be twice what they are here. ✉ *A2, Hong Kwong Mansion., 25–29 Hankow Rd., Tsim Sha Tsui, Kowloon* ☎ *2275–3392* Ⓜ *Tsim Sha Tsui.*

Initial. This team of local designers creates simple but whimsical women's clothing with a trendy urban edge. The bags and accessories strike a soft vintage tone, fitting the store's fashionably worn interiors, casually strewn secondhand furniture and sultry jazz soundtrack. ✉ *Ground fl., China Insurance Bldg., 48 Cameron Rd., Tsim Sha Tsui, Kowloon* ☎ *3402–4499* ⊕ *www.initialfashion.com* Ⓜ *Tsim Sha Tsui* ✉ *Ground fl., Style House, 310 Gloucester Rd., Causeway Bay* Ⓜ *Causeway Bay* ✉ *68 Des Voeux Rd., Central* Ⓜ *Central.*

CRAFTS AND CURIOS

Tittot. This Taiwanese brand has taken modern Chinese glass art global. Glass works here are made using the laborious lost-wax casting technique, used by artists for centuries to create a bronze replica of an original wax or clay sculpture. The collection includes tableware, paperweights and decorative pieces, glass Buddhas, and jewelry. ✉ *Unit E, 5th fl., World Wide Ctr., 123 Tung Chau St., Tsim Sha Tsui, Kowloon* ☎ *2397–3021* ⊕ *www.tittot.com* Ⓜ *Tsim Sha Tsui.*

GIZMOS, GADGETS, AND ACCESSORIES

CDS, DVDS, AND VCDS

Hong Kong Records. Although this company from way back hasn't updated its look in years, you'll find a good selection of current local and international CDs and DVDs. The lower profile also means prices are sometimes lower than in flashier retailers. ✉ *Gateway Arcade, Harbour City, 3 Canton Rd., Tsim Sha Tsui, Kowloon* ☎ *2175–5700* Ⓜ *Tsim Sha Tsui* ✉ *Festival Walk, 80 Tat Chee Ave., Kowloon Tong, Kowloon* Ⓜ *Kowloon Tong.*

JEWELRY

WATCHES

Artland Watch Co Ltd. Elegant but uncomplicated, the interior of this established watch retailer is like its service. The informed staff will guide you through the countless luxury brands on show and in the catalogs from which you can also order. Prices here aren't the best in Hong Kong, but they're still lower than at home. ✉ *Ground fl., Mirador Mansion, 54–64B Nathan Rd., Tsim Sha Tsui, Kowloon* ☎ *2366–1074* Ⓜ *Tsim Sha Tsui* ✉ *Ground fl., New Henry House, 10 Ice House St., Central* Ⓜ *Central.*

WATCHES

Prince Jewellery And Watch Company. This shop carries timepieces made by more than 50 international brands such as Franck Muller, Omega, Chopard, and Piaget, in addition to other jewelry, which may entertain those accompanying the avid watch-shopper. ✉ *Ground fl., Bo Yip Bldg, 10 Peking Rd., Tsim Sha Tsui, Kowloon* ☎ *2369–2123.*

DIAMONDS

TSL Jewellery. One of the big Hong Kong chains, TSL (Tse Sui Luen), specializes in diamond jewelry, and manufactures, retails, and exports its designs. Its range of 100-facet stones includes the Estrella cut, which reflects nine symmetrical hearts and comes with international certification. Although its contemporary designs use platinum settings, TSL also sells pure, bright, yellow-gold items targeted at Chinese customers. ✉ *G9–10, Park Lane Shopper's Blvd., Nathan Rd., Tsim Sha Tsui, Kowloon* ☎ *2332–4618* ⊕ *www.tsljewellery.com* Ⓜ *Tsim Sha Tsui* ✉ *Ground fl., 1 Yee Woo St., Causeway Bay* Ⓜ *Causeway Bay.*

TAILOR-MADE CLOTHING
MEN'S TAILORS

David's Shirts Ltd. Customers have been enjoying the personalized service of David Chu since 1961. All the work is done in-house by Shanghainese tailors with at least 20 years' experience each. There are more than 6,000 imported European fabrics to choose from, each prewashed. Examples of shirts, suits, and accessories—including 30 collar styles, 12 cuff styles, and 10 pocket styles—help you choose. Single-needle tailoring, French seams, 22 stitches per inch, handpicked, double-stitched shell buttons, German interlining—it's all here. Your details, down to on which side you wear your wristwatch, are kept on file should you wish to use its mail-order service in the future. ⊠ *Ground fl., Wing Lee Bldg., 33 Kimberley Rd., Tsim Sha Tsui, Kowloon* ☎ *2367–9556* ⊕ *www.davidsshirts.com* ⊠ *Mezzanine, Mandarin Oriental, 5 Connaught Rd., Central* Ⓜ *Central.*

Maxwell's Clothiers Ltd. After you've found a handful of reputable, high-quality tailors, one way to choose between them is price. Maxwell's is known for its competitive rates. It's also a wonderful place to have favorite shirts and suits copied and for straightforward, structured women's shirts and suits. It was founded by third-generation tailor Ken Maxwell in 1961 and follows Shanghai tailoring traditions, while also providing the fabled 24-hour suit upon request. The showroom and workshop are in Kowloon, but son Andy and his team take appointments in the United States, Canada, and Europe twice annually. The motto of this family business is, "Simply let the garment do the talking." ⊠ *7th fl., Han Hing Mansion, 38–40 Hankow Rd., Tsim Sha Tsui, Kowloon* ☎ *2366–6705* ⊕ *www.maxwellsclothiers.com* Ⓜ *Tsim Sha Tsui.*

Fodor's Choice ★ **Sam's Tailor.** Unlike many famous Hong Kong tailors, you won't find the legendary Sam's in a chic hotel or sleek mall. But don't be fooled. These digs in humble Burlington House, a tailoring hub, have hosted everyone from U.S. presidents (back as far as Richard Nixon) to performers such as the Black Eyed Peas, Kylie Minogue, and Blondie. This former uniform tailor to the British troops once even made a suit for Prince Charles in a record hour and 52 minutes. The men's and women's tailor does accept 24-hour suit or shirt orders, but will take about two days if you're not in a hurry. Founded by Naraindas Melwani in the 1950s, "Sam" is now his son, Manu Melwani, who runs the show with the help of his own son, Roshan, and about 55 tailors behind the scenes. In 2004 Sam's introduced a computerized bodysuit that takes measurements without a tape measure. (It uses both methods, however.) These tailors also make annual trips to Europe and North America. (Schedule updates are listed on the Web site). ⊠ *Burlington House, 90–94 Nathan Rd., Tsim Sha Tsui, Kowloon* ☎ *2367–9423* ⊕ *www.samstailor.com* Ⓜ *Tsim Sha Tsui.*

W. W. Chan & Sons Tailors Ltd. Chan is known for excellent-quality suits and shirts, classic cuts, and has an array of fine European fabrics. It's comforting to know that you'll be measured and fitted by the same master tailor from start to finish. The Kowloon headquarters features a mirrored, hexagonal changing room so you can check every angle. Tailors from here travel to the United States several times a year to fill

Don't skimp on custom clothing. Rely on the expert tailors listed in this chapter for classic, tailor-made Chinese clothing.

orders for its customers; if you have a suit made here and leave your address, they'll let you know when they plan to visit. ✉ *2nd fl., Burlington House, 92–94 Nathan Rd., Tsim Sha Tsui, Kowloon* ☎ *2366–9738 or 2366–2634* ⊕ *www.wwchan.com* Ⓜ *Tsim Sha Tsui.*

WOMEN'S TAILORS

Irene Fashions. In 1987 the women's division of noted men's tailor W. W. Chan branched off and was renamed Irene Fashions. You can expect the same level of expertise and a large selection of fine fabrics. Experienced at translating ideas and pictures into clothing, in-house designers will sketch and help you develop concepts. Like its parent company, Irene promises that the same tailor will take you through the entire process, and most of the work is done on-site. ✉ *Burlington House, 2nd fl., 92–94 Nathan Rd., Tsim Sha Tsui, Kowloon* ☎ *2367–5588* ⊕ *www. wwchan.com* Ⓜ *Tsim Sha Tsui.*

Mode Elegante. Don't be deterred by the somewhat dated mannequins in the windows. Mode Elegante is a favorite source for custom-made suits among women and men in the know. Tailors here specialize in European cuts. You'll have your choice of fabrics from the United Kingdom, Italy, and elsewhere. Your records are put on file so you can place orders from abroad. It'll even ship the completed garment to you almost anywhere on the planet. Alternatively, you can make an appointment with director Gary Zee, one of Hong Kong's traveling tailors who make regular visits to North America, Europe, and Japan. ✉ *11th fl., Star House, 3 Salisbury Rd., Tsim Sha Tsui, Kowloon* ☎ *2366–8153* ⊕ *www. modeelegante.com* Ⓜ *Tsim Sha Tsui.*

YAU MA TAI, MONG KOK, AND NORTHERN KOWLOON

The bright-lights-big-city look of Tsim Sha Tsui gives way to housing blocks and tenements hung with aging signs north of Jordan Road. Streets are crowded and traffic is manic, but this down-to-earth chaos is what makes shopping in these north Kowloon neighborhoods rewarding. Well, that and all the bargains at the area's markets. Yau Ma Tei has jade and pearls at Kansu Street; and bric-a-brac and domestic appliances fill atmospheric Temple Street nightly. Farther north are blocks and blocks of brandless clothes and accessories at the Fa Yuen Street Ladies' Market. Parallel Tung Choi Street has cut-price sporting goods. Goldfish, flowers, and birds each have their own dedicated market in Prince Edward, north of Mong Kok. Yue Hwa's five-story Jordan shop is one of the best places in Hong Kong for cheap gifts. The arrival of the cavernous Langham Place changed the local landscape here; the user-friendly megamall has lashings of natural light and a sanctuary-like food hall.

DEPARTMENT STORES

Fodor'sChoice **Yue Hwa Chinese Products Emporium.** Five floors contain Chinese goods,
★ ranging from clothing and housewares through tea and traditional medicine. The logic behind the store's layout is hard to fathom, so go with time to rifle around. As well as the predictable tablecloths, silk pajamas, and chopstick sets, there are cheap and colorful porcelain sets and offbeat local favorites like mini-massage chairs. The top floor is entirely given over to tea—you can pick up a HK$50 packet of leaves or an antique Yixing teapot stretching into the thousands. ⊠ *301–309 Nathan Rd., Jordan, Kowloon* ☎ *3511–2222* ⊕ *www.yuehwa.com* Ⓜ *Jordan, Exit A* ⊠ *55 Des Voeux Rd., Central* Ⓜ *Central, Exit B* ⊠ *1 Kowloon Park Dr., Tsim Sha Tsui, Kowloon* Ⓜ *Tsim Sha Tsui, Exit E.*

MALLS AND CENTERS

Fodor'sChoice **Festival Walk.** Don't be put off by Festival Walk's location in residential
★ Kowloon Tong—it's 20 minutes from Central on the MTR. Make the effort to get here: Festival Walk has everything from Giordano (Hong Kong's answer to the Gap) to Vivienne Tam. By day the six floors sparkle with sunlight, which filters through the glass roof. Marks & Spencer and Esprit serve as anchors; Armani Exchange and Calvin Klein draw the elite crowds; while Camper and agnès b. keep the trend spotters happy. Hong Kong's best bookstore, Page One, has a big branch downstairs. The mall also has one of the city's largest ice rinks, as well as a multiplex cinema, perfect if you're shopping with kids who want a respite from the sometimes scorching-hot weather. ⊠ *80 Tat Chee Ave., Kowloon Tong, Kowloon* ⊕ *www.festivalwalk.com.hk* Ⓜ *Kowloon Tong, Exit C2.*

Langham Place. This mall's light beige sandstone stands in stark contrast to the pulsating neon signs and crumbling residential blocks around it. Yet Langham Place has fast become a fixture of Mong Kok's chaotic shopping scene, with nearly 300 shops packed into 15 floors. It's especially popular with hipsters, who come for the local and Japanese labels in offbeat boutiques ranged around a spiral walkway on the 11th and 12th floors. Extra-long escalators—dubbed "Xpresscalators"—whisk you quickly up four levels at a time. ⊠ *8 Argyle St., Mong Kok,*

Kowloon ⊕ *www.langhamplace.com.hk* Ⓜ *Mong Kok, Exit C3.*

Mega Box. This 18-story mall is a great option for family shopping expeditions: those with minimal shopping stamina can amuse themselves at the video arcade, the IMAX theater, or the skating rink, and there are also numerous eateries. Shops include B&Q, a U.K.-based company that is equivalent to Home Depot in the United States. However, unlike other malls that are walking distance from MTR stations, visitors need to take its free shuttle from the Kowloon Bay MTR station. To catch the shuttle, exit the MTR station at Exit A and go through Telford Plaza; you can always ask the Plaza concierge if you're confused. Shuttles run about every 10 minutes. ⊠ *38 Wang Chiu Rd., Kowloon Bay, Kowloon* ☏ *2989–3000* ⊕ *www.megabox.com.hk/tc* Ⓜ *Kowloon Bay, Exit A.*

MARKETS

Flower Market. Huge bucketfuls of roses and gerbera spill out onto the sidewalk along Flower Market Road, a collection of street stalls selling cut flowers and potted plants. Delicate orchids and vivid birds of paradise are some of the more exotic blooms. During Chinese New Year there's a roaring trade in narcissi, poinsettias, and bright yellow chrysanthemums, all auspicious flowers. ⊠ *Flower Market Rd., off Prince Edward Rd. W, Mong Kok, Kowloon* ☉ *Daily 7AM–7:30PM* Ⓜ *Prince Edward, Exit B1.*

Goldfish Market. Goldfish are considered auspicious in Hong Kong (though aquariums have to be positioned in the right place to bring good luck to the family), and this small collection of shops is a favorite local source. Shop fronts are decorated with bag upon bag of glistening, pop-eyed creatures, waiting for someone to take them home. Some of the fishes inside shops are serious rarities and fetch unbelievable prices. ⊠ *Tung Choi St., Mong Kok, Kowloon* ☉ *Daily 10–6* Ⓜ *Mong Kok, Exit B2.*

Kansu Street Jade Market. Jade in every imaginable shade of green, from the milkiest apple tone to the richest emerald, fills the stalls of this Kowloon market. If you know your stuff and haggle insistently, you can get fabulous bargains. Otherwise, stick to cheap trinkets. Some of the so-called "jade" sold here is actually aventurine, bowenite, soapstone, serpentine, and Australian jade—all inferior to the real thing. ⊠ *Kansu St. off Nathan Rd., Yau Ma Tei, Kowloon* ☉ *Daily 10–4* Ⓜ *Yau Ma Tei, Exit C.*

Ladies' Market. Block upon block of tightly packed stalls overflow with clothes, bags, and knickknacks along Tung Choi Street in Mong Kok. Despite the name, there are clothes for women, men, and children here. Most offerings are imitations or no-name brands; rifle around enough and you can often pick up some cheap and cheerful basics. Haggling is the rule here: a poker face and a little insistence can get you dramatic

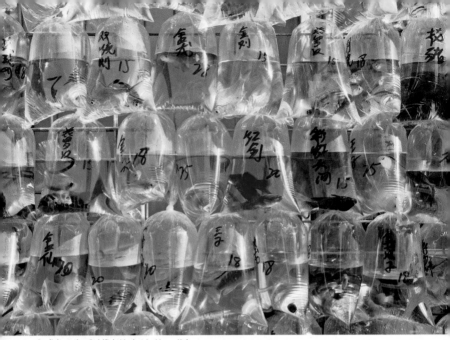

Go fish at the Goldfish Market in Mong Kok.

discounts. At the corner of each block and behind the market are stands and shops selling the street snacks Hong Kongers can't live without. Pick a place where locals are munching and point at whatever takes your fancy. Parallel **Fa Yuen Street** is Mong Kok's unofficial sportswear market. ⊠ *Tung Choi St., Mong Kok, Kowloon* ⊙ *Daily noon–11* PM Ⓜ *Mong Kok, Exit E.*

Fodor'sChoice
★

Temple Street Night Market. Each night, as it gets dark, the lamps strung between the stalls of this Yau Ma Tei street market slowly light up, and the air fills with the smells wafting from myriad food carts. Hawkers try to catch your eye by flinging clothes up from their stalls. Cantonese opera competes with pop music, and vendors' cries and shoppers' haggling fills the air. Adding to the color here are the fortune-tellers and the odd magician or acrobat who has set up shop in the street. Granted, neither the clothes nor cheap gadgets on sale here are much to get excited about, but it's the atmosphere people come for—any purchases are a bonus. The market stretches for almost a mile, and is one of Hong Kong's liveliest nighttime shopping experiences. ⊠ *Temple St., Mong Kok, Kowloon* ⊙ *Daily 5* PM–*midnight; best after 8* PM Ⓜ *Jordan, Exit A.*

CLOTHING
HONG KONG CASUAL

Bossini. A Giordano competitor, Bossini takes a very similar, light approach to casual clothing, as

ITS GOOD TO BE JADED

The Chinese believe that jade brings luck, and it's still worn as a charm in amulets or bracelets. A jade bangle is often presented to newborns, and homes are often adorned with jade statues or other carved decorative items.

indicated by its brand philosophy, "Be Happy." Expect colorful collections for women, men, and children. ✉ *6–12A Sai Yeung Choi St., Mong Kok, Kowloon* ☎ *2710-8466* ⊕ *www.bossinibehappy.com* Ⓜ *Mong Kok* ✉ *Ground fl., On Lok Yuen Bldg., 27A Des Voeux Rd., Central* Ⓜ *Central* ✉ *Cityplaza, 18 Tai Koo Shing Rd., Tai Koo, Eastern* Ⓜ *Tai Koo.*

F.C.K. (Fashion Community Kitterick). One of the trendiest local chains sells several brands including Kitterick, Z by Kitterick, indu homme, K-2, a.y.k., and the Lab. These are clothes that Hong Kong's brand-conscious youth are happy to wear. ✉ *6th fl, Langham Place Mall, 8 Argyle St., Mong Kong, Kowloon* ☎ *2721–0836* ⊕ *www.kitterick.com.hk* Ⓜ *Mong Kok* ✉ *Silvercord 30 Canton Rd.,Tsim Sha Tsui, Kowloon* Ⓜ *Tsim Sha Tsui.*

La Nue Lingerie. Tucked into a residential building on a busy shopping street, these two small apartments are stocked with lingerie of all sizes, including plus-size bras up to an F cup. The products include samples of lines exported to Europe, though the quality is a little hit-or-miss. Stock turns over fast, and with prices hovering around HK$250, a good rummage can turn up gems. ✉ *Flat D, 4/F, Lung Fei Bldg., 36–38 Argyle St., Mong Kok, Kowloon* ☎ *2398–3312* ⊕ *www.lanue.com* ⊙ *10–8.*

Me & George. Anyone who enjoys a good thrift-store rummage will delight in the messy abandon of Me & George (also known as Mee & Gee), not to mention the rock-bottom prices. Clothing items here start at HK$10. Yes, you heard right! Expect a mix of poorly made factory rejects and vintage dresses, shoes, and handbags, and enjoy trying to discern between the two. Fitting is not usually allowed (as is the case with most small fashion import outlets), but staff are often tolerant of quick try-ons in front of a mirror. ✉ *64 Tung Choi St., Mong Kok, Kowloon.*

GIZMOS, GADGETS, AND ACCESSORIES

Golden Computer Arcade. It's the most famous—some would say infamous—computer arcade in town. Know what you want before you go to avoid being dazed by the volume of computer equipment and software. ✉ *146–152 Fuk Wa St., Sham Shui Po, Kowloon* ☎ *2729–2101* ⊕ *www.goldenarcade.org* Ⓜ *Sham Shui Po.*

Kubrick. This is the closest thing to a bilingual community bookshop you're likely to find in Hong Kong, with its stock of alternative-spirited books, graphic novels, magazines, music, and DVDs in a variety of foreign languages. It's also attached to a cinema that regularly shows art-house flicks and a casual café serving basic pastas and panini, and hosting occasional poetry readings or music gigs. Come here to get a good, if slightly unpolished, sense of the city's art culture, and pick up an interesting gift—perhaps book exploring "a Swiss-Chinese Intercultural

---

SHAM SHUI PO

Two stops from Mong Kok on the MTR is Sham Shui Po, a labyrinth of small streets teeming with flea markets and wholesale shops where you can buy anything from electronics to computers to clothing. The Golden Computer Arcade, stuffed with small computer hardware shops, is favored by local mouse potatoes. Prices are competitive, but parts usually come without a warranty.

CLOSE UP

Shopping Hong Kong's Markets

Chinese markets are hectic and crowded, but great fun for the savvy shopper. The intensity of the bargaining and the variety of goods available are well worth the detour.

Nowadays Hongkongers may prefer to flash their cash in department stores and designer boutiques, but generally, markets are still the best places to shop. Parents and grandparents, often toting children, go to their local neighborhood wet market almost daily to pick up fresh items such as tofu, fish, meat, fruit, and vegetables. Food markets are also great places to mix with the locals and engage with the touts.

Some markets have a mish-mash of items, whereas others are more specialized, dealing in one particular ware. Prices paid are always a great topic of conversation. A compliment on a choice article will often elicit the price paid in reply, and a discussion may ensue on where to get the same thing at an even lower cost.

GREAT FINDS
The prices we list below are meant to give you an idea of what you can expect to pay for certain items. Actual post-bargaining prices will of course depend on how well you haggle, while prebargaining prices are often based on how much the vendor thinks he or she can get out of you.

Pearls. Many freshwater pearls are grown in Taihu; seawater pearls come from Japan or the South Seas. Some have been dyed and others mixed with semi-precious stones. Designs can be pretty wild and the clasps are not of very high quality, but necklaces and bracelets are cheap. Post-bar-gaining, a plain, short strand of pearls should cost around Y40.

"Maomorabilia." The Chairman's image is readily available on badges, bags, lighters, watches, ad infinitum. Pop-art–like figurines of Mao and his Red Guards clutching red books are kitschy but iconic. For soundbites and quotes from the Great Helmsman, buy the Little Red Book itself. Prebargaining, a badge costs Y25, a bag Y50, and a ceramic figurine Y380. Just keep in mind that many posters are fakes.

Retro Finds. Odd items from the prewar '30s to the booming '70s include treasures like antique furniture, wooden toys, and tin advertising signs. Small items such as teapots can be bought for around Y250. Retro items are harder to bargain down for than mass-produced items.

Jade. A symbol of purity and beauty for the Chinese, jade comes in a range of colors. Subtle and simple bangles vie for attention with large sculptures on market stalls. A lavender jade Guanyin (Goddess of Mercy) pendant runs at Y260 and a green jade bangle about Y280 before bargaining.

Propaganda and Comic Books. Follow the adventures of Master Q, or look for scenes from Chinese history and lots of *gongfu* (Chinese martial arts) stories, like *Longfumun* (Dragon Tiger Gate). Most titles are in Chinese and often in black and white, but can be bargained down to around Y15.

Silk. Items made from silk, from purses to slippers to traditional dresses, are available at some markets. Silk brocade costs around Y35 per meter, a price that is generally only negotiable if you buy large quantities.

Mah-Jongg Sets. The clack-clack of mah-jongg tiles can be heard late into the night in many public housing estates during the summer. Cheap plastic sets go for about Y50. Far more aesthetically pleasing are ceramic sets in slender drawers of painted cases. These run about Y250 after bargaining, from a starting price of Y450.

SHOPPING KNOW-HOW

When to Go: Avoid weekends if you can and try to go early in the morning, from 8 AM to 10 AM, or early evening for the night markets. Rainy days are also good bets for avoiding the crowds and getting better prices.

Bringin' Home the Goods: Although that faux-Gucci handbag is tempting, remember that some countries have heavy penalties for the import of counterfeit goods. Likewise, that animal fur may be cheap, but you may get fined a lot more at your home airport than what you paid for it. Counterfeit goods are generally prohibited in the United States, but there's some gray area regarding goods with a "confusingly similar" trademark. Each person is allowed to bring in one such item, as long as it's for personal use and not for resale.

At the Markets: Make sure to put money and valuables in a safe place. Pickpockets and bag-slashers are becoming common. When purchasing, check for fake items, for example, silk and pearls.

HOW TO BARGAIN

Successful bargaining requires knowing your prices and never losing your cool. Here's a step-by-step guide to getting the price you want and having fun at the same time.

Do's

■ Start by deciding how much you're willing to pay for an item.

■ Let the vendor know you're interested.

■ The vendor will quote you a price, sometimes using a calculator.

■ At this point it's up to you to express either incredulity or loss of interest. But be forewarned, the vendor plays this game, too.

■ Name a price that's around 70% of the original price—or lower if you feel daring.

■ Pass the calculator back and forth until you reach an agreement, hopefully closer to your price than the vendor's.

Don'ts

■ Don't enter into negotiations if you aren't seriously considering the purchase.

■ Don't haggle over small sums of money.

■ If the vendor isn't budging, walk away; he'll likely call you back.

■ It's better to bargain if the vendor is alone. He's unlikely to come down on the price if there's an audience.

■ Saving face is everything in China. Remain pleasant and smile often.

■ Buying more than one of something can get you a better deal.

■ Dress down and leave your jewelry and watches in the hotel safe on the day you go marketing. You'll get a lower starting price if you don't flash your wealth.

4

Encounter about the Culture of Food" or a photo documentary of Hong Kong's informal rooftop communities. When seeking directions, ask for the Broadway Cinemateque. You'll find a small, upscale commercial branch with a posh café in the IFC Mall. ⊠ *Shop H2, Prosperous Garden, 3 Public Square St., Yau Ma Tei, Kowloon* ☎ *2384–8929* ⊕ *www.kubrick.com.hk* ☉ *11:30–10* Ⓜ *Yau Ma Tei* ⊠ *L6–1a, 6th fl., Millennium City 5 APM, 418 Kwun Tong Rd., Kwun Tong, Kowloon* Ⓜ *Kwun Tong.*

HOME FURNISHINGS

ASIAN LIFE-STYLE STORES **Yuen Po Street Bird Garden.** Though mostly built as a neighborhood park in which bird-owning residents can meet and "walk" their caged pets, the Urban Renewal Authority also included some 70 stalls to be used by those who lost trade when the famous Hong Lok Street songbird stalls were demolished in a revitalization project in the late nineties. Though it sells various kinds of feathered creatures, you can also pick up the picturesque, empty carved cages and put them to better (empty) use in your home decor. Access the garden Hong Lok Street from Boundary Street, a short walk from the Prince Edward MTR station. ⊠ *Yuen Po St., Mong Kok, Kowloon* ☎ *2302–1762* ⊕ *www.lcsd.gov.hk/parks/ ypsbg/en* ☉ *7 AM–8 PM* Ⓜ *Prince Edward.*

JEWELRY

PEARLS **Sandra Pearls.** You might be wary of the lustrous pearls hanging at this little Jade Market stall. The charming owner, Sandra, does, in fact, sell genuine and reasonably priced cultured and freshwater pearl necklaces and earrings. Some pieces are made from shell, which Sandra is always quick to point out, and could pass muster among the snobbiest collectors. ⊠ *Stalls 381 and 447, Jade Market, Kansu St., Yau Ma Tei, Kowloon* ☎ *9485–2895* Ⓜ *Yau Ma Tei.*

SHOES AND BAGS

Right Choice Export Fashion Co. Take a moment to look past the plastic stilettos worthy of an exotic dancer, and you might just discover unfathomably cheap yet stylish shoes (even if they'll only last one season). The sandals are especially pretty and can cost as little as HK$60. Look for shops like this near most market streets. ⊠ *Ground fl., 187 Fa Yuen St., Mong Kok, Kowloon* ☎ *2394–6953* Ⓜ *Prince Edward.*

Sportshouse. Come here for trendy sneakers and other casual footwear by brands like Nike, Adidas, Crocs, Converse, Havaianas, Playboy, Red Wing, and Birkenstock. The shop also offers athletic and casual apparel, and bags. C.P.U. and Match Box, two other chains, are under the same management and carry similar goods. ⊠ *Ground fl., 61 Fa Yuen St., Mong Kok, Kowloon* ☎ *2332–3099* ⊕ *www.sportshouse.com* Ⓜ *Mong Kok* ⊠ *Shop B01, Basement fl., The Elegance, Sheraton Hong Kong Hotel and Towers, 20 Nathan Rd., Tsim Sha Tsui, Kowloon* Ⓜ *Tsim Sha Tsui* ⊠ *3rd fl., New Town Plaza Phase 1, 18 Sha Tin Centre St., Sha Tin, New Territories* Ⓜ *Shatin.*

Where to Eat

WORD OF MOUTH

"For Peking duck, try Spring Deer. Like a restaurant out of the '40s (and I don't think they've changed the curtains since) with florescent lighting, older waiters in white coats, lots of locals at big tables, ducks coming out of the kitchen by the dozens, and only a wee smattering of tourists."

—LAleslie

Updated by
Dorothy So

No other city in the world boasts quite as eclectic a dining scene as the one in Hong Kong. Luxurious fine-dining restaurants opened by celebrity chefs, such as Gray Kunz and Joël Robuchon, are just a stone's throw away from humble local eateries doling out thin noodles served with some of the best wonton shrimp dumplings, or delicious slices of tender barbecued meat piled atop bowls of fragrant jasmine rice.

Never judge a book by its cover—the most unassuming eateries are often the ones that provide the most memorable meals. At noodle-centric restaurants, fishball soup with ramen noodles is an excellent choice, and the goose, suckling pig, honeyed pork, and soy-sauce chicken are good bets at the roast-meat shops. A combination plate, with a sampling of meats and some greens on a bed of white rice, is a foolproof way to go. Street foods are another must-try; for just a couple of bucks, sample curry fishballs, skewered meats, stinky tofu, and all sorts of other delicious tidbits. If you have the chance, visit a *dai pai dong* (outdoor food stall) and try the local specialties.

For fine dining with a unique Hong Kong twist, you can always hit up places like the exclusive and extravagant Krug Room or try Alvin Leung's one-of-a-kind "X-treme Chinese" fare at Bo Innovation.

Finally, remember that Hong Kong is the world's epicenter of dim sum. While you're here you must have at least one dim sum breakfast or lunch in a teahouse. Those steaming bamboo baskets you see conceal delicious dumplings, buns, and pastries—all as comforting and delicious as they are exotic.

CHEUNG
SHA WAN

MONG
KOK
Street food
central

THE NEW
TERRITORIES
Great seafood
eateries off the
beaten path

SAN PO
KONG

YAU MA TEI
Budget eats
along famous
Temple Street

KOWLOON

HUNG
HOM

JORDAN
Home to some
of the city's
best Nepalese
restaurants

Western Kowloon Hwy.

Eastern Corridor

TSIM SHA
TSUI
Eclectic choices
from high-end
to the
basics

Eastern
Harbour
Crossing

Western Harbour Crossing

Harcourt Rd.

NORTH
POINT

Victoria
Harbour

Cross-Harbour
Tunnel

Alphur Channel

WESTERN
Eclectic range of
foreign cuisine
and local eats

CENTRAL
Celebrity chefs
and Michelin
stars

CAUSEWAY
BAY
Trendy restaurants
call this bustling
district home

SAI WAN PO

EASTERN
Cheap eats

PEAK
DISTRICT

HAPPY
VALLEY

JARDINE'S
LOOKOUT

POK FU
LAM

WAN CHAI
Choices abound
from five-star luxury
to noodle-shop
dives

Pok Fu Lam Rd.

Aberdeen Tunnel

HONG KONG
ISLAND

LANTAU
ISLAND
Perfect spot for
dining with kids

SOUTHSIDE
Open-air joints
along the beach

WAH FU

Aberdeen Praya Rd.

Ap Lei
Chau

Deep
Water
Bay

Middle
Island

Repulse
Bay

East Lamma Channel

Luk Chau
Wan

George Island

Chung Hom
Wan

Ngan
Chau

LAMMA
ISLAND

Ha Mei
Wan

Stanley
Bay

Picnic
Bay

0   1 mile

0   1 kilometer

WHERE TO EAT PLANNER

Dining Strategy

Where should we eat? With thousands of Hong Kong eateries competing for your attention, it may seem like a daunting question. But fret not—the 90-plus selections here represent the best the region has to offer. Search "Best Bets" for top recommendations by price, cuisine, and experience. Sample local flavor in the neighborhood features. Or find a review in the listings, organized alphabetically within neighborhoods. Delve in, and enjoy!

Share and Share Alike

In China food is meant to be shared. Instead of ordering individual main dishes, it's usual for those around a table—whether 2 or 12 people—to share several. Four people eating together, for example, might order a whole or half chicken, another type of meat, a fish dish, a vegetable, and fried noodles—all of which would be placed on the table's lazy Susan. Restaurants may adjust portions and prices according to the number of diners.

Western-style cutlery is common in many—but not all—upmarket Chinese restaurants in Hong Kong, but what better place to practice your chopstick skills? Serving chopsticks are usually provided for each dish. You should use these to serve yourself and others. If no serving chopsticks are provided, serve yourself using your own chopsticks; just be sure to use the ends that you haven't put into your mouth.

Reservations

Book ahead during Chinese holidays and the eves of public holidays, or at high-end hotel restaurants like the Krug Room or Caprice. Certain classic Hong Kong preparations (e.g., beggar's chicken, whose preparation in a clay pot takes hours) require reserving not just a table but the dish itself. Do so at least 24 hours in advance. You'll also need reservations for a meal at one of the so-called private kitchens—unlicensed culinary speakeasies, which are often the city's hottest tickets. Book several days ahead, and be prepared to pay a deposit. Reservations are virtually unheard of at small, local restaurants.

Hours

A typical Hong Kong breakfast is often congee (a rice porridge), noodles, or plain or filled buns. Most hotels serve western-style breakfasts, however, and coffee, pastries, and sandwiches are readily available at local coffee-shop chains and western cafés. Lunchtime is between noon and 2 PM; normal dinner hours are from 7 until 11 PM, but Hong Kong is a 24-hour city, and you'll be able to find a meal here at any hour. Dim sum can begin as early as 7:30 AM, but it's unusual to find it served in the evening.

What to Wear

Casual dress—sports shirts, T-shirts, clean jeans, and the like—is acceptable almost everywhere in Hong Kong, although shorts and sneakers or flip-flops will feel out of place at trendy venues and five-star restaurants where people dress to impress. Generally, the dress code in Hong Kong is stylish but quite conservative.

Cru or Brew?

Traditionally, markups on wine have been high here, and wine lists uninspired. French reds have long had a cachet in Hong Kong, but wine lists increasingly include selections from Australia, New Zealand, and South America that are often better suited to the local cuisine and the climate. More people are also getting interested in pairing wine with Asian cuisine, and it's not uncommon to see Chinese restaurants—especially the higher-end ones—create tasting menus designed specifically to go with various wines. Many midrange restaurants and private kitchens allow you to bring your own wine for a corkage fee.

For Cantonese food, tea is traditional, but Hong Kong likes its beer—before, during, or after dinner. It's generally light stuff, like Heineken, the locally brewed San Miguel, or a Chinese lager such as immensely popular Tsing Tao. Several English and Irish pubs have Guinness and Harp on tap. When it's time to hit the karaoke bars or clubs, though, people switch to whiskey and cocktails. With whiskey, it's commonly sipped on the rocks or mixed with sweetened, iced, green tea. Beware: this local concoction goes down very easily.

In This Chapter

Best Bets, p. 164
Restaurant reviews, p. 172
Hong Kong Island, p. 172
Western, p. 172
Central, p. 173
Wan Chai, Causeway Bay, and Beyond, p. 183
Southside, p. 189
Lantau Island, p. 191
Kowloon Peninsula, p. 192
Tsim Sha Tsui, p. 192
Yau Ma Tei, Mong Kok, and Northern Kowloon, p. 201
The New Territories, p. 204

Spotlight On

Central, p. 166
Causeway Bay, p. 168
Yau Ma Tei, Mong Kok, and Jordan, p. 170

Prices, Tipping, and Tax

The ranges in our chart reflect actual prices of main courses on dinner menus (unless dinner isn't served). That said, the custom of sharing dishes affects the ultimate cost of your dinner. Further, we exclude outrageously expensive dishes—abalone, bird's-nest soup, shark's-fin soup.

Don't be shocked that you've been charged for everything, including tea, rice, and those side dishes placed automatically on your table. At upmarket and western-style restaurants tips are appreciated (10% is generous); the service charge on your bill doesn't go to the waitstaff.

WHAT IT COSTS IN HK$

	¢	$	$$	$$$	$$$$
At dinner	under HK$50	HK$50–HK$100	HK$100–HK$200	HK$200–HK$300	over HK$300

Prices are per person for a main course at dinner and exclude the customary 10% service charge.

Using the Maps

Throughout the chapter, you'll see mapping symbols and coordinates (✛ 3:F2) after property names or reviews. To locate the property on a map, turn to the Hong Kong Dining and Lodging Atlas at the end of this chapter. The first number after the ✛ symbol indicates the map number. Following that is the property's coordinate on map grid.

BEST BETS FOR HONG KONG DINING

Fodor's writers and editors have listed their favorite restaurants by price, cuisine, and experience below. In the first column the Fodor's Choice properties represent the "best of the best" across price categories. You can also search by neighborhood in the following pages.

Fodor'sChoice ★

8 ½ Otto e Mezzo, $$$$, p. 173
Bo Innovation, $$$$, p. 183
Café Gray Deluxe, $$$–$$$$, p. 174
The Drawing Room, $$$$, p. 187
Go Koong, $$, p. 196
L'Atelier de Joël Robuchon, $$$$, p. 179
Ta Pantry, $$$$, p. 186
Thai BBQ 2, ¢–$, p. 203
Tim Ho Wan, ¢, p. 203
Tim's Kitchen, $$–$$$, p. 172
Tung Po, $, p. 188

By Price

¢

Mak's Noodles Limited, p. 181
Thai BBQ 2, p. 203
Tim Ho Wan, p. 203
Tsui Wah Restaurant, p. 182

$

Chuan Shao, p. 193
Tung Po, p. 188

$$

Din Tai Fung, p. 193
Gaylord, p. 196
Go Koong, p. 196
Spices, p. 190
Tim's Kitchen, p. 172
Wu Kong, p. 188

$$$

Café Gray Deluxe, p. 174
Fusion 5th Floor, p. 172
Liberty Exchange Kitchen & Bar, p. 180
Sushi U, p. 182

$$$$

8 ½ Otto e Mezzo, p. 173
Bo Innovation, p. 183
The Drawing Room, p. 187
L'Atelier de Joël Robuchon, p. 179
Ta Pantry, p. 186

By Cuisine

ASIAN

Gaylord, p. 196

Go Koong, p. 196
Spices, p. 190
Thai BBQ 2, p. 203

CANTONESE

The Chairman, p. 175
Ko Lau Wan Hotpot and Seafood Restaurant, p. 202
Lung King Heen, p. 181
Tim's Kitchen, p. 172
Tung Po, p. 188
Yung Kee, p. 183

DIM SUM

Crystal Lotus, p. 191
Tim Ho Wan, p. 203
Yan Toh Heen, p. 201

FRENCH

Amber, p. 173
L'Atelier de Joël Robuchon, p. 179
Caprice, p. 175
The French Window, p. 176
Restaurant Pétrus, p. 181

JAPANESE

Santouka, p. 188

Sushi Hiro, p. 187
Sushi U, p. 182

SICHUAN

Da Ping Huo, p. 176
San Xi Lou, p. 182
Yunyan Sichuan, p. 201

By Experience

BUSINESS DINING

8 ½ Otto e Mezzo, p. 173
DiVino, p. 176
Gaia, p. 178
Grappa's, p. 178
H One, p. 178

CHILD-FRIENDLY

Crystal Lotus, p. 191
Main St. Deli, p. 197
Top Deck, p. 190
Zaks, p. 191

GREAT VIEW

Café Deco, p. 174
The French Window, p. 176
Hutong, p. 196
Pearl on the Peak, p. 181
Restaurant Pétrus, p. 181

MOST ROMANTIC

Caprice, p. 175
Lucy's, p. 190
Pearl on the Peak, p. 181
The Verandah, p. 190

CENTRAL

This neighborhood is one of Hong Kong's hottest dining districts. Options are eclectic, from cheap to pricy; Asian to western; good to bad to downright ugly.

(top) Outdoor dining at a dai pai dong; (right, top) The egg tart, a favorite Hong Kong pastry; (right, bottom) Guests enjoy tea time at the Mandarin Oriental's Clipper Lounge.

The Central business district offers classic and generally safer dining options, understandable since it houses some of the city's most luxurious hotels and the restaurant-laden International Finance Centre Mall.

But it's a whole different story when you hit Lan Kwai Fong. Mostly known as a drinking hole with mediocre dining options, LKF has stepped up its game recently by installing some serious restaurants—most of which are tucked away in commercial buildings, away from the hustle and bustle of the street-level bars.

For a wider array of choices, head up to SoHo, but be wary of where you go. A lot of the places are your average, cookie-cutter variety in terms of food and service quality. NoHo is a bit more bohemian, with some truly awesome hidden, independent culinary gems, especially along Gough Street.

AFTERNOON TEA

The Mandarin Oriental's **Clipper Lounge** (✉ *Mandarin Oriental, 5 Connaught Rd., Central* ☎ *2825– 4007*) has long been lauded for having one of the best afternoon tea sets in town. Sandwiches, savories, and miniature cakes cascade down a multitier stand. Classic scones are served with clotted cream and the restaurant's famed rose-petal jam.

DAI PAI DONG DINING

Once a mainstay of the Hong Kong streets, there are now only a little more than 20 licensed dai pai dongs—that is, open-air food stalls specializing in various types of local dishes. These outdoor eateries are popular for their dirt-cheap prices, minimal service, and—of course—their awesome food. There's usually no English menu, so be prepared to point to the dishes at neighboring tables.

Sing Heung Yuen (✉ *2 Mei Lun St., NoHo* ☎ *2544–8368*): This iconic dai pai dong has been in operation for well over 30 years. The canopied tables are pretty much always packed from 8 AM to 5:30 PM, when they close up shop. The iconic dishes here are the instant ramen noodles with beef, served in a sweet tomato broth, as well as the toasted, crispy buns drizzled with condensed milk.

Shui Kee (✉ *2 Gutzlaff St, Central* ☎ *2541–9769*): Fold-up tables and stools are scattered around this small stall, which specializes in cow offal. Tender beef brisket and deep-fried wontons are also popular options.

Shing Kee (✉ *9–10 Stanley St., Central* ☎ *2541–5678*): This is one of the rare dai pai dongs in the area that stay open late into the evening. The menu is pretty extensive, with the home-style stir-fries being particularly good. Chewy calamari in spicy salt is a classic favorite. The adventurous should try the soy-sauce goose intestines.

Leaf Dessert (✉ *2 Elgin St., SoHo* ☎ *2544–3795*): Visit this outdoor stall for authentic Chinese desserts. Sweet soups made with red bean or ground black sesame are served in both hot and chilled versions. Warmed, chewy glutinous rice balls heaped with sugar, crushed peanuts, and desiccated coconut, are messy but delicious.

Ball Kee (✉ *Staveley St., Central* ☎ *2544–5923*): The stir-fried noodle dishes here are especially good. Thin noodles are cooked until crispy and topped with strips of pork and bean sprouts.

AND FOR DESSERT . . .

Tai Cheong (✉ *35 Lyndhurst Terr.* ☎ *2544–3475*) is an ultrapopular bakery that was close to shutting down for good in 2005. But due to immense public support, the bakery reopened shortly afterward and has since expanded to a multichain company with outlets all across the city. Here you'll find all sorts of packaged and oven-fresh baked goods. Crunchy, thin egg biscuit rolls are served by the boxload. Other local delicacies include sugar-dusted Chinese donuts. But it's the egg tarts that steal the show with their buttery crust and custardy rich centers. For western treats, head to **Antique Patisserie** (✉ *46 Lyndhurst Terrace* ☎ *2542–2816*) just across the street, which offers a rainbow selection of macarons, dainty cakes, and other delicate French desserts. Grab a box to go or enjoy the sweets in their beautiful tearoom.

5

CAUSEWAY BAY

One of the most popular hangout spots among the younger crowd is Causeway Bay, which is often compared with Tokyo's Shibuya district. Here you'll find many mid-price eateries.

(top) Hotpot cooking in action; (right, top) The signature "b" logo atop a pastry from agnès b. café; (right, bottom) The Japanese-style pancake, okonomiyaki, on the grill.

For those who aren't sure where to begin, Times Square's Food Forum is a good starting point, with more than a dozen different eateries distributed over several floors. The area behind the giant SOGO department store houses some great street snacking options. If you fancy a tall glass of milk tea dotted with black tapioca pearls, this is the place to go. But Causeway also has its fair share of high-end eateries. They're mainly concentrated in the area surrounding Lee Gardens Two, home to many luxury fashion stores.

Some of the most exciting dining options in the area are the upstairs eateries. Hidden away from street view, these venues rely mainly on foodies in the know, but house some of the best eats in the neighborhood.

HOTPOT

Hotpot is immensely popular in Hong Kong, and places like **Hotpot Instinct** (✉ *52 Tang Lung St.* ☎ *2573–2844*) are packed even during the hot and humid summer months. The large menu offers thinly sliced beef, pork, seafood, and a range of house-made fish- and meatballs, which diners then dip into a boiling vat of broth at their table.

TURNING JAPANESE

Causeway Bay houses some of the best Japanese eats in town. Here are some of our favorites:

Sushi Hiro (✉ *10th fl., Henry House, 42 Yun Ping Rd.* ☎ *2882–8752*): Often lauded as one of the best Japanese joints in town, Sushi Hiro offers fresh sashimi and noteworthy tempura dishes. If you don't want to spend too much on dinner, the restaurant offers good lunch deals, the most popular being the choose-your-own sushi set.

Xenri no Tsuki (✉ *6th fl., Jardine Centre, 50 Jardine's Bazaar* ☎ *2576–1880*): A hidden gem in this always-bustling neighborhood, Xenri no Tsuki follows a strict philosophy of seasonal eating, and their selection of in-season fish is particularly impressive.

Tonkichi Tonkatsu Seafood (✉ *Shop 412, World Trade Centre, 280 Gloucester Rd.* ☎ *2577–6617*): The restaurant specializes in *tonkatsu*—panko-crusted and deep-fried pork cutlet. The pork is crispy on the outside but remains tender and juicy on the inside. The fillet is sliced up and served with an appetizing, tangy tonkatsu sauce, and goes perfectly with a bowl of steamed rice.

Bang Bang Pan Pan (✉ *34 Leighton Rd.* ☎ *2203–4009*): You can make your own meal here, where the signature dish is the do-it-yourself *okonomiyaki* (Japanese-style pancake). Diners are presented with the basic batter and a choice of raw ingredients, ranging from pork belly and squid, to mushrooms to kimchi. Then they mix together their desired ingredients and then place the batter onto a heated grill until cooked through.

Iroha (✉ *2nd fl., Jardine Centre, 50 Jardine's Bazaar* ☎ *2882–9877*): Experts in the art of *yakiniku* (grilled meats), the restaurant stocks top-quality ingredients for the tabletop grills. Go for the premium Wagyu beef selection, but seafood choices are also worth trying. Remember to order the legendary thick-sliced beef tongue.

AND FOR DESSERT...

The **agnès b. café** (✉ *Shop 1–2A, 2–4 Kingston St.* ☎ *2577–0370*) is a great spot to rest your heels after a full day of shopping, with a cup of tea and a slice of cake. Some of the petit cakes are marked with the brand's iconic "b." logo to reel in the fashionista-foodies. Try the dense cheesecake or the zesty lemon tart. Chocoholics should make a beeline to **Awfully Chocolate** (✉ *Shop 15, 2–4 Hysan Ave.* ☎ *2577–0370*). The chocolate cake is near perfection—dark, dense, and divine. It's cocoa at its best. The cakes are available in several flavors—original dark fudge, chocolate banana, or choco with rum and cherry. The dark-chocolate ice cream also deserves special mention, especially since it contains less sugar than your average ice cream but remains as sinfully rich.

YAU MA TEI, MONG KOK, AND JORDAN

These three close-knit areas house some of the best cheap eats in town. While it may not seem like the most tourist-friendly of places (non-English menus, impatient waiters, etc.), you're more likely to score an interesting meal here than anywhere else.

(top) The streets of Yau Ma Tei; (right, top) Pudding from Yee Shun Dairy Company; (right, bottom) The infamous street snack, stinky tofu.

Yau Ma Tei's famed Temple Street is a good place to start. The street hides dai pai dongs and wallet-friendly noodle shops amid the many DVD shops and souvenir stores. Venture a little farther to Mong Kok—the most continually crowded of all Hong Kong districts. It's popular especially for its dirt-cheap street eats. The Tung Choi Street vicinity is especially rich in eateries of this type, selling everything from spicy *Chongqing* noodles to curry fishballs on bamboo skewers.

Jordan is the least chaotic of the three places, but you should still expect a lot of small, independently owned culinary gems wedged in the side streets. There's also a fairly high Nepalese population in this neighborhood, so look out for awesomely authentic ethnic eats.

TASTE OF NEPAL

For a dose of authentic Nepalese food, head to **Yak & Yeti** (⊠ *54 Jordan Rd.* ☎ *2311–1415*). The restaurant serves up all the essentials—sautéed spinach and cottage cheese with herbs and spices; steamed momo dumplings (the pork-filled ones are the best)—complete with an awesome atmosphere and live bands performing Nepalese hits late into the night.

EATING ALONG TEMPLE STREET

This jungle of souvenir shops hides some great local eats. Don't expect any red-carpet service though, and remember to bring cash, as most of these eateries don't accept credit cards.

Temple Spice Crabs (⊠ *210 Temple St.*): Seafood dishes take center stage at this evening-only local eatery. Tables are often crowded with stir-fried razor clams in black bean sauce, prawns in spicy salt, and steamed scallops served on the half-shell and piled high with vermicelli and pungent garlic. It's the type of food that necessitates an ice-cold beer to wash it down.

Lung Kee (⊠ *226 Temple St.* ☎ *2770-9108*): A meal here will probably set you back less than $20. Order yellow noodles topped with their signature wontons, which are sized like Ping-Pong balls and are filled with succulent shrimp. The beef and pork balls are also worth trying.

Tan Ngan Lo (⊠ *151 Temple St.* ☎ *2384-3744*): Chinese herbal teas are served by the bowl at this Temple Street institution. Some of the bittersweet beverages may not be to everyone's taste, but most of them—such as the five flower tea—have beneficial medicinal properties and are especially refreshing on a hot day.

STREET EATS

The street stalls of Hong Kong are filled with interesting snacks of all shapes and sorts. The intrepid should trek over to **Delicious Food** (⊠ *30–32 Nullah Rd.* ☎ *2142–7468*) for their infamous stinky tofu. Dundas Street in Mong Kok is littered with street eats. **Fei Jie Snacks Stall** (⊠ *55 Dundas St.*) is one of the best, with its dizzying selection of skewered choices—from chewy squid, pig intestine (best eaten with a squirt of mustard), and duck gizzard. Egg waffles are another local specialty. **Egg Waffles Specialist** (⊠ *43 Dundas St.*) offers this sweet snack in several flavors—original, strawberry, chocolate, taro, and cheese.

AND FOR DESSERT...

Expect to wait in line if you want to try the famed milk desserts from **Yee Shun Dairy Company** (⊠ *63 Pilkem St.* ☎ *2730–2799*). The velvety-smooth double-boiled milk pudding is rich and comforting. The ginger-flavored milk pudding has a nice spicy kick, making it the perfect stomach warmer—a must-try if you're visiting Hong Kong in the wintertime. Chocolate and coffee puddings are also available. For a summer-perfect treat, drop by **Tong Pak Fu** (⊠ *99 Hak Po St.* ☎ *2866–6380*) for their Taiwanese-style shaved snow ice. Blocks of flavored ice (chocolate, milk, fruit) are put into a special machine that shaves them into thin, ribbonlike sheets that fold upon one another in a mountainous heap. The texture is reminiscent of a shaved creamsicle, richer and denser than regular shaved ice.

HONG KONG ISLAND

Reviews listed alphabetically within neighborhoods.

WESTERN

$$$$ ╳ **Corner Kitchen.** This charming cottagelike space started off originally
ECLECTIC as a boutique cooking school for the amateur chef. It was recently
transformed into a semi-private kitchen, offering private dinners (usually HK$800 per person, including welcome drinks), in addition to
their regular classes. The dining area has a spacious open kitchen,
where the friendly chefs prep the meal with maximum interaction with
the guests; you'll feel like you're at a friend's place for dinner. The
menu is extremely flexible—work out preferred specifications with the
chefs, or have them design it for you. Book at least three days ahead
for dinner. The private kitchen opens only on request, so reservations
are a must. ⊠ *20 Po Hing Fong, Sheung Wan, Western* ☎ *2803–2822*
⊕ *www.corner-kitchen.com* ☖ *Reservations essential* ▭ *No credit cards*
Ⓜ *Sheung Wan* ✛ *1:B3.*

$$$–$$$$ ╳ **Fusion 5th Floor.** A culinary gem in the oft-overlooked Sheung Wan
ECLECTIC district, this restaurant does modern fusion western cuisine sans the
pretentious gimmicks. The food is well thought out and expertly exe-
cuted in a constantly changing, market-driven menu. The lamb rack is
always done to perfection, as are the Wagyu steaks. Reasonably priced
set lunch and dinner menus are available, but the tasting menu (six or
eight course) is the way to go. Their Sunday brunch is legendary in
Hong Kong, and requires several weeks' advanced booking. The food
is paired with friendly and attentive service, adding to the allure of
Fusion 5th. For those looking for a less formal dining experience, the
Fusion owners have opened a gourmet grocery store and café in the
building's first floor, serving artisan breads, desserts, and other fantastic
small bites. ⊠ *5th fl., The Pemberton, 22–26 Bonham Strand, Sheung
Wan, Western* ☎ *2854–1801* ⊕ *www.fusion5thfloor.com* ☖ *Reserva-
tions essential* ▭ *AE, MC, V* Ⓜ *Sheung Wan* ✛ *1:C2.*

$$–$$$ ╳ **Tim's Kitchen.** Most of the homespun dishes at this award-winning
CANTONESE restaurant require at least a day's advanced ordering. But the little extra
Fodor's Choice fuss is worth it. One signature dish pairs a meaty crab claw with winter
★ melon—a clean and simple combo that allows the freshness of the ingre-
dients to shine. The fist-size "glassy" king prawn looks unassuming,
paired with nothing but a slice of Yunnan ham on a plain, ungarnished
plate. Take a bite though, and you'll be amazed at how succulent and
delectably creamy it is. Word of warning—some of the more intricate
dishes can get pretty pricy. But simpler (and cheaper) options are also
available, such as pomelo skin sprinkled with shrimp roe, and stir-fried
flat rice noodles with beef. ⊠ *84–90 Bonham Strand E, Sheung Wan,
Western* ☎ *2543–5919* ⊕ *www.timskitchen.com.hk* ☖ *Reservations
essential* ▭ *MC, V* ☾ *Closed Sun.* Ⓜ *Wan Chai* ✛ *1:C2.*

CENTRAL

One of Hong Kong's busiest areas is particularly crazy at lunchtime, when office workers crowd the streets and eateries. Most restaurants have set lunches—generally good values—with speedy service, so everyone gets in and out within an hour. At night the norm is either a formal dinner or a quick bite followed by many drinks, especially in Central's nightlife center, a warren of cobbled backstreets called Lan Kwai Fong. If you want to sample the expat party scene, you might want to eat elsewhere and head to LKF after dinner; restaurants in this district tend to have a contrived quality, with stylized themes and menus along with relatively steep prices. Admiralty, wedged between Central and Wan Chai, is home to large shopping malls, and much of the food is aimed at meeting the lunch needs of workers and shoppers. It is also home to several large hotels and their respective high-end restaurants.

> ### WORD OF MOUTH
>
> "Lunch at Amber in the Landmark Hotel is a set tasting menu with wine matched. What a great restaurant; service was the best from all the staff. The food was amazing. It really was the best meal!"
> —aussiedreamer

$$$$ ✕ **8½ Otto e Mezzo.** Spearheaded by chef Umberto Bombana (the ex-Ritz
ITALIAN Carlton chef, often lauded as "the best Italian chef in Asia"), this glitzy
Fodor'sChoice space delivers everything it promises. The service is hotel grade, the wine
★ list is extensive, and the interior is nothing less than glamorous. Most importantly, the authentic Italian food here is truly magnificent. Chef Bombana's famed handmade pastas continue to inspire, with the burrata cheese ravioli in black-olive and eggplant sauce being particularly stellar. Mains are solid—the beef tongue and beef cheek is excellently executed, but seafood options fare even better; the lobster cassoulet with sea urchin is absolutely delicious. If you can't make up your mind, the degustation menu offers a neat sampling of Bombana's best. ⊠ *Shop 202, Alexandra House, 18 Chater Rd., Central* ☎ *2537–8859* ⊕ *www.otto-e-mezzo.com* ⊲ *Reservations essential* ⊟ *AE, MC, V* ⊘ *Closed Sun.* Ⓜ *Central* ✛ *1:E3.*

$$$ ✕ **agnès b. le pain grillé.** This IFC restaurant is the most extravagant of
FRENCH all the pain grillé outlets in the city. The restaurant is in the center of the giant agnès b. La Loggia flagship store, and is right next to the faux al fresco patisserie and coffee shop. Pass the reception desk and you are led into the dining salon, which is inspired by an elegant study room. The food is, of course, classic French cuisine. Seafood dishes are particularly well made, with the bouillabaisse being a hearty, no-fail favorite. ⊠ *Shop 3096–3097, La Loggia, Podium Level 4, International Finance Center Mall, Central* ☎ *2805–0798* ⊟ *AE, MC, V* Ⓜ *Central* ✛ *1:E2.*

$$$$ ✕ **Amber.** When the Landmark Mandarin Oriental hotel opened in 2005,
FRENCH its aim was to be seen as the preeminent hotel on Hong Kong Island. It made sense that it would contain a flagship power-lunch restaurant that aspires to a similar level of impeccable, modern style. Chef Richard Ekkebus's menu includes creative dishes such as line-caught amadai with orange and fennel confit and "bottarga" grated potatoes bouillabaisse, as well as sea urchin in lobster gelatin with cauliflower, caviar, and

5

seaweed waffle. ⊠ *Landmark Mandarin Oriental Hotel, 15 Queen's Rd., Central* ☎ *2132–0066* ⊕ *www.amberhongkong.com* ⊟ *AE, DC, MC, V* Ⓜ *Central* ✛ *1:E3.*

$$$–$$$$
ITALIAN

✕ **Bistecca.** Touting itself as Hong Kong's "first authentic Italian steak house," Bistecca has become one of the hottest go-to places for delectable beef. The space is charmingly rustic, decorated with butcher knives, hanging herbs, and a giant display case to show off the restaurant's premium cuts imported from only the best suppliers around the globe. The steaks are all aged to tenderness and are flavored with flecks of sea salt and peppercorns, then prepped simply by charcoal grilling before being drizzled with a little Tuscan olive oil and lemon. ⊠ *2nd fl., Grand Progress Bldg.,15–16 Lan Kwai Fong, Central* ☎ *2525–1308* ⊕ *www.diningconcepts.com.hk* ⊟ *AE, DC, MC, V* Ⓜ *Central* ✛ *1:C5.*

> ### ABOVE-IT-ALL DINING
>
> Central is the place to catch the tram up to the legendary Victoria Peak. A meal in a restaurant at the city's highest point has to be on everyone's itinerary. The trip is justified many times over on clear days, when the views from the top (and en route) are unparalleled. When the clouds are thick and low, though, you won't be able to see a thing—you'll just hear the sounds of the city beneath you.

$$
ECLECTIC

✕ **Café Deco Bar & Grill.** As is often the case where there's a captive audience, dining up at the Peak Galleria mall is a crapshoot. This huge eatery is no exception: you come for the views, not the food. The best strategy might be to come here in time for sunset, hit Café Deco just for drinks and appetizers, and enjoy the vistas; then head down to the city for dinner. Dishes on the overly ambitious menu traverse five or six continents, and are dramatically prepared by chefs in open kitchens (which will, at least, amuse the kids). Oysters are good, and the pizzas and pastas are okay, but you should avoid the insipid Southeast Asian fare and overpriced steaks. When you book (and you must), be sure to request a table with a view, as many tables in the place have none, which defeats the purpose of coming. ⊠ *1st fl., Peak Galleria, 118 Peak Rd., The Peak, Central* ☎ *2849–5111* ⊕ *www.cafedecogroup.com* ✍ *Reservations essential* ⊟ *AE, DC, MC, V* ✛ *1:C6.*

$$$–$$$$
ECLECTIC
Fodor's Choice
★

✕ **Café Gray Deluxe.** In the new boutique hotel, the Upper House, celebrated chef Gray Kunz's restaurant offers expertly prepared modern European fare in a casual and relaxed 49th-floor locale that offers stunning views of Victoria Harbor. A fan of fresh, seasonal ingredients, chef Gray incorporates local ingredients into the ever-evolving menu whenever possible. Steak tartare with Kunz ketjap and chips shines among the lineup of stellar "first plates," which also include the signature saffron pasta fiore served with tangy tomatoes and lemon thyme. Also worth noting are the Asian influences, which creep up here and there to excellent effect. Steamed grouper swims in a Chinese-esque ginger bouillon, sharing menu space with dishes such as roast curry chicken. The bar also offers a unique menu of delicious drinks. So even if you can't stop by for a sit-down meal, drop by the bar for a tipple. ⊠ *The Upper House, 49th fl., Pacific Place, 88 Queensway, Admiralty, Central* ☎ *3968–1106* ⊕ *www.cafegrayhk.com* ✍ *Reservations essential* ⊟ *AE, DC, MC, V* Ⓜ *Admiralty* ✛ *1:F4.*

Lobster and mozzarella salad served at 8 ½ Otto e Mezzo

$$$$
FRENCH

✕ **Caprice.** The Four Seasons spared no expense in creating this stunning space, bringing in well-known designers and feng shui masters, which has resulted in a private dining room that is quite possibly one of the most spectacular in the world: you sit next to an indoor garden, looking through the entire open kitchen, floor-to-ceiling glass, and the great harbor beyond. Crystal chandeliers sparkle in the main dining hall. Chef Vincent Thierry sets himself apart with the details: the menu changes seasonally, but dishes such as steamed foie gras with saffron fennel, licorice, and orange-blossom foam, and hamachi tartare with caviar and watercress coulis are heavenly. The talented sommelier seems to be able to pick the best wine to go with any dish. ⊠ *Four Seasons Hotel, 8 Finance St., Central* ☎ *3196–8888* ⊕ *www.fourseasons.com* ⌂ *Reservations essential* ▤ *AE, DC, MC, V* Ⓜ *Central* ✛ *1:E2.*

$$$–$$$$
CANTONESE

✕ **The Chairman.** The restaurant celebrates a return to authentic Cantonese fare. Using only fresh, top-quality ingredients—from locally reared free-range chicken to wild-caught seafood—and sticking with their no-msg policy, The Chairman celebrates the intrinsic, beautiful flavors of each ingredient. Appetizers are creative—shredded pig's ear and tripe salad is given an extra crunchy edge with the addition of freshly sliced guava; yellow croaker fish are deep-fried and served with aged balsamic vinegar. But it gets even better with the mains. The signature soy-sauce chicken is flavored with 18 different fragrant Chinese herbs. Also recommended is the steamed fresh crab, which is steeped in the delicate and delicious flavors of aged ShaoXing wine. ⊠ *18 Kau U Fong, NoHo, Central* ☎ *2555–2202* ⊕ *www.thechairmangroup.com* ⌂ *Reservations essential* ▤ *AE, MC, V* Ⓜ *Central* ✛ *1:C3.*

$$$$
CANTONESE

✕ **Cuisine Cuisine.** This Cantonese restaurant is one of the best, already gaining praise for its traditional menu (albeit with some nouvelle liberties), like the braised abalone dish served with mushrooms and vegetables. Other winners include the sautéed assorted seafood prepared on a fish boat, and the sautéed crystal king prawns. ⊠ *3101–3107, podium level 3, International Finance Center Mall, Central* ☎ *2393–3933* ⊕ *www.cuisinecuisine.hk* ▭ *AE, DC, MC, V* Ⓜ *Central* ⊹ *1:E2.*

$$–$$$
SICHUAN

✕ **Da Ping Huo.** If you can find the semi-hidden door to this restaurant speakeasy, one of Hong Kong's famed private kitchens, the rewards are great indeed. It begins with a multicourse meal (usually consisting of 13–14 dishes) that takes you on a spicy tour of the Sichuan province and ends with live Chinese opera, courtesy of the chef. The menu varies day to day—it's whatever the chef feels like preparing—so leave your food phobias and quirks at the door, especially if those phobias include a burning mouth: this is some of the spiciest food in town. ⊠ *49 Hollywood Rd., SoHo, Central* ☎ *2559–1317* ▭ *No credit cards* ⊗ *No lunch* Ⓜ *Central* ⊹ *1:B5.*

$$$
ITALIAN

✕ **DiVino.** This ultracool wine bar serves small plates for casual snacking, and mixed platters ideal for sharing. Not surprisingly, it's popular with the drinks-after-work crowd—and you get complimentary savory treats with any drink from 6 to 8 PM. But don't underestimate the cuisine: the tailor-made cold-cut platters, for starters, are superb. The cheese board is served with crusty, oven-warm bread. Pasta main courses include Gorgonzola and black-truffle penne, and lobster linguine with fresh tomatoes. The place also stays open for revelry late into the evening. ⊠ *Shop 1, 73 Wyndham St., Central* ☎ *2167–8883* ⊕ *www.divino.com.hk* ▭ *AE, DC, MC, V* ⊗ *No lunch Sun.* Ⓜ *Central* ⊹ *1:C5.*

$$$
SPANISH

✕ **FoFo by el Willy.** This is Hong Kong's outpost of Shanghai's super-popular el Willy Spanish restaurant. The snow-white interior is all sorts of cute, decked out with designer Kartell chairs and chubby fiberglass animal figurines. For the food side of things, authentic and traditional tapas share menu space with creatively contemporary Spanish dishes. The 36-month aged Iberian ham served with crusty tomato bread, sautéed prawns with garlic, and cold gazpacho soup represent the classic side of the menu. Although these are all well executed, the modern end of the menu offers much more excitement. The scallop ceviche is laid on a bed of creamy avocado and topped with crispy fried shallots, while foie gras is paired with beets and popcorn powder. The "inspired" juicy rice paellas are also worth trying, whether steeped in the flavors of Boston lobster or bathed in the essence of chewy cuttlefish and jet-black squid ink. ⊠ *20th fl., M88,2–8 Wellington St., Lan Kwai Fong, Central* ☎ *2900–2009* ▭ *AE, MC, V* ⊗ *Closed Sun.* Ⓜ *Central* ⊹ *1:C5.*

$$$$
FRENCH

✕ **The French Window.** Style and sophistication are happily married in this modern European restaurant. From the reception desk guests are led through a dimly lit, chateau-inspired hallway before being seated in the restaurant's slicked up main dining room. The harbor view is stunning, and so is the food. Dishes appear like pieces of artwork on a plate—from the seared lamb with pesto sauce, served on a rectangular potato fondant and fit into a crunchy potato "tunnel," to the tiny green baubles of avocado filled with shrimp. If there is one complaint,

CHINA'S CUISINES

To help you navigate China's many cuisines we have used the following terms in our restaurant reviews.

Cantonese: A diverse cuisine that roasts and fries, braises and steams. Spices are used in moderation. Notable dishes include fried rice, sweet-and-sour pork, and roasted goose.

Chinese: Catch-all term used for restaurants that serve cuisine from multiple regions of China; pan-Chinese.

Chinese fusion: Any type of Chinese cuisine with international influences.

Chiu chow: Known for its vegetarian and seafood dishes, which are mostly poached, steamed, or braised. Signature dishes include *popiah* (nonfried spring rolls), baby oyster congee, and fish ball noodle soup.

Hunan: Stewing, frying, braising, and smoking are featured cooking methods. Flavors are spicy, incorporating chili peppers, shallots, and garlic, along with dried and preserved condiments. Signature dishes are Mao's braised pork, steamed fish head with shredded chilies, and spicy eggplant in garlic sauce.

Macanese: An eclectic blend of southern Chinese and Portuguese cooking, featuring the use of salted dried fish, coconut milk, turmeric, and other spices. Common dishes are "African" barbecued chicken with spicy piri piri sauce, pork buns, and curried baked chicken.

Mandarin (Beijing): China's capital city, Beijing, features cuisine from all over the country. Dishes from the city typically are snack-size, featuring ingredients like dark soy paste, sesame paste, and sesame oil. Regional specialties include Peking duck, moo shu pork, and quick-fried tripe.

Northern Chinese (inner Mongolia and environs): Staples are lamb and mutton, preserved vegetables, and noodles, steamed breads, pancakes, stuffed buns, and dumplings. Common dishes are cumin-scented lamb, congee porridge with pickles, and Mongolian hotpot.

Sichuan (central province): Famed for bold flavors and spiciness resulting from liberal use of chilies and Sichuan peppercorns. Regional dishes include "dan dan" spicy rice noodles, twice-cooked pork, and tea-smoked duck.

Shanghainese: Cuisine characterized by rich flavors produced by braising and stewing, and the use of alcohol in cooking. Dumplings, noodles, and bread are served more than rice. Signature dishes are baby hairy crabs stir-fried with rice cake slices, steamed buns and dumplings, and "drunken chicken."

Taiwanese: Diverse cuisine owing to its history and subtropical location. Seafood, pork, rice, soy, and fruit form the backbone of the cuisine. Specialties include "three cups chicken" with a sauce made of soya, rice wine, and sugar; oyster omelets; cuttlefish soup; and dried tofu.

Yunnan (southernmost province): This region is known as the "kingdom of plants and animals." Its cuisine is noted for its use of vegetables, fruit, bamboo shoots, and flowers in its spicy preparations. Signature dishes include rice noodle soup with chicken, pork, and fish.

5

it is that certain dishes may appear overly ambitious, with substance being sacrificed for style. Still, the food is solid, the service is impeccable, and the wine list is impressively extensive. ⊠ *3101, podium level 3, International Finance Center Mall, Central* ☎ *2393–3812* ⊕ *www. thefrenchwindow.com* ⊟ *AE, DC, MC, V* Ⓜ *Central* ✛ *1:E2.*

$$$
ITALIAN
✕ **Gaia.** The concept here at this trendy restaurant is a re-creation of Rome's Spanish steps, complete with alfresco seating. The restaurant is particularly popular with the business crowd, many of whom come especially for the excellent antipasti buffet. The authentic pan-Italian fare includes *pappardelle* (wide pasta noodles) in a Sangiovese-marinated rabbit ragout, and beef carpaccio with the signature Roman-style thin-crust pizzas. ⊠ *Ground fl., The Piazza, Grand Millennium Plaza, 181 Queen's Rd., Central* ☎ *2167–8200* ⊕ *www.gaiaristorante.com* ⊟ *AE, DC, MC, V* Ⓜ *Sheung Wan* ✛ *1:C4.*

$$
ITALIAN
✕ **Grappa's Ristorante.** Don't let this restaurant's banal location put you off. It may be inside a shopping mall, but Grappa's lively atmosphere will make you forget your surroundings as soon as you're inside. The menu offers a wide selection of tasty Italian fare: pizzas, pastas, seafood antipasti, and plenty of meat dishes, all served in generous portions on oversized plates. Choose from inventive dishes like porcini mushroom and goose-liver risotto or *salsiccia luganega*—homemade savory Italian sausage served with polenta and stewed vegetables. The decor is light and modern, with jazz playing in the background, and service is smart and efficient. Book a booth for more privacy, or a terrace-style table if you want to watch the shoppers and strollers and pretend you're on a city sidewalk. Hip, talkative, international types like it here, which means you could happily dine alone and people-watch. ⊠ *Shop 132, Pacific Place, 88 Queensway, Admiralty Central* ☎ *2868–0086* ⊕ *www. elgrande.com.hk* ⊟ *AE, DC, MC, V* Ⓜ *Admiralty* ✛ *1:F4.*

$$$–$$$$
ECLECTIC
✕ **H One.** Inside the swanky International Finance Centre mall, which houses more than 200 fashion brands and high-end eateries, this chic restaurant combines great harbor views with an eclectic menu offering everything from oysters to Mediterranean, and Thai dishes. Surprisingly, the team of chefs here manages to pull off the ambitious menu with great skill, aided by the friendly staff. The charcoal-grilled sirloin is done to perfection and one of the best in town. Diners can also opt for tasting menus of five to eight courses, which cost HK$680 and up, and include dishes such as sautéed US Manila clams, Wagyu beef carpaccio, angel-hair pasta with scampi tails, and Wagyu short ribs braised in Barolo wine. Tip: the tasting menus do not typically include Thai dishes unless you request them. Reservations are recommended for window seats. ⊠ *Shop 4008–10, podium level 4, International Finance Center Mall, 8 Finance St., Central* ☎ *2805–0638* ⊕ *www.jcgroup.hk* ⊟ *AE, DC, MC, V* Ⓜ *Central* ✛ *1:E2.*

$$$
ITALIAN
✕ **Isola.** In the shadow of the world's sixth-tallest building, flowing Isola is everything that the new Hong Kong is all about, especially the outdoor seats amid an urban jungle of concrete, manicured glass, and potted trees in front of the open harbor. But Isola's regional Italian cuisine is authentic, with selections like hand-twisted pasta with Parma ham, black truffle, fava beans, and Norcia cheese; simple and

well-executed stone-baked pizzas; or whole sea bass baked in sea-salt crust, served with vegetables. Even so, Isola is as much of a nighttime bar scene as anything else, and it's worth coming just to sample cocktails in the equally trendy Isobar upstairs. ⊠ *Levels 3 and 4, International Finance Center Mall, Central* ☎ *2383–8765* ⊕ *www.isolabarandgrill. com* ⊟ *AE, DC, MC, V* Ⓜ *Central* ✛ *1:E2.*

$$$
ECLECTIC

✕ **Jimmy's Kitchen.** One of the oldest restaurants in Hong Kong, Jimmy's opened in 1928 and serves comfort food from around the world to a loyal clientele in a private-club atmosphere. The restaurant underwent a major renovation in 2006, adding a full British bar to complement their new look. Its handy location just off Queen's Road in Central and a menu that offers a wide selection of both western and Asian dishes including steak, borscht, goulash, bangers and mash, curry, and burgers have made Jimmy's a favorite with both Chinese locals and tourists looking for a taste of home. It's not cheap, but it's a good choice for a night out with friends, especially if your group's cravings are pulling you in different directions. ⊠ *Ground fl., South China Bldg., 1–3 Wyndham St., Central* ☎ *2526–5293* ⊟ *AE, DC, MC, V* Ⓜ *Central* ✛ *1:C5.*

$$$$
INTERNATIONAL

✕ **JW's California.** Lobster and raw fish are the draw at this sleek, trendy flagship of the JW Marriott Hotel. Slide up to the sushi bar and leave your fate in the hands of the virtuoso sushi chef, who serves up pricey but artistic plates of sushi and sashimi made with incredibly fresh fish. You might also try king crab linguine with chorizo, lava stone–grilled Japanese Wagyu, and finish with the liquid chocolate cake with vanilla-ginger ice cream. ⊠ *5th fl., JW Marriott Hotel, Pacific Place, 88 Queensway, Admiralty, Central* ☎ *2841–3899* ⊕ *www.jwmarriotthk. com* ⊟ *AE, DC, MC, V* Ⓜ *Admiralty* ✛ *1:F4.*

$$$$
CONTEMPORARY

✕ **Krug Room.** This private dining room is a must-visit for the serious epicure. The experience is surreal—guests are led through the hotel's legendary Chinnery Bar and into the back, where a single black door announces the exclusive Krug Room. The long communal table seats up to 12 diners and gives full view of the hotel's most impressive kitchen, where chef Uwe Opocensky and his team are busy at work. The Krug Room is essentially the creative workshop of chef Opocensky, who trained at El Bulli. He labels his cuisine "progressive gastronomy"—perfectly fitting when dishes such as the signature "Rain" salad appear like potted plants with edible soil (usually made with arugula or anchovy purée). Equally fun is the "Meat Fruit"—foie gras disguised as a pear, served with warmed bread. The "Bounty Bar" takes inspiration from the childhood classic candy and combines chocolate, coconut and pop rocks. The menu changes according to chef Opocensky's creative whims, but it is possible to ask him to tailor-make a menu. A meal here isn't cheap; it costs at least HK$2,000 to dine here, but that's for 10–14 courses (sometimes more!) and the first glass of bubbly. ⊠ *1st fl., Mandarin Oriental, 5 Connaught Rd., Central* ☎ *2825–4014* ⊕ *www. mandarinoriental.com* ⌀ *Reservations essential* ⊟ *AE, DC, MC, V* ⊙ *No lunch, closed Sun.* Ⓜ *Central* ✛ *1:E3.*

$$$$
FRENCH
Fodor'sChoice
★

✕ **L'Atelier de Joël Robuchon.** Though his creations come at an astronomical price, Robuchon, the most Michelin-starred chef in the world, claims that his atelier (or "artist's workshop") is for contemporary casual dining. Diners sit on red-leather-and-chrome barstools around a square,

Dessert served at L' Atelier de Joël Robuchon

black marble counter, designed like a modern Japanese sushi bar so that everyone can watch the chef and his staff painstakingly preparing the food in the open kitchen. Though entrées are available, diners typically order several small plates designed for sharing. Everything from the freshly baked bread, stacked in a coral-shape basket, to desserts like the creamy dark Valrhona chocolate sorbet on an Oreo biscuit, topped with raspberry–mango sauce, is immaculately presented. The crispy langoustine papillote with basil; the free-range quail with foie gras, served with the deservedly famous mashed potatoes; and the sea urchin in a lobster jelly, topped with cauliflower cream, are all standouts. Those who do not want to splurge on a full meal should try the superb croissants, cakes, and coffee at the tea salon one floor down from the restaurant. ⊠ *Shop 315 (salon) and 401 (restaurant), The Landmark, 15 Queen's Rd., Central* ☎ *2166–9000* ⊕ *www.robuchon. hk* ▭ *AE, DC, MC, V* Ⓜ *Central* ✢ *1:E3.*

$$$–$$$$
AMERICAN

✗ **Liberty Exchange Kitchen & Bar.** This two-level restaurant and bar fuses comfort food with fine-dining execution and finesse. It's unabashedly casual, from the stylish young waitstaff decked out in clean white shirts and skinny black ties to the menu dotted with dishes such as baked mac 'n' cheese, free range chicken, and waffles. The team behind Liberty Exchange also runs a reservations-only private kitchen in Lan Kwai Fong called Liberty Private Works, which offers a more personal (and more expensive) fine-dining experience. ⊠ *2 Exchange Sq., 8 Connaught Pl., Central* ☎ *2810–8400* ⊕ *www.lex.hk* ▭ *AE, DC, MC, V* Ⓜ *Central* ✢ *1:E3.*

$$$$
SEAFOOD

✗ **Lobster Bar and Grill.** The giant tropical-fish tank at the entrance sets the scene here. As the name suggests, lobster is the featured ingredient, whipped into soups, stuffed into appetizers, and presented in full glory in numerous entrées. Lobster bisque is creamy yet light, with great chunks of meat at the bottom. The seafood platter—half a lobster thermidor, whole grilled langoustine, shrimp, baked oysters, creamy scallops, crab cakes, black cod—doesn't disappoint. Decorated in blue and gold, with mahogany timbers, leather upholstery, and the sparkle of stained glass, the restaurant has a vibe that is at once formal and cozy—and as such, the place is also great for before- or after-dinner drinks at the bar. ⊠ *Lobby level, Island Shangri-La, Pacific Place, Supreme Court Rd., Admiralty, Central* ☎ *2820–8560* ⊕ *www.shangri-la.com* ⊰ *Reservations essential* ▤ *AE, DC, MC, V* Ⓜ *Admiralty* ✛ *1:F4.*

$$$
CANTONESE

✕ **Lung King Heen.** It's made a serious case for being the best Cantonese restaurant in Hong Kong. Where other contenders tend to get too caught up in prestige dishes and name-brand chefs, Lung King Heen focuses completely on taste. When you try a little lobster-and-scallop dumpling, or a dish of house-made XO sauce that is this divine, you will be forced to reevaluate your entire notion of Chinese cuisine. ⊠ *Podium 4, Four Seasons Hotel, 8 Finance St., Central* ☎ *3196–8880* ⊕ *www. fourseasons.com* ⊰ *Reservations essential* ▤ *AE, DC, MC, V* Ⓜ *Central* ✛ *1:E2.*

¢
CANTONESE

✕ **Mak's Noodles Limited.** Mak's looks like any other Hong Kong noodle shop, but it's one of the best-known in town, with a reputation that belies its humble decor. The staff is attentive, and the menu includes some particularly inventive dishes, such as tasty pork-chutney noodles. The real test of a good noodle shop, however, is its wontons, and here they're fresh, delicate, and filled with whole shrimp. And don't miss the *sui kau*, filled with minced chicken and shrimp. ⊠ *77 Wellington St., Central* ☎ *2854–3810* ▤ *No credit cards* Ⓜ *Central* ✛ *1:C4.*

$$$
ECLECTIC

✕ **Pearl on the Peak.** Sitting atop the Peak, one of Hong Kong's must-see attractions, this restaurant offers a 270-degree view of the glittering city far below through its floor-to-ceiling windows. Though the stunning view alone is reason to come, this lofty place has more than a sensational view—it serves good modern international cuisine. For starters, try the seared Japanese jumbo scallops or the carpaccio of Wagyu with leeks, chives, and thyme dressing. The signature entrée—panfried Norwegian salmon with mango salad, cherry tomato, and macadamia nuts—is heavenly. For desserts, try the half-baked chocolate cake with white-chocolate ice cream. The menu changes seasonally. Make sure to book well in advance for window-side tables. For those who just want to enjoy the view, the restaurant has a bar area on the terrace. ⊠ *Shop 2, level 1, The Peak Tower, 128 Peak Rd., Central* ☎ *2849–5123* ▤ *AE, DC, MC, V* Ⓜ *Admiralty or Central* ✛ *1:C6.*

$$$$
FRENCH

✕ **Restaurant Pétrus.** Commanding breathtaking views atop the Island Shangri-La, Restaurant Pétrus scales the upper Hong Kong heights of prestige, formality, and price. This is one of the city's few flagship hotel restaurants that have not attempted to reinvent themselves as fusion; sometimes traditional French haute cuisine is the way to go. Likewise, the design of the place is in the old-school restaurant-as-ballroom mode. The kitchen has a particularly good way with foie gras, and the wine list is memorable, with verticals of Chateau Pétrus among the roughly

1,500 celebrated vintages. The dress here is business casual—no jeans or sneakers. ⊠ *56th fl., Island Shangri-La, Pacific Place, Supreme Court Rd., Admiralty, Central* ☏ *2820–8590* ⊕ *www.shangri-la.com* ⚑ *Reservations essential* ⊟ *AE, DC, MC, V* Ⓜ *Admiralty* ⊹ *1:F4.*

$$
SICHUAN

✕ **San Xi Lou.** This Midlevels eatery is known for the high quality of its spicy Sichuan cuisine. The famous Chongqing spicy chicken is heaped with dried red chili peppers for a sensational tingling, mouth-numbing effect. Another unique creation is the homemade silken tofu, which is bathed in a bright red spicy broth speckled with chunks of whitefish, chopped scallions, and crunchy roasted peanuts. Those in town during the cold winter months should go for the yinyang hotpot—the fiery hot side is perfect for dunking with thin slices of fat marbled beef and the local favorite, deep-fried fish skin. ⊠ *7th fl., Coda Plaza, 51 Garden Rd., Central* ☏ *2838–8811* ⊟ *AE, MC, V* Ⓜ *Central* ⊹ *1:D5.*

$$$
JAPANESE

✕ **Sushi U.** Tucked away in one of Central's commercial buildings, Sushi U is one of the best Japanese joints in the area. The interior is simple—bathed in natural wood tones reminiscent of traditional sushi bars in Japan. Grab a seat at the sushi bar for the best experience. If you (and your wallet) are up for it, go for the omakase (chef's recommendation), which will have the freshest jet-flown items on your plate. Otherwise, the many set-menu and à la carte items are also satisfying. The sake list is also extensive. Ask for their recommendations if you want a good sake to go with your food. ⊠ *3rd fl., Century Square,1–13 D'Aguilar St., Lan Kwai Fong, Central* ☏ *2537–9393* ⊟ *AE, MC, V* Ⓜ *Central* ⊹ *1:C5.*

$$
INDIAN

✕ **Tandoor.** A hidden gem of an Indian restaurant, Tandoor's location slightly away from the main nightlife areas means it risks being overlooked by all but Indian regulars in the know. Look no further for excellent food from a classic, wide-ranging menu and gentle, efficient service. Appetizers and tandoori dishes are particularly good. The large screen showing Bollywood movies and music is the one odd aspect of an otherwise elegant interior, but the effect is not overbearing. There's a lunch buffet on weekdays and a great value dinner buffet Monday through Thursday. Live classical Indian music plays here every night except Sunday. ⊠ *1st fl., Lyndhurst Tower, 1 Lyndhurst Terr., Central* ☏ *2845–2262* ⊕ *www.hktandoor.com* ⊟ *AE, DC, MC, V* Ⓜ *Central* ⊹ *1:C5.*

¢
ASIAN

✕ **Tsui Wah Restaurant.** Finding a hearty meal in Central doesn't mean you have to spend a fortune—especially not if you head here first. Join the locals and order milk tea, and then move on to the extensive menu, which ranges from toasted sandwiches to noodles, fried rice, and Malaysian curries. Although it's not quite what typical Hong Kongers would make at home, it's as close as you can come to Chinese comfort food. Noodles and fried rice are some of the safest bets for timid palates. There's also a wide range of set meals with very reasonable prices. ⊠ *15–19 Wellington St., Lan Kwai Fong, Central* ☏ *2525–6338* ⊕ *www.tsuiwahrestaurant.com* ⊟ *No credit cards* Ⓜ *Central* ⊹ *1:C5.*

$$$–$$$$
SHANGHAINESE

✕ **Yè Shanghai.** This nostalgic replica of Old Shanghai is part of a chain expanding across Asia. The old-fashioned setting includes 1950s furnishings and ceiling fans. First there are the dumplings: an exemplary version of steamed pork soup dumplings, for instance; then entrées like pork knuckle braised in sweet soy sauce, or braised meatballs ("lion's head"). For dessert, try the Shanghai staple, deep-fried egg white stuffed with banana and mashed red-bean paste. Be sure to reserve ahead for the comfortable booths or window tables. ✉ *Shop 332, level 3, Pacific Place, 88 Queensway, Admiralty, Central* ☎ *2918–9833* ⊕ *www.elite-concepts.com* 🖃 *AE, DC, MC, V* Ⓜ *Admiralty* ✛ *1:F4.*

$$–$$$
CANTONESE
✕ **Yung Kee.** Close to Hong Kong's famous bar and dining district of Lan Kwai Fong, Yung Kee has turned into a local institution since it first opened shop as a street-food stall in 1942. It serves authentic Cantonese cuisine amid riotous decor and writhing gold dragons. Locals come here for roast goose with beautifully crisp skin and tender meat, as well as dim sum. Other award-winning dishes include the "cloudy tea" smoked pork, which needs to be reserved a day in advance, and deep-fried prawns with mini crab roe. More adventurous palates may wish to check out the thousand-year-old preserved eggs. ✉ *32–40 Wellington St, Lan Kwai Fong, Central* ☎ *2522–1624* ⊕ *www.yungkee.com.hk* 🖃 *AE, DC, MC, V* Ⓜ *Central* ✛ *1:C5.*

$$$$
JAPANESE
✕ **Zuma.** This funky *izakaya* has been serving good (though pricey) Japanese food since it opened here in 2007 following the huge success of its London restaurant. Located in the heart of Hong Kong's financial district, Zuma's Hong Kong branch makes abundant use of wood and stone in its design, creating a hip but relaxing atmosphere. Chefs concoct primarily Japanese food with a creative twist in an open kitchen. The sushi and sashimi are fresh and beautifully presented on a slab of ice with chrysanthemum-flower petals sprinkled on top. The dessert platter, which includes a chocolate cake that has a melted chocolate center and exotic Asian fruits, is equally stunning. An outdoor balcony allows diners to take in the surrounding Central night view. ✉ *Levels 5 and 6, The Landmark Atrium, 15 Queen's Rd., Central* ☎ *3657–6388* ⊕ *www.zumarestaurant.com* 🖃 *AE, DC, MC, V* Ⓜ *Central* ✛ *1:E3.*

WAN CHAI, CAUSEWAY BAY, AND BEYOND

The range of dining options in Wan Chai is extreme—from five-star luxury to noodle-shop dives open into the wee hours. Right next door is Causeway Bay, which is one of Hong Kong's busiest shopping districts and houses some of the trendiest restaurants in town. Adjoining Causeway Bay on its southern edge is Happy Valley. Though known mainly for its racing track, the area also has some great culinary gems.

WAN CHAI

$$$$
CONTEMPORARY
Fodor's Choice
★
✕ **Bo Innovation.** The mastermind behind this deservedly renowned and upscale "private kitchen" is Alvin Leung, who dubbed himself the "demon chef" and had that moniker tattooed on his arm. Leung entered the dining scene back in 2003 with a private kitchen named Bo InnoSeki in Central. From there, he set up Bo Innovation, which serves what he calls "X-treme Chinese" cuisine, applying molecular gastronomy, French, and Japanese cooking techniques to traditional Cantonese dishes. The restaurant has moved to a bigger spot in Wan Chai with outdoor seating, but Leung's cooking remains quirky and hard to define. The Australian Wagyu strip loin with black-truffle *cheung fun*, or rice roll, is a winner, as well as the signature molecular *xiao long bao* (soup

dumpling). At dinner, choose between the eight-course tasting menu (HK$680) or the 12-course chef's menu (HK$1,080); à la carte dining is not available. Tables are often full on Friday and Saturday, so book in advance. ⊠ *Shop No. 13, 2nd fl., J Residence, 60 Johnston Rd., Wan Chai* ☏ *2850–8371* ⊕ *www.boinnovation.com* ⌂ *Reservations essential* ▭ *AE, DC, MC, V* ⊘ *Closed Sun. No lunch Sat.* Ⓜ *Wan Chai* ✛ *2:B4.*

$–$$
CANTONESE
✕ **Che's Cantonese Restaurant.** Smartly dressed locals in the know head for this casually elegant dim sum specialist, which is in the middle of the downtown bustle yet well concealed on the fourth floor of an office building. From the elevator, you'll step into a classy Cantonese world. It's hard to find a single better dim sum dish than Che's crispy pork buns, whose sugary baked pastry conceals the brilliant saltiness of stewed pork within. Other dim sum to try include panfried turnip cake; rich, tender braised duck web (foot) in abalone sauce; and a refreshing dessert of cold pomelo and sago with mango juice for a calming end to an exciting meal. ⊠ *4th fl., The Broadway, 54–62 Lockhart Rd., Wan Chai* ☏ *2528–1123* ▭ *AE, DC, MC, V* Ⓜ *Wan Chai* ✛ *2:B3.*

$$$
ITALIAN
✕ **Cinecittà.** Come here for fine Roman cuisine in this foodie enclave just around the corner from Pacific Place. As the name suggests, the theme is Italian cinema, centered on Fellini and his works. The interior is mostly white and glass, the atmosphere trendy and elegant, and the food always top-notch. Order from the menu or ask the chef to compose a tasting selection for you. Pastas are homemade and excellent. ⊠ *9 Star St., Wan Chai* ☏ *2529–0199* ⊕ *www.elite-concepts.com* ▭ *AE, DC, MC, V* Ⓜ *Wan Chai* ✛ *2:A3.*

$$$$
CANTONESE
☼
✕ **Dynasty.** Dining on haute Cantonese cuisine at the highest Chinese restaurant in Hong Kong, with panoramic views over Victoria Harbor, is indeed a memorable experience. The expert chefs here are famed for adapting family-style recipes into works of art, and the service here is impeccable yet friendly. The menu changes with the seasons and leans heavily toward fresh seafood. With its high ceilings, Old World charm, and laid-back tempo, Dynasty is one of the rare top-notch restaurants where you can comfortably linger over a meal. Ask for a table with a view of the harbor. ⊠ *3rd fl., Renaissance Harbour View, 1 Harbour Rd., Wan Chai* ☏ *2802–8888 Ext. 6971* ▭ *AE, DC, MC, V* Ⓜ *Wan Chai* ✛ *2:C2.*

¢
ASIAN
✕ **Kam Fung.** The space is dingy, the tables are cramped, the staff is brash—but the food makes it all worth it. Kam Fung has been around for more than five decades, serving traditional Hong Kong café fare, such as crumbly crusted freshly baked egg tarts, and pineapple buns wedged with a thick slab of butter. Wash everything down with their famous velvety smooth milk tea after a meal that's cheap, quick, and absolutely satisfying. ⊠ *41 Spring Garden La., Wan Chai Kok* ☏ *2572–0526* ▭ No credit cards Ⓜ *Wan Chai* ✛ *2:C4.*

$
FRENCH
✕ **La Crêperie.** This French-owned spot specializes in authentic, thin Breton pancakes filled with all sorts of sweets (crêpe) and savories (galette). The space is decked out in a cute nautical theme, with photos of ships adorning the walls and lighthouse-shape salt-and-pepper shakers at each table. Most of the clientele are French, which is a good sign of the authenticity of the food here. Fillings for these made-fresh-to-order

Diners gather at The Pawn.

pancakes range from traditional to fresh and experimental; La Complète buckwheat galette is loaded with a classic combination of egg, ham, and deliciously gooey melted cheese, while L'Italienne is topped off with tomato, mozzarella cheese, anchovies, and olives. The dessert crêpes selection is just as wide-ranging. Le Defi is a winning combination of caramel ice cream, cooked bananas, and salted caramel. Also recommended is La Krompouz—an autumn-appropriate concoction with stewed apples and cinnamon. La Crêperie also carries a delicious sweet apple cider—the traditional drink of choice for accompanying galettes in Brittany. ✉ *1st fl., 100 Queen's Rd. E, Wan Chai* ☎ *2529–9280* ▭ *MC, V* Ⓜ *Wan Chai* ⊹ *2:B4.*

$$$$
CANTONESE
✕**One Harbour Road**. It's hard to say what's more impressive at the Grand Hyatt's Cantonese showpiece—the interior design (two terraced indoor levels, the sound of the lily pond's rushing water, and an incredible sense of space and motion), or the view over the harbor from the restaurant's floor-to-ceiling windows. Unlike many harborside establishments, you don't need a window seat to catch the view. And the Cantonese cuisine is traditional but excellent—for best results, order from among the rotating seasonal dishes. ✉ *7th and 8th fl., Grand Hyatt Hong Kong, 1 Harbour Rd., Wan Chai* ☎ *2584–7938* ⊕ *www. hongkong.grand.hyatt.com* ▭ *AE, DC, MC, V* Ⓜ *Wan Chai* ⊹ *2:C2.*

$$
CANTONESE
✕**OVOlogue**. In one of Hong Kong's last remaining colonial buildings, this stylish and innovative Cantonese restaurant offers an elegant respite from the hectic shopping streets of Wan Chai. The menu includes dim sum with a few novel additions, as well as a selection of popular Cantonese dishes. The decor—1920s Shanghai style—is exquisitely executed and evokes a bygone Chinese era. This is a good choice for diners

who want to try Cantonese cuisine and dim sum in beautiful surroundings. ⊠ *66 Johnston Rd., Wan Chai* ☎ *2527–6088* ⊟ *AE, DC, MC, V* Ⓜ *Wan Chai* ✛ *2:C3.*

$$–$$$
BRITISH

✕ **The Pawn.** In the same refurbished old heritage pawn shop as OVOlogue, the Pawn serves high-end British gastropub fare in stunning environs. The first floor "living room" bar and lounge is a great drinking spot with its wide array of beers, cocktails, and whiskies. The upstairs dining room is the best place to enjoy the full food potential of the restaurant. The signature fish-and-chips is stellar, served with their homemade tartar sauce. The third-floor open-air rooftop terrace affords breathtaking views of the busy Wan Chai district. ⊠ *62 Johnston St., Wan Chai* ☎ *2866–3444* ⊕ *www.thepawn.com.hk* ⊟ *AE, MC, V* Ⓜ *Wan Chai* ✛ *2:C3.*

$$$$
ECLECTIC
Fodor's Choice
★

✕ **Ta Pantry.** In a quiet residential building, chef Esther Sham's private kitchen is one of the coziest and most charming places in town. The space is decorated with cookbooks, cooking utensils, wine bottles, and many of the chef's other prized possessions. Diners can choose from five different themed menus, including Japanese, Shanghainese, New American, Indochine, and a menu De Luxe. The crabmeat ravioli in lemongrass-scented chicken jus from the Indochine menu is stunning, as is the coco balsamic linguine with mushrooms. The signature melting onion duck is deliciously rich and worth every penny of the supplementary HK$150. Only one table, seating a maximum of 10 people, is served per evening, so reservations are compulsory (one week advance notice is recommended). Also note that there is a minimum charge (HK$4,400–HK$5,500 for dinner; HK$2,200 for weekday lunch). ⊠ *1C, Moon Star Ct., 2D Star St., Wan Chai* ☎ *9403–6430* ✍ *Reservations essential* ⊟ *No credit cards* Ⓜ *Wan Chai* ✛ *2:A3.*

$$$
SEAFOOD

✕ **Victoria City Seafood.** This perennially popular restaurant excels at Cantonese dim sum, Shanghainese, and seafood. It's a big, bright, banquet-style space, generally packed with large groups. Not to be missed are the spectacular soup dumplings with hairy-crab roe and stir-fried rice rolls with XO sauce. Seafood, which you select live from the tank, might include whitebait in chili sauce, steamed prawns in vinegar sauce, or crab cooked with fried garlic. ⊠ *Sun Hung Kai Center, 30 Harbour Rd., Wan Chai* ☎ *2827–9938* ⊠ *5th fl. Citic Tower, 1 Tim Mei Ave., Admiralty* ☎ *2877–2211* ⊟ *AE, DC, MC, V* Ⓜ *Wan Chai* ✛ *2:D2.*

CAUSEWAY BAY

¢
ASIAN

✕ **Café Match Box.** The decor, staff uniforms, and—of course—the food all capture the retro vibe of the typical 1960s Hong Kong *cha chaan teng* (local café). Classic Cantonese pop songs from that era play over the sound system while diners relish bowls of rice vermicelli or elbow macaroni served in soup and topped with spam and fried eggs. Other *cha chaan teng* staples include fluffy egg and ham sandwiches, baked rice, and spaghetti served in chicken broth with green peas. But it's the pastries and sweets that stand out the most. The freshly baked egg tarts are rich and custardy, and the French toasts are served with a giant slab of butter, ready to be doused with golden syrup. For the best item in the house, go for the hotcakes stack—a delicious concoction topped with sliced bananas, buttered walnuts, and soft-serve ice cream drizzled with caramel sauce. ✉ *8 Cleveland St., Causeway Bay* ☎ *2868–0363* ▭ *MC, V* Ⓜ *Causeway Bay* ✥ *2:G2.*

$–$$
CANTONESE

✕ **Dim Sum.** This elegant jewel breaks with tradition and serves dim sum during the day and in the nighttime. The original menu goes beyond common Cantonese morsels like *har gau* (steamed shrimp dumplings), embracing dishes more popular in the north, including chili prawn dumplings, Beijing onion cakes, and steamed buns. Luxury dim sum items, such as siu mai topped with shark's fin and abalone dumplings are particularly popular. Lunch reservations are not taken on weekends, so there's always a long line. Arrive early, or admire the antique telephones and old Chinese posters while you wait. Even if it feels somewhat contrived, it's worth it. ✉ *63 Sing Woo Rd., Happy Valley, Causeway Bay* ☎ *2834–8893* ▭ *AE, MC, V* Ⓜ *Causeway Bay* ✥ *2:F6.*

$$$$
ITALIAN
Fodor'sChoice
★

✕ **The Drawing Room.** Within the stylish Philippe Starck-designed JIA boutique hotel, the Drawing Room serves contemporary Italian fare in a slicked up, artfully decorated space. The menu is tweaked every few days depending on what's fresh and the kitchen team's creative culinary whims. Several popular signatures are almost always available though, such as the panfried quail and foie gras, and the inspiring trio of Wagyu short rib, Wagyu beef tenderloin, and ox tongue. Two different tasting menu options are offered every night, but the dishes are also available for à la carte ordering. The place is a dining hot spot, so reservations are a definite must. ✉ *1st fl., JIA Boutique Hotel,1–5 Irving St., Causeway Bay* ☎ *2915–6628* ⊕ *www.thedrawingroom.com.hk* ⌕ *Reservations essential* ▭ *AE, MC, V* ☉ *Closed Sun.* Ⓜ *Central* ✥ *2:G3.*

$$
HUNAN

✕ **Hunan Garden.** Run by Hong Kong's largest restaurant chain, Maxim's, this eatery serves Hunan cuisine that has been watered down for Hong Kongers' mild palates. The elegant black-and-white decor resembles a European restaurant more than a typical Chinese joint. Dishes may not be spicy-hot, but the signature dish—codfish fillet with fried minced beans, a chewy and nutty bean paste—is well worth trying. So is the smooth Hunan chicken soup with minced chicken and pork, served in a small porcelain container. Those who like the orange-color sweet-and-sour sauce may want to try the Beijing-style deep-fried prawns in chili sauce. ✉ *Shop 1302, 13th fl., Food Forum, Times Square, Causeway Bay* ☎ *2506–9288* ▭ *AE, DC, MC, V* Ⓜ *Causeway Bay* ✥ *2:F3.*

$–$$
JAPANESE

✕ **Nan Tei.** One of the most established and best izakayas in town, this place is always buzzing. The aproned waitstaff serves up plate upon plate of *yakitori* and *kushiyaki* (grilled skewered items) amidst a raucously jovial atmosphere. A seat at the bar gives full view of the busy chefs working the grill. The skewered ox tongue is exceptional—succulent, soft, and flavored with just the right pinch of salt. Kushiyaki staples, such as grilled chicken wings and shiitake mushrooms are also all up to standard. Nightly specials are displayed on a chalkboard. And in true izakaya fashion, Nan Tei offers a well-ranging sake list to accompany the bite-sized nosh. A great place for a casual Japanese meal with good food and a couple of drinks. ✉ *6–10 Sun Wui Rd., Causeway Bay* ☎ *3118–2501* ▭ *AE, MC, V* Ⓜ *Causeway Bay* ✥ *2:F3.*

$$$
JAPANESE

✕ **Sushi Hiro.** *Uni* (sea urchin), *shirako* (blowfish sperm), *o-toro* (the fattiest of fatty tuna). If these words make you drool, then you should make a beeline for Sushi Hiro, buried within an office building, and quite possibly the best place for raw fish in Hong Kong. The minimalist interior stays faithful to Japanese style, unlike some more opulent Hong Kong restaurants. But what really draws in the Japanese crowd is the freshness of the fish, which you can watch being filleted in front of you at the sushi bar. Dinner may get a little pricey, but the restaurant also does some fantastic lunch deals. ⊠ *10th fl., Henry House, 42 Yun Ping Rd., Causeway Bay* ☎ *2882–8752* ▤ *AE, DC, MC, V* Ⓜ *Causeway Bay* ✛ *2:F3.*

$$ ╳ **Wu Kong.** This chain restaurant right next to Hunan Garden serves
SHANGHAINESE good Shanghainese fare at reasonable prices. Pigeon in wine sauce is an excellent appetizer, and the honey-ham and crispy bean-curd skin wrapped in soft bread is delicious and authentic. Be sure to try their tofu dumplings, which require advanced ordering. The Shanghai-style doughnut on the dessert menu is a deep-fried sweet ball whipped up with fluffy egg whites and stuffed with red bean and banana. The set lunch, which includes an appetizer, a main dish, dim sum of your choice, and free dessert, is a great value. ⊠ *13th fl., Food Forum, Times Square, 1 Matheson St., Causeway Bay* ☎ *2506–1018* ⊕ *www.wukong.com.hk* ▤ *AE, DC, MC, V* Ⓜ *Causeway Bay* ✛ *2:F3.*

EASTERN

¢ ╳ **Santouka.** This Hokkaido-imported chain does some of the best Japa-
JAPANESE nese ramen in town. The noodles are thick, glossy, and perfectly al dente. But it's the sensational savory broths that set Santouka apart. The signature *shio* (soy sauce) broth coats each strand of noodle to flavor perfection. The salt- and miso-flavored broths are also delicious. Topped with slices of fatty *chasiu* (Japanese roast pork) and kelp, this a simple bowl of noodles worth making a special trip to try. Even better, we recommend topping the glistening yellow noodles with a Japanese-style poached egg—the runny yolk adds an indescribable dimension to the already amazing noodles. ⊠ *Jusco, Kornhill Plaza, 1 Kornhill Rd., Quarry Bay, Eastern* ☎ *2967–4044* ▤ *MC, V* Ⓜ *Tai Koo* ✛ *2:H3.*

$$–$$$ ╳ **Tapeo.** This is the second outpost of this über-popular modern tapas
SPANISH bar (the original one is in SoHo). The Eastern District branch is bigger than the original, and boasts an awesome harborside location, which adds to the chill, laid-back vibe. Authentic Spanish tapas, with dishes such as ham croquettes and sautéed mushrooms with sherry, are perfect for sharing. The crispy pork belly served with quince aioli rocks, and hearty paellas are an expansion from the original menu. ⊠ *GA01– 03,55 Tai Hong St., Sai Wan Ho, Eastern* ☎ *2513–0199* ⊕ *www. conceptcreations.hk* ▤ *AE, MC, V* Ⓜ *Sai Wan Ho* ✛ *2:H3.*

$ ╳ **Tung Po.** Arguably Hong Kong's most famous—if not most perpetu-
CANTONESE ally packed—indoor dai pai dong. Tung Po takes over five stall spaces
Fodor's Choice in Java Road market's cooked food center, boasting tables large enough
★ to fit 18 guests and with walls scribbled with their ever-growing list of specials. The food is Hong Kong cuisine with a few fusion innovations. Try the spaghetti with chewy rounds of cuttlefish, which is flavored and dyed with aromatic jet-black fresh squid ink and sprinkled with chopped herbs. The seafood dishes and stir-fries are all satisfying, but it's really the atmosphere that makes Tung Po a must-visit spot. Owner

CLOSE UP

Sharks Fin Soup

It makes sense that soup made from shark's fin—said to be an aphrodisiac—costs so much. Only the promise of increased virility would lead someone to pay HK$1,000 or more for a bowl of the stuff. It actually consists of cartilage from the great beast's pectal, dorsal, and lower tail fins that has been skinned, dried, and reconstituted in a rich stock form. This cartilage has almost no taste on its own, and is virtually indistinguishable from *tun fun* (cellophane) noodles that are used to create "mock shark's-fin soup."

Selling shark's fins is a big business, and Hong Kong is said to be responsible for 50% of the global trade. The soup is a fixture at banquets, weddings, and state dinners here. Love potion, elixir, vitality booster, or not, at the very least the dish is high in protein. Recently, however, conservation groups have pointed out that it's also high in mercury. But of even greater concern is the practice of "finning." Since shark meat as a whole isn't valuable, fishermen often clip the fins and dump the rest of the animal back into the sea.

So, is eating shark's-fin soup a not-to-be-missed Hong Kong experience or a morally reprehensible act? Well, we don't need to take sides in the debate to warn you away from it. Let us repeat: the shark's-fin cartilage *has no taste*. This makes it—and bird's-nest soup, that other tasteless Cantonese delicacy—one of the biggest wastes of money in the culinary universe.

5

Robby Cheung is one of the friendliest and most delightful characters in the Hong Kong food and beverage industry. Later in the evening, he'll blast the latest pop songs from the sound system. And if you're lucky, you might just catch him in one of his moonwalking moods. ✉ *2nd fl., Java Road Cooked Food Centre, 99 Java Rd., North Point, Eastern* ☎ *2880–9399* ▭ *No credit cards* Ⓜ *North Point* ✛ *2:H3.*

SOUTHSIDE

The south side of Hong Kong Island is a string of beaches, rocky coves, and luxury developments; Repulse Bay, 20 minutes away by bus from Central, is comprised of all three. The Repulse Bay complex also has some good restaurants, most of which boast alfresco seating so diners can take full advantage of the sea breeze. A visit to Stanley Village reveals another side of Hong Kong, with a much slower pace of life than the one you see in the city. After exploring the market, historic sights, and beaches, take a leisurely meal at one of the top-notch restaurants scattered around, some of which have harbor views. Stanley is 30 minutes by bus or taxi from Central.

Also on Southside, Shek O is a tiny seaside village with a few decent open-air restaurants. Once you've made the trek—the longest overland trip possible from Central—you'll need some sustenance.

$$$–$$$$

MEDITERRANEAN

✕ **The Boathouse.** The cozy Boathouse has a lovely view of the seafront, making it the perfect spot to hang out with friends and family. A bucket of mussels, served with nicely toasted garlic bread, goes down well with a glass of chilled white wine. Sandwiches and pastas are good bets for casual dining. ⊠ *86–88 Stanley Main St., Stanley, Southside* ☎ *2813–4467* ⊟ *AE, DC, MC, V* ✛ *2:E6.*

$$$
MEDITERRANEAN

✕ **Lucy's.** Turn left after Delifrance to find this warm, intimate eatery hidden inside the famous Stanley Market and rarely uncovered by tourists. You may feel like you've walked into someone's house when you enter the small, shabby-chic dining room, but Lucy's is a professionally run restaurant offering excellent, home-cooked food. The daily specials are a very safe bet, and often include risottos and grilled or roasted meat; there are also plenty of fresh fruits and veggies on the menu. Desserts, especially the pecan pudding with toffee cream sauce, are not to be missed. More upscale than most of the beachside restaurants here and with oodles more character, Lucy's is a perfect end to a relaxed day browsing in the market, and easily your best bet in Stanley. ⊠ *Ground fl., 64 Stanley Main St., Stanley, Southside* ☎ *2813–9055* ⊟ *AE, MC, V* ✛ *2:E6.*

$
ASIAN

✕ **Shek O Chinese & Thai Seafood Restaurant.** The seaside village of Shek O lies past Stanley, and is worth a trip for the large sandy beach and fresh local seafood. For the quality and variety of food, this casual eatery is an all-time favorite. Come here for simple seaside dining at its best—the menu is extensive, and everything's good and fresh—but prepare for plastic tables and toilets that are best approached with caution. This is a great spot for relaxing and dining with friends or family for a very reasonable price. ⊠ *303 Shek O Village, main intersection, next to bus stop, Shek O, Southside* ☎ *2809–4426 or 2809–2202* ⊟ *AE, DC, MC, V* ✛ *2:F5.*

$$
ASIAN

✕ **Spices.** Inside the Repulse Bay luxury residential complex, Spices is a staunch favorite among well-heeled locals in search of relaxed dining. The menu offers favorites from throughout Asia. Service is friendly and professional. The mango salad and deep-fried prawn cakes are excellent. Other choices include tandoori dishes, satay, and fried noodles; everything here is a safe bet. The indoor dining room, with high ceilings and wooden tables and floors, can get noisy. If the weather permits, reserve an outdoor table in the evocative colonial courtyard for the full tropical experience. ⊠ *Ground fl., The Repulse Bay, 109 Repulse Bay Rd., Southside* ☎ *2292–2821* ⊟ *AE, DC, MC, V* ✛ *2:D5.*

$$$–$$$$
ECLECTIC
☺

✕ **Top Deck.** For a long time the Jumbo Floating Restaurant and Dragon Court were the only places to eat at Aberdeen's famed Jumbo Kingdom. But now there's Top Deck, a classier, less kitschy, if equally pricey alfresco option on the roof deck of the big boat, beneath a three-story pagoda. It has a vastly better view (and breeze) than the indoor restaurants beneath. If the weather permits, you should sit outdoors. The menu is somewhat haphazard (Thai, Japanese, Indian, Italian, steak) but generally good. The raw bar is the best option, if you like seafood. There's a Saturday and Sunday brunch every week. ⊠ *Shum Wan Pier Drive, Wong Chuk Hang, Aberdeen, Southside* ☎ *2552–3331* ⊕ *www. cafedecogroup.com* ⊟ *AE, MC, V* ☾ *Closed Mon.* ✛ *2:B5.*

$$$$
CONTINENTAL

✕ **The Verandah.** You will not forget an evening at The Verandah. From the well-spaced, candlelit tables overlooking the bay to the menu of delicious classics (French onion soup, baked milk-fed veal, slow-cooked duck breast) and excellent, unobtrusive service, this is an unabashedly colonial experience that delivers with finesse at every turn. A live pianist sets the scene for romance, while slow-moving ceiling fans add to that hazy feeling that time is standing still. The food doesn't disappoint, and the wine list is more reasonably priced than you might expect. Note that shorts aren't allowed during dinner. ✉ *1st fl., The Repulse Bay, 109 Repulse Bay Rd., Southside* ☎ *2292–2882* ⊕ *www.therepulsebay.com* ⊟ *AE, DC, MC, V* ⊙ *Closed Mon.* ✛ *2:D5.*

LANTAU ISLAND

You'll wind up on Lantau Island if you're visiting Disneyland Hong Kong. There are several restaurants within the Disneyland park itself, none of them distinguished, but good if you're traveling with children. The best restaurants are in the hotels. You can reach Lantau by ferry or by one of the many airport-bound buses. But the easiest way to reach the island is by MTR. The Tung Chung line connects from Central and transfers straight to the Disneyland Resort.

$$$
CANTONESE
⊙

✗ **Crystal Lotus.** The first thing you'll notice in the Disneyland Hotel's flagship restaurant is also the most Disney-ish touch: a computer-animated koi pond, where electronic fish deftly avoid your feet, darting out of the way as you walk across. Once inside the glittering, crystal-studded yet warm and inviting space, you'll choose from a well-thought-out menu that's really more pan-Chinese than Cantonese, with careful preparations of dishes like barbecue fillets of eel glazed with Osmanthus honey, gently stewed king prawns with spicy Sichuan sauce, and perfectly executed XO seafood fried rice. Crystal Lotus is also the only Disney restaurant that offers "Character dim sum" dishes, such as barbecue pork buns shaped like the three little pigs, and seafood glutinous pancakes bearing the likeness of Mickey Mouse. If you wind up in Disneyland—perhaps on your way to or from the airport—this is by far the best way to dine (unless the kids demand a character meal at the Enchanted Garden in the hotel's lower level). ✉ *Hong Kong Disneyland Hotel, Hong Kong Disneyland, Lantau Island* ☎ *3510–6000* ⊕ *park.hongkongdisneyland.com* ⊟ *AE, DC, MC, V* Ⓜ *Disneyland Resort* ✛ *3:C1.*

$$
INTERNATIONAL
⊙

✗ **Zak's.** A large, laid-back, beachfront dining terrace and an extensive international menu make this one of the best outdoor restaurants in Hong Kong. Perched on the Discovery Bay promenade a 25-minute ferry ride from Central, Zak's sea and beach views alone are easily worth the trip. Signature dishes are surf and turf and baby back ribs, and there's a wide choice of lightly prepared fresh seafood as well as pizzas and Asian and Mexican favorites, all served in generous portions. Come early to enjoy the great beach, and stay to catch a free view of nearby Disneyland's nightly fireworks display at 8 PM. If you spend more than HK$100, you get a free ticket back to Central. ✉ *Shop G03, D Deck, Discovery Bay Plaza, Discovery Bay, Lantau Island* ☎ *2987–6232* ⊕ *www.zaks.com.hk* ⊟ *MC, V* Ⓜ *Disneyland Resort* ✛ *3:C2.*

5

A food stall near the Ladies' Market in Kowloon.

KOWLOON PENINSULA

Parts of Kowloon are among the most densely populated areas on the planet, and support a corresponding abundance of restaurants. Many hotels, planted here for the view of Hong Kong Island (spectacular at night), also have excellent restaurants, though they're uniformly expensive. Some of the best food in Kowloon is served in backstreet eateries, where immigrants from Vietnam, Thailand, and elsewhere in Asia keep their native cooking skills sharp.

TSIM SHA TSUI

Tsim Sha Tsui is a foodie's paradise. The high density of hotels here—from the legendary Peninsula Hotel to the chic and modern Mira Hotel—means that there is no shortage of luxury dining options. This district also has several large shopping malls, all filled with restaurants, some better than others. The area is also known for its authentic Korean and Indian cuisine. For the best local eats though, head to neighboring Jordan and Mong Kok. The eateries here tend to be cramped and noisy, but its worth exploring for those who want to immerse themselves in the city's local culture.

$$$ ✕ **Aqua.** This trendy restaurant and bar is in the penthouse of the One ECLECTIC Peking Road building, and goes by many names (Aqua Tokyo, Aqua Roma, Aqua Spirit). The menu brings together the East and the West—the Japanese kitchen plates up fresh sashimi, tempura, and innovative sushi and maki rolls, while the restaurant's Italian side offers risottos and pastas. The Japanese offerings usually fare better than the Italian ones,

but the thing really worth going to Aqua for is the superb view from the windows of the Hong Kong skyline. You might just stop in for a drink—the bar stays open until 2 AM weeknights, and 3 AM on weekends. ✉ *Penthouse, 1 Peking Rd., Tsim Sha Tsui Kowlooni* ☎ *3427–2288* ⊕ *www.aqua.com.hk* ▭ *AE, DC, MC, V* Ⓜ *Tsim Sha Tsui* ✣ *3:D5.*

$$$–$$$$
ITALIAN
✗ **Aspasia.** Stepping into the Luxe Manor's signature Italian restaurant is like entering another world. Stunning purple pillars and tiger-print chairs show off Aspasia's fun and eccentric side, culminating in the restaurant's three beautifully decorated Heaven, Hell, and Eden VIP dining rooms. The menu is another demonstration of creativity, with inspired dishes anchored by the freshest ingredients and classic Italian influences. The à la carte and tasting menus change regularly, according to the seasons, but surprises abound every time, whether it's in the form of a lobster carpaccio salad with mint and mustard vinaigrette or a perfectly charred and juicy Wagyu sirloin served sizzling on a hot Luserna stone. ✉ *1st fl., The Luxe Manor, 39 Kimberley Rd, Tsim Sha Tsui., Kowloon* ☎ *3763–8800* ⊕ *www.aspasia.com.hk* ▭ *AE, DC, MC, V* Ⓜ *Tsim Sha Tsui* ✣ *3:F4.*

$–$$
SICHUAN
✗ **Chuan Shao.** The hip and young staff here wear tailor-made tees reading either "beef" or "beer" in Chinese characters. That should give some indication of what this place is about. Chuan Shao fires up the grill with robatayaki-like skewered items—only they draw flavor inspiration from Sichuan. The menu is extensive, capping in at more than 60 different choices on any given day (including daily and seasonal specials). The handmade octopus and shrimp seafood sticks are grilled to crunchiness on the edges but retain a lovely, fluffy soft bounce on the inside. Grilled shisamo is perfect with beer, as is the crisped bacon wrapped around chewy, grilled Korean rice cake. When in season, order grilled fresh oysters and other seafood items. The innovative folks at Chuan Shao also have grilled banana and pineapple on the menu as "dessert." The restaurant is open until late, and there's plenty of beer (Hoegaarden and Tsing Tao are served on tap) so those staying at a hotel in the nearby area might just want to keep this place in mind. ✉ *29–31 Chatham Rd., Tsim Sha Tsui, Kowloon* ☎ *2311–8101* ▭ *AE, MC, V* Ⓜ *Tsim Sha Tsui* ✣ *3:F5.*

$$
TAIWANESE
✗ **Din Tai Fung.** Originally from Taiwan, this global restaurant chain is most famous for their expertly made dumplings. They're serious about their craft—each dumpling is made from a specified amount of dough and kneaded to a uniform thinness to ensure maximum quality control. The signature steamed *xiaolongbao* dumplings arrive piping hot at the table, filled with delectable fatty pork and slurpfuls of flavorful broth. The sweet-toothed should try the taro-paste dumpling. The awesome food is paired with VIP treatment from the friendly staff, making Din Tai Fung completely worthy of its immense popularity. ✉ *Shop 130, 3rd fl., Silvercord, 30 Canton Rd., Tsim Sha Tsui, Kowloon* ☎ *2730–6928* ▭ *AE, MC, V* Ⓜ *Tsim Sha Tsui* ✣ *3:E5.*

$$$$
INTERNATIONAL
✗ **Felix.** It's not for the faint of stomach, this Philippe Starck–designed, preposterously fashionable scene atop the Peninsula. The floor-to-ceiling walls do have breathtaking views of Hong Kong, unless the blinds are drawn, as they sometimes are. The dinner menu is artistic, and might

CLOSE UP

The Dim Sum Experience

Dim sum restaurants have always been associated with noise, so don't be dissuaded by the boisterous throngs of locals gathered around large round tables. At one time big metal carts filled with bamboo baskets were pushed around the restaurant by ladies who would shout out the names of the dishes and stamp a mark onto a table's check when it ordered a basket of this or that. This is still the typical dim sum experience outside of China, but in Hong Kong most restaurants require you to order off a form, creating a more sedate and efficient dining experience. Thankfully, many places offer English-translated order forms or menus, although you should ask your waiter about daily specials that might not appear in translation, as those are often some of the most exciting dim sum options. And never forget that most basic principle of Hong Kong ordering: simply point to something you see at a nearby table.

Although dim sum comes in small portions, it's still intended for sharing between three or four people. When all is said and done, a group can expect to try about 10 or 12 dishes, but don't order more than one of any single item. Most dim sum restaurants prepare between 15 and 100 varieties of the more than 2,000 kinds of dim sum in the Cantonese repertoire, daily. These can be dumplings, buns, crepes, cakes, pastries, or rice; they can be filled with beef, shrimp, pork, chicken, bean paste, or vegetables; and they can be bamboo-steamed, panfried, baked, or deep-fried. More esoteric offerings vary vastly from place to place. Abandon any squeamish tendencies and try at least one or two unusual plates, like duck web (foot) in

abalone sauce, tripe, liver dumplings, or dried pork bellies.

You'll be able to find dim sum from before dawn to around 5 or 6 PM, but it's most popular for breakfast (from about 7:30 to 10 AM) and lunch (from about 11:30 AM to 2:30 PM). Dim sum is served everywhere from local teahouses to high-concept restaurants, but it's often best at casually elegant, blandly decorated midrange spots that cater to Chinese families.

The following is a guide to some of our favorite common dim sum items, but don't let it narrow your mind. It's almost impossible to find a bite of dim sum that's anything less than delicious, and the more unique house specialties can often be the best.

BUNS

■ **Cha siu so:** baked barbecued pork pastry buns; they're less common than the steamed cha siu bao, but arguably even better.

■ **Cha siu bao:** steamed barbecued pork buns are an absolute must. With the combination of soft and chewy textures and sweet and salty tastes, you might forget to remove the paper underneath before eating.

DUMPLINGS

■ **Ha gow:** steamed dumplings with a light translucent wrap that conceals shrimp and bamboo shoots.

■ **Siu mai:** steamed pork dumplings are the most common dumplings, and you'll find them everywhere, easily recognizable by their bright yellow wrappers; some are stuffed with shrimp.

MEATS

■ **Ngau yuk yuan:** steamed beef balls, like meatballs, placed on top of thin bean-curd skins; not the most flavorful option, but a good one for kids or picky eaters.

■ **Pie gwat:** bite-size pieces of succulent pork spare ribs in a black-bean and chili-pepper sauce.

RICE CREATIONS

■ **Ha cheong fun:** shrimp-filled rice rolls, whose dough is made in a rice-noodle style; the thick, flat rice rolls are drowned in soy sauce. Other versions include ngau yuk cheong fun (beef filled) and cha siu cheong fun (barbecued pork filled; if available, these are not to be missed).

■ **Ja leung:** similar to cheong fun but filled with a crunchy, deep-fried pastry. The rice-noodle dough is sometimes dotted with chopped scallions. These are also served with soy sauce but should also be dunked in sweet sauce and peanut paste.

■ **Ho yip fan:** delicious sticky rice, which is usually cooked with chopped Chinese mushrooms, Chinese preserved sausage, and dried shrimp, and wrapped and steamed in a lotus leaf to keep it moist (don't eat the leaf).

DON'T BE AFRAID OF . . .

■ **Woo tao go:** a glutinous panfried taro cake, sweet enough for dessert but eaten as a savory dish, with delicate undertones that come from preserved Chinese sausage, preserved pork belly, and dried shrimp. Another version of this is *lau bak go*, which is made with turnip instead of taro.

■ **Foong jow:** marinated chicken feet, whose smooth, soft texture is unlike any other. Once you get past the idea that you're sucking the cartilage off a foot, the sensation is wonderful.

■ **Gam cheen to:** cow's stomach served with chunks of daikon and doused in an addictive black-bean sauce with chili.

SWEETS

■ **Dan taht:** tarts with a custard filling, generally served for dessert.

■ **Mong gwor bo deen:** mango pudding that has a consistently glassy texture. The pudding itself is not too sweet and needs to be eaten with condensed milk.

■ **Ma lai go:** This soft and spongy steamed cake is served warm and is popular for its eggy, custardy aroma.

5

include Asian-influenced items such as plancha-seared ahi with truffle purée. The food here is generally good but a little pricey. Many people come just for cocktails—or to try out the most celebrated pissoir in Asia, whose views across Tsim Sha Tsui are superior to those in the restaurant itself. ✉ *28th fl., Peninsula Hong Kong, Salisbury Rd.,Tsim Sha Tsui Kowloon* ☎ *2315–3188* ⊕ *www.hongkong.peninsula.com* ✍ *Reservations essential* 🖃 *AE, DC, MC, V* Ⓜ *Tsim Sha Tsui* ✛ *3:E6.*

$$
INDIAN

✕ **Gaylord.** Opened in the early 1970s, this was one of the first Indian restaurants to crop up in the Hong Kong dining scene. The atmosphere is intimate and fun, especially with the live musical performances every night. The food is packed with all the authentic spices and there's also an extensive menu for vegetarians. The chowpatty chaat is a winning combination of potatoes, chickpeas, and crisp wafers in a spiced-up dressing. The chicken tikka masala here is almost legendary. Lamb dishes are also done well, especially those in fragrant curry sauce, perfect for scooping up with bits of naan bread, or for spooning over plates of fragrant basmati rice. The restaurant also offers several set and buffet lunch and dinner menus at excellent value. ✉ *1st fl., Ashley Centre, 23–25 Ashley Rd., Tsim Sha Tsui, Kowloon* ☎ *2376–1001* ⊕ *www. chiram.com.hk* 🖃 *AE, DC, MC, V* Ⓜ *Tsim Sha Tsui* ✛ *3:E5.*

$$
KOREAN
Fodor's Choice
★

✕ **Go Koong.** Go Koong is one of the best Korean restaurants in town. The menu covers extensive ground, from raw meats and seafood sizzling on the tabletop barbecue grill to hearty kimchi stews and thick egg-based pancakes studded with shrimp, squid, and scallions. The complimentary *banchans* (Korean appetizers) are a feast in themselves, with over ten different items available every day. Order the smoked duck-breast salad to start before moving onto more substantial fare, such as the tender beef ribs steamed in whole pumpkin. Korean classics, including *japchae* glassy noodles and *bibimbap* stonepot rice are all awesome, so prepare to be spoilt for choice. If you still have room at the end of the meal, remember to try the pat *bingsoo*—a giant bowl of crunchy shaved ice laced with sweetened red beans and fresh fruit. ✉ *Shop 202, Toyomall, 9 Granville Rd., Tsim Sha Tsui East, Kowloon* ☎ *2311–0901* 🖃 *AE, V* Ⓜ *Tsim Sha Tsui* ✛ *3:G4.*

$$$–$$$$
NORTHERN
CHINESE

✕ **Hutong.** It's not hard to see why Hutong is one of the hottest tables in Hong Kong: it has some of the most imaginative food in town, yet it's completely Chinese. Meanwhile, its spot at the top of the dramatic One Peking Road tower overlooks the entire festival of lights that is the Island skyline. Best among a sensational selection of northern Chinese creations are crispy, deboned lamb ribs, whose crackling skin conceals a deep, tender gaminess within. More subtle are Chinese spinach in a well-developed herbal ginseng broth, and delicate scallops with fresh pomelo. Hutong is a good choice for a memorable meal in Hong Kong. Make sure to reserve well in advance. ✉ *28th fl., 1 Peking Rd., Tsim Sha Tsui, Kowloon* ☎ *3428–8342* ⊕ *www.aqua.com.hk* ✍ *Reservations essential* 🖃 *AE, DC, MC, V* Ⓜ *Tsim Sha Tsui* ✛ *3:D4.*

$
VEGETARIAN

✕ **Kung Tak Lam.** Health-conscious diners will appreciate this simple Shanghainese vegetarian food. The interior is light and airy, in keeping with the ultramodern One Peking Road tower feel. Still, it's the food that makes this place so popular. The menu revels in its vegetarianism,

Aqua's expansive windows allow for breathtaking views of the Hong Kong skyline.

rather than trying to emulate meat; highlights include the Golden Treasure Cold Platter, which includes delicious sweet gluten with mushrooms; the Shanghai-style cold noodles with seven different sauces; and gentle bean-curd dumplings. Good, too, are the sweet panfried cakes. Set-price meals are incredibly cheap, but beware the high prices on the à la carte menu, which can add up. ⊠ *7th fl., 1 Peking Rd., Tsim Sha Tsui, Kowloon* ☎ *2312–7800* ⊟ *AE, DC, MC, V* Ⓜ *Tsim Sha Tsui* ⊹ *3:D5.*

$$-$$$
AMERICAN
Ⓒ
✕ **Main St. Deli.** Inspired by New York's 2nd Avenue Deli, with a tiled interior to match, Main St. Deli introduced traditional Big Apple neighborhood favorites to Hong Kong and found immediate popularity with visitors and locals alike. It continues to make lunch favorites such as hot dogs, bagels, and pastrami on rye and hot corned-beef sandwiches. Reuben sandwiches and Matzo-ball soup satisfy homesick New Yorkers. Serious-size lemon meringue pie makes an ideal accompaniment to afternoon coffee. ⊠ *Ground fl., Langham Hong Kong, 8 Peking Rd., Tsim Sha Tsui, Kowloon* ☎ *2375–1133* ⊕ *hongkong.langhamhotels. com* ⊟ *AE, DC, MC, V* Ⓜ *Tsim Sha Tsui* ⊹ *3:D5.*

$$$
ITALIAN
✕ **Osteria.** This underrated restaurant does some excellent, homestyle Italian fare in a sophisticated yet relaxed and inviting environment. The charmingly traditional cuisine has won over many homesick Italian expats. The pizzas and pastas are done with respect to classic, authentic recipes without being tired; the recommended carbonara *mezze maniche* is a satisfyingly hearty dish of short tube pasta mixed with pork cheek and egg. Starters also hold ample ground—the beef carpaccio with house-smoked salmon and arugula salad is tender and flavorful, and the other favorite starter, Ligurian octopus salad, is a balance of delectable chewiness and delightful herby freshness from the basil

pesto. ✉ *Holiday Inn Golden Mile, 50 Nathan Rd., Tsim Sha Tsui, Kowloon* ☎ *2315–1010* 🟰 *AE, DC, MC, V* ⊘ *No lunch Sun.* Ⓜ *Tsim Sha Tsui* ✛ *3:E5.*

$$$$
SEAFOOD

✕ **Oyster & Wine Bar.** Atop the Sheraton Hong Kong Hotel & Towers, against the romantic backdrop of Hong Kong's twinkling harbor, this is the top spot in town for oyster lovers. More than 30 varieties are flown in daily and kept alive on ice around the horseshoe oyster bar, ready for shucking. Staff cheerfully explain the characteristics of the available oysters and guide you to ones to suit your taste. Also on the aphrodisiac menu is the oyster chowder with a hint of dry Vermouth, as well as clams, mussels, crab, and panfried cod. The Dungeness crabcake is another standout, made with sweet and succulently delicious crabmeat. Wine aficionados are also spoilt for choice here, with the extensive wine selection that line the walls. ✉ *Sheraton Hong Kong Hotel & Towers, 20 Nathan Rd., Tsim Sha Tsui, Kowloon* ☎ *2369–1111 Ext. 3145* 🟰 *AE, DC, MC, V* ⊘ *No lunch* Ⓜ *Tsim Sha Tsui* ✛ *3:F6.*

$$
JAPANESE

✕ **Rakuen Tsim Sha Tsui.** Stepping away from the more commonplace Japanese eateries, Rakuen serves authentic Okinawan cuisine. Start with the umi-budo—an interesting variety of sea kelp shaped like bunches of grapes (the bubble-like appearance has also won it its "green caviar" nickname). Other regional specialties include the homemade peanut tofu. Despite the name, it's not a tofu dish but rather, a gelatinized mixture of peanuts that has a chewy but firm texture and discerning nutty flavor, which is drawn out by a drizzling of soy sauce. Okinawan ingredients—such as bitter gourd and squid-ink noodles—are equally impressive, and the melt-in-the-mouth grilled ox tongue is a definite must-order. ✉ *1st fl., Golden Dragon Centre, 38–40 Cameron Rd., Tsim Sha Tsui, Kowloon* ☎ *3428–2500* ⊕ *www.en.com.hk* 🟰 *AE, DC, MC, V* ⊘ *No lunch* Ⓜ *Tsim Sha Tsui* ✛ *3:F4.*

$$$$
ITALIAN

✕ **Sabatini.** Run by the Sabatini family (who have restaurants in Rome, Japan, and Singapore), this small corner of Italy with sponge-painted walls and wooden furnishings has a cult following among those who crave authentic Italian cuisine. Linguine Sabatini, the house specialty, is prepared according to the original Roman recipe in a fresh-tomato-and-garlic marinara sauce, served with an array of seafood. For dessert, try homemade tiramisu or refreshing wild-berry pudding. ✉ *3rd fl., The Royal Garden, 69 Mody Rd., Tsim Sha Tsui Kowloon* ☎ *2733–2000* ⊕ *www.rghk.com.hk* ⚑ *Reservations essential* 🟰 *AE, DC, MC, V* Ⓜ *Tsim Sha Tsui* ✛ *3:G5.*

$$
MANDARIN

✕ **Spring Deer.** With shades of pastel blue and green in a somber interior and waiters in bland uniforms, this Peking duck specialist looks like something out of 1950s communist Beijing. The crowd, too, is hilariously old-school, which only adds to your duck experience. You'll see locals with noodle dishes, stir-fried wok meat dishes, and so forth, but the Peking duck is the showstopper—it might be the best in town. Even the peanuts for snacking, which are boiled to a delectable softness, go above and beyond the call of duty. ✉ *1st fl., 42 Mody Rd., Tsim Sha Tsui, Kowloon* ☎ *2366–4012 or 2366–5839 or 2723-3673* 🟰 *AE, DC, MC, V* ⚑ *Reservations essential* Ⓜ *Tsim Tsa Shui* ✛ *3:F5.*

$$$$
STEAK

✕ **The Steak House winebar + grill.** This restaurant with its lively, informal din, salad buffet, and gleaming harbor views, serves the best steak in the city. After being seated, you can choose from among 10 steak knives, 12 mustards, and eight kinds of rock salt—gimmicky, but fun. But the main event is of course the meat: Wagyu steaks from Japan and Australia are grain-fed for more than a year (400 days), and the results are shockingly tender, buttery, and flavorful. In addition, the restaurant now features its own dry-aged beef and smoke dry-aged beef. Other delicious cuts are flown in from the United States; and all of it is lovingly seared on a charcoal grill. There isn't a jacket-and-tie policy but note that shorts are not allowed. ✉ *Lower level, Hotel InterContinental Hong Kong, 18 Salisbury Rd., Tsim Sha Tsui, Kowloon* ☎ *2313–2323* ⊕ *hongkong-ic.intercontinental.com* ✍ *Reservations essential* ⊟ *AE, DC, MC, V* Ⓜ *Tsim Sha Tsui* ✛ *3:F6.*

$$$$
EUROPEAN

✕ **St. George.** Hullett House—the former marine police headquarters turned bespoke hotel—was designed with maxed-out luxury in mind. So it was to be expected that its signature fine-dining restaurant would be a no-expenses-spared venture. The restaurant is decked out in colonial era–inspired duds, complete with chandeliers and comfy leather sofas. But while the decor pays homage to days gone by, the cuisine—designed by executive chef Philippe Orrico (who trained with Pierre Gagnaire)—is modern, creative, and totally inspired. The crispy 63-degree eggs are served with creamy crabmeat velouté and sweet potato puree; soups are interesting, with concoctions such as foie-gras soup with black pudding and pineapple sorbet. Most of the dishes are offered in regular and small portions, which give diners flexibility to try more things. Two tasting menus are also available (five or eight courses), for those who want the full St. George experience. ✉ *2A Canton Rd., Tsim Sha Tsui, Kowloon* ☎ *3988–0220* ⊕ *www.hulletthouse.com* ✍ *Reservations essential* ⊟ *AE, DC, MC, V* ☾ *Closed Sun.* Ⓜ *Tsim Sha Tsui* ✛ *3:E6.*

¢
ASIAN

✕ **Sun Kee.** This grotty little café might not be the easiest of places to locate, being tucked away in an old complex filled mainly with second-hand camera and wristwatch stores. The place has a bit of a cult following, with photos of local celebrity patrons adorning almost every inch of wall space. Most customers come for one thing—the instant noodles blanketed in a rich and creamy melted cheese sauce. The coiled noodles are best eaten topped with tender slices of grilled pork neck meat. It's not exactly healthy eating, but definitely satisfying. ✉ *Shop 13, Ground fl., Champagne Court, 16–20 Kimberley Rd., Tsim Sha Tsui, Kowloon* ☎ *2722–4555* ⊟ *No credit cards* Ⓜ *Tsim Sha Tsui* ✛ *3:F4.*

$–$$
ECLECTIC

✕ **Tai Ping Koon.** This is one of the oldest established restaurants in the city, and also one of the first places to serve "soy sauce" Hong Kong-styled western cuisine. The decor, staff, and menu seem to have remained unchanged since day one, adding to the interesting nostalgic charm of the place. Steaks are served to dramatic effect on hot, sizzling iron plates and are served by waiters clad in waistcoats. Other highlights include the baked Portuguese chicken, a near-perfect stir-fried rice noodles with beef (a classic Hong Kong dish), chicken wings doused in "swiss sauce" (which, funnily enough, has no real Swiss associations), and the enormous baked soufflé which takes 20 minutes

A Spot of Tea

Legend has it that the first cup dates from 2737 BC, when Camellia sinensis leaves fell into water being boiled for Emperor Shenong. He loved the result, tea was born, and so were many traditions.

Historically, when a girl accepted a marriage proposal she drank tea, a gesture symbolizing fidelity (tea plants die if uprooted). Betrothal gifts were known as "tea gifts," engagements as "accepting tea," and marriages as "eating tea." Traditionally the bride and groom kneel before their parents, offering cups of tea in thanks.

Serving tea is a sign of respect. Young people proffer it to their parents or grandparents; subordinates do the same for their bosses. Pouring tea also signifies submission, so it's a way to say you're sorry. When you're served tea, show your thanks by tapping the table with your index and middle fingers.

Even modern medicine acknowledges that tea's powerful antioxidants reduce the risk of cancer and heart disease. It's also thought to be such a good source of fluoride that Mao Zedong eschewed toothpaste for a green-tea rinse.

TEA TYPES

Pu'er tea, which is known here as Bo Lei, is the beverage of choice at dim sum places. In fact, another way to say dim sum is yum cha, meaning "drink tea."

Afternoon tea is another local fixation—neighborhood joints with Formica tables, grumpy waiters, and often, menus written only Chinese. Most people go for nai cha made with evaporated milk. A really good cup is smooth, sweet, and hung with drops of fat. An even richer version, cha chow, is made with condensed milk. If yuen yueng (yin yang, half milk tea and half instant coffee) sounds a bit much, ling-mun cha (lemon tea) is also on hand. Don't forget to order peanut-buttered toast or daan-ta (custard tarts).

The bubble (or boba) tea craze is strong. These cold brews contain pearly balls of tapioca or coconut jelly. There's also been a return to traditional teas with chains such as Chinese Urban Healing Tea, which serves healthy blends in MTR stations all over town.

FLAGSTAFF HOUSE MUSEUM OF TEA WARE

All that's good about British colonial architecture is exemplified in the simple white facade, wooden monsoon shutters, and colonnaded verandas of Flagstaff House Museum of Tea Ware. Over 600 pieces of delicate antique teaware from the Tang (618–907) through the Qing (1644–1911) dynasties fill rooms that once housed the commander of the British forces.

The best place to put your tea theory into practice is the **Lock Cha Tea-Shop** (☎ *2801–7177*) in the K.S. Lo Gallery annex of Flagstaff House. It is half shop, half teahouse, so you can sample brews before you buy. ■TIP➔ **The Hong Kong Tourist Board runs tea appreciation classes at Lock Cha TeaShop—phone the shop to book a place.** ✉ *Hong Kong Park, 10 Cotton Tree Dr., Central* ☎ *2869–0690* ⊕ *www. lcsd.gov.hk/CE/Museum/Arts/english/ tea/tea.htmlAFree* ⊘ *Wed.–Mon. 10–5* Ⓜ *Admiralty MTR, Exit C1.*

to prepare and at least three people to devour. ⊠ *40 Granville Rd., Tsim Sha Tsui, Kowloon* ☎ *2721–3559* ⊕ *taipingkoon.com* ☰ *MC, V* Ⓜ *Tsim Sha Tsui* ✛ *3:F4.*

$$$–$$$$
EUROPEAN

✕ **Whisk.** Award-winning Singaporean chef Justin Quek's first dining venture in Hong Kong is housed comfortably in the sleek and stunning Mira Hotel. Seasonal ingredients are turned into creative European dishes specifically designed to impress. Wagyu beef carpaccio is sprinkled with truffle salt and served with aged Parmesan for a savory kick that draws out the freshness of the beef. The highlight has to be chef Quek's signature roasted suckling pig—a layer of melt-in-the-mouth, fatty meat covered in a layer of deliciously crispy skin. This is one pig worth trying. For diners wanting to sample the best of Whisk's offerings, go for the superb-value five-course set dinner menus ($680–$1080) or the six-course wine-pairing menu. ⊠ *5th fl., The Mira Hotel, 118 Nathan Rd., Tsim Sha Tsui, Kowloon* ☎ *2315–5999* ⊕ *www.themirahotel.com* ☰ *AE, DC, MC, V* Ⓜ *Tsim Sha Tsui* ✛ *3:E4.*

$$$$
CANTONESE

✕ **Yan Toh Heen.** This Cantonese restaurant in the InterContinental Hong Kong sets formal elegance against expansive harbor views, and its food is at the top of its class in town. Exquisite is hardly the word for the place settings, all handcrafted with green jade. Equally successful are dim sum, sautéed Wagyu beef with mushrooms and shishito pepper (a mild green chili pepper), and exemplary braised whole abalone in oyster sauce. The vast selection of seafood transcends the usual tank to offer a selection of shellfish like red coral crab, cherrystone clam, and sea whelk. There is also a selection of "health" dishes, showcasing the hotel's innovative preventative health concept with delicious and nutritious dishes created by Chef Lau Yiu Fai. Shorts are not allowed. ⊠ *Lower level, Hotel InterContinental Hong Kong, 18 Salisbury Rd., Tsim Sha Tsui, Kowloon* ☎ *2313–2323* ⊕ *hongkong-ic.intercontinental.com* ⌖ *Reservations essential* ☰ *AE, DC, MC, V* Ⓜ *Tsim Sha Tsui* ✛ *3:F6.*

$$
SICHUAN

✕ **Yunyan Sichuan.** This is one of Hong Kong's most popular Sichaun restaurants. Veteran chef Kenny Chan is generous with the chili spices in dishes such as his famed crispy chicken with red chilies and Sichuan peppercorns. The poached sliced Mandarin fish with crispy soybeans is another classic. For something with a little less heat but still equally delicious, go for the roasted duck, which is marinated in sweet honey and stuffed with bean sprouts, shallots, and sliced meats and then roasted to crispiness. ⊠ *4th fl., Miramar Shopping Centre, 132–134 Nathan Rd., Tsim Sha Tsui, Kowloon* ☎ *2375–0800* ⊕ *www.miramar-group.com* ☰ *AE, DC, MC, V* Ⓜ *Tsim Sha Tsui* ✛ *3:E4.*

YAU MA TEI, MONG KOK, AND NORTHERN KOWLOON

This district is known for its cheap but delicious eats. Visit Yau Ma Tei's famous Temple Street—a long stretch of clothing and souvenir stores dotted with wonton noodle shops and no-frills eateries. For the best street snacks in town, look no further than Mong Kok, where you'll find curry fishballs and fragrant egg waffles, among other snacks. Also part of this busy district, Norther Kowloon is home to an assortment of interesting ethnic cuisines. Some of the city's best Nepalese and Indian fare can be found in the nooks and crannies of Jordan.

Moon cakes served at Yan Toh Heen

¢–$

SHANGHAINESE

✕ **Best Noodle Restaurant.** Just beyond the northern boundary of Tsim Sha Tsui, on a side street off Nathan Road near the Jordan MTR station, this humble place is popular among locals seeking a quick bowl of noodles or a simple, tasty Shanghainese dish. Try a dish of Shanghainese rice with vegetables, topped with your choice of meat, or the fried noodles, soup noodles, and sweet spareribs. ⊠ *105 Austin Rd., Jordan, Kowloon* ☎ *2369–0086* ▭ *No credit cards* Ⓜ *Tsim Sha Tsui* ✛ *3:F3.*

$$

CANTONESE

✕ **Ko Lau Wan Hotpot and Seafood Restaurant.** Those seeking authentic Cantonese hotpot need look no further. Locals flock here for the tender beef and a wide selection of seafood, served in thin slices that you cook at your table in a piping-hot soup (the soup selection is quite extensive, but the satay broth and the fish stock with crab are particularly tasty.) The owner runs his own fish farm in the seaside district of Sai Kung—no wonder the cuttlefish or shrimp balls and the sea urchin, amberjack, and abalone sashimi are all so tantalizingly fresh. The adventurous should try the geoduck, a giant clam, popular among Hong Kongers, which can be eaten raw with soy sauce and wasabi or slightly cooked in a soup. ⊠ *1st fl., 21–23 Hillwood Rd., Jordan Kowloon* ☎ *3520–3800* ⊕ *www.hotpotexpress.com* ▭ *MC, V* ☉ *No lunch; open from 6 PM to 3 AM daily* Ⓜ *Jordan* ✛ *3:E3.*

$–$$

VIETNAMESE

✕ **Lo Chiu Vietnamese Restaurant.** The spartan interior may not impress, but pay no heed, because what you're here for is the hearty authentic food. Take your time and try not to burn your tongue on the sizzling-hot and wonderfully flavorsome lemongrass chicken wings. Deep-fried sugarcane with minced shrimp is sweet and juicy. There is also a good variety of noodles and vermicelli served in soup or with fish sauce. A bottle of imported French beer is just the thing to wash it all down. ⊠ *Ground* *fl., shop 1, Diamond Court, 10–12 Hillwood Rd., Jordan, Kowloon* ☎ *2314–7966 or 2314–7933* ⊟ *MC, V* Ⓜ *Jordan* ✛ *3:E3.*

$–$$
SHUNDE

✕ **Siu Shun Village Cuisine.** This is one of the few restaurants in town specializing in authentic Shunde cuisine. Often lauded as "the hometown of Cantonese chefs," Shunde food is famed for its unique use of ingredients and its spectrum of flavors—all of which are well captured by the kitchen team at Siu Shun. The restaurant has enjoyed plenty of success; it currently has seven outlets across the city, but the MegaBox one is the original. A collection of fish tanks at the front of the restaurant display various types of freshwater fish, which can be ordered steamed, fried, baked, or sautéed. The whole steamed fish in broth is one of the best ways to enjoy the freshwater selection—the fish soaks up the flavors of the broth and in turn, the fish fortifies the soup as it boils. The sautéed fresh milk is one of Shunde's most renowned dishes. At Siu Shun, it's made with fresh soy milk, solidified with egg whites and combined with fresh prawns and conpoy. Don't skip dessert—the double boiled sweetened milk is reminiscent of a rich, custardy pudding and is a perfectly comforting closure to a meal at Siu Shun. ⊠ *Shop 6, 7th fl., MegaBox, 38 Wang Chiu Rd., Kowloon Bay, Kowloon* ☎ *2798–9738* ⊕ *www. siushun.com* ⊟ *MC, V* Ⓜ *Kowloon Bay* ✛ *3:H1.*

¢–$
THAI
Fodor's Choice
★

✕ **Thai BBQ 2.** This might not be the prettiest of places to have your meal, but the Thai food here is truly awesome, and about as authentic you can get in Hong Kong. This is literally a point-and-order place, since some of the best items are the ones that aren't on the menu. One of these is the moo kata; various raw meats and offal are cooked on a raised, dome-shape charcoal powered grill, which is surrounded by a mote of boiling broth. The meat juices trickle down from the grill to flavor the broth, which can also be used to cook the meats or accompanying greens, mushrooms, and vermicelli. The moo kata is designed to share, especially over a few rounds of cold Singha beer. ⊠ *17 Nam Kok Rd., Mong Kok, Kowloon* ☎ *2718–6219* ⊟ *No credit cards* Ⓜ *Mong Kok* ✛ *3:H1.*

¢
DIM SUM
Fodor's Choice
★

✕ **Tim Ho Wan.** Don't let the undiscerning storefront fool you— Tim Ho Wan is an award-winning eatery that serves up some of the city's best dim sum. Opened by a former Four Seasons Hotel chef, this humble Mong Kok eatery makes all of its shrimp dumplings, roast pork–filled rice rolls, siu mai pork dumplings, and such, fresh to order. It's top-quality food at dirt-cheap prices. But be warned—the shop is small, and its popularity is immense. So go at off hours between 2:30 PM and 5 PM, or you might find yourself waiting up to half an hour for a seat. ⊠ *2–8 Kwong Wah St., Mong Kok, Kowloon* ☎ *2332–2896* ⊟ *No credit cards* Ⓜ *Mong Kok* ✛ *3:F1.*

¢–$
CANTONESE

✕ **Tso Choi Koon.** If you have a delicate constitution, or prefer fine food, take a pass on this home-style Cantonese restaurant. Tso Choi (which translates as "rough dishes") is not everyone's cup of

> **WORD OF MOUTH**
>
> "Tim Ho Wan is awesome! We went there a few months ago and the wait is super long (get there early in the morning to get your number if you hope to wait less than two hours) but it's very delicious. Pork buns are their specialty."
> —katrinab

5

tea. Tripe lovers and haggis fans, however, might like to try the Chinese versions of some of their favorites: fried pig tripe, fried pig brain (served as an omelet), double-boiled pig brain—you get the idea. The older Hong Kong generation still likes this stuff; younger folks may demur. The wary can still opt for creamy congee, fried chicken, or a fish fillet. ✉ *17–19 Nga Tsin Wai Rd., Mong Kok, Kowloon* ☎ *2383–7170* ▭ *No credit cards* Ⓜ *Mong Kok* ✛ *3:H1.*

THE NEW TERRITORIES

Sai Kung in the New Territories is worth a visit, if only for a meal. The many restaurants lining the main street and the giant fish tanks with the dizzying selection of fresh fish, crabs, prawns, clams, and oysters are a sight to behold. Point to your catch of choice and have the kitchen cook it up in any way your stomach desires (stir-fried with spicy salt is the no-fail way to go).

¢   ✕ **Honeymoon Dessert.** Though it's expanded into a multistore chain
CANTONESE   across the city, Honeymoon Dessert's first ever store in Sai Kung still draws in droves of loyal and new fans alike. The store made a name for itself in the beginning with its homemade traditional desserts such as the smooth-as-butter black sesame sweet soup, the milky white almond tea, and the refreshing mango pomelo sweet soup with sago. The store is constantly adding new items to their menu—nibble on chewy glutinous round rice dumplings dusted with desiccated coconut and filled with fresh mango or, in the summertime, don't miss out on the wide selection of cooling grass jelly items. You can dine in at one of the many small tables here, or order your desserts to-go. ✉ *10 Po Tung Rd., Sai Kung, New Territories* ☎ *2792–4991* ⊕ *www.honeymoon-dessert.com* ▭ *No credit cards* Ⓜ *Hang Hau* ✛ *3:F1.*

$$ ✕ **Jaspa's.** What could be better than heading straight to a cozy restau-
ECLECTIC   rant after a day out in the countryside? The food here is delicious and
☺   filling, perfect after a day walking in the hills or enjoying the water and sun. Sit out on the terrace or indoors. The chicken fajitas arrive on your table sizzling hot; bay bugs (large crayfish, available in season) and lamb chops are also delicious. ✉ *13 Sha Tsui Path, Sai Kung, New Territories* ☎ *2792–6388* ▭ *AE, MC, V* Ⓜ *Hang Hau* ✛ *3:F1.*

$$$ ✕ **Tung Kee Seafood Restaurant.** Lobsters, clams, abalone, crabs, prawns,
SEAFOOD   fish, and everything else from the deep blue sea is here for the tasting on Sai Kung's picturesque harbor. Crustaceans and fish are quickly cooked by steaming and wok-frying, and are presented whole, leaving no doubt as to the freshness of your food. A quick look inside the tank is like a lesson in marine biology. Pick your favorites, and leave the rest to the chef. Then just prepare yourself for a feast *de la mer.* ✉ *96–102 Man Nin St., Sai Kung, New Territories* ☎ *2792–7453* ▭ *AE, DC, MC, V* Ⓜ *Hang Hau* ✛ *3:F1.*

Hong Kong Dining and Lodging Atlas

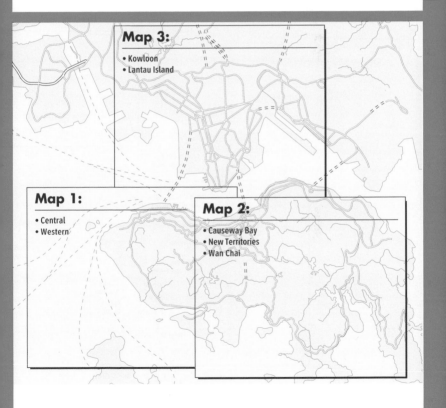

Map 3:
- Kowloon
- Lantau Island

Map 1:
- Central
- Western

Map 2:
- Causeway Bay
- New Territories
- Wan Chai

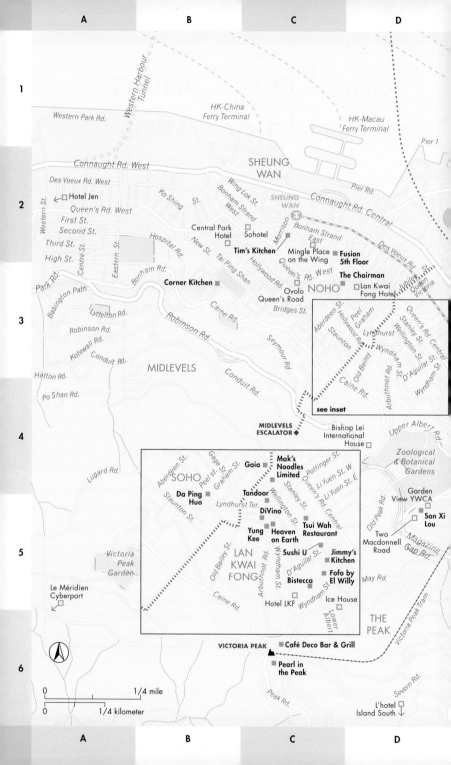

A   **B**   **C**   **D**

1

Western Harbour Tunnel

Western Park Rd.

HK-China
Ferry Terminal

HK-Macau
Ferry Terminal

Pier 1

SHEUNG
WAN

Connaught Rd. West

2

Des Voeux Rd. West

Western St.

Hotel Jen

Queen's Rd. West

First St.

Second St.

Third St.

High St.

Park Rd.

Ko Shing St.

Wing Lok St.

Bonham Strand
West

Morrison St.

SHEUNG
WAN

Connaught Rd. Central

Pier Rd.

Bonham Strand
East

Des Voeux Rd.

Central Park
Hotel

Sohotel

Tim's Kitchen

Mingle Place
on the Wing

Fusion
5th Floor

Hospital Rd.

New St.

Tai Ping Shan

Hollywood Rd.

Queen's Rd. West

The Chairman

Eastern St.

Centre St.

Bonham Rd.

Corner Kitchen

Ovolo
Queen's Road

NOHO

Lan Kwai
Fong Hotel

Jubilee St.

Queen Victoria

3

Babington Path

Lyttelton Rd.

Robinson Rd.

Bridges St.

Caine Rd.

Robinson Rd.

Kotewall Rd.

Conduit Rd.

Seymour Rd.

Aberdeen St.

Peel St.

Hollywood Rd.

Graham St.

Lyndhurst

Staunton St.

Wyndham St.

Queen's Rd. Central

Stanley St.

Wellington St.

D'Aguilar St.

Wyndham St.

Hatton Rd.

MIDLEVELS

Conduit Rd.

Old Bailey St.

Arbuthnot Rd.

Po Shan Rd.

Caine Rd.

see inset

4

MIDLEVELS
ESCALATOR ◆

Bishop Lei
International
House ☐

Upper Albert Rd.

Zoological
& Botanical
Gardens

Lugard Rd.

SOHO

Aberdeen St.

Gage St.

Peel St.

Graham St.

Gaia

Mak's
Noodles
Limited

Pottinger St.

Li Yuen St. W

Old Peak Rd.

Garden
View YWCA

Da Ping
Huo

Tandoor

Lyndhurst Ter.

Stanley St.

Wellington St.

Li Yuen St. E

Queen's Rd. Central

San Xi
Lou

DiVino

Magazine Gap Rd.

5

Victoria
Peak
Garden

Le Méridien
Cyberport

Yung
Kee

Heaven
on Earth

Tsui Wah
Restaurant

Sushi U

Jimmy's
Kitchen

Two
Macdonnell
Road

LAN
KWAI
FONG

Old Bailey St.

Arbuthnot Rd.

Wyndham St.

D'Aguilar St.

Fofo by
El Willy

May Rd.

Bistecca

Caine Rd.

Hotel LKF

Ice House

Wyndham St.

Lower
Albert

THE
PEAK

Victoria Peak Tram

6

N

VICTORIA PEAK ▲

Café Deco Bar & Grill

Pearl in
the Peak

Severn Rd.

Peak Rd.

L'hotel
Island South ↓

0   1/4 mile

0   1/4 kilometer

A   **B**   **C**   **D**

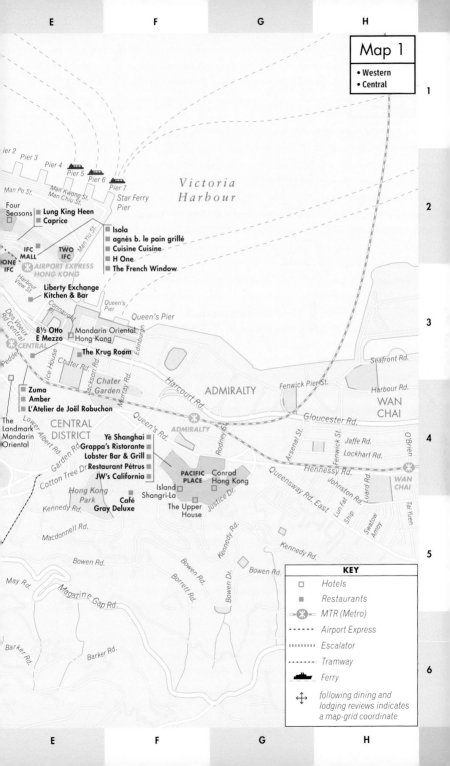

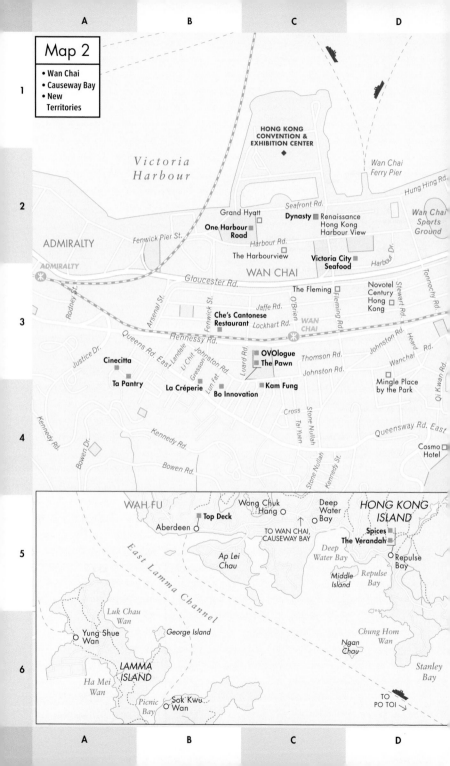

Map 2

- Wan Chai
- Causeway Bay
- New Territories

Victoria Harbour

HONG KONG CONVENTION & EXHIBITION CENTER

Wan Chai Ferry Pier

Hung Hing Rd.

Wan Chai Sports Ground

Seafront Rd.

Grand Hyatt

Dynasty

Renaissance Hong Kong Harbour View

One Harbour Road

Fenwick Pier St.

Harbour Rd.

ADMIRALTY

ADMIRALTY

The Harbourview

Victoria City Seafood

Harbou

WAN CHAI

Gloucester Rd.

The Fleming

Novotel Century Hong Kong

Stewart Rd.

Tonnochy Rd.

Rodney

Arsenal St.

Fenwick St.

Jaffe Rd.

O'Brien

WAN CHAI

Fleming Rd.

Queens Rd. East

Che's Cantonese Restaurant

Lockhart Rd.

Johnston Rd.

Heard Rd.

Hennessy Rd.

Justice Dr.

Thomson Rd.

Wanchai

IQ Kwan Rd.

Cinecitta

Landale

Li Chit

Gresson St.

Luard Rd.

OVOlogue

The Pawn

Johnston Rd.

Ta Pantry

Lun Fat

La Créperie

Bo Innovation

Kam Fung

Mingle Place by the Park

Cross

Stone Nullah

Kennedy Rd.

Queensway Rd. East

Bowen Dr.

Kennedy Rd.

Stone Nullah

Kennedy St.

Cosmo Hotel

Bowen Rd.

WAH FU

Wong Chuk Hang

Deep Water Bay

HONG KONG ISLAND

Top Deck

TO WAN CHAI, CAUSEWAY BAY

Spices

Aberdeen

Deep Water Bay

The Verandah

East Lamma Channel

Ap Lei Chau

Middle Island

Repulse Bay

Repulse Bay

Luk Chau Wan

George Island

Chung Hom Wan

Yung Shue Wan

Ngan Chau

LAMMA ISLAND

Stanley Bay

Ha Mei Wan

Picnic Bay

Sok Kwu Wan

TO PO TOI

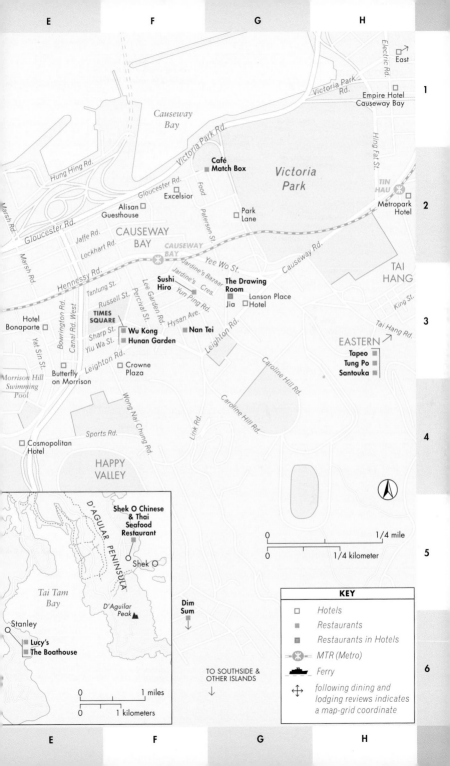

E   **F**   **G**   **H**

East

Electric Rd.

Victoria Park Rd.

1

Empire Hotel
Causeway Bay

*Causeway
Bay*

Hung Hing Rd.

Victoria Park Rd.

Hing Fat St.

*Victoria
Park*

Café
Match Box

Gloucester Rd.

Food

TIN
HAU

2

Excelsior

Metropark
Hotel

Alisan
Guesthouse

Marsh Rd.

Gloucester Rd.

Jaffe Rd.

CAUSEWAY
BAY

Paterson St.

Park
Lane

Lockhart Rd.

CAUSEWAY
BAY

Yee Wo St.

Causeway Rd.

TAI
HANG

Marsh Rd.

Hennessy Rd.

Jardine's Bazaar

Jardine's Cres.

The Drawing
Room

Sushi
Hiro

Lanson Place

King St.

Hotel
Bonaparte

Tantung St.

Russell St.

Lee Garden Rd.

Percival St.

Yun Ping Rd.

Jia

Hotel

Tai Hang Rd.

3

Bowrington Rd.

Canal Rd. West

TIMES
SQUARE

Hysan Ave.

Wu Kong

Nan Tei

Leighton Rd.

EASTERN

Hunan Garden

Sharp St.

Tapeo

Yiu Wa St.

Caroline Hill Rd.

Tung Po

Yat Sin St.

Leighton Rd.

Santouka

Butterfly
on Morrison

Crowne
Plaza

*Morrison Hill
Swimming
Pool*

Wong Nai Chung Rd.

Link Rd.

Caroline Hill Rd.

4

Cosmopolitan
Hotel

Sports Rd.

*HAPPY
VALLEY*

D'AGUILAR PENINSULA

Shek O Chinese
& Thai
Seafood
Restaurant

Shek O

0		1/4 mile
0		1/4 kilometer

5

*Tai Tam
Bay*

*D'Aguilar
Peak*

Dim
Sum
↓

Stanley

Lucy's

The Boathouse

TO SOUTHSIDE &
OTHER ISLANDS
↓

KEY	
☐	*Hotels*
■	*Restaurants*
■	*Restaurants in Hotels*
✳	*MTR (Metro)*
⬛	*Ferry*
⬌	*following dining and lodging reviews indicates a map-grid coordinate*

6

0		1 miles
0		1 kilometer

E   **F**   **G**   **H**

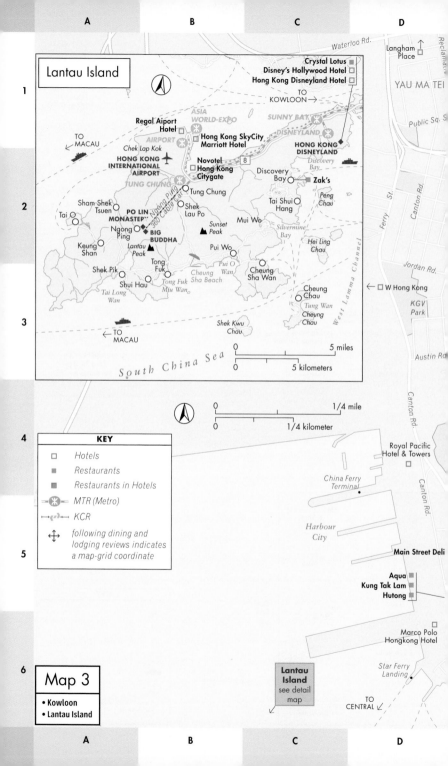

Lantau Island

Crystal Lotus ■
Disney's Hollywood Hotel □
Hong Kong Disneyland Hotel □

TO KOWLOON →

ASIA WORLD-EXPO

Regal Aiport Hotel □

AIRPORT

Chek Lap Kok

Hong Kong SkyCity Marriott Hotel □

HONG KONG INTERNATIONAL AIRPORT

TUNG CHUNG

SUNNY BAY

DISNEYLAND

HONG KONG DISNEYLAND ◆

Discovery Bay

Novotel □
Hong Kong Citygate □

8

Discovery Bay ■ Zak's

← TO MACAU

Tung Chung

Sham Shek Tsuen ○

Tai ○

PO LIN MONASTERY

Shek Lau Po ○

Peng Chau

Tai Shui Hang ○

Mui Wo

Silvermine Bay

Ngong Ping ◆ BIG BUDDHA

Lantau Peak ▲

Sunset Peak ▲

Hei Ling Chau

Keung Shan ○

Shek Pik ○

Tong Fuk ○

Pui Wo

Cheung Sha Wan

Shui Hau ○

Tong Fuk Mju Wan

Pui O Wan

Cheung Sha Beach

Tai Long Wan

Cheung Chau ○

Tung Wan

Cheung Chau

West Lamma Channel

← TO MACAU

Shek Kwu Chau

South China Sea

0   5 miles

0   5 kilometers

---

0   1/4 mile

0   1/4 kilometer

KEY

□ *Hotels*

■ *Restaurants*

■ *Restaurants in Hotels*

⊛⊗ *MTR (Metro)*

—•— *KCR*

⟷ *following dining and lodging reviews indicates a map-grid coordinate*

Waterloo Rd.

Langham Place □

YAU MA TEI

Public Sq. S

Canton St.

Ferry St.

Jordan Rd.

← □ W Hong Kong

KGV Park

Austin Rd

Royal Pacific Hotel & Towers □

China Ferry Terminal •

Canton Rd.

Harbour City

Main Street Deli

Aqua ■
Kung Tak Lam ■
Hutong ■

Marco Polo Hongkong Hotel □

Star Ferry Landing

TO CENTRAL ↙

Lantau Island see detail map

Map 3

• Kowloon
• Lantau Island

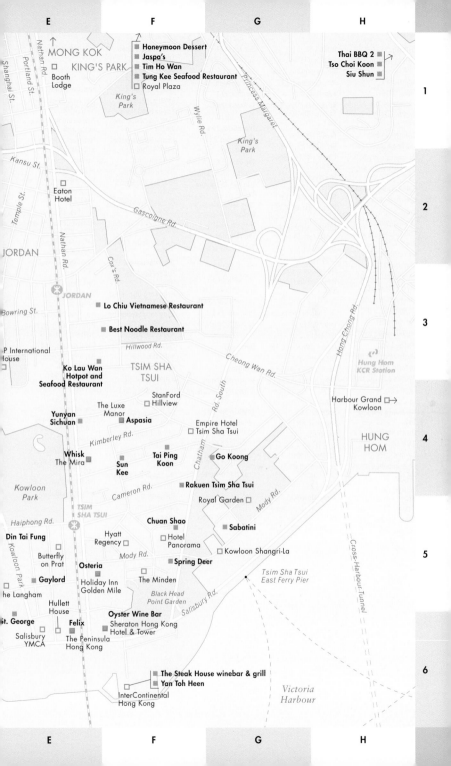

E

MONG KOK

KING'S PARK

Booth
Lodge

King's
Park

Nathan Rd.

Portland St.

Shanghai St.

Kansu St.

Temple St.

Eaton
Hotel

Nathan Rd.

JORDAN

JORDAN

Bowring St.

P International
House

Ko Lau Wan
Hotpot and
Seafood Restaurant

TSIM SHA
TSUI

Yunyan
Sichuan

The Luxe
Manor

■ Aspasia

Whisk
The Mira

Sun
Kee

Kowloon
Park

TSIM
SHA TSUI

Haiphong Rd.

Din Tai Fung

Butterfly
on Prat

Osteria

Kowloon Park

■ Gaylord

Holiday Inn
Golden Mile

he Langham

Hullett
House

St. George

■ Felix

Salisbury
YMCA

The Peninsula
Hong Kong

F

■ Honeymoon Dessert
■ Jaspa's
■ Tim Ho Wan
■ Tung Kee Seafood Restaurant
□ Royal Plaza

Wylie Rd.

Gascoigne Rd.

Cox's Rd.

■ Lo Chiu Vietnamese Restaurant

■ Best Noodle Restaurant

Hillwood Rd.

StanFord
□ Hillview

Kimberley Rd.

Tai Ping
Koon

Cameron Rd.

Empire Hotel
□ Tsim Sha Tsui

■ Go Koong

■ Rakuen Tsim Sha Tsui

Royal Garden □

Chuan Shao

Hyatt
Regency □

Mody Rd.

□ Hotel
Panorama

■ Spring Deer

The Minden

Black Head
Point Garden

Oyster Wine Bar
Sheraton Hong Kong
Hotel & Tower

■ The Steak House winebar & grill
■ Yan Toh Heen

InterContinental
Hong Kong

G

Princess Margaret

King's
Park

Cheong Wan Rd.

Rd. South

Chatham Rd.

■ Sabatini

□ Kowloon Shangri-La

Tsim Sha Tsui
East Ferry Pier

Salisbury Rd.

Victoria
Harbour

H

Thai BBQ 2 ■
Tso Choi Koon ■
Siu Shun ■

Hong Chong Rd.

Hung Hom
KCR Station

Harbour Grand □→
Kowloon

HUNG
HOM

Mody Rd.

Cross-Harbour Tunnel

1

2

3

4

5

6

Dining

agnès b. le pain grillé, 1:E2
Amber, 1:E3
Aqua, 3:D5
Aspasia, 3:F4
Best Noodle Restaurant, 3:F3
Bistecca, 1:C5
The Boathouse, 2:E6
Bo Innovation, 2:B4
Café Deco Bar & Grill, 1:C6
Café Gray Deluxe, 1:F4
Café Match Box, 2:G2
Caprice, 1:E2
The Chairman, 1:C3
Che's Cantonese Restaurant, 2:B3
Chuan Shao, 3:F5
Cinecittà, 2:A3
Corner Kitchen, 1:B3
Crystal Lotus, 3:C1
Cuisine Cuisine, 1:E2
Da Ping Huo, 1:B5
Dim Sum, 2:F6
Din Tai Fung, 3:E5
DiVino, 1:C5
The Drawing Room, 2:G3
Dynasty, 2:C2
8½ Otto e Mezzo, 1:E3
Felix, 3:E6
Fofo by El Willy, 1:C5
The French Window, 1:E2
Fusion 5th Floor, 1:C2
Gaia, 1:C4
Gaylord, 3:E5
Go Koong, 3:G4
Grappa's Ristorante, 1:F4
Honeymoon Dessert, 3:F1
H One, 1:E2
Hunan Garden, 2:F3
Hutong, 3:D5

Isola, 1:E2
Jaspa's, 3:F1
Jimmy's Kitchen, 1:C5
JW's California, 1:F4
Kam Fung, 2:C4
Ko Lau Wan Hotpot and Seafood Restaurant, 3:E3
Krug Room, 1:E3
Kung Tak Lam, 3:D5
L'Atelier de Joël Robuchon, 1:E3
La Crêperie, 2:B4
Liberty Exchange Kitchen & Bar, 1:E3
Lobster Bar and Grill, 1:F4
Lo Chiu Vietnamese Restaurant, 3:E3
Lucy's, 2:E6
Lung King Heen, 1:E2
Main St. Deli, 3:D5
Mak's Noodles Limited, 1:C4
Nan Tei, 2:F3
One Harbour Road, 2:C2
Osteria, 3:E5
OVOlogue, 2:C3
Oyster & Wine Bar, 3:F6
The Pawn, 2:C3
Pearl in the Peak, 1:C6
Rakuen Tsim Sha Tsui, 3:F4
Restaurant Petrus, 1:F4
Sabatini, 3:G5
Santouka, 2:H3
San Xi Lou, 1:D5
Shek O Chinese & Thai Seafood Restaurant, 2:F5
Siu Shun Village Cuisine, 3:H1
Spices, 2:D5
Spring Deer, 3:F5
The Steak House Wine Bar & Grill, 3:F6
St. George, 3:E6

Sun Kee, 3:F4
Sushi Hiro, 2:F3
Sushi U, 1:C5
Tai Ping Koon, 3:F4
Tandoor, 1:C5
Ta Pantry, 2:A3
Tapeo, 2:H3
Thai BBQ 2, 3:H1
Tim Ho Wan, 3:F4
Tim's Kitchen, 1:C2
Top Deck, 2:B5
Tso Choi Koon, 3:H1
Tsui Wah Restaurant, 1:C5
Tung Kee Seafood Restaurant, 3:F1
Tung Po, 2:H3
The Verandah, 2:D5
Victoria City Seafood, 2:D2
Whisk, 3:E4
Wu Kong, 2:F3
Yan Toh Heen, 3:F6
Yè Shanghai, 1:F4
Yung Kee, 1:C5
YunYan Sichuan, 3:E4
Zak's, 3:C2
Zuma, 1:E3

Lodging

Alisan Guesthouse, 2:F2
Bishop Lei International House, 1:D4
Booth Lodge, 3:E1
BP Internationa House, 3:E3
Butterfly on Morrison, 2:E3
Butterfly on Prat, 3:E5
Central Park Hotel, 1:B2
Conrade Hong Kong, 1:G4
Cosmo Hotel, 2:D4
Cosmopolitan Hotel, 2:E4

Crowne Plaza Hong Kong, 2:F3
Disney's Hollywood Hotel, 3:C1
East, 2:H1
Eaton Hotel, 3:E2
Empire Hotel Hong Kong, Causeway Bay, 2:H1
Empire Hotel Kowloon, Tsim Sha Tsui, 3:F4
Excelsior, 2:F2
The Fleming, 2:C3
Four Seasons Hong Kong, 1:E2
Garden View—YWCA, 1:D5
Grand Hyatt Hong Kong, 2:C2
Harbour Grand Kowloon, 3:H4
The Harbourview, 2:C2
Holiday Inn Golden Mile, 3:E5
Hong Kong Disneyland Hotel, 3:C2
Hong Kong Skycity Marriott Hotel, 3: B1
Hotel Bonaparte, 2:E3
Hotel Jen, 1:A2
Hotel LFK, 1:C5
Hotel Panorama, 3:F5
Hullett House, 3:E6
Hyatt Regency, 3:F5
Ice House, 1:C5
InterContinental Hong Kong, 3:F6
Island Shangri-La, 1:F4
JIA, 2:G3
Kowloon Shangri-La, 3:G5
The Landmark Mandarin Oriental, 1:E3
The Langham, 3:E5
Langham Place, 3:D1
Lan Kwai Fong Hotel, 1:D3
Lanson Place Hotel, 2:G3

Le Méridien Cyberport, 2:A5
L'hotel Island South, 2:D6
The Luxe Manor, 3:F4
Mandarin Oriental Hong Kong, 1:E3
Marco Polo Hongkong Hotel, 3:D6
Metropark Hotel Causeway Bay, 2:H2
The Minden, 3:F5
Mingle Place by the Park, 2:D3
Mingle Place on the Wing, 1:C2
The Mira, 3:E4
Novotel Century Hong Kong, 2:D3
Novotel Hong Kong Citygate, 3:B2
Ovolo Queen's Road, 1:C3
Park Lane, 2:G2
The Peninsula Hong Kong, 3:E6
Regal Airport Hotel, 3:B1
Renaissance Hong Kong Harbour View, 2:C2
Royal Garden, 3:G5
Royal Pacific Hotel & Towers, 3:D4
Royal Plaza, 3:F1
Salisbury YMCA, 3:E6
Shama Causeway Bay, 2:E3
Sheraton Hong Kong Hotel & Tower, 3:F6
Sohotle, 1:C2
StanFord Hillview, 3:F4
Two Macdonnell Road, 1:D5
The Upper House, 1:F5
W Hong Kong, 3:D3

6

Where to Stay

WORD OF MOUTH

"There are some who prefer staying on Hong Kong Island, and some on Kowloon. If you want the million-dollar harbor view, then get a hotel in Tsim Sha Tsui, like the InterContinental, Peninsula, or Sheraton. Otherwise, stay at a hotel that's within short walking distance of any MTR stops."

—rkkwan

Updated by
Cherise Fong

Whether you're a business traveler or a casual tourist, you'll inevitably be caught up with the manic pace of life here. Luckily, Hong Kong's hotels are constantly increasing their efforts to make you feel at home, so you can enjoy wonderful views of either city life or the world-famous harbor, free from stress.

From the standard budget stays to the centrifugal views emanating from the luxurious upper-level suites of the Peninsula's flagship hotel over Victoria Harbour, you're sure to find a style and site to fit your fancy. Prices tend to reflect quality of service and amenities more than location, so it's worth choosing neighborhood over notoriety. Business-oriented hotels may tout more in-room tech gadgets and eco-friendly options, but better upgrade to executive club privileges if you appreciate free Wi-Fi and complimentary buffets in the VIP lounge.

The rock stars of Hong Kong's hotel industry are perfectly situated around Victoria Harbour, where unobstructed harbor views, sumptuous spas, and reputable service all compete for the patronage of business-suited jet-setters, status-sensitive mainland tourists, and any visitor willing to splurge on uncompromised, premium service and accommodations. Farther up the hills, on both Kowloon and Hong Kong Island sides, tony boutique hotels have opened over the past five years seducing travelers who simply want a safe and cozy place to crash in a trendy locale. And as hip new shopping malls and arcades of all shapes and sizes continue their conquest of Hong Kong's dense real estate, brand-name hotels are coming along. While most big hotels are already attached to a mall, watch for the resurrected Ritz-Carlton on the 102nd to 118th floors of West Kowloon's International Commerce Centre. And with innovations in hospitality on the horizon, look out for Hotel ICON in Tsim Sha Tsui East, unconventionally associated with Polytechnic University's School of Hotel and Tourism Management.

WHERE SHOULD I STAY?

	NEIGHBORHOOD VIBE	PROS	CONS
Western	A sprawling neighborhood with hidden alleyways, antique shops, Chinese medicine markets and temples.	Western is akin to the residential extension of Central, with less traffic and similarly spectacular views. Most accessible on foot, and a leisurely tram ride during off-peak hours.	May require steep footwork if your destination is not near the main road, where the trams and MTR run. Even taxis have difficulty navigating many narrow, one-way streets.
Central	A dense international finance center full of banks, shopping malls, and footbridges above traffic. High up the escalators, Midlevels is an exclusive residential getaway.	Home to major luxury brands' flagship stores, as well as grand hotels, fine restaurants, and famous nightlife area Lan Kwai Fong. Midlevels offers quiet views from above the fray.	Congested streets by day, crowded bars by night. Midlevels escalators only run uphill after morning rush hour.
Wan Chai, Causeway Bay, and Beyond	Wan Chai hosts a strip of street-level bars in addition to the designer Star Street area. Causeway Bay is the haven of hip young locals who come to eat, shop, and hang out in upstairs cafes.	Wan Chai has stylish restaurants, the convention center, and some performing-arts venues. Causeway Bay, home to Victoria Park, is conveniently situated with hotels in all price ranges.	The Wan Chai bar strip can get seedy, while Causeway Bay is extremely crowded on weekends. Eastern is mostly for business or residents.
Southside	Lower building density means more space and fewer people, with a fishing-village atmosphere around Aberdeen.	Proximity to great beaches right on Hong Kong Island, as well as to Stanley Market and Cyberport.	Be prepared for a lot of car and bus rides along winding roads, often in slow traffic.
Lantau Island	Hong Kong's largest island hosts disparate attractions: an international airport, an outlet shopping mall, natural scenery, Hong Kong Disneyland, and AsiaWorld-Expo.	MTR end-of-the-line town Tung Chung is the point of access to the Ngong Ping scenic cable-car ride and Citygate outlet shopping. Some may prefer a more resortlike setting inside Disneyland.	Inconvenient for exploring the rest of Hong Kong, as even Tung Chung is a half-hour MTR ride out from Central.
Kowloon	The "wild" side of Hong Kong, culminating in the commercial centers of Mong Kok and Tsim Sha Tsui—if not the air-conditioned mall in West Kowloon.	Shopping paradise indeed, for both malls and markets. The TST promenade, including the touristy Avenue of Stars, offers postcard views of the Hong Kong skyline.	Kowloon is not everyone's idea of a holiday—outside residential areas the streets (even pedestrian) are generally noisy, crowded and congested.

6

HONG KONG LODGING PLANNER

Lodging Strategy

Where should we stay? With hundreds of hotels, it may seem like a daunting question. But fret not—our expert writers and editors have done most of the legwork. The 60-plus selections here represent the best this city has to offer. Scan "Best Bets" on the following pages for top recommendations by price and experience. Reviews are arranged alphabetically within neighborhood. Happy hunting!

Reservations

Most hotels have reliable online booking systems, but phone reservations are also accepted, and receptionists speak English.

Specify arrival and departure dates; number of guests; room type (standard, deluxe, suite); and any specific preferences. Make sure to find out what is, and what is not, included in the room rate, such as breakfast, in-room Wi-Fi, and local calls. A credit-card deposit is generally required to secure reservations.

Flights from the United States often arrive in the evening, so it's a good idea to inform the hotel when you plan to arrive. Some hotels will not otherwise hold a booking after 6 PM.

Rooms with a View

It's no secret that the prime waterfront properties have the best views in Hong Kong. On the Kowloon side, hotels in Tsim Sha Tsui generally have the most compelling views of the most distinctive area of skyline from across Victoria Harbour. Because of the curvature of the bay, hotels in Causeway Bay can also have an equally exhilarating view down the coast of Hong Kong Island, as well as of Kowloon. Remember that silence speaks loudly; if the hotel doesn't advertise views, no matter how hip on the inside, it probably has none. And while more low-profile boutique hotels interior-design their rooms specifically to optimize their smaller square footage, nothing opens up a room like a far-reaching view, be it harbor (preferably) or city (high-rise horizons).

Executive Privilege

Most high-end hotels have a VIP executive floor or lounge. Complimentary breakfast and cocktails are usually served in these clubs, which can range from modest private rooms with a few tables, newspapers, and a fridge full of drinks to lavish halls with rotating buffets and top-floor views. The business facilities tend to include unlimited high-speed Internet, laser printing, special dedicated concierges, and sometimes a mini-conference room. Entry to these clubs and lounges is based on the type of room you book, although some hotels allow guests staying in less expensive rooms to pay an additional fee for executive privileges.

Children

Many hotels allow children under a certain age to stay in their parents' room at no extra charge, but be sure to ask about the cutoff age. Some hotels can make special arrangements for children, while many offer a babysitting service. The hotels that are especially accommodating to those traveling with children are marked with the ☺ symbol.

Facilities

Unless stated otherwise in the review, hotels are equipped with elevators, and all guest rooms have air-conditioning, TV, telephone, and private bathroom. Note that bathrooms with showers but no bathtubs are common in smaller hotels, so be sure to check if this is a concern. Almost all hotels have designated no-smoking rooms or floors, or even premises. Many also have designated "special access" rooms for guests in wheelchairs.

Note that we use "Internet" to designate the presence of genuine high-speed broadband and mention wireless (Wi-Fi) access where available. Most moderately priced hotels will offer up-to-date technologies such as plasma screens, entertainment on demand, iPod docks, and sometimes even cell phones. However, unless you have executive privileges, in-room Internet or Wi-Fi access often costs extra, and is usually charged by the hour, for a few hours, or by the day. Most hotels that are not conveniently situated near the MTR also provide free shuttle service to the nearest station, as well as to popular downtown destinations.

Prices

Prices vary dramatically depending on season and occupancy, and most hotels also guarantee the "Best Available Rate" or "Lowest Internet Rate" that you can find online. You can usually check the hotel's own Web site for a calendar of quoted rates around the dates of your stay, along with various other discounted conditions. Almost all hotels offer timely promotions, discounts for longer stays or advance purchase, and special packages catered to families, couples, and business travelers, so always check first before you book. Hong Kong's high season ranges from October through April, covering both family holidays and business conventions.

WHAT IT COSTS IN HK$

	¢	$	$$	$$$	$$$$
For two people	under HK$700	HK$700–HK$1,100	HK$1,100–HK$2,100	HK$2,100–HK$3,000	over HK$3,000

Prices are for two people in a standard double room in high season, excluding 10% service charge and a 3% government tax.

In This Chapter

Best Bets, p. 218
Hotel Reviews, p. 219
Hong Kong Island, p. 219
Western, p. 219
Central, p. 220
Wan Chai, Causeway Bay, and Beyond, p. 225
Southside, p. 232
Lantau Island, p. 233
Kowloon, p. 236
Tsim Sha Tsui, p. 236
Yau Ma Tei, Mong Kok, and Northern Kowloon, p. 245

Checking In

6

Typical check-in and check-out times are 2 PM and noon, respectively, although most hotels will be flexible if they are not fully booked, and if you request earlier or later times in advance. Many large hotel chains have privilege clubs that allow their members to extend their checkout times until the evening.

Using the Maps

Throughout the chapter, you'll see mapping symbols and coordinates (✛ 3:F2) after property names or reviews. To locate the property on a map, turn to the Hong Kong Dining and Lodging Atlas at the end of the Where to Eat chapter. The first number after the ✛ symbol indicates the map number. Following that is the property's coordinate on the map grid.

BEST BETS FOR HONG KONG LODGING

Fodor's offers a selective listing of quality lodgings at every price range, from the city's best budget guesthouses to its most sophisticated luxury hotels. We've compiled our top recommendations by price and experience. The best properties are designated in the listings with a Fodor's Choice logo.

Fodor's Choice ★

Alisan Guest House, ¢, p. 227

Bishop Lei International House, $, p. 220

Butterfly on Morrison, $, p. 227

Hotel Panorama, $$, p. 238

InterContinental Hong Kong, $$$$, p. 240

JIA, $$, p. 231

Lan Kwai Fong Hotel, $$, p. 222

The Luxe Manor, $$, p. 241

The Peninsula, Hong Kong, $$$$, p. 243

The Upper House, $$$, p. 224

W Hong Kong, $$$, p. 248

By Price

¢

Alisan Guesthouse, p. 227

Booth Lodge, p. 245

$

Bishop Lei International House, p. 220

Butterfly on Morrison, p. 227

Central Park Hotel, p. 219

Mingle Place by the Park, p. 219

Sohotel, p. 220

$$

Hotel Panorama, p. 238

JIA, p. 231

Langham Place, p. 247

Lan Kwai Fong Hotel, p. 222

The Luxe Manor, p. 241

$$$

Crowne Plaza Hong Kong, p. 228

Hotel LKF, p. 222

Kowloon Shangri-La, p. 240

The Upper House, p. 224

W Hong Kong, p. 248

$$$$

Four Seasons Hotel, Hong Kong, p. 221

Hullett House, p. 238

InterContinental Hong Kong, p. 240

Island Shangri-La, p. 222

The Peninsula Hong Kong, p. 243

By Experience

BEST VIEW

Bishop Lei International House, p. 220

InterContinental Hong Kong, p. 240

The Peninsula Hong Kong, p. 243

The Upper House, p. 224

BEST LOCATION

Bishop Lei International House, p. 220

The Excelsior, p. 229

Hullett House, p. 238

Langham Place, p. 247

BEST INTERIOR DESIGN

Hullett House, p. 238

JIA, p. 231

Landmark Mandarin Oriental, p. 224

The Luxe Manor, p. 241

BEST SPA

InterContinental Hong Kong, p. 240

Landmark Mandarin Oriental, p. 224

Mandarin Oriental Hong Kong, p. 224

The Peninsula, Hong Kong, pg. 243

Regal Airport Hotel, p. 235

BEST POOL

InterContinental Hong Kong, p. 240

Four Seasons Hotel, Hong Kong, p. 221

The Peninsula Hong Kong, p. 243

Royal Plaza, p. 248

BEST FOR BUSINESS

East, p. 232

Four Seasons Hotel, Hong Kong, p. 221

Kowloon Shangri-La, p. 240

Le Méridien Cyberport, p. 233

The Upper House, p. 224

BEST FOR KIDS

Disney's Hollywood Hotel, p. 234

Hong Kong Disneyland Hotel, p. 234

Salisbury YMCA, p. 244

Cosmopolitan Hotel, p. 228

HONG KONG ISLAND

Reviews listed alphabetically within neighborhood.

WESTERN

The old-fashioned tram ride and steep, narrow streets characteristic of Western District have attracted a growing number of boutique hotels catering to those who favor originality over opulence. Hotels situated in Sheung Wan combine transport convenience with neighborhood character, while hotels located further out on the main drive focus on sleek efficiency and minimalist style. However, getting here usually means passing through high-traffic Central or navigating congested streets, steps, and alleyways.

$ **Central Park Hotel.** You might get the wrong idea when you enter the lobby and see a glitzy chandelier above bright red furniture and a winding black staircase; rest assured that the rest of the hotel is decorated in a minimalist style, with soothing white, green, and earth tones offsetting low ceilings with big windows and low beds. Garden-view rooms overlook the historic Hollywood Road Park, which is a plus if you are partial to morning birdsong. The upstairs lounge area combines indoor and outdoor spaces. The hotel has no restaurant of its own, but it can offer room service from the award-winning restaurant, Wagyu, right next door. **Pros:** relaxing decor in a peaceful location. **Cons:** few in-hotel facilities, although guests may use the gym at the sister Lan Kwai Fong Hotel. ⊠ *263 Hollywood Rd., Sheung Wan, Western* ☎ *2850-8899* ⊕ *www.centralparkhotel.com.hk* ✎ *142 rooms* ☖ *In-room: safe, kitchen (some), refrigerator (some), Internet, Wi-Fi. In-hotel: room service, laundry service, Internet terminal, Wi-Fi hotspot* ⊟ *AE, DC, MC, V* Ⓜ *Sheung Wan* ⊹ *1:B2.*

$$ **Hotel Jen.** This business hotel, which opened in early 2008, has a sleek, Zen-like atmosphere, with lots of white and other calming neutral colors, beige wood, glass-walled bathrooms, and plenty of natural light. Rooms have daybeds in front of their large windows, which are perfect for reading or enjoying the view—be it harbor, city, or mountain—while long desks accommodate those with work to get done. The bright and uncluttered Sky Lounge, reserved exclusively for hotel guests, is generally not crowded, and makes a nice place to relax. The 52-foot outdoor rooftop pool, with its expansive views of the bay, is another soothing destination. The hotel's immediate vicinity shuts down after dark, but in the morning it's only a short walk to the galleries and antique shops around Hollywood Road. **Pros:** secluded residential location; relaxing atmosphere; free Wi-Fi. **Cons:** an approximate 20-minute walk to the closest MTR stop; no nearby nightlife. ⊠ *508 Queen's Rd. W, Western* ☎ *2974–1234* ⊕ *www.hoteljen.com* ✎ *280 rooms* ☖ *In-room: safe, DVD (some), Internet, Wi-Fi. In-hotel: 3 restaurants, room service, bar, pool, gym, laundry service, Wi-Fi hotspot, parking (paid)* ⊟ *AE, DC, MC, V* Ⓜ *Sheung Wan* ⊹ *1:A2.*

$ **Mingle Place on the Wing.** Here, podlike rooms have white walls and mattress beds that help soften the cutting edge of the hotel's digital gadgetry: fingerprint identification that recalls your spoken language and room settings (temperature, lighting, surround-sound music); in-room Skype phone; and a dedicated Intelligent Hotel System, which handles everything from room service to billing. Some rooms have outdoor patios, and the ground-floor café may provide further relief for social claustrophobics. On the Wing caters primarily to singles, students, and minimalist business travelers. **Pros:** free Wi-Fi; high-tech gadgets. **Cons:** tiny rooms; no views; hands-off service. ⊠ *105 Wing Lok St., Sheung Wan, Western* ☎ *2581–2329* ⊕ *www.mingleplace.com* ↪ *47 rooms* ⚭ *In-room: refrigerator, DVD, Internet, Wi-Fi. In-hotel: restaurant, room service, Internet terminal, Wi-Fi hotspot* ▤ *MC, V* Ⓜ *Sheung Wan* ✛ *1:C2.*

$ 🏨 **Sohotel.** While many similar "no-frills" hotels in trendy locations settle for merely functional interior design, Sohotel's subdued sleekness makes you feel more like an executive rather than a penny-pinching tourist. The slim building features a built-in curve that offers corner rooms a playfully concave city view. The location, just far up enough the hill to be away from the chaos, is close enough to the MTR to be convenient. **Pros:** stylish corner rooms with curved windows; free Wi-Fi and local calls. **Cons:** few in-hotel facilities. ⊠ *139 Bonham Strand, Sheung Wan, Western* ☎ *2851–8818* ⊕ *www.sohotel.com.hk* ↪ *37 rooms* ⚭ *In-room: safe, refrigerator, Internet, Wi-Fi. In-hotel: room service, laundry service, Internet terminal, Wi-Fi hotspot* ▤ *AE, MC, V* Ⓜ *Sheung Wan* ✛ *1:C2.*

CENTRAL

As Hong Kong's financial nerve, Central has attracted many fine restaurants, luxury boutiques, and swank hotels, where deals are hatched, closed, and celebrated; so prepare to pay top prices for uncompromising service amid glamorous skyline views. Just up the hill, Lan Kwai Fong nightlife beckons with rowdy release; farther up the escalators, Midlevels offers peaceful respite. Admiralty is a busy traffic hub extension of Central that climbs into the gentrified heights of Pacific Place, above shopping malls and embassies, to more remote palatial hotel offerings with panoramic views.

$ 🏨 **Bishop Lei International House.** Owned and operated by the Catholic diocese of Hong Kong, this deluxe guesthouse is off the Midlevels Escalator (exit left on Mosque Street). If you've ever dreamed of living a life of privilege in Midlevels, this is your chance to do it in style, complete with red-clad concierge standing in front of world city clocks. Many of the rooms were renovated in 2008 but remain small, so best book one of the 120-numbered rooms and suites with harbor views. Although the hotel is economically priced in a residential area, it has a fully equipped business center, workout room with view, pleasant outdoor pool, and restaurant serving Chinese and western meals, in addition to buffet breakfast. **Pros:** unique perch near escalators; good value. **Cons:** lots of walking down steps after morning rush hour, if not you'll have to take a taxi, bus or shuttle. ⊠ *4 Robinson Rd., Midlevels, Central* ☎ *2868–0828* ⊕ *www.bishopleihtl.com.hk* ↪ *227 rooms* ⚭ *In-*

Fodor's Choice
★

room: safe, refrigerator, Internet, Wi-Fi. In-hotel: restaurant, pool, gym, laundry service, Wi-Fi hotspot ⊟ *AE, DC, MC, V* Ⓜ *Central* ✛ *1:D4.*

$$$$ 🏨 **Conrad Hong Kong.** This luxurious hotel occupies part of a gleaming-white, oval-shape tower rising from the upscale Pacific Place complex. Along with the neighboring Shangri-La and JW Marriott, the Conrad enjoys a reputation for reliable, high-quality service. Spacious but relatively low-ceilinged rooms have dramatic views of either the harbor or the Peak, and standard high-tech amenities and creature comforts. Five executive floors have their own private elevator, lounge, and gym. The heated outdoor pool, tucked beneath an apocalyptic skyscraper-scape, is legendary. Nicholini's, the hotel's top-floor signature restaurant specializing in North Italian cuisine, is popular with city executives, who can fill up on fresh pasta as they look down on Hong Kong. **Pros:** urban poolscape. **Cons:** not the most distinctive of Pacific Place hotels. ⊠ *Pacific Place, 88 Queensway, Admiralty, Central* ☎ *2521–3838* ⊕ *www.conrad.com.hk* ⤵ *513 rooms* ♿ *In-room: safe, refrigerator, DVD, Internet, Wi-Fi (some). In-hotel: 4 restaurants, room service, bar, pool, gym, spa, laundry service, Wi-Fi hotspot, parking (paid)* ⊟ *AE, D, DC, MC, V* Ⓜ *Admiralty* ✛ *1:G4.*

$$$$ 🏨 **Four Seasons Hotel Hong Kong.** The opening of the Four Seasons Hotel Hong Kong in September 2005 brought an air of civilized class to the International Finance Centre complex, proving that top-quality customer service could soften the glare of commercial luxury-brand shops and faceless investment banks. Home to two award-winning restaurants and a lavish spa, the hotel's most attractive feature may be its outdoor infinity pool, heated in winter, which lets you swim right up to the horizon to contemplate the harbor from above. While the pool terrace is a destination in itself, be sure to enjoy the pool's complimentary mini-spa amenities, exclusive to guests. All rooms are comfortably spacious and elegantly decorated with TV over the bathtub, no luxury is overlooked. **Pros:** spacious rooms; great views; attention to detail. **Cons:** hot breakfast not included; views are of the less exciting side of Victoria Harbour. ⊠ *International Finance Centre, 8 Finance Rd., Central* ☎ *3196–8888* ⊕ *www.fourseasons/hongkong* ⤵ *399 rooms* ♿ *In-room: safe, refrigerator, DVD, Internet, Wi-Fi. In-hotel: 5 restaurants, room service, bar, pools, gym, spa, laundry service, Wi-Fi hotspot* ⊟ *AE, DC, MC, V* Ⓜ *Hong Kong* ✛ *1:E2.*

$$ 🏨 **The Garden View – YWCA.** This attractive cylindrical guesthouse on a hill overlooks the Hong Kong Zoological and Botanical Gardens and beyond. Its clean, well-designed rooms make excellent use of small irregular shapes and emphasize each room's picture windows. If you want to do your own cooking, ask for a suite, which comes with a kitchenette; if not, the coffee shop serves European and Asian food. You can also use the outdoor pool and gym in the adjacent YWCA. The Garden View is a five-minute drive, or an uphill 20-minute walk, from Central. **Pros:** zoo and aviary views; within walking distance of Central. **Cons:** traffic can get bad during rush hours due to a nearby school. ⊠ *1 MacDonnell Rd., Midlevels, Central* ☎ *2877–3737* ⊕ *hotel.ywca.org.hk* ⤵ *141 rooms* ♿ *In-room: kitchen (some), Internet. In-hotel: restaurant, pool, gym, laundry service* ⊟ *AE, MC, V* Ⓜ *Central* ✛ *1:D5.*

$$$ 🏨 **Hotel LKF.** Too often confused with the Lan Kwai Fong Hotel far-ther west, thanks to their identical Chinese name, this newer high-end boutique hotel is also truer to its title. Its obvious advantage is its loca-tion—in the beating heart of Lan Kwai Fong, in a tower full of restau-rants and bars—but there's more to it than convenience for partygoers. Despite the small lobby with its dizzying array of wavy and circular patterns, guest rooms are decorated in deep, soothing colors and are surprisingly spacious,. Expect the most high-tech amenities, including 42-inch plasma screens, surround sound, and ergonomic Aeron chairs. The spectacular rooftop bar, Azure, invites you to literally tower over Lan Kwai Fong, as live DJs spin the show. **Pros:** at the towering cen-ter of Hong Kong's nightlife. **Cons:** noise through the walls; rowdy neighborhood streets. ⊠ *33 Wyndham St., Lan Kwai Fong, Central* ☎ *3518–9688* ⊕ *www.hotel-lkf.com.hk* ⤵ *95 rooms* ♿ *In-room: safe, kitchen (some), refrigerator, DVD, Internet, Wi-Fi. In-hotel: restau-rant, room service, bar, gym, laundry service, Wi-Fi hotspot, some pets allowed* ⊟ *AE, DC, MC, V* Ⓜ *Central* ✛ *1:C5.*

$$$$ 🏨 **Island Shangri-La.** This trademark elliptical building has become an icon of Hong Kong, as has *The Great Motherland of China*, the world's largest Chinese silk painting, which is housed in its glass atrium. The painting, which spans 16 stories, can be viewed from elevators soaring up and down through the atrium, carrying guests to their rooms. The lobby of this deluxe hotel sparkles with 771 Austrian crystal chandeliers hanging from high ceilings and huge, sun-drenched windows. Take the elevator up from the 39th floor and see the mainland's misty moun-tains drift by. Rooms are some of the largest on Hong Kong Island, and have magnificent views of the harbor, city, or Peak; all boast opulent furniture and tasteful design, a chandelier, as well as all-in-one bedside control panels. For upscale dining there's the scenic, formal French restaurant Pétrus on the top floor. **Pros:** dazzling lobby; quality service; free Wi-Fi. **Cons:** no real spa. ⊠ *Two Pacific Place, Supreme Court Rd., Admiralty, Central* ☎ *2877–3838* ⊕ *www.shangri-la.com/island* ⤵ *565 rooms* ♿ *In-room: safe, DVD, Internet, Wi-Fi. In-hotel: 7 restaurants, room service, bar, pool, gym, laundry service, Wi-Fi hotspot, parking (paid)* ⊟ *AE, DC, MC, V* Ⓜ *Admiralty* ✛ *1:F4.*

$$
Fodor'sChoice
★
🏨 **Lan Kwai Fong Hotel.** Opened west of the famous nightlife district in 2006, this oriental-themed boutique hotel is popular with westerners who appreciate its Chinese decor and more friendly SoHo location. Inspired by the cozy feel of an old Hong Kong apartment building, the relatively small rooms are enlarged by bay windows with plunging views of both the harbor and surrounding cityscape, while tiny bath-rooms are gracefully outfitted with wooden ladder towel racks and faux antique Chinese doors. Inner walls may be thin, but the outdoor Breeze lounge is a pleasant place to relax in a neighborhood already crawling with art galleries, cafés, and design shops. Look for the live turtles on either side of the modest entranceway. **Pros:** hotel and neigh-borhood have lots of character. **Cons:** narrow roads surrounding the hotel are often congested. ⊠ *3 Kau U Fong, Soho, Central* ☎ *3650–0000* ⊕ *www.lankwaifonghotel.com.hk* ⤵ *163 rooms* ♿ *In-room: safe, kitchen (some), Internet, Wi-Fi. In-hotel: 2 restaurants, room service, bar, gym, laundry service* ⊟ *AE, DC, MC, V* Ⓜ *Sheung Wan* ✛ *1:D3.*

The Upper House exterior.

Harbour view from a suite at The Upper House

$$$$ ⌐ **The Landmark Mandarin Oriental.** The interior design of this boutique-size hotel is dazzling, with spacious rooms featuring seven-foot round spa bathtubs placed in the center of giant bathrooms with city views. Everything from iPod docks to surround-sound speakers is controlled through your TV remote. Upstairs, the 25,000-square-foot holistic spa includes vitality pools, aromatherapy steam rooms, and Roman, Turkish, and Moroccan baths; the MO Bar offers all-day fine dining, cocktails, and live music till late. And all of this is implausibly concealed within the financial mitochondrion of the city, inside Hong Kong's most exclusive shopping arcade. **Pros:** you can't get more central in Central. **Cons:** no harbor views, not even from the spa. ⊠ *15 Queen's Rd., Central* ☎ *2132–0188* ⊕ *www.mandarinoriental.com/landmark* ⤳ *113 rooms* ⌂ *In-room: refrigerator, DVD, Internet, Wi-Fi. In-hotel: 3 restaurants, room service, bar, pool, gym, spa, laundry service, Wi-Fi hotspot* ⊟ *AE, DC, MC, V* Ⓜ *Central* ✛ *1:E3.*

$$$$ ⌐ **Mandarin Oriental Hong Kong.** In September 2006, the legendary Mandarin, which has served the international elite since 1963, completed a top-to-bottom renovation that included the installation of one of the city's most elaborate spas. The hotel is such a symbol of Hong Kong's colonial and financial history that rumors of the renovations sparked fierce debate amongst the business set. However, the Mandarin has not lost its characteristic charm in the face of modernization; sumptuous materials and furnishings, including silky cognac drapes, honey leather armchairs, and Black Forest Chinese marble bathrooms, are the norm in guest rooms, but now so are flat-screen TVs and iPod docks. The Mandarin can even provide children's slippers and bathrobes, while adults can choose from a pillow menu. On the 25th floor, rising high above the Central skyline, Michelin-starred French restaurant Pierre and the panoramic M bar continue to sparkle at night, while the downstairs Clipper Lounge is a long-standing venue for traditional high tea. Exploring the spa area is a delight in itself, as every corridor, alleyway, and room feels like a classic Oriental boudoir, concealing hidden delights. **Pros:** every room feels luxuriously spacious and exquisite; Statue Square views. **Cons:** in-room Wi-Fi isn't free. ⊠ *5 Connaught Rd., Central* ☎ *2522–0111* ⊕ *www.mandarinoriental.com/hongkong* ⤳ *501 rooms* ⌂ *In-room: safe, DVD, Wi-Fi. In-hotel: 9 restaurants, room service, bars, pool, gym, spa, laundry service, Wi-Fi hotspot* ⊟ *AE, DC, MC, V* Ⓜ *Central* ✛ *1:E3.*

$$$ ⌐ **The Upper House.** The hotel's vertically inclined architecture invites
Fodor's Choice   guest to journey upward to the House, where an elevator opens at
★   the 42nd-floor Sky Lounge lobby. But the real breakthrough experience takes place inside each and every spacious guestroom, equipped with both 42- and 19-inch TVs, surround sound and video-on-demand, not to mention splendid bay-window harbor and city views. Paperless minimalism is embodied in a single iPod Touch, which serves as reception check-in and -out, hotel directory, and information concierge. Additional services are personalized rather than centralized (also available by phone). Meanwhile, the House does its best to make you feel at home by offering in-room complimentary cookies, candies, beer, juice, and a full espresso machine. **Pros:** relaxing space in eco-friendly

environment; great views. **Cons:** "uphill" access to a location with limited pedestrian appeal. ✉ *Pacific Place, 88 Queensway, Admiralty, Central* ☎ *2918–1838* ⊕ *www.upperhouse.com* ⤴ *117 rooms* ⌂ *In-room: safe, refrigerator, Internet, Wi-Fi. In-hotel: restaurant, room service, bar, gym, laundry service, Wi-Fi hotspot, parking (paid)* ⊟ *AE, DC, MC, V* Ⓜ *Admiralty* ✛ *1:F5.*

WAN CHAI, CAUSEWAY BAY, AND BEYOND

Wan Chai, the neighborhood made famous in *The World According to Suzie Wong*, still has its nightlife (and red-light activity), in addition to 24-hour noodle joints and hip new wine bars. Hotels around the Hong Kong Convention & Exhibition Centre may offer great views, but nights can get noisy around Lockhart Road. Causeway Bay is the choice of the young and trendy for food and fashion, but is overcrowded with pedestrians around Times Square every weekend. It also includes the recreational green spaces of Victoria Park and the Happy Valley racecourse. Eastern is strictly business.

WAN CHAI

$$ ⬚ **The Fleming.** The cubist stand-alone gray building is a fresh face in a neighborhood defined mostly by red-light clubs and bars on Lockhart Road. Don't be alarmed by The Fleming's singular "female-only" floor, where the feminine-theme rooms feature beauty kits, jewelry boxes, facial steamers, herbal teas, and a leg-massage machine upon request. Other rooms are decorated in subdued earth tones, with views of the bustling streets below. Some include yoga mats, and even kitchenettes, while all guests have free access to the California Fitness gym around the corner. But the hotel's discreet location, within elevated walking distance of the ferry pier and just around the corner from the MTR, is most welcome in Wan Chai. **Pros:** boutique Wan Chai location. **Cons:** the hotel's only restaurant is on the ground floor with no views. ✉ *41 Fleming Rd., Wan Chai* ☎ *3706-2288* ⊕ *www.thefleming.com.hk* ⤴ *66 rooms* ⌂ *In-room: safe, kitchen (some), refrigerator (some), DVD (some), Internet, Wi-Fi. In-hotel: restaurant, room service, laundry service, Wi-Fi hotspot* ⊟ *AE, DC, MC, V* Ⓜ *Wan Chai* ✛ *2:C3.*

$$$$ ⬚ **Grand Hyatt Hong Kong.** A ceiling painted by Italian artist Paola Dindo tops the Hyatt's art-deco-style lobby, and black-and-white photographs of classic Chinese scenes hang on the walls. Elegant guest rooms have sweeping harbor views above the convention center, accented by curving wooden desks and black-marble bathroom counters. The One Harbour Road Cantonese restaurant is notable, but the breakfast and dessert buffets at Tiffin are decadent, where a pianist and live trio play throughout the day. The Plateau spa establishes a Zen-like calm, with soothing views across the harbor, while outdoor sports facilities include a curvaceous swimming pool, tennis and squash courts, and a driving range. The hotel is especially convenient if you're spending time at the Hong Kong Convention & Exhibition Centre, which is connected to the building. **Pros:** sports facilities; nice spa. **Cons:** quiet outside the hotel at night. ✉ *1 Harbour Rd., Wan Chai* ☎ *2588–1234* ⊕ *www. hongkong.grand.hyatt.com* ⤴ *553 rooms* ⌂ *In-room: safe, Internet,*

6

Wi-Fi. In-hotel: 9 restaurants, room service, bars, tennis courts, pool, gym, spa, laundry service, Wi-Fi hotspot, parking (paid) ▭ *AE, DC, MC, V* Ⓜ *Wan Chai* ✛ *2:C2.*

$$ ⊞ **The Harbourview.** This waterfront YMCA property has small but relatively inexpensive rooms near the Wan Chai Star Ferry pier. Rooms are pleasantly decorated and offer enviable harbor views. The hotel is well placed if you want to attend cultural events in the evening: both the Arts Centre and the Academy for Performing Arts are next door. It's also opposite the Hong Kong Convention & Exhibition Centre. The pedestrian overpass will get you across Wan Chai or to the Star Ferry quickly without stepping down into the traffic, that is, until you get to Hennessy Road. For a small fee, you can also use the Salisbury YMCA's excellent indoor sports facilities just across the harbor. **Pros:** use of Salisbury YMCA facilities; affordable rates for reliable service and decent rooms. **Cons:** not right next to the MTR. ⊠ *4 Harbour Rd., Wan Chai* 🕾 *2802–0111* ⊕ *www.theharbourview.com.hk* ↝ *320 rooms* ⚘ *In-room: safe, refrigerator, Wi-Fi. In-hotel: 2 restaurants, room service, laundry service, Wi-Fi hotspot* ▭ *AE, DC, MC, V* Ⓜ *Wan Chai* ✛ *2:C2.*

$ ⊞ **Mingle Place by the Park.** Housed in a renovated Wan Chai residential building from the 1960s, Mingle Place by the Park relaunched in late 2008, preserving the original staircase, raw concrete walls, and stone railings, while restoring the floor tiles typical of that period. Some rooms, while authentically diminutive, also feature an outdoor balcony or patio, and all rooms are furnished with vintage household items like a 1960s telephone, mechanical alarm clock, Chinese almanac calendar, or spittoon. Not to worry, however, in-room high-tech conveniences include a 26-inch flat-screen TV with surround sound, Internet access, and the group's Intelligent Hotel System in guise of the front desk. Its private rooftop garden will also appeal to backpackers and wandering expats seeking a place to meet fellow travelers. **Pros:** historical interest; rooms with balconies; free Wi-Fi. **Cons:** small, stark rooms in a walk-up building situated more than a few steps away from the MTR. ⊠ *143 Wan Chai Rd., Wan Chai* 🕾 *2838–1109* ⊕ *www.mingleplace. com/hotels/park* ↝ *25 rooms* ⚘ *In-room: refrigerator, DVD, Internet, Wi-Fi. In-hotel: Internet terminal, Wi-Fi hotspot* ▭ *MC, V* Ⓜ *Wan Chai* ✛ *2:D3.*

$$ ⊞ **Novotel Century Hong Kong.** This hotel was redesigned to suit the needs of business travelers, but it also accommodates many group tours, and the vertical glass lobby can get extremely crowded with crossing arrivals and departures. Rooms are simply and sparsely furnished, with no particular interior design to speak of, even though some have decent harbor views. Although situated on old Jaffe Road, the rooftop gym and outdoor pool lend it a more resortlike atmosphere. Watch out for the suits, as it's just a short walk by covered pedestrian overpass to the Hong Kong Convention & Exhibition Center. **Pros:** near the MTR. **Cons:** nondistinctive rooms; can get crowded. ⊠ *238 Jaffe Rd., Wan Chai* 🕾 *2598–8888* ⊕ *www.novotelhongkongcentury.com* ↝ *511 rooms* ⚘ *In-room: safe, refrigerator, Internet, Wi-Fi. In-hotel: 4 restaurants, room service, bar, pool, gym, laundry service, Wi-Fi hotspot* ▭ *AE, DC, MC, V* Ⓜ *Wan Chai* ✛ *2:D3.*

$$$$ 🏨 **Renaissance Hong Kong Harbour** ⟳ **View.** Sharing the Hong Kong Convention & Exhibition Centre complex with the Grand Hyatt is this more modest but attractive hotel. Guest rooms are medium in size with plenty of mirrors that reflect the modern decor. Many rooms have harbor views, but others overlook the hotel's 11,000-square-foot recreational area, featuring a voluptuously sprawling outdoor pool, driving range, jogging trails, and playground, which should also keep the kids busy. The wonderfully scenic, soaring lobby lounge hosts a live jazz band in the evening and is a popular rendezvous spot for locals and visiting businesspeople. **Pros:** harborside recreational garden. **Cons:** a little walk away from the MTR, but the Star Ferry is accessible via pedestrian overpass. ✉ *1 Harbour Rd., Wan Chai* ☎ *2802–8888* ⊕ *www.renaissancehotels.com/ hkghv* ⇆ *862 rooms, 53 suites* ⟷ *In-room: safe, refrigerator, Internet, Wi-Fi. In-hotel: 4 restaurants, room service, tennis courts, pool, gym, laundry service, Wi-Fi hotspot, parking (paid)* ☰ *AE, DC, MC, V* Ⓜ *Wan Chai* ✛ *2:C2.*

CAUSEWAY BAY

¢ 🏨 **Alisan Guest House.** There are many upstairs guest houses with tiny rooms nestled in the old apartment buildings of Causeway Bay, but Alisan is one of the few that prioritize cleanliness, safety, and friendly hospitality, all for a budget price. The no-frills rooms are furnished with single, double, or triple beds, and some of these have views of the yachts just across Gloucester Road. It's almost like staying in a real Hong Kong apartment, with the convenience of an en-suite washroom and shower. Book early and opt to pay in cash or via PayPal, as there is a 5% service charge for credit cards. Look for the entrance to Hoi To Court on Cannon Street, and take the elevator to the 5th-floor reception. **Pros:** friendly staff; good location; free Wi-Fi. **Cons:** small rooms and windows; surcharge to pay with credit card. ✉ *Flat A, 5/F, Hoi To Court, 275 Gloucester Rd., Causeway Bay* ☎ *2838–0762* ⊕ *home. hkstar.com/~alisangh* ⇆ *30 rooms* ⟷ *In-room: Wi-Fi. In-hotel: Internet terminal, Wi-Fi hotspot* ☰ *MC, V* Ⓜ *Causeway Bay* ✛ *2:F2.*

Fodor's Choice ★

$ 🏨 **Butterfly on Morrison.** Opened in 2009 and tucked away behind Times Square, this second Butterfly hotel, in between Wan Chai and Causeway Bay, offers pleasing views of Happy Valley and surroundings from its ultramodern rooms with wall-to-wall windows. Standard rooms run small and there is no restaurant on the premises, not even a gym, but every room has a refrigerator and electric kettle, and the hotel's Internet lounge offers free coffee and tea. Besides, the hotel is not far from Causeway Bay's own low-profile bar scene. It is a good choice for independent travelers who aren't fussy about facilities but love a great view. **Pros:** new, modern rooms with good views of the neighborhood **Cons:**

Fodor's Choice ★

6

no in-hotel facilities. ✉ *39 Morrison Hill Rd., Wan Chai* ☎ *3962–8333* ⊕ *www.butterflyhk.com/butterfly-on-morrison* ↪ *93 rooms* ⚏ *In-room: safe, refrigerator, DVD, Internet. In-hotel: laundry service, Internet terminal* ▭ *AE, DC, MC, V* Ⓜ *Causeway Bay* ✛ *2:E3.*

$ 🏨 **Cosmo Hotel.** The Cosmopolitan's little sister invites a younger, more style-conscious crowd to share in the prestige. Each room has a comforting contemporary design emphasizing one of three mood colors— acridine orange, modo-green, or pastel yellow—but it's the ground-floor Nooch Bar, with its lush red-velvet booths, giant sports screen, and cocktail expertise, that defines the hotel as a destination in itself. The city views may not be as spectacular as those from next door, but Cosmo guests are free to enjoy the Cosmopolitan's business center and gym facilities. **Pros:** cheerful rooms; Nooch Bar. **Cons:** situated next to a very high-traffic intersection. ✉ *375–377 Queen's Rd. E, Wan Chai* ☎ *3552-8388* ⊕ *www.cosmohotel.com.hk* ↪ *142 rooms* ⚏ *In-room: safe, kitchen (some), refrigerator (some), DVD (some), Internet, Wi-Fi. In-hotel: room service, bar, laundry service, Wi-Fi hotspot* ▭ *AE, DC, MC, V* Ⓜ *Causeway Bay* ✛ *2:D4.*

$$ 🏨 **Cosmopolitan Hotel.** In its previous incarnation this building was occu-
☾   pied by the Xinhua News Agency, Beijing's de facto embassy in Hong Kong until the handover in 1997. Since 2004, however, the Cosmopolitan Hotel holds its own, where the only visible reference to its historical past is its eponymous Xinhua banquet room. The hotel's emphasis is on personalized service and amenities, from a pillow menu and housekeeping card bearing the name of the person who cleans your room to several different types of complimentary bottled water and varied shuttle service. But its main attractions are its signature theme suites, stocked with a range of Osim massage chairs, and the family-friendly Toy Suite, full of stuffed animals, miniature vehicles, a DVD player, and a big-screen gaming console. For the adults, most rooms have views of the Happy Valley horse-racing track, which lights up spectacularly on Wednesday race nights. **Pros:** theme suites; kid-friendly; Happy Valley views. **Cons:** access requires driving or walking through (and passing under) a sprawling intersection with high vehicle traffic. ✉ *387–397 Queen's Rd. E, Wan Chai* ☎ *3552–1111* ⊕ *www.cosmopolitanhotel. com.hk* ↪ *454 rooms* ⚏ *In-room: safe, refrigerator (some), DVD (some), Internet, Wi-Fi. In-hotel: restaurant, room service, bar, gym, children's programs (ages 2–11), laundry service, Wi-Fi hotspot* ▭ *AE, DC, MC, V* Ⓜ *Causeway Bay* ✛ *2:E4.*

$$$ 🏨 **Crowne Plaza Hong Kong.** This international brand opened its first hotel in Hong Kong in late 2009, featuring sleek executive rooms equipped with surround-sound DVD systems and 42-inch flat screens, all encased in a tall black tower overlooking Happy Valley. While its racecourse views are not as intimate as those from the nearby Cosmopolitan Hotel, rooms from the 13th floor and upward have floor-to-ceiling double-glazed windows offering sweeping views of both the track and Leighton Hill greenery. Suites afford a truly panoramic view of the hills, with windows on all three sides. Although it's situated just around the corner from Causeway Bay's low-key bar street, the hotel comes alive at night with its own rooftop bar Club @28. **Pros:** suites

with three-sided Happy Valley views. **Cons:** great outdoor pool has a nice view, but no privacy in the evening. ✉ *8 Leighton Rd., Causeway Bay* ☎ *3980–3980* ⊕ *www.cphongkong.com* ↘ *263 rooms* ⚲ *In-room: safe, DVD, Internet, Wi-Fi. In-hotel: 3 restaurants, room service, bar, pool, gym, laundry service, Wi-Fi hotspot* ▭ *AE, DC, MC, V* Ⓜ *Causeway Bay* ✛ *2:F3.*

$$ ⛩ **Empire Hotel Hong Kong, Causeway Bay.** This newest Empire Hotel, designed by Japanese architect Koichiro Ikebuchi and launched in 2009, is adventurously located just east of Victoria Park in its own quiet Tin Hau neighborhood. It has only one restaurant, but Electric Road around the corner is full of cheap eats. It has no pool or gym, but nearby Victoria Park has a public pool and plenty of outdoor sports facilities. Certain rooms have free access to the new Life Spa opened in 2010, built around five treatment suites based on the five elements (metal, wood, water, fire, earth) of Chinese medicine. **Pros:** quiet neighborhood; beautiful west-looking views; new spa. **Cons:** small rooms and windows; no pool or gym; situated away from the action. ✉ *8 Wing Hing St., Causeway Bay* ☎ *3692–2333* ⊕ *www.empirehotel.com.hk* ↘ *280 rooms* ⚲ *In-room: safe, Internet, Wi-Fi. In-hotel: restaurant, room service, spa, laundry service* ▭ *AE, DC, MC, V* Ⓜ *Tin Hau* ✛ *2:H3.*

$$ ⛩ **Excelsior.** Despite its 1970s furnishings and interior, this hotel remains a favorite with travelers, mainly because its prices are moderate compared with other high-end hotels, especially in the center of Causeway Bay. A lively English pub is in the basement of the hotel, which may explain its popularity with the British. Some rooms are spacious, with splendid views of the bay; other rooms are smaller and have street views. But all have a light, contemporary design and include high-tech amenities. The hotel has no pool, but it does have its own spa and fitness center. The location, adjacent to Victoria Park, is ideal for recreation, shopping, and dining. On a historical note, the hotel sits on the first plot of land auctioned by the British government when Hong Kong became a colony in 1841. **Pros:** excellent location. **Cons:** no pool. ✉ *281 Gloucester Rd., Causeway Bay* ☎ *2894–8888* ⊕ *www.excelsiorhongkong.com* ↘ *864 rooms* ⚲ *In-room: safe, refrigerator, Internet, Wi-Fi. In-hotel: 7 restaurants, room service, bar, gym, spa, laundry service, Wi-Fi hotspot, parking (paid)* ▭ *AE, DC, MC, V* Ⓜ *Causeway Bay* ✛ *2:F2.*

$ ⛩ **Hotel Bonaparte.** At this "micro-luxury" boutique hotel, which opened in 2008, rooms range in size from 100 to 300 square feet; almost two-thirds are mid-sized business rooms, and only two exclusive executive rooms occupy the 25th floor. Yet all rooms include the standard items (safe, minibar, laundry service, 24-hour concierge, etc.) expected of a luxury hotel. The adjacent street-level A Café x Lounge serves basic breakfast, a variety of alcoholic beverages, and snacks, where guests and locals can enjoy the macro-size 52-inch HD screen, free Wi-Fi and computers. **Pros:** free local cell-phone use; tiny tony rooms **Cons:** luxuriously claustrophobic. ✉ *11 Morrison Hill Rd., Wan Chai* ☎ *3518–6688* ⊕ *ww.hotelbonaparte.com.hk* ↘ *82 rooms* ⚲ *In-room: safe, refrigerator, Internet, Wi-Fi. In-hotel: restaurant, room service, bar, laundry facilities, laundry service, Internet terminal, Wi-Fi hotspot* ▭ *AE, DC, MC, V* Ⓜ *Causeway Bay* ✛ *2:E3.*

6

The reception area at JIA.

A guestroom at JIA.

$$ \text{ }$$

$$ JIA. The first boutique hotel designed by Philippe Starck in Asia
is a destination in itself, beginning with the dark lobby and its sur-
real silver, antiquelike sculptural furniture. This is also where guests
can enjoy complimentary afternoon tea and cakes, evening wine, and
soft drinks. Accommodations consist of studios or one-bedroom suites,
plus two-bedroom duplex penthouses. All rooms are decorated in airy
white, with sheer-curtain separations and marble-finish bathrooms and
kitchenettes equipped with dining tables and cookware. Hot breakfast
is served downstairs in the all-wood decor of Madera tapas and wine
bar, while the award-winning Drawing Room restaurant offers con-
temporary Italian cuisine in an art gallery setting. Guests receive free
access to the California Fitness gym around the corner, as well as an
exclusive Insider Access Card, which gives membership privileges at
several nightlife venues, not to mention evening harbor tours on the
famous Aqua Luna junk. **Pros:** designer rooms at a reasonable price,
which includes free Wi-Fi, breakfast, and selected drinks in the lobby.
Cons: no views; trendy lobby and surrounding venues feel more like
a nightclub. ⊠ *1–5 Irving St., Causeway Bay* ☎ *3196–9000* ⊕ *www.
jiahongkong.com* ⤵ *54 rooms* ⚹ *In-room: safe, kitchen, refrigera-
tor, DVD, Internet, Wi-Fi. In-hotel: 2 restaurants, room service, bars,
laundry facilities, laundry service, Wi-Fi hotspot* ⊟ *AE, DC, MC, V*
Ⓜ *Causeway Bay* ⊹ *2:G3.*

$$ **Lanson Place Hotel.** The ground floor of this boutique business hotel
poses as an empty garden café, while just upstairs the reception, lobby
lounge, and library comprise a space that reflects neoclassical elegance.
The hotel feels like an exclusive apartment building, and all rooms have
kitchenettes and living areas, thanks to clever design for a small space.
Each room is decorated with a unique painting, and is astonishingly
quiet, given the building's busy location. While there's no restaurant,
buffet breakfast and evening cocktails are served in the piano lounge,
along with live jazz every Wednesday night. **Pros:** personalized privacy
right in Causeway Bay. **Cons:** no harbor views; no substantial dining.
⊠ *133 Leighton Rd., Causeway Bay* ☎ *3477–6888* ⊕ *www.lansonplace.
com* ⤵ *194 rooms* ⚹ *In-room: safe, kitchen, refrigerator, DVD, Internet, Wi-Fi. In-hotel: bar, room service, gym, laundry facilities, laundry
service, Wi-Fi hotspot* ⊟ *AE, DC, MC, V* Ⓜ *Causeway Bay* ⊹ *2:G3.*

$$ **Metropark Hotel Causeway Bay.** This contemporary hotel offers simple
but effectively designed rooms, which have extensive views of the park,
the harbor, or the hills. The tiny lobby leads into Vic's bar; the Café
du Parc serves French-Japanese fusion cuisine. The rooftop pool may
be small, but offers a spectacular view of Victoria Park and beyond.
Besides, this hotel is situated on the quieter side of Victoria Park, near the
public swimming pool and Tin Hau's street food of Electric Road. **Pros:**
spectacular views for less. **Cons:** limited hotel facilities. ⊠ *148 Tung Lo
Wan Rd., Causeway Bay* ☎ *2600–1000* ⊕ *www.metroparkhotel.com*
⤵ *266 rooms* ⚹ *In-room: safe, refrigerator, Internet, Wi-Fi (some). In-
hotel: restaurant, room service, bar, pool, gym, spa, laundry service,
Wi-Fi hotspot* ⊟ *AE, DC, MC, V* Ⓜ *Tin Hau* ⊹ *2:H2.*

$$ **Park Lane.** This elegant hotel overlooks Victoria Park from the Causeway Bay side, backing into Hong Kong Island's busiest pedestrian

streets for shopping and entertainment, especially on weekends. Rooms have smart glass-top tables, a glass-walled bathroom, sitting area, and marvelous views of the harbor, Victoria Park, or the city, looking east. The rooftop restaurant offers an even more panoramic view, serving international cuisine with a touch of Asian flavor. **Pros:** eastward Victoria Park views. **Cons:** often crowded; no pool. ⊠ *310 Gloucester Rd., Causeway Bay* ☎ *2293–8888* ⊕ *www.parklane.com.hk* ⤴ *810 rooms* ⌂ *In-room: safe, Internet. In-hotel: 4 restaurants, room service, bar, gym, laundry service, Wi-Fi hotspot, parking (paid)* ⊟ *AE, DC, MC, V* Ⓜ *Causeway Bay* ✛ *2:G2.*

EASTERN

$$ Ⓣ **East.** East caters to business travelers who appreciate a well-rounded experience including culinary, bodily and social pleasures. The fitness center, Beast, tends to the body with a heated outdoor pool and high-tech gym; and the in-house restaurant, Feast, features a casual all-day buffet of international dishes. Don't leave without sipping a cocktail at the open rooftop Sugar bar lounge, which offers panoramic sunset views. **Pros:** free Wi-Fi; dynamic atmosphere. **Cons:** not much of interest around the hotel for nonbusiness travelers. ⊠ *29 Taikoo Shing Rd., Easternt* ☎ *3968-3968* ⊕ *www.east-hongkong.com* ⤴ *345 rooms* ⌂ *In-room: safe, Internet, Wi-Fi. In-hotel: restaurant, room service, bar, pool, gym, laundry service, Wi-Fi hotspot* ⊟ *AE, DC, MC, V* Ⓜ *Tai Koo* ✛ *2:H1.*

SOUTHSIDE

Southside feels relatively far removed from the more frequented northern coast of Hong Kong Island, due to less direct transport routes. The area's only major hotel is situated within Cyberport, which was initially launched in 2004 as a high-tech business hub. Today the complex also includes residential, commercial, and even educational facilities, but it's still pretty lifeless at night. On the upside, it's only a short drive to popular south-coast destinations such as Aberdeen, Ocean Park, Repulse Bay beach, and Stanley Market.

$ Ⓣ **L'hotel Island South.** Aberdeen's first major hotel is the youngest member of the L'hotel group. Situated among industrial buildings and factories on Aberdeen's main road, the hotel is hardly a waterfront property, but its towering 37 floors offer clean and modern rooms with hardwood floors and views of Ap Lei Chau, Deep Water Bay, Aberdeen Country Park, and the city below. Four grand terrace suites have the exclusive privilege of panoramic southern coastline and hill views. The hotel itself projects a casual atmosphere to suit its surroundings, and an in-room touch-screen digital concierge provides high-tech privacy for those seeking a fuss-free retreat. The relaxing landscape includes an outdoor pool, and a separate children's pool. **Pros:** free Wi-Fi; south coast views; proximity to Ocean Park. **Cons:** high road traffic; industrial location. ⊠ *55 Wong Chuk Hang Rd., Aberdeen, Southside* ☎ *3968–8888* ⊕ *www. lhotelislandsouth.com* ⤴ *432 rooms* ⌂ *In-room: safe, Internet, Wi-Fi. In-hotel: restaurant, room service, bar, pool, gym, laundry service, Wi-Fi hotspot, parking (paid)* ⊟ *AE, DC, MC, V* ✛ *2:D6.*

A look inside Le Méridien Cyberport

$$ ▦ **Le Méridien Cyberport.** This relatively small, boutique-style hotel was the first high-profile hotel to open in two decades on the southern side of Hong Kong Island, in 2004. Although professionals doing business at Cyberport make up a large portion of the clientele, the hotel maintains a resort-like atmosphere, given its isolated location, which may also appeal to families. Guest rooms are spacious and bright, with 42-inch plasma TVs, big windows mostly facing out to the sea, and glass-walled bathrooms with rain showers. Each room also has a "soothing corner," where you'll find a stone bowl filled with fresh flower petals, essential oils, and floating candles. Some of the suites on the corner of the building have incredible 270-degree panoramic views of the sea, perfect for watching the sunset. The property includes hip bars, fine restaurants, and a chic outdoor pool area. You can also request a private boat to take you to Lamma Island for seafood. **Pros:** successful combination of business and resort facilities; Cyberport exclusivity; Telegraph Bay and Southside sea views. **Cons:** relatively isolated location on Hong Kong Island. ⌧ *100 Cyberport Rd., Pok Fu Lam, Southside* ☎ *2980–7778* ⊕ *www.lemeridien.com/hongkong* ⟿ *170 rooms* ⌂ *In-room: safe, Internet, Wi-Fi. In-hotel: 5 restaurants, room service, bars, pool, laundry service, Wi-Fi hotspot* ▭ *AE, DC, MC, V* ✛ *2:A5.*

LANTAU ISLAND

The main advantage to staying on Lantau Island is its proximity to the airport and SkyPier, for late-night arrivals or early-morning departures, or to AsiaWorld-Expo, if you're here on business. Most come to Lantau by MTR as a day trip; popular attractions include Disneyland, the

Ngong Ping cable-car ride, the Great Buddha, scenic hikes and beaches, and outlet shopping at Citygate mall. For the more adventurous, the island is also home to remote fishing villages by way of ferry and other roads less traveled. Note that gentrified Discovery Bay beach, easily accessible by ferry from Central, hosts Dragon Boat races every spring.

$$ ⛄ **Disney's Hollywood Hotel.** Like its sister, the Disneyland Hotel, Disney's Hollywood Hotel could theoretically be viewed simply as one of Asia's best airport hotels. But that would hardly do justice to the creativity and attention to detail that so brightly color every aspect of your stay here. The theme is the golden age of Hollywood, and you may smile at its loving display of Americana, from the New York–theme restaurant to the art deco frontage of the cocktail lounge. Of course, this is Disneyland, and there are the Chef Mickey restaurants, too. There's a playroom, Malibu Toy Shop, as well as a number of activities for kids. Rooms are on the smaller side, and a bit more "Goofy" than they are at the Disneyland Hotel, with perhaps even greater appeal for the children. **Pros:** great value. **Cons:** cut off from other Hong Kong attractions. ⊠ *Hong Kong Disneyland Resort, Lantau Island* ☎ *3510–5000* ⊕ *www. hongkongdisneyland.com* ⇥ *600 rooms* ⚘ *In-room: safe, refrigerator, Internet. In-hotel: 3 restaurants, room service, bars, tennis court, pool, gym, spa, children's programs (ages 2–12), laundry service* ▭ *AE, DC, MC, V* Ⓜ *Disneyland* ✛ *3:C1.*

$$ ⛄ **Hong Kong Disneyland Hotel.** Modeled in Victorian style after the Grand Floridian in Florida's Walt Disney World Resort, this top-flight hotel is beautifully executed on every level, from the spacious rooms with balconies overlooking the sea to the topiary of Mickey's Maze, and grand, imposing ballrooms that wouldn't be out of place in a fairy-tale castle. There's a daily schedule of activities, many for children, although adults may enjoy the horticulture tours; downstairs, Disney characters meet and greet guests during the enormous buffet breakfast. Don't overlook Disneyland as a place to stay before or after your early-morning or late-night flight—it's minutes from the airport. **Pros:** great for kids. **Cons:** cut off from the rest of Hong Kong. ⊠ *Hong Kong Disneyland Resort, Lantau Island* ☎ *3510–6000* ⊕ *www.hongkongdisneyland.com* ⇥ *400 rooms* ⚘ *In-room: safe, refrigerator, Internet. In-hotel: 3 restaurants, room service, bars, tennis court, pool, gym, spa, children's programs (ages 2–12), laundry service, parking (free)* ▭ *AE, DC, MC, V* Ⓜ *Disneyland* ✛ *3:C1.*

$$ ⛄ **Hong Kong SkyCity Marriott Hotel.** Opened in late 2008, this newest airport hotel conveniently crosses over to AsiaWorld-Expo via footbridge, with free shuttle service to Citygate shopping mall in Tung Chung and SkyPlaza mall at the airport. The hotel can also provide access to the adjacent Nine Eagles Golf Course, and there are fun classes for the kids right on the premises. Blue-carpeted rooms overlook the golf course or the bay. But this airport hotel's best feature is its casual fine dining at Man Ho Chinese restaurant, which offers traditional dishes with tasty innovative twists. While most guests will be here on business, SkyCity Marriott also hosts the occasional student summer retreat, and beware of boy-band groupies camping out before a concert at AsiaWorld-Expo. **Pros:** business atmosphere; Man Ho restaurant; golf course; connection to AsiaWorld-Expo. **Cons:** tiny spa; low-ceilinged indoor pool. ⊠ *1 Sky City Rd. E, Hong Kong International Airport, Lantau Island* ☎ *3969–1888* ⊕ *www.skycitymarriott.com* ⇆ *658 rooms* ⬧ *In-room: safe, DVD, Internet, Wi-Fi. In-hotel: 5 restaurants, room service, bar, golf course, pool, gym, spa, children's programs (ages 4–12), laundry service, Wi-Fi hotspot, parking (paid)* ▭ *AE, DC, MC, V* Ⓜ *Asia World Expo* ⊹ *3:B1.*

$$ 🏨 **Novotel Hong Kong Citygate.** This hotel's out-of-the-way location on
⏱ Lantau Island may not immediately strike you as desirable: it's not next to either the airport (though it's only a short bus ride away) or Disneyland, and it's quite a way from the city center. However, Lantau has been developing as a tourist attraction in its own right, and the island's natural beauty is finally getting the publicity it deserves. Situated right at the island's main transport hub, Novotel Citygate is perfectly placed for exploring Lantau's sights. Buses to Tai O, a remote fishing village on the other side of the island, leave just five minutes from here on foot; the Ngong Ping 360 cable car is also close by. Experienced trekkers can even try walking the Lantau hills from here, although there aren't yet many trails designated easy. The concierge can organize white dolphin sightseeing trips, which depart from the nearby pier. Guest rooms are spacious and bright, with large windows and open bathroom, offering spectacular views of either the sea or the Lantau hills and cable cars. Should the weather not hold up, you may find other pleasures in the adjoining Citygate outlet mall and cinemas, not to mention the 30-minute MTR ride from Tung Chung to Central. **Pros:** ideal location for exploring the island. **Cons:** remote from more urban pursuits. ⊠ *51 Man Tung Rd., Tung Chung, Lantau Island* ☎ *3602–8888* ⊕ *www. novotel.com* ⇆ *440 rooms* ⬧ *In-room: safe, kitchen (some), Internet, Wi-Fi. In-hotel: 4 restaurants, room service, bar, pool, gym, laundry service, Wi-Fi hotspot, parking (paid)* ▭ *AE, DC, MC, V* Ⓜ *Tung Chung* ⊹ *3:B2.*

$$$ 🏨 **Regal Airport Hotel.** Ideal for passengers in transit, this is one of the largest airport hotels in the world. The Airport Express can deliver you to Hong Kong Island in about 25 minutes, and a free shuttle bus can take you to Tsim Sha Tsui in a little more time depending on traffic. It's also connected directly to the passenger terminal by an air-conditioned, moving walkway. Consistently voted one of the best airport hotels in the world, it has a Thai-themed spa with an impressive range of treatments. Some rooms have terrific views of planes landing from afar; those with balconies overlook the hotel's two swimming pools and make you feel like you're staying in a resort. **Pros:** direct access to the airport on foot; refreshing pool and spa facilities. **Cons:** far removed from Hong Kong sights. ⊠ *9 Cheong Tat Rd., Hong Kong International Airport, Lantau Island* ☎ *2286–8888* ⊕ *www.regalhotel.com* ⇆ *1,171 rooms* ⬧ *In-room: safe, refrigerator, Wi-Fi. In-hotel: 6 restaurants, room service, bars, pool, gym, spa, laundry service, parking (paid)* ▭ *AE, DC, MC, V* Ⓜ *Airport* ⊹ *3:B1.*

KOWLOON

If you enjoy rubbing elbows with the locals in chatty all-day noodle stalls just as much as shuffling through touristy pedestrian night markets and malls, Kowloon is the place to be. Postcard skyline views abound from harborfront hotels in Tsim Sha Tsui, a 10-minute ferry ride away from Hong Kong Island, with a calmer atmosphere heading eastward toward Hung Hom.

TSIM SHA TSUI

The southern tip of the Kowloon peninsula is the birthplace of the Golden Mile, and upholding its reputation is the territory's greatest density of luxury hotels around the southern end of Nathan Road. Postcard skyline views from posh suites overlooking Victoria Harbour provide an oasis of serenity above the bustling and boisterous neighborhood below.

$$ ⛆ **BP International House.** Built by the Boy Scouts Association, this grand hotel on the northern side of Kowloon Park offers excellent value. A portrait of association founder Baron Robert Baden-Powell, hangs in the spacious, modern lobby. The rooms are small and spartan but not uncomfortable, and all have standard hotel amenities. Some rooms are bigger than others, so but sure to inquire before you're assigned a room. A multipurpose hall hosts exhibitions, conventions, and concerts. Another attraction for budget travelers is the self-service coin laundry. **Pros:** affordable panoramic harbor views from the Kowloon side. **Cons:** can get crowded with business and tour groups. ⊠ *8 Austin Rd., Tsim Sha Tsui, Kowloon* ☎ *2376–1111* ⊕ *www.bpih.com.hk* ⤴ *529 rooms* ⌂ *In-room: safe, refrigerator, Internet, Wi-Fi. In-hotel: 3 restaurants, bar, laundry facilities, laundry service, Internet terminal, Wi-Fi hotspot, parking (paid)* ⊟ *AE, DC, MC, V* Ⓜ *Austin or Jordan* ✛ *3:E3.*

$ ⛆ **Butterfly on Prat.** Opened in late 2008, the Butterfly provides bright rooms decorated in soothing hues and natural wood, which are all equipped with a refrigerator, electric kettle, and microwave. The hotel has a tiny reception area and no restaurants, so the idea is that guests make their own breakfast and spend most of their time out and about in bustling Tsim Sha Tsui and beyond. This could be a good option for longer-term stays or families. **Pros:** friendly staff; colorful rooms with microwave and fridge. **Cons:** very limited street views; no restaurant. ⊠ *21 Prat Ave., Tsim Sha Tsui, Kowloon* ☎ *3962–8888* ⊕ *www.butterflyhk.com/butterfly-on-prat* ⤴ *122 rooms* ⌂ *In-room: safe, kitchen, refrigerator, DVD, Internet. In-hotel: gym, laundry service, Internet terminal* ⊟ *AE, DC, MC, V* Ⓜ *Tsim Sha Tsui* ✛ *3:E5.*

$$ ⛆ **Empire Hotel Kowloon, Tsim Sha Tsui.** Although the Island-side Empire Hotel in Tin Hau has its new Life Spa, this Kowloon-side property, housed in a glamorous cylindrical skyscraper, has its serene atrium pool area, with accompanying sauna and steam rooms. Standard rooms are small but posh, and only upper-level suites have those gorgeous harbor views worth the upgrade. The bed is near the windows, while the bathroom is encased in walls of titillating "magic glass," which turns from opaque to transparent at the flick of a switch. **Pros:** gorgeous views from suites; atrium pool. **Cons:** no spa. ⊠ *62 Kimberley Rd.,*

CLOSE UP

Lodging Alternatives

Almost every hotel will offer you a special discount or custom rate for longer-term stays of a week or more—and some, like JIA and Lanson Place Hotel in Causeway Bay, are especially equipped for residential guests. So be sure to compare prices first if it's savings you're after. But if you prefer a more hands-off atmosphere in which to relax during your sojourn, consider renting a serviced apartment. The following properties, which are all licensed to accommodate tenants by the week or by the day, were chosen for their compelling locations, boutique-style qualities, and cozy but comfortable interiors. However, as most of these are inhabited year-round by monthly renting expatriates, it's best to call early and discuss dates, rates and conditions with sales well in advance.

Ice House. Sunlight is plentiful in all 64 studio apartments, which face southwest toward the hills, and the glass-cube showers are an amusing touch. Select luxury rooms are reserved for daily stays. Fingerprint security is applied 24 hours a day and renovations are scheduled for late 2010. Pros: ideal location. Cons: no sea views. ⊠ *38 Ice House St., Central* ☎ *2836–7333* ⊕ *www.icehouse. com.hk* ⚷ *Kitchen, Internet, laundry facilities* ⊟ *AE, DC, MC, V* Ⓜ *Central* ✛ *1:C5.*

Ovolo Queen's Road. Ovolo specializes in serviced apartments in Central and Western District, but among these only this location rents 500-square-foot studios by the day. Rooms have hardwood floors in a refreshing olive and white decor, with rounded furniture and a minimalist wooden counter attached to the kitchen. ⊠ *286 Queen's Rd. Central,* *Central* ☎ *2910–0700* ⊕ *www.ovolo. hk* ⚷ *Safe, kitchen, DVD, Internet, Wi-Fi, laundry facilities, laundry service* ⊟ *AE, DC, MC, V* Ⓜ *Sheung Wan* ✛ *1:C3.*

Shama Causeway Bay. Shama manages several serviced-apartment locations across Hong Kong Island, but its Causeway Bay property is the first to obtain a guesthouse license. With 110 flats ranging from studios to two-bedroom suites directly across from the Times Square shopping mall, this location is also the most popular, if not the most spectacular. Rooms have a Japanese-influenced design with low, square furniture, Nepalese carpets, and original Asian artwork. The property includes a pleasant rooftop garden, and residents receive privilege cards entitling them to discounts at dining and leisure venues around town, as well as gym membership. ⊠ *8 Russell St., Causeway Bay* ☎ *3100–8555* ⊕ *www.shama.com* ⚷ *Kitchen, DVD, Internet, Wi-Fi, laundry facilities, laundry service* ⊟ *AE, DC, MC, V* Ⓜ *Causeway Bay* ✛ *2:E3.*

Two Macdonnell Road. Offering sweeping views of the Hong Kong Zoological and Botanical Gardens and beyond from its Midlevels perch, this property offers six different apartment layouts, ranging from studios to two-bedroom suites. Two Macdonnell Road has its own business center, gym, and café, and provides free shuttle service to Central and Admiralty during weekday rush hours. ⊠ *2 Macdonnell Rd., Mid-Levels* ☎ *2132–2132* ⊕ *www. twomr.com.hk* ⚷ *Kitchen, Internet, gym, laundry service* ⊟ *AE, DC, MC, V* ✛ *1:D5.*

6

Tsim Sha Tsui, Kowloon ☎ *3692–2222* ⊕ *www.empirehotel.com.hk* ⤵ *343 rooms* ⚿ *In-room: safe, Internet, Wi-Fi. In-hotel: restaurant, room service, bar, pool, gym, laundry service* ▭ *AE, DC, MC, V* Ⓜ *Tsim Sha Tsui* ✢ *3:F4.*

$$ 🛏 **Holiday Inn Golden Mile.** On the Golden Mile of Nathan Road, the
Ⓢ main commercial artery of Kowloon, stands this straightforward hotel, whose friendly service has ensured its popularity with tourists and business travelers. The medium-size rooms are designed for comfort, with a sofa and coffee table, but unfortunately, no views. However, the refreshing outdoor pool area serves drinks and also includes sauna, steam, and massage rooms. The hotel has multiple dining options, including a Cantonese restaurant and German deli, but the Osteria Ristorante Italiano provides a more polished fine-dining setting. **Pros:** friendly service; pleasant pool area; kids under the age of 12 eat free in the four in-house restaurants. **Cons:** no views; no spa; can get crowded. ✉ *50 Nathan Rd., Tsim Sha Tsui, Kowloon* ☎ *2369–3111* ⊕ *holidayinn.com/ hongkong-gldn* ⤵ *614 rooms* ⚿ *In-room: safe, refrigerator, Internet, Wi-Fi. In-hotel: 4 restaurants, room service, bar, pool, gym, laundry service, Wi-Fi hotspot* ▭ *AE, DC, MC, V* Ⓜ *Tsim Sha Tsui* ✢ *3:E5.*

$$ 🛏 **Hotel Panorama.** This Tsim Sha Tsui hotel, opened in 2008, borrows
Fodor'sChoice many boutique qualities from its sister property Hotel LKF, such as the
★ contemporary interior design and hip venues that attract local residents to join in the fun. Its compact vertical structure allows for desirable destinations at the top, including the Santa Lucia Restaurant & Sky Bar, which offers fine international dining, as well as the executive breakfast buffet, with floor-to-ceiling views of the harbor. Meanwhile the open Sky Garden alcove provides a more intimate lounge area to view the skyline. Rooms have a tastefully modern decor, and the building's architecture treats almost all guests to concave corner windows. About two-thirds of the rooms face the harbor, while the others have still-interesting views of the crawling, neon-lit streets and alleys of Kowloon. **Pros:** boutique luxury in an old neighborhood at a reasonable price. **Cons:** no gym, even no-smoking rooms may smell of smoke. ✉ *8A Hart Ave., Tsim Sha Tsui, Kowloon* ☎ *3550–0388* ⊕ *www.hotelpanorama. com.hk* ⤵ *324 rooms* ⚿ *In-room: safe, Internet. In-hotel: 2 restaurants, room service, bar, laundry service, Wi-Fi hotspot, some pets allowed* ▭ *AE, DC, MC, V* Ⓜ *Tsim Sha Tsui* ✢ *3:F5.*

$$$$ 🛏 **Hullett House.** Hong Kong's former Marine Police Headquarters, a three-storey white-stucco structure originally built in 1881, now accommodates 10 luxury suites, each named after one of Hong Kong's bays. The distinctively themed suites are all equipped with the latest technology in surround audio-visual systems, hidden flat screens, and remote-controlled mood lighting. Most eye-catching is the Casam suite, decorated like an art gallery with hardwood floors and famous artworks by Yue Minjun and Nikki de Saint Phalle, among others. The more relaxing Stanley suite features birdcages and a mural of 26 hand-painted native birds of China, as well as the building's original fireplace. Due to the exclusive nature of the property, guests receive exceptionally personalized service, including a 24-hour butler. **Pros:** historic site prestige. **Cons:** extreme decor evokes a theme-park environment.

The sushi bar at the InterContinental Hong Kong.

Aerial view of the Peninsula lobby.

The lobby at the Luxe Manor

✉ *2A Canton Rd., Tsim Sha Tsui, Kowloon* ☎ *3988–0000* ⊕ *www.hulletthouse.com* ⤴ *10 suites* ☝ *In-room: safe, DVD, Wi-Fi. In-hotel: 5 restaurants, room service, bar, laundry service* ▭ *AE, DC, MC, V* Ⓜ *Tsim Sha Tsui* ✥ *3:E6.*

$$$ ⌖ **Hyatt Regency Hong Kong, Tsim Sha Tsui.** Since its opening in late 2009, this business hotel's new incarnation within the gimmicky K11 Art Mall complex has been successfully working around the hype to reassert its own brand. The legendary Hugo's restaurant, a permanent fixture of the hotel since it first opened on Nathan Road in 1969, has been minutely re-created, while The Chinese Restaurant attracts locals for its dim sum. The Café entertains guests with an open-kitchen buffet, and the Chin Chin Bar shows off its whiskey collection as it hosts live jazz every night. Rooms are decorated in reassuring olive and brown tones, with burgundy armchairs and black-and-white photos of Hong Kong on the wall. However, given its boxed-in location among other commercial and residential high-rises, only upper-floor rooms have memorable views, most notably the Regency suites, whose curved windows offer a panoramic half-circle view of the harbor. **Pros:** excellent views. **Cons:** dense shopping-mall location; no outdoor horizon-view terraces. ✉ *18 Hanoi Rd., Tsim Sha Tsui, Kowloon* ☎ *2311–1234, 800/492–8804 in U.S. and Canada* ⊕ *www.hongkong.tsimshatsui.hyatt.com* ⤴ *381 rooms* ☝ *In-room: safe, refrigerator (some), DVD (some), Internet, Wi-Fi. In-hotel: 4 restaurants, room service, bar, pool, gym, laundry service, Wi-Fi hotspot, parking (paid)* ▭ *AE, DC, MC, V* Ⓜ *Tsim Sha Tsui* ✥ *3:F5.*

$$$$
Fodor's Choice
★
⌖ **InterContinental Hong Kong.** Given its exceptional location at the protruding tip of the Kowloon peninsula, the InterContinental is often listed as one of the most desirable hotels in Asia, as it affords a truly panoramic front-row view of the entire coast of Hong Kong Island from its palatial yet ultramodern five-star environment. The restaurant line-up features Spoon by Alain Ducasse and Nobu, while the lower-level lobby lounge tea sets and Harbourside buffets keep passersby drooling as they ogle the property from the Avenue of Stars. Contemporary rooms designed with Asian accents include deep-sunken tubs in the marbled bathrooms, while corner suites enjoy spacious outdoor terraces with their own Jacuzzi. **Pros:** exceptional views; modern design; extravagant spa. **Cons:** exclusive location offers little retreat from the touristy Avenue of Stars. ✉ *18 Salisbury Rd., Tsim Sha Tsui, Kowloon* ☎ *2721–1211* ⊕ *www.hongkong-ic.intercontinental.com* ⤴ *495 rooms* ☝ *In-room: safe, refrigerator, DVD, Internet, Wi-Fi. In-hotel: 6 restaurants, room service, bar, pool, gym, spa, laundry service, parking (paid)* ▭ *AE, DC, MC, V* Ⓜ *Tsim Sha Tsui* ✥ *3:F6.*

$$$ ⌖ **Kowloon Shangri-La.** You'll feel like a tycoon in the golden lobby, with its crystal chandeliers, marble floors and fountain, live piano and violin music, and the two famously restored murals of the Shangri-La Valley. Catering mainly to business travelers, this upscale hotel boasts 24-hour "IT butler service" and live teleconferencing facilities. Always up-to-date, the elevator carpets are changed every night at midnight to indicate the day of the week. The spacious rooms are decorated in warm colors, with an armchair, rich wooden furniture, concave bay windows, a pillow menu, and TVs in the marbled bathroom. Many

suites have magnificent harbor views facing Wan Chai. The expansive hotel premises host five distinctive restaurants, plus afternoon tea in the lounge. Heath facilities include an indoor pool, sauna, massage, and facial services. Exit the lobby through the upstairs footbridge and take a scenic walk down the east side of the promenade to reach the hot spots of Tsim Sha Tsui. **Pros:** warm hospitality; attention to detail; free Wi-Fi; quality restaurants. **Cons:** less exciting garden views on lower floors. ⊠ *64 Mody Rd., Tsim Sha Tsui East, Kowloon* ☎ *2721–2111* ⊕ *www. shangri-la.com/kowloon* ➥ *688 rooms* ⏴ *In-room: safe, kitchen (some), refrigerator, DVD (some), Internet, Wi-Fi. In-hotel: 5 restaurants, room service, bar, pool, gym, spa, laundry service, Wi-Fi hotspot* ⊟ *AE, DC, MC, V* Ⓜ *Tsim Sha Tsui East* ✛ *3:G5.*

$$$ 🏨 **The Langham.** A wide marble staircase leads up to the opulent lobby under high-ceiling chandeliers, just as swirling red glass Chihuly sculptures hang above the reception desk. The rooms are warmly decorated, though a bit dark, with limited views. However all rooms feature soothing marble bathrooms with deep tubs behind wooden doors, which adds to the atmosphere of classic luxury. Linked directly to the DFS Galleria, the hotel sometimes partners with luxury brands, and many guests are serious shoppers from mainland China. But the Langham's stronghold is the quality of its dining venues: award-winning T'ang Court offers authentic Cantonese dishes in a classic setting; the Bostonian serves only sustainable seafood amid a personal collection of contemporary paintings; and Main St. Deli makes Reuben sandwiches and giant slices of cheesecake. If you don't have time for traditional high tea in the lobby, at least be sure to indulge in the lavish breakfast buffet at L'Eclipse. **Pros:** possibly the best buffet breakfast in Hong Kong. **Cons:** limited city views; no spa. ⊠ *8 Peking Rd., Tsim Sha Tsui, Kowloon* ☎ *2375–1133* ⊕ *www.hongkong.langhamhotels.com* ➥ *495 rooms* ⏴ *In-room: safe, DVD (some), Internet, Wi-Fi. In-hotel: 5 restaurants, room service, pool, gym, laundry service, Wi-Fi hotspot, parking (paid)* ⊟ *AE, DC, MC, V* Ⓜ *Tsim Sha Tsui* ✛ *3:E5.*

$$ 🏨 **The Luxe Manor.** This midrange manor, which opened in late 2006, adds a fresh dose of fantasy to the Knutsford Terrace neighborhood with its chic surrealist flair. The elusive lobby sets the tone with white line drawings of penny farthings, compasses, and clocks against dark magentas, purples, gold, and black, all centered around a bright red armchair. Rooms are predominantly white, with empty picture frames painted on the wall above the bed, a funky faux-drawer cupboard and gold-framed flat-screen TV, all of which help to compensate for the total lack of views. Six theme suites offer six different interior experiences, but the most fun is the Mirage suite, with its four door handles, tilted nightstand, and fake-silhouette closets. Upstairs, the lush Dada bar and lounge hosts stand-up comedy, art exhibits, and a resident jazz band that plays Thursday through Saturday nights. On the first floor the white-walled Aspasia restaurant features very fine Italian cuisine. **Pros:** price includes buffet breakfast; free Wi-Fi; attentive service. **Cons:** no views. ⊠ *39 Kimberley Rd., Tsim Sha Tsui, Kowloon* ☎ *3763–8880* ⊕ *www.theluxemanor.com* ➥ *159 rooms* ⏴ *In-room: safe, Internet, Wi-Fi. In-hotel: 2 restaurants, room service, bars, gym, laundry service, Wi-Fi hotspot* ⊟ *AE, DC, MC, V* Ⓜ *Tsim Sha Tsui* ✛ *3:F4*

Fodor's Choice
★

6

$$$ ⊡ **Marco Polo Hongkong Hotel.** This is the largest of three Marco Polo hotels situated along Canton Road within the wharf-side Harbour City shopping complex, which share pool, gym, and spa facilities. The hotel's location on the western edge of Tsim Sha Tsui means that most rooms have sweeping views of Hong Kong Island, the sea, and West Kowloon, although windows aren't exactly floor-to-ceiling. The Marco Polo Hongkong enjoys a long-standing reputation among European and American travelers, and is the official hotel for the Hong Kong Sevens rugby players. The largest Oktoberfest in town also takes place here, with more than 1,000 beer-swilling participants, so be sure to check out the hotel's Guinness World Record-setting collection of rum in the Lobby Lounge before they get there. **Pros:** westward views; Harbour City convenience. **Cons:** full in late March during the Hong Kong Sevens tournament; boisterous crowds during Oktoberfest. ⊠ *Harbour City, Canton Rd., Tsim Sha Tsui, Kowloon* ☎ *2113–0088* ⊕ *www.marcopolohotels. com* ⇙ *664 rooms* ♿ *In-room: safe, refrigerator, Internet, Wi-Fi. In-hotel: 3 restaurants, room service, bar, pool, laundry service, parking (paid)* ⊟ *AE, DC, MC, V* Ⓜ *Tsim Sha Tsui* ✛ *3:D6.*

$ ⊡ **The Minden.** The coolest thing about this boutique hotel in Tsim Sha Tsui's lower-key bar district is Courtney's, the Minden's distinctive bar and lounge. It's named after Australian artist Pauline Courtney, whose colorful original paintings are permanently exhibited on the walls. In the morning, it serves a buffet breakfast for guests; in the evening, the bar comes alive with the chatter of local patrons. Inside, an old-style jukebox plays contemporary pop tunes, which can also be heard on the cozy outdoor garden terrace. The Minden's lobby is quietly conservative in contrast, resembling an old English gentleman's study. The small guest rooms and their tiny bathrooms have a similarly subdued decor, and some also have a painting hanging on the wall. But their lack of views in this already dense location makes them feel somewhat stifling. **Pros:** Courtney's character; free breakfast, Internet, and local calls. **Cons:** small rooms; no views; some noise at night. ⊠ *7 Minden Ave., Tsim Sha Tsui, Kowloon* ☎ *2739–7777* ⊕ *www.theminden.com* ⇙ *64 rooms* ♿ *In-room: safe, Internet. In-hotel: room service, laundry service* ⊟ *AE, D, DC, MC, V* Ⓜ *Tsim Sha Tsui* ✛ *3:F5.*

$$$ ⊡ **The Mira.** When it opened in 1948 this building, formerly known as the Miramar, was owned by the Spanish Catholic Mission, which intended to use the structure to shelter missionaries expelled from China. As tourism blossomed here, the priests changed their plan and turned the premises into a hotel. In 2008 the Miramar underwent a comprehensive renovation. Now known as The Mira, the hotel has a thoroughly contemporary feel, with unsettlingly opaque black-glass doors that lead into a reflecting white and gray lobby with flowing wave patterns creating an iceberg effect. Off the maze-like corridors, silvery rooms are decorated in mood colors of burgundy, olive, or violet, with a seventies-style chair and glass-walled bathrooms. High-tech gadgets include the Sony Entertainment Center, featuring a 500 GB personal computer with wireless keyboard, 40-inch flat screen, and Bose sound system. Some suites have an outdoor terrace, while renovated spa-type rooms are equipped with a Jacuzzi and deluxe massage showers. The

spa itself is sleek, but with low ceilings and no windows it feels claustrophobic, as does the indoor pool. **Cons:** low-ceilinged rooms feel almost like refurbished office space. ⊠ *118 Nathan Rd., Tsim Sha Tsui, Kowloon* ☎ *2368–1111* ⊕ *www.themirahotel.com* ⊅ *492 rooms* ⚲ *In-room: safe, refrigerator, DVD, Internet, Wi-Fi. In-hotel: 4 restaurants, bar, pool, gym, laundry service, Internet terminal, Wi-Fi hotspot, parking (paid)* ⊟ *AE, DC, MC, V* Ⓜ *Tsim Sha Tsui* ✛ *3:F4.*

$$$$
Fodor's Choice
★

🏨 **The Peninsula Hong Kong.** Established in 1928, The Peninsula is an oasis of Old World glamour amid the chaos of Tsim Sha Tsui. Anyone who has savored classic high tea with live chamber music in the lobby, or sipped cocktails at the bar of the Philippe Starck–designed Felix restaurant with its panoramic views of the territory, can attest to this. When staying here, guests have a choice of accommodations in the original building, with its high-ceiling apartment-like suites, or in the newer upper wing, where Kowloon and harbor views from suites equipped with iron telescopes make you feel like you own Hong Kong. All rooms are furnished to reflect the territory's colonial heritage, complete with marbled bathrooms, but also include modern audio-visual systems, outside weather indicators, mood lighting, and remote-controlled curtains. In celebration of its 81st anniversary, the Peninsula added two MINI Clubman cars to its already famous fleet of Rolls-Royce Phantoms, so grab the included iPhone with GPS and go for a complimentary scenic ride far away from the crowds. **Pros:** Old World glamour; impeccable service; unrivalled views from upper-level rooms; free Wi-Fi; helicopter rides. **Cons:** not for those on a budget. ⊠ *Salisbury Rd., Tsim Sha Tsui, Kowloon* ☎ *2920–8888* ⊕ *peninsula.com* ⊅ *354 rooms* ⚲ *In-room: safe, DVD, Internet, Wi-Fi. In-hotel: 9 restaurants, room service, bars, pool, gym, spa, laundry service, parking (free)* ⊟ *AE, DC, MC, V* Ⓜ *Tsim Sha Tsui* ✛ *3:E6.*

$$$
🏨 **Royal Garden.** This aptly named hotel's garden atrium features lush greenery and running water, which rises from the basement restaurant, through the lobby, and all the way up to the rooftop. Glass elevators, live classical music, trailing vines, and trickling streams create a sense of serenity. Spacious rooms decorated in sleek grays or soothing earth tones surround the atrium. Rooftop health facilities feature a heated outdoor pool fashioned after an ancient Roman bath, plus fountains, Jacuzzi, sauna, gym, putting green, and tennis court. **Pros:** illuminated rooftop tennis court; inspired pool facilities; distinguished restaurants. **Cons:** no harbor views from the rooms. ⊠ *69 Mody Rd., Tsim Sha Tsui East, Kowloon* ☎ *2721–5215* ⊕ *www.rghk.com.hk* ⊅ *420 rooms* ⚲ *In-room: safe, Internet, Wi-Fi. In-hotel: 6 restaurants, room service, bar, tennis court, pool, gym, laundry service, Wi-Fi hostpot, parking (paid)* ⊟ *AE, DC, MC, V* Ⓜ *East Tsim Sha Tsui* ✛ *3:G5.*

$$
🏨 **Royal Pacific Hotel & Towers.** As part of the China Hong Kong City complex, which includes a terminal for ferries to mainland China and Macau, the Royal Pacific sits literally on the western edge of Tsim Sha Tsui. Guest rooms are arranged in two blocks: hotel and tower wings. Tower-wing rooms, renovated in mid-2010, have large harbor views and are luxuriously furnished, while the smaller hotel-wing rooms have Kowloon Park and city views. The small lobby already seems

far removed from the Harbour City crowds, as it opens out to restaurants on long and peaceful rooftop decks facing West Kowloon. In the other direction, a footbridge connects the hotel directly to Kowloon Park, which has a giant outdoor swimming-pool complex. **Pros:** both Kowloon-Park and quiet westward sea views; footbridge to the park. **Cons:** no outdoor rooftop pool. ⊠ *China Hong Kong City, Canton Rd., Tsim Sha Tsui, Kowloon* ☎ *2736–1188* ⊕ *www.royalpacific.com.hk* ⤵ *673 rooms* ♿ *In-room: safe, kitchen (some), refrigerator (some), Internet, Wi-Fi (some). In-hotel: 4 restaurants, room service, bar, gym, laundry service, Wi-Fi hotspot, parking (paid)* ☰ *AE, DC, MC, V* Ⓜ *Tsim Sha Tsui* ✛ *3:D4.*

$$

$$ 🏨 **Salisbury YMCA.** This upscale YMCA is Hong Kong's most popular and is a great value for your money. Across the street from the Peninsula and opposite the Cultural Centre, Space Museum, and Museum of Art, it's ideally situated for theater, art, and concert crawls. Most rooms, decorated in a chirpy yellow, have at least partial harbor views of the ferry pier, but it's worth the small upgrade to full harbor view, or even to suites with wider views through bigger windows. Alternatively, you could also crash in one of seven four-bed dorm rooms. The Y premises also consist of a rooftop garden, chapel, hair salon, bookshop, and excellent health and fitness facilities, including a large indoor pool, squash courts, and climbing walls. **Pros:** prime views at modest prices; indoor activities to occupy the whole family. **Cons:** busy lobby reflects the Y's recreational roots. ⊠ *41 Salisbury Rd., Tsim Sha Tsui, Kowloon* ☎ *2368–7888* ⊕ *www.ymcahk.org.hk* ⤵ *363 rooms* ♿ *In-room: safe, refrigerator, Internet, Wi-Fi. In-hotel: 2 restaurants, room service, pool, gym, laundry facilities, laundry service, Internet terminal, Wi-Fi hotspot* ☰ *AE, DC, MC, V* Ⓜ *Tsim Sha Tsui* ✛ *3:E6.*

$$$ 🏨 **Sheraton Hong Kong Hotel & Towers.** At the dense and congested southern end of Nathan Road, the Sheraton is often ungraciously bypassed, but its expansive lobby with sweeping staircase is filled with artwork and sometimes enhanced with live guitar music. Rooms have a warm yet modern feel, with slick glass desktops and glass-bowl sinks in the marbled bathroom. Choose from private harbor, city, or courtyard views, but be sure to check out the panoramic views from the Sky Lounge and trendy Oyster & Wine Bar at the top. Or ascend straight to the rooftop outdoor pool and terrace via the exterior glass elevator to enjoy precious moments of respite from the crowds below while sipping champagne in a bubbling Jacuzzi. **Pros:** modern and comfortable facilities. **Cons:** congested area as soon as you set foot out the door. ⊠ *20 Nathan Rd., Tsim Sha Tsui, Kowloon* ☎ *2369–1111* ⊕ *www.sheraton.com/hongkong* ⤵ *782 rooms* ♿ *In-room: safe, refrigerator, DVD, Wi-Fi.*

In-hotel: 7 restaurants, room service, bars, pool, gym, laundry service, Wi-Fi hotspot ⊟ *AE, DC, MC, V* Ⓜ *Tsim Sha Tsui* ✛ *3:F6.*

$$ ⛶ **Stanford Hillview Hotel.** On the far eastern end of Knutsford Terrace, this simple but stately hotel rises above the neighborhood's trendy dining and nightlife venues to offer more subdued small, and straightforward rooms with views of a hill. Of course, this is not just any hill, but the hill on which is perched the Hong Kong Observatory, the city's famous white weather-predicting globe. Renovated in late 2009, every room features concave bay windows, which serve to better frame the dramatic hillscape. The rooftop has two outdoor golf-driving nets and offers local-style barbecue packages in the Sky Garden, where everyone grills their own skewers over the fire. The bright Hillview Café hosts buffet breakfast, lunch, tea, and dinner with more classic international cuisine. **Pros:** quieter hillside location. **Cons:** small, simple rooms. ⊠ *Observatory Rd. on Knutsford Terr., Tsim Sha Tsui, Kowloon* ☎ *2722–7822* ⊕ *www.stanfordhillview.com* ⤳ *177 rooms* ⛨ *In-room: safe, refrigerator, DVD, Wi-Fi. In-hotel: 3 restaurants, room service, bar, gym, laundry service, Internet terminal, Wi-Fi hotspot, parking (paid)* ⊟ *AE, DC, MC, V* Ⓜ *Tsim Sha Tsui* ✛ *3:F4.*

YAU MA TEI, MONG KOK, AND NORTHERN KOWLOON

As you venture up and off Kowloon's central artery of Nathan Road through Yau Ma Tei, accommodations tend to be older and cheaper, until you reach the grand hotels dominating shopping malls in Mong Kok. West Kowloon, centered around the classier Elements shopping mall and ICC tower, is the air-conditioned, up-and-coming exception.

¢ ⛶ **Booth Lodge.** This surprisingly pleasant retreat, which is off Nathan Road on a dead-end side street across from Temple Street Market, has been operated by the Salvation Army for the past quarter of a century. Everything here is bright and fresh, from the walls to the starched sheets on the double beds. The lobby may resemble an office, but the rooms are bigger than their location would suggest. The coffee shop serves mainly buffets, with a small outdoor balcony offering nice views of the neighborhood. There's a busy bus stop right around the corner, and the Yau Ma Tei MTR station is across the street. **Pros:** clean lodgings at a bargain price. **Cons:** noisy vehicle and foot traffic on the main street. ⊠ *11 Wing Sing La., Yau Ma Tei, Kowloon* ☎ *2771–9266* ⊕ *boothlodge.salvation.org.hk* ⤳ *60 rooms* ⛨ *In-room: refrigerator, Wi-Fi. In-hotel: restaurant, laundry service, Wi-Fi hotspot* ⊟ *AE, MC, V* Ⓜ *Yau Ma Tei* ✛ *3:E1.*

$$ ⛶ **Eaton Hotel.** Housed in a brick-red shopping and cinema complex in the middle of Nathan Road, the Eaton is just a stone's throw away from Kowloon's most famous night market on Temple Street. Its location is about equidistant between the lively nighttime street scene in Mong Kok to the north and the more touristy attractions of Tsim Sha Tsui to the south, but it's at least a 15-minute walk in either direction. The hotel's comfortable, modern rooms have beige walls, dark-wood furniture, and accentuated frames that make the best of relatively small windows, while suites feature floor-to-ceiling bay views of the city. The rooftop

Modern décor within the W Hong Kong

The W Hong Kong stands tall in Kowloon.

outdoor heated pool, just outside the glass-walled gym, is designed like a roman bath, and has large windows overlooking Kowloon on all sides. **Pros:** comfortable rooms in a relatively convenient location. **Cons:** Nathan Road can be overwhelming with the traffic and noise. ✉ *380 Nathan Rd., Yau Ma Tei, Kowloon* ☎ *2782–1818* ⊕ *hongkong. eatonhotels.com* 🛏 *465 rooms* ⚘ *In-room: safe, Internet. In-hotel: 6 restaurants, room service, bar, pool, gym, laundry service, Wi-Fi hot-spot, parking (paid)* ▭ *AE, DC, MC, V* Ⓜ *Jordan* ✚ *3:E2.*

$$ 🖼 **Harbour Grand Kowloon.** The Harbour Grand features a sweeping atrium lobby, lounges on two levels, and the spectacular Promenade buffet. Rooms are large, comfortable, and contemporary, and more than two-thirds of them have harbor views, albeit facing the less inter-esting side of the Hong Kong Island coastline. Dining venues include the traditional Japanese Robatayaki restaurant and the Waterfront Bar & Terrace, featuring Italian cuisine, an outdoor terrace, and a live band playing six days a week. If you prefer to cook, the hotel's 48-ser-viced suites have fully equipped kitchens. The setting would be idyllic, if it weren't for its deceptively removed location. Although shuttles, taxis, buses, and ferries all run to and from nearby traffic hubs and hot spots, it's a long walk from the MTR, which is the only reliable means of transportation at rush hours, on Sunday and holidays, or in bad weather. **Pros:** harborfront location on the peaceful, nontouristy side of the promenade; gorgeous glass-walled outdoor pool. **Cons:** no easy access to the MTR. ✉ *20 Tak Fung St., Whampoa Garden, Hung Hom, Kowloon* ☎ *2621–3188* ⊕ *www.harbourgrand.com/kowloon* 🛏 *554 rooms* ⚘ *In-room: safe, kitchen (some), refrigerator (some), DVD (some), Wi-Fi. In-hotel: 7 restaurants, room service, bars, pool, gym, spa, laundry service, Wi-Fi hotspot* ▭ *AE, MC, V* Ⓜ *Hung Hom* ✚ *3:H4.*

$$ 🖼 **Langham Place.** When Hong Kong's second Langham hotel opened in March 2005 as part of the shiny new Langham Place Shopping Center, it ushered in an era of prestige and prominence for its once seedy, but still refreshingly unwesternized Mong Kok neighborhood. Contempo-rary sculptures of Mao's Red Guards greet you at the entrance to this sleek, cyberage hotel made of glass and steel; it's a great exemplar of that specific science-fiction feel that defines much of modern Hong Kong. All luxurious guest rooms feature 10-foot-high floor-to-ceiling windows, mirrored walls, and tastefully low beds, with mood lighting, 42-inch plasma TVs, and an in-hotel mobile phone. Glass-walled mar-ble bathrooms include an oversized bathtub and separate rain shower. A lavish buffet breakfast is served in the light-drenched, open-kitchen The Place, while the Michelin-starred Cantonese restaurant Ming Court has private dining rooms. The hotel's top three floors are consumed by Chuan spa, with panoramic city views to accompany treatments, and the open rooftop atrium is dominated by a heated outdoor 65-foot-long pool. **Pros:** Langham luxury at a Mong Kok price; free Wi-Fi. **Cons:** no real sense of retreat from the mall. ✉ *555 Shanghai St., Mong Kok, Kowloon* ☎ *3552–3388* ⊕ *hongkong.langhamplacehotels.com* 🛏 *665 rooms* ⚘ *In-room: safe, DVD, Internet, Wi-Fi. In-hotel: 5 restaurants, room service, bar, pool, gym, spa, laundry service, Wi-Fi hotspot, park-ing (paid)* ▭ *AE, DC, MC, V* Ⓜ *Mong Kok* ✚ *3:D1.*

\$\$ ▦ **Royal Plaza.** The Royal Plaza is easily accessed from the connecting Mong Kok East MTR station, and is probably the northernmost location up Nathan Road any tourists would travel on their own, just across the street from the morning Flower Market. As part of the massive Grand Century Place complex, the environment may be overwhelming. The mall is almost always swarming with dense crowds of shoppers navigating through narrow spaces, and it's easy to get lost in the maze. The hotel is less significant for its seamless integration within the mall than for its singular location in Kowloon. The Bird Market lies at the end of Flower Market Road, and pedestrian overpasses will lead you past the Goldfish Market and into the Ladies Market, where you can also duck into the Mong Kok MTR station. Simply but comfortably furnished rooms have views of Lion Rock and the rest of Kowloon, and are surprisingly quiet. Another hotel highlight is the rooftop 130-foot-long Roman-style pool with underwater music. **Pros:** easy access to MTR; proximity to Flower, Bird, Goldfish, and Ladies' markets. **Cons:** Grand Century Place overkill. ⊠ *193 Prince Edward Rd. W, Mong Kok, Kowloon* ☎ *2928–8822* ⊕ *www.royalplaza.com.hk* ↘ *693 rooms* ♿ *In-room: safe, DVD (some), Internet, Wi-Fi (some). In-hotel: 4 restaurants, room service, pool, gym, laundry service, Wi-Fi hotspot, parking (paid)* ⊟ *MC, V* Ⓜ *Mong Kok East* ✛ *3:F1.*

\$\$\$ ▦ **W Hong Kong.** The pioneer hotel of the up-and-coming indoor com-
Fodor'sChoice mercial district of West Kowloon, W Hong Kong's main asset is its
★ seamless connection to the Elements shopping mall directly above the Kowloon MTR station, as well as to the adjacent International Commerce Centre. Although its guests are almost exclusively businesspeople, the hotel emphasizes a hip young vibe. Public spaces feature leathery and velvety furniture, funky sculptures, and even antique typewriters. If the 76th-floor outdoor heated pool and Jacuzzi area feels more like an open solarium decorated with the hotel's iconic butterfly fantasy mural; Bliss spa offers an intimate retreat from the party, with cozy views of the Hong Kong Island horizon. The veritable urban oasis, however, lies inside the rooms—soundproof and spacious, alternately colorful or sleek on even and odd floors, with mood lighting, surround audiovisual systems connected to 52-inch screens, big mirrors, and even bigger views of the harbor like you've never seen it before. **Pros:** friendly service; spacious and colorful rooms; panoramic views show a very different side of Victoria Harbour from the west. **Cons:** frigid air-conditioning and noisy atmosphere outside rooms; removed shopping-mall location. ⊠ *1 Austin Rd. W, Kowloon Station, Kowloon* ☎ *3717–2222* ⊕ *www.whotels.com/hongkong* ↘ *393 rooms* ♿ *In-room: safe, DVD, Internet, Wi-Fi. In-hotel: 4 restaurants, room service, bars, pool, gym, spa, laundry service, Wi-Fi hotspot, parking (paid)* ⊟ *AE, DC, MC, V* Ⓜ *Kowloon* ✛ *3:D3*

After Dark

WORD OF MOUTH

"A trip on Aqua Luna includes a drink and some hors d'ourves. The wooden junk is lovely and goes back and forth and around the harbour. It takes about an hour and is a good thing to do at sunset or in the afternoon."

—Cicerone

AFTER DARK PLANNER

Mug or Martini Glass

From champagne decadence to sports bars lined with peanut shells, each of Hong Kong's districts has its own distinct nighttime personality. Even on one street, dress codes and drink prices can vacillate wildly. The bar- and pub-lined streets of Lan Kwai Fong, Wan Chai, and Kowloon are a fairly casual affair, though shorts and flip-flops will limit your options. A beer or a mixed drink will cost from HK$50 to HK$80.

The Central, SoHo, and Wyndham Street areas are home to classy bars and glamorous nightclubs where a cosmopolitan mix of high rollers and partiers comes out to play. Drinks are expensive; a fresh-fruit martini will set you back more than HK$100. If you're prepared to pay a steep minimum for bottle service (HK$1,000 to HK$10,000 depending on the club), you can reserve a table for your party at some of these swanky establishments. Door trolls abound, so dress up to get in and blend in—shorts, flip-flops, and sneakers are definite no-nos.

Members Only

Many bars and clubs have a "members-only" policy, but don't let this deter you. It's mostly a way of prioritizing the guest list on busy nights. It can also mean that you're required to pay a cover charge, usually in the region of HK$150 to HK$200 and including a drink on the house.

Nightlife Savvy

HK magazine is distributed free each Friday. Listings authority *Time Out Hong Kong* costs HK$18 and is published every other Wednesday. Another good source of nightlife and cultural information is the daily English-language newspaper the *South China Morning Post,* whose Going Out supplement is released every Thursday.

Tickets for most big cultural events are on sale through citywide branches of **URBTIX** (☎ 2111–5999 ⊕ *www.urbtix. hk*). **HK Ticketing** (☎ 3128–8288 ⊕ *www.hkticketing.com*) sells tickets to many shows.

Hours

Twenty-four-hour liquor licenses are common, so strict closing times are not. Bars start closing around 2 AM, clubs around 4 AM, with some seeing in the sunrise. Happy hours are from midafternoon to 8 or 9 PM on weekdays. Closing times listed refer to Friday, Saturday, and the eves of public holidays; you can expect things to wind down an hour or two earlier midweek. Bars are typically open nightly, but nightclubs are closed or quiet on Sunday and Monday.

Dancing

Nightclubs range from down-to-earth dives with boisterous cover bands to hermetically sealed hip-hop dungeons packed with models and millionaires. The venues listed here tend to be smaller and more intimate than their high-octane megaplex cousins. Cover charges, if levied, can be steep, from HK$120 to HK$250, but often include a drink or two. Information and tickets for international DJ events can be found at ⊕ www.hkclubbing.com or ⊕ www.hiphongkong.com. Some bars and restaurants also hold weekly or monthly club nights, where music ranges from jazz to drum-and-bass.

Hostess Clubs

Many hostess clubs found in Hong Kong are clubs in name only. Some of these are multimillion-dollar operations with plush interiors and hundreds of hostess-companions working for them. Hostess clubs are a stage for showgirls and tycoons, designed to sweeten lucrative deals and lubricate business relationships. Expect to see exhibitions of arguably tasteless extravagance as patrons pay up to HK$1,000 per hour for the privilege of drinking in the company of attractive women. Between minimum drink charges, drinks for the hostesses, tips, and the possibility of spending upwards of five figures on a bottle of wine, you're looking at an HK$100,000-plus tab, a sum that does not faze the regulars. Indeed, legend has it that the biggest security problem faced by bouncers is breaking up fights over who gets to pay the bill.

The better clubs are on a par with music lounges in deluxe hotels, though they cost a little more. Dance floors are often large, with live bands and a lineup of both pop and cabaret singers. Their happy hours start in the afternoon, when many have a sort of tea-dance ambience, and continue through to mid-evening. Peak hours are 10 PM to 4 AM.

Many so-called hostess clubs, however, are in fact fronts for prostitution. In Wan Chai, for instance, hostess clubs—too many to mention by name—are dotted among regular bars. Most if not all of them are sad little places full of leering men watching girls with vacant expressions, dressed in leotards, performing halfhearted pole dances. These houses of prostitution are not the same as establishments such as the upmarket Club BBoss in Tsim Sha Tsui.

Better Safe than Sorry

All premises licensed to serve alcohol are supposedly subject to stringent fire, safety, and sanitary controls, although at times this is hard to believe, given the overcrowding at the hippest places. Think twice before succumbing to the city's raunchier hideaways. If you stumble into one, check out cover and table charges *before* you get too comfortable. If you don't have a table, pay for each round of drinks as it's served (by cash rather than credit card).

Hong Kong is a surprisingly safe place, but as in many destinations, the art of the out-of-towner rip-off has been perfected. If you're unsure, visit places signposted as approved by the Hong Kong Tourism Board (HKTB).

After the Party

The clean and reliable subway (MTR) shuts down at around 1 AM, depending on your location. Taxis are your only way home after that. They are relatively cheap and can easily be flagged down on the street; when the light on the car roof is on, it's available for hire. If the cab has an OUT OF SERVICE sign over its round FOR HIRE neon sign on the dashboard, it means it's a cross-harbor taxi. Fares start at HK$18.

Updated by
Samantha
Leese

A riot of neon, heralding frenetic after-hours action, announces Hong Kong's nightlife districts. Clubs and bars fill to capacity, evening markets pack in shoppers looking for bargains, restaurants welcome diners, cinemas pop corn as fast as they can, and theaters and concert halls prepare for full houses.

The neighborhoods of Wan Chai, Lan Kwai Fong, and SoHo are packed with bars, pubs, and nightclubs that cater to everyone from the hippest trendsetters, to bankers ready to spend their bonuses, and more laid-back crowds out for a pint. Partying in Hong Kong is a way of life; it starts at the beginning of the week with a drink or two after work, progressing to serious barhopping and clubbing on the weekends. Wednesday is a big night out here—so much so that the staff at one famous club sport "Thursday Sucks" T-shirts on the quiet day after. Work hard, play harder is the motto in Hong Kong, and people follow it seriously.

Because each district has so much to offer, and since they're all quite close to each other, it's perfectly normal to pop into two or three bars before heading to a nightclub. At the other end of the spectrum, the city's arts and culture scene is equally lively, with innovative music, dance, and theater. Small independent productions as well as large-scale concerts take to the stage across the territory every weekend. You simply cannot go home without a Hong Kong nightlife story to tell!

HONG KONG ISLAND

WESTERN

BARS

Club 71. This bohemian diamond-in-the-rough was named in tribute to July 1, 2003, when half a million Hong Kongers successfully rallied against looming threats to their freedom of speech. Tucked away on a terrace down a market side street, the quirky, unpretentious bar is a

HONG KONG'S TOP FIVE NIGHTLIFE SPOTS

dragon-i: The door's clipboard-wielding glamazons will not make entry easy, but this is easily the kingpin of the big Central clubs, and second home to the city's extravagant elite.

Felix: Aqua Spirit may be trendier, but Phillipe Starck–designed Felix is an institution. The best view of the skyline is marketing currency in Kowloon, and this penthouse bar really matches its claim.

The Pawn: Modern panache and history's charm combine to make this one of the most unique establishments in town. Order a bottle of wine and settle onto one of the vintage couches in the ever-popular "living room."

Solas: Unofficial epicenter of Wyndham Street's seismic after-dark action, Solas is dfifficult to beat if you're looking for somewhere loud and lively to meet new people over well-mixed drinks.

Volume: A fun, friendly, and diverse crowd distinguishes Volume from many of the city's more aloof gay establishments. The Wednesday evening happy hour is the best mixer on the scene.

mainstay of artists, journalists, and left-wing politicians. The outdoor area closes around midnight. ⊠ *B/F, 67 Hollywood Rd., Sheung Wan, Western* ☎ *2858–7071* ⊙ *Closes 2* AM Ⓜ *Central.*

GAY AND LESBIAN SPOTS

Volume. Down a leafy residential staircase where Hollywood Road meets Aberdeen Street, Volume feels a little like the backstage of a small-town cabaret with faux tiger-fur seats, red-velvet curtain, dancer's pole, and mirror ball dominating the decor. The club hosts a friendly, mixed crowd of gays, lesbians, and their friends, thanks to free entry and an open-door policy. New Arrivals Wednesdays are a staple of the scene, welcoming tourists and newbies, and attracting locals with free vodka between 7 and 9:30 PM. Weekends are reliably hyper, with dance anthems filling the floor till the wee hours. The entrance is just below street level, around the corner from the main road. ⊠ *83–85 Hollywood Rd., Sheung Wan, Western* ☎ *2857–7683* ⊙ *Closes late* Ⓜ *Sheung Wan.*

CENTRAL

On weekends the streets of Lan Kwai Fong are liberated from traffic, and the swilling hordes from both sides of the street merge into one heaving organism. A five-minute walk uphill is SoHo. Back in the '90s it took local businesses some effort to convince district councillors that the sometimes vice-associated moniker (which in this case stands for South of Hollywood Road) was a good idea, but Hong Kong is now proud of this *très* chic area, a warren of streets stuffed with commensurately priced restaurants, bars, and late-night boutiques. Midway between Lan Kwai Fong's madness and SoHo's bohemian glamour is Wyndham Street, home to an array of sophisticated bars, nightclubs, and restaurants and strict domain of the over 25s.

CLOSE UP

Lan Kwai Fong

A curious, L-shape cobblestone lane in Central is the pulsating center of nightlife and dining in Hong Kong. Lan Kwai Fong, or just "the Fong," is a spot that really shines after the sun sets. You can start with a pre-dinner drink at any number of bars, then enjoy some of the territory's finest dining before stopping at a nightclub to dance the night away.

For such a small warren, Lan Kwai Fong has an incredibly broad range of nightlife to offer, with dozens of bars, restaurants, and clubs within just a few blocks. Since most of the ground-floor establishments spill out onto the pavement, there's an audible buzz about the place, lending it a festive air that's unmatched elsewhere in Hong Kong. Whether it's corporate financiers celebrating their latest million-dollar deals at La Dolce Vita or more humble office workers having drinks with their buddies at Le Jardin, there's a place here to suit everyone.

The same "something for everyone" motto extends to the plethora of upmarket restaurants in Lan Kwai Fong. From Asia, there are Chinese, Thai, Japanese, and Vietnamese restaurants, while European food can be found at French and Italian establishments. If your wallet's feeling a little light from your latest shopping expedition, take heed of the excited waiters waving to potential customers along Wing Wah Lane (affectionately known as Rat Alley). Here you'll find rowdy Indian, Thai, and Malaysian restaurants that serve piping-hot dishes at reasonable prices.

Lan Kwai Fong used to be a hawkers' neighborhood before World War II. Its modern success is largely due to Canadian expatriate Allan Zeman, an

eccentric figure who has been dubbed the "King of Lan Kwai Fong" by the local media. He opened his first North American–style restaurant here 20 years ago; today he not only owns dozens of other restaurants and bars, but also the buildings they're in. He claims to have about 100 restaurants, and although he doesn't actually own them all, he acts as the landlord for most of them. The Fong restaurants are now simply a hobby for Zeman, whose business empire includes everything from property development to fashion.

New Year's Eve (December 31) is undoubtedly the busiest time for Lan Kwai Fong. Thousands of people line the tiny area to celebrate and party. You'll notice a strong police presence moving the human traffic through the streets and keeping an eye out for any troublemakers. This is mainly to prevent another tragedy such as the one in the early 1990s when 21 people were crushed to death as a massive throng went out of control as they ushered in a new year. Now when large crowds are anticipated—usually New Year's Eve, Christmas Eve, and also Halloween—the police carefully monitor the number of people entering the area.

Call it progress or a type of survival-of-the-strongest evolution, but this trendy neighborhood has seen as many establishments open as close down. New spots are constantly in development, or old places under refurbishment. Regardless of the changes, Lan Kwai Fong is always alive with scores of people and places to be merry.

—Eva Chui Loiterton

Partiers vie for elbow room on Lan Kwai Fong, Central's nightlife hub.

BARS

Barco. Had enough of the crowds and looking for a quiet drink and conversation that you can actually hear? Barco is the place. It's cozy, with a small lounge area and an even smaller courtyard in the back, and an assortment of board games if you're feeling playful. ⊠ *42 Staunton St., SoHo, Central* ☎ *2857–4478* ⊗ *Closes 1* AM Ⓜ *Central.*

F.I.N.D.S. The name of this supercool restaurant and bar is an acronym of Finland, Iceland, Norway, Denmark, and Sweden. Inspired by Scandinavian winters, the striking decor is pale blue and white, with sparkling granite walls. There's a large outdoor terrace with comfortable seating. About 30 premium vodkas are served. You can also try a cocktail from the adventurous molecular mixology menu. ⊠ *2nd fl., LKF Tower, 33 Wyndham St., Central* ☎ *2522–9318* ⊗ *Closes 3* AM Ⓜ *Central.*

Goccia. Beautiful people both young and not-so-young flock to this Italian bar (with a restaurant upstairs), and it's packed wall-to-wall most nights. *Goccia*—which means "drop" in Italian—occupies a long room on the ground floor, and if it had a VIP table it would be one by the open front facing the street, where you can see and be seen. ⊠ *73 Wyndham St., Central* ☎ *2167–8181* ⊗ *Closes 3* AM Ⓜ *Central.*

La Dolce Vita. Crowds at this Lan Kwai Fong mainstay, beneath its sister restaurant **Post 97** and next to its other sibling **Club 97**, often spill onto the pavement. One of the first modern bars to pop up when the area gained popularity, La Dolce Vita has a sleek interior and is a popular stomping ground for the moneyed masses. ⊠ *9 Lan Kwai Fong, Lan Kwai Fong, Central* ☎ *2810–9333* ⊗ *Closes 3* AM Ⓜ *Central.*

Le Jardin. For an otherworldly, cosmopolitan vibe, check out this casual bar with a lovely outdoor terrace overlooking the gregarious alfresco dining lane known locally as Rat Alley. Walk through the dining area and up a flight of steps. It's a little tricky to find, but the leafy, fairy-lit setting is worth it. ✉ *1st fl., 10 Wing Wah La., Central* ☎ *2877–1100* ⊙ *Closes 4* AM Ⓜ *Central*.

Lei Dou. Meaning simply "here" in Cantonese, this boudoir-styled spot, hidden away in the heart of the action, is where those in the know (and those seeking discretion) come to wind down in style. Lei Dou's fans love it for its decadent, low-lit decor, down-tempo jazz, and comfortable seating. ✉ *Ground fl., 20–22 D'Aguilar St., Central* ☎ *2525–6628* ⊙ *Closes 3* AM Ⓜ *Central*.

Lux. The well-heeled drink martinis and designer beers at this swanky corner spot. It has a prime location in Lan Kwai Fong and is a great bar for people-watching; it also serves excellent food in booths at the back. ✉ *California Tower, 30–32 D'Aguilar St., Lan Kwai Fong, Central* ☎ *2868–9538* ⊙ *Closes 4* AM.

MO Bar. This plush bar in the Landmark Mandarin Oriental is where the banking set goes to relax. You'll pay top dollar for the martinis (up to HK$150), but the striking interior makes it worthwhile. A huge, red-light circle dominates an entire wall, the "O" being a Chinese symbol of shared experience. ✉ *The Landmark Mandarin Oriental, 15 Queen's Rd. Central, The Landmark, Central* ☎ *2132–0077* ⊙ *Closes 2* AM Ⓜ *Central*.

RED Bar. Although its shopping mall location, outdoor terrace self-service policy, and incongruous affiliation with the next-door gym may not seem appealing, once you arrive, you'll throw all your preconceived notions into the harbor. On the roof of IFC Mall, RED has breathtaking views of the city, making it a great place to grab an early dinner and relax with a cocktail while watching the sunset. ✉ *Level 4, Two IFC, 8 Finance St., Central* ☎ *8129–8882* ⊙ *Closes 2* AM Ⓜ *Hong Kong*.

Sevva. With a view onto Central's glittering valley of skyscrapers, this cool and elegant rooftop bar is always busy on Friday and Saturday nights. If you're feeling indulgent, come for dessert (the cakes are among the city's best) and stay for cocktails. Most of Sevva's well-heeled clientele prefer to drink outside on the spacious, slatted terrace, but there are couches inside too. ✉ *25th fl., Prince's Bldg., 10 Chater Rd., Central* ☎ *2537–1388* ⊙ *Closes 2* AM Ⓜ *Central*.

Fodor's Choice ★ **Solas.** Positioned a floor below super-club dragon-i, this red-lit, always crowded bar is Wyndham Street's party central. Expect a mostly expat crowd of twenty- and thirtysomethings, who come straight from work on weekdays. To avoid the excited crush on Wednesday's ladies night and on weekends, head for the booths along the walls and leave before the DJ starts to spin at around 11 PM. ✉ *60 Wyndham St., SoHo, Central* ☎ *3162–3710* ⊙ *Closes 4* AM Ⓜ *Central*.

Staunton's Wine Bar & Cafe. Adjacent to Hong Kong's famous outdoor escalator is this popular bistro-style café and bar. Partly alfresco, it's the perfect place to people-watch, whether from the balcony or from the steps, where you can hang out on foam picnic mats. You can come

Art Spaces

CLOSE UP

Fringe Club. The pioneer of Hong Kong's alternative arts scene has been staging excellent independent theater, music, and art productions since opening in 1983. The distinctive brown-and-white-stripe colonial structure was built as a cold-storage warehouse in 1892. It was derelict when the Fringe moved in; and the painstaking renovation has earned awards. Light pours through huge windows into the street-level Economist Gallery, with its small, well-curated exhibitions.

The übercool Fotogalerie, upstairs, is Hong Kong's only photography gallery. Downstairs, meat and cheese were once sold in the space that now houses the Fringe Theatre. The lighting box of the smaller Studio Theatre was once a refrigeration unit, built to preserve not food but winter clothes from summer mildew. Fringe productions are sometimes in Cantonese, so check the program carefully. ⊠ *2 Lower Albert Rd., Central* ☎ *2521-7251 general inquiries, 3128-8288 box office* ⊕ *www.hkfringe.com.hk* ⊠ *Galleries free* ⊘ *Art galleries and box office: Mon.–Sat. noon–10. Fotogalerie: Mon.–Thurs. noon–midnight, Fri. and Sat. 10:30* AM*–3* AM. *Fringe Gallery Bar: Mon.–Thurs. 4* PM*–midnight, Fri. and Sat. 4* PM*–3* AM Ⓜ *Central, Exit D2.*

Hong Kong Arts Centre. A hodgepodge of activities takes place in this deceptively bleak concrete tower, financed with horse-racing profits donated by the Hong Kong Jockey Club. Intriguing contemporary art exhibitions are held in the 14th-floor Goethe Gallery, a white-cube space. Thematic cycles of art-house flicks run in the basement Agnès b. CINEMA! Community theater groups are behind much of the fare at the Shouson Theatre and smaller McAulay Studio, though international drama and dance troupes sometimes appear. Quality is hit and miss, so check newspaper reviews for advice. From Wan Chai MTR, cross the footbridge to Immigration Tower, then dogleg left through the open plaza until you hit Harbour Road: the center is on the left. ⊠ *2 Harbour Rd., Wan Chai* ☎ *2582-0200, 2802-0088 Goethe Gallery* ⊕ *www.hkac.org.hk* ⊠ *Free* ⊘ *Center: daily 10–8. Goethe Gallery: weekdays 10–8, Sat. 2–6* Ⓜ *Wan Chai, Exit C.*

Ma Tau Kok Cattle Depot. A former slaughterhouse in industrial To Kwa Wan has become a happening hub of independent art. It's divvied up into spaces run by different groups. In July 1997—as Hong Kong was handed back to China—a group of young local artists formed the **Artists' Commune** (⊠ *Unit 12* ☎ *2104-3322* ⊕ *www.artist-commune.com* ⊠ *Free* ⊘ *Tues.–Sun. 2–8),* whose massive loftlike premises showcase offbeat works. Expect funky, well-curated pickings at **1aspace** (⊠ *Unit 14* ☎ *2529-0087* ⊕ *www.oneaspace.org.hk* ⊠ *Free* ⊘ *Tues.–Sun 2–8),* a cool, sleek gallery. The easiest way to get here is by taxi from Tsim Sha Tsui (around HK$50) or from Lok Fu MTR (around HK$35). ⊠ *63 Ma Tau Kok Rd., To Kwa Wan, Kowloon.*

—Victoria Patience

7

for a drink at night or for coffee or a meal during the day. It's also a Sunday-morning favorite for nursing hangovers over brunch. ⊠ *10–12 Staunton St., SoHo, Central* ☎ *2973–6611* ⊘ *Closes 3* AM Ⓜ *Central.*

DISCOS AND NIGHTCLUBS

Azure. Head skyward to this cosmopolitan, bi-level club at the top of the 30-story Hotel LKF. The downstairs lounge is a sophisticated space with pool tables, couches, and a soundtrack of ambient tunes. Upstairs, take in a 270-degree panorama of the harbor from the smoker's terrace, or dance to funky-house music inside. ⊠ *29th fl., Hotel LKF, 33 Wyndham St., Central* ☎ *3518–9330* ⊘ *Closes 2* AM Ⓜ *Central.*

Cliq. Cliq has garnered plaudits as one of the city's top clubbing venues. Its 6,000 square feet contain an unusually spacious dance floor and are decorated with a wall of TV screens, black chandeliers, polished concrete surfaces, and a large platform for visiting DJs. ⊠ *2nd fl., On Hing Bldg., On Hing Terrace, Central* ☎ *2868–3111* ⊘ *Closes 3* AM Ⓜ *Central.*

Fodor's Choice
★

dragon-i. The entrance is marked by an enormous birdcage (filled with real budgies and canaries) made entirely of bamboo poles. Have a drink on the busy alfresco deck by the doorway or step inside the rich, red playroom, which doubles as a restaurant at lunchtime and in the early evening. The club's notorious Model's Night takes place on Wednesdays, and is a playground for the city's young and beautiful. ⊠ *The Centrium, 60 Wyndham St., Central* ☎ *3110–1222* ⊘ *Closes 5* AM Ⓜ *Central.*

Drop. This pint-size gem is where celebrities party—usually until sunrise—when they're in town. Hidden down an alley beside a late-night food stand, its location only adds an air of exclusivity to the speakeasy feel. Excellent fresh-fruit martinis are its forte. Drop has two incarnations: after-dinner cocktail lounge before midnight, and impenetrable fortress later on, so arrive early to avoid disappointment. ⊠ *Basement, On Lok Mansion, 39–43 Hollywood Rd., entrance off Cochrane St., Central* ☎ *2543–8856* ⊘ *Closes 6* AM Ⓜ *Central.*

MINT. This Hollywood Road hot spot attracts a more sophisticated crowd than Central's other big clubs. While it can get packed when big-name DJs perform, it usually provides a break from Wyndham Street's nighttime swell. Look out for soirées that are thrown regularly here, such as jazz series or networking nights. Table bookings are advised for the VIP area, where you can enjoy your bottle under the glow from a shark tank. ⊠ *108 Hollywood Rd., Central* ☎ *2261–1111* ⊘ *Closes at 3* AM Ⓜ *Sheung Wan.*

Philia. With regular events aimed at the artistic community, Philia has become a trendy hub for the city's creative minds. With a neo-Victorian interior and a name that means friendship, the green-lit space is a favorite spot for networking while having a drink to the sounds of an up-and-coming DJ, MC, or a live band. Check the schedule for the monthly events like the "Speak Up!" open mike night and performances by hyperactive DJ duo Songs for Children. ⊠ *4 Arbuthnot Rd., Central* ☎ *2147–2389* ⊘ *Closes 2* AM Ⓜ *Central.*

Volar. By midnight the line outside this club is more like a scrimmage, as die-hard clubbers claw through the fray to face the meanest door staff

CLOSE UP

Late-Night Bites

Nix that looming hangover with a greasy fry-up *before* you hit the sack. **The Flying Pan** (⊠ *Ground fl., 9 Old Bailey St., Central* ☎ *2140–6333* ⊠ *3rd fl., 81–85 Lockhart Rd., Wan Chai* ☎ *2528–9997*) is a popular 24-hour breakfast diner, equally busy at 3 AM and 3 PM on weekends. Eggs any style come with your two picks from a huge list of sides including grits, blintzes, baked beans, and fruit salad. The truly greedy can order a Kitchen Sink, which is a taste of everything.

A decent late-supper spot is **Post 97** (⊠ *1st fl., 9 Lan Kwai Fong, Lan Kwai Fong, Central* ☎ *2810–9333* Ⓜ *Wan Chai*), where the kitchen is open until 2 AM on Friday and Saturday. The all-day menu has consistently good grub from focaccia and salads to chicken wings and hearty breakfasts. Grab a window seat to peer down at the other late-night revelers of Lan Kwai Fong.

While locals head to **Tsui Wah** (⊠ *15–19 Wellington St., Central* ☎ *2525–6338* Ⓜ *Central*), a large, three-story Chinese restaurant, at any time of the day, the late-night crowds are the happiest. Service is quick, there's a huge menu of typical Chinese fare such as fried rice and noodles, as well as western dishes such as steak and pasta. It's noisy, smoky, and bright, but the crowds just keep on coming. You may even find the odd celebrity chowing down on beef brisket noodles at 2 AM. The place closes for an hour at 4 AM.

—Eva Chui Loiterton

7

in town. The maze of low-ceilinged basement rooms features a young, hip crowd, and a genuinely eclectic mix of music, from electro-house to hip-hop to rock and roll mash-ups. The monthly bassline night (a popular party featuring electronic music heavy on the bass), Hype Nasty, is run by local DJ doyens Kid Fresh and Enso, and usually happens on the last Friday of the month. ⊠ *Basement, 39–44 D'Aguilar St., Lan Kwai Fong, Central* ☎ *2810–1272* ☉ *Closes 5* AM Ⓜ *Central.*

Yumla. This tiny, alternative club is the den of local DJ talent, and the only noncommercial music space in Central (you won't hear this music on the radio). As such, it has garnered a band of fiercely loyal regulars, which can make the casual visitor feel out of place. Even with a cover charge of HK$100 on weekends, the place can get mercilessly packed. But if you're there for the music, it's worth it. Check the Web site for schedules and promotions. ⊠ *Lower basement, 79 Wyndham St., Central* ☎ *2147–2382* ⊕ *www.yumla.com* ☉ *Closes late* Ⓜ *Central.*

GAY AND LESBIAN SPOTS

Propaganda. Off a quaint but steep cobblestone street is one of *the* most popular gay clubs in Hong Kong. Propaganda holds a near-monopoly on the late-night scene. The art deco bar area hosts quite the flirt-fest, while the sunken dance floor has poles on either side for go-go boys to flaunt their wares. It's pretty empty during the week, despite the free-entry happy hour Tuesday through Thursday nights; the crowds arrive well after midnight on weekends. The entrance is in an alleyway, Ezra

The Globe offers a bit of Britain in SoHo.

Lane, which runs parallel to Hollywood Road and is best accessed from Pottinger Street. ⊠ *1 Hollywood Rd., Central* ☎ *2868–1316* ⊘ *Closes 5:30* AM Ⓜ *Central.*

MUSIC CLUBS

The Cavern. This large bar at the top of Lan Kwai Fong is a laid-back space where locals and out-of-towners alike come to drink beer, eat peanuts, tap their feet to the lively cover bands, and watch the swelling streets from the pavement tables. ⊠ *Shop 1, ground fl., LKF Tower, 33 Wyndham St., entrance on D'Aguliar St., Central* ☎ *2121–8969* ⊘ *Closes 4* AM Ⓜ *Central.*

Fodor's Choice
★
Fringe Club. The arts-minded mingle in this historic redbrick building that also houses the members-only Foreign Correspondents' Club, next door. The Fringe is the headquarters for Hong Kong's alternative arts scene, and normally stages live music twice a week. The outdoor roof bar, with its potted plants and fairy lights, is laid-back and serves reasonably priced drinks. If the weather is unfriendly, go to the ground-floor gallery bar to rub shoulders with regulars, from students to the city's who's who in arts and film. ⊠ *2 Lower Albert Rd., Central* ☎ *2521–7251* ⊘ *Closes 3* AM.

Grappa's Cellar. This cavernous basement restaurant clears its tables regularly for some of the best live music gigs in town. Whether the performers are visiting indie bands or homegrown Dixieland jazz talent, the huge dance floor and rowdy second-level bar make it difficult not to have fun. Swing kings Stray Katz Big Band play on the first Saturday of each month. City magazines like HK and Time Out sometimes host sponsored multi-band events here, so look out for these year round.

☒ *Basement, Jardine House, 1 Connaught Pl., Central* ☎ *2521–2322* ⏲ *Closes midnight* Ⓜ *Central.*

PUBS

Fodor's Choice
★

Globe. This gastropub and perennial British expat hangout has switched shop and upped stakes. The large, now trendy SoHo space brings the feel of southwest London with it. You can book the sectioned off "chill-out" area to watch live sports coverage with a private party. Good luck trying to get the proprietors to turn on the World Series or the Super Bowl, though. Soccer and rugby reign supreme here, and you have to share the TV. ☒ *45–53 Graham St., SoHo, Central* ☎ *2543–1941* ⏲ *Closes 2 AM* Ⓜ *Central.*

LES PECHES

Though Central has a relatively open gay scene, Hong Kong's lesbians are notoriously low profile. For newcomers, Les Peches Lounge is an oasis of sorts: a monthly get-together, open to lesbians, bisexual women, and their friends, with a good mix of ages and ethnic backgrounds. Les Peches takes place on the first Tuesday of every month at Tavis Club (☒ *20th fl. Century Square, 1-13 D'Aguilar St., Lan Kwai Fong* ✉ *lespechesinfo@yahoo.com* Ⓜ *Central*) from 8 PM to 2 AM; the HK$80 cover includes one drink.

The Keg. As its name implies, beer and more beer is the beverage of choice at this small pub. It is designed to resemble the inside of a keg, with interiors finished in wood, copper, and polished steel. Large wooden barrels serve as tables, and the floors are covered with discarded peanut shells. Sports coverage rules the TV screens. ☒ *52 D'Aguilar St., Lan Kwai Fong, Central* ☎ *2810–0369* ⏲ *Closes 3 AM* Ⓜ *Central.*

WINE BAR

Tastings. Oenophiles will discover like minds at this marble-accented retreat, a vanguard of the city's blossoming (and very serious) wine scene. Tucked in an alley off Wellington Street, the bar stocks more than 160 wines. A rotating 40 are available for sampling through the Enomatic wine dispenser, which the sommeliers use to draw from rare wines without uncorking the entire bottle. Head toward the doorway's chichi blue glow to find the place. Enjoy the spread of fine cheeses and Italian antipasti before the tasting begins. ☒ *27 and 29 Wellington St., Central* ☎ *2523–6282* ⏲ *Closes 2 AM* Ⓜ *Central.*

WAN CHAI

Wan Chai is the pungent night flower of the nocturnal scene, where the way of life served as inspiration for the novel *The World of Suzie Wong*. It now shares the streets with hip wine bars, salsa nights, old men's pubs, and after-parties that continue past sunrise. The seedy "hostess bars" in this neighborhood are easy to spot and avoid, with curtained entrances guarded by old ladies on stools and suggestive names in neon. But some things never change: the busiest nights are still when there's a navy ship in the harbor on an R&R stopover. Wednesday's ladies' night, with half-price drinks, is also a big draw.

CLOSE UP

Chinese Opera

For a unique evening out, nab tickets to a Chinese Opera performance.

There are 10 **Cantonese opera** troupes headquartered in Hong Kong, as well as many amateur singing groups. Some put on performances of "street opera" in, for example, the Temple Street Night Market almost every night, while others perform at temple fairs, in City Hall, or in playgrounds under the auspices of the Urban Council. Those unfamiliar with Chinese opera might find the sights and sounds of this highly complex and sophisticated art form a little strange. Every gesture has its own meaning; in fact, there are 50 gestures for the hand alone.

Props attached to the costumes are similarly intricate and are used in exceptional ways. For example, the principal female often has 5-foot-long pheasant-feather tails attached to her headdress; she shows anger by dropping the head and shaking it in a circular fashion so that the feathers move in a perfect circle. Surprise is shown by what's called "nodding the feathers." You can also "dance with the feathers" to show a mixture of anger and determination. Orchestral music punctuates the singing. It's best to attend with someone who can translate the gestures for you; or you can learn more at the Cantonese Opera Halls in the Hong Kong Heritage Museum.

The highly stylized **Peking opera** employs higher-pitched voices than Cantonese opera. Peking opera is an older form, more respected for its classical traditions; the meticulous training of the several troupes visiting Hong Kong from the People's Republic of China each year is well regarded. They perform in City Hall or at special temple ceremonies. You can get the latest programs from the Hong Kong Cultural Centre.

—Eva Chui Loiterton

BARS

Mes Amis. In the heart of Wan Chai, on the corner of Lockhart and Luard roads, Mes Amis is a friendly, high-ceilinged bar that also serves food. Its corner setting and open bi-fold doors mean that none of the action outside is missed, and vice versa—the perpetual crowd inside is on display to those on the street. ⊠ *83 Lockhart Rd., Wan Chai* ☎ *2527–6680* ⊙ *Closes 5 AM* Ⓜ *Wan Chai.*

1/5 nuevo. Once one of Hong Kong's slickest nightspots, 1/5 moved down to street level in 2007 and morphed into a tapas lounge and cocktail bar, hence the addition of "nuevo" to its name. High-flyers, financiers, and expats populate this dark, sophisticated Star Street hangout. ⊠ *9 Star St., Wan Chai* ☎ *2529–2300* ⊙ *Closes 2 AM* Ⓜ *Wan Chai.*

Fodor's Choice ★ **The Pawn.** In a district plagued by controversial redevelopment, this attractive historic building, a former pawnshop, has been preserved with minimal fuss. The stylish interior is outfitted with retro furniture, while carefully selected vestiges from its less salubrious days give the space a decadent, vintage feel. The long balcony overlooking the iconic Hong Kong tramway is a great place for spying on bustling everyday life below. Upstairs is the restaurant, serving quality gastro-pub fare. Above that is the pretty, wood-accented roof garden—a favorite of the art and journalist crowds. ⊠ *62 Johnston Rd., Wan Chai* ☎ *2866–3444* ⊙ *Closes 2 AM* Ⓜ *Wan Chai.*

Vertigo Ultralounge. A few streets away from Wan Chai's seedy neon strip, closer to Admiralty and fashionable, upmarket Star Street, this skyscraping bar has a DJ booth in the main arena and three private party rooms, one with a full-size American pool table, another with a karaoke setup. The dress code is strictly smart casual. ⊠ *26th fl., 202 Queen's Rd. E, Wan Chai* ☎ *2575–8980* ⊙ *Closes 3 AM* Ⓜ *Wan Chai.*

Wooloomooloo. This sleek rooftop bar, the name of which is the Australian aboriginal word for "young male kangaroo," provides a respite from the Wan Chai crowds. The downstairs steak house had its original branch in Lan Kwai Fong, and has done well enough to open three more branches. Here it's the alfresco bar that's the real draw. The breezy terrace and a panoramic view over Happy Valley have made it a favorite among the after-work crowd. The catch? Licensing woes mean that the only drinks served up here are wines from the restaurant's New World–heavy wine list. ⊠ *31/F, 256 Hennessy Rd., entrance on 211 Johnson Rd., Wan Chai* ☎ *2893–6960* ⊙ *Closes midnight* Ⓜ *Wan Chai.*

ARTFUL DATES

Hong Kong City Fringe Festival (January and February): Theater, dance, comedy, film, visual arts, and new media take place in venues across town. ⊕ *www.hkfringe.com.hk.*

Hong Kong Arts Festival (February and March): Past visitors have included Mikhail Baryshnikov, Pina Bausch, and José Carreras. The focus is on performing arts. ⊕ *www.hk.artsfestival.org.*

Hong Kong International Film Festival (April): Asian cinema accounts for many of the 200 new films shown in this festival. ⊕ *www.hkiff.org.hk.*

7

CLOSE UP

Performance Places

City Hall. From Isaac Stern, Yo-Yo Ma, and the New York Philharmonic to the Bee Gees; from the Royal Danish Ballet to the People's Liberation Army Comrade Dance Troupe, the offerings here are varied, but consistently excellent. Two buildings make up the chunky '60s complex, divided by a World War II memorial garden and shrine. The 1,500-seat concert hall and a smaller theater are in the low-rise block, as is Maxim's City Palace, a massive clattering restaurant with really good dim sum. The high-rise building has an exhibition space and a smaller recital hall, as well as a public library and marriage registry office. Performances are usually held Friday and Saturday at 8 PM. ✉ *5 Edinburgh Pl., Central* ☎ *2921–2840, 2734–9009 box office* ⊕ *www.lcsd.gov.hk* ⊘ *Daily 9–9; box office daily 10–8* Ⓜ *Central, Exit K.*

Hong Kong Academy for Performing Arts. Many of Hong Kong's most talented performers studied at this academy's schools of drama, music, dance, television, and film. It also has five theaters and a gallery. Large-scale productions are staged in the huge Lyric Theatre and the smaller Drama Theatre; offerings are often in the round at the dinky Studio Theatre. The two concert halls host choice classical or traditional Chinese music performances. ■TIP→ **When the weather's good, inquire about shows in the garden amphitheater.** ✉ *1 Gloucester Rd., Wan Chai* ☎ *2584–8580* ⊕ *www.hkapa.edu* ⊘ *Box office Mon.–Sat. noon–6 PM; on performance nights, the box office remains open until 30 minutes after the last performance starts* Ⓜ *Wan Chai, Exit C.*

Hong Kong Cultural Centre. Superlatives abound here: the massive oval concert hall, which seats 2,000, is Asia's biggest; its 8,000-pipe Austrian organ is one of the world's largest. Only slightly smaller, the tiered Grand Theatre often hosts visiting Broadway musicals and opera and ballet productions. Cozier plays take place in the Studio Theatre. Look out for performances by the world-class **Hong Kong Philharmonic Orchestra** (☎ *2721–2030* ⊕ *www.hkpo.com*), which performs everything from classical to avant-garde to contemporary music by Chinese composers. Past soloists have included Vladimir Ashkenazy, Rudolf Firkusny, and Maureen Forrester. Exhibits are occasionally mounted in the atrium. ✉ *10 Salisbury Rd., Tsim Sha Tsui, Kowloon* ☎ *2734–2010; 2734–9009 box office* ⊕ *www.lcsd.gov.hk* ⊘ *Daily 9–11; box office daily 10–9:30* Ⓜ *Tsim Sha Tsui, Exit E.*

Kwai Tsing Theatre. It might be in the sticks, but it's a major player in the cultural scene. Sunlight pours into the atrium through a curving glass facade that looks onto a plaza where performances are often held. Inside, the 900-seat theater provides a much-needed middle ground between the massive spaces and tiny studio theaters at other venues. And if the likes of Phillip Glass and the Royal Shakespeare Company can schlep out here, 20 minutes from Central, to perform, you can certainly get out here to watch. ✉ *12 Hing Ning Rd., Kwai Chung, New Territories* ☎ *2408–0128, 2406–7505 box office* ⊕ *www.lcsd.gov.hk* ⊘ *Daily 9 AM–11 PM; box office daily 9 AM–5 PM* Ⓜ *Kwai Fong, Exit C.*

—Victoria Patience

Rock out at Carnegie's, a pub in Wan Chai.

DISCOS AND NIGHTCLUBS

Dusk Till Dawn. Loud, energetic cover bands get the dance floor jumping on Wednesday to Saturday nights. Popular with expats, it can be seedy, but patrons are usually having too much fun to notice or care. ⊠ *76–84 Jaffe Rd., Wan Chai* ☎ *2528–4689* ⊘ *Closes 6 AM* Ⓜ *Wan Chai.*

Joe Bananas. This disco and bar has a reputation for all-night partying and general good times. People dressed too casually are strictly excluded: no shorts, sneakers, or T-shirts (the only exception is the Rugby Sevens weekend, when even Joe can't turn away the thirsty swarm). Arrive before 11 PM to avoid the line. ⊠ *23 Luard Rd., Wan Chai* ☎ *2529–1811* ⊘ *Closes 5 AM* Ⓜ *Wan Chai.*

PUBS

Carnegie's. Named after the Scotsman and steel baron Andrew Carnegie, whose family sailed to America in the late 1800s, this rock-and-roll bar lives up to its name. Although Carnegie himself probably didn't imagine bar-top dancing to classic rock tunes at an establishment bearing his name, the Scottish owners feel that the spirit of his love of music lives on regardless. ⊠ *53–55 Lockhart Rd., Wan Chai* ☎ *2866–6289* ⊘ *Closes 3 AM* Ⓜ *Wan Chai.*

The Canny Man. In the basement of the nondescript Wharney Guang Dong Hotel on Wan Chai's heaving Lockhart Road is an oasis of relative calm, with a dart board, a pool table, and live sports coverage, as well as a full menu that involves Haggis balls. It's Hong Kong's only old-school Scottish pub, decked out in timber and red-tartan furnishings. The bar serves an impressive collection of 180 single malts and 28 artisan beers, alongside a roster of guest ales that changes regularly.

⊠ *Basement, Wharney Guang Dong Hotel, 57–73 Lockhart Rd., Wan Chai* ☎ *2861–1935* ⊘ *Closes 3* AM Ⓜ *Wan Chai.*

CAUSEWAY BAY

BARS

ToTT's Asian Bar and Grill. Also known as Talk of the Town, this full-floor restaurant and bar was once more famous for its weird and wacky decor than the 270-degree vista, but has become sleeker and more sophisticated, with neutral tones that complement, rather than distract from, the skyline. ⊠ *34th fl., The Excelsior, 281 Gloucester Rd., Causeway Bay* ☎ *2837–6786* ⊘ *Closes 2* AM Ⓜ *Causeway Bay.*

GAY AND LESBIAN SPOTS

Virus. Girls come here in groups to play drinking games, drink cheap beer, and sing along to Canto-pop—not a great scene for a foreigner looking to meet people, but typical of Hong Kong's under-the-radar lesbian scene. For something more inviting, check out Les Peches (⇨ *box, above*). ⊠ *6th fl., 468 Jaffe Rd., Causeway Bay* ☎ *2904–7207* ⊘ *Closes 5* AM Ⓜ *Causeway Bay.*

PUBS

East End Brewery. Deep in the veritable beer desert of Hysan Avenue lies a pub with the refreshing motto "Let No Man Thirst For Want Of Real Ale" displayed on its wall. Here, you will find dozens of brews, accompanied by live sports coverage and a reassuring ocean of peanut shells underfoot. ⊠ *Sunning Plaza, 10 Hysan Ave., Causeway Bay* ☎ *2577–9119* ⊘ *Closes 1:30* AM Ⓜ *Causeway Bay.*

KOWLOON

Central and Wan Chai are undoubtedly the king and queen of nightlife in Hong Kong. If you're staying in a hotel, however, or having dinner across the water in Kowloon, Ashley Road and Knutsford Terrace still make for a fun night out.

BARS

Fodor'sChoice **Aqua Spirit**. Inside One Peking, an impressive curvaceous skyscraper,
★ this very cool bar is on the mezzanine level of the top floor. The high ceilings and raking glass walls offer up unrivaled views of Hong Kong Island and the harbor filled with ferries and ships. ⊠ *29th fl. and 30th fl., One Peking, 1 Peking Rd., Tsim Sha Tsui, Kowloon* ☎ *3427–2288* ⊘ *Closes 2* AM Ⓜ *Tsim Sha Tsui.*

All Night Long. The classier cousin to Wan Chai's bawdy Dusk til Dawn, this Knutsford Terrace staple hosts a talented Filipino cover band, which mainly works hits from the '80s and '90s. Drinks are a little overpriced, but acoustics are supported by an impressive sound system and a loud sing-along from the crowd is standard. Spanish-style artwork adorns the red and yellow walls. ⊠ *9 Knutsford Terr., Tsim Sha Tsui, Kowloon* ☎ *2367–9487* ⊘ *Closes 6* AM Ⓜ *Tsim Sha Tsui.*

Bahama Mama's. You'll find tropical rhythms at the Caribbean-inspired bar, where world music plays and the kitsch props include a surfboard

Drinks come with a spectacular view of Hong Kong at Felix, high up in the Peninsula Hotel.

over the bar and the silhouette of a curvaceous woman showering behind a screen over the restroom entrance. ✉ *4–5 Knutsford Terr., Tsim Sha Tsui, Kowloon* ☎ *2638–2121* ⊙ *Closes 4 AM* Ⓜ *Tsim Sha Tsui.*

Balalaika. Vodka is served in a –20°C (–36°F) room at this Russian-theme bar, but don't be alarmed at the freezing temperature—it provides fur coats and traditional Russian fur hats. Take your pick from the 15 varieties of vodka from five different countries. ✉ *2nd fl., 10 Knutsford Terr., Tsim Sha Tsui, Kowloon* ☎ *2312–6222* ⊙ *Closes 1 AM.*

Dada. This bar in the eccentric Luxe Manor hotel is a tribute to anarchic surrealism and works hard to be weird in a turn-of-the-century kind of way. A side gallery boasts two original etchings by Salvador Dalí. References to the artist and other greats like Magritte abound. A dark and spacious bar area is anchored by a central counter, from which cast resin ponies sprout and bottles of absinthe glimmer. ✉ *39 Kimberly Rd., Tsim Sha Tsui, Kowloon* ☎ *3763–8778* ⊙ *Closes 2 AM* Ⓜ *Tsim Sha Tsui.*

Fodor'sChoice ★ **Felix.** High up in the Peninsula Hotel, this bar is immensely popular with visitors; it not only has a brilliant view of the island, but the interior was designed by the visionary Philippe Starck. Don't forget to check out the padded mini-disco room. Another memorable feature is the male urinals, situated right by glass windows overlooking the city. ✉ *28th fl., Peninsula Hong Kong, Salisbury Rd., Tsim Sha Tsui, Kowloon* ☎ *2920–2888* ⊙ *Closes 2 AM* Ⓜ *Tsim Sha Tsui.*

The Living Room. On the 6th floor of the slick W hotel is a sprawling bar designed to feel like a stylised living room. Coffee-table tomes lie artfully in low bookcases set around the space. Chess and checker boards are available for use, and whimsical sculptures hang among funhouse mirrors from the two-storey-high ceiling. On Wednesday from 8 PM pay HK$198 for all the New World wine you can sample. Otherwise, the lychee martinis are excellent. ⊠ *1 Austin Rd. W, Kowloon Station, Kowloon* ☎ *3717–2222* ⊗ *Closes 2* AM Ⓜ *Kowloon.*

The Lobby. You'll feel well taken care of at the Peninsula's classically colonial lobby bar. Society watchers linger here; sit to the right of the hotel entrance to observe the crème de la crème. ⊠ *Peninsula Hotel, Salisbury Rd., Tsim Sha Tsui, Kowloon* ☎ *2920–2888* ⊗ *Closes 1* AM.

HOSTESS CLUBS

Fodor's Choice
★

Club BBoss. It's hard to fathom the size of a club that can accommodate 3,000 people, but with more than 60,000 square feet of space, more than a thousand staff, a rotating stage, and three nightly cabaret shows to entertain a crowd of moneyed execs, Club BBoss is hostess paradise. Women are welcome, provided they are accompanying male customers. ⊠ *Mandarin Plaza, Tsim Sha Tsui East, Kowloon* ☎ *2369–2883* ⊗ *Closes 4* AM Ⓜ *Tsim Sha Tsui East.*

Club Kokusai. As its name implies, this place appeals to visitors from the Land of the Rising Yen. Interestingly, there's no karaoke here, just the shows—and girls, of course. ⊠ *81 Nathan Rd., Tsim Sha Tsui, Kowloon* ☎ *2367–6969* ⊗ *Closes 3* AM Ⓜ *Tsim Sha Tsui.*

SOMETHING DIFFERENT

Aqua Luna. As the city's last traditionally crafted vessel, or junk, *Aqua Luna*'s dramatic appearance and red sails make her easy to spot. Step off dry land from either pier, in Kowloon or Central, order a G&T, and take in the shimmering harbor sights for 45 minutes, with snack menus, and plush seating. The HK$180 price tag includes one drink. The ferry runs every hour from 5.30 PM daily. ■TIP➔ **Catch the slightly more expensive 7:30 cruise to watch the city's nightly Symphony of Lights show from the harbor.** ⊠ *Cultural Centre Pier, Tsim Sha Tsui* ⊠ *Pier No. 1, Tsim Sha Tsui* ⊠ *Pier No. 9, Central* Ⓜ *Central* ☎ *2116–8821* ⊗ *Last sail 10:30 PM, Tsim Sha Tsui; 10:45 PM, Central.*

PUBS

Delaney's. Both branches of Hong Kong's pioneer Irish pub have interiors that were shipped here from the Emerald Isle, and the mood is as authentic as the furnishings. Guinness and Delaney's ale (a specialty microbrew) are on tap, and there are corner snugs (small private rooms) and an Irish menu. The crowd includes some genuine Irish regulars; get ready for spontaneous outbursts of fiddling and other Celtic traditions. Happy hour runs from 5 to 9 PM daily. ⊠ *Basement fl., 71–77 Peking Rd., Tsim Sha Tsui, Kowloon* ☎ *2301–3980* Ⓜ *Tsim Sha Tsui* ⊠ *Ground fl., One Capital Place, 18 Luard Rd., Wan Chai* ☎ *2804– 2880* ⊗ *Closes 3* AM Ⓜ *Wan Chai.*

Ned Kelly's Last Stand. Come to this boisterous Australian watering hole, named for the continent's notorious bushranger, for pub meals and an exuberant Dixieland jazz and comedy outfit. They are popular among visitors and expats from Down Under and often leading the crowd in a rowdy singalong. The band plays from 9:30 PM to 1 AM nightly. Arrive early for decent seats. ⊠ *11A Ashley Rd., Tsim Sha Tsui, Kowloon* ☎ *2376–0562* ⊗ *Closes 2* AM Ⓜ *Tsim Sha Tsui.*

Side Trip to Macau

WORD OF MOUTH

"There's a day's worth of walking around hilly narrow streets of ancient housing to various fortifications, churches, and a hill-top museum on Macau's history, which is well-done. The Portuguese [influence has] quite a different type of charm from Hong Kong . . ."
—PeterN_H

WELCOME TO MACAU

TOP REASONS TO GO

★ **Ruins of São Paulo.** The church facade is a symbol of Macau. En route to it, sample regional cuisine and experience local charm in Senado Square.

★ **A-Ma Temple.** It's steeped in Macau's culture and history. Search for the Lucky Money Pool, then wash your hands in the blessed water before heading to the casinos.

★ **Place Your Bets.** Even if you don't gamble, take a peek inside the Lisboa, a classic Macau landmark, or the much newer Venetian, whose sprawling complex includes singing gondoliers on indoor canals and high-luxury shopping.

★ **Relax on Hác-Sá Beach.** Sunbathe on charcoal-gray sands before taking a stroll, heading out on Jet Skis, or feasting on seafood.

★ **Spaaahhh.** Macau's spas have ultra-indulgent treatments and world-class facilities—with prices to match. But who cares? You're on vacation.

1 Downtown Macau. You'll experience authentic Macau in a downtown square, with its European-style paving and sidewalk cafés, as well as in a Buddhist temple, with its red lanterns and fragrant joss sticks. But perhaps even more authentic is that pink colonial Portuguese building that houses a Chinese herbal medicine shop.

2 Taipa Island. Although the Portuguese presence on Macau dates from the mid-1500s, Taipa wasn't occupied until the mid-1800s. The island remained a garrison and a pastoral retreat until the 1970s, when it was linked to Macau by bridge. Today some parts retain a village feel, while other parts are crowded with soulless high-rises.

3 Cotai. The 3-km (2-mi) causeway that once separated Coloane from Taipa has been bridged by a massive land-reclamation and development project that includes casinos and casino hotels, resorts, and shopping malls.

0 — 1/2 mi
0 — 800 meters

Inner Harbour

GUANDONG PROVINCE (CHINA)

A Ma Temple

Av. d Conselheir Bor

GUANDONG PROVINCE (CHINA)

CHINA

↑
TO
ZHUHAI

Av. do
Almante
Laceida

*Macau
Island*

Reservoir

Macau
Ferry Terminal

*Outer
Harbour*

Av. Almeida
Ribeira

1

Friendship Bridge

Macau-Taipa Bridge

*ZHUJIANG
KOU*

Taipa Island

Taipa Ferry
Terminal

2

✈
Macau
International
Airport

Venetian

Avenida de Cofai

Taipa-Coloane Causeway

Lotus Bridge

3

4
Coloane Island

Hác-Sá Beach

Estrada de Cheoc Van

Cheoc Van Beach

4 **Coloane Island.** The larger island remains less populated and more intimate than Taipa, and few tourists venture this far south. It's also known for its parks, beaches, and golf club, as well as its unchanged Portuguese architecture and cobblestone streets.

GETTING ORIENTED

Macau, a Special Administrative Region (SAR) of the People's Republic of China, is on the western bank of the Pearl River Delta, about an hour from Hong Kong by hydrofoil. It consists of the Macau Peninsula and Taipa and Coloane islands. The Cotai area, a glitzy, Vegas-like strip of hotels and casinos that began development in 2006, lies between Taipa and Coloane and virtually merges the two. Most people visit Macau to gamble, eat cheap seafood, and shop. But don't overlook its timeless charms and unique culture, born from centuries of both Portuguese and Chinese influence.

8

MACAU PLANNER

The Basics

The Macau Government Tourist Office (MGTO) is well managed. **Macau Government Tourist Office** (*MGTO ⊠ Macau Ferry Terminal, Macau* ☎ *853/2833–3000* ⊕ *www.macautourism.gov. mo* ⊠ *Shun Tak Centre, 200 Connaught Rd., Central, Hong Kong* ☎ *2857–2287*).

To enter Macau, Americans, Canadians, and EU citizens need only a valid passport for stays of up to 90 days.

The Macanese pataca (MOP) has a fixed exchange rate of MOP$1.032 to HK$1 and roughly MOP$7 to US$1. Patacas come in 10, 20, 50, 100, 500, and 1,000 MOP banknotes plus 1, 5, and 10 MOP coins. A pataca is divided into 100 avos, which come in 10-, 20-, and 50-avo coins. Hong Kong dollars are accepted in Macau on a 1:1 basis.

Language

Chinese and Portuguese are Macau's official languages. Cantonese and Mandarin are widely spoken. English is unreliable outside tourist areas. It's best to print your destination in Chinese characters for taxi drivers.

Getting to Macau

BY AIR

International flights (from Asia) come into Macau, but there are no planes from Hong Kong. Fifteen-minute helicopter flights fly between Hong Kong's Shun Tak Centre and the Macau Ferry Terminal on Sky Shuttle; they leave every 30 minutes from 9 AM to 11 PM daily. Prices are HK$2,600 Monday to Thursday with a HK$200 surcharge on Friday, Saturday, Sunday, and holidays. Reservations are essential. **Sky Shuttle** (☎ *853/2872–7288 Macau Terminal; 2108–9898 Shun Tak Centre* ⊕ *www.skyshuttlehk.com*).

Macau International Airport (☎ *853/2886–1111* ⊕ *www. macau-airport.gov.mo*).

BY FERRY

Ferries run every 15 minutes with a reduced schedule from midnight to 7 AM. Prices for economy/ordinary and super/deluxe run HK$134–HK$275. VIP cabins begin at HK$944 (four seats) to HK$1,416 (six seats). Weekday traffic is usually light, so you can buy tickets right before departure. Weekend tickets often sell out, so make reservations. You can book tickets up to 90 days in advance with China Travel Service (⊕ *www.ctshk.com*) agencies or directly with CotaiJet or TurboJET by phone or online. Booking by phone requires a Visa card. You must pick up tickets at the terminal at least a half hour before departure.

Most ferries leave from Hong Kong's Shun Tak Centre Sheung Wan MTR station in Central, though limited service is available from First Ferry at Kowloon's Tsim Sha Tsui terminal. In Macau most ferries disembark from the main Macau Ferry Terminal, but CotaiJet services the terminal on Taipa Island. The trip takes one hour one way. Buses, taxis, and free shuttles to most casinos and hotels await on the Macau side.

CotaiJet (☎ *853/2885–0595 in Macau, 2359–9990 in Hong Kong* ⊕ *cotaijet.com.mo*). **First Ferry** (☎ *2131–8181* ⊕ *www.nwff.com.hk*). **TurboJET** (☎ *2859–3333 information, 2921–6688 reservations* ⊕ *www.turbojet.com.hk*).

Getting Around Macau

BY BUS

Public buses are clean and affordable; trips to anywhere in the Macau Peninsula cost MOP$3.20. Service to Taipa Island is MOP$4.20, service to Coloane is MOP$5, and the trip to Hác Sá is MOP$6.40. Buses run 6:30–midnight and require exact change upon boarding. But you can get downtown for free, via casino shuttles, from the official Border Gate crossing just outside mainland China, from the airport, and from the Macau Ferry Terminal.

BY CAR

As in Hong Kong, Macau motorists drive on the left-hand side of the road. Road signs are in Chinese and Portuguese only. Rental cars with Avis are available at the Grand Lapa Hotel. Regular cars start at MOP$499 on weekdays and MOP$599 on weekends. Book three to four days in advance for weekend rentals.

Avis (☎ 853/2833–6789 in Macau, 2926–1126 in Hong Kong ⊕ www.avis.com).

BY TAXI

Taxis are inexpensive but not plentiful in Macau. The best places to catch a cab are the major casinos—the Wynn, Sands, and Venetian. Carry a bilingual map or ask the concierge at your hotel to write the name of your destination in Chinese. All taxis are metered, air-conditioned, and reasonably comfortable. The base charge is MOP$13 for the first 1.6 km (1 mi) and MOP$1.50 per additional 230 m. Trips between Coloane and either the Macau Peninsula or Taipa incur respective surcharges of MOP$5 or MOP$2. Drivers don't expect a tip.

WHAT IT COSTS IN MOP$

	¢	$	$$	$$$	$$$$
Restaurants	under $50	$51–$100	$101–$200	$201–$300	over $300
Hotels	under MOP$700	$701–$1,100	$1,101–$2,100	$2,101–$3,000	over $3,000

Restaurant prices are per person for a main course at dinner and exclude the customary 10% service charge. Hotel prices are for two people in a standard double room in high season, excluding 10% service charge and 3% government tax.

Tours

Depending on your mind-set, tours of Macau can either be spontaneously joined or meticulously made-to-order. If you're just debarking for the day at the main ferry terminal, find the **New Sintra Tours** (✉ Macau Ferry Terminal, Av. da Amizade ☎ 853/2872–8050) counter, where you can book tours for the day.

For a tour of the islands, **Cotai Travel** (✉ Shop 1028, Venetian Macao-Resort-Hotel ☎ 853/8118–2930 or 853/8118–2833) hosts daily tours from 9 to 1 that include the Taipa Houses Museum and the A-Ma Cultural Village on Coloane for MOP$270 per person.

Book at least one day in advance from one of many travel agents in Hong Kong. Browse your options at the travel counters of the main ferry terminals in either Macau or Hong Kong, or check ⊕ www.macautourism.gov.mo for a list of authorized travel agencies in Macau; some offer tours in multiple languages.

Estoril Tours (✉ Shop 3711, 3rd fl., Shun Tak Centre, 200 Connaught Rd., Central, Hong Kong ☎ 2559–1028 ⊕ www. estoril.com.mo) will customize a private group tour, from bungee-jumping off the Macau Tower to wandering through Coloane Village or a day visiting museums.

8

Updated by
Doretta Lau

Enter the desperate, smoky atmosphere of a Chinese casino, where frumpy players bet an average of five times more than the typical Vegas gambler. Sit down next to grandmothers who smoke like chimneys while playing baccarat—the local game of choice—with visiting high rollers. Then step out of the climate-controlled chill and into tropical air that embraces you like a warm, balmy hug. Welcome to Macau.

The many contrasts in this tiny enclave of 559,000 people serve as reminders of how very different cultures have embraced one another's traditions for hundreds of years. Though Macau's population is 95% ethnic Chinese, there are still vibrant pockets of Portuguese and Filipino expats. And some of the thousands of Eurasians—who consider themselves neither Portuguese nor Chinese, but something in between—can trace the intermarriage of their ancestors back a century or two.

Macau's old town, while dominated by the buildings, squares, and cobblestone alleyways of colonial Portugal, is tinged with eastern influences as well, as in the Buddhist temple at the intersection of the Travessa de Dom Quixote and Travessa de Sancho Panca. In Macau you can spend an afternoon strolling the black sands of Hác-Sá Beach before feasting on a dinner of *bacalhau com natas* (dried codfish with a cream sauce), grilled African chicken (spicy chicken in a coconut-peanut broth—a classic Macanese dish), Chinese lobster with scallions, or fiery prawns infused with Indian and Malaysian flavors. Wash everything down with *vinho verde*, the crisp young wine from northern Portugal, and top it all off with a traditional Portuguese *pastel de nata* (egg-custard tart) and dark, thick espresso.

EXPLORING MACAU

Macau is a small place, where on a good day you could drive from one end to the other in 30 minutes. This makes walking and bicycling ideal ways to explore winding city streets, nature trails, and long stretches of beach. Most of Macau's population lives on the peninsula attached to mainland China. The region's most famous sights are here—Senado Square, the Ruins of St. Paul's, A-Ma Temple—as are most of the luxury hotels and casinos. As in the older sections of Hong Kong, cramped older buildings stand comfortably next to gleaming new structures.

DOWNTOWN MACAU

Chances are you'll arrive at the Macau Ferry Terminal after sailing from Hong Kong. There's not much to see around the terminal itself, so hop into one of the many waiting casino or hotel shuttles and head straight downtown, less than 10 minutes away. From there it's a short walk to the city's historic center, along the short stretch of road named Avenida Almeida Ribeiro, more commonly known as San Ma Lo, which is Macau's commercial and cultural heart.

TOP ATTRACTIONS

Fodor's Choice
★
Fortaleza da Guia. The Guia Fortress, built between 1622 and 1638 on Macau's highest hill, was key to protecting the Portuguese from invaders. You can walk the steep, winding road up to the fortress or take a five-minute cable-car ride from the entrance of Flora Garden on Avenida Sidónio Pais. Once inside the fort, notice the gleaming white Guia Lighthouse (you can't go inside, but you can get a good look at the exterior) that's lit every night. Next to it is the Guia Chapel, built by Clarist nuns to provide soldiers with religious services. The chapel is no longer used for services, but restoration work in 1998 uncovered elaborate frescoes mixing western and Chinese themes. They're best seen when the morning or afternoon sun floods the chapel. ✉ *Guia Hill, Downtown* ☎ *853/8399–6699* ✆ *Free* ☼ *Daily 9–5:30.*

Fodor's Choice
★
Largo do Senado. The charming Senado Square, Macau's hub for centuries, is lined with neoclassical-style colonial buildings painted bright pastels. Only pedestrians are allowed on its shiny black-and-white tiles, and the alleys off it are packed with restaurants and shops. Take your time wandering. There are plenty of benches on which to rest after shopping and sightseeing. Come back at night, when locals of all ages gather to chat and the square is beautifully lit.

The magnificent yellow **Igreja de São Domingos** (*St. Dominic's Church* ✉ *Largo de São Domingos, Downtown* ☎ *No phone* ☼ *Daily 8–6*) beckons you to take a closer look. After a restoration in 1997, it's again among Macau's most beautiful churches, with a cream-and-white interior that takes on a heavenly golden glow when illuminated for services. The church was originally a convent founded by Spanish Dominican friars in 1587. In 1822 China's first Portuguese newspaper, *The China Bee,* was published here. The church became a repository for sacred art in 1834 when convents were banned in Portugal.

It's hard to ignore the imposing white facade of **Santa Casa da Misericordia** (⊠ *2 Travessa da Misericordia* ☎ *853/2857–3938 or 853/8399–6699* 🖾 *MOP$5* ⏱ *Mon.–Sat. 10–1 and 2–5:30*). Founded in 1569 by Dom Belchior, Macau's first bishop, the Holy House of Mercy is the China coast's oldest Christian charity, and it continues to take care of the poor with soup kitchens and health clinics, as well as providing housing for the elderly. The exterior is neoclassical, but the interior is done in a contrasting opulent, modern style. A reception room on the second floor contains paintings of benefactress Marta Merop.

> ## WORLD HERITAGE
>
> In 2005 "The Historic Centre of Macau" was listed as China's 31st UNESCO World Heritage Site. The term "center" is misleading, as the site is really a collection of churches, buildings, and neighborhoods that colorfully illustrate Macau's 400-year history. Included in it are China's oldest examples of western architecture and the region's most extensive concentration of missionary churches.

The neoclassical **Edifício do Leal Senado** (*Senate Bldg.* ⊠ *163 Av. de Almeida Ribeiro, Downtown* ☎ *853/2833–7676* 🖾 *Free* ⏱ *Tues.–Sun. 9–9*) was built in 1784 as a municipal chamber and continues to be used by the government today. An elegant meeting room on the first floor opens onto a magnificent library based on one in the Mafra Convent in Portugal, with books neatly stacked on two levels of shelves reaching to the ceiling. Art and historical exhibitions are frequently hosted in the beautiful foyer and garden. ⊠ *Downtown*.

NEED A BREAK?

Not far off the main drag but somewhat hidden down an alleyway, Margaret's Café e Nata (⊠ *Rua Comandante Mata e Oliveira, Downtown* ☎ *853/2871–0032*) offers a cool place to sit, outside under fans and awnings, with some of the best custard tarts in town, plus fresh juices, homemade tea blends, and pizza slices.

Look for the small cow sign marking the out-of-the-ordinary Leitaria i Son (⊠ *Largo do Senado 7, Downtown* ☎ *853/2857–3638*) milk bar. The decor is cafeteria-style and spartan, but the bar whips up frothy glasses of fresh milk from its dairy and blends them with all manner of juices: papaya, coconut, apricot, and more.

Macau Canidrome. The greyhound track looks rundown and quaint compared to the bigger Jockey Club and glitzy casinos, but it offers a true taste of Macau in a more popular neighborhood near the China border crossing. The Canidrome opened in 1932; it tends to attract a steady crowd of older gamblers several times a week for the slower-pace, lower-stakes gambling rush of betting on fast dogs chasing an electronic rabbit. Check out the parade of race dogs before each race. You can sit on benches in the open-air stadium, at tables in the air-conditioned restaurant, or in an upstairs box seat. ⊠ *Av. do Artur Tamagnini Barbosa at Av. General Castelo Branco, Downtown* ☎ *853/2833–3399, 853/2826–1188 to place bets* ⊕ *www.macauyydog.com* 🖾 *Public stands MOP$10,*

Pedestrian-only Largo do Senado preserves the Portuguese influence that shaped Macau for centuries.

private boxes MOP$120 ⊗ Mon., Thurs., and weekends 6 PM–11 PM; first race at 7:30.

Fodor's Choice **Macau Tower Convention & Entertainment Centre.** Rising 1,000 feet above
★ the peaceful San Van Lake, the world's 10th-largest freestanding tower
recalls Sky Tower, a similar structure in. And it should, as both were
designed by New Zealand architect Gordon Moller. The Macau Tower
offers a variety of thrills, including the Mast Climb, which challenges
the daring and strong of heart and body with a two-hour climb on steel
rungs 344 feet up the tower's mast for incomparable views of Macau
and China. Other thrills include the Skywalk, an open-air stroll around
the tower's exterior—without handrails; the SkyJump, an assisted,
decelerated 765-foot descent; and the classic bungee jump. More sub-
dued attractions inside the tower are a mainstream movie theater and
a revolving lunch and dinner buffet at the 360 Café. ⊠ *Largo da Torre
de Macau, Downtown* ☎ *853/2893–3339* ⊕ *www.macautower.com.
mo* ⊠ *MOP$588 for the Skywalk to MOP$1; 888 for the Mast Climb;
photos extra ⊗ Observation deck: weekdays 10–8:45, weekends and
holidays 9–8:45.*

Fodor's Choice **Ruínas de São Paulo** (*Ruins of St. Paul's Church*). Only the magnificent,
★ towering facade, with its intricate carvings and bronze statues, remains
from the original Church of Mater Dei, built between 1602 and 1640
and destroyed by fire in 1835. The church, an adjacent college, and
Mount Fortress, all Jesuit constructions, once formed East Asia's first
western-style university. Now the widely adopted symbol of Macau, the
ruins are a primary tourist attraction, with snack bars and antiques and
other shops at the foot of the site.

Behind the facade of São Paulo is the **Museum of Sacred Art and Crypt** (☎ *No phone* ✉ *Free* ☉ *Daily 9–6*), which holds statues, crucifixes, and the bones of Japanese and Vietnamese martyrs. There are also some intriguing Asian interpretations of Christian images, including samurai angels and a Chinese Virgin and Child.

The **Templo de Na Tcha** is a small Chinese temple built in 1888, during the Macauan plague. The hope was that Na Tcha Temple would appeal to a mythical Chinese character who granted wishes and could save lives. The **Troco das Antigas Muralhas de Defesa** (Section of the Old City Walls) is all that remains of Macau's original defensive barrier, and borders the left side of the Na Tcha Temple. These crumbling yellow walls were built in 1569 and illustrate the durability of *chunambo*, a local material made from compacted layers of clay, soil, sand, straw, crushed rocks, and oyster shells. ✉ *Top end of Rua de São Paulo, Downtown* ☎ *853/8399–6699* ☉ *Daily 8–5*.

WORD OF MOUTH

"I do enjoy the old town parts of Macau city, and also find that Taipa and Coloane (especially Coloane), have much less of a city feel, offer some nice beaches and parks, and are mostly devoid of the hordes of tourists you can find in the old town in Macau. The little town near Hác Sá is cute and the village of Coloane itself has a Tin Hau temple and the famous and very good egg tarts at the Lord Stow Bakery. In Macau city itself, once you get out of the main historic core around the cathedral and the steps of St Paul's, it can be very quiet indeed and much less crowded."

—Cicerone

Fodor's Choice ★ **Templo de A-Ma** (*A-Ma Temple*). Thought to be Macau's oldest building, this temple, properly Ma Kok Temple but known to locals as simply A-Ma, is also one of Macau's most picturesque. The structure had its origins in the Ming Dynasty (1368–1644), and was influenced by Confucianism, Taoism, and Buddhism, as well as local religions. Vivid red calligraphy on large boulders tells the story of the goddess A-Ma (also known as Tin Hau), the patron of fishermen. A small gate opens onto prayer halls, pavilions, and caves carved directly into the hillside. ✉ *Rua de São Tiago da Barra, Largo da Barra, Downtown* ☉ *Daily 7–6*.

WORTH NOTING

Camões Garden. Macau's most popular park is frequented from dawn to dusk by tai chi enthusiasts, lovers, students, and men huddled over Chinese chessboards with their caged songbirds nearby. The gardens, which were developed in the 18th century, are named after Luís de Camões, Portugal's greatest poet, who was banished to Macau for several years during the 16th century. A rocky niche shelters a bronze bust of the poet in the park's most famous and picturesque spot, Camões Grotto. At the grotto's entrance a bronze sculpture honors the friendship between Portugal and China. A wall of stone slabs is inscribed with poems by various contemporary writers, praising Camões and Macau.

Alongside Camões Garden is a smaller park, the **Casa Garden** (☎ *853/2855–4699* ✉ *Free* ☉ *Weekdays 10–12:30 and 3–5:30*),

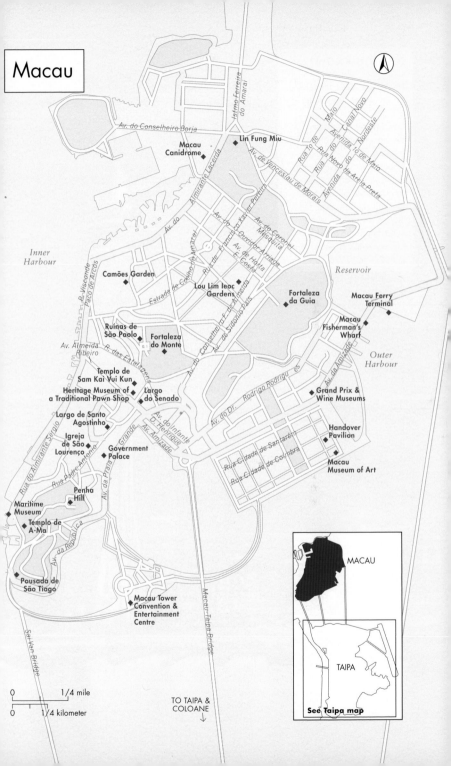

Macau

Av. do Conselheiro Borja

Istmo Ferreira do Amarai

Canal Novo

Rua de Maio

Avenida do de Maio

Rua Novo da Areia Preta

Av. de Venceslau de Morais

Macau Canidrome

Lin Fung Miu

Av. do Almirante Lacerda

Inner Harbour

Estrada de Coelho do Amaral

Av. do Coronel Mesquita

Av. da Xavier Pereira

Rua do Ouvidor Arriaga

Av. de Horta E. Costa

Reservoir

Camões Garden

R. Visconde Paço de Arcos

Lou Lim Ieoc Gardens

Rua de Francis Xavier Pereira

Fortaleza da Guia

Macau Ferry Terminal

Ruínas de São Paolo

Av. Almeida Ribeiro

R. das Estalagens

Fortaleza do Monte

Av. do Conselheiro F. de Almeida

Rua de Sidónio Pais

Macau Fisherman's Wharf

Outer Harbour

Templo de Sam Kai Vui Kun

Av. da Amizade

Heritage Museum of a Traditional Pawn Shop

Largo do Senado

Av. do Infante D. Henrique

Rua do Dr. Rodrigo Rodrigues

Grand Prix & Wine Museums

Largo de Santo Agostinho

Av. da Praia Grande

Handover Pavilion

Igreja de São Lourenço

Government Palace

Rua Cidade de Santarém

Rua Cidade de Coimbra

Macau Museum of Art

Rua do Almirante Sergio

Rua Padre Antonio

Penha Hill

Maritime Museum

Templo de A-Ma

Av. da República

Macau-Taipa Bridge

Pousada de São Tiago

Macau Tower Convention & Entertainment Centre

San Van Bridge

0 ____ 1/4 mile

0 ____ 1/4 kilometer

TO TAIPA & COLOANE ↓

MACAU

TAIPA

See Taipa map

The Macau Tower, modeled on Sky Tower in Auckland, offers thrills just like its Down Under counterpart. Do the Mast Climb up the side of the tower to reach Macau's highest point. Nowhere else in the world you can scale a freestanding building to its top. You can also walk the around the outside of the outer rim of the tower on the Skywalk X or bungy jump from 233 m. (765 ft.) up.

originally the grounds of a merchant's estate. Today, the estate's villa, which was built in 1770, is the headquarters for the Orient Foundation, a private institution involved in community, cultural, and arts affairs. The grounds are lovingly landscaped with a variety of flora and bordered with a brick pathway. There's also a central pond stocked with lily pads and lotus flowers. ✉ *13 Praça Luis de Camões, Downtown* ☉ *Daily 6 AM–10 PM.*

Fortaleza do Monte *(Mount Fortress).* On the hill overlooking the ruins of São Paulo and affording great peninsular views, this renovated fort was built by the Jesuits in the early 17th century. In 1622 it was the site of Macau's most legendary battle, when a priest's lucky cannon shot hit an invading Dutch ship's powder supply, saving the day. The interior buildings were destroyed by fire in 1835, but the outer walls remain, along with several large cannons and artillery pieces. Next to the fort, exhibits at the **Macau Museum** (✉ *112 Praceta do Museu de Macau, Monte Hill, Downtown* ☎ *853/2835–7911* 💵 *MOP$15; free on 15th of each month* ☉ *Tues.–Sun. 10–6*) take you through Macau's history, from its origins to modern development. ✉ *Monte Hill, Downtown* ☎ *853/2833–5141* 💵 *Free* ☉ *Tues.–Sun. 10–7.*

🎡 **Grand Prix Museum.** Inaugurated in 1993 to celebrate the 40th anniversary of the Macau Grand Prix and renovated 10 years later, this museum tells the stories of the best drivers from every year, but the highlights are the actual race cars on display. More than 20 Formula vehicles are exhibited in the hall, of which the centerpiece is the red-and-white Formula Three car driven by the late champion Aryton Senna. ✉ *431 Rua Luis Gonzaga Gomes, Downtown* ☎ *853/8798–4108* 💵 *MOP$10, MOP$20 with Wine Museum* ☉ *Wed.–Mon. 10–6.*

Heritage Exhibition of a Traditional Pawn Shop. This impressive re-creation documents the important role that pawnshops have played in Macau for hundreds of years. ✉ *396 Av. Almeida Ribeiro, Downtown* ☎ *2892– 1811* 💵 *MOP$5* ☉ *Daily 10:30–7; closed 1st Mon. of month.*

Igreja de São Lourenço. One of Macau's three oldest churches, the Church of St. Lawrence was founded by Jesuits in 1560 and has been lovingly rebuilt several times. Its present appearance dates to 1846. It overlooks the South China Sea amid pleasant, palm-shaded gardens. Families of Portuguese sailors used to gather on the front steps to pray for the sailors' safe return; hence its Chinese name, Feng Shun Tang (Hall of the Soothing Winds). Focal points of its breathtaking interior are the elegant wood carvings, a baroque altar, and crystal chandeliers. ■ TIP➡ Admission to all churches and temples is free, though donations are suggested. ✉ *Rua de São Lourenço, Downtown* ☎ *8399–6699* ☉ *Weekdays 10–4, Sat. 10–1*

Largo de Santo Agostinho. Built in the pattern of traditional Portuguese squares, St. Augustine Square is paved with black-and-white tiles laid out in mosaic wave patterns and lined with leafy overhanging trees and lots of wooden benches. It's easy to feel as if you're in a European village, far from South China.

One of the square's main structures is the **Teatro Dom Pedro V** (✉ *Calçada do Teatro, Downtown* ☎ *8399–6699*), a European-style

8

theater with an inviting green-and-white facade built in 1859. It's an important cultural landmark for Macanese and was regularly used until World War II, when it fell into disrepair. It was renovated in 1993 by the Orient Foundation, and the 300-seat venue once again hosts concerts and recitals—especially during the annual Macau International Music Festival—as well as important public events, which is the only time you can go inside. It does, however, have a garden that's open daily 10 am to 11 pm, and admission is free.

Igreja de Santo Agostinho (*St. Augustine's Church* ⊠ *Largo de Santo Agostinho, Downtown* ☎ *2851–0331* ۞ *Daily 10–6*) dates from 1814, and has a grand, weathered exterior and a drafty interior with a high wood-beam ceiling. There's a magnificent stone altar with a statue of Christ on his knees, bearing the cross, with small crucifixes in silhouette on the hill behind him. The statue, called Our Lord of Passos, is carried in a procession through the streets of downtown on the first day of Lent. ⊠ *Off R. Central, Downtown.*

Lin Fung Miu. Built in 1592, the Temple of the Lotus honors several Buddhist and Taoist deities, including Tin Hau (goddess of the sea), Kun Iam (goddess of mercy), and Kwan Tai (god of war and wealth). The front of the temple has awesome clay bas-reliefs of renowned figures from Chinese history and mythology. Inside are several halls, shrines, and courtyards. The temple is best known as a lodging place for Mandarins traveling from Guangzhou. Its most famous guest was Commissioner Lin Zexu, whose confiscation and destruction of British opium was largely responsible for the First Opium War. ⊠ *Av. do Almirante Lacerda, Downtown* ☎ *No phone* ۞ *Daily dawn–dusk.*

Lou Lim Ieoc Gardens. These beautiful gardens were built in the 19th century by a Chinese merchant named Lou Kau. Rock formations, water, vegetation, pavilions, and sunlight were all carefully considered when planning this garden. Balanced landscapes are the hallmark of Suzhou garden style. The government took possession and restored the grounds in the late 1970s, so that today you can enjoy tranquil walks among delicate flowering bushes framed with bamboo groves and artificial hills. A large auditorium frequently hosts concerts and other events, most notably recitals during the annual Macau International Music Festival. Adjacent to the gardens, a European-style edifice contains the **Macau Tea Culture House** (⊠ *10 Estrada de Adolfo Loureiro, Downtown* ☎ *853/2882–7103* ▣ *Free* ۞ *Tues.–Sun. 9–7*), a small museum with exhibits on the tea culture of Macau and China. ⊠ *Estrada de Adolfo Loureiro, at Av. do Conselheiro Ferreira de Almeida, Downtown* ▣ *MOP$1 (free Fri.)* ۞ *Daily* 6 AM–9 PM.

Macao Museum of Art. The large, boxy museum is as well known for its curving, rectangular framed roof as it is for its calligraphy, painting, copperware, and international film collections. It's Macau's only art museum, and has five floors of eastern and western works, as well as important examples of ancient indigenous pottery found at Hác-Sá Beach. While you're there, check out the program for the rest of the **Macao Cultural Centre** (☎ *853/2870–0699* ⊕ *www.ccm.gov.mo*), which often hosts edgy bands and theater troupes, in addition to the classic performances. ✉ *Macao Cultural Centre, Av. Xian Xing Hai, Outer Harbour* ☎ *853/8791–9814 or 853/8791–9800* ⊕ *www.artmuseum.gov.mo* ✉ *MOP$5 (free Sun.)* ☉ *Tues.–Sun. 10–7.*

☺ **Macau Fisherman's Wharf.** More of a distraction than an amusement park, this developing complex of minor attractions nonetheless has an Old World decadence. Its center-piece is the Roman Amphitheatre, which hosts outdoor performances, but its main draws are the lively themed restaurants on the west side, such as AfriKana B.B.Q and Camões. Across from the toylike

DISCOUNT PASS

To make Macau's museums more accessible, the Macau Government Tourist Office (MGTO) offers the Macau Museum Pass, which entitles you to a single entry into all of the following: the Grand Prix Museum, Lin Zexu Memorial Museum, Maritime Museum, Museum of Art, Museum of Macau, and Wine Museum. The five-day pass is MOP$25, and can be purchased at the MGTO or any at any participating museum.

Babylon Casino, the Rocks Hotel heralds a series of themed accommodations to come. Children's rides and games, on the east end, include a role-playing war game and an underground video-game arcade. Come for the food, and stay after dark, as Fisherman's Wharf is even more active at night. ✉ *Av. da Amizade, at Av. Dr. Sun Yat-Sen, Downtown* ☎ *853/8299–3300* ⊕ *www.fishermanswharf.com.mo* ✉ *Admission free, rides and games MOP$20–MOP$200* ☉ *Open 24 hours.*

Maritime Museum. Across from the A-Ma temple, this museum is a great place to spend an interesting hour brushing up on seafaring history. The handsome white building looks like a ship, thanks to jutting white slats and porthole windows. A row of fountains out front soothes you almost as much as the calm, cool interior. Multimedia exhibits cover fishermen, merchants, and explorers from Portugal, South China, and Japan. Look for compasses, telescopes, and sections of ships. There's even a small aquarium gallery with local sealife. Try your hand at astronomic navigation—which sailors have used for thousands of years—by looking up at the top floor's nifty celestial dome ceiling. ✉ *1 Largo do Pagode da Barra, Inner Harbour* ☎ *853/2859–5481* ⊕ *www.museumaritimo.gov.mo* ✉ *MOP$10 (MOP$5 Sun.)* ☉ *Wed.–Mon. 10–5:30.*

Quartel dos Mouros. The elegant yellow-and-white building with Moorish architectural influences built onto a slope of Barra Hill is the Moorish Barracks. It now houses the Macau Maritime Administration, but was originally constructed in 1874 for Indian police regiments brought into the region, a reminder of Macau's historic relationship with the Indian city of Goa. The barracks are not open to the public but visitors can tour the ornamented veranda. ✉ *Barra Hill, Inner Harbour* ☎ *853/8399–6699* ✉ *Free* ☉ *Veranda open 24 hours.*

Templo de Sam Kai Vui Kun. Built in 1750, this temple is dedicated to Kuan Tai, the bearded, fierce-looking god of war and wealth in Chinese mythology. Statues of him and his two sons sit on an altar. A steady stream of people comes to pray and ask for support before they go wage battle in the casinos. May and June see festivals honoring Kuan Tai throughout Macau. ⊠ *Rua Sui do Mercado de São Domingos, Downtown* ⊙ *Daily 8–6.*

Wine Museum. In the same building as the Grand Prix Museum, this museum has more than 1,100 wines on display; some are almost 200 years old. You'll learn about production techniques and the importance of *vinho* (wine) in Portuguese culture. More than 50 varieties are on hand for impromptu tastings. ⊠ *431 Rua Luis Gonzaga Gomes, Downtown* ☎ *853/8798–4109* 🏷 *MOP$15, MOP$20 with Grand Prix Museum* ⊙ *Wed.–Mon. 10–6.*

TAIPA ISLAND

The island directly south of peninsular Macau was once two small islands that were, over time, joined by deposits from the Pearl River Delta. It's connected to peninsular Macau by three long bridges. The region's two universities, horse-racing track, scenic hiking trails, and its international airport are all here.

Like downtown Macau, Taipa has been greatly developed in the past few years, yet it retains a visual balance between old Macau charm and modern sleekness. Try to visit on a weekend, so you can shop for clothing and crafts in the traditional flea market that's held every Sunday from morning to evening in Taipa Village.

Macau Jockey Club. After Dr. Stanley Ho bought the Macau Jockey Club (MJC) in 1991, he transformed what was a quiet trotting track into a lucrative high-stakes racing facility. However horse racing is now a more retro gambling option in Asia's rising casino hotspot of Macau, and the local MJC pales in comparison to the truly world-class Hong Kong Jockey Club. Nonetheless the MJC continues to operate year-round, hosting an average of 100 races and entertaining a majority of local middle-aged men, as well as some younger, more curious spectators who come to see the horses close up in between races (every 30 minutes). If you're game, you can place bets at a number of stations throughout Macau and Hong Kong, as well as by phone and on the Internet. ⊠ *Estrada Governador Albano de Oliveira, Taipa* ☎ *853/2882–0868* ⊕ *www.macauhorse.com* 🏷 *Grandstand seating MOP$20.*

Pou Tai Un Buddhist Monastery. The region's largest temple is part of a functioning monastery with several dozen monks. The classically designed structure has an ornate main prayer hall and central pavilions with sculptures, fish ponds, and banyan trees. Monks tend the vegetable plots that supply the popular on-site vegetarian restaurant. The monastery is next to the Macau Jockey Club and near the Four Faces Buddha statue. ⊠ *Estrada Almirante Marques Esparteiro, Taipa* ☎ *853/2881–1007* 🏷 *Free* ⊙ *Daily noon–6.*

Fodor's Choice
★

Taipa Village. Its narrow, winding streets are packed with restaurants, bakeries, shops, temples, and other buildings with traditional South Chinese and Portuguese design elements. The aptly named Rua do Cunha (Food Street) has many great Chinese, Macanese, Portuguese, and Thai restaurants. Several shops sell homemade Macanese snacks,

A BIT OF HISTORY

Macau's current economic surge mirrors a long history of ebb and flow. When trading began through the Silk Road, farmers from Guangdong and Fujian settled in the area. By 1557 the Portuguese had taken Macau and made it the first European colony in East Asia. Macau was known as "A Ma Gao" in honor of the patron goddess of sailors, A-Ma. The Portuguese adapted this Chinese name to "Macau," and for more than a century the port thrived as the main intermediary in the trade between Asia and the rest of the world. Ships from Italy, Portugal, and Spain came here to buy and sell Chinese silks and tea, Japanese crafts, Indian spices, African ivory, and Brazilian gold.

In addition to international trade, Macau became an outpost for western religions. St Francis Xavier successfully converted large numbers of Japanese and Chinese to Christianity and used Macau as a base of operations. In the 1500s and 1600s many churches were built, including an ambitious Christian college. Today in Macau this religious legacy can be seen in the array of well-preserved churches.

Macau's age of prosperity ended in the 1800s, when the Dutch and British gained control of most trading routes to East Asia. After the British victory over China in the 1814 Opium War, the huge, deep-water port of Hong Kong was established, and Macau was relegated to a quiet, sleepy port town. Macau did, however, remain important to Chinese refugees of World War I and World War II and the Cultural Revolution. With the widespread introduction of legalized gambling in the 1960s, Macau became a freewheeling place, where gambling, espionage, and crime reigned in the long shadow of modern, wealthy Hong Kong.

Today textile, furniture, electronics, and other exports join a world-class tourism industry in making Macau prosperous. Just before the 1999 handover to the Chinese government, the Portuguese administration launched a staggering number of public works. A huge international airport was built on a reclaimed island, and two new bridges were built to connect Macau's two islands. These years also saw the construction of two artificial lakes in the Outer Harbour along the Praia Grande.

Yet another phase of development in Cotai nearly complete, with construction slated to end in December 2011; the project has transformed Macau into a location of choice for casinos and luxury resorts.

8

including steamed milk pudding, almond cakes, beef jerky, and coconut candy.

Atop a small hill overlooking Taipa Village, the beautiful **Carmel Garden** (⌧ *Av. de Carlos da Maia, Taipa* ⛁ *Free* ☉ *Daily 24 hours*) has a number of palm trees that provide great shade. Within the garden stands the brilliant white-and-yellow Nossa Senhora do Carmo (Church of Our Lady of Carmel), built in 1885 and featuring a handsome single-belfry tower. Paths lead down from the Carmel Garden to the **Taipa Houses-Museum** (⌧ *Av. da Praia, Carmo Zone, Taipa*

READY, SET, GO!

Grand Prix racing, which began in Macau in 1953, is the region's most glamorous annual sporting event. During the third or fourth weekend of November the city is pierced with the sound of supercharged engines testing the 6-km (4-mi) Guia Circuit, which follows city roads along the Outer Harbour to Guia Hill and around the reservoir. The route is as challenging as that of Monaco, with rapid gear changes demanded at the right-angle Statue Corner, the Doña Maria bend, and the Melco hairpin. Cars achieve speeds of 224 kph (140 mph) on the straightaways, with the lap record approaching two minutes, 20 seconds. The premier event is the Formula Three Championship, with cars competing from around the world in what's now the official World Cup of Formula Three. Winners qualify for Formula One licenses. There are also races for motorcycles and production cars. If you plan to travel during this time, beware of the logistical disruption it causes, including rerouting of main roads and lack of hotel vacancies.

☎ 853/2882–7103 💳 MOP$5; free Sun. ☉ Tues.–Sun. 10–6). These five sea-green houses were originally residences of wealthy local merchants, and were converted into small museums and exhibition spaces. They were all fully restored shortly before the Macau handover, and are interesting examples of Porto-Chinese architecture. Official receptions are often held here, as are changing art exhibitions. The Venetian Casino and the Cotai complex construction block a once marvelous view of Coloane and the South China Sea.

OUTDOOR ACTIVITIES

Whether you prefer a leisurely walk though a park or conquering steep hills on foot or by bike, Taipa Island has the region's best trails. The rewards for heading up Taipa Grande and Taipa Pequena, the island's two largest hills, are majestic views. The Taipa Grande trail starts at Estrada Colonel Nicolau de Mesquita, near the United Chinese Cemetery. The Taipa Pequena trail starts at Estrada Lou Lim Ieoc (Lou Lim Ieoc Gardens) behind the Regency Hotel. Be sure to wear rugged hiking shoes, use bug repellent, and, if possible, bring a mobile phone for emergency calls. The most popular place to rent bicycles is the shop at the bus stop outside the Civic and Municipal Affairs Bureau in Taipa Village on Largo Camões, where you can also find trail maps.

COLOANE ISLAND

Centuries ago, Coloane was a wild place, where pirates hid in rocky caves and coves, awaiting their chance to strike at cargo ships on the Pearl River. Early in the 20th century the local government sponsored a huge planting program to transform Coloane from a barren place to a green one. The results were spectacular—and enduring. Today this island is idyllic, with green hills and clean sandy beaches.

Once connected to Taipa Island by a thin isthmus, Coloane is now almost completely fused with Taipa via the huge Cotai reclaimed land

DID YOU KNOW?

According to the Portuguese, their heralded five-centuries-old colony is spelled "Macau," and the Macau Government Tourist Office has since adopted this spelling. However, the anglicized "Macao" is still used in some (usually) English names and titles, even within the local government.

So why is it Wynn Macau and Venetian Macao? Just as you say "tom-ay-to" and I say "tom-ah-to"—in the private sector, anything goes. Nonetheless, most new ventures here have reverted to the source: Macau.

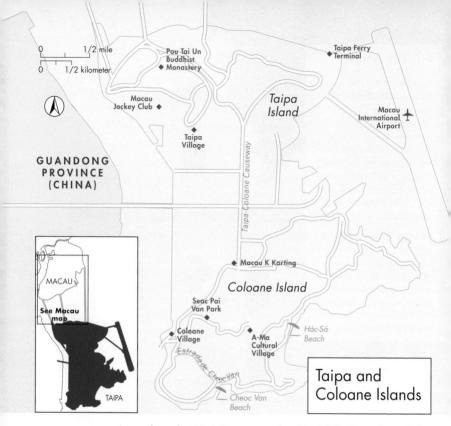

See Macau map

project, where the "Strip" was completed in 2010. Regardless of the recent development boom, Coloane remains the destination of choice for anyone seeking natural beauty and tranquility.

TOP ATTRACTIONS

A-Ma Cultural Village. A path just south of Seac Pai Van Park leads to A-Ma Cultural Village, a huge complex built in a traditional Qing Dynasty style. It pays homage to Macau's namesake, the goddess of the sea. The vibrancy and color of the details in the bell and drum towers, the tiled roofs, and the carved marble altars are truly awe-inspiring. It's as if you've been transported back to the height of the Qing Empire and can now see temples in their true state of greatness. Other remarkable details include the striking rows of stairs leading to Tian Hou Palace at the entrance. Each row features painstakingly detailed marble and stone carvings of auspicious Chinese symbols: a roaring tiger, double lions, five cranes, the double phoenix, and a splendid imperial dragon. The grounds here also have a recreational fishing zone and an arboretum with more than 100 species of local and exotic flora.

Behind A-Ma Cultural Village is the 560-foot-tall **Coloane Hill,** crowned by a gleaming white-marble statue of A-Ma (commemorating the year of Macau's handover), soaring 65 feet and visible from miles away. You can make the short hike up to the top or take one of the shuttle buses that leave from the foot of the hill every 30 minutes. ⊠ *Off Estrada de Seac Pai Van Coloane Island South* ⊘ *Daily 8–6.*

Fodor's Choice ★ **Coloane Village.** Quiet, relaxed Coloane Village is home to traditional Mediterranean-style houses painted in pastels, as well as the baroque-style Chapel of St. Francis Xavier and the Taoist Tam Kung Temple. The surrounding narrow alleys have surprises at every turn; among many things you may encounter are fishermen repairing their junks or a local baptism at the chapel.

The village's heart is a small square around a fountain with a bronze Cupid. The surrounding Macanese and Chinese open-air restaurants are among the region's best; some are the unheralded favorites of chefs visiting from Hong Kong and elsewhere in Asia.

WORTH NOTING

Cheoc Van Beach. Perfect for romantic walks, this beach is in a sheltered cove, with a nice seafood restaurant to one side, the Marine Club with kayak rentals on the other side, and a charming pousada (historic inn) overlooking the ocean. Be warned that there are lots of stray, though generally friendly, dogs on this beach. ⊠ *Off Estrada de Cheoc Van, Coloane Island South* ⊘ *Open 24 hours.*

🄲 **Hác-Sá.** Translated from the Chinese, hác-sá means "black sand," although the sands of the area's biggest beach are actually a deep gray. Playgrounds, picnic areas, and restaurants are all within walking distance. Even if you don't stay at the resident five-star Westin Resort, you can use the public sports complex, which is equipped with an Olympic-size swimming pool, tennis courts, and other sports facilities, for a fee. Also nearby is the Hác-Sá Reservoir BBQ park with picnic and barbecue facilities, boat rentals, and water-sports outfitters. ⊠ *Off Estrada de Hác Sá, Coloane Island South* ⊘ *Open 24 hours.*

Macau Kartodromo. Race enthusiasts and thrill-seekers alike should head to the Macau Motor Sports Club, opposite Coloane Park, the only go-kart track in both Macau and Hong Kong. Drivers must be at least 16 years old, as 200-cc-engine go-karts can speed up to 50 kmph on the 1.2 km-long, 10 meter-wide track with 10 challenging curves. Aim for a lap time under 50 seconds on a sunny day. ⊠ *Estrada de Seac Pai Van, Coloane Island West* ☎ *853/2888–2126* ⊠ *MOP$180 for 20 mins* ⊘ *Weekdays 11:30–7, weekends 11–8.*

🄲 **Seac Pai Van Park** *(Coloane Park).* This large park has extensive gardens, ponds, and waterfalls, and a large walk-in aviary with more than 200 bird species chirping and flying about. There are lots of things of interest to children, including playgrounds, a mini zoo, and an interactive museum with exhibits on nature and agriculture. ⊠ *Off Estrada de Seac Pai Van, Coloane Island West* ⊘ *Daily 8–6.*

CASINOS

In February 2006 Macau surpassed Las Vegas in gambling revenue. By June 2008 Macau's casinos were turning over 2.6 times the revenue of their Vegas Strip counterparts. Small wonder that international casino

Rickshaws await the gamblers leaving the Casino Lisboa, the gambling den that started it all.

groups have swarmed the region, and they continue to drive Macau's explosive double-digit growth.

From the late 1960s until 2001, Macau native Dr. Stanley Ho owned all the casinos, helping him to become one of the world's wealthiest people. One of the first steps the Chinese government took after the 1999 handover was to break up Dr. Ho's monopoly and award casino licenses to several consortiums from Las Vegas. The grand plan to transform Macau from a quiet town that offered gambling into one of the world's top gaming destinations has become a reality.

THE SCENE

Gambling is lightly regulated, so there are only a few things to remember. No one under age 18 is allowed into casinos. Most casinos use Hong Kong dollars in their gaming and not Macau patacas, but you can easily exchange currencies at cashiers. High- and no-limit VIP rooms are available on request, where minimum bets range from HK$50,000 to HK$100,000 per hand. You can get cash from credit cards and ATMs 24 hours a day, and every casino has a program to extend additional credit to frequent visitors. Most casinos don't have strict dress codes outside of their VIP rooms, but men are better off not wearing shorts or sleeveless shirts. Minimum bets for most tables are higher than those in Las Vegas, but there are lower limits for slots and video gambling.

The players here may not look sophisticated, but don't be fooled. Many of Macau's gamblers are truly hard-core. Average bets are in the hundreds per hand, and many people gamble until they're completely exhausted or completely broke, usually the latter.

Macau is also famous for gambling's sister industries of pawnshops, loan sharks, seedy saunas, and prostitution. This underbelly is hidden, though. You won't encounter such things unless you seek them out.

THE CASINOS

Gone are the days of Macau's dark and dingy underground gaming parlors. One is no longer bound by Stanley Ho's iron grip on the gambling scene, and there's now an emerging dreamland of opportunity for the bigwigs of Las Vegas to move in and spice up the competition. Over the past few years American-style casinos have been mushrooming like mad, primarily in Macau's NAPE (zona Nova de Aterros do Porto Exterior), or New Reclamation Area, in the Outer Harbour district between the main ferry terminal and the historic center. The foreign exports are most likely to please both casual tourists and serious players for their variety of gaming and other entertainment, relatively clean, well-lit atmosphere, free 24/7 accessibility, and overall glamour-resort experience.

DOWNTOWN

Casino Lisboa. Welcome to the casino that started it all. First opened in 1965 by Dr. Stanley Ho, this iconic Macau gaming den is replete with ancient jade ships in the halls, gilded staircases, and more baccarat tables than you can shake a craps stick at. It's great for a few rounds of HK$50 dai-siu—dice bets over cups of iced green tea. Most of the gamblers are from neighboring Guangdong province, and Cantonese is the lingua franca. Other popular pastimes at this storied casino revolve around international fine-dining venues and colorful coffee shops, if you care to wander around a maze of marbled floors and low ceilings. Make the Old Lisboa your first casino stop in Macau to get a perspective on how far this city has come since 2004, when the Sands Macao jump-started "Asia's Las Vegas." ⊠ *Av. de Lisboa, Downtown* ☎ *853/2837–5111* ⊕ *www.hotelisboa.com.*

Galaxy StarWorld. As you enter the StarWorld empire you're greeted by tall girls in high heels, while a mariachi band serenades you from across the lobby. Up the escalator, locals typically lay it all down for baccarat, but the upstairs stud poker tables are also picking up momentum. The gaming floors are small and have a couple of Chinese-style diners if you get peckish, but the cool Whisky Bar (⇨ *After Dark*) on the 16th floor of the adjacent hotel is an atmospheric place to either begin or wind down your evening. The neon-blue building is just across from the Wynn and down the block from the MGM

ASIA'S VEGAS

Sheldon Anderson, CEO of the Las Vegas Sands, spearheaded a $13 billion venture to transform the Cotai area into "Asia's Las Vegas." The huge Venetian Macao-Resort-Hotel has already made its mark, along with other development partners including: Hilton, Conrad, Four Seasons, Sheraton, St. Regis, Shangri-La, and Mandarin Oriental. The Cotai area now boasts more than 20 luxury properties; more than 6,000 gaming tables; 29,000 hotel rooms; and 4,000,000 square feet of retail space.

Grand. Its live lobby entertainment and local holiday attractions add a kitschy, friendly feel. ✉ *Av. da Amizade, Downtown* ☎ *853/2838–3838* ⊕ *www.galaxyentertainment.com.*

Grand Lisboa. Meet the veteran Casino Lisboa's younger, more spectacular sister. Opened by Dr. Stanley Ho, this casino has taken Macau by storm with its giant disco ball–like orb, the "precious pearl" at the base of a spouting lotus tower of glitz. With more than 300 tables and about 500 slot machines, the Grand Lisboa's main gaming floor is anchored with a glowing egg statue and a leggy Paris cabaret show every 15 minutes. For more serious spectators, the one-hour, HK$380 "Tokyo Nights" show entertains six times a day in a separate theater. The second floor features craps and sports betting, and has a great bar. True to Lisboa tradition, the Grand also has a variety of dining choices, from the baroque Don Alfonso Macau 1890 to the Round the Clock Coffee Shop and a deli between the first and second gaming floors. ✉ *2–4 Av. de Lisboa, Downtown* ☎ *853/2838–5111* ⊕ *www.grandlisboa.com.*

MGM Grand. Opened in December 2007, the MGM Grand is a stylish addition to Macau's gambling scene. The lavish lounges, Dale Chihuly glass sculptures, Portuguese-inspired architecture, and fine dining of the 1,088-square-meter Grande Praça arcade add to the gaming ambience. The gambling floor itself is popular with high rollers from Hong Kong, including business tycoons who are just in for a few days. One of the main owners, Pansy Ho (like her brother Lawrence Ho), is often cast as the product of her father, the "gambling godfather," Dr. Stanley Ho, but is a high-octane business professional in her own right. The glitz-and-glam energy and high-society appeal are evidence that this is the only casino in Macau with a woman's classy touch. ✉ *Av. Dr. Sun Yat Sen, Downtown* ☎ *853/8802–8888* ⊕ *www.mgmgrandmacau.com.*

Fodor's Choice ★ **Sands Macao**. Thanks to Paul Steelman's design, the Sands Macao has one of the largest parking entrances on earth. And until its sibling, the Venetian, stole the spotlight, this casino was the largest on earth. It's the first casino you'll see on the peninsula even before debarking from the ferry. Past the sparkling 50-ton chandelier entrance, its grand gaming floor is anchored with a live cabaret stage above an open bar and under a giant screen. Several tiers are tastefully linked with escalators leading to the high-stakes tables upstairs, just outside the 888 Buffet and food court. Its relatively friendly atmosphere and location, just across from Fisherman's Wharf and near the bar street in NAPE, is well suited as a warm-up to your night out. ✉ *203 Largo de Monte Carlo, Downtown* ☎ *853/2888–3333* ⊕ *www.sands.com.mo.*

Fodor's Choice ★ **Wynn Macau**. Listen for theme songs such as "Diamonds are Forever," "Luck Be a Lady," or "Money, Money" as you watch the Wynn's outdoor Performance Lake dazzle you with flames and fountain jets of whipping water, which entrance gamblers and tourists every 15 minutes from 11 AM to midnight. Inside the "open hand" structure of Steve Wynn's Macau resort, the indoor Rotunda Tree of Prosperity also wows guests with feng shui glitz. Opened in several stages beginning in 2006, the Wynn's expansive, brightly lit gaming floor, fine dining, buffet meals, luxury shops, deluxe spa, and trendy suites make it one of the more

The opulent Wynn Macau is both luxurious and family friendly.

family-friendly resorts to visit. ✉ *Rua Cidade de Sintra, Downtown* ☎ *853/2888–9966* ⊕ *www.wynnmacau.com.*

MACAU INNER HARBOUR

Ponte 16. In the swinging seaside days of the 1950s, Macau's western port, or Ponte 16, is where all the action took place. When the eastern port opened in the mid-1960s, this area of the Macau Peninsula fell into decay. The 2008 phase-one opening of Ponte 16 changed all that. Taking its cue from the good old days, Ponte 16's winning combination is gorgeous views of the Inner Harbour, with 105 gaming tables and 300 modern slot machines. Popular with Hong Kong and Taiwanese pop stars, the Macanese-owned Ponte 16 is also gaining ground with mainland mass-market gamblers and VIPs from Beijing and Shanghai. Probably because of the casino's relatively isolated location, the atmosphere tends to be casual, but that doesn't limit the minimum bet amounts on the floor. A new shopping arcade replaced the crumbling buildings across the street, so Ponte 16 can be credited for breathing new life into this legendary Latin Quarter. ✉ *4th fl., Rua do Visconde Paço de Arcos, Inner Harbour* ☎ *853/8861–8888* ⊕ *www.ponte16.com.mo.*

TAIPA

Fodor's Choice
★
Altira Macau. Touting itself as Macau's first "six-star" integrated resort, the Altira is indeed stellar. Previously known as Crown Macau, its five swank, '70s-style gaming floors are decked out in browns and taupes with mod-style chandeliers. Opened in May 2007, this is the only classy casino on the island of Taipa. Facing the glow of casinos to the north on the peninsula, the strength of the Altira casino rests in its abundant selection of game play, from baccarat to straight-up slots to posh VIP

Transport yourself to Renaissance Italy at the Venetian Macao-Resort-Hotel.

gaming rooms. Its VIP resort suites and fine-dining components Aurora and Kira (⇨ *Where to Eat*), not to mention the elegantly discreet 38 Lounge on the roof, with outdoor seating open 24 hours, add to the overall ambience. It is equidistant from the peninsula and Cotai. ⊠ *Av. de Kwong Tung, Taipa* ☎ *853/2886–8888* ⊕ *www.altiramacau.com/.*

COTAI

City of Dreams. Upon entering City of Dreams, the underwater theme is quickly apparent, with giant screens flashing images of mermaids swimming to and fro. Cotai's glitzy entertainment complex boasts a 420,000-square-foot casino with 400 gaming tables and 1,300 gaming machines, and more than 20 cafés, restaurants, and bars. Kids will love the free multimedia show "Dragon's Treasure," as well as Kid's City, a playground. "House of Dancing Water," an aquatic-based spectacle that cost HK$2 billion to mount, plays in the Theater of Dreams. Once you're tired out, you can elect to stay at one of the three attached hotels: Grand Hyatt, Hard Rock Hotel, and Crown Towers. ⊠ *Estrada do Istmo, Cotai* ☎ *8868–6688* ⊕ *www.cityofdreamsmacau.com.*

Fodor's Choice
★
Venetian Macao-Resort-Hotel. With 10.5 million square feet of space for gambling, shopping, eating, and sleeping, the Venetian is twice the size of its sister property in Las Vegas. The faux-Renaissance decoration, built-in canals plied by crooning gondoliers, live carnival acts, and upscale luxury brands are sheer spectacle, with more than a touch of pretension. The 550,000-square-foot gaming floor has some 3,000 slot machines and more than 750 tables of casino favorites. The sprawling property also includes 3,000 suites, a 15,000-seat arena, and Cirque du Soleil's ZAIA Theater. So it's no wonder the Venetian is the

must-see megacomplex that everyone's talking about. ✉ *Estrada da Baía de N. Senhora da Esperança, Cotai* ☎ *853/2882–8888* ⊕ *www. venetianmacao.com.*

WHERE TO EAT

Macau's medley of Portuguese and Cantonese cuisine—spicy and creamy Macanese interpretations of traditional Cantonese dishes such as baked prawns, braised abalone, and seafood stews—has made it one of Asia's top fine-dining destinations for decades.

Now, thanks to the spate of new casino-hotels, Macau has also become an exciting world-class culinary frontier. Cases in point: one of Asia's only sake sommeliers can be found at the Wynn's Okada Japanese restaurant. But Macau dining isn't all highbrow. Near the Largo do Senado, in the villages of Taipa or Coloane, wander the back alleys for *zhu-bao-bao,* a slap of fried pork on a toasted bun served with milk tea, or the signature *pasteis de nata* (custard tart): simple and delicious, and classic Macau.

PLANNING

Expect to shell out MOP$90 to MOP$150 per person per meal without wine, though you can always go to a hole-in-the-wall noodle shop for MOP$25–MOP$30. Budget MOP$500 per person for an unforgettable dinner. A 10% service charge is added automatically, but, depending on the service quality, it's common for customers to round up the total. While major credit cards are accepted at most restaurants, cash is preferred at the smaller eateries.

Despite the surge in upscale dining accompanying casino development in Macau, the pace is still siesta style, with serious lunches lasting a few hours. The hotels serve breakfast early, but corner coffee shops start serving ham and cheese on croissants with espresso by around 11 AM. Cocktails begin at around 6:30, and dinner at around 8.

DOWNTOWN MACAU

$$ ✕**Afonso III.** After four years at
PORTUGUESE the Hyatt Regency, Chef Afonso Carrao decided to open his own place and cook the way his grandmother did. The result is his modest café in the heart of downtown near Senado Square, with an intimate space downstairs of dark wood and stucco, and a more expansive upstairs. The food consists of simple, hearty, traditional dishes served in huge portions, mostly to Portuguese expatriates and Macanese locals. Your best bets are the daily specials, which invariably include

8

SWEET SOUVENIRS

Walking toward the Ruins of St. Paul's, you will likely be accosted by salespeople forcing Macanese snacks into your hands. Have a taste or two—competition is fierce and you're expected to shop around. Of this street's several *pastelarias* (pastry shops) with traditional almond cakes, ginger candy, beef jerky, and egg rolls, one of the oldest and best is Pastelaria Koi Kei (✉ *70–72 Rua Felicidade, Downtown* ☎ *853/2893-8102* ⊕ *www.koikei.com*). Other branches are on nearby Rua de São Paulo and on Rua do Cunha in Taipa. Cash is preferred.

bacalhau (Portuguese salted codfish), braised pork, or beef stew probably better than any other you'll taste in Macau. The wine list is extensive, and comes in generous goblets or by the bottle. ✉ *11A Rua Central, Downtown* ☎ *853/2858–6272* ▭ *No credit cards* ☉ *Closed Sun.*

$$$$
FRENCH

✕ **Aux Beaux Arts.** Styled after a 1930s Parisian brasserie, the MGM Grand's Aux Beaux Arts is one of the trendiest restaurants in Macau. Chinese clients are particularly fond of its fresh, catch-of-the-day seafood—the lobster is especially choice. So, too, are the French mains, such as steak with potatoes au gratin. Oysters and caviar are also exclusive, at prices reaching MOP$7,800 for 125 grams. In-house sommeliers are at hand to pair the latest wines with dishes. The tan wood, private booth, and piazza deck tables are other draws. In fact, the decor is as much old French Concession Shanghai as it is old Paris. Either way, it has raised the bar for Macau's restaurant reputation. ✉ *MGM Grand, Av. Dr. Sun Yat Sen, Downtown* ☎ *853/8802–3888* ▭ *AE, MC, V.*

$$$
PORTUGUESE

✕ **Clube Militar de Macau (The Macau Military Club).** Founded in 1870 as a private military club, the stately pink-and-white structure was restored in 1995 and reopened as a restaurant. The languid Old World atmosphere perfectly complements the extensive list of traditional Portuguese dishes offered, such as *bacalhau dourado* ("golden cod," a specialty of fried cod and potatoes), African chicken, and and*arroz de marisco* (flavored rice and seafood). Leave room for dessert—the Portuguese platter includes almond cake, sponge cake, and egg pudding, or go for warm chestnut tart or coconut ice cream with caramelized pineapple. For those with less of a sweet tooth, try the Portuguese cheddar cheese. ✉ *975 Av. da Praia Grande, Downtown* ☎ *853/2871–4010* ▭ *AE, MC, V.*

$$
PORTUGUESE
Fodor's Choice
★

✕ **Dom Galo.** "Quirky" springs to mind when describing the colorful decor of Dom Galo, from plastic monkey puppets to funky chicken toys hanging from the ceilings. Located near the MGM Grand, it draws a wide clientele, from graphic designers to gambling-compliance lawyers to 10-year-old Cantonese kids celebrating birthdays. The waitstaff is from the Philippines and the owner is Portuguese—which means service is usually spot-on. And the food is good: *insalada de polvo* (octopus salad), king prawns, and steak fries served with a tangy mushroom sauce. Pitchers of sangria are essential with any meal here. So, too, are reservations, as this place becomes increasingly popular with tourists. ✉ *Av. Sir Andars Ljung Stedt, Downtown* ☎ *853/2875–1383* ⟁ *Reservations essential* ▭ *MC, V.*

$$$$
CANTONESE

✕ **The Eight.** Executive chef Andy Ng Chi-Kai dishes up Cantonese and Huaiyang in the opulently decorated the Eight, designed by Hong Kong's Alan Chan. Signature dishes include steamed crab claw with ginger and Chinese yellow wine, and deep-fried Macau sole with spicy salt. The wine cellar contains more than 6,800 different vintages, while teetolers can enjoy teas from an extensive menu that includes a *pu er* that has been aged for 49 years. The lunch menu boasts over 50 types of dim sum. ✉ *2/F, Grand Lisboa Hotel, Av. De Lisboa, Downtown* ☎ *853/8803–7788* ▭ *AE, MC, V* ☉ *Mon.–Sat. 11:30–2:30, 6:30–10:30, Sun. and holidays 10–3, 6:30–10:30.*

$$ **×Fat Siu Lau.** Well known to both locals and Hong Kong visitors, Fat
CANTONESE Siu Lau has kept its customers coming back since 1903 with delicious
Fodor's Choice Macanese favorites and modern creations. For best results, try ordering
★ whatever you see the chatty Cantonese stuffing themselves with at the
surrounding tables, and you won't be disappointed. It will probably be
whole curry crab, grilled prawns in a butter garlic sauce, and the famous
roasted pigeon marinated in a secret marinade. The newer Fat Siu Lau
2 is on Macau Lan Kwai Fong Street and offers the same great food.
⊠ *64 Rua da Felicidade, Downtown* ☎ *853/2857–3580* ⌕ *Reservations
essential* ▭ *MC, V.*

$$$$ **×Il Teatro.** With its dedicated view of (and music wafting in from) the
ITALIAN Wynn's Performance Lake show, and the flashing glows of the Lis-
boa casinos providing ambience, Il Teatro is one of the most roman-
tic restaurants in Macau, where Hong Kong pop stars and jet-setting
millionaires from Malaysia hobnob. Popular among the impeccable
southern Italian delights are melon-and-prosciutto starters, Parma ham-
and-lobster gnocchi, accompanied by chilled wine from an exhaustive
list. Desserts range from rich chocolate cakes to homemade sorbets and
ice cream imported straight from Italy. Window seats in particular are
at a premium, and are best reserved three weeks in advance. The dress
code is "casual elegance," which means long pants, closed-toe shoes,
and no open shirts for men; it's not the place for children under five.
⊠ *Wynn Macau, Rua da Sintra, Downtown* ☎ *853/8986–3648* ▭ *AE,
DC, MC, V* ⊘ *No lunch.*

$$ **×Long Kei.** One of the oldest and most popular Cantonese restaurants
CANTONESE in Macau, Long Kei is in busy Senado Square, in a handsome pink
building a few meters from the fountain. The huge menu includes many
daily specials printed only in Chinese, so ask your waiter to translate.
The restaurant is noisy and chaotic, and makes no attempt at glamour
or sophistication. The focus is on the food, and for good reason, as
it rarely disappoints. Be sure to sample the shrimp toast, congee, and
the in-house roasted pork and chicken dishes. ⊠ *7B Largo do Senado,
Downtown* ☎ *853/2857–3970* ▭ *MC, V.*

$$–$$$ **×Portas do Sol.** Originally a Portuguese restaurant, Portas do Sol has
SHANGHAINESE been transformed into a destination for exquisite dim sum and Chinese
cuisine. Tiny, sweet Shanghainese pork buns, turnip cakes, steamed rice-
flour crepes, and soup dumplings are some of the traditional fare, and
there are some innovative new creations that look like miniature jewels
on the plate. For dessert you can choose from a wide variety of Chinese
sweets, including coconut-milk sago pudding, double-boiled papaya
with snow fungus (a tasteless mushroom that becomes gelatinous when
cooked), and sweet red-bean porridge with ice cream. Evening diners
may or may not appreciate the cabaret show and ballroom dancing.
Reservations are a good idea on weekends, as this place fills up with
Hong Kong and mainland visitors. ⊠ *Hotel Lisboa, Av. da Amizade,
Downtown* ☎ *853/8803–3100* ▭ *AE, MC, V.*

$$ **×Praia Grande.** This classic Portuguese restaurant retains its Mediter-
PORTUGUESE ranean beauty inside and outside, with a gleaming white facade open-
ing into a dining room with graceful arches, terra-cotta floors, and
wrought-iron furniture. The menu is creative, with dishes ranging

8

from Portuguese dim sum, African chicken, mussels in white wine, and pork and clams *cataplana* (in a stew of onions, tomatoes, and wine). Guitarists serenade you every night. ✉ *10A Praça Lobo d'Avila, Av. da Praia Grande, Downtown* ☎ *853/2897–3022* ▭ *AE, MC, V.*

$$$$
FRENCH

✕ **Robuchon a Galera**. A slice of Paris in the heart of Macau, this restaurant on the third floor of the Hotel Lisboa is a must, particularly if you just hit it big in the casino. In the ornate interior, with rich velvets

> ## LOVE OF VINHO
>
> Wine lovers should take full advantage of Macau's intimate love of *vinho*. Some restaurants have wine lists as thick as phone books. Most places list at least a couple of bottles of delicious Portuguese wine—usually a hearty red from the Dão region or a slightly sparkling *vinho verde* from the north.

and dark woods, a Swarovski crystal star field twinkles on the ceiling. Signature dishes are a heavenly mille-feuille of tomato and crabmeat, duck breast with turnips and foie gras, and lamb served with creamy potato puree. But Robuchon's 12-course tasting menus, including two desserts, are the best way to experience the restaurant's gastronomic offerings. The wine list is as thick as an encyclopedia, and includes some rare wines. ✉ *Hotel Lisboa, Av. da Amizade, Downtown* ☎ *853/8803–7878* ⌕ *Reservations essential* ▭ *AE, MC, V.*

MACAU OUTER HARBOUR

$$
AFRICAN

✕ **AfriKana B.B.Q. Restaurant**. It's one of the few places in Macau where you can eat roasted coconut chicken under thatched huts, and where Macau's historical contacts with Africa, especially Angola and Mozambique, come into sharp focus. Scores of Portuguese-speaking residents who were born in Portugal's African colonies come here for parties or cultural events. The eight pavilions of thatched huts feature resilient colors, from dark blues to mustard yellows to sandy reds. The all-you-can-eat evening buffets are particularly popular, with staples such as seared fish, barbecued steak, steamed carrots, and other grilled dishes. Buffet prices range from MOP$188 to MOP$188 per person, depending on the day. ✉ *Fisherman's Wharf, Outer Harbour* ☎ *853/8299–3678* ▭ *AE, MC, V.*

$$
PORTUGUESE

✕ **Camões**. Named after the famed Portuguese poet Luis de Camões, this restaurant serves traditional Portuguese dishes in a Mediterranean ambience. The whitewashed walls are accented by dark-wood tables and chairs, and wall tiles are blue-inked with images of old schooners and Chinese junks. *Pata negra* ham (similar to prosciutto) on toasted bread, cold crab, diced pork with lime juice, and whipped potatoes are among the culinary delights. The large selection of Portuguese wines includes several labels from the famous Alentejo region of southern Portugal. Among the desserts are drunken pear and *serradura* (layers of cream and biscuits). ✉ *1st fl., Lisboan building, Fisherman's Wharf, Outer Harbour* ☎ *853/2872–8818* ▭ *AE, MC, V.*

$$$$
STEAK
Fodor's Choice
★

✕ **Copa Steakhouse**. The first traditional American steak house in Macau, the Copa has a selection of premium quality steaks and seafood, along with a range of cigars and cocktails in an interior that looks like 1960s Las Vegas. Sip a cocktail at the bar near the grand piano, and get ready for huge slabs of American and Australian beef, grilled to juicy perfection before your eyes in the open kitchen. The Japanese Kagoshima beef tops the list at MOP$2,188. Other dishes include sautéed sea scallops and fresh oysters when in season. For dessert, try the sinfully rich crème brûlée. ⊠ *Sands Casino, 203 Largo de Monte Carlo, Outer Harbour* ☎ *853/8983–8222* ⊟ *AE, MC, V* ☉ *Closed Sun. No lunch.*

$$$ ✕ **Naam.** The Grand Lapa's Thai restaurant is set amid the hotel's land-
THAI scaped tropical gardens. Start your meal off with a refreshing *yam som-o* (herbed pomelo salad with chicken and prawns) or aromatic *tom kha gai* (herbed coconut soup with chicken). Then move on to main courses such as the fried lobster with sweet basil and young peppercorns or the traditional favorite *moo phad bai ga praow* (spicy pork with chilies and hot basil leaves). For dessert, there's a melt-in-your-mouth *kluey thod krub bai toey* (deep-fried banana with sweet pandanus-fruit sauce). It's a popular lunch spot for local casino managers, and a hot ticket at dinnertime. ⊠ *Grand Lapa, 956–1110 Av. da Amizade, Outer Harbour* ☎ *853/8793–4818* ⌕ *Reservations essential* ⊟ *AE, DC, MC, V.*

MACAU INNER HARBOUR

$$$ ✕ **A Lorcha.** Vastly popular A Lorcha (the name means "wooden ship")
PORTUGUESE celebrates the heritage of Macau as an important port with a maritime
Fodor'sChoice theme for the menu. Don't miss the signature dish, Clams Lorcha Style,
★ with tomato, beer, and garlic. Other classics include *feijoada* (Brazilian pork-and-bean stew), steamed crab, and perfectly smoky and juicy fire-roasted chicken. Excellent desserts include thick mango pudding and sinfully dense serradura. Watch for racers during the Grand Prix, as the Macanese owner Adriano is a fervent Formula fan. ⊠ *289 Rua do Almirante Sérgio, Inner Harbour* ☎ *853/2831–3193* ⌕ *Reservations essential* ⊟ *AE, MC, V* ☉ *Closed Tues.*

$$$ ✕ **Litoral.** One of the most popu-
MACANESE lar local restaurants, Litoral serves authentic Macanese dishes that are simple, straightforward, and deliciously satisfying. It is tastefully decorated with whitewashed walls and dark-wood beams. Must-try dishes include the tamarind pork with shrimp paste, as well as codfish baked with potato and garlic, and a Portuguese vegetable cream soup. For dessert, try the *bebinca de leite*, a coconut-milk custard, or the traditional egg pudding, *pudim abade de priscos*. Variously priced set menus are also available, and reservations are recommended on weekends. ⊠ *261 Rua do Almirante Sergio, Inner Harbour* ☎ *853/2896–7878* ⊟ *AE, MC, V.*

$$ ✕ **O Porto Interior.** Come here for
MACANESE traditional Portuguese food that

A COLONIAL FEAST

The Macanese like hearty Portuguese fare. Most restaurants serve the beloved *bacalhau* (salt cod) baked, boiled, grilled, deep-fried with potato, or stewed with onion, garlic, and eggs. Other dishes include sardines, sausages, and *caldo verde* (vegetable soup). Giant prawns in a curry sauce recall the cuisine of Goa, India—another Portuguese colony. Indeed, there are dishes drawn from throughout the colonial empire, including Brazilian *feijoada* (a stew of beans, pork, and vegetables) and Mozambique chicken, baked or grilled and seasoned with piri-piri chili, tangy spices, and coconut.

8

relies on meats, seafood, and heavy sauces, with excellent renditions of grilled prawns, African chicken, and various curries. For dinner parties, the Macanese owner Carlos will be happy to design a set-price menu on request. It's the design, however, that makes the place so special, with an elegant two-story facade, upstairs private room, brilliant white colonnades, and Iberian arches tiled with azulejos (glazed and painted Portuguese tiles) complemented by marble steps and bridges. Reservations are a good idea on weekends. ⊠ *259B Rua do Almirante Sergio, Inner Harbour* ☎ *853/2896–7770* ▭ *AE, MC, V.*

TAIPA

$$$$
ITALIAN
✕ **Aurora.** With its southern Italian fare inspired by the Puglia Region and sweeping views of the Macau Peninsula, Aurora is popular with a high-level business clientele and those seeking modern romance. Chef Michele dell'Aquila's menu focuses on seafood, spotlighting Japanese sea bass, Boston lobster, crabs, prawns, and oysters, but there are plenty of pastas and meats as well. The massive wine cellar holds 600–700 wines, and there is a wine tasting every Friday 6–8. Buffet brunch is served from 11 to 4 on Sunday and costs MOP$388. ⊠ *Altira Macau, Av. de Kwong Tung, Taipa* ☎ *853/8803–6622* ⌕ *Reservations essential* ▭ *AE, MC, V* ☺ *No lunch.*

$$$$
CHINESE
✕ **Beijing Kitchen.** Inspired by its sister restaurant Made In China in Grand Hyatt Beijing, Beijing Kitchen features northern Chinese cuisine. Every chef on staff is from the capital city. One of the signature dishes is the Peking duck, which is cooked in a wood-burning oven, burning away the fat and leaving the skin crispy. The home-style panfried pork dumplings have a delicately thin skin. The open kitchen, exposed brick, high ceilings, dark-wood furnishings, and modern Chinese decor give the eatery a sophisticated, yet comfortable, atmosphere. The dessert menu contains Chinese sweets such as mango and passion-fruit pudding, as well as homemade ice cream. ⊠ *Grand Hyatt, City of Dreams, Estrada do Istmo, Cotai* ☎ *853/8868–1930* ⊕ *macau.grand.hyatt.com* ▭ *DC, MC, V* ☺ *Daily 10:30–midnight.*

$$$–$$$$
PORTUGUESE
✕ **Belcanção.** Located next to the Bali-inspired poolside at Four Seasons, Belcanção offers an impressive buffet spread featuring Portuguese, Indian, Chinese, Italian, and a smaller selection of Japanese. The dessert and salad bars are amply stocked, and the service is impeccable. Try the codfish with chickpeas salad, have a slice of thin-crust pizza, and wash it all down with a delectable mango juice. Follow up with an egg tart or a serradura, which is a Portuguese dessert containing cookies and cream.

KING OF TARTS

Originally a modest, traditional bakery opened by a young Englishman named Andrew Stow in 1989, **Lord Stow's Bakery** (⊠ *1 Rua da Tassara, Coloane Village Sq.* ☎ *853/2888–2534* ⊕ *www.lordstow.com*) is now a culinary landmark in Coloane, just off the town square. Locals sit on nearby benches munching the signature hot and flaky *pasteis de nata* (custard tarts) straight from the oven. Inside the little shop, breads, muffins, cookies, flapjacks, and other homemade goods are on offer, but be sure to walk out with at least one tart. The neighboring Lord Stow's Café (☎ *853/2888–2174*) has sit-down meals.

Make sure to sample one (or more) of Lord Stow's sought after tarts.

Lunch is MOP$288, plus 10% service charge. ⊠ *Four Seasons, Estrada da Baía de N. Senhora da Esperança, Cotai* ☎ *853/2881–8888* ⊕ *www.fourseasons.com/macau* 🖻 *AE, DC, MC, V* ⏱ *Breakfast 6:30–11, lunch noon–2:30, dinner 6–10, Sunday brunch noon–3.*

$$$$

JAPANESE

✕ **Kira.** Next to Aurora and with the same stunning views of the peninsula, Kira serves immaculate Japanese meals by chef Hiroshi Kagata. Its wasabi, for example, comes fresh and doesn't burn badly—truly sublime mustard is a sign that something fresh is taking place in the kitchen. Outdoor deck seating is nice way to enjoy Kira's carefully cut sashimi and subtle seaweed soups, if not fine cuts of Wagyu beef. There are also private booths for intimate or amorous dining. It's an excellent choice for entertaining guests and for family dining. ⊠ *Altira Macau, Av. de Kwong Tung, Taipa* ☎ *853/8803–6633* 🖋 *Reservations essential* 🖻 *AE, DC, MC, V* ⏱ *No lunch.*

COLOANE

$$

PORTUGUESE

Fodor's Choice

★

✕ **Fernando's.** Everyone in Hong Kong and Macau knows about Fernando's, but the vine-covered entrance close to Hác-Sá Beach is difficult to spot. The open-air dining pavilion and bar have attracted beachgoers for years now, and the enterprising Fernando has built a legendary reputation for his tiny Portuguese restaurant. The menu focuses on seafood paired with homegrown vegetables, and diners choose from among the bottles of Portuguese reds on display rather than from a wine list. The informal nature of the restaurant fits in with the satisfying, home-style food such as grilled fish, baked chicken, and huge bowlfuls of spicy clams, all eaten with your fingers and washed down with crisp vinho verde. ⊠ *Hác-Sá Beach 9, Coloane Island South* ☏ *853/2888–2531* ⌂ *Reservations not accepted* ▭ *No credit cards.*

$$
PORTUGUESE
✗ **Restaurante Espaço Lisboa.** A favorite among local Portuguese, this Portuguese-owned restaurant with a Portuguese chef is a converted two-story house with a small but pleasant outdoor balcony for alfresco dining overlooking Coloane Village. Menu highlights include codfish cakes, savory duck rice, monkfish rice, boiled bacalhau with cabbage, sausage flambé, steak topped with ham and fried egg, and smoked ham imported from Portugal. Take your pick from an extensive list of hearty Portuguese wines, and finish the meal with homemade mango ice cream with a cherry flambé. ⊠ *8 Rua das Gaivotas, Coloane Island West* ☏ *853/2888–2226* ▭ *MC, V.*

WHERE TO STAY

The Altira. The Venetian. The MGM Grand. Since late 2006, an influx of luxury hotels has transformed Macau into a posh place to stay. The suites at the integrated resorts complement the likes of the Grand Lapa on the peninsula and the Westin Resort on Coloane. The musty three-stars are still out there, but the five-stars are generally worth the splurge. For a true Macau experience, try staying in *pousadas,* restored historic buildings that have been converted into intimate hotels with limited facilities but lots of character.

PLANNING

When choosing a hotel, consider the surroundings. In pulsating downtown Macau (or in the Outer Harbour, connected to Downtown via frequent casino shuttles), historic and cultural sites, casinos, and restaurants are all within walking distance. Hotels in more residential Taipa, just a short bus or taxi ride away, often have incomparable sea and bright-lights views. Cotai offers one-stop sleeping, shopping, eating, and gambling. Outside the resorts, it's still a construction field, with new, glitzy hotels opening frequently. The peaceful Inner Harbour has excellent sea views, but for true otherworldly quiet, head to Coloane, where you can hit the beach and hiking trails.

For discounted rates in the grand hotels, book a package through a Hong Kong travel agency. Or, subject to availability, an agent at the Macau hydrofoil terminal can book you a room at a three- to five-star hotel for a discount price. Macau hotels are busiest during the Grand Prix (third week of November) and all official Chinese holidays. Book at least a couple of weeks in advance at these times. Year-round, weekends fill up fast and walk-ins can be prohibitively expensive. Weekday rates are often half price.

DOWNTOWN MACAU

$$$
🏨 **Galaxy StarWorld Hotel.** If it's good enough for China's 2008 Olympic gold medalists, it must have some appeal. And it does, at least in the luminous open "studio" suites with high ceilings, Jacuzzi tubs, and panoramic bay windows. Even the deluxe rooms, with their high-quality bedding and dark wood furniture, make you feel like you're somewhere special. At the happening Whisky Bar (⇨ *After Dark*) on the 16th floor,

as well as downstairs in the lobby, StarWorld brings you flashy dancers, live bands, and even a Chaplin impersonator. The dazzling blue building was designed by Rocco Yim, also known for designing Hong Kong's towering Two IFC. **Pros:** celestially designed suites; live entertainment in the lobby and lounge bar; free Internet access in every room. **Cons:** high energy at all hours; in a heavy-traffic area. ⊠ *Av. da Amizade, Downtown* ☎ *853/2878–1111* ⊕ *www.starworldmacau.com* ⇙ *465 rooms, 44 suites* ⬧ *In-room: safe, DVD (some), Internet. In-hotel: 5 restaurants, room service, bars, pool, gym, spa, laundry service, Internet terminal, parking (paid), no-smoking rooms* ⊟ *AE, DC, MC, V.*

$$ ⊡ **Hotel Lisboa.** Macau's infamous landmark, with its distinctive, labyrinthine interior architecture, rumored connections to organized crime, open prostitution, and no-limit VIP rooms, now stands in the shadow of its Grand Lisboa sister. The two are connected by a bridge and share facilities, such as the Grand's modern pool, gym, and spa. The advantages to staying in the older structure are nostalgic value and lower price. And though the Grand Lisboa opened in early 2007, the Hotel Lisboa was renovated one year later, so the rooms are just as luxurious, with hardwood floors and Jacuzzi baths. Take your time to wander through the hotel's corridors displaying jade and artworks from Dr. Stanley Ho's private collection, before running into an ostentatiously gilded staircase. Many people come to the Lisboa expressly for its restaurants: Robuchon a Galera and Portas do Sol (⇨ *Where to Eat*). **Pros:** historical interior; central location; superior restaurants; linked to the Grand Lisboa. **Cons:** old building; low ceilings; smoky casino. ⊠ *2–4 Av. de Lisboa, Downtown* ☎ *853/2888–3888, 800/969–130 in Hong Kong* ⊕ *www.hotelisboa.com* ⇙ *1,000 rooms, 28 suites* ⬧ *In-room: safe, DVD, Internet. In-hotel: 5 restaurants, room service, pool, gym, spa, laundry service, no-smoking rooms* ⊟ *AE, DC, MC, V.*

$ ⊡ **Hotel Sintra.** Minutes away from Senado Square and right down the street from the New Yaohan department store, the Sintra is a good three-star antechamber to the Lisboan kingdom, with its own built-in Mocha minicasino accessible through the lobby. Its cosy, carpeted rooms are decorated in soothing brown-and-cream color schemes, while the staff is smartly dressed and helpful. Breakfast is an extra MOP$99 for an American buffet. **Pros:** in the heart of downtown; simple but tasteful decor. **Cons:** small rooms; small casino. ⊠ *Av. De Dom João IV, Downtown* ☎ *853/2871–0111, 800/969–145 in Hong Kong* ⊕ *www. hotelsintra.com* ⇙ *240 rooms, 11 suites* ⬧ *In-room: safe, refrigerator, Internet. In-hotel: restaurant, room service, Wi-Fi hotspot, no-smoking rooms* ⊟ *AE, DC, MC, V.*

$$$ ⊡ **MGM Grand.** In Macau, the golden lion statue stands guard on the
Fodor's Choice peninsula's southern coast, as guests penetrate into the MGM's spec-
★ tacular Grande Praça (Grand Square), an 82-foot-tall floor-to-glass-ceiling space modeled after a Portuguese town square that serves as an inner courtyard and has fine dining under the stars. A few million Hong Kong dollars were invested in the permanent chandelier sculpture and original drawings by Dale Chihuly decorating the hotel lobby and reception. Chihuly's glassworks line the hall linking the art gallery to the patisserie, giving it a warm pink glow, while the M Bar plays soft jazz

8

Luxury Spas

The Spa at the Grand Lapa scrubs and rubs customers into relaxation.

Macau is well known for its casinos and restaurants, but it's also rapidly gaining a reputation for its luxury spa and sauna facilities, offering a huge range of treatments. Almost every luxury hotel has its own spa, with special packages and offers for hotel guests. Many visitors opt for spa treatments at luxury hotels, but Macau's independent spas have become a major force, offering equally exquisite service at lower prices than hotels. All spas offer services for couples, and provide a great opportunity to relax in a peaceful space with someone special.

Treatments begin at around MOP$300 and up for 60 minutes of service. The following are some of the more impressive spa facilities available:

THE SPA AT THE GRAND LAPA MACAU

The largest and best-known spa in town takes advantage of the Grand Lapa's sumptuous Mediterranean architecture and lets in lots of natural sunlight for a bright and airy spa experience. It offers numerous Chinese, European, Thai, and Japanese treatments, including its signature 2½-hour, three-part Macanese Sangría Ritual, which includes a full body scrub using fresh grapes, sangria bath in a private outdoor Jacuzzi, and grape-seed-oil massage, for MOP$1,720. Reserve ahead. ⊠ *Grand Lapa, 956–1110 Av. da Amizade, Outer Harbour* ☎ *853/8793–4824 or 800/968–886* ⊕ *www. mandarinoriental.com/grandlapa/spa.*

NIRVANA SPA

In a quiet area of town near the Nam Van Lake, the Asian-inspired Nirvana has rooms decorated in Chinese, Thai, Balinese, Indian, Macau, and various other eastern themes, where therapists from Thailand and the Philippines are trained in deep-tissue, ayurvedic, herbal, shiatsu, and aromatherapy massages. ⊠ *Ground fl., China Law Bldg., 403 Av. da Praia Grande, Downtown* ☎ *853/2833–1521* ⊕ *www.nirvanaspamacau.com.*

and lounge music. The rooms are everything you'd expect in the way of comfort and elegance from a luxury accommodation, with the decor adhering to a muted cream, brown, and beige color palette, but it's the classy world around them, outside the casino, that distinguishes this hotel from the rest. **Pros:** tasteful architecture; Chihuly artwork; refined dining and lounge options. **Cons:** inseparable from the casino, which can get smoky and loud; high-traffic location. ⊠ *Av. Dr. Sun Yat Sen, Downtown* ☎ *853/8802–8888* ⊕ *www.mgmgrandmacau.com* ⤳ *494 rooms, 99 suites* ⎘ *In-room: safe, refrigerator (some), DVD (some), Wi-Fi. In-hotel: 8 restaurants, room service, bars, pool, spa, laundry service, Wi-Fi hotspot, parking (paid), no-smoking rooms* ⊟ *AE, MC, V.*

$ **Pousada de Mong-Há.** Restored by the MGTO in 1979, and renovated in 2010, this secluded pousada halfway up Mong-Há Hill was once a Portuguese military barracks, before being used to house foreign civil servants, and is now a training hotel entirely run by students of the attached Institute for Tourism Studies. Accommodation and service are exemplary, spacious rooms are delicately decorated with hand-stitched carpets, and the restaurant shows off its traditional azulejos at breakfast and teatime. Kun Iam and Lin Fung temples are nearby, as is the famous Canidrome. **Pros:** historic charm; hillside walks and views. **Cons:** half-hour walk north from city center; no pool. ⊠ *Colina de Mong-Há, Downtown* ☎ *853/2851–5222* ⊕ *www.ift.edu.mo/pousada* ⤳ *16 rooms* ⎘ *In-room: safe, refrigerator, Internet, Wi-Fi. In-hotel: restaurant, gym, laundry service, no-smoking rooms* ⊟ *AE, MC, V.*

$$$$ **Wynn Macau.** If you just can't get enough of the Wynn's Performance Lake by merely admiring it at ground level, the hotel offers rooms with a plunging view of the fire-and-water spectacle, as well as of the peaceful Nam Van Lake. Alternatively, you can opt for a glittering city view of the outdoor pool and neighboring Lisboa casinos, as all rooms have floor-to-ceiling windows. Hotel extras include buffet breakfast at the Café Esplanada and a daily Macau heritage tour. The Wynn resort is also home to such fine dining options as Il Teatro and Okada, which has one of Asia's only resident sake sommeliers. **Pros:** exclusive VIP club space; Nam Van and Performance Lake views. **Cons:** light pollution from neighboring casinos; lowest rooms on 5th floor. ⊠ *Rua Cidade de Sintra, Downtown* ☎ *853/2888–9966, 800/966–963 in Hong Kong* ⊕ *www.wynnmacau.com* ⤳ *460 rooms, 140 suites* ⎘ *In-room: safe, refrigerator, Internet, Wi-Fi. In-hotel: 5 restaurants, room service, bar, pool, gym, spa, laundry service, Wi-Fi hotspot, no-smoking rooms* ⊟ *AE, MC, V.*

MACAU OUTER HARBOUR

$$$ **Grand Lapa Hotel.** The hotel, formerly the Mandarin Oriental, is elegant, with an understated opulence. The rooms feature bright Portuguese decor, with views of the city or of the resort itself. The Grand Lapa is also widely known for deluxe treatments in the enormous spa complex next to the gorgeous, tropical swimming pool on the landscaped grounds. You'll feel like you're in a lush rain forest as you look out from the traditional Mediterranean architecture of the hotel. The hotel's renowned restaurants include the Café Bela Vista for its endless buffet, and Naam, the exquisite Thai restaurant popular with locals

and visitors alike. **Pros:** classic luxury facilities; on-site rock climbing; kid's club. **Cons:** old casino; high-traffic location. ⊠ *956–1110 Av. da Amizade, Outer Harbour* ☎ *853/8793–3261, 2881–1288 in Hong Kong, 800/526–6567 in U.S.* ⊕ *www.mandarinoriental.com/grandlapa* 🛏 *388 rooms, 28 suites* ♻ *In-room: safe, refrigerator, Internet, Wi-Fi. In-hotel: 4 restaurants, room service, bar, tennis courts, pools, gym, spa, water sports, children's programs (ages 3–12), laundry service, Wi-Fi hotspot, no-smoking rooms* ⊟ *AE, DC, MC, V.*

$$ **Rocks Hotel.** The posh-yet-quaint five-story Rocks Hotel is modeled after the charm of 18th-century Victorian England. Each room and suite is individually decorated, with a novelty old-fashioned bathtub in addition to a modern shower stall. Balconies offer low sea views on all sides. The extensive Asian and American breakfast buffet will keep you fueled during your day's adventures. The foyer itself is impressive, with its grand staircase under sparkling chandeliers, although it could use some real birds in the giant gilded cage to liven up the lobby. **Pros:** distinctive decor; low-key fine dining. **Cons:** no pool or spa; inside an amusement park. ⊠ *Macau Fisherman's Wharf, Outer Harbour* ☎ *853/2878–2782, 800/962–863 in Hong Kong* ⊕ *www.rockshotel.com.mo* 🛏 *66 rooms, 6 suites* ♻ *In-room: safe, Internet. In-hotel: restaurant, room service, bar, gym, laundry service, parking (free), no-smoking rooms* ⊟ *AE, DC, MC, V.*

$$$ **Sands Macao.** Las Vegas casino tycoon Sheldon Anderson's first venture in Macau, the Sands is nothing if not luxurious. Spacious rooms have deep, soft carpets, large beds, and huge marble bathrooms with Jacuzzis. If you opt to become a high-rolling member, you can stay in one of the 51 deluxe or executive suites, ranging in size from 650 to 1,300 square feet, with all-in-one remote-control plasma TV, karaoke, curtains, and lighting, plus personal butler service on request. VIP members also have privileges such as high-limit gaming rooms at both the Sands and Venetian casinos. But all guests can enjoy the outdoor heated pool on the 6th floor, as well as the exclusive sauna, spa, and salon. **Pros:** heated outdoor pool; across the street from Fisherman's Wharf. **Cons:** not as new as the Venetian; near lots of vehicle traffic. ⊠ *203 Largo de Monte Carlo, Outer Harbour* ☎ *853/2888–3388* ⊕ *www. sands.com.mo* 🛏 *258 rooms, 51 VIP suites* ♻ *In-room: safe, DVD. In-hotel: 6 restaurants, room service, bar, pool, spa, laundry service, parking (paid)* ⊟ *AE, MC, V.*

MACAU INNER HARBOUR

$$$$ **Pousada de São Tiago.** The spirit of the structure's past life as a 17th-century fortress permeates every part of this romantic and intimate lodging, making it ideal for a honeymoon or wedding. Even the front entrance is impressive: an ascending stone tunnel carved into the mountainside with water seeping through in quiet trickles. The pousada reopened in mid-2007 after a major renovation that consolidated accommodations into 12 modern luxury suites, each with Jacuzzi bathrooms and large balconies for room-service breakfast. Stop for high tea in the mirrored lounge, or sip a cocktail on the terrace under 100-year-old trees. **Pros:** all the modern comfort of a luxury hotel inside a 17th-century fortress; intimate, sunset views of the Inner Harbour.

Fodor'sChoice
★

Cons: small pool; limited facilities; you'll need to call a taxi to go out. ⊠ *Fortaleza de São Tiago da Barra, Av. da República, Inner Harbour* ☎ *853/2837–8111, 800/969–153 in Hong Kong* ⊕ *www.saotiago.com. mo* ⤳ *12 suites* ⚷ *In-room: Internet, Wi-Fi. In-hotel: restaurant, room service, bar, pool, laundry service, Wi-Fi hotspot, parking (free), no-smoking rooms* ⊟ *AE, MC, V.*

$$
Fodor'sChoice
★

🏨 **Sofitel Macau at Ponte 16.** Ever since its February 2008 opening, Ponte 16 has pioneered the revamp of Macau's retro western port into an emerging casino and commercial pole. The neighborhood may not be there yet, but Sofitel is Ponte 16's jewel in the crown, with lush, sleek suites and a giant, curvaceous pool, complete with cocktail and juice bar, just outside the indoor buffet lounge. Adventurous and up-and-coming, it has all the edgy perks—grab it while it's hot. **Pros:** giant outdoor pool with bar serving everything from fresh fruit to fine wine; some rooms have unique views of the Inner Harbour. **Cons:** in a still-developing neighborhood; heavy traffic outside. ⊠ *Rua do Visconde Paço de Arcos, Inner Harbour* ☎ *853/8861–0016* ⊕ *www.sofitel.com* ⤳ *389 rooms, 19 suites* ⚷ *In-room: safe, DVD, Internet. In-hotel: restaurants, room service, bar, pool, gym, spa, laundry service, parking (free), no-smoking rooms* ⊟ *AE, DC, MC, V.*

TAIPA

$$$$
Fodor'sChoice
★

🏨 **Altira.** Towering over northern Taipa, the Altira offers stunning sea views of the Macau Peninsula from each and every room, suite, and villa. Even standard rooms are like suites, with a dedicated lounge, walk-in wardrobe, and circular stone bath. There's a panoramic-view swimming pool, a two-level spa with 12 treatment rooms, Aurora's Sunday buffet brunch, classy VIP gaming rooms, and the 24-hour Crystal Club, which provides starlight seating on the rooftop for cool cocktails in a romantic setting. The vertically designed Altira reaches high to set its own standard of chic above and beyond all the mushrooming kitsch. **Pros:** glowing sea views from every room; panoramic-view pool; open-air rooftop bar. **Cons:** may sometimes be noisy from nearby construction; still a taxi (or shuttle) ride from the peninsula. ⊠ *Av. de Kwong Tung, Taipa* ☎ *853/2886–8888* ⊕ *www.crown-macau.com* ⤳ *184 rooms, 24 suites, 8 villas* ⚷ *In-room: safe, refrigerator (some), DVD (some), Internet, Wi-Fi. In-hotel: 6 restaurants, room service, bar, pool, gym, spa, laundry service, parking (paid), no-smoking rooms* ⊟ *AE, MC, V.*

$$$$
🏨 **Crown Towers.** The lobby of the Crown Towers is filled with fine art, alluding to the luxury within. The bright rooms are spacious at 47 to 60 square meters, with soft carpeting, sleek furnishings, and huge bathrooms. The spa, with an indoor heated pool and fully equipped fitness center nearby, has an extensive menu of relaxing treatments and a Jacuzzi, steam room, and sauna. **Pros:** plenty of privacy; luxurious spa **Cons:** part of a themed complex; near construction. ⊠ *City of Dreams, 1 Estrada do Istmo, Cotai* ☎ *853/8868–6888* ⊕ *www.cityofdreamsmacau.com/?q=hotel/crown-towers* ⤳ *300 rooms* ⚷ *In-room: safe, refrigerator, Wi-Fi. In-hotel: restaurant, room service, bar, pool, gym, spa, laundry service, Internet terminal, Wi-Fi hotspot, parking (paid)* ⊟ *AE, MC, V.*

8

MGM Grand

Westin Resort

Sofitel Macau at Ponte 16

$$$$ 🏨 **Four Seasons Hotel.** Opened in October 2008, the Four Seasons conscientiously upholds its brand-name reputation with this property. Nestled in the southeast corner of the Venetian complex, it is independently managed, and without a casino to worry about, the focus is on providing guests with the best possible accommodation and well-being experience. The understated luxurious decor in the rooms is a welcome respite from the overwrought design of the nearby Venetian. Witness its comprehensive spa treatments and facilities, as well as separate pools for the kids. The Shoppes at Four Seasons luxury boutiques await you just outside the lobby, as you rejoin the tourist flow. **Pros:** focus on service; extensive spa treatments. **Cons:** attached to the Venetian; beside a shopping mall. ✉ *Estrada da Baía de N. Senhora da Esperança, Cotai* ☎ *853/2881–8888* ⊕ *www.fourseasons.com/macau* ⤢ *276 rooms, 84 suites* ♿ *In-room: safe, refrigerator (some), DVD, Internet, Wi-Fi. In-hotel: 5 restaurants, room service, bar, pools, gym, spa, laundry service, Wi-Fi hotspot, parking (paid), no-smoking rooms* ▭ *AE, DC, MC, V.*

$$$ 🏨 **Hard Rock Hotel.** For the music enthusiastic, this may be the perfect hotel, with some 700 pieces of memorabilia displayed in various spots throughout and a suite devoted to Cantopop megastar Jacky Cheung. The rooms are hip and cozy, boasting floor to ceiling windows that let in ample natural light and a lovely minimalist bathroom with. You can select your very own soundtrack from the streaming tunes to set the mood for your vacation, or plug in your own MP3 player. Because it is part of the City of Dreams complex, restaurants, bars and shops are accessible without even stepping foot outside. Near the pool there's an artificial beach, complete with set up for beach volleyball. **Pros:** youthful appeal; makes use of new technology **Cons:** music theme may not appeal to everyone. ✉ *City of Dreams, 2 Estrada do Istmo, Cotai* ☎ *853/8868–3338* ⊕ *www.hardrockhotelmacau.com* ⤢ *256 rooms; 66 suites* ♿ *In-room: safe, Internet, Wi-Fi. In-hotel: 2 restaurants, room service, bars, pool, gym, spa, laundry service, Internet terminal, Wi-Fi hotspot, parking (paid)* ▭ *AE, MC, V.*

$$$ 🏨 **Grand Hyatt.** The Grand Hyatt arrived in style. The two towers of the hotel were inspired by waves, in keeping with the aquatic City of Dreams theme. The elegant interior has both Portuguese and Chinese decorative elements, and the rooms are comfortable, rather than ostentatious, with simple soft white sheets, plush brown carpeting, and a sleekly designed bathroom. Express check-in and check-out make the trip smooth, and breakfast is complimentary. **Pros:** stunning pool area; large spa with extensive menu. **Cons:** nearby construction; surrounding neighborhood lacks character. ✉ *City of Dreams, Estrada do Istmo, Cotai* ☎ *853/8868–1234* ⊕ *macau.grand.hyatt.com* ⤢ *503 rooms, 288 suites* ♿ *In-room: safe, Internet, Wi-Fi. In-hotel: 2 restaurants, room service, bars, pools, gym, spa, laundry service, Internet terminal, Wi-Fi hotspot, parking (paid)* ▭ *AE, MC, V.*

$$$ 🏨 **Venetian Macao-Resort-Hotel.** You either love it or you hate it. The Venetian's strong presence in the Cotai area is both its draw and its bane. It's not everywhere you have singing gondoliers in manmade canals leading to clowns on stilts under an always-blue sky—but the other place you find it is Vegas, not Venice. Service is geared toward mainland

8

Chinese gamblers, confirming that the Venetian is first a casino, second a shopping mall, third a convention and entertainment venue, and only last a hotel. On the upside, the Venetian's Royale, Bella, and Rialto suites are spacious enough for family-sized comfort, and the extra TV with cable in every room, variety of swimming pools, and miniature 18-hole golf course make the difference with the kids. Come for the over-the-top environment, but be prepared to share it with a round-the-clock flow of tourists. **Pros:** living rooms; comprehensive shopping and dining. **Cons:** pretentious decor; gambling and convention crowds; lack of intimacy outside the suite. ⊠ *Estrada de Baía de Nossa Senhora da Esperança, Cotai* ☎ *853/2882–8888* ⊕ *www. venetianmacao.com* ⏎ *2,531 hotel suites, 374 casino VIP suites* ⚒ *In-room: safe, Internet, Wi-Fi. In-hotel: 19 restaurants, room service, bars, golf course, pools, gym, spa, laundry service, Wi-Fi hotspot, parking (paid), no-smoking rooms* ▭ *AE, MC, V.*

> ## MACAU GOLF AND COUNTRY CLUB
>
> Macau's most famous golf course is at the **Macau Golf and Country Club**, and the only way to play there, unless you become a member, is to book a package and stay at the Westin. The beautiful 18-hole, PGA Tour–level course has breathtaking sea views from atop a plateau. ⊠ *Westin Resort, 1918 Estrada de Hác-Sá, Coloane Island South* ☎ *853/2887–1188* ⊠ *Packages around MOP$5,000* ⏰ *Daily 7:30 AM–8 PM, call for tee times* ⊕ *www.macaugolfandcountryclub.com.*

COLOANE

$ 🏨 **Pousada de Coloane.** At Cheoc-Van Beach at the southernmost tip of Coloane Island, Pousada de Coloane offers a quiet, natural setting, nestled within the lush hills and mountains of Macau's south. There are ample opportunities for kayaking, hiking, and swimming. A long winding path paved with Portuguese azulejo tiles leads you to the spacious terrace overlooking the beach, and is ideal for outdoor wedding receptions and other celebrations. The open terrace garden and restaurant offers traditional Portuguese, Macanese, and Chinese favorites cooked in a heavy, home-style tradition, but there are also other seafood restaurants down on the beach. All 30 rooms have private hot tubs, cable TV, and balconies overlooking the beach, with the mountains of mainland China in the distance. **Pros:** intimate coastal location; sea-view balconies. **Cons:** limited facilities; no in-room Internet. ⊠ *Cheoc Van Beach, Coloane Island South* ☎ *853/2888–2143* ⊕ *www.hotelpcoloane.com.mo* ⏎ *30 rooms* ⚒ *In-room: safe (some), Internet. In-hotel: restaurant, room service, bar, pool, laundry service, Wi-Fi hotspot, parking (free)* ▭ *MC, V.*

$$ 🏨 **Westin Resort.** Built into the side of a cliff, the Westin is surrounded
⟳ by the black sands of Hác-Sá Beach and lapping waves of the South
FodorśChoice China Sea. This is where you truly get away from it all. Every room
★ faces the ocean; the place glows as much because of the sunny tropical color scheme as from the sunshine. The vast private terraces are ideal for alfresco dining and afternoon naps. Guests also receive access to Macau's renowned golf club, the PGA-standard, 18-hole Macau Golf and Country Club, which was built on the rocky cliffs and plateaus

Hác-Sá is one of Macau's two most accessible beaches and is usually crowded on weekends.

above the hotel. There are half day and full day programs for kids that include arts and crafts, games, sports, and treasure hunts. **Pros:** green surroundings; golf-club access; fun for kids. **Cons:** isolated location; limited access. ⊠ *1918 Estrada de Hác Sá, Coloane Island South* 🕭 *Box 1429* 🕾 *853/2887–1111, 800/228–3000 in Hong Kong* ⊕ *www. starwoodhotels.com/westin* 🖙 *208 rooms, 20 suites* 🛆 *In-room: safe, Internet. In-hotel: 3 restaurants, room service, bars, golf course, tennis courts, pools, gym, spa, beachfront, bicycles, children's programs (ages 3–12), laundry service, parking (free), no-smoking rooms* 🚭 *AE, DC, MC, V.*

AFTER DARK

Old movies, countless novels, and gossip through the years have portrayed Macau's nightlife as a combustible mix of drugs, wild gambling, violent crime, and ladies of the night. Up until the 1999 handover back to mainland China, this image of Macau was mostly accurate, and worked to drive away tourists.

Outside of the casinos and a few restaurants, today's Macau shuts down after 11 PM. You can slip into any dark, elegant lounge bar inside the larger hotels and enjoy live music and expensive cocktails, but don't expect much energy or big crowds. And most late-night saunas are glorified brothels, with "workers" from China, Vietnam, Thailand, and Russia. Because casino-hotel lounges often double as coffee shops in the morning or around midday, some "nightlife" hot spots may open as early as 7 AM.

DOWNTOWN MACAU
LOUNGES AND PUBS

Bar Cristal. An antique French chandelier from the 19th century is the centerpiece of the opulent interior, which is designed to look like a life-size jewelry box. Sip on cocktails or sample one of the many champagnes in stock. ✉ *G/F, Encore at Wynn Macau, Rua Cidade de Sintra, Downtown* ☎ *853/8986–3663* ⊙ *Sun.–Thurs 2 PM–1 PM, Fri.–Sat. 2 PM–2 AM.*

Whisky Bar. Depending on the time of day or night, the bar on the 16th floor of the StarWorld Hotel provides either upbeat cabaret entertainment or a cool moment of respite from the clinking casinos all around. Happy hour is daily from 5 to 10, and the Star Band starts playing nightly at 7:30. In addition to a full selection of the usual hard stuff, the bar has 75 different kinds of whisky, including the ultra-rare Macallan 1946. ✉ *StarWorld Hotel, Av. da Amizade, Downtown* ☎ *853/8290–8698* ⊙ *Closes 2 AM.*

MACAU OUTER HARBOUR
LOUNGES AND PUBS

Macau's Lan Kwai Fong. A modest collection of bars lines a small stretch of street in NAPE, within sight of the huge golden Guan Yin statue in Macau's Outer Harbour. Although it takes its name from the legendary bar area in Hong Kong, in reality, it's a bunch of nice, quiet bars where you can meet with friends or watch sports on a big-screen TV. A large number of expats come to this area to relax and drink in the evenings, but don't expect the wild times and thumping music you might find in the original LKF in Hong Kong. ✉ *Edifício Vista Magnífica Court, Av. Dr. Sun Yat-Sen, Outer Harbour.*

MP3. Chandeliers hang over red vinyl booths, and there is a giant TV tuned to sporting events. Happy hour runs from 6 to 9, during which time it's all you can drink for MOP$120. The stage set up for pole dancing is a highlight; it becomes the focus at 9 every night when go-go dancers from various parts of Europe, as well as Brazil and Vietnam, perform. ✉ *1333 Av. Dr. Sun Yat Sen, Outer Harbour* ☎ *853/2875–1306* ⊕ *www.mp3barlounge.com* ⊙ *Closes 4 AM.*

TAIPA
LOUNGES AND PUBS

38 Lounge. When you're finally done with the casinos and ready to look down on the rest of the world, hop over to Taipa and take the Altira elevator straight up the to this lofty spot just around the corner from the lobby. Sip cocktails under the stars on the outdoor terrace, where tapas are served from 6 PM to 1 AM. Indoors, a live band plays from 10 PM to 2 AM nightly. ✉ *38th fl., Altira Macau, Av. De Kwong Tung, Taipa* ☎ *853/8803–6868* ⊕ *www.crown-macau.com* ⊙ *24 hours.*

COTAI
LOUNGES AND PUBS

Blue Frog Bar & Grill. For a family-friendly nighttime option, head to this grill, which serves big breakfasts and buy-one-get-one burgers, and even has a children's menu. While live music is lacking from this Shanghai export, the atmosphere turns to live-broadcast sports and cocktails in the evening. Happy hour is Sunday to Friday 4–8 and two-for-one drinks begin at 8 PM every Wednesday, Ladies' Night. ⊠ *Shop 1037, Grand Canal Shoppes, Venetian Macao, Estrada de Baía de Nossa Senhora da Esperança, Cotai* ☎ *853/2882–8281* ⊕ *www.bluefrog.com. cn/macao* ◷ *Closes 2* AM.

Cafe Deco. The lively restaurant and bar is in the center of the Grand Canal Shoppes, and features live music on Thursday and Friday nights. Happy hour runs from 5:30 to 8:30, and the deal is buy one drink, get one free. Kick back with a cold drink, or partake in a game of pool. ⊠ *Shop 1036, Grand Canal Shoppes, Venetian Macao, Estrada de Baía de Nossa Senhora da Esperança, Cotai* ☎ *853/2882–3326* ⊕ *www. cafedecogroup.com* ◷ *Open 24 hours.*

City Bar. Mixologists are on hand to make champagne cocktails, martinis, and classic drinks, such as mai tais and mojitos, while live bands play in this City of Dreams hot spot. ⊠ *Level 1, City of Dreams, Estrada do Istmo, Cotai* ☎ *No phone* ◷ *24 hours.*

SHOWS

The House of Dancing Water. At this writing, Franco Dragone, former star director at Cirque du Soleil, plans to open a resident aquatic show at the City of Dreams underwater-themed casino-hotel on September 17, 2010. Check the Web site for updates. ⊠ *Estrada do Istmo, Cotai* ☎ *8868–6688* ⊕ *www.dragone.be.*

ZAIA. Cirque du Soleil pounced on the opportunity to create the first resident full-scale Vegas-style show at the Venetian in 2008. Staged in a meticulously engineered, cosmic-themed theater, the show follows the narrative of a girl traveling through space with the aid of over-the-top props—such as floating bicycles—and captivating human performances. Upper midrange seats offer the best view of the swooping dancers, dangling equilibrists, and quick-change clown routines. ⊠ *Venetian Macao, Estrada de Baía de Nossa Senhora da Esperança, Cotai* ☎ *853/2882– 8818, 6333–6660 in Hong Kong* ⊕ *www.cirquedusoleil.com/zaia.*

8

SHOPPING

Macau, like Hong Kong, is a free port for most items, which leads to lower prices for electronics, jewelry, and clothing than other international cities. But the experience is completely different, with a low-key atmosphere, small crowds, and compact areas. It is a hub for traditional Chinese arts, crafts, and even some antiques (but be aware that there are many high-quality reproductions in the mix, too). Macau's major shopping district is along its main street in the downtown area, Avenida Almeida Ribeiro, more commonly known by its Chinese name, **San Ma Lo**; there are also shops downtown on **Rua Dos Mercadores** and its side streets; in **Cinco de Outubro**; and on the **Rua do Campo**.

Most of Macau's shops operate year-round with a short break in late January for Chinese New Year and are open from 10 AM to 8 PM and later on weekends. While most shops accept all major credit cards, specialty discount shops usually ask for cash, and street vendors accept only cash. For most street vendors and some smaller stores, some friendly bargaining is expected; ask for the "best price," which ideally produces instant discounts of 10%–20%. The shopping mantra here is "bargain hard, bargain often."

DOWNTOWN MACAU

DEPARTMENT STORE **New Yaohan.** Originally a Japanese-owned department store, this failing shop was taken over by Stanley Ho several years ago and transformed into a popular shopping destination for locals. Relocated in 2008, it can still call itself "Macau's only department store," with a good mix of shops selling household goods, clothing, jewelry, and beauty products. It also has an extensive food court, a well-stocked supermarket, and a large bakery on the first floor. ⊠ *Av. Doutor Mario Soares, Downtown* ☎ *853/2872–5338* ⊕ *www.newyaohan.com.*

WINE **Pavilions.** In tandem with rich, hearty Portuguese cooking, Macanese have also adopted a love for wine, and little-known Portuguese wines in particular. The basement wine cellar at Pavilions has a wide and varied selection, especially from Portugal and France. Although Hong Kong customs allows only one bottle per passenger, it doesn't vigorously enforce this rule, especially if you're discreet. ⊠ *417–425 Av. da Praia Grande, Downtown* ☎ *853/2837–4026.*

ANTIQUES **Wing Tai.** This large, well-established antiques dealer in the heart of downtown gives visitors a convenient introduction to Macau's variety of antique styles. A general rule of thumb when purchasing antiques is to bargain hard and bargain soft, and then bargain again. ⊠ *1A Av. Almeida Ribeiro, Downtown.*

COTAI

MALL **The Grand Canal Shoppes.** The Venetian's vision of a gentrified megamall comes complete with cobblestone walkways, arched bridges, and working canals manned by singing gondoliers (rides are MOP$88). All the big-name brands and luxury shops in fashion, accessories, gifts, services, and sporting goods are among its 350 retailers; it also has a spa, 19 restaurants, and an international food court. Don't be surprised to see wandering stilt walkers, violinists, and juggling jesters, especially around St. Mark's Square, which hosts four daily live performances. The mall connects with the Shoppes at Four Seasons, adding even more exclusive luxury shops to the arcade, such as Autore, which carries jewelry set with its own cultivated South Sea pearls. ⊠ *Venetian Macao, Av. Xian Xing Hai, Cotai* ☎ *853/2882–8888.*

COLOANE

ANTIQUES **Asian Artifacts.** Specializing in detailed restorations of authentic antiques, the shop provides "before" and "after" pictures, a personal history, and a story from the friendly British owner for each piece. ⊠ *9 Rua dos Negociantes, Coloane Island West* ☎ *853/2888–1022.*

Travel Smart Hong Kong

WORD OF MOUTH

"Arrival into HK airport. HUGE lines at customs . . . but I had remembered that last time we discovered that there is another section that is to the right of where the crowds of people are heading. The section is just on the other side of the huge columns. And guess what? I was right (YAY for me!)"

—kooba

GETTING HERE AND AROUND

Public transportation options are many and varied—all are good, too. An Octopus stored-value card is by far the most convenient way to get around Hong Kong. It's used on all forms of public transport: simply "beep" it over the farebox or turnstile sensor to deduct your fare, which will automatically be cheaper than a single ticket. In fact, it doesn't even require physical contact to register the transaction, so you never need to remove it from a plastic holder or even a wallet. You can buy an Octopus card in any MTR or Airport Express Station. It costs HK$150, of which HK$50 is a refundable deposit, and the other HK$100 is for you to use. (If you return it in less than a month, you forfeit HK$7 of your deposit as a processing fee.) There are also special one-day or three-day passes available for tourists. You can refill the cards at any ticket counter, at speedy machines in stations, or at a 7-Eleven, OK convenience store, or Wellcome supermarket—where you can also use it to pay for purchases. It also works in most Starbucks, fast-food restaurants, and vending machines around Hong Kong.

Information Octopus Cards (☎ 2266–2222 ⊕ www.octopus.com.hk).

▌ BY AIR

Flying time to Hong Kong is around 16 hours direct from Newark/New York, 13½ hours direct from Los Angeles, or 13 hours direct from San Francisco.

Airlines and Airports Airline and Airport Links.com (⊕ www.airlineandairportlinks.com) has links to many of the world's airlines and airports.

Airline Security Issues Transportation Security Agency (⊕ www.tsa.gov/public) has answers for almost every question that might come up.

AIRPORTS

The sleek, sophisticated Hong Kong International Airport (HKG) is also commonly known as Chek Lap Kok, which is where it's located. At almost a mile long, the Y-shape passenger Terminal 1 is the world's second-largest terminal, while the new Terminal 2 is just as modern and well-equipped, but smaller. Terminal 2 handles departures for selected airlines; all flights arrive at Terminal 1.

Chek Lap Kok is one of the friendliest, cleanest, most efficient airports around. Walkways connect the check-in and arrival halls with nearby gates, while electric trains glide to gates at the end of the terminals. Restaurants, fast-food outlets, juice joints, and bars abound. Most eateries are open from 7 AM to 11 PM or midnight; local chain Café de Coral and Ajisen Ramen (Japanese noodles) in the east departures hall are the only outlets open 24 hours.

There's free Wi-Fi access throughout the terminals, but data transfer is often slow. A telecom and business center, Connect Zone, is in the Level 6 Departures Hall near Gate 24. It provides Wi-Fi and Internet access on computers, free local phone calls, select TV programs, and other business support services. If you're going to be overnighting at Chek Lap Kok, consider buying a package from the Plaza Premium Traveler's Lounges, which has four locations at the airport. The 15,000-square-foot flagship lounge is in Terminal 1 Level 6 Departures Hall before Gate 1. Most of the lounges have rest areas, showers, massages, Internet access, newspapers, and a 24-hour buffet—an overnight package costs HK$780. Note that the airport has no other public showers or spa or massage facilities.

Check in at least two hours before departure. Most major airlines let you use the In-Town check-in service at the Hong Kong or Kowloon Airport Express stations. You can check your bags up to 24 hours before your flight—a boon if you're flying at night and don't want to return to your hotel to get your bags. The service is available until 1½ hours before your flight time.

Airport tax is normally included in your ticket price. If it's not, hold on to HK$120 for the airport tax, payable on departure from the country. It's only levied on those 12 years and older and is waived for all transit and transfer passengers who arrive and leave on the same day. When you go through immigration, have your Hong Kong entry slip (given to you on arrival) ready to show officials along with your passport.

Airport Information Hong Kong International Airport (☎ 2181–8888 ⊕ *www. hongkongairport.com*). **Plaza Premium Lounge** (☎ 2261–0888 ⊕ *www.plaza-asia. com*).

GROUND TRANSPORTATION

The Airport Express train service is the quickest and most convenient way to and from the airport. Gleaming, high-speed trains whisk you to Kowloon in 19 minutes and Central in 24 minutes. Trains run every 12 minutes between 5:50 AM and 1:15 AM daily. There's plenty of luggage space, legroom, and comfortable seating with video screens on the backs of the passenger seats showing tourist information and the latest news. Although it's the most expensive public transport option, the speed and efficiency make it well worth the extra cost.

The Airport Express station is connected to the MTR's AsiaWord-Expo, Tsing Yi, Kowloon, and Hong Kong (Central) stations—however, the latter is via a long, underground walkway with no guarantee of a luggage cart. One-way or same-day return fare to or from Central is HK$100; from Kowloon, HK$90. Round-trip tickets valid for one month cost HK$180 for Central and HK$160 for Kowloon. The Airport Express also provides its customers with free shuttle buses every 12

or 20 minutes between major hotels and its Hong Kong and Kowloon stations—there are seven routes. To board, you must show your Airport Express ticket and airline ticket/boarding pass.

GROUND TRANSPORTATION TO CENTRAL		
Transport Mode	Time	Cost
Airport Express	24 mins	HK$100
Citybus Line A (Cityflyer)	50 mins	HK$40
Citybus Line E (Regular)	70 mins	HK$21
Coach	45 mins	HK$150
Limo	45 mins	HK$750
Taxi	45 mins	HK$280
Tung Chung (S1 bus) + MTR (train)	10 mins + 36 mins	HK$3.50 + HK$21

Citybus runs five buses ("A" precedes the bus number) from the airport to popular destinations. They have fewer stops than regular buses, which have an "E" before their number, so are more expensive. Two useful routes are the A11, serving Central, Admiralty, Wan Chai, and Causeway Bay; and the A21, going to Tsim Sha Tsui, Jordan, and Mong Kok. There's plenty of space and onboard announcements in English, so you won't miss your stop.

Several small shuttle buses with an "S" before their number run to the nearby Tung Chung MTR station, where you can get the MTR to Central and Kowloon. The trains follow the airport express route, but make more stops, so are a little slower but a quarter of the cost.

Taxis from the airport are reliable and plentiful, and cost around HK$280 for Hong Kong Island destinations and HK$230 for Kowloon destinations, plus HK$5 per piece of luggage stored in the trunk. Trans-Island runs leather-seated coaches to 104 hotels every 30–60 minutes for HK$150 on Hong Kong Island,

HK$130 in Kowloon. Parklane offers Mercedes Benz limousine transfers for HK$550–HK$850, depending on the destination and type of car.

GROUND TRANSPORTATION TO TSIM SHA TSUI		
Transport Mode	Time	Cost
Airport Express	19 mins	HK$90
Citybus Line A (Cityflyer)	45 mins	HK$33
Citybus Line E (Regular)	60 mins	HK$14
Coach	35 mins	HK$130
Limo	35 mins	HK$700
Taxi	35 mins	HK$230
Tung Chung (S1 bus) + MTR (train)	10 mins + 38 mins	HK$3.50 + HK$15.50

Contacts Airport Express (☏ 2881–8888 for MTR hotline ⊕ www.mtr.com.hk). **City-bus** (☏ 2873–0818 ⊕ www.nwstbus.com.hk). **Parklane Limousine** (☏ 2261–0303 ⊕ www. hongkonglimo.com). **Trans-Island Limousine Service** (☏ 3193–9333 ⊕ www.trans-island. com.hk).

FLIGHTS
Cathay Pacific is Hong Kong's flagship carrier. It maintains high standards, with friendly service, good food, an extensive in-flight entertainment system, and an excellent track record for safety—while also offering the most competitive prices for direct flights. Cathay has nonstop flights from both Los Angeles and San Francisco on the west coast and from New York–JFK on the east coast, with connecting services to many other U.S. cities. The Taiwanese carrier China Airlines provides reasonably priced flights with a stopover in Taipei. Several other airlines offer service from the United States to Hong Kong, sometimes with connections in Asia.

If you're planning to travel to three or four Asian destinations, One World's Visit Asia Pass is an excellent deal. Cities are grouped into zones, and there's a flat rate for each zone. It doesn't include flights from the United States, however. Inquire through American Airlines, Cathay Pacific, or any other One World member.

Airline Contacts Cathay Pacific Airways (☏ 800/233–2742 in U.S., 800/268–6868 in Canada, 2747–1888 in Hong Kong ⊕ www. cathay-usa.com). **China Airlines** (☏ 800/227–5118 in California, 800/368–2003 in New York, 2868–2299 in Hong Kong ⊕ www.china-airlines.com). **Visit Asia Pass** (One World ⊕ www.oneworld.com).

▌ BY BOAT AND FERRY
With fabulous views of both sides of Victoria Harbour, the Star Ferry is so much more than just a boat. It's an iconic Hong Kong landmark in its own right, and has been running across the harbor since 1888. Double-bowed, green-and-white vessels connect Central and Wan Chai with Kowloon in less than 10 minutes, daily from 6:30 AM to 11:30 PM; the ride costs HK$2.50 on the upper deck on weekdays, making it the cheapest scenic harbor tour in town.

New World First Ferry (NWFF) Services Ltd. runs nine routes from Central to the outlying islands of Lantau and Cheung Chau. There are ordinary ferries and there are fast ferries, which travel at twice the speed for twice the price. Pick up printed schedules at the Hong Kong Tourist Board (HKTB) info center at the Tsim Sha Tsui Star Ferry Concourse, call the HKTB Visitor Hotline, or simply ask for a schedule at the ferry ticket counters.

(For information about ferry service to Macau, see Chapter 8, Macau.)

FERRY TRAVEL			
Line/ Route	Frequency	Travel Time	Fare
DBTPL Central–Discovery Bay (Lantau)	20–30 mins	25 mins	HK$31
NWFF Central–Cheung Chau	30 mins	35–60 mins	HK$11.30–HK$32.20
NWFF Central–Mui Wo (Lantau)	40 mins	35–55 mins	HK$13.0–HK$36.70
Star Ferry Central–Tsim Sha Tsui	6–12 mins	7 mins	HK$2.00–HK$3.00
Star Ferry Central–Wan Chai	10–14 mins	8 mins	HK$2.50–HK$3.00

Information Discovery Bay Transportation Services Limited (☎ *2238–1188* ⊕ *www. discoverybay.com.hk*). **HKTB Visitor Hotline** (☎ *2508–1234*). **New World First Ferry** (☎ *2131–8181* ⊕ *www.nwff.com.hk*). **Star Ferry** (☎ *2367–7065* ⊕ *www.starferry.com.hk*).

▌ BY BUS

An efficient network of double-decker buses covers most of Hong Kong. Figuring them out, however, is a tricky business. Drivers don't usually speak English, and routes listed at bus stops are complicated. There are also several companies, and no central Web site or pocket bus map with every company's service exist (although at least now companies share Web sites).

In general, bus numbers starting with the letter "M" connect to an MTR station; "A" buses go to the airport; "N" lines run the night service; and buses ending with the letter "X" are express.

Rattling along Hong Kong's roads at breakneck speed are numerous minibuses, which seat 16 people. They're cream-color, with green or red roofs, and prominently display the route number and the price. They usually stop at designated spots, but often need to be flagged down; if you want to get off, you'll need to shout out to the driver and hold on tight as he screeches to a halt. Slightly more expensive than buses, minibuses are faster because of their small size, but also have a reputation for dangerous speeding.

Citybus runs Hong Kong Island, cross-harbor, and airport routes. Kowloon Motor Bus mainly serves Kowloon and the New Territories, while Long Win Bus Company serves north Lantau, including Tung Chung. New World First Bus has services on Hong Kong Island and in New Kowloon (the southern section of the New Territories).

FARES

Double-decker bus fares range from HK$2.50 to HK$48; minibus fares from HK$2 to HK$20. Only some minibus drivers give change when you pay in cash, but it's best pay with exact change on all buses, or better yet, use an Octopus card.

Bus Information Citybus (☎ *2873–0818* ⊕ *www.nwfb.com.hk*). **Kowloon Motor Bus** (☎ *2745–4466* ⊕ *www.kmb.com.hk*). **Long Win Bus Company** (☎ *2261–2791* ⊕ *www.kmb. com.hk*). **New World First Bus** (☎ *2136–8888* ⊕ *www.nwfb.com.hk*).

▌ BY CAR

Frankly, you'd be mad to rent a car on Hong Kong Island or Kowloon. Maniac drivers, traffic jams, and next to no parking make driving here severely stress-inducing, and gasoline costs up to twice what it does in the United States. So why bother, when public transportation is excellent and taxis inexpensive? If you must have your own wheels, consider hiring a driver. Most top-end hotels can arrange this; the Peninsula in Kowloon and the Island Shangri-La even have their own fleets of Rolls-Royces and Mercedes available for hourly rental by guests.

If you're determined to drive yourself, your driver's license is valid in Hong Kong if you're 18 to 70 years old (those over 70 must pass a physical examination before driving). You'll need an International Driver's Permit for long stays. Check the AAA Web site for more info as well as for IDPs ($10) themselves. Rental rates begin at HK$450 per day and HK$2,250 per week for an economy car with air-conditioning, automatic transmission, and unlimited mileage.

Hawk Rent-a-Car has lots of models and prices; there are special rates for weekends and longer-term rentals. Parklane Limousine rents Mercedes with drivers.

Information Hawk Rent-a-Car (☎ 2516–9822 ⊕ www.hawkrentacar.com.hk). **Parklane Limousine** (☎ 2730–0662 ⊕ www. hongkonglimo.com).

PARKING

There's next to no on-street parking in Central and Tsim Sha Tsui. Most people use multistory or mall parking garages, which cost up to HK$22 per hour in prime locations. The Hong Kong traffic police are extremely vigilant, and hand out copious parking tickets.

RULES OF THE ROAD

Cars drive on the left-hand side of the road in Hong Kong. Wearing a seat belt is mandatory in the front and back of private cars, and the standard speed limit is 50 kph (30 mph) unless road signs say otherwise. The Hong Kong Police spend a lot of time setting up photographic speed traps and giving out juicy fines. Likewise, using handheld cell phones while driving is forbidden. You can't make a right turn on a red light, and you should scrupulously obey lane markings regarding turns. Drunk driving is taken very seriously: the legal limit is 50 mg of alcohol per 100 ml of blood (or 22 micrograms of

alcohol per 100ml of breath), and there are penalties of up to HK$25,000 and three years in prison for those who disobey. You can get highly detailed information on Hong Kong's road rules on the Transport Department's Web site.

Road Rules Hong Kong Government Transport Department Road Safety Code (☎ 2804–2600 hotline ⊕ www.td.gov.hk).

■ BY CRUISE

Star Cruises has trips through Southeast Asia that start from, or call at, Hong Kong. The crème de la crème of cruisers, Cunard, docks in Hong Kong on its round-the-world trips. Princess Cruises has a wide variety of packages that call at Hong Kong and many other Asian destinations. Holland America has two-week Asian cruises as well as round-the-world options.

Cruise Lines Cunard (☎ 800/728–6273 ⊕ www.cunard.com). **Holland America** (☎ 877/932–4259 ⊕ www.hollandamerica. com). **Princess Cruises** (☎ 800/774–6237 ⊕ www.princess.com). **Star Cruises** (☎ 2317–7711 Hong Kong ⊕ www.starcruises.com).

■ BY SUBWAY

By far the best way to get around Hong Kong is on the Mass Transit Railway (MTR). Since merging with the former Kowloon-Canton Railway (KCR) in late 2007, the MTR network now provides all subway and train services in Hong Kong.

There are five main subway lines. The Island line runs along the north coast of Hong Kong Island; the Tsuen Wan line goes from Central under the harbor to Tsim Sha Tsui, then up to the western New Territories. Mong Kok links Tsim Sha Tsui to eastern New Kowloon via the Kwun Tong line; also serving this area is the Tseung Kwan O line, which crosses back over the harbor to Quarry Bay and North Point. Finally, the Tung Chung line connects Central and West Kowloon to Tung Chung on Lantau, near the airport.

The MTR's highly modern, efficient trains are clean and very safe, as are the stations. Entrances, platforms, and exits are clearly marked and signposted, and all MTR areas are air-conditioned. Most stations have wheelchair access, and all have convenience stores and other shops or services. Trains run every 2 to 8 minutes between 6 AM and 1 AM daily.

FARES AND SCHEDULES
You can buy tickets from ticket machines (using coins or notes) or from English-speaking staff behind glass-windowed customer service counters near the turnstile entrances. Fares are not zoned, but depend on which stations you're traveling between. There are no monthly or weekly passes, but if you plan to make more than a few trips on public transport during your stay, it's worth getting a rechargeable Octopus card. It saves time lining up for tickets and generally fussing for change, gives you a discounted fare on each trip, and can also be used for small purchases around Hong Kong.

Fares range from HK$3.70 to HK$42.50, depending how far you travel and whether you use Octopus or not. The special Tourist MTR One-Day Pass (HK$50) allows you unlimited rides in a day. The three-day Airport Express Tourist Octopus passes (HK$220–HK$300) include one or two Airport Express rides and unlimited MTR travel for three days.

Information HKTB Visitor Hotline (☎ 2508–1234). **MTR** (☎ 2881–8888 ⊕ www.mtr.com.hk). **Octopus Cards** (☎ 2266–2222 ⊕ www.octopuscards.com).

▌ BY TAXI

While there are some 18,000 taxis in Hong Kong, heavy daytime traffic in Central and Tsim Sha Tsui means they aren't the best option. Outside these areas, or after dark, they're much more useful. Drivers usually know the terrain well, but as many don't speak English, having your destination written in Chinese is a good idea. You can hail cabs on the street,

provided it's a stopping area (i.e., not on double yellow lines). The white TAXI sign is lit when the cab is available. Note that it's sometimes hard to find a taxi around 4 PM, when the drivers switch shifts.

Fares for the red taxis operating in urban areas start at HK$18 for the first 2 km (1½ mi), then HK$1.50 for each .2 km (.1 mi) or minute of waiting time (so fares add up fast in bumper-to-bumper traffic). There's a surcharge of HK$5 for each piece of luggage you put in the trunk. The Cross-Harbour Tunnel, Eastern Harbour Crossing, and Western Harbour Crossing all incur surcharges of the toll plus HK$10 or HK$15 return toll. The surcharge for crossing the Tsing Ma Bridge over to Lantau is HK$30. Passengers must pay the toll amount for other tunnels and roads.

In the New Territories taxis are green; on Lantau they're blue. Fares are slightly lower than in urban areas, but while urban taxis may travel into rural zones, rural taxis can't cross into urban zones.

Passengers are required by law to wear a seat belt when available. Most locals don't tip; however, if you round up the fare by a few Hong Kong dollars you're sure to earn yourself a winning smile from your underpaid and overworked driver. Taxis are usually reliable, but if you have a problem, note the taxi's license number, which is usually on the dashboard, and call the Transport Complaints Unit.

In urban areas it's as easy and safe to hail a cab on the street as to call one. There are hundreds of taxi companies, so it's usually best to get your hotel or restaurant to call a company it works with. If you need to call one yourself, try Hong Kong Kowloon Taxi. Note that there's a HK$5 surcharge for phone bookings.

Complaints Transport Complaints Unit (☎ 2889–9999). **Hong Kong Kowloon Taxi & Lorry Owners Association Ltd.** (☎ 2574–7311).

▋ BY TRAIN

Since the former Kowloon–Canton Railway (KCR) merged with the MTR subway system in 2007, all trains now run under the MTR name. The ultra-efficient train network connects Kowloon to the eastern and western New Territories. Trains run every 5–8 minutes, and connections to the subway are relatively quick. It's a commuter service and, like the subway, has sparkling clean trains and stations—smoking and eating are forbidden in both.

The train network has three main lines. The East Rail line begins at Hung Hom, with notable stops at Mong Kok, Kowloon Tong, Sha Tin, Racecourse, Chinese University, and Tai Po on its way to Lo Wu at the Chinese border. East Rail is the fastest way to get to Shenzhen—it's a 40-minute trip from Hung Hom to Lo Wu. The Hung Hom train station terminus connects via a series of walkways with East Tsim Sha Tsui; you can also transfer to the subway at Kowloon Tong.

The short Ma On Shan Rail service starts at Tai Wai and has eight stops in the northeastern New Territories.

West Rail starts at East Tsim Sha Tsui, moves on to Tsim Sha Tsui for a possible connection to the subway, then extends westward through 10 more stops to Tuen Mun, in the New Territories. Here West Rail connects with the local Light Rail Transit, an above-ground train serving mainly residential and industrial areas in the western New Territories.

Fares range from HK$3.10 to HK$42.50; you can pay by Octopus card or buy tickets from sales counters or ticket machines.

Train Information MTR (☎ 2881–8888 ⊕ www.mtr.com.hk).

▋ BY TRAM

PEAK TRAM

It's Hong Kong's greatest misnomer—the Peak Tram is actually a funicular railway. Since 1888 it's been rattling the 1,365 feet up the hill from Midlevels to the Victoria Peak tram terminus. As well as a sizeable adrenaline rush due to the steepness of the ascent, on a clear day it offers fabulous panoramas. Most passengers board at the Lower Terminus between Garden Road and Cotton Tree Drive. (The tram has five stations.) The fare is HK$25 one way, HK$36 round-trip, and it runs every 10–15 minutes between 7 AM and midnight daily. Bus 15C shuttles passengers between the Lower Terminus and the Star Ferry.

STREET TRAMS

Old-fashioned double-decker trams have been running along the northern shore of Hong Kong Island since 1904. Most routes start in Kennedy Town or Western Market, and go eastward all the way through Central, Wan Chai, Causeway Bay, North Point, and Quarry Bay to Shau Kei Wan. A branch line turns off in Wan Chai toward Happy Valley, where horse races are held in season.

Destinations are marked on the front of each tram; you board at the back and get off at the front, paying HK$2 regardless of distance (by Octopus or with exact change) as you leave. Avoid trams at rush hours, which are generally weekdays from 7:30 to 9:30 AM and 5 to 7:30 PM. Although trams move slowly, for short hops between Central and Western or Admiralty they can be quicker than going underground to take the MTR. A leisurely top-deck ride from Western to Causeway Bay is a great city tour.

Tram Information Hong Kong Tramways (☎ 2548–7102 ⊕ www.hktramways.com). **Peak Tram** (☎ 2849–6754 ⊕ www.thepeak.com.hk).

ESSENTIALS

▮ BUSINESS AND TRADE SERVICES

BUSINESS CENTERS

Hong Kong has many business centers outside hotels, and some are considerably cheaper than hotel facilities. Others cost about the same but offer private desks (from HK$250 per hour for desk space to upward of HK$8,000 a month for a serviced office). Amenities include a private address and phone-answering and forwarding services. Many centers are affiliated with accountants and lawyers who can expedite company registration. Some will even process visas and wrap gifts for you.

Harbour International Business Centre provides typing, secretarial support, and office rentals. Reservations aren't required. The Executive Centre and Regus are two international business services companies with several office locations in Hong Kong. They provide secretarial services, meeting and conference facilities, and office rentals.

The American Chamber of Commerce can arrange a Breakfast Briefing Program at your hotel for a fee based on group size. The chamber hosts luncheons and seminars, its Young Professionals Committee holds cocktail parties about once a month, and it also provides China trade services.

Information American Chamber of Commerce (✉ *Bank of America Tower, 12 Harcourt Rd., Room 1904, Central* ☎ *2530–6900* ⊕ *www. amcham.org.hk*). **The Executive Centre** (☎ *2293–2600* ⊕ *www.executivecentre.com*). **Harbour International Business Centre** (☎ *2529–0356* ⊕ *www.hibc.com*). **Regus** (☎ *2166–8000* ⊕ *www.regus.hk*).

CONVENTION CENTER

The Hong Kong Convention & Exhibition Centre (HKCEC) is a state-of-the-art, five-level complex located on the Wan Chai waterfront. The HKCEC houses six exhibition halls, two convention halls, two theaters, and 52 meeting rooms, totaling 985,000 square feet of rentable space. The center is adjacent to the Convention Plaza, which includes the 829-room Renaissance Harbour View Hotel, the 553-room Grand Hyatt, a 39-story office tower, an apartment tower, a shopping arcade, and an underground parking garage.

Information Hong Kong Convention & Exhibition Centre (✉ *1 Expo Dr., Wan Chai* ☎ *2582–8888* ⊕ *www.hkcec.com.hk*).

MESSENGERS

Most business centers offer delivery service, and you can sometimes arrange a delivery through your hotel concierge. Courier services such as City-Link International will pick up from your hotel, as will FedEx and DHL, who also have drop-off points all over Hong Kong. Price is based on weight and distance.

Information City-Link International Courier Co. Ltd (☎ *2382–8289* ⊕ *www.citylinkexpress. com*). **DHL** (☎ *2400–3388* ⊕ *www.dhl.com.hk*). **Federal Express** (☎ *2730–3333* ⊕ *www.fedex. com/hk_english*).

TRADE INFORMATION

Information Hong Kong General Chamber of Commerce (☎ *2529–9229* ⊕ *www. chamber.org.hk*). **Hong Kong Trade Development Council** (☎ *1830–668* ⊕ *www. hktdc.com*). **Hong Kong Trade & Industry Department** (☎ *2392–2922* ⊕ *www.tid.gov. hk*). **Innovation & Technology Commission** (☎ *2737–2208* ⊕ *www.itc.gov.hk*).

TRANSLATION SERVICES

Information Polyglot Translations (☎ *2851–7232* ⊕ *www.polyglot.com.hk*). **Translation Business** (☎ *2893–5000* ⊕ *www. translationbusiness.com.hk*). **Venture Language Training** (☎ *2507–4985* ⊕ *www. languageventure.com*).

∎ COMMUNICATIONS

INTERNET

Hong Kong is an Internet-friendly place for those bearing laptops. Almost all hotels have in-room Internet access; Wi-Fi is common both in hotels and in public places, including many cafés, bars, and restaurants. All business centers have high-speed access.

Laptops and smartphones are so ubiquitous in Hong Kong that things can get tough if you haven't got one. Internet cafés are practically nonexistent; the only places to log on to a wired terminal for free are at a public library or one of the many branches of Pacific Coffee or Mix cafés. Just remember to buy a coffee or juice first (HK$20–HK$30).

Contacts Hong Kong Public Librar-ies (⊕ hkpl.gov.hk). **Mix** (⊕ www.mix-world. com). **Pacific Coffee Company** (⊕ www. pacificcoffee.com).

PHONES

The good news is that you can now make a direct-dial telephone call from virtually any point on earth. The bad news? You can't always do so cheaply. Calling overseas from a hotel is almost always the most expensive option; hotels usually add huge surcharges to all calls, particularly international ones. In some countries you can phone from call centers or even the post office. Calling cards usually keep costs to a minimum, but only if you purchase them locally. And then there are mobile phones (⇨ below), which are sometimes more prevalent—particularly in the developing world—than landlines; as expensive as mobile-phone calls can be, they are still usually a much cheaper option than calling from your hotel.

Hong Kong was the first city in the world with a fully digitized local phone network, and the service is efficient and cheap. Even international calls are inexpensive relative to those in the United States. You can expect clear connections and helpful directory assistance. Don't hang up if you

hear Cantonese when calling automated and prerecorded hotlines; English is usually the second or third language option. The country code for Hong Kong is 852; there are no local area codes.

CALLING WITHIN HONG KONG

Hong Kong phone numbers have eight digits: landline numbers usually start with a 2 or 3; mobiles with a 9, 6, or 5.

If you're old enough to talk in Hong Kong, you're old enough for a cell phone, which means public phones can be difficult to find. MTR stations usually have one: local calls to both land- and cell lines cost HK$1 per five minutes. If you're planning to call abroad from a pay phone, buy a phone card. Convenience stores such as 7-Eleven sell stored-value phone cards (a PIN-activated card you can use from any phone). Some pay phones accept credit cards.

Restaurants and shopkeepers may let you use their phone for free, as the phone company doesn't charge for individual local calls. Some hotels may charge as much as HK$5 for a local call, while a few others include them for free in your room rate.

Dial 1081 for directory assistance from English-speaking operators. If a number is constantly busy and you think it might be out of order, call 109 and the operator will check the line. The operators are very helpful, if you speak slowly and clearly.

CALLING OUTSIDE HONG KONG

International rates from Hong Kong are reasonable, even more so between 9 PM and 8 AM. The international dial code is 001, then the country code.

The country code is 1 for the United States.

So to call the United States you dial 0011. You can dial direct from many hotel and business centers, but always with a hefty surcharge. Dial 10013 for international inquiries and for assistance with direct dialing. Dial 10010 for collect and operator-assisted calls to most countries, including the United States. Dial 10011 for credit-card, collect, and international conference calls.

Access Codes AT&T Direct (☏ *800/96–1111*). **MCI** (☏ *800/96–1121*).

MOBILE PHONES

If you have a multiband phone (some countries use different frequencies than what's used in the United States) and your service provider uses the world-standard GSM network (as do T-Mobile, Cingular, and Verizon), you can probably use your phone abroad. Roaming fees can be steep, however: 99¢ a minute is considered reasonable. And overseas you normally pay the toll charges for incoming calls. It's almost always cheaper to send a text message than to make a call, since text messages have a very low set fee (often less than 5¢).

If you just want to make local calls, consider buying a new prepaid rechargeable SIM card (note that your provider may have to unlock your phone for you to use a different SIM card). You'll then have a local number and can make local calls at local rates. ■TIP➔ If you travel internationally frequently, save one of your old mobile phones or buy a cheap one; ask your cell phone company to unlock it for you, and take it with you as a travel phone, buying a new SIM card with pay-as-you-go service in each destination.

Most GSM-compatible mobile handsets work in Hong Kong. If you can unlock your phone, buying a SIM card locally is the cheapest and easiest way to make calls. Local phone company PCCW sells them from around HK$50 from their shops all over town. Local calls cost around HK$0.25 a minute.

Otherwise, you can rent handsets from CSL (HK$150 per week plus HK$230 registration) with prepaid SIM cards (HK$48–HK$1,000). There's a stand at the airport and shops all over town. If you're in town for a week, this is a good-value option.

Cellular Abroad rents and sells GMS phones and sells SIM cards that work in many countries. **Mobal** rents mobiles and sells GSM phones (starting at $49) that will operate in 190 countries. Per-call rates vary throughout the world. **Planet Fone** rents cell phones, but the per-minute rates are expensive.

Contacts Cellular Abroad (☏ *800/287–5072* ⊕ *www.cellularabroad.com*). **Planet Fone** (☏ *888/988–4777* ⊕ *www.planetfone.com*).

■ CUSTOMS AND DUTIES

You're always allowed to bring goods of a certain value back home without having to pay any duty or import tax. But there's a limit on the amount of tobacco and liquor you can bring back duty-free, and some countries have separate limits for perfumes; for exact figures, check with your customs department. The values of so-called "duty-free" goods are included in these amounts. When you shop abroad, save all your receipts, as customs inspectors may ask to see them along with the items you purchased. If the total value of your goods is more than the duty-free limit, you'll have to pay a tax (most often a flat percentage) on the value of everything beyond that limit.

Except for the usual prohibitions against endangered species, narcotics, explosives, firearms, and ammunition, and modest limits on alcohol, tobacco products, and perfume, you can bring anything you want into Hong Kong, including an unlimited amount of money. Nonresidents may bring in, duty-free, 19 cigarettes or 1 cigar or 25 grams of tobacco, and 1 liter of alcohol.

Information in Hong Kong Hong Kong Customs & Excise Department (☏ *2815–7711 or 2545–6182 customs hotline* ⊕ *www.customs. gov.hk*).

U.S. Information U.S. Customs and Border Protection (⊕ *www.cbp.gov*).

LOCAL DOS AND TABOOS

CUSTOMS OF THE COUNTRY

Face is ever important. Never say anything that will make people look bad, especially in front of superiors. Having said that, Hong Kongers call it as they see it—sometimes with an honesty that westerners find brutal. You may be told how fat you're looking or that your mobile phone is a very old model. Take it in stride; it's not meant aggressively. Hong Kongers like to talk about money—salaries, stocks, insurance, and real estate—so don't be surprised to be asked about these things.

GREETINGS

Hong Kongers aren't touchy-feely. Be discreet. Stick to handshakes and low-key greetings.

SIGHTSEEING

By and large Hong Kongers are a rule-abiding bunch. Avoid jaywalking, eating on public transport, and feeding birds. Legislation has banned smoking in restaurants, most bars, workplaces, schools, and even public areas such as beaches, sport grounds, and parks. A whopping fine of HK$1,500 should deter even the most hardened smoker.

Hong Kong is *crowded*; pushing and nudging are common, especially on public transport.

OUT ON THE TOWN

Meals are a communal event, so food in a Chinese restaurant is always shared. You usually have a small bowl or plate in which to transfer food from the center platters. Although cutlery is common in Hong Kong, chopsticks are ubiquitous. Be sure not to mistake the communal serving chopsticks (usually black or a different color) with your own.

It's fine to hold the bowl close to your mouth and shovel in the contents. Noisily slurping up soup and noodles is acceptable, as is picking your teeth with a toothpick while covering it with your other hand when you're done. Leaving crumbs, drips, and even spat-out bones on the tablecloth is a sign you've enjoyed your meal. Avoid leaving your chopsticks standing up in a bowl of rice—they look like the two incense sticks burned at funerals.

Young Hong Kongers dress quite smartly when going out on the town. Things get pretty glam at bars and clubs, too.

DOING BUSINESS

Make appointments well in advance and be punctual. Hong Kongers have a keen sense of hierarchy in the office: egalitarianism is often insulting. Let the tea lady get the tea and coffee—that's what she's there for. If you're visiting in a group, let the senior member lead proceedings.

Suits are the norm, regardless of the outside temperature. Local businesswomen are immaculately groomed. Pants are acceptable.

When entertaining, locals may insist on paying: after a slight protest, accept, as this lets them gain face.

Business cards are a big deal: not having one is like not having a personality. If possible, have yours printed in English on one side and Chinese on the other. Proffer your card with both hands, and receive one in the same way, handling it with respect.

■ ELECTRICITY

The current in Hong Kong is 220 volts, 50 cycles alternating current (AC), so most American appliances can't be used without a transformer. Most plugs have three square prongs, like British plugs, but you can buy adapters in just about every supermarket and at electronics stalls in street markets.

Consider making a small investment in a universal adapter, which has several types of plugs in one lightweight, compact unit. Most laptops and mobile phone chargers are dual voltage (i.e., they operate equally well on 110 and 220 volts), and thus require only an adapter. These days the same is true of small appliances such as hair dryers. Always check labels and manufacturer instructions to be sure. Don't use 110-volt outlets marked FOR SHAVERS ONLY for high-wattage appliances such as hair dryers.

Steve Kropla's Help for World Travelers has information on electrical and telephone plugs around the world. **Walkabout Travel Gear** has a good coverage of electricity under "adapters."

Contacts Steve Kropla's Help for World Travelers (⊕ www.kropla.com). Walkabout Travel Gear (⊕ www.walkabouttravelgear.com)

■ EMERGENCIES

Locals and police are usually very helpful in emergencies. Most officers speak some English or will contact someone who does. For police, fire, and ambulance, dial 999. There are 24-hour accident and emergency services at the Caritas, Prince of Wales, and Queen Mary hospitals. Queen Mary Hospital also has a 24-hour pharmacy. Local drugstore/pharmacy chains Watsons and Mannings have shops throughout the city; closing times generally vary between 7:30 PM and 10:30 PM. Most of the 12 private hospitals in Hong Kong have only primary and secondary medical services. The 41 government-run public hospitals cover all three types.

Most treatments in public hospitals are heavily subsidized or free (⊕ www.ha.org. hk).

Consulate U.S. Consulate General (✉ 26 Garden Rd., Central ☎ 2523–9011 ⊕ hongkong. usconsulate.gov).

General Emergency Contacts Police, fire, & ambulance (☎ 999). **Hong Kong Police Hotline** (☎ 2527–7177).

Hospitals and Clinics Caritas Medical Centre (public) (✉ 111 Wing Hong St., Sham Shui Po, Kowloon ☎ 3408–7911 ⊕ www. ha.org.hk). **Hong Kong Adventist Hospital** (private) (✉ 40 Stubbs Rd., Happy Valley, Causeway Bay ☎ 3561–8888 ⊕ www.hkah. org.hk). **Hong Kong Baptist Hospital** (private) (✉ 222 Waterloo Rd., Kowloon ☎ 2339–8888 ⊕ www.hkbh.org.hk). **Hong Kong Central Hospital** (private) (✉ 1 Lower Albert Rd., Central ☎ 2522–3141 ⊕ www.hkch.org). **Matilda International Hospital** (private) (✉ 41 Mount Kellet Rd., The Peak, Central ☎ 2849–0111 ⊕ www.matilda.org). **Prince of Wales Hospital** (public) (✉ 30–32 Ngan Shing St., Sha Tin, New Territories ☎ 2632–2211 ⊕ www.ha.org. hk/pwh). **Queen Elizabeth Hospital** (public) (✉ 30 Gascoigne Rd., Yau Ma Tei, Kowloon ☎ 2958–8888 ⊕ www.ha.org.hk/qeh). **Queen Mary Hospital** (public) (✉ 102 Pok Fu Lam Rd., Pok Fu Lam, Western ☎ 2255–3838 ⊕ www. ha.org.hk/qmh).

Pharmacies Mannings (☎ 2299–3381 ⊕ www.mannings.com.hk/eng). **Watsons** (☎ 2868–4388 ⊕ watsons.com.hk).

GOVERNMENT ADVISORIES

As different countries have different worldviews, look at travel advisories from a range of governments to get more of a sense of what's going on out there. And be sure to parse the language carefully. For example, a warning to "avoid all travel" carries more weight than one urging you to "avoid nonessential travel," and both are much stronger than a plea to "exercise caution." A U.S. government travel warning is more permanent (though not necessarily more serious) than a so-called public announcement, which carries an expiration date.

The U.S. Department of State's Web site has more than just travel warnings and advisories. The consular information sheets issued for every country have general safety tips, entry requirements (though be sure to verify these with the country's embassy), and other useful details.

■TIP➔ Consider registering online with the State Department (https://travelregistration.state.gov), so the government will know to look for you should a crisis occur in the country you're visiting.

Hong Kong is a highly safe place as far as crime goes. Besides a few random acid attacks in Mong Kok and Causeway Bay, the only large-scale safety threats were health-related: the SARS outbreak in 2003, intermittent fears over Influenza A virus subtype H5N1 (avian flu), and H1N1 (swine flu) in 2009. A massive awareness program stopped the spread of the illnesses, but it's worth checking to be sure there have been no new outbreaks.

General Information and Warnings U.S. Department of State (⊕ www.travel.state. gov).

▌ HEALTH

It's a good idea to be immunized against typhoid and hepatitis A and B before coming to Hong Kong. In winter, a flu vaccination is also smart, especially if you're infection-prone or are a senior citizen.

Water from government mains satisfies World Health Organization (WHO) standards, but most locals don't drink water straight from the tap. Expect to pay HK$10 to HK$20 for a 1½-liter bottle of distilled or mineral water, or drink boiled tap water.

Condoms can help prevent most sexually transmitted diseases, but they aren't absolutely reliable, and their quality varies from country to country. Speak with your physician and/or check the CDC or

World Health Organization Web sites for health alerts, particularly if you're pregnant, traveling with children, or have a chronic illness.

Health Warnings National Centers for Disease Control & Prevention (CDC ☎ 800/232-4636 24-hr hotline ⊕ www.cdc.gov/travel). World Health Organization (⊕ www.who.int).

HONG KONG–SPECIFIC ISSUES
Severe Acute Respiratory Syndrome (SARS), also known as atypical pneumonia, is a respiratory illness caused by a strain of coronavirus that was first reported in parts of Asia in early 2003. Symptoms include a fever greater than 100.4°F (38°C), shortness of breath, and other flu-like symptoms. The disease is thought to spread by close person-to-person contact, particularly respiratory droplets and secretions transmitted through the eyes, nose, or mouth. To prevent SARS, the Hong Kong Health Department recommends maintaining good personal hygiene, washing hands frequently, and wearing a face mask in crowded public places. SARS hasn't returned to Hong Kong, but many experts believe that it or other contagious, upper-respiratory viruses will continue to be a seasonal health concern. It is also worth noting that the World Health Organization declared Hong Kong SARS-free in 2003.

Avian influenza, commonly known as bird flu, is a form of influenza that affects birds (including poultry) but can be passed to humans. It causes initial flu symptoms, followed by respiratory and organ failure. Although rare, it's often lethal. The Hong Kong Government now exercises strict control over poultry farms and markets, and there are signs warning against contact with birds. Pay heed to them, and make sure that any poultry or eggs you consume are well cooked.

In May 2009 Hong Kong's response level to Influenza A (H1N1), commonly known as swine flu, was raised from "serious" to "emergency" when a man traveling from Mexico through Shanghai to Hong

Kong was confirmed to be the first case found in the city—and the first case in Asia. The patient was isolated in hospital, while the 173-room Metropark Hotel in Wan Chai where he had been staying was quarantined for a week. In June 2009 all primary schools, kindergartens, and special schools were closed for two weeks; by November 2009 more than 32,300 people in Hong Kong had tested positive for the virus, of which the overwhelming majority were under the age of 14. In May 2010 the response level was lowered from "emergency" to "alert," with the public advised to stay vigilant and continue to practice good personal and environmental hygiene habits.

Although you will find hand-sanitizing dispensers in office buildings and other public areas, it's relatively rare to see people wearing face masks, and health alerts have not further disrupted daily life in Hong Kong.

Local Health Information Department of Health Hotline (☎ 2961–8989 ⊕ www.dh.gov. hk). Travel Health Service (☎ 2961–8840 on Hong Kong Island; 2150–7235 in Kowloon ⊕ www.travelhealth.gov.hk).

OVER-THE-COUNTER REMEDIES

You can easily find most familiar over-the-counter medications (like aspirin and ibuprofen) in pharmacies such as Watsons or Mannings, and usually in supermarkets and convenience stores, too. Acetaminophen—or Tylenol—is often locally known as paracetamol. Oral contraceptives are also available without prescription.

▌ HOURS OF OPERATION

Banks are open weekdays from 9 to 4:30 and Saturday from 9 to 12:30. Office hours are generally from 9 to 5 or 6, although working longer hours is common. Some offices are open from 9 to noon on Saturday. Lunch hour is 1 PM to 2 PM; don't be surprised if offices close during lunchtime. Museums and sights are usually open six days a week from 9 to 5. Each site picks a different day, usually a Monday or Tuesday, to close. Pharmacies are generally open from about 10 AM until about 9 PM. For a 24-hour pharmacy go to Queen Mary Hospital. (⇨ *Emergencies, above*).

HOLIDAYS

Public holidays in Hong Kong are: New Year's (January 1), Chinese New Year (three days in late January/early February), Ching Ming (April 4 or 5), Good Friday and Easter Monday (April), Labor Day (May 1), Buddha's Birthday (May), Dragon Boat Festival (late May/early June), Hong Kong SAR Establishment Day (July 1), Mid-Autumn Festival (late September/early October), National Day (October 1), Chung Yeung (October), and Christmas and Boxing Day (December 25 and 26).

▌ MAIL

Hong Kong's postal system is generally efficient. Airmail letters to any place in the world should take three to eight days, but receiving international mail in Hong Kong is much less reliable. The Kowloon Central Post Office in Yau Ma Tei is open 9:30 AM to 6 PM Monday through Friday and 9:30 AM to 1 PM on Saturday; the General Post Office in Central is open 8 AM to 6 PM Monday through Saturday and 9 AM to 5 PM on Sunday and holidays.

Airmail sent from Hong Kong is classified by destination into one of two zones. Zone 1 covers all of Asia except Japan. Zone 2 is everywhere else. International airmail costs HK$2.40 (Zone 1) or HK$3 (Zone 2) for a letter or postcard weighing less than 20 grams. To send a letter within Hong Kong, the cost is HK$1.40. The post office also has an overnight international courier service called Speedpost.

Main Postal Branches General Post Office (✉ 2 Connaught Rd., Central ☎ 2921–2222 ⊕ www.hongkongpost.com). Kowloon Central Post Office (✉ 405 Nathan Rd., Yau Ma Tei, Kowloon).

SHIPPING PACKAGES

Packages sent via airmail to the United States can take up to two weeks. Airmail shipments to the United Kingdom—both packages and letters—arrive within three or five days, while mail to Australia often arrives in as little as three days.

You are probably best off shipping your own parcels instead of letting shop owners do this for you, both to save money and to ensure that you are actually shipping what you purchased and not a quick substitute—though most shop owners are honest and won't try to cheat you in this way. The workers at Hong Kong Post are extremely friendly, and will sell you all the packaging equipment you need, at unbelievably reasonable prices. Large international couriers in Hong Kong include DHL and Federal Express.

Express Services DHL (☎ *2400–3388* ⊕ *www. dhl.com.hk*). **Federal Express** (☎ *2730–3333* ⊕ *www.fedex.com/hk_english*).

▮ MONEY

Cash and plastic are the way to go. Very few shops or restaurants accept U.S. dollars, so either change in bulk or draw Hong Kong dollars direct from an ATM. Traveler's checks aren't accepted in most shops, and can be a pain to cash—avoid them, if possible. Getting change for large bills isn't usually a problem.

SAMPLE PRICES	
Cup of Coffee/ Tea	HK$25/HK$20
Glass of Wine	HK$45–HK$70
Glass of Beer	HK$40–HK$60
Sandwich	HK$25–HK$40
Fresh Juice from a Stall	HK$10
Bowl of Noodle Soup	HK$20

Prices throughout this guide are given for adults. On public transport and for attractions, reduced fees are almost always available for children, students, and senior citizens.

▮TIP➔ Banks never have every foreign currency on hand, and it may take as long as a week to order. If you're planning to exchange funds before leaving home, don't wait until the last minute.

ATMS AND BANKS

Your own bank will probably charge a fee for using ATMs abroad; the foreign bank you use may also charge a fee. Nevertheless, you'll usually get a better rate of exchange at an ATM than you will at a currency-exchange office or when changing money in a bank. And withdrawing funds as you need them is a safer option than carrying around a large amount of cash.

Reliable, safe ATMs are widely available throughout Hong Kong. MTR stations are also a good place to look, where you'll always find at least one Hang Seng Bank ATM. If your card was issued from a bank in an English-speaking country, the instructions on the ATM machine will appear in English. You can withdraw cash in multiples of HK$100. ▮TIP➔ PIN numbers with more than four digits are not recognized at ATMs in many countries. If yours has five or more, remember to change it before you leave.

CREDIT CARDS

Major credit cards are widely accepted in Hong Kong, though they may not be accepted at small shops, and in some shops you get better rates paying in cash. When adding tips to restaurant bills, be sure to write "HK$" and not just "$."

Throughout this guide, the following abbreviations are used: **AE**, American Express; **D**, Discover (very rarely accepted); **DC**, Diners Club; **MC**, MasterCard; and **V**, Visa.

It's a good idea to inform your credit-card company before you travel, especially if you're going abroad and don't travel internationally very often. Otherwise, the credit-card company might put a hold on your card owing to unusual activity—not a good thing at the beginning of your trip. Record all your credit-card numbers—as well as the phone numbers to call if your cards are lost or stolen—in a safe place, so you're prepared should something go wrong. Both MasterCard and Visa have general numbers you can call (collect if you're abroad) if your card is lost, but you're better off calling the number of your issuing bank, as Master-Card and Visa usually just transfer you to your bank; your bank's number is usually printed on your card.

If you plan to use your credit card for cash advances, you'll need to apply for a PIN at least two weeks before your trip. Although it's usually cheaper (and safer) to use a credit card abroad for large purchases (so you can cancel payments or be reimbursed if there's a problem), note that some credit-card companies *and* the banks that issue them add substantial percentages to all foreign transactions, whether they're in a foreign currency or not. Check on these fees before leaving home, so there won't be any surprises when you get the bill.

■ TIP➔ Before you charge something, ask the merchant whether he or she plans to do a dynamic currency conversion (DCC). In such a transaction the credit-card *processor* (shop, restaurant, or hotel, not Visa or MasterCard) converts the currency and charges you in U.S. dollars. In most cases you'll pay the merchant a 3% fee for this service in addition to any credit-card company and issuing-bank foreign-transaction surcharges.

Dynamic currency conversion programs are becoming increasingly widespread. Merchants who participate in them are supposed to ask whether you want to be charged in dollars or the local currency, but they don't always do so. And even if they do offer you a choice, they may well avoid mentioning the additional surcharges. The good news is that you *do* have a choice. And if this practice really gets your goat, you can avoid it entirely

thanks to American Express; with its cards, DCC simply isn't an option.

Reporting Lost Cards American Express (☎ *800/528-4800 in U.S., 336/393-1111 collect from abroad* ⊕ *www.americanexpress. com*). **Diners Club** (☎ *800/234-6377 in U.S., 2860-1888 in Hong Kong* ⊕ *www.dinersclub. com*). **MasterCard** (☎ *800/627-8372 in U.S., 636/722-7111 collect from abroad* ⊕ *www. mastercard.com*). **Visa** (☎ *800/847-2911 in U.S., 800/96-7025 in Hong Kong* ⊕ *www.visa. com*).

CURRENCY AND EXCHANGE

The only currency used is the Hong Kong dollar, divided into 100 cents. There are bronze-color coins for 10, 20, and 50 cents; silver-color ones for 1, 2, and 5 dollars; and chunky bimetallic 10-dollar pieces. Bills can be confusing, as there are a range of designs and issuing banks. There are new purple and a few remaining older green 10-dollar bills in circulation, as well as bills for HK$20 (blue-green), HK$50 (purple), HK$100 (red), HK$500 (brown), and HK$1,000 (yellow). Don't be surprised if two bills of the same value look different: three local banks (HSBC, Standard Chartered, and Bank of China) all issue bills, and each has its own design. Although the image of Queen Elizabeth II doesn't appear on new coins, old ones bearing her image are still valid.

The Hong Kong dollar has been pegged to the U.S. dollar at an exchange rate of HK$7.8 to US$1 since 1983. There are no currency restrictions in Hong Kong. You can exchange currency at the airport, in hotels, in banks, and through private money changers scattered through the tourist areas. Banks usually have the best rates, but as they charge a fee of up to HK$50 for non-account holders, it's better to change large sums infrequently. Currency exchange offices have no fees, and are open conveniently late hours, but this is offset with relatively poor rates. Stick to ATMs wherever you can.

▌ PACKING

Appearances in Hong Kong are important. This is a city where suits are still de rigueur for meetings and business functions, and women are expected to look elegant (or at least cute). Slop around in flip-flops and shorts and you *will* feel there's a neon "tourist" sign over your head. Pack your nicer pairs of jeans, slacks, or skirts for sightseeing—there are plenty of fake handbags around to dress them up with, come dinner.

From May through September it's seriously hot and sticky, but air-conditioning in hotels, restaurants, museums, and movie theaters can be arctic—keep a crushproof sweater or shawl in your day pack. Don't forget your swimsuit and sunscreen; many large hotels have pools, and you may want to spend some time on one of Hong Kong's many beaches. In October, November, March, and April, a jacket or sweater should suffice, but from December through February bring a light overcoat, preferably waterproof. Compact folding umbrellas can come in handy to protect against either rain or sun, but hotels will also lend you bigger ones for the day.

PASSPORTS AND VISAS

Citizens of the United States need only a valid passport to enter Hong Kong for stays up to three months. You need at least six months' validity on your passport before traveling to Asia. All minors regardless of age, including newborns and infants, must also have their own passport. Upon arrival, officials at passport control will give you a Hong Kong entry slip. Keep this slip safe; you must present it with your passport for your return trip home. If you're planning to pop over the border into mainland China, you must first get a visa *(⇨ below)*.

PASSPORTS

U.S. passports are valid for 10 years for adults, five years for minors under 16. You must apply in person if you're getting a passport for the first time; if your

previous passport was lost, stolen, or damaged; or if your previous passport has expired and was issued more than 15 years ago; or issued when you were under 16. All children under 18 must appear in person to apply for or renew a passport. Both parents must accompany any child under 16 and provide proof of their relationship to the child.

There are 18 regional passport offices, as well as 9,400 passport acceptance facilities in post offices, public libraries, and other governmental offices. If you're renewing a passport, you can do so by mail. Forms are available at passport acceptance facilities and online.

The cost to apply for a new passport is $135 for adults, $102 for children under 16; renewals are $75. Allow four to six weeks for processing, both for first-time passports and renewals. For an expediting fee of $60 you can reduce this time to two to three weeks. If your trip is less than two weeks away, you can get a passport even more rapidly by going to a passport office with the necessary documentation. Private expediters can get things done in as little as 24 hours, but charge hefty fees.

▌TIP➡ Before your trip, make two copies of your passport's data page (one for someone at home and another for you to carry separately). Or scan the page and e-mail it to someone at home and/or yourself.

VISAS

A visa is essentially formal permission to enter a country. Visas allow countries to keep track of you and other visitors—and generate revenue (from application fees). You *always* need a visa to enter a foreign country; however, many countries routinely issue tourist visas on arrival, particularly to U.S. citizens. When your passport is stamped or scanned in the immigration line, you're actually being issued a visa. Sometimes you have to stand in a separate line and pay a small fee to get your stamp before going through immigration, but you can still do this at the airport on arrival. Getting a visa isn't always that easy. Some countries require that you arrange for one in advance of your trip. There's usually—but not always—a fee involved, and said fee may be nominal ($10 or less) or substantial ($100 or more).

If you must apply for a visa in advance, you can usually do it in person or by mail. When you apply by mail, you send your passport to a designated consulate, where your passport will be examined and the visa issued. Expediters—usually the same ones who handle expedited passport applications—can do all the work of obtaining your visa for you; however, there's always an additional cost (often more than $50 per visa).

Most visas limit you to a single trip—basically during the actual dates of your planned vacation. Other visas allow you to visit as many times as you wish for a specific period of time. Remember that requirements change, sometimes at the drop of a hat, and the burden is on you to make sure that you have the appropriate visas. Otherwise, you'll be turned away at the airport or, worse, deported after you arrive in the country. No company or travel insurer gives refunds if your travel plans are disrupted because you didn't have the correct visa.

Travel agents in Hong Kong can issue visas to visit mainland China. Costs for U.S. citizens range from $130 for a visa issued within two to three working days to $160 for a same-day service. Note: The visa application will ask your occupation. The Chinese don't look favorably on those who work in publishing or the media. People in these professions routinely state "teacher" under "occupation." Some applications ask for a business card. Before you go, contact the embassy or consulate of the People's Republic of China to gauge the current mood.

China Visa Information Chinese Consulate in New York (☎ 212/244–9456 ⊕ www. nyconsulate.prchina.org/eng). **Chinese Embassy in the U.S.** (☎ 202/338–6688 or 202/337–1956 ⊕ www.china-embassy.org/ eng). **Visa to Asia** (☎ 888/821–8472 ⊕ visa-toasia.com/china.html) provides up-to-date information on visa applications for China.

Hong Kong General Information Hong Kong Immigration Department (☎ 2824–6111 ⊕ www.immd.gov.hk).

Hong Kong Travel Agents China Travel Service (☎ 2315–7188 ⊕ www.ctshk.com) has more than 20 branches all over Hong Kong.

U.S. Passport Information U.S. Department of State (☎ 877/487–2778 ⊕ travel.state.gov/ passport).

U.S. Passport and Visa Expediters A. Briggs Passport & Visa Expeditors (☎ 800/806–0581 or 202/338–0111 ⊕ www.abriggs.com). **American Passport Express** (☎ 800/455–5166 ⊕ www.americanpassport.com). **Travel Document Systems** (☎ 800/874–5100 or 202/638–3800 ⊕ www.traveldocs.com). **Travel the World Visas** (☎ 866/886–8472 ⊕ www. world-visa.com).

▌ RESTROOMS

Hong Kong was once renowned for its lack of public restrooms, but things are improving. When sightseeing in the city, dip into malls or the lobbies of big international hotels to use their facilities. Since SARS and the influenza alerts, the government has been particularly active in keeping public facilities clean, but toilet paper can be hit-and-miss: bring your own tissues in case.

Find a Loo The Bathroom Diaries (⊕ www.thebathroomdiaries.com) is flush with unsanitized info on restrooms the world over—each one located, reviewed, and rated.

▮ SAFETY

Hong Kong is an incredibly safe place—day and night. The police do a good job maintaining law and order, but there are still a few pickpockets about, especially in Tsim Sha Tsui. So exercise the same caution you would in any large city: be aware and avoid carrying large amounts of cash or valuables with you, and you should have no problems.

Nearly all consumer dissatisfaction in Hong Kong stems from the electronics retailers in Tsim Sha Tsui. Get some reference prices online before buying, and always check the contents of boxed items before you leave the shop.

▮TIP➜ Distribute your cash, credit cards, IDs, and other valuables between a deep front pocket, an inside jacket or vest pocket, and a hidden money pouch. Don't reach for the money pouch once you're in public.

▮ TAXES

Hong Kong levies a 10% service charge and a 3% government tax on hotel rooms. There's no other sales tax or V.A.T.

▮ TIME

Hong Kong is 12 hours ahead of Eastern Standard Time and eight hours ahead of Greenwich Mean Time. There is no daylight savings time in Hong Kong, so remember to add an hour to the time difference between the U.S. or other countries that observe it.

Time Zones Timeanddate.com (⊕ www.timeanddate.com/worldclock) can help you figure out the correct time anywhere in the world.

▮ TIPPING

Tipping isn't a big part of Hong Kong culture. That said, hotels are one of the few places where tips are expected. Hotels and restaurants usually add a 10% service charge; however, in almost all cases, this money does not go to the waiters and waitresses. Add on up to 10% more for good service, or simply round up the tab. Tipping restroom attendants is common, but it is generally not the custom to leave an additional tip in taxis and beauty salons, and unheard of in theaters and cinemas.

TIPPING GUIDELINES FOR HONG KONG	
Bartender	HK$10–HK$20 per round of drinks, depending on the number of drinks
Bellhop	HK$5–HK$20 per bag, depending on the level of the hotel
Hotel Concierge	HK$20–HK$50, more if he or she performs a service for you
Hotel Doorman	HK$5 if he helps you get a cab
Restroom Attendants	HK$2–HK$5
Porter at Airport or Train Station	HK$2–HK$5 per bag
Waiter	5%–10% if service was good

▮ VISITOR INFO

ONLINE TRAVEL TOOLS

For a guide to what's happening in Hong Kong, check out the Hong Kong Tourist Board's excellent site. For weather info, check out the Hong Kong Observatory.

For political information plus news and interesting business links try the Hong Kong government site.

Business in Hong Kong is a government-run site packed with advice, and Centamap provides online Hong Kong street maps so detailed they give street numbers and building names. The Hong Kong Government, Hong Kong Tourist Board (HKTB), and Hong Kong Observatory all provide practical information for preparing for your trip to Hong Kong.

For cultural activities check out *HK* magazine, an online version of a quirky weekly rag with the lowdown on just about everything happening in town. The government portal Hong Kong Leisure and Cultural Services Department provides access to the Web sites of all of Hong Kong's museums and parks. Time Out Hong Kong, the well-known city guide magazine, offers both features and detailed listings.

Google does currency conversion. Just type in the amount and currencies to be converted (e.g., "600 HKD to USD"), and voilà. Oanda.com offers comprehensive currency tools, charts, and services. XE.com provides quick and straightforward currency conversion.

For some local insight, go to Eat Drink Hong Kong, an excellent online guide to Hong Kong's bars and restaurants, or GLB Hong Kong, a catchall site to gay and lesbian resources and venues. Geoexpat collects wisdom from Hong Kong's large expat community. Hong Kong Outdoors is the authority on hiking, camping, and all things wild in Hong Kong. Love HK Film.com will tell you all you need to know about Hongkollywood.

The Standard is a free English-language tabloid focused on business, but the South China Morning Post is Hong Kong's leading local English-language daily.

All About Hong Kong Business in Hong Kong (⊕ www.gov.hk/en/business). Centamap (⊕ www.centamap.com). Hong Kong Government (⊕ www.gov.hk). Hong Kong Tourist Board (*HKTB* ⊕ www.discoverhongkong.com). Hong Kong Observatory (⊕ www.weather.gov.hk).

Cultural Activities HK Magazine (⊕ hk.asiacity.com). Hong Kong Leisure and Cultural Services Department (⊕ www.lcsd.gov.hk). Time Out Hong Kong (⊕ www.timeout.com.hk).

Currency Conversion Google (⊕ www.google.com). Oanda.com (⊕ www.oanda.com). XE.com (⊕ www.xe.com).

Local Insight Eat Drink Hong Kong (⊕ www.eatdrinkhongkong.com). GLB Hong Kong (⊕ sqzm14.ust.hk/hkgay). Geoexpat (⊕ www.geoexpat.com). Hong Kong Outdoors (⊕ www.hkoutdoors.com). Love HK Film.com (⊕ lovehkfilm.com).

Newspapers South China Morning Post (⊕ www.scmp.com). The Standard (⊕ www.thestandard.com.hk).

INDEX

A

A Lorcha ✕, 299
Aberdeen, 67
Addresses, 13
Admiralty, 132–135
Advisories, 327–328
Afonso III ✕, 295–296
AfriKana B.B.Q. Restaurant
    ✕, 298
agnès b. café ✕, 169
agnès b. le pain grillé ✕, 173
Air travel, 316–318
    airports and transfers, 18,
    317–318
    Macau, 272
Alisan Guesthouse 🖫, 227
Altira 🖫, 307
Altira Macau (casino), 292–293
A-Ma Cultural Village,
    288–289
A-Ma Temple, 270
Amandarling (shop), 107, 122
Amber ✕, 173–174
Amusement parks, 35–37
    Lantau Island, 71
    Macau, 277, 283
    Southside, 66
Antique Patisserie ✕, 167
Antiques, shopping for
    Hong Kong Island, 111–112,
    116–118, 144
    Macau, 314
    SoHo and NoHo, 107
Ap Lei Chau Island (Duck's
    Tongue Island), 32, 67
Apartment rentals, 237
Aqua ✕, 192–193
aqua luna (bar), 32
Aqua Spirit (bar), 266
Arch Angel Antiques (shop),
    107, 116
Architecture, 20–21, 44, 47,
    283
Aroma Natural Skin Care
    (shop), 109
Art, shopping for, 58, 107,
    113, 114, 116–119, 121, 148
Art galleries, 16, 80, 87, 257
    New Territories, 92, 93
    SoHo and NoHo, 107
    Wan Chai, 58
    Western District, 43
Artists' Commune (art gallery),
    257
Arts. ⇨ See Nightlife and the
    arts

Arts & Crafts Fair, 148
Asian Art Archive, 113
Aspasia ✕, 193
ATMs, 330
Auction houses, 135
Aurora ✕, 300
Aux Beaux Arts ✕, 296
Avenue of the Stars, 81
Aviaries, 36–37, 52
Awfully Chocolate ✕, 169

B

Bags, shopping for, 127–128,
    135, 136, 141–142, 157, 158
Bahçe ✕, 73
Ball Kee ✕, 167
Bang Bang Pan Pan ✕, 169
Bank of China building, 49
Bank of China Tower, 20
Banks, 330
Bargaining, 103, 115, 157
Bars, 32, 250
    Causeway Bay, 266
    Central District, 57, 253,
    255–256, 258
    Kowloon, 266–268
    Macau, 312–313
    Wan Chai, 263
    Western, 252–253
Bathing Ape, A (shop), 140
Bauhaus (shop), 109
Beaches
    Lantau Island, 28–29, 71
    Macau, 270, 278
    New Territories, 27–28, 97,
    100
    Southside, 26–27, 67
Beauty and cosmetics, shop-
    ping for, 112, 121, 138
Beijing Kitchen ✕, 300
Belcançáo ✕, 300–301
Best Noodle Restaurant ✕, 202
Bird cages, shopping for, 88,
    105, 158
Bird Garden, 36, 88, 105, 158
Bird-watching, 16, 36–37
Bishop Lei International House
    🖫, 220–221
Bishop's House, 52
Bistecca ✕, 174
Black Sheep Restaurant ✕, 69
Bo Innovation ✕, 183–184
Boat and ferry travel, 14, 19,
    32, 318–319
    Central District, 48, 51
    Kowloon, 83

Lantau Island, 73
    Macau, 272
    Wan Chai, Causeway Bay and
    beyond, 61
    Western District, 45
Boathouse, The ✕, 189–190
Bonham Strand, 24–25
Bookstores, 111–112
Booth Lodge 🖫, 245
BP International House 🖫, 236
Bread Tree Express ✕, 61
Broadway Cinematheque, 38
Bunn's Divers Institute, 27
Bus travel, 319–320
    Kowloon, 83, 95
    Lantau Island, 73
    Macau, 273
Business and trade services,
    323
Business hours, 162, 250, 329
Butterfly on Morrison 🖫,
    227–228
Butterfly on Prat 🖫, 236

C

Café Deco Bar and Grill ✕,
    174
Café Gray Deluxe ✕, 174
Café Match Box ✕, 186–187
Café O ✕, 45
Calligraphy supplies, shopping
    for, 102
Cameras, shopping for, 140
Camões ✕, 298
Camões Garden, 278
Cantonese cuisine, 177
Cantonese opera, 92, 262
Cantonese Opera Hall, 92
Caprice ✕, 57, 175
Car racing, 286
Car travel and rentals, 95,
    273, 319–320
Carmel Gardens, 285
Carpets and rugs, shopping
    for, 124, 145
Casa Garden, 278, 281
Cashmere, shopping for, 145,
    148
Casino Lisboa, 274, 291
Casinos, 274, 289–295
Cattle Depot Artist Village, 87
Causeway Bay, 10, 62–63
    hotels, 215, 227–229, 231–232
    nightlife and the arts, 62, 266
    restaurants, 62, 63, 168–169,
    186–188

shopping, 62, 63, 108–109,
137–142
spas, 109
sports and outdoor activi-
ties, 62
transportation, 61
Causeway Bay Typhoon
Shelter, *62*
CDs, DVDs and VCDs, shopping
for, *123, 149*
Central District, *10, 48–57*
guided tours, 51
hotels, 215, 220–222, 224–225
nightlife and the arts, 49, 54,
57, 166–167
restaurants, 49, 50, 57, 173–
176, 178–181
shopping, 49, 113–132
spas, 55, 57
sports and outdoor activities,
55, 57
transportation, 48, 51, 52
Central Ferry Pier, *52*
Central Park Hotel ⚊ , *219*
Central Plaza, *58–59*
Central Police Station, *52*
Central Star Ferry Pier, *36, 48*
Ceramics, shopping for, *124*
Chairman, The ✕ , *175*
Charlie's Acupressure and
Massage Centre of the
Blind, *24*
Chek Lap Kok Airport, *18*
Cheoc Van Beach, *289*
Che's Cantonese Restaurant
✕ , *184*
Cheung Chau Bun Festival, *17*
Cheung Chau Island, *30*
Cheung Sha Beach, *28–29, 71*
Chi Lin Nunnery, *86*
Children
activities for, 12, 22, 35–37, 49,
66, 71, 81, 92, 153
hotels, 216, 224, 227, 228,
234–235, 238, 244, 305–306,
310–311
Macau, 281, 283, 288, 289,
305–306, 310–311
restaurants, 164, 184, 190, 191,
197, 204
Children's clothing, shopping
for, *121*
Children's Discovery Gallery, *92*
Chinese Antiquities Gallery, *80*
Chinese Arts & Crafts (department store), *133*
Chinese Fine Art Gallery, *80*
Chinese medicine, *23–25, 112,*
129

Chinese New Year, *17*
Chinese opera, *92, 262*
Chinese University of Hong
Kong Art Museum, *93*
Ching Chung Koon Taoist
Temple, *93*
Ching Ming Festival, *17*
Chopsticks, shopping for, *102*
Chuan Shao ✕ , *193*
Chuan Spa, *105*
Chungking Mansions, *84*
Cinecittà ✕ , *184*
Cinema, *38–39*
City Hall, *264*
City of Dreams (casino), *294*
City'super (department store),
113–114
Classified ✕ , *45*
Climate, *13*
Clocks, shopping for, *106*
Cloth Haven (shop), *114*
Clothing, shopping for, *112,*
121–123, 129–133, 135,
138–140, 142, 144–145,
154–155
Club BBoss (hostess club),
268
Clube Militar de Macau (The
Macau Military Club) ✕ ,
296
Coloane Island, *271, 278, 286,*
288–289, 301–302, 310–311,
314
Coloane Village, *289*
Comic books, shopping for,
156
Communications, *324–325*
Computers, shopping for,
135–136, 140
Connoisseur Art Gallery, *107,*
118
Conrad Hong Kong ⚊ , *221*
Contemporary Hong Kong Art
Gallery, *80*
Copa Steakhouse ✕ , *298–299*
Corner Kitchen ✕ , *172*
Cosmo Hotel ⚊ , *228*
Cosmopolitan Hotel ⚊ , *228*
Cotai, *270, 294–295, 312–313,*
314
Crafts and curios, shopping
for, *113, 123, 145*
Credit cards, *7, 330–331*
Cricket, *17*
Crown Towers ⚊ , *307*
Crowne Plaza Hong Kong ⚊ ,
228–229
Cruises, *320*
Crystal Lotus ✕ , *191*

Cuisine, *177*
Cantonese, 177
dim sum, 194–195
Mandarin, 177
Nepalese, 170
Portuguese, 299
Shanghainese, 177
shark's fin soup, 189
Szechuan (Sichuan), 164
Cuisine Cuisine ✕ , *176*
Culture classes, *16*
Curios, shopping for, *113,*
123, 145
Currency, *272, 331*
Customs and duties, *325*

D

Da Ping Huo ✕ , *176*
Dance clubs, *251*
Deep Water Bay, *26, 69*
Department stores, *113–115,*
133–134, 137, 152, 312
Des Voeux Road West, *25*
Diamonds, shopping for,
125–126, 149
Dim sum, *194–195*
Dim Sum ✕ , *187*
Din Tai Fung ✕ , *193*
Dining. ⇨ *See* Cuisine;
Restaurants
Discos, *258–259, 265*
Discounts and deals, *115, 283*
Disney's Hollywood Hotel ⚊ ,
234
DiVino ✕ , *176*
D-mop (shop), *109*
Dog racing, *276–277*
Dolphin watching, *72*
Dom Galo ✕ , *296*
Downtown Macau, *270,*
275–278, 281–284, 295–299,
302–305, 312, 314
Dragon Boat Festival, *17*
dragon-i ✕ , *57, 253, 258*
Dragon's Back (park), *33*
Drawing Room, The ✕ , *187*
Drop (nightclub), *57*
Duck's Tongue Island, *32, 67*
Duk Ling (fishing junk), *15, 32*
Duties, *325*
DVDs, shopping for, *123, 149*
Dynasty ✕ , *184*

E

East ⚊ , *232*
Eastern District, *64–65*
restaurants, 188–189
shopping, 142–143
Eaton Hotel ⚊ , *245, 247*

Edificio do Leal Senado (Senate Building), *276*
Edward Youde Aviary, *36–37, 52*
Eight, The ✕ , *296*
8½ Otto e Mezzo ✕ , *173*
Electricity, *327*
Electronic goods, shopping for, *123, 136–136, 140, 149, 155*
Elements (mall), *147*
Emergencies, *327–328*
Empire Hotel Hong Kong, Causeway Bay 🖫 , *229*
Empire Hotel Kowloon, Tsim Sha Tsui 🖫 , *236, 238*
Enchanted Garden ✕ , *191*
Etiquette and behavior, *326*
Eu Yan Sang Medical Hall, *23, 112*
Excelsior 🖫 , *229*

F

Fa Yuen Street, *105*
Fabrics, shopping for, *102, 156*
Fang Fong (shop), *107*
Fashion Walk, *62*
Fat Siu Lau ✕ , *297*
Felix ✕ , *193, 196, 253, 266*
Feng shui, *20–21*
Fernando's ✕ , *301–302*
Ferries. ⇨ *See* Boat and ferry travel
Festival Walk (mall), *152*
Festivals and seasonal events, *17, 263, 282*
Film, *38–39*
Film festivals, *263*
Flagstaff House Museum of Tea Ware, *48–49, 56, 200*
Fleming, The 🖫 , *225*
Flower Market, *87*
Flying Pan ✕ , *65, 259*
Flying Pan Wan Chai, The ✕ , *61*
Fo Fo by el Willy ✕ , *176*
Former French Mission Building, *53–54*
Fortaleza da Guia, *275*
Fortaleza do Monte, *281*
Fortress (shop), *140*
Forts
Lantau Island, 75
Macau, 275, 281
Four Seasons Hotel (Macau) 🖫 , *309*
Four Seasons Hotel Hong Kong 🖫 , *221*
Free attractions, *16*

French Window, The ✕ , *176, 178*
Fringe Club, *257, 260*
Fusion 5th Floor ✕ , *172*

G

G.O.D. (shop), *106, 141*
Gaia ✕ , *178*
Galaxy StarWorld (casino), *291–292*
Galaxy StarWorld Hotel 🖫 , *302–303*
Gambling, *40, 270, 289–295*
Garden View YWCA, The 🖫 , *221*
Gardens. ⇨ *See* Parks and gardens
Gay and lesbian nightlife, *253, 259–260, 261, 266*
Gaylord ✕ , *196*
Genki Sushi ✕ , *50*
Globe (pub), *261*
Go Koong ✕ , *196*
Go-cart racing, *289*
Goldfish Market, *87, 153*
Golf, *17, 69*
Macau, 310
tournaments, 17
Government advisories, *327–328*
Government House, *53*
Government Publications Centre (shop), *33*
Grand Hyatt (Macau) 🖫 , *309*
Grand Hyatt Hong Kong 🖫 , *225–226*
Grand Lisboa (casino), *292*
Grand Prix Museum, *281*
Grappa's Ristorante ✕ , *178*
Great Outdoor Clothing Company (shop), *33*
Greyhound racing, *276–277*
Guided tours
art galleries, 80, 92
Central District, 51
Kowloon, 80, 83, 84
Lantau Island, 726
Macau, 273, 283
New Territories, 95
shopping, 102

H

H One ✕ , *178*
Hác Sá Beach, *270, 289*
Hakka people, *31, 75*
Handicrafts, shopping for, *113, 123, 145*

Happy Feet Reflexology Center, *24, 129*
Happy Foot (spa), *107*
Happy Valley Racetrack, *40, 62*
Harbour City (mall), *147*
Harbour Grand Kowloon 🖫 , *247*
Harbourview, The 🖫 , *226*
Hard Rock Hotel 🖫 , *309*
Harvey Nichols (department store), *114*
Health, *23–25, 328–329*
Heritage Exhibition of a Traditional Pawn Shop, *281*
High Island Reservoir, *97*
Hiking. ⇨ *See* Walking and hiking
Hillier Street, *25*
Historic Centre of Macau, The, *276*
Holiday Inn Golden Mile 🖫 , *238*
Hollywood Road, *43*
Homeless (shop), *106*
Honeymoon Dessert Shop ✕ , *94, 204*
Hong Kong Academy for Performing Arts, *264*
Hong Kong Art Walk, *133*
Hong Kong Arts Centre, *58, 257*
Hong Kong Arts Festival, *263*
Hong Kong City Fringe Festival, *263*
Hong Kong Convention and Exhibition Centre, *59*
Hong Kong Cricket Festival, *17*
Hong Kong Cultural Centre, *79, 264*
Hong Kong Disneyland, *35, 71*
Hong Kong Disneyland Hotel 🖫 , *234*
Hong Kong Dolphinwatch, *72*
Hong Kong Fashion Week, *147*
Hong Kong Film Archive, *39*
Hong Kong Heritage Museum, *16, 91, 92*
Hong Kong International Film Festival, *263*
Hong Kong Island
Admirality, 132–135
beaches, 26–29, 67, 71, 97, 100
Central District, 10, 48–57
children, activities for, 12, 22, 35–37, 49, 66, 71, 81, 92, 153
climate, 13
Eastern District, 64–65

guided tours, 51, 72, 80, 83, 84, 95, 102
hotels, 219–235
Lantau Islnd, 71–75
Nathan Road, 84, 104–105
neighborhoods, 42–75
New Territories, 11, 91–100
nightlife and the arts, 16, 250–268
price categories, 163, 217
restaurants, 172–191
shopping, 14–15, 23, 24–25, 33, 111–145
Southside, 66–70
spas, 128–129
sports and outdoor activities, 12, 16, 26–34, 40, 62, 63, 66, 69, 71, 75, 97, 99, 100
transportation, 13, 18–19, 45, 48, 51, 52, 60, 61, 68, 73, 74, 83, 95
Wan Chai, Causeway Bay and beyond, 58–65
Western District, 43–47
Hong Kong Museum of Art, 79–81
Hong Kong Museum of History, 79
Hong Kong Museum of Medical Sciences, 23–24, 46
Hong Kong Park, 49
Hong Kong Philharmonic Orchestra, 264
Hong Kong Science Museum, 81
Hong Kong Sky City Marriott Hotel ⊡ , 234–235
Hong Kong Space Museum, 81
Hong Kong Tourist Board (HKTB), 12
Hong Kong Trail, 22
Hong Kong University Chinese Medicine Clinic and Pharmacy, 24
Hong Kong Wetland Park, 37
Hong Kong Zoological & Botanical Gardens, 37, 53
Hongkong & Shanghai Bank (HSBC) **Main Building,** 21
Horse racing, 40
Macau, 284
New Territories, 99
Wan Chai, Causeway Bay and beyond, 62
Hostess clubs, 250, 268
Hotel Bonaparte ⊡ , 229
Hotel Jen ⊡ , 219
Hotel Lisboa ⊡ , 303
Hotel LKF ⊡ , 222
Hotel Panorama ⊡ , 238

Hotel Sintra ⊡ , 303
Hotels, 7
Central District, 215, 220–222, 224–225
Hong Kong Island, 219–235
hotel atlas, 205–212
Kowloon, 215, 236, 238, 240–245
Lantau Island, 215, 233–235
Macau, 302–311
price categories, 217, 273
reservations, 216
Southside, 215, 232–233
Tsim Sha Tsui, 236, 238, 240–245
Wan Chai, Causeway Bay and beyond, 215, 225–229, 231–232
Western District, 215, 219–220
Yau Me Tei and Mong Kok, 245, 247–248
Hotpot Instinct ✕ , 168
HSBC building, 20, 53
Hullett House ⊡ , 238, 240
Hungry Ghosts Festival, 17
Hutong ✕ , 196
Hyatt Regency Hong Kong, Tsim Sha Tsui ⊡ , 240

I

IFC Mall, 115
Igreja de Santo Agostinho, 282
Igreja de São Domingos, 275
Igreja de São Lourenço, 281
Il Teatro ✕ , 297
Inner Harbour (Macau), 293, 299–300, 306–307
InterContinental Hong Kong ⊡ , 240
International Finance Centre, 53
Internet service, 324
Iroha ✕ , 169
Island Beverley (mall), 109
Island Shangri-La ⊡ , 222
Isola ✕ , 178–179

J

Jade, shopping for, 87, 126, 136, 154, 156
Jade Garden ✕ , 83
Jamia Mosque, 53–54
Jardine House, 54
Jaspa's ✕ , 204
Jet skiing, 270
Jewelry, shopping for, 124–127, 136, 141, 149, 158
JIA ⊡ , 231
Jimmy's Kitchen ✕ , 179
Johnston Road, 59

Jordan, 170
Joyce Beauty (shop), 144
Joyce Boutique (shop), 144
Joyce Warehouse (outlet shop), 144
JP Cinema, 39
Junks and sampans, 32
JW's California ✕ , 179

K

Kam Fung ✕ , 184
Kansu Street Jade Market, 87
Kira ✕ , 301
Ko Lau Wan Hotpot and Seafood Restaurant ✕ , 202
Kowloon, 11, 78–100
guided tours, 80, 83
hotels, 215, 236, 238, 240–245, 247–248
Mong Kok, 14–15, 152–158, 170–171, 201–204, 245, 247–248
nightlife and the arts, 266–268
restaurants, 83, 93, 192–193, 196, 199, 201
shopping, 87–88, 89, 145, 146–158
spas, 89
Tsim Sha Tsui, 79–84, 192–193, 196–199, 201, 236, 238, 240–245
transportation, 83, 94
Yau Ma Tei, 84–88, , 170–171, 201–204, 245, 247–248
Kowloon Mosque, 81
Kowloon Park, 15, 81
Kowloon Shangri-La ⊡ , 240–241
Kowloon Walled City Park, 84
Krug Room ✕ , 179
Kubrick Bookshop Café ✕ , 83
Kung Fu Supplies Co. (shop), 102
Kung Tak Lam ✕ , 196–197
Kwai Tsing Theatre, 264

L

La Crêperie ✕ , 184–185
La Nue Lingerie (shop), 105
Lam Tsuen Wishing Trees, 93
Lamma Island, 30
Lan Kwai Fong, 54, 254
Landmark, The (mall), 115
Landmark Mandarin Oriental ⊡ , 224
Lane Crawford (department store), 133
Langham, The ⊡ , 241
Langham Place ⊡ , 247

Langham Place (mall), *105*
Language, *12, 272*
Lanson Place Hotel 🏨 , *231*
Lantau Island, *71–75*
  beaches, 28–29, 71, 75
  guided tours, 72
  hotels, 215, 233–235
  restaurants, 73, 74, 75, 191
  *sports and outdoor activities,
    71, 72, 75*
  transportation, 73, 74
Lantau Peak, *75*
Lantern Festival, *17*
Largo de Santo Agostinho,
  281–282
Largo do Senado, *275*
L'Atelier de Joël Robuchon ✕ ,
  179–180
Law Uk Folk Museum, *64*
Le Méridien Cyberport 🏨 , *233*
Leaf Dessert ✕ , *167*
Lee Gardens One and Two
  (malls), *109*
Les Peches Lounge (lesbian
  club), *261*
L'hotel Island South 🏨 , *232*
Liberty Exchange Kitchen & Bar
  ✕ , *181*
Lin Fung Miu (temple), *282*
Lin Heung Lau Tea House ✕ ,
  45, 47
Lion Rock, *33–34*
Litoral ✕ , *299*
Liu Man Shek Tong, *96*
Lo Chiu Vietnamese Restaurant
  ✕ , *202–203*
Lobster Bar & Grill ✕ , *180–181*
Lock Cha Tea Shop, *49*
Lodging. ⇨ *See* Hotels
Lok Man Rare Books, *111–112*
Long Kei ✕ , *297*
Lou Lim Ieoc Gardens, *282*
Lowland Gardens, *36*
Lucy's (Hong Kong Island)
  ✕ , *190*
Lung Kee ✕ , *171*
Lung King Heen ✕ , *181*
Luxe Manor, The 🏨 , *241*

M

Ma Tau Kok Cattle Depot (art
  gallery), *257*
Macao Cultural Centre,
  282–283
Macao Museum of Art,
  282–283
Macau, *270–314*
  beaches, 270, 278, 289
  casinos, 270, 289–295

children, activities for, *281,
  283, 288, 289, 305–306,
  310–311*
Coloane Island, *271, 278, 286,
  288–289, 301–302, 310–311,
  314*
Cotai, *270, 294–295, 312–313,
  314*
currency, *272*
discount passes, *283*
Downtown, *270, 275–278,
  281–284, 312, 314*
guided tours, *273*
history, *285*
hotels, *302–311*
Inner Harbour, *293, 299–300,
  306–307*
language, *272*
nightlife and the arts, *311–313*
Outer Harbour, *298–299,
  305–306, 312*
passports and visas, *272*
price categories, *273*
restaurants, *276, 295–302*
shopping, *295, 313–314*
spas, *270*
sports and outdoor activities,
  276–277, 286
Taipa Island, *270, 278, 284–
  286, 293–294, 300–301, 307,
  309–310, 312*
transportation, *272–273*
visitor information, *272*
Macau Canidrome, *276–277*
Macau Fisherman's Wharf, *283*
Macau Golf and Country Club,
  310
Macau International Music
  Festival, *282*
Macau Jockey Club, *284*
Macau Kartodromo, *289*
Macau Museum, *281*
Macau Tea Culture House, *282*
Macau Tower & Convention &
  Entertainment Centre, *277*
MacLehose Trail, *34*
Madame Tussaud's
  (museum), *22*
Mah-jongg sets, shopping for,
  157
Mail and shipping, *329–330*
Main Street Deli ✕ , *197*
Mak's Noodles Limited ✕ , *181*
Man Mo Temples, *46, 96*
Mandarin Beauty Salon and
  Barber Shop, *129*
Mandarin cuisine, *177*
Mandarin Oriental Hong Kong
  🏨 , *224*

Mandarin Spa & the Oriental
  Spa, The, *129*
Marco Polo Hongkong Hotel
  🏨 , *242*
Margaret's Café e Nata ✕ ,
  276
Marine Land, *36*
Maritime Museum, *283*
Markets and bazaars, *14–15,
  156–157*
  Causeway Bay, 138
  *Kowloon, 87–88, 153–154,
    156*
  Nathan Road, 84
  New Territories, 99
  Western District, 111
Marks & Spencer (department
  store), *114–115*
Massage, *24, 107, 128–129*
Me & George (shop), *105, 155*
Meal plans, *7*
Metropark Hotel Causeway
  Bay 🏨 , *231*
MGM Grand (casino), *292*
MGM Grand 🏨 , *303, 305*
Mid-Autumn Festival, *17*
Midlevels Escalator, *14, 18, 44,
  45, 49*
Milan Station (shop), *108, 141*
Minden, The 🏨 , *242*
Mingle Place by the Park 🏨 ,
  226
Mingle Place on the Wing 🏨 ,
  219–220
Mira, The 🏨 , *242–243*
Miu Fat Buddhist Monastery
  ✕ , *94*
MO Bar, *57*
Monasteries
  Lantau Island, 74
  Macau, 284
  New Territories, 94
Money matters, *330–331*
Mong Kok, *14–15, 84–88*
  hotels, 245, 247–248
  *restaurants, 170–171,
    201–204*
  shopping, 152–158
Mosques, *53–54, 81*
Movies, *88–89*
Mui Wo, *75*
Museum of Coastal Defence, *64*
Museum of Sacred Art and
  Crypt, *278*
Museums, *16, 22, 25–26*
  Central District, 48–49, 56
  Kowloon, 79–81
  *Macau, 278, 281, 282–283,
    284*

New Territories, 91, 92, 93, 96
*Wan Chai, Causeway Bay and
beyond, 64*
Western District, 43, 46
Music, 260–261

N

Naam ✕ , 299
Nan Tei ✕ , 187
Nathan Road
shopping, 84, 104–105
spas, 105
Nepalese cuisine, 170
New Territories, 11, 91–100
beaches, 27–28, 97
guided tours, 92, 95
nightlife and the arts, 92
restaurants, 94, 100, 204
shopping, 99
*sports and outdoor activi-
ties,* 99
transportation, 95, 100
**New Territories Heritage
Hall,** 92
Neway Karaoke, 109
Ngong Ping *360 Skyrail,*
18–19, 73
Ngong Ping Village, 74
Nightlife and the arts, 16,
250–268
Central District, 57, 253–261
Kowloon, 266–268
Macau, 311–313
New Territories, 92
safety, 251, 334
*Wan Chai, Causeway Bay
and beyond,* 65, 261, 263,
265–266
NoHo, 106–107
Noonday Gun, 62–63
Novotel Century Hong Kong
⊡ , 226
Novotel Citygate Hong Kong
⊡ , 235
Nunnery, 86

O

O Porto Interior ✕ , 299–300
Ocean Park (amusement park),
35, 66
1/5 nuevo (bar), 65, 263
One Harbour Road ✕ , 185
Opera, Chinese, 92, 262
Oriental Spa, 55, 57
Osteria ✕ , 197–198
Outer Harbour (Macau), 312
Outer Islands, 11, 30–31.
⇨ *See also* specific islands
Ovolo ⊡ , 237

OVOlogue ✕ , 185–186
Oyster & Wine Bar ✕ , 198

P

Packing for Hong Kong,
332–333
Pak Tai Temple, 96–97
Palace IFC (cinema), 39
Park Lane ⊡ , 231–232
Parks and gardens, 15, 30–31,
34–36, 37, 53
Central District, 49, 53
Kowloon, 15, 81, 84, 87
in Macau, 278, 281, 282, 285,
289
*Wan Chai, Causeway Bay and
beyond,* 62
Passports and visas, 272,
332–333
Pastelaria Koi Kei ✕ , 295
Patrick's Waterskiing, 27
Pawn, The ✕ , 59, 186, 253,
263
Peak Café Bar ✕ , 107
Peak Tower, 22
Peak Tram, 19
Pearl on the Peak ✕ , 181
Pearls, shopping for, 126–127,
158
Pearls & Cashmere (shop),
148
Pedder Building (mall), 116
Peking opera, 262
Peninsula Hong Kong, The ⊡ ,
84, 89, 243
Pink Martini (shop), 109
Po Lin Monastery, 74
Po Toi Island, 31
Ponte 16 (casino), 293
Portas do Sol ✕ , 297
Portobello ✕ , 107
Portuguese cuisine, 299
Possession Street, 46
Post 97 ✕ , 259
**Pou Tai Un Buddhist Monas-
tery,** 287
Pousada de Coloane ⊡ , 310
Pousada de Mong-Há ⊡ , 305
Pousada de São Tiago ⊡ ,
306–307
Praia Grande ✕ , 297–298
President Theatre, 39
Price categories
dining, 163, 273
lodging, 217, 273
Propaganda, shopping for, 156
Pubs, 261, 265–266, 268,
312–313
Pure Yoga, 55

Q

**Quality Chinese Medical
Centre,** 24
Quartel dos Mouros, 283
Queen's Road, 54
Queen's Road West, 25

R

Rakuen Tsim Sha Tsui ✕ , 198
RED Bar + Restaurant ✕ , 57
Regal Airport Hotel ⊡ , 235
**Renaissance Hong Kong Har-
bour** ⊡ , 227
Repulse Bay, 26, 67
**Repulse Bay Verandah
Restaurant & Bamboo Bar**
✕ , 69
Restaurant Pétrus ✕ , 181–182
Restaurante Espaco Lisoboa
✕ , 302
Restaurants, 7, 160–204. ⇨ *See
also* Cuisine
Central District, 49, 50, 57,
166–167, 173–176, 178–181
dining atlas, 205–212
hours, 162
Kowloon, 83, 93, 192–193,
196, 199, 201
Lantau Island, 73, 74, 75, 191
Macau, 276, 295–302
Mong Kok, 170–171, 201–204
New Territories, 94, 100, 204
price categories, 163, 273
reservations, 162
SoHo and NoHo, 107
Southside, 67, 69, 189–191
tipping, 163
Tsim Sha Tsui, 83, 192–193,
196–199, 201
*Wan Chai, Causeway Bay and
beyond,* 59, 61, 62, 63, 64,
65, 168–169, 183–189
Western District, 45, 47, 50,
172
Yau ma Tei, 170–171, 201–204
Restrooms, 333–334
Robuchon a Galera ✕ , 298
Rocks Hotel ⊡ , 306
Royal Garden ⊡ , 243
**Royal Hong Kong Yacht
Club,** 63
Royal Pacific Hotel & Towers
⊡ , 243–244
Royal Plaza ⊡ , 248
Rugby, 17
Rugby Sevens, 17
Ruinas de São Paulo, 270,
277–278

S

Sabatini ✕ , *198*
Safety, *251, 334*
Sai Kung Peninsula, *26, 97*
Sailing, *32*
St. George ✕ , *199*
St. John's Cathedral, *54*
Salisbury YMCA 🖭 , *244*
Sam Tung Uk Museum, *96*
Sampans and junks, *32*
Sam's Tailor (shop), *150*
San Xi Lou ✕ , *182*
Sands Macao (casino), *292*
Sands Macao 🖭 , *306*
Santa Casa da Misericordia, *276*
Santouka ✕ , *188*
Schoeni Art Gallery, *107, 119*
Scuba diving, *27*
Seac Pai Van Park, *289*
Seals, shopping for, *102*
Sha Ha (beach), *27–28*
Sha Tin, *99*
Sha Tin Racecourse, *40, 99*
Shama Causeway Bay 🖭 , *237*
Shanghai Street, *87–88*
Shanghai Tang (department store), *122–123*
Shanghai Tang-Imperial Tailors (shop), *130*
Shanghainese cuisine, *177*
Shark's fin soup, *189*
Shek O, *26–27, 67*
Shek O Chinese & Thailand Seafood Restaurant ✕ , *190*
Sheraton Hong Kong Hotel & Towers 🖭 , *244–245*
Shoe repair shops, *129*
Shoes and bags, shopping for, *127–128, 136, 141–142, 158*
Shopping, *14–15, 23, 24–25, 33, 102–158*
 Causeway Bay, *62, 63, 108–109, 137–142*
 Central District, *49, 113–132*
 Kowloon, *87, 145–158*
 Lantau Island, *75*
 Macau, *295, 313–314*
 Nathan Road, *84, 104–105*
 New Territories, *99*
 SoHo and NoHo, *106–107*
 Southside, *66, 143–145*
 tips for, *102–103, 131, 156–157*
 tours, *102*
 Western District, *44, 46–47, 111–113*

Shopping centers and malls, *111, 115–116, 134, 137–138, 147, 152–153*
Shows, *313*
Shui Hu Ju ✕ , *47*
Shui Kee ✕ , *167*
Shuing Kee ✕ , *167*
Shun Dairy Company ✕ , *171*
Sichuan (Szechuan) cuisine, *164*
Sik Sik Yuen Wong Tai Sin Temple, *85, 87*
Silk, shopping for, *102, 156*
Silvermine Beach, *29*
Silverstrand (beach), *26*
Sincere (department store), *115*
Sing Heung Yuen ✕ , *167*
Sistyr Moon (shop), *140*
Siu Shun Village Cuisine ✕ , *203*
Sofitel Macau at Ponte 16 🖭 , *307*
SoHo, *49, 106–107*
Sohotel 🖭 , *220*
Solas (nightclub), *253, 256*
Sole Town (shop), *109*
Southside, *10–11*
 beaches, *26–27, 67*
 hotels, *215, 232–233*
 restaurants, *67, 69, 189–191*
 shopping, *66, 143–145*
 sports and outdoor activities, *69*
 transportation, *68*
Spa at the Grand Lapa Macau, The, *304*
Spa by mtm, *109*
Spas, *128–129*
 Causeway Bay, *109*
 Central District, *55, 57*
 Kowloon, *89*
 Macau, *270, 304*
 Nathan Road, *105*
 SoHo and NoHo, *107*
Specialty shops, *111–112, 116–118, 135, 144*
Spices ✕ , *190*
Sports and outdoor activities, *12, 16, 26–34, 40.* ⇨ *See also* specific sports
 Lantau Island, *71, 75*
 Macau, *276–277, 286*
 Southside, *66, 69*
 New Territories, *97, 99, 100*
 Wan Chai, Causeway Bay and beyond, *62*
Spring Deer ✕ , *198*
Standard Chartered Bank, *54*

Standard Chartered Hong Kong Marathon, *17*
Stanford Hillview Hotel 🖭 , *245*
Stanley, *15, 27, 66*
Stanley Village Market, *69, 142*
Star Ferry, *14, 19, 51*
Star Ferry piers, *79*
Statue Square, *54–55*
Steak House winebar + grill, The ✕ , *199*
Stoep, The ✕ , *73*
Subway travel, *83, 95, 251, 320–321*
Sun Kee ✕ , *199*
Sushi Hiro ✕ , *169, 187–188*
Sushi U ✕ , *182*
Symbols, *7*
Symphony of Lights, *16*
Szechuan (Sichuan) cuisine, *164*

T

T.T. Tsui Gallery of Chinese Art, *92*
Ta Pantry ✕ , *186*
Tai Cheong ✕ , *167*
Tai Fu Tai, *99*
Tai Mo Shan, *99*
Tai O, *75*
Tai Ping Koon ✕ , *199, 201*
Tai Po, *99*
Tailor-made clothing, shopping for, *129–132, 142, 150–151*
Taipa Houses Museum, *285–286*
Taipa Island, *270, 278, 284–286, 293–294, 300–301, 307, 309–310, 312*
Taipa Village, *284–286*
Tan Ngan Lo ✕ , *171*
Tandoor ✕ , *182*
Tap Mun Island, *31, 100*
Tapeo ✕ , *188*
Tasty Congee and Noodle Wonton Shop ✕ , *65*
Taxes, *163, 334*
Taxis, *73, 83, 95, 273, 321*
Tea, *102, 166, 200*
Tea and tea equipment, shopping for, *102*
Teatro Dom Pedro V, *281–282*
Telephones, *324–325*
Temple of Ten Thousand Buddhas, *91, 93*
Temple Spice Crabs ✕ , *171*
Temple Street, *88, 171*

Temple Street Night Market, *105*, *154*
Temples and shrines, *16*
Kowloon, 85, 87
Macau, 270, 278, 282, 283–284
New Territories, 91, 93, 96–97
Western District, 46
Templo de A-Ma, *278*
Templo de Na Tcha, *278*
Templo de Sam Kai Vui Kun, *283–284*
Textile Society of Hong Kong, The, *114*
Thai BBQ *2* ✕, *203*
Theater, *281–282*
Tian Tan Buddha, *15, 71, 74*
Tim Ho Wan ✕, *203*
Timberland (shop), *33*
Time, *334*
Times Square (mall), *63, 138*
Timing the trip, *13*
Tim's Kitchen ✕, *172*
Tin Hau Temple, *88*
Tipping, *163, 334*
Tong Pak Fu ✕, *171*
Tong Ren Tang (Chinese medicine company), *24*
Tonkichi Tonkatsu Seafood ✕, *169*
Top Deck ✕, *69, 190*
Top Shoes Repair & Lock Centre (shop), *129*
Traditional Chinese Medicine (TCM), *23*
Train travel, *19, 322*
Trams, *14, 18, 322*
Transportation, *13, 18–19, 316–322*
Central District, 48, 51, 52
Kowloon, 83
Lantau Island, 73, 74
Macau, 272–273
New Territories, 95
Southside, 68
Wan Chai, Causeway Bay and beyond, 60, 61
Western District, 45, 51
Troco das Antigas Muralhas de Defesa, *278*
Tsim Sha Tsui
hotels, 236, 238, 240–245
restaurants, 83, 192–193, 196–199, 201
shopping, 145, 146–151
Tsing Ma Bridge, *75*
Tso Choi Koon ✕, *203–204*
TST East Promenade, *79*

Tsui Wah Restaurant ✕, *50, 57, 182, 259*
Tung Choi Ladies' Market, *88*
Tung Chung Fort, *75*
Tung Chung New Town, *75*
Tung Kee Seafood Restaurant ✕, *204*
Tung Ping Chau, *30–31*
Tung Po ✕, *188–189*
Turkish Café Bahçe ✕, *73*
Two Macdonnell Road 📷, *237*

U

UBS Hong Kong Open Golf Championship, *17*
University Museum and Art Gallery, *43*
University of Hong Kong, *46*
Upper House, The 📷, *224–225*

V

VCDs, shopping for, *123, 149*
Venetian Macao-Resort-Hotel 📷, *294–295, 309–310*
Verandah, The ✕, *190–191*
Victoria City Seafood ✕, *186*
Victoria Peak, *14, 22, 49*
Visas, *272, 332–333*
Visitor information, *12, 334–335*
Macau, 272
Volar (nightclub), *57, 258–259*
Volume (nightclub), *253*

W

W Hong Kong 📷, *248*
Walking and hiking, *15, 16, 22, 33–34, 83*
Wan Chai, *10*
guided tours, 60
hotels, 215, 225–229, 231–232
nightlife and the arts, 62, 63, 65, 261, 263, 265–266
restaurants, 59, 61, 63, 64, 65, 183–189
shopping, 62, 63, 135–136
sports and outdoor activities, 62
transportation, 60, 61
Wanchai Computer Centre (shop), *135–136*
Watches, shopping for, *127, 149*
Waterskiing, *27*
Weather, *13*

Web sites, *334–335*
Western District, *10, 43–47*
hotels, 215, 219–220
restaurants, 45, 47, 50, 172
shopping, 44, 46–47, 111–113
transportation, 45, 51
Western Market, *111, 114*
Westin Resort 📷, *310–311*
Whisk ✕, *201*
Wilson Trail, *34*
Windsurfing, *27, 28*
Wine, *163, 298*
Wine, shopping for, *314*
Wine bars, *261*
Wine Museum, *284*
Wing Lee Street, *47*
Wing Lok Street, *25*
Wing On (department store), *111*
Wisdom Path, *74*
Woodlands ✕, *83*
World Sports Co., Ltd. (shop), *33*
Wu Kong ✕, *188*
Wynn Macau (casino), *292–293*
Wynn Macau 📷, *305*

X

Xenri na Tsuki ✕, *169*

Y

Yan Toh Heen ✕, *201*
Yan Yuen Shek (Lovers' Rock), *59*
Yau Ma Tei, *84–88*
hotels, 245, 247–248
restaurants, 170–171, 201–204
shopping, 152–158
Yé Shanghai ✕, *182–183*
Yee Shun Milk Company ✕, *61*
Yoga classes, *55*
Yue Hwa Chinese Products Emporium (department store), *105, 152*
Yuen Kee ✕, *47*
Yuen Po Street Bird Garden, *36, 88, 105, 158*
Yuen Yuen Institute, *100*
Yung Kee ✕, *183*
Yunyan Sichuan ✕, *201*

Z

Zak's ✕, *191*
Zoos, *37, 53*
Ztampz (shop), *140*
Zuma ✕, *183*

PHOTO CREDITS

1, Jose Fuste Raga / age fotostock. 2-3, Alvaro Leiva / age fotostock. **Chapter 1: Experience Hong Kong.** 8-9, Walter Bibikow / age fotostock. 10, Hong Kong Tourism Board. 11 (left), Ian Muttoo/Flickr. 11 (right), Ella Hanochi/iStockphoto. 14 (left), claudio zaccherini/Shutterstock. 14 (top center), Hong Kong Tourism Board. 14 (bottom center), K.C. Tang/wikipedia.org. 14 (top right), Hong Kong Tourism Board. 14 (bottom right), maveric2003/Flickr. 15 (left), karendotcom127/Flickr. 15 (top center), James Cridland/Flickr. 15 (bottom right), Hong Kong Tourism Board. 15 (top right), amybbb/Shutterstock. 16, Hong Kong Tourism Board. 17, John Leung/Shutterstock. 18, Sze Kit Poon/iStockphoto. 19 (left), oksana.perkins/Shutterstock. 19 (right), Andrew Kerr/Shutterstock. 21 (left and right), Michael Weber. 23, tiltti/Flickr. 24 (bottom), Anna Jurkovska/Shutterstock. 24 (top), charles taylor/Shutterstock. 25 (bottom), Andrew Baron/Flickr. 25 (top left), Marc van Vuren/Shutterstock. 25 (top right), Marek Brzezinski/iStockphoto. 26, Li lin hk - Imaginechina. 27 (left), Hong Kong Tourism Board. 27 (right), Victor Fraile/Hong Kong Tourism Board. 29 (left), wong chi kin/iStockphoto. 29 (right), Khoroshunova Olga/Shutterstock. 30, Hong Kong Tourism Board. 31 (left), Keith Molloy/iStockphoto. 31 (right), Jess Yu/Shutterstock. 32, deb22/Shutterstock. 33, Ian D Walker/Shutterstock. 35, Hong Kong Tourism Board. 36, leungchopan/Shutterstock. 37 (left), winhorse/iStockphoto. 37 (right), Ewan Chesser/Shutterstock. 39 (left), AndyYip/Shutterstock. 39 (right), Sam DCruz/Shutterstock. 40, Li Wa/Shutterstock. **Chapter 2: Hong Kong Neighborhoods.** 41, Hemis / Alamy. 42, Laoshi/iStockphoto. 45, Hong Kong Tourism Board. 48, Hong Kong Tourism Board. 51, Hong Kong Tourism Board. 52, Dallas & John Heaton / age fotostock. 55, Hemis / Alamy. 56, MAISANT Ludovic / age fotostock. 58, Hippo Studio/iStockphoto. 61, claudio zaccherini/Shutterstock. 63, Gavin Hellier / age fotostock. 66, Hong Kong Tourism Board. 69, Let Ideas Compete/Flickr. 70, David Ewing / age fotostock. 71, Oksana Perkins/iStockphoto. 73, AngMoKio/wikipedia.org. 74, Hong Kong Tourism Board. 76, Ron Yue / Alamy. **Chapter 3: Kowloon Neighborhoods.** 77, Pat Behnke / Alamy. 78, LungSanLau/wikipedia.org. 80, Ian Muttoo/Flickr. 83, Hong Kong Tourism Board. 86, cozyta/Shutterstock. 89, Iain Masterton / Alamy. 90, James Montgomery / age fotostock. 91, Hong Kong Heritage Museum. 92, wikipedia.org. 95, Ella Hanochi/iStockphoto. 97, Doug Houghton / Alamy. 98, Ian Trower / age fotostock. **Chapter 4: Shopping.** 101, Ian Cumming / age fotostock. 104, Greg Elms / age fotostock. 105, OzMark17/Flickr. 106, John Warburton-Lee Photography / Alamy. 107, Jack Rosenfeld/Flickr. 108 and 109, Roger Price/Flickr. 110, Grotto Fine Art. 112, Amanda Hall / age fotostock. 117, VH / age fotostock. 120, Doco Dalfiano / age fotostock. 127, Hong Kong Tourism Board. 134, Sylvain Grandadam / age fotostock. 143, Hong Kong Tourism Board. 146, Gavin Hellier / age fotostock. 151, Douglas LeMoine/Flickr. 154, Jochen Tack / age fotostock. **Chapter 5: Where to Eat.** 159, Picture Contact / Alamy. 160, The Pawn. 165, JTB Photo / Alamy. 166, Hong Kong Tourism Board. 167 (bottom), George Apostolidis. 167 (top), Chiu Pong Ng/iStockphoto. 168, Florian/Flickr. 169 (bottom), Shintaro MORIGUCHI/iStockphoto. 169 (top), chinnian/Flickr. 170, Tomasz D. Dunn/Flickr. 171 (bottom), Yali Shi/iStockphoto. 171 (top), perry_marco/Flickr. 175, 8 1/2 Otto e Mezzo. 180, macglee/Flickr. 185, The Pawn. 192, BrokenSphere/wikipedia.org. 195, Hong Kong Tourism Board. 197, Aqua Spirit. 202, InterContinental Hong Kong. **Chapter 6: Where to Stay.** 213, Worldhotels. 214, flowerego/flickr. 223 (top and bottom) and 230 (top), Michael Weber. 230 (bottom), Jia Hong Kong. 233, Graham Uden. 239 (top), InterContinental Hong Kong/flickr. 239 (bottom left), bryangeek/flickr. 239 (bottom right), The Luxe Manor. 246 (top and bottom), Starwood Hotels and Resorts. **Chapter 7: After Dark.** 249, Francisco Diez/Flickr. 252, Hong Kong Tourism Board. 255, Fumio Okada / age fotostock. 260, The Globe. 262, K. Koroda / age fotostock. 265, Picture Contact / Alamy. 267, Peninsula Hotels. **Chapter 8: Side Trip to Macau.** 269, Steve Vidler / age fotostock. 270 (top), Lance Lee I AsiaPhoto.com/iStockphoto. 270 (bottom), Cloodlebing and Great Kindness/Flickr. 271 (top), Roger Price/Flickr. 271 (bottom), Lauri Silvennoinen/wikipedia.org. 274, leungchopan/Shutterstock. 277, Iain Masterton / Alamy. 280, Tito Wong/Shutterstock. 287 and 290, Christian Goupi / age fotostock. 293, Barbara Kraft. 294, Jimmy Yao/Flickr. 301, dbimages / Alamy. 304, George Apostolidis. 308 (top), dadokit, INC. 308 (bottom left), Starwood Hotels and Resorts. 308 (bottom right), Dennis Wong/Flickr. 311, LOOK Die Bildagentur der Fotografen GmbH / Alamy.

NOTES

NOTES

NOTES

NOTES

NOTES

NOTES